Rumba on the River

Also by Gary Stewart
Breakout: Profiles in African Rhythm

Rumba on the River

A history of the popular music of the two Congos

◆

GARY STEWART

V
VERSO
London · New York

First published by Verso 2000
© Gary Stewart 2000
Paperback edition first published by Verso 2003
All rights reserved

1 3 5 7 9 10 8 6 4 2

The moral rights of the author have been asserted

Verso
UK: 6 Meard Street, London W1F OEG
USA: 180 Varick Street, New York, NY 10014-4606

Verso is the imprint of New Left Books

ISBN: 978-1-85984-368-0

British Library Cataloguing in Publication Data
Stewart, Gary
 Rumba on the river : a history of the popular music of the two Congos
 1. Popular music – Congo (Democratic Republic) – History and criticism
 I. Title.
 781.6'3'096751
 ISBN 1859843689

Library of Congress Cataloging-in-Publication Data
A catalog record for this book is available from the Library of Congress

Designed and typeset in Monotype Joanna by Illuminati, Grosmont
Printed and bound in Great Britain by Bath Press Ltd, Avon

For Les Immortel(le)s:
Abeti
Bill Alexandre
Bavon Marie Marie
Franklin Boukaka
Léon Bukasa
Franco
J.S. Huey
Nicolas Jeronimidis
Jhimmy
Joseph Kabasele
Pepe Kalle
Paul Kamba
Vicky Longomba
D.V. Moanda
Pamelo Mounk'a
M'Pongo Love
Mujos
Docteur Nico
Frères Soki
et les autres

Contents

    Prologue: A mighty sound   1
    Mobutu and the musicians, 1997

1   **Difficult delivery**   3
    Bowane, Leopold II, Stanley, Brazza, Kamba, Feruzi, and Wendo, 1946 and before

2   **Why don't you make a record?**   23
    Olympia, Ngoma, Opika, and Loningisa, 1946–1950

3   **The brains of the music**   34
    Jhimmy, Kabasele, and African Jazz, 1950–1955

4   **In need of a name**   49
    Essous, Franco, and O.K. Jazz, 1955–1956

5   **A change in mentality**   60
    Kasavubu, Lumumba, Rock'a Mambo, O.K. Jazz, and Orchestre Bantou, 1957–1959

6   **Celebrations and sorrows**   83
    Kasavubu, Lumumba, African Jazz, and O.K. Jazz, 1960–1961

7	**Congo music** Orchestre Bantou and Ry-Co Jazz, 1960–1963	101
8	**Money changes everything** African Jazz, African Fiesta, Moïse Tshombe, O.K. Jazz, and Orchestre Bantou, 1963–1965	110
9	**Revolution** Mobutu, Franco, Bavon Marie Marie, Kwamy, Docteur Nico, Rochereau, and Essous, 1965–1967	122
10	**Dances and disorder** Docteur Nico, Rochereau, Sam Mangwana, and Franco, 1968–1969	135
11	**Rhythm of the time** Franco, Verckys, Bella Bella, Zaïko Langa Langa, Bavon Marie Marie, Franklin Boukaka, and Rochereau, 1969–1970	148
12	**The name game** Vévé, Trio Madjesi, Afrisa, Fiesta Sukisa, O.K. Jazz, and Bantous de la Capitale, 1971–1973	169
13	**The guys have it** Abeti, Franco, and Mobutu, 1973–1974	188
14	**What goes up...** Mobutu, George Foreman, Muhammad Ali, Tabu Ley, Bella Bella, and Zaïko Langa Langa, 1974–1976	206
15	**...Must come down** Abeti, M'Pongo Love, Papa Wemba, Franco, and Tabu Ley, 1975–1978	219
16	**Exodus** Bantous de la Capitale, Mobutu, African All Stars, Verckys, Koffi Olomide, and Docteur Nico, 1977–1980	235

17	**Paris**	254
	Franco, Pamelo Mounk'a, Bopol, Pablo, M'Pongo Love, Kosmos, Kanda Bongo Man, and Les Quatre Etoiles, 1979–1982	
18	**Article 15**	276
	Kabasele, Sam Mangwana, Franco, Tabu Ley, Mbilia Bel, and Docteur Nico, 1980–1985	
19	**You can't tell the players without a program**	300
	Empire Bakuba and Clan Langa Langa, 1979–1985	
20	**Crossroads**	314
	Tshala Muana, Abeti, Rigo Star, Les Quatre Etoiles, Loketo, Kanda Bongo Man, Tabu Ley, and Mbilia Bel, 1985–1988	
21	**Get out your program again**	333
	Clan Langa Langa, Koffi Olomide, and Empire Bakuba, 1985–1989	
22	**Matters of life and death**	350
	Bantous de la Capitale and O.K. Jazz, 1985–1989	
23	**The gray nineties**	369
	O.K. Jazz, Wenge Musica, Bantous de la Capitale, Soukous Stars, Abeti, Papa Wemba, and Tabu Ley, 1989 and after	
	Notes	393
	Bibliography	404
	Select discography	410
	Acknowledgments	416
	Index	419

Author's note

In so many ways this book is also the work of Beth G. Raps. Over the dozen years that have passed since we first met, Beth translated two complete books and an uncountable number of articles from French for me as I gathered information about Congolese music. She accompanied me on my research trips to Europe and Africa and interpreted nearly all of my interviews with French-speaking musicians and producers. As the author of this book, the selection of material and the writing is my own, but Beth smoothed my rudimentary translations of quotations and suggested important structural changes and edits that helped shape the final work. Her contributions have made this a far better book than I could have produced by myself. For that I am enormously grateful.

'African music was and remains a music of encounters; in this lies its attractive power.'

Manu Dibango

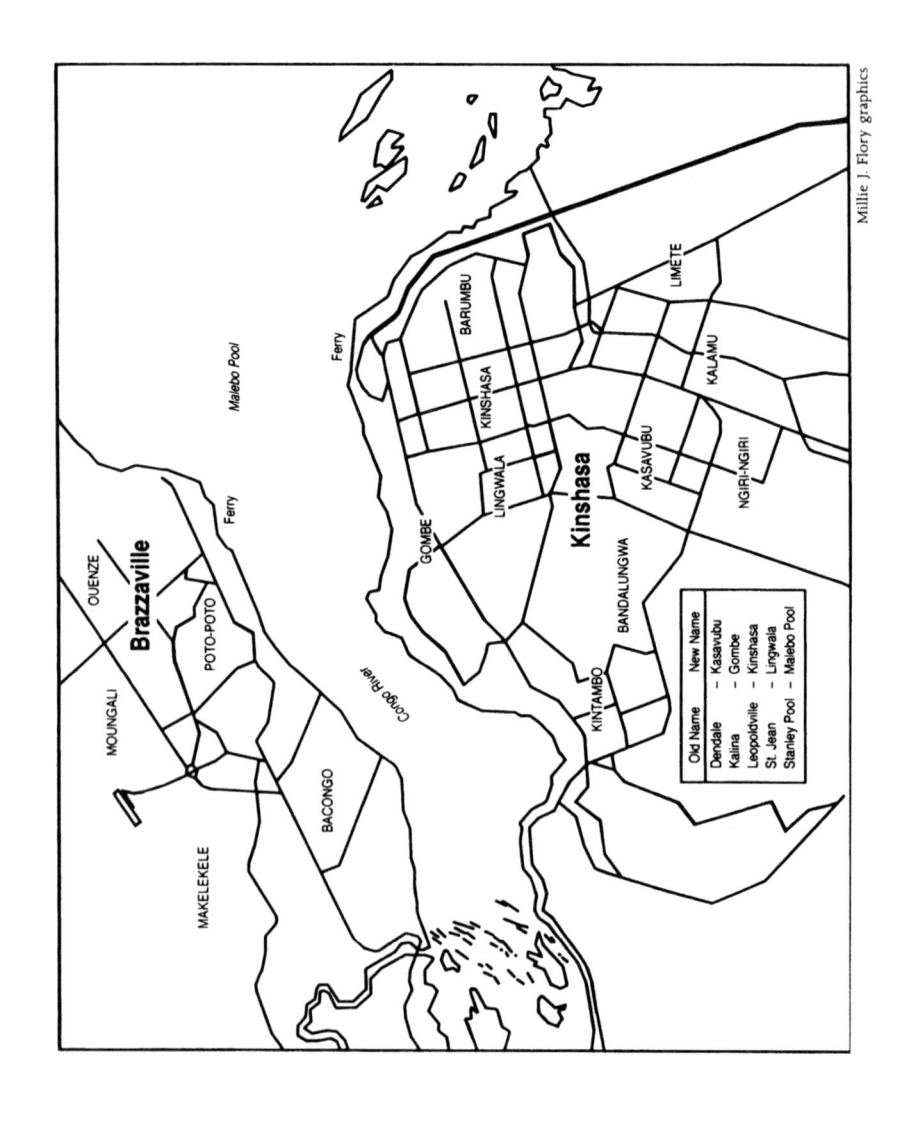

Old Name	New Name
Dendale	– Kasavubu
Kalina	– Gombe
Leopoldville	– Kinshasa
St. Jean	– Lingwala
Stanley Pool	– Malebo Pool

Millie J. Flory graphics

PROLOGUE
A mighty sound

Mobutu and the musicians, 1997

In the early morning hours of Friday, May 16, 1997, Zaïre's president, Mobutu Sese Seko, left his stronghold at Camp Tshatshi on Kinshasa's western outskirts for the last time. He slipped into the back seat of an inconspicuous sedan for a hasty motorcade to the capital's international airport where a jetliner waited to carry him into exile. Only a few short miles beyond the airport's perimeter the soldiers of Laurent Kabila's rebellion readied themselves for one final campaign – a celebratory parade really – to take the capital and put an end to nearly thirty-two years of Mobutu's corrupt dictatorship.

Mobutu was embarking, albeit in more luxurious fashion, on a journey that many of his country's musicians had already taken. Theirs was compelled by a collapsing economy which in turn forced his at gunpoint. The former Zaïrean president would settle into his comfortable villa in Morocco to live out the days numbered by a spreading cancer.

The musicians whose livelihoods he all but destroyed had moved to more modest surroundings in Paris and Brussels. Sam Mangwana, Abeti Masikini, Tabu Ley Rochereau, Papa Wemba, Tshala Muana, and scores of others joined their counterparts from across the river in Congo-Brazzaville and from West Africa and the Caribbean to transform the former metropolises of Europe's colonial empires into fertile musical crossroads. The confluence of styles and ideas produced another music industry flavor of the moment, 'world beat.'

Despite the misleading label, most 'world beat' recorded in Paris and Brussels is African. Much of that comes from Congo and Zaïre – the latter called Congo too since Mobutu's departure. The ironic truth is that the inroads

2 Rumba on the River

made by Congolese music abroad developed in proportion to how badly things went at home. Like canaries in a coal mine whose silence foreshadows disaster, the flight of Congolese musicians presaged the chaos that would consume both Congos in the decade of the nineties.

That the migration of musicians would serve as a warning seemed only natural. Congolese music itself was the product of upheavals that had engulfed central Africa for hundreds of years. The encounters that gave it life were often less joyful than their offspring. Some played out in the spirit of curiosity and good will. Others bore the scars of ignorance and greed. Together they produced a legacy of suffering, and of joy, and a new popular music that would reach far beyond the boundaries of its birthplace.

1
Difficult delivery

Bowane, Leopold II, Stanley, Brazza, Kamba, Feruzi, and Wendo, 1946 and before

The two cities gleamed like diamonds washed up on opposite banks of the Congo River, one cut with the precision of a lapidary's chisel, the other rough and sandy, still bearing nature's scars. But like the smile of the confidence man the glint of gems deceives. These two were costume jewels molded by the hands of African laborers and the power of European brute force. The triumph in this lay not in the quick-to-dull spit and polish of transplanted European façades but rather in the astonishing character of human adaptability. For in these artificial creations, twin capitals of two even more unlikely domains, Africans met the European world of Christianity and commerce and in the process produced a flowering of musical creativity to rival that of old New Orleans.

Near the beginning of a series of tumultuous cataracts some 240 miles from the Atlantic, clumps of water hyacinth float lazily along the river, a perpetual procession of efflorescence from deep in the interior of central Africa. There, at a wide place in the river known as Stanley Pool, the Belgians and the French chose to establish the capitals of their respective central African colonies. Léopoldville in the Belgian Congo on the river's southeast bank was the cut and polished gem. 'It reflects strongly the Belgian national character,' wrote journalist John Gunther in the 1950s. 'People are hardheaded, hardworking, frugal, bourgeois, and successful. There is no nonsense about aesthetics.'

Brazzaville, on the northwest bank in the French Congo, part of French Equatorial Africa, was the rough, uncut gem. Gunther described it as 'still an

4 Rumba on the River

African city, loosely constructed, colorful, relaxed, to which has been magically added a dash of Paris.' Graham Greene found

> Brazzaville a far prettier, more sympathetic place than Leo – Europe in Leo weighs down on the African soil in the form of skyscrapers: here [in Brazzaville] Europe sinks into the greenery and trees of Africa. Even the shops have more chic than Leo.

Through force or through fancy, rural Africans flocked to these new capitals to do the bidding of the Europeans and make what they hoped would be a better life for themselves. Like slaves brought to America, Africans entering the colonial cities on their own continent were urged to leave Africa at the door. This was the white man's world of clocks and order, of identity cards and regular jobs. But on both sides of the Atlantic, African music sneaked inside and, to paraphrase historian Basil Davidson, modernized out of its own traditions and history, borrowing from the whites what was useful, rejecting what was not.

The new city dwellers brought with them the languages and traditions of their peoples and the music that metered their everyday existence. Away from the protection of the close-knit village, these elements began to mix. New associations developed blurring ethnic ties. Roving minstrels took up the cheap guitars that flooded into Africa and bridged the gap from traditional to modern music. From this urban conglomeration there emerged a new music style which, for Africans, was as revolutionary as the birth of American jazz. 'Congo music' it came to be known throughout most of the African continent; today in the West many call it 'soukous.'

•

Henri Bowane boarded a Congo riverboat in 1946 and headed for the city. Growing up in Coquilhatville, 400-odd miles up-river from Stanley Pool, he had listened as travelers told stories about the good life in 'Lipopo,' Léopoldville. He had listened to musicians who came from there, vocal groups and guitar-playing troubadours. Some of them had come up-river to perform. Now, the seventeen-year-old Bowane would meet them on their home ground. He would become an *ngembo*, a bat, one of the droves of young people who hung from trees or clung to walls surrounding the capital's open-air 'dancing bars' in order to get a glimpse of the action.

The Léopoldville Bowane found was a city divided. White people lived along the river in an eight- to ten-block-wide strip some seven miles in length, known in popular parlance as the ville. Its splendid, palm-lined boulevards linked Kalina, the seat of government in the ville's center, with the commercial district of Léo East on one side and residential Léo West on the other. To the south, across a 'cordon sanitaire' made up of Fernand de Bock Park, a zoo, and a golf course, African laborers and servants occupied the cité indigène. The cité comprised two rapidly expanding districts, Kinshasa on the east side and Kintambo to the west, separated by a military camp and assorted schools and factories. Belgian authorities, fearing the influx of Africans from the countryside, tried to control the cité's growth as much as possible. Early-morning raids to rout out 'illegals' occurred with regularity. Bowane needed a passport to make his journey, although he, like many others, may have evaded the requirement.

By day the white ville bustled with activity as people of all races mingled in the commercial east end where they worked and traded at shops owned by Belgian, Greek, and Portuguese businessmen. But as an African, Bowane would best be out of the ville when the bugle call sounded at nine in the evening. Only Africans who worked as servants for white families could stay legally in the ville between nine and four-thirty the next morning, and then only as long as they lived on the property of their employers. Even in the cité Africans were forbidden to move about from ten until four.

•

Central Africa's encounter with the white man had begun in 1483 when the Portuguese explorer Diogo Cão sailed into the mouth of an nzadi, a great river – mistakenly called zaïre by the Portuguese – known today as the Congo. The nzadi ran through the country of the Kongo people who were ruled by a mani (king) headquartered at Mbanza in the northern part of today's Angola. What began, in Davidson's words, as a 'different but equal' partnership between Europeans and Africans rapidly degenerated into a one-sided operation which enriched Europe and the Americas at the expense of African people and the bounty of their land. In the process, justified by the most outrageous rationalizations, Africans came to be regarded as 'sub-human,' 'savages,' 'heathens,' by slavers who packed their fellow human beings into dank ships' holds for the harrowing Atlantic passage to tobacco, sugar, and cotton plantations in the Americas.

In a holocaust of unparalleled proportions European and American slave traders sapped the strength of West and central Africa for more than four centuries, from about 1450 to the 1880s. Some twenty million of the continent's hardiest souls – perhaps as many as five million from the area of the Congo river-mouth alone – were captured or killed in a grim business that fractured African institutions and de-humanized both black and white.

In East Africa, Arabs from Egypt, Sudan, and the Arabian Peninsula conducted their own trade for black slaves. At its peak, according to one estimate, the Arab-run trade took as many as 10,000 captives a year from the Swahili Coast and 12,000 a year from the Red Sea Coast.

With the rise of abolitionist movements in the late eighteenth and early nineteenth centuries, Europeans gradually turned their attention to what the explorer David Livingstone termed the '3Cs' as an antidote to the slave trade. Commerce, Christianity, and 'civilization' would be Africa's salvation. Those who had ravaged the continent would come to its rescue.

For the makers of Congo music and their ancestors, the most important of these 'rescuers' were the explorers Henry Morton Stanley and Pierre Savorgnan de Brazza. Working independently of each other, indeed in competition, the Welsh-born American Stanley and the Italian-turned-Frenchman Brazza explored the territory that would one day become the two Congos. Stanley set out in November of 1874 to cross the continent from Zanzibar to the mouth of the Congo River. Supported by three white companions and a half-mile-long caravan of some 350 African warriors, porters, and servants toting eight tons of supplies and the sections of a forty-foot boat, Stanley's three-year expedition cost the lives of countless Africans who resisted his belligerent intrusion into their territory.

A year after Stanley began, Brazza departed for the coast of Gabon in the company of three other whites and a few Senegalese sailors. Traveling slowly up the Ogowé River with only a tiny fraction of the entourage Stanley employed, Brazza presented a less menacing specter than his extravagant competitor. By August of 1877, while Stanley stumbled into Boma near the Atlantic Ocean, Brazza came within a hundred or so miles of the Congo River, where he was driven back by the local people.

The exploits of Stanley, Brazza, and others brought Africa to the consciousness of the European world. Stanley spoke to the British of forty million naked Africans, 'and the cotton-spinners of Manchester are waiting to clothe them ... and the ministers of Christ are zealous to bring them, the poor benighted heathen, into the Christian fold.' But British leaders, preoccupied with economic recession and struggling with France for influence in Egypt, seemed uninterested. Brazza found little more enthusiasm for such ideas in

France. It was King Leopold II of the Belgians who dreamed the dreams of Brazza and Stanley.

Leopold II, of German descent and cousin to Queen Victoria, presided over a country of quarreling peoples, the Flemings and Walloons, which had won independence from its Dutch neighbors only a scant thirty-four years before his accession to the throne in 1865. Restricted by a constitution that gave power to the politicians, Leopold was relegated to performing ceremonial duties. That failed to stop the ambitious king, who wanted an overseas colony for his tiny country, or perhaps for his own personal profit. Central Africa looked like a good prospect.

The king had avidly followed Africa's exploration. In 1876 he had organized the International African Association, a grouping of eminent European scientists and explorers, for the purported purpose of opening Africa to further exploration and study. He summoned Stanley and Brazza to the royal palace on separate occasions in an effort to engage them in his enterprise. Brazza, hoping that his adopted France would take up the challenge in central Africa, refused. Stanley, having been rebuffed by the British, signed on. He polished off his two-volume, soon-to-be-bestselling book, *Through the Dark Continent*, and set out again for Africa, this time in the service of the Belgian king.

Unbeknown to Stanley, he was in a race. While he recruited assistants in Zanzibar, Brazza was drumming up support in France for a new expedition of his own. Meanwhile, Leopold's high-minded International African Association quietly became the Comité d'Etudes du Haut Congo (Committee for the Study of the Upper Congo), supported by a group of prominent businessmen whose involvement made it look suspiciously like a commercial venture. By August of 1879, Stanley and his Zanzibari laborers worked feverishly to set up trading stations along the Congo estuary and to blast a rocky road around the cataracts between the Atlantic and Stanley Pool. The locals called Stanley *bula matadi* (corrupted to *bula matari*), breaker of rocks, a term that would later become synonymous with white men and the colonial Congolese state. Five months after Stanley started, Brazza, underwritten by hard-won French support, paddled his way up the Ogowé River from the Gabonese coast.

While Stanley struggled with the tasks of construction, Brazza wasted little time. He tramped out of the bush in August of 1880 in sight of the Congo River. There he met the *makoko* (king) of the Téké people on the north shore of Stanley Pool. After more than a month of comradeship and negotiation with Brazza, the *makoko* put his mark on a treaty placing him and his people under French protection. Stanley reached the pool in July of 1881 to find the

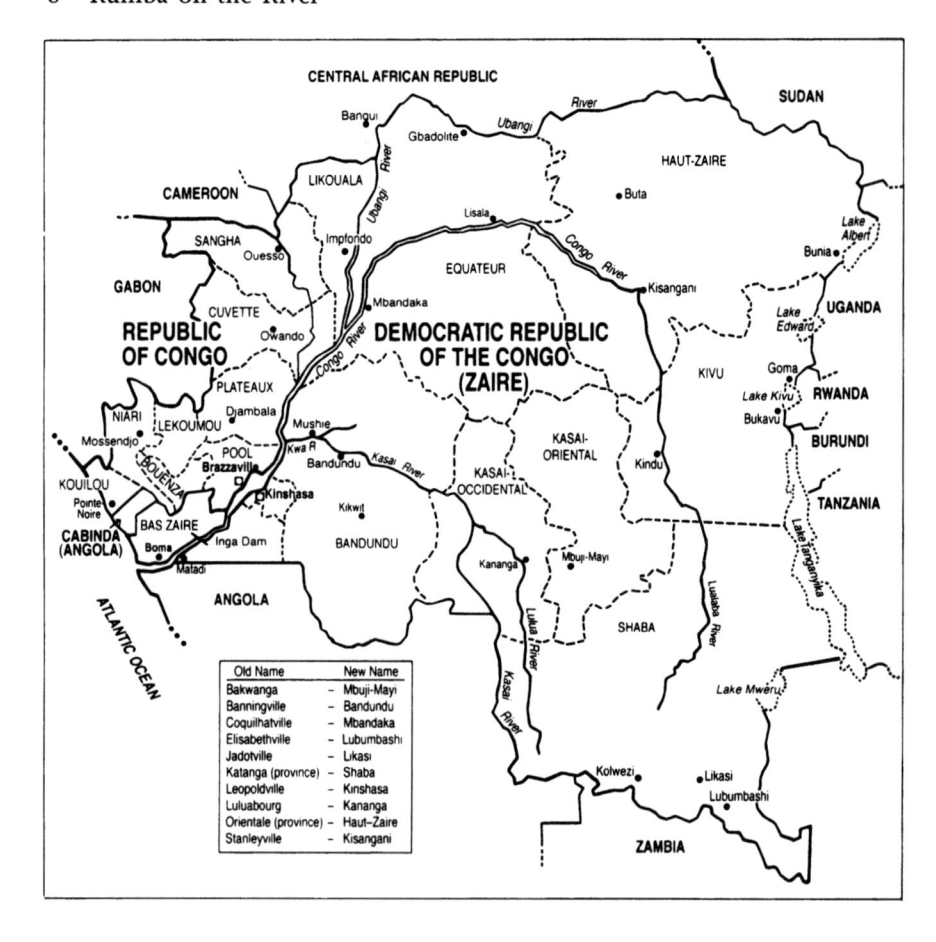

Since assuming power in the Democratic Republic of the Congo, the Kabila government has changed several names bestowed by the Mobutu regime. The province of Bas Zaïre has been changed to Bas Congo. Haut Zaïre has reverted to its original name, Orientale. Shaba Province has reverted to its original name, Katanga. Kivu has been transformed into three provinces, Nord Kivu, Sud Kivu, and Maniema.

French flag fluttering over a hastily built station in the village of N'tamo, soon to become known as Brazzaville.

Shaken and angry that a portion of his pool had been stolen almost from under his nose, Stanley set about securing the south shore for Leopold's Comité d'Etudes from another Téké king named Ngaliema. A large station called Léopoldville was built near the village of Nshasha – Europeanized as Kinshasa. (Stanley would later find he had been bilked by Ngaliema and be forced to renegotiate with Kinshasa's genuine ruler.)

Historians have employed the term 'scramble for Africa' to describe what took place in the 1880s. After some initial hesitation, European politicians began to see Africa, a continent about which they knew almost nothing, as a place where they might play their power games with little or no risk. In September of 1882, Stanley delivered his pact with Ngaliema to Brussels. The French Chamber of Deputies ratified Brazza's treaty with the *makoko* early the next year. Both explorers returned to Africa to consolidate their positions through a new round of treaty negotiation and coercion. These activities alarmed the British, who had augmented territorial claims in western and southern Africa with extensive commercial interests along the Gabonese coast and the lower Congo River. Meanwhile Germany, which for years had scoffed at any talk of colonies, shocked everyone in 1884 by claiming Togo, Cameroon, and South-west Africa. Clearly the scramble was becoming unseemly. To tidy things up, Germany's chancellor, Otto von Bismarck, proposed a conference of the competing powers be held in Berlin.

Fourteen countries, many of which had little or no stake in Africa, answered Bismarck's invitation. The U.S., Russia, and several smaller nations attended as observers, while the major combatants, Britain, France, and Germany, haggled. Unseen in all this, but clearly felt, was the skillful hand of Leopold II, who, although not invited to the conference, manipulated the powers like his personal collection of marionettes. Leopold and his agents and intermediaries had been working for months before the conference, deceiving and dealing the powers one against another until each country's self-interest was revealed to correspond to Leopold's vision. He had reinvented his Comité d'Etudes as the International Association of the Congo, a philanthropic organization dedicated to the suppression of slavery and the preservation of free trade for all nations in the Congo. This new line won Leopold recognition for the Association from the United States. Next he maneuvered France into recognizing his venture by wisely explaining how such an act would keep their British rivals out of central Africa. The British and the Germans, not wanting

France in central Africa any more than the French wanted Britain, also supported Leopold's International Association.

The pieces fell into place as the Berlin West Africa Conference opened in November of 1884. After a few weeks of pleasantries and platitudes about free trade and civilization for Africa, the conference recessed while negotiators hammered out territorial claims in private. Reconvened in February of 1885, the delegates had only to ratify what had been agreed during the recess and paper over a few nagging differences with a nebulous document of diplomatese. With a few pen strokes and the firepower to enforce them, the old nations of Africa were sundered and fused into counterfeit states to be run from the capitals of Europe.

Two Congos were created at Berlin. France had secured Brazza's well-explored Congo territory north and west of Stanley Pool, and Leopold's ambition was fulfilled. Under the guise of philanthropy he had acquired Africa's vast center for his own personal plantation. It would be called the Congo Free State – free from taxes on trade but not from the tyranny of European occupation. What did the Africans think of all this? No one knew or cared. No African had been consulted. None had been invited to the proceedings. Few Africans had heard of Berlin, let alone the conference that would decide their future.

In the ensuing years rubber and ivory brought Leopold a fortune, but Africans and elephants paid the bitter price. Thousands upon thousands of elephants were slaughtered for their valuable tusks. Millions of Africans were enslaved anew to extract the Congo Free State's wealth for Europe. A network of state agents who earned commissions on the collection of ivory and rubber administered the Congo. African soldiers and police enforced the agents' demands. Some Africans went directly from slavery at the hands of the Arabs to that of the Europeans. As political scientist Ali Mazrui put it, 'When Leopold's ambition arrived in the Congo, it was not the natives who needed to be civilized; it was the newly arrived white man.'

Mustering opposition to the horrors of the Congo proved a difficult task, but a few scattered voices were heard in the wilderness. Gradually, at the beginning of the twentieth century, they became a rousing chorus. The solution to the Congo Free State problem was all too obvious, although far short of leaving Africa to the Africans. It had been talked about on and off for years: Belgium should relieve the Congo from Leopold's reign of terror by annexing the territory for itself. Belgium's public and its politicians, wanting no part of any colony, had long resisted such an idea, but British and American pressure, along with internal revulsion at the king's excesses, forced a collective change of mind. On November 15, 1908, Belgium reluctantly took control of the Congo from its discredited sovereign. Leopold died the following year without once setting foot in that faraway land where for twenty-four years he had caused so much misery.

The 900,000 square miles of central Africa Stanley had carved out for the king covered eighty times the area of tiny Belgium. The saddened land sustained an estimated five to six million people of more than 200 national groups, many of whom were cut off from their brothers and sisters by colonialism's illogical, arbitrary boundaries. The remnants of the once proud Kongo Kingdom that Diogo Cão had met now found themselves in territories ruled by Belgium, France, and Portugal.

France combined its central African territories – Congo (called Moyen-Congo or Middle Congo), Gabon, Oubangui-Chari (today's Central African Republic), and Chad – in 1910 to form the Federation of French Equatorial Africa. The new colony was roughly equivalent in size to the Belgian Congo, although more thinly populated. And on the banks of Stanley Pool the small outposts of Brazzaville and Léopoldville grew steadily into modern cities.

•

As the visiting Henri Bowane would soon find out, curfew in Léopoldville's cité indigène was enforced less rigorously than the one imposed on Africans in the whites-only ville. The cité's night life had begun to blossom as more and more people crowded into town. Bars catered to a variety of tastes; they served up beer and live music, or dancing to the sounds of imported records. Even a few adventurous whites went to the cité in search of entertainment. The most popular bars were found in the Kinshasa district near Avenue Prince Baudouin, the main artery which began in the ville at Boulevard Albert I (named for Leopold II's successor) and ran south through the cité to the edge of town near the airport, Sabena Aerodrome. Avenue Baudouin, Kinshasa's lone paved and lighted street, provided the only glimpse of the cité that most Europeans ever got as they drove from Léo East out to the whites-only swimming club on the tiny Funa River.

The Kongo Bar, Siluvangi, Quist, Congo-Moderne, Macauley, and several other bars could all be found within a few blocks of each other just east of the Avenue. This was where Bowane would spend his nights in Léopoldville. It's doubtful he envisioned the prominent role he would play in the development of modern Congo music, but in time Bowane would become a catalyst

12 Rumba on the River

Map legend (boxed):
1. Esengo
2. Golf Club
3. Gombe Cemetery
4. Loningisa
5. MAZADIS
6. Ngoma
7. O.K. Bar
8. Opika
9. Palais du Peuple
10. Palladium
11. Park/Zoo
12. Perruche Bleue
13. Siluvangi Bar
14. Stadium 20 May
15. Type K
16. Un-Deux-Trois
17. Vévé Centre
18. Vis-à-Vis

Old Name / New Name:

Old Name	New Name
Aerodrome Sabena	Aeroport de Ndolo
Av Prince Baudouin	Av President Kasavubu
Av Princesse Charlotte	Av du 24 Novembre
Boulevard Albert I	Boulevard du 30 Juin
Boulevard Leopold III	Boulevard Lumumba
Dendale	Kasavubu
Foncobel	Kimbangu
Kalina	Gombe
Mount Stanley	Mount Ngaliema
Renkin	Matonge
St. Jean	Lingwala
Stanley Pool	Malebo Pool

Millie J. Flory graphics

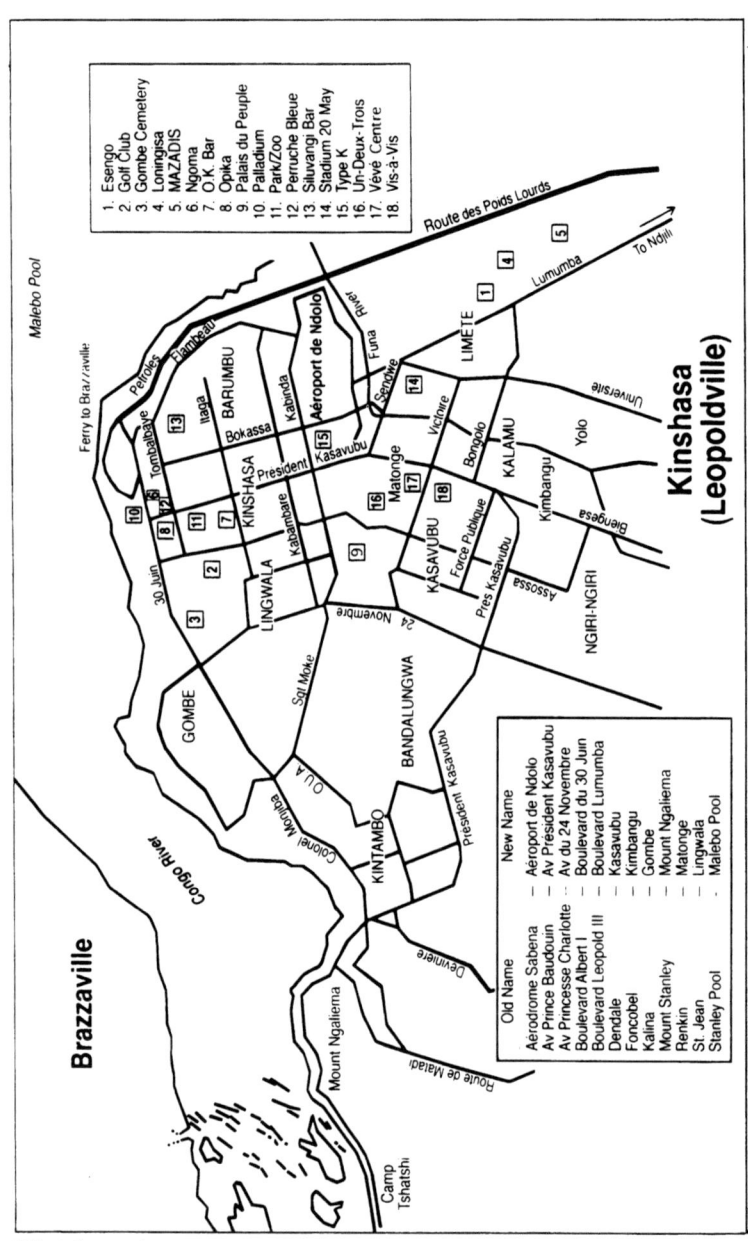

Several names have been changed in Kinshasa (Léopoldville) under the Kabila government. For example, Avenue 24 Novembre, which commemorated Mobutu's coup d'état, has been renamed 17 Mai in honor of Kabila's takeover. Similarly, Stadium 20 May has reverted to its earlier name, Tata Raphael.

whose talent and ambition would help to push music firmly into the realm of commerce. He would fit in nicely with the musical ingredients that had already assembled on the banks of Stanley Pool.

•

A magazine picture from 1904 shows one of the first phonographs in the Belgian Congo. Its spring-driven turntable lies atop a square wooden box with a wind-up crank poking out of the right side. The playing arm, a pickup needle protruding from one end, is mounted on the left side. On top of that sits a large, bell-shaped horn, poised to broadcast the sound extracted from grooves pressed into brittle black platters made of powdered slate and shellac. The first trickle of European classical and religious records which seeped into Africa swelled, in the 1920s and 1930s, to a babbling brook of King Oliver, Louis Armstrong, and the jazz of black America, torch ballads of European charm singers like Tino Rossi, music from other parts of Africa, and the music of Latin America.

'South American music, the records we had here, especially on the GV label, distributed works that Congolese people picked up on right away,' said Guy-Léon Fylla, a musician and painter who came of age as Congo music began to develop. 'They had much more of a taste for this South American music, because [in it] they found their own music.' Those records were part of a series launched in 1933 by the English label His Master's Voice, which brought together recordings made by the American company Victor and England's Gramophone Company – thus, presumably, the GV prefix. (Congolese came up with their own etymology, *grands vocalistes*.) The 10-inch, 78 r.p.m. discs sporting a distinctive magenta label with the famous logo of Nipper the dog, his head cocked listening to a gramophone, presented music of mostly Cuban origin. Early GV recordings by guitarist Miguel Matamoros and his Trio Matamoros, the Sexteto Habanero of Guillermo Castillo and Gerardo Martinez, the more polished Don Azpiazu and his Havana Casino Orchestra, and many others, brought the African-influenced music of Latin America back home.

If the Latin rhythms seemed familiar, so did the language of the vocals. The melodic, rolling vowels of Spanish, especially at the ends of words, sounded like many of the languages on both banks of the Congo River, including the emerging vernacular, Lingala. Whether or not they understood the words, Congolese singers sometimes sang in Spanish, and indeed several learned Spanish basics and wrote their own songs with Spanish lyrics.

14 Rumba on the River

Other foreign instruments had come to central Africa before the new mechanical gadget and its magical spinning discs. Guitars, banjos, horns of all kinds, even organs and pianos, were borne on the backs of African porters toting the baggage of explorers, missionaries and traders. A lieutenant of Stanley's, Edward Pocock, roused the members of one expedition with the call of his bugle – that is, until he succumbed to typhus. Stanley himself often entertained his troops with tunes on his accordion. During a reunion with the *makoko* in 1884, Brazza presented him with a harmonium and a music box. In later years, the colonial armies – Force Publique on the Belgian side, Gendarmerie on the French – mounted European-style brass bands to muster the troops.

Africans soon adopted these new instruments into their own, already impressive, panoply. *Chicago Tribune* reporter Frederick Starr, who visited the Belgian Congo in 1906, observed that

> there are native instruments in plenty, drums of every size and form, from the small hand drum, made by stretching a skin across an earthen pot three or four inches in diameter, up to the great cylindrical, horizontal drum made by hollowing logs a yard in diameter and ten feet long. There are horns, fifes, pipes, and whistles, and a great series of stringed instruments, ranging from the musical bow with but one cord to lutes with ten or twelve.

One instrument that Starr failed to mention, perhaps the most important of all to Congo music, was the thumb piano, found in wide variety throughout most of Africa and known in the two Congos as *likembe* or *sanza*. The likembe consists of a series of keys made of metal strips of varying length mounted on a flat board, or for better resonance a hollowed-out piece of wood or gourd. A player plucks the keys with the thumbs in a fashion that, as music historian John Storm Roberts has pointed out, is remarkably similar to the modern Congolese musician's rhythmic, one-note-at-a-time guitar picking.

Mission schools taught their African students European-style choral and instrumental music for use in the performance of Christian hymns. They discouraged the use of African instruments, which were closely associated with local ritual and often didn't fit the European musical scheme. Missionaries translated the words of standard hymns into African languages, with varying degrees of success. Best results were achieved when they composed new hymns based in the local culture. Some set their sacred texts to melodies of indigenous folk songs; others wrote words in local languages first and then composed music to fit so as not to violate the tonal qualities of the language.

Difficult delivery 15

On the heels of explorers, missionaries, and colonial administrators, another group of foreigners, Africans from Dahomey (today's Benin), Gold Coast (Ghana), Sierra Leone, and other colonies along the west coast, moved into central Africa in the 1920s and 1930s. They worked as dock-hands and teachers, and staffed the Congolese branches of European trading firms like Ollivant and Lever that had first established themselves in West Africa. Stuffed in their baggage was their own array of musical instruments, including the guitars of Europe which they had already embraced.

Since many of these African 'foreigners' came from the towns of Grand Popo and Petit Popo on the Dahoman coast, the Congolese called them *popo*, or by the English term *coastmen*. Many of the coastmen lived together in a neighborhood at Léopoldville's east end called Citas (the acronym for Compagnie Industrielle et de Transports au Stanley Pool, a Belgian company operating at the port which employed many of the coastmen). Away from their day jobs, they organized parties for their own amusement that quickly attracted the attention of Congolese on both sides of the river.

Many an aspiring Congolese musician learned the trade by mimicking foreign songs and instrumental styles. The coastmen could be observed first hand at a neighborhood bar called the Siluvangi. Some of them took the time to show their Congolese friends how to play. Imported records could be listened to over and over while a nascent guitarist or trumpeter played along. According to Guy-Léon Fylla, unintelligible English or Spanish lyrics were replaced by words in Kikongo or Lingala or some other of the local languages to fit the melody. 'El Manicero' (the peanut vendor), a song from the GV series that enjoyed immense popularity, might become 'Eh Marie' as Congolese musicians composed their own stories to fit the music. People learned to play imported instruments and imported music, but they also listened to their own songs again. This, said Fylla, was how traditional elements worked their way into the music. 'He tries it out on his instrument. But with the transformation that he's already had from listening to French melodies, American melodies ... it makes quite a salad up there in your head.'

Early forms of indigenous entertainment included the agbaya, a dance favored by members of many of the ethnic groups who had migrated to Léopoldville. Agbaya gatherings featured dancing to the accompaniment of likembes, drums, and other percussion instruments. Similar to agbaya in its multi-ethnic appeal was the kebo, a dance popular among women and girls. Participants often danced single-file, each holding the shoulders of the woman in front of her and singing in unison to percussion accompaniment.

GV series label

The 1920s saw the rise of maringa, a music style attributed variously to the Katanga region of southeastern Belgian Congo and Loango on the French Congolese coast. The maringa, played with likembe or accordion, a square frame drum called patenge, and a bottle, also lacked a clear ethnic identity, which hastened its spread. Musicologist Herbert Pepper described it as being 'more openly Europeanized' than its predecessor, malinga (so named for another type of frame drum), because the maringa included accordion and 'rhythms borrowed from fandangos, polkas, schottisches; Protestant hymns or military marches; its subject any local event, past or current.' Other imported dances like the French quadrille found some favor, and along with the polka from Bohemia via France came its more staccato variant, the polka piqué.

The confluence at Stanley Pool of indigenous African music, Afro-Spanish songs brought home to Africa on records, and European music of colonial French and French-speaking Belgians, recalled turn-of-the-century New Orleans and the mixing of African, Afro-Spanish, and French musical elements into jazz. Both new musical forms employed instruments of European origin. Where jazz evolved on the pianos, brass, and woodwinds of America's dominant European culture, modern Congolese music embraced the guitar, the instrument that played and sounded closest to the lutes and likembes of traditional African music. Brass bands marched on both banks of the Congo, and even a few pianos survived the tropical humidity. But the budding musicians of Léo and Brazza for the most part chose the guitar.

•

As Africans assimilated European forms of music, dance, religion, wage labor, and the rest, they couldn't escape the baggage of their colonial rulers' politics. The scramble for Africa had been only a preview of Europe's economic and territorial rivalries. In 1914 and again in 1939, those simmering conflicts exploded into world wars. The outbreaks of fighting in Europe produced additional burdens in the colonies.

Africans in the French Congo were recruited for the armies of the Allies and the zinc and lead mines of the Compagnie Minière du Congo Français. Men, women, and children mobilized for cultivation and harvest. Small factories sprang up to produce soap, shoes, cement, matches, and other essentials. The Congo–Ocean railway from Brazzaville to the Atlantic coast, built with forced labor after World War I, rushed food crops, palm oil, lumber, cotton, and ore to the Allied ships that choked the harbor at Pointe Noire during World War II.

In the Belgian Congo, Africans and Europeans alike were enlisted to fight alongside the Allies in both wars. Colonial administrators expanded their policy that required rural Congolese to cultivate the land. In the mineral-rich southern province of Katanga, the Belgian mining company Union Minière du Haut Katanga intensified its extraction of tin, copper, and other strategic materials. To the north, the mines of Kivu and Orientale provinces contributed millions of dollars in gold to the war efforts. The rubber harvest was pushed to its limit. Manufacturing plants opened, and the railroads clattered with produce-laden freight cars. By 1944 the Belgian Congo boasted factories for the smelting of copper and production of textiles, sugar, and wood products for export. Others manufactured consumer goods for local consumption.

Mass mobilization of Africans for the two war efforts only deepened the dislocation of what was left of traditional life. What was initially a smattering of people leaving the burdens forced upon them in the countryside grew into a multitude. Léopoldville – the small village of Kinshasa in Stanley's time – had grown by the end of World War II into a city of 100,000 people. Brazzaville – tiny N'tamo with a handful of people when Brazza first planted the French flag – contained nearly 70,000, perhaps one-tenth of the French

Congo's entire population. 'The growth is so rapid that, at best, the native quarters look like villages which have suddenly contracted elephantiasis, and more commonly resemble camps with an endless stream of new arrivals,' wrote French anthropologist Georges Balandier in the late fifties. These burgeoning cities

> bear witness less to a civilization than to its absence. In the confusion and uncertainty, ethnic groups collide and customs tend to erase each other like overlapping waves. Here Negro citizens camp in the hope of attaining wealth which the industrial powers distribute only sparingly, and many must be content to catch the crumbs and leftovers that fall their way.

Still, growing numbers of Africans found jobs in the cities, and as they did the consumer goods of Europe became more affordable. Musical instruments, guitars and horns, and the new technological marvels, radios, gramophones, and records, were high on the list of desirability. Soon the sounds of Europe, America, and, more importantly, Latin America permeated Congolese cities. African rhythms exported on slave ships echoed from the grooves of 78 r.p.m. records and crackling radio loudspeakers. Africans in the two Congos embraced them like a kidnapped offspring suddenly released from captivity.

A club of Europeans founded the first radio station in Brazzaville in 1935, a low-power transmitter that became an early voice of the Free French in 1940. By 1943, in government hands and refurbished with 50-kilowatt transmitters, Radio Brazzaville could broadcast to occupied France and around the world.

Léopoldville got its first station in 1937 when the rector of the city's Albert College launched Radio Léo. Two years later a second station known as Congolia took to the air. Congolia was owned by a businessman and radio enthusiast named Jean Hourdebise who dealt in film production and projection equipment and later ran the Albertum Cinema. Unlike Radio Léo, whose broadcasts were limited to Sundays and holidays and largely aimed at Europeans, Congolia broadcast daily programs in French and four local languages: Lingala, Swahili, Kikongo, and Tshiluba. Congolia augmented its listenership in the African cité, where most residents couldn't afford radios, by installing loudspeakers at several public locations so people could hear the broadcasts. Imported jazz and pop records – especially the popular Latin GV series – made up a sizeable portion of the station's programing, but time was allotted for local talent as well. Every Sunday groups of musicians would gather at the station to record songs for later broadcast.

Difficult delivery 19

Hourdebise's idea of recording Africans for an African audience was a relatively new one. Whatever recording that had taken place in central Africa up to this point had largely been done for white consumption, often as scholarly research or cultural preservation. But as Congolia's success demonstrated, there was, not surprisingly, an African audience for African music. Léopoldville's merchants, hoping to attract additional customers, paid to become patrons of certain programs in order to have the names of their firms announced on the air.

During World War II, Radio Congo Belge was set up in Léopoldville to relay programs from the British Broadcasting Corporation, the voice of the Allies, back home to occupied Belgium. (The Germans found short-wave broadcasts from faraway Léopoldville more difficult to jam than those emanating from London.) Later in the war a new, more powerful station, Radiodiffusion Nationale Belge, assumed this function, and Radio Congo Belge began to program for the colony. By playing foreign records, and in Congolia's case music recorded locally, the Belgian stations and Radio Brazzaville contributed to the critical mix of music taking shape on the banks of the Congo River.

Most early, non-traditional Congolese musicians worked alone, moving from place to place to play guitar, mandolin, banjo, or accordion and sing for free drinks or pocket change. But toward the end of the thirties, bands – known by the French term *orchestre* – began to form. The coastmen organized a group in Léopoldville called Orchestre Excelsior, named for an old Ghanaian band that had begun in Accra in the early 1900s, which in turn was the namesake of a New Orleans brass band. A Frenchman from the Antilles named Jean Réal came to Brazzaville with the French military around the beginning of World War II and pulled several local guitarists together into a band called Congo Rumba. Singers also pooled their talents in a rapidly multiplying array of vocal groups.

Albert Loboko of Brazzaville played piano, guitar, mandolin, banjo and saxophone, and possessed a voice to match his prodigious instrumental talent. He liked to organize dance parties where he would play and sing accompanied by another musician who tapped out rhythms on an empty bottle. In 1939 Loboko put together an all-woman vocal ensemble called Bonne Espérance (good hope) and recruited another talented singer named Paul Kamba away from his job as a clerk for a mining company in western French Congo to manage the group.

Kamba stayed with his mentor for little more than two years before he stoked the fires of competition by striking out on his own. Around 1942 he created an all-male vocal group called Victoria Brazza, whose music and words so captivated music lovers on both sides of the river that, according to Guy-Léon Fylla, 'We even said he made a pact with the devil to create his works.'

Brazzavilleans were separated by race when it came to housing. A tiny enclave of whites found itself sandwiched between the exploding African quarters of Poto-Poto and Bacongo. In general, however, Africans and Europeans mixed easily without the attitude of animosity and the irritant of curfews that prevailed among their neighbors in Léopoldville. Paul Kamba's domain was Poto-Poto, an area of mixed African classes and ethnicities on the northeast side of the city's white *ville*. Southwest of the *ville* the more homogeneous Bacongo, largely inhabited by the Lari subgroup of the Kongo people, had its own musical king in the person of Bernard Massamba, better known as 'Lebel.' Massamba Lebel and his mentor François Bamanabio triggered a crosstown rivalry by forming their own powerful vocal group called Jazz Bohème.

All these groups played weddings, funerals, and private parties for whatever fees could be negotiated, plus *matabisi* (tips) from appreciative partygoers. Songs composed specific to the occasion, for the couple to be wed or in honor of the deceased, were interspersed with each group's more general repertoire of songs of satire and social commentary. The singers animated their performances with small *tam-tams* (drums), maracas, bottles, and scrapers. By the mid-forties Brazzaville was awash with live music.

While Brazzaville advanced its vocal groups, Léopoldville championed instrumental bands. One of the first was the combo belonging to accordionist Camille Feruzi. At home in Stanleyville more than a thousand miles up-river, Feruzi learned from his father how to play maringas on the accordion. In the late twenties, the teenaged Feruzi boarded a riverboat bound for Léopoldville. A decade later, around 1938 or 1939, his quartet, featuring accordion, piano, guitar, and saxophone, made its debut. Prompted, perhaps, by its Guadeloupean saxophone player, the group began to replace the familiar maringas with subtly swinging rumbas from Latin America.

•

The 'rumbas' heard in the two Congos were actually a Cuban style known as *son*. The real rumba had developed in nineteenth-century Cuba among slaves from West and central Africa. Several variations evolved, all of which coupled drums and other percussion instruments with call-and-response singing between a leader and chorus. One of the more popular variants, the *guaguancó*, served, in the words of Cuban journalist Leonardo Acosta, 'as a social chronicle of the dispossessed.' But above all the rumba was born to be danced. In the guaguancó, couples performed a pantomime of sexual seduction closely resembling the *yuka* fertility dance found in parts of central Africa. Latter-day orchestrated ballroom versions which enthralled devotees to the north bore little resemblance to the boisterous sensuality of the original. Musicologist Charley Gerard points out that the ballroom version was often spelled "rhumba with an H" to distinguish it from the rhythmically volatile and percussive music.'

The *son*, on the other hand, married African call-and-response singing, percussion, and thumb piano – the latter called *marimbula* in Cuba – with an indigenous, guitar-like instrument of Spanish descent called the *tres*. Songs were more structured, and the instrumentation produced a melodic feel closer to what is termed 'modern' music. By the 1930s, when the *sones* (plural of *son*) of the Sexteto Habanero came to Africa on the GV series records, the band's line-up featured string bass in place of the marimbula, a guitar in tandem with the tres, hand drums, maracas, and claves. This style, which the Congolese began to incorporate, also came to be known as 'rumba.'

It is difficult to pinpoint how the naming confusion arose. Mexico's Eduardo Llerenas, who has spent a quarter-century collecting *sones* for his Corason label, attributes it to mis-labeling by record companies. Don Azpiazu's version of 'El Manicero' – issued as part of the GV series under its English title 'The Peanut Vendor' – bore the description 'Rumba Fox-trot' on its label, for example. But many other GV releases are correctly marked *son*. It may be that music consumers, Congolese and otherwise, simply liked the nearly onomatopoeic *rumba*, whose very utterance seemed to command the hips to move. After all, to the French-speaking Congolese (and to Spanish speakers too), *son* simply meant the bland, generic word *sound*. Whatever the cause, Congolese began to lump all Cuban music under the rumba rubric in much the same way that we have come to call the many styles of Congolese popular music 'soukous.' Congolese musicians temporarily experimented with the biguine, merengue, and the rest that Latin America offered, but the rumba would soon win over them and their followers. 'The rumba,' one journalist remarked, 'seems to be the dance which most reveals the African soul.'

•

Following the lead of Camille Feruzi, a group of Belgian Congolese musicians formed Orchestre Odéon Kinois in the mid 1940s. Other bands sprang up around the same time – Orchestre Americain, named in honor of a nearby

American military encampment; Orchestre Martiniquais, saluting the soldiers of the French Antilles; and Orchestre Kasongo, named for its leader, saxophonist Antoine Kasongo. These were mostly brass bands of saxophone, trumpet, tuba, and trombone along with some percussion – maracas, a small drum, or a bottle. They played polkas, interpretations of American and Caribbean songs, and their own compositions, which echoed these foreign styles.

Daily steamers chugging between the two capitals fostered a growing musical commerce. Paul Kamba took his Victoria Brazza to Léopoldville. Odéon Kinois returned the honor by playing its own engagements in Brazzaville. These exchanges gave birth to imitators on both sides of the river. One of Brazzaville's leading intellectuals, Emmanuel Dadet, created an instrumental group called Melo-Congo, while in Léopoldville singer Antoine 'Wendo' Kolosoyi formed a vocal group he called Victoria Kin. All these bands were made up of amateur musicians in the sense that few of them played exclusively to earn a living. Most had day jobs as clerks or mechanics or drivers and pursued their musical careers only at night and weekends.

Wendo and Kamba were the musicians whom Henri Bowane saw on his first trip to Léopoldville in 1946. 'They gave me the taste for music,' he declared. 'When they performed they wore jackets and baggy trousers and carried a white streamer in their hands.... I imported their stage outfits and the songs I learned [to Coquilhatville].' Bowane started his own group, Victoria Coquilhatville, to re-create for the home-town public what he had seen. Nearly three years later, by then an accomplished musician, he would repeat the river journey to the capital, this time with the intention of staying.

2
Why don't you make a record?

Olympia, Ngoma, Opika, and Loningisa, 1946–1950

Reflecting on the presence of his fellow Greeks in the world's farthest corners a Congo veteran once remarked, 'We like to say that when the Americans went to the moon and climbed out of their spaceship, they found a Greek guy standing there in front of his taverna.' In that spirit many Greeks had come to the Congo, beginning in King Leopold's time, and stayed on to build their lives and businesses far removed from the political and economic turmoil of Europe. One person would arrive, get established, then send home for friends and relatives. Nearly every Congolese city on the Belgian side had residents from particular regions of Greece. Old hands could tell by people's names what part of the Congo they lived in and where in Greece they had come from. Greeks worked for the mines, in agriculture, set up commercial enterprises, and during the boom following World War II they established most of Léopoldville's first recording studios.

In 1930 as the Great Depression settled over the United States and began to infect the nations of Europe, Nicolas Jeronimidis left his family in Alexandria and set out for the Belgian Congo. A short, compact man with a flair for business, Jeronimidis had been born in Egypt to parents of Greek extraction who had emigrated from the island of Cyprus. Now, at the age of twenty seven, he headed down the Nile through Wadi Halfa and Khartoum to where real money could be found, the gold mines of Kilo-Moto not far from the town of Bunia and the western shores of Lake Albert. Jeronimidis quickly mastered the mode of trading in eastern Congo and contracted with

Kilo-Moto to furnish the mines with an assortment of supplies. By 1934 his Bunia-based business had grown to the point where he no longer needed the mines. He sent for his younger brother Alexandros, in Egypt, to come help operate Firme Jeronimidis, a thriving enterprise engaged in the import and wholesale of a wide range of manufactured goods from Europe and Japan.

Leaving Alexandros in charge in Bunia, Nicolas moved to Léopoldville following the end of World War II to take advantage of the boom that had begun to develop in the mushrooming capital. He settled into a large building on Avenue Beernaert in Léo East, just off Boulevard Albert I and a convenient walk down Avenue Prince Baudouin for Congolese customers from the cité. But Nico Jeronimidis had more than run-of-the-mill trading on his mind. He had fallen in love with the songs of traditional musicians he had heard at the mines and in the streets of Bunia. 'My brother ... liked music a lot,' Alexandros Jeronimidis recalled. 'He had recorded some African music for his own pleasure. He played the recorded music for some friends who said to him that that was something that would likely interest a lot of people. "Why don't you make a record?"'

One such venture had already demonstrated the idea's feasibility. At the end of World War II, with travel between Belgium and the Congo once again unimpeded, a Belgian entrepreneur named Fernand Janssens had come to Léopoldville with a portable, direct-to-disc recording machine. Janssens owned a company called Société Belge du Disque (SOBEDI), whose labels, Olympia and Novelty, issued records by a number of European, mostly Belgian, musicians. With another Belgian, a Mr. Patou, in charge, SOBEDI technicians toured the colony recording traditional groups and a few of the emerging modern musicians. The acetate masters were then shipped to the SOBEDI factory in Ghent for pressing into 78 r.p.m. records as part of Olympia's new African series.

By 1948, the Olympia catalog contained some 200 records by scores of artists, including a choir from the Force Publique, the Chanteurs à la Croix de Cuivre (singers of the copper cross, from the mines in Katanga), Antoine Wendo and his Victoria Kin, Orchestre Odéon Kinois, and Camille Feruzi, along with a twenty-lesson Lingala language course. Although Olympia's African series appeared to have been conceived for consumption by whites in Belgium, records on Olympia and its associated labels, Kongo Bina and Lomeka, were shipped back to the Congo, where they enjoyed considerable popularity. This experiment confirmed what the entrepreneur Jean Hourdebise

Nicolas Jeronimidis

had discovered with his Congolia radio station: there was indeed a market for African music among urban, working-class Africans.

Olympia's success and the marked increase in sales of gramophones and records – closely linked to Léopoldville's population explosion – made the opening of a recording studio seem like a sensible risk. Nico Jeronimidis emptied a small storage building behind his shop and covered its interior walls with soundproofing material. He ordered a professional direct-to-disc recording machine and microphones from the United States, installing them in the building with the help of a friend from one of the city's radio stations (possibly Hourdebise). Jeronimidis called his new studio Ngoma, the Kikongo word for drum.

'We had, of course, auditioned several musicians and chose those we believed to be the best,' said Alexandros Jeronimidis, who had left Bunia to join his brother in Léopoldville. The studio tried to record traditional music, but transporting the troupes into town and paying large numbers of musicians proved to be too costly. Besides, the new recording technology seemed ill suited to traditional music. The bands, who in the village sometimes played for hours without stopping, were just getting warmed up when, three minutes after they had started, the recorder's cutter head hit the center of the disc. Smaller, more modern groups suited recording technology better, because their songs were more easily tailored to fit the medium's limits. The three-minutes-or-less format forced a tighter structure and stricter discipline on the newly evolving pop music and seemed a good match for the European-style, workaday world of the city.

A few months after Ngoma's 1948 opening, Nicolas Jeronimidis met Henri Bowane. Bowane had settled into the *cité* sometime in 1949 following his second journey down-river from Coquilhatville. He was now a lean twenty-year-old with an amiable disposition and the apparent skills of a diplomat, both of which served to blunt the barbs awaiting a black man in colonial Léopoldville. Armed with a repertoire of original compositions, improving guitar-picking skills, and a more than adequate voice, he sang his songs from time to time on Radio Congo Belge. The radio exposure earned him a number of admirers and a shot at making a record. 'I went to knock at Ngoma's door,' he recalled.

> I went into the studio and recorded some songs. But as I didn't know how to handle the guitar very well my boss asked me to call on an expert. The only guitar virtuoso I knew at the time was Wendo, but he was traveling. Upon his return I went to introduce him to Ngoma.

Wendo was the tall, bushy-haired musician Bowane had seen on his first visit to Léopoldville three years earlier. His real name was Antoine Kolosoyi, and he had come to Léopoldville in the early forties from Mushie, his birthplace on the Kwa River, a tributary of the Congo 150 miles up-river from the capital. To earn his living he traveled the colony on riverboats working as a mechanic and buying and selling goods on the side to supplement his salary.

As Wendo told it, his mother, who had died when he was a young boy, came to him in a dream and said, 'You're going to play the guitar.' He took

Antoine 'Wendo' Kolosoyi in a publicity shot from Ngoma in the early fifties

the message to heart, learning first on a friend's guitar and then playing his own for audiences along the course of his riverboat journeys. He composed songs about everyday life in the country's various regions, most of which he had visited, and in the words of a colleague, 'about women who didn't want to respect their husbands.' Sometime during the years of World War II, he formed the band Victoria Kin, an echo of Paul Kamba's Victoria Brazza.

In his early twenties, shortly after the war's end, Wendo sang on Radio Congolia, a break that spread his popularity still further. Next, Olympia's Mr. Patou came calling. Wendo recorded a dozen solo sides for the label and twenty more with Victoria Kin. But his first big success came in the company of Henri Bowane.

Wendo and Bowane complemented each other. Bowane, in spite of his modest self-assessment, possessed a special flair for the guitar, Wendo the superior voice. Each possessed a gift for musical composition, a quality not lost on Nicolas Jeronimidis. He signed them both to contracts.

According to some who worked at Ngoma, musicians under contract received a monthly salary for their exclusive services plus three or four hundred Belgian francs (six to eight dollars) for each composition that was recorded. 'At that time we would buy the rights,' explained Nikiforos Cavvadias, a brother-in-law to Jeronimidis who handled the company's legal affairs. 'We paid an amount, and they signed a document saying that they were assigning all rights to us.' Coming at a time when the daily minimum wage had only reached the equivalent of twenty-two cents (U.S.) in 1946 and wouldn't climb to one dollar until 1959, six to eight dollars for a song looked like good money to most musicians. Other house musicians who backed up the principal artist on a recording would be paid accompanists' fee in addition to their salaries. 'I don't know how many of my records were sold,' Wendo said. 'My publisher just told me, "If you need money, go to the cashier." He bought me a whole pile of stuff and even a car and a house. I wondered just how much my work was worth.'

Wendo and Bowane worked together at Ngoma for nearly a year recording several songs, including the massive hit 'Marie-Louise.' Those old enough to remember say the song 'brought the spirits out of the cemetery to listen.' When Wendo and Bowane played the local bars, 'even the sick got up to go dancing.' 'Marie-Louise,' a joint composition with Wendo on vocals accompanied by Bowane's guitar, tells of Wendo's love for a woman whose father does not approve of him as a potential son-in-law. Bowane also takes a turn on vocals to offer advice:

> Wendo, you talk for nothing
> We have our car
> We have our guitars
> We have our voices
> We are going to run away with her to Kingabwa.

'Yoka sebene,' listen to the sebene, Bowane cries as he launches into a guitar solo. Almost on the strength of that one small command in one of the era's most popular songs, the word *sebene* (pronounced say-ben) came to be synonymous with an extended instrumental bridge. Sebene, according to several Congolese musicians, originated with the coastmen. While the singer

Ngoma catalog cover

rested, the guitarists liked to work the seventh chord into their solos and would often cry 'seven' to signal each other. Congolese musicians repeated the word as 'sebene.' Others place the sebene's origins farther back in transitional genres like the *kebo*. According to them, the part where most of the dancing occurred was called the sebene. Indeed, at least one Lingala dictionary defines 'sebene' as dance, but it can't be said with certainty when the word entered the language. Whatever its origins, sebene became the name of Congo music's extended instrumental sections, more generous during live performances when the musicians were free from the time constraints of recording technology.

'Marie-Louise' and a follow-up called 'Nato Mama' bumped Wendo and Bowane to the top of Ngoma's expanding roster of talent. Paul Kamba and his Victoria Brazza crossed the river to make their first recordings at Ngoma. Jeronimidis also signed accordionist Camille Feruzi and several singer-guitarists: Manoka De Saio, Adou Elenga, and Léon Bukasa, along with Manuel D'Oliveira and Georges Edouard who formed a band called San Salvador.

The Ngoma studio flourished as the war years receded from memory and the boom of the late forties beckoned confidently to a new decade. Brazzaville's population nearly doubled from some 45,000 in 1940 to around 84,000 in 1950. Léopoldville leaped from 50,000 to over 200,000 during the same period. Flush with new immigrants who had jobs and money in their pockets, the twin capitals brimmed with possibilities for the business and pleasure of an entertainment industry.

Bowane, for one, could see the prospects. 'He was a star,' said his friend Guy-Léon Fylla. 'He was like a beautiful woman, courted by everyone. The heart belongs to the highest bidder. The person who pays the most gets the woman.' But Bowane was not above doing some courting of his own. He watched as two cousins named Papadimitriou successfully established their dry goods business on Avenue Charles de Gaulle just across Fernand de Bock Park from the *cité*.

Basile Papadimitriou, a skinny, dark-haired boy from Macedonia, had followed the African trail blazed by his relatives. In July of 1938, as Hitler's Germany began to threaten the rest of Europe, fifteen-year-old Basile boarded ship for a crossing of the Mediterranean to Alexandria. From there he caught a train to Cairo and followed the Nile to Juba in southern Sudan. Together with some Greek compatriots, he crossed the border into the Belgian Congo for a reunion with his cousin Athanase in Bambili, a hundred or so miles from the town of Buta.

Athanase had come to the Congo the previous year to take up employment with a well-established older cousin. Basile moved easily into the business, working at its shop in Dembia selling cloth and other supplies and learning Lingala. The cousins worked together in the Dembia–Dakwa–Bambili area until 1942, when Basile and Athanase moved to nearby Buta to form their own wholesale and retail dry goods company, A. & B. Papadimitriou. As business improved they relocated to the larger city of Stanleyville, and, following the end of World War II, moved on to Léopoldville. It was in the capital in 1950 that the cousins Papadimitriou met Henri Bowane.

The A. & B. Papadimitriou company specialized in selling *lipopela*, wrap-

Athanase Papadimitriou (left) and his cousin Basile Papadimitriou at Buta in eastern Congo in the 1940s

skirt cloth for women, also popularly known by the French *pagne*. The Papadimitrious' exclusive designs, imported from Holland, England, Switzerland, France, and Japan, gave them an edge on the competition. According to Basile, Bowane approached him one day. 'He asked me why we didn't also handle Congolese music publishing like the other publishers did.... I thought it over with my cousin Athanase, and we decided to consider the matter.' Apart from business considerations and Bowane's powers of persuasion, Basile 'loved music, having had mandolin lessons when I was young in Greece, and having learned to play accordion by myself when I was selling in the store in Dakwa.' The cousins agreed to open their own recording studio in a new part of town called Foncobel. The Kinshasa district of the cité had become so crowded that the Belgians had split it into three administrative districts, St. Jean, Kinshasa, and Barumbu, and were presently hard at work laying out a completely new cité south of the old one to handle the influx from the countryside. Foncobel, where the new recording studio was constructed, lay just west of the Funa River about a mile south of the Sabena Aerodrome.

The Papadimitrious called their studio Loningisa from the Lingala *ningisa*, which means to shake or to move. The name, Basile explained, was coined by Bowane, who officially left the company of Wendo and Ngoma to help launch the new enterprise. 'It means a human being or a band which by its actions can become a disturbance, for evil or for good, depending on the case. Loningisa disturbed the dancers, the listeners, on the dance floor or in the yards of their houses.' In a deal with Fernand Janssens, SOBEDI furnished the recording equipment and pressed the finished 78 r.p.m. records at its factory in Ghent. Loningisa recorded its first songs direct to acetate discs on September 1, 1950.

The Papadimitrious provided money, equipment, and marketing. Bowane recruited much of the talent. He brought in a young singer-guitarist named Honoré Liengo, three women singers called Les Trois Amies, and contributed his own considerable musical skills. Among Loningisa's first releases came Bowane's 'Liwa' (death), a lively rumination on human mortality. The record labels the song a polka piqué, but it sounds a lot like the old maringas (which borrowed from the polka piqué). A chorus of predominantly female voices responds to the call of Bowane's lead vocal while he plays his guitar in tandem with a guitar accompanist. A patenge drum or an empty packing box struck with a fist or a mallet supplies a steady bass line side by side with the rhythm of a struck bottle. Another song, 'Kotiya Zolo Te' (don't mess around with us), has Bowane singing in unison with a chorus touting the group's prowess on the dance floor. Bowane and an accompanist strum the guitar lines backed by maracas, a scraper, and what sounds like two wood blocks of differing pitch each contributing a separate rhythm. When word of the new studio spread, would-be professional musicians flocked to Foncobel in hopes of gaining an audition. Ngoma began to feel Loningisa's heat.

In studios like Ngoma and Loningisa, urbanization and commerce combined to transform the communal music of the village into a saleable commodity created and performed by professionals who were paid salaries like teachers or drivers or the clerks who pushed the papers of business and the colonial apparatus. And more than any other element, apart from the musicians' own curiosity and creativity, the studios forced the music to modernize. Records had to be sold to pay salaries and generate profits. Economics demanded new songs and experimentation to create variety. Studios imported other instruments to augment the guitars and accordions of the first wave of modernization. 'We had all the musical instruments sent from France,' Alexandros Jeronimidis said.

> We already had a piano, and we had all the wind instruments, all of them. We imported [acoustic] guitars from Germany, I think, but that was the business side. We sold guitars. But for our musicians we had better guitars sent from France. And the wind instruments were Selmer.

An increasing stream of new releases reduced a record's shelf life to the span of a few weeks or at most a few months. Records were a disposable commodity to be enjoyed only until new replacements arrived in the shops. It didn't hurt that the brittle 78s were easily broken or their songs grooved into unrecognizability by repeated spins under the gramophone's heavy needle. Traditional music could still be heard in the streets of Léo and Brazza, but the rising class of urban Congolese workers eagerly adopted the newfangled music of the studios.

Ngoma and Loningisa weren't alone in pushing the new music. In Léo East, around the same time that Bowane and Wendo first got together, two brothers said to have come from the Greek island of Rhodes had opened yet another studio. Like their compatriots, Gabriel Moussa Benetar and his brother Joseph had come to the Belgian Congo to do business. They set up a successful trading firm on Avenue Baron Van Eetvelde near the park, and, eyeing the brothers Jeronimidis and their achievements at Ngoma, founded their own studio around 1949. They called it Opika, from the Lingala expression *opika pende*, resist or stand firm, as if to say, 'When we come to you with our guitars, you'd better be prepared.'

Closely resembling Ngoma in size, Opika occupied a room about the equivalent of a medium-sized parlor. At one end the musicians would arrange themselves around a large microphone which fed the music to a recording machine set up at the other. But what Opika lacked in technological pizazz it made up with an unparalleled stable of talent. Wendo carried the Ngoma banner. Bowane was building Loningisa. But Opika boasted a promising young singer named Joseph Kabasele and the era's greatest star, Jhimmy 'The Hawaiian.'

3
The brains of the music

Jhimmy, Kabasele, and African Jazz, 1950–1955

Barely twenty years old, the slight, nattily dressed youth tooled around Léopoldville on his big Norton motorcycle looking for all the world like the rude-boy protagonist from the Jamaican film *The Harder They Come*. But this was 'Jhimmy Too Bad,' not 'Johnny,' and he brandished a guitar instead of a gun. As 1949 dissolved into 1950, he captured the crown of Congolese pop.

The Benetars had lucked out. They had signed this kid Zacharie Elenga from Brazzaville, who called himself 'Jhimmy' with an h, almost as soon as they'd opened the doors of their new Opika studio. He came complete with star-quality attractiveness, compelling compositions, and a penchant for picking solo displays on his acoustic guitar the likes of which had never been heard before. Jhimmy strung his guitar with two E strings, the second in place of the normal D string. Since Congolese musicians prefer solmization to letter names for notes, E was mi, and the tuning scheme came to be known as the *mi-composé*. Jhimmy clamped a homemade capo at the fourth fret to raise the pitch, and when he played, picking the strings with thumb and forefinger, he produced a distinctive natural vibrato that made him the envy of other guitarists. He called his style 'Hawaiian,' and although it had little in common with authentic Hawaiian music, his fans accepted the label. He sang about women like 'Henriette' and 'Marie Lompengo' and praised himself in 'Na Kombo ya Jhimmy Putulu,' literally sweep Jhimmy's dust (because he's so good).

Because of his education, Jhimmy was regarded as an intellectual by Congolese musicians and their followers. Born in Brazzaville to a Congolese father and a mother from the Oubangui-Chari territory to the north, he had attended seminary for a time with the aim of becoming a priest. Rumor had it that the fathers had kicked him out, which explained his return to Brazzaville, where he worked for a short time as an office clerk. But music filled his head, and the spirited new recordings of Wendo and Bowane from studios across the river held out the tantalizing notion that one needn't work an office job in order to earn a living.

At Opika Jhimmy joined a small but talented group of young musicians. Guitarists Georges Doula, Albert Yamba-Yamba, and François 'Gobi' Boyimbo; singer Paul Mwanga; and percussion player Etienne 'Baskis' Diluvila had been among the first to sign on with Opika. When he played for parties, Jhimmy usually performed as a one-man-band, singing, playing his guitar, and making the sounds of rhythm instruments with his mouth. But in the studio he could call on other musicians to fill out his sound. Paul Mwanga added a harmonic second voice. Gobi's guitar accompaniment meshed nicely with Jhimmy's lead. Baskis buttressed the mix on percussion, especially maracas.

Jhimmy's recordings created a sensation on both banks of the river. His was music for the young, vigorous and brash. 'Jhimmy revolutionized the music,' declared Jean Serge Essous, a teenager during Jhimmy's era. 'The music Jhimmy played is the music people play today.... The current style they're doing now, with the cries [of animation] and all that, Jhimmy did that fifty years ago.' Opika's sales boomed. The Benetars rewarded Jhimmy with the big Norton cycle on which he shamelessly cruised the main streets of Léo, much to the delight of his fans. Competition among the studios heated up, and the citified new popular music began to fly.

Congolese writer Sylvain Bemba described Jhimmy's role as that of a musical 'pyromaniac' who created songs 'in which he totally sacrificed the text to the tyranny of the rhythm.' His distinctive style, which nearly always included a guitar solo, fired the imaginations of Congolese youth. On both banks of the Congo River more and more young boys wanted to learn guitar.

•

In 1949, fourteen-year-old Charles Mwamba fit that description. Like thousands of others, his parents had abandoned rural life – Mikalayi in Kasai province – following World War II to try their luck in Léopoldville. They had two children who, in the tradition of many Congolese ethnic groups, carried different last names. Charles had been named Mwamba after an uncle, and his younger brother Nicolas was given his grandfather's name, Kasanda. The family settled into a house on Avenue de la Croix Rouge in the Kinshasa district of the African cité, where the boys attended school and began to learn the lessons of city life.

Charles and Nicolas both had an ear for music. Back in the village their father played accordion, and their mother performed traditional songs and dances of the Luba people. Around the corner from their house in Léopoldville a small record shop spun the latest imports and current releases from the city's new recording studios. Charles loved the guitar playing of Ngoma's Georges Edouard. He tried to teach himself guitar but had better luck with his voice, still a lovely, clear soprano.

Word of his singing soon spread beyond the neighborhood to Opika's Paul Mwanga and Baskis, who were looking for a third voice to complement the duo of Jhimmy and Mwanga. Charles's parents wouldn't hear of it. They were working hard to see that he and his brother got a good education. That was the key to success in their modern, European-imposed social order. Léopoldville differed from the village, where music accompanied the routines and rituals of daily life. In the city, music was the devil's work, the tinder of profligate parties and dancing bars. Charles chose the devil. He ran away from home and went to live with Jhimmy.

They formed an imposing quintet, Jhimmy and his band, Mwanga, Gobi, Baskis, and young Charles Mwamba. Opika's Gabriel Benetar dressed them in T-shirts, each with a different letter emblazoned on the front that together spelled OPIKA. Music fans lined the 'beach' to greet the great Jhimmy when he strode off the ferry to play dates in Brazzaville. His fame spread as far west as Gabon, where it was said that people were charged admission to the house he stayed in just to get a glimpse of him. Congo Films produced a short film, eventually shown in Europe, called *Jhimmy Chante* (Jhimmy sings), spotlighting Jhimmy, Gobi, and Charles playing a four-song set.

One Congolese journalist likened Jhimmy to a shooting star. He seemed to explode from nowhere to outstrip his rivals, but in less than four years the flames subsided when Jhimmy inexplicably banished himself back to the bureaucracy of Brazzaville. In 1952 he recorded some songs with another Opika singer named Joseph Kabasele. The event symbolized the passing of the torch to one who would bear it for the long haul.

Like Jhimmy, Kabasele was considered to be an intellectual since he had completed three years of secondary school before – again like Jhimmy – running afoul of school administrators, who expelled him. He had come to Léopoldville with his parents shortly after his birth at Matadi on the lower

Jhimmy 'the Hawaiian' (right) with Charles Mwamba (left) and
François 'Gobi' Boyimbo from the film Jhimmy Chante

Congo in 1930. Despite his rough edges, being born to a prominent family – his uncle, Abbé Joseph Malula, would one day be elected to the College of Cardinals at the Vatican – gave Kabasele a certain cachet. He worked for several of Léopoldville's commercial establishments as a shorthand typist, but music was his true calling.

Those who knew him say Kabasele was born to be a singer. Taller than most, with placid good looks and a waggish glint in his eyes, he refined his talent in church choirs, where, according to one promotional brochure, he became 'the darling of the faithful.' Around 1950, soon after Opika had opened its doors, Kabasele began to hang around the studio after work. He met Jhimmy and the other players, sang their songs, and auditioned his own.

In precisely this way, the new recording studios nourished the music. They provided instruments and a congenial place for artists to mingle and exchange ideas. When someone had a song, he would call on others to arrange and rehearse it with him to audition for the boss. The studio purchased the rights to those that passed muster, then recorded and issued them, usually under the composer's name with the back-up musicians listed below. Groups of musicians worked more and more regularly together to the point that many became permanent, full-fledged bands.

Opika's Groupe Doula Georges (following the French custom of putting family names first) evolved in this fashion. Guitarists Georges Doula and Albert Yamba-Yamba had signed with Opika early on as studio players. Singer Marcelin Laboga worked with them, and when Joseph Kabasele came along he fit in nicely as the second voice. The group played shows at the Astra Cinema and for other functions around the cité. In 1951 Doula and his band starred in a publicity film for the former Radiodiffusion Nationale Belge, now known as Voix de la Concorde operating under the call letters OTC. The resulting notoriety prompted the musicians to change their group's name to OTC, which they said in their case stood for Orchestre de Tendance Congolaise (band of a Congolese bent).

While Kabasele matured in OTC, Charles Mwamba's apprenticeship with Jhimmy began to pay off. He strung his guitar with a second E string, like Jhimmy, and worked on playing rhythm parts. The youngster's skills developed to the point where he displaced Gobi as Jhimmy's accompanist. His Opika brothers began to call him 'Dechaud' (hot one), because his playing heated up the music. Jhimmy's lengthy tutorial yielded another dividend when Dechaud, after nearly a year's absence, moved back home and began to teach guitar to his little brother Nicolas.

Nicolas Kasanda was a natural. What his brother had acquired through the sweat of hard work, 'little Nico' seemed to absorb with the effort of a sponge. He had already been fooling around with his own guitar, which he had fashioned from a chunk of wood and scraps of string and nails. But practicing with the sleek, imported model that Dechaud brought home from Jhimmy's was like sliding behind the wheel of one of Léopoldville's shiny Cadillacs. Nico said that he felt a strong affinity for the guitar, because 'in the Kasai region ... we have several stringed musical instruments. When the guitar came to [Congo], I got inspired.'

Just as they had with Dechaud, their parents strongly opposed Nico's interest in music. Undeterred, he began to hang around Opika with his brother after school. Gabriel Benetar took notice. 'When I started scratching [at the guitar], he gave me a guitar,' Nico recalled. 'He said, "That little guy over there, he's good." ... He gave me a guitar and a little bike ... to encourage

Congolese record labels of the fifties often carried a photo of the principal artist, in this case Joseph Kabasele

me.' Around 1950 or 1951 Nico made his recording debut singing behind Paul Mwanga. A year or so later he was guitar-wise enough to back Kabasele with his fingers on a rumba called 'Para-Fifi' (paradise Fifi), sung to a woman who announced for Radio Brazzaville. 'Félicité ... my passion for you, makes my blood pound.' Kabasele draws his delivery out like the Corsican crooner Tino Rossi, whose music was very much the vogue. 'Ah, your face/ It drives me crazy.' A wheezing Solovox organ and percussion accompany Nico's surprisingly nimble debut. With tongues in cheeks, his amazed colleagues (grizzled veterans in their early twenties) called him Nico mobali, 'the real man.' The short, scrawny wisp of a youth was all of thirteen years old.

•

Congo music in the early fifties bubbled with the exuberance of youthful prodigies like Nico and Kabasele and the waning king, Jhimmy. These were educated city kids largely divorced from the village life that shaped their elders. They were attuned to the technology of radio and records and the echoes of Africa that returned from abroad. But an invention of another sort delivered the next musical innovation to the twin capitals.

Despite the depression, Belgium's airline Sabena had inaugurated a regular passenger service between Brussels and Léopoldville in 1935. Air travel within and to the Belgian Congo rapidly expanded following the end of World War II, and to accommodate the increasing numbers of flight personnel, business people, and tourists, Sabena opened a hotel in Léopoldville's east end called the Guest House. Its management made the place seem more like a little slice of home by flying in European musicians to provide entertainment.

Opika's Gabriel Benetar employed a Belgian musician named Gilbert Warnant as a kind of artists and repertoire (A&R) man. A piano player who contributed the organ passages to 'Para-Fifi,' Warnant auditioned talent for the studio and supervised recording sessions in addition to his keyboard contributions. He and Benetar sometimes spent evenings at the Guest House listening to European jazz combos, perhaps comparing them to their own aggregations. Up to this point most Congolese pop bands employed only acoustic guitarists and singers with a smattering of percussion. They lacked the variety and versatility of foreign groups. During their excursions to the Guest House, Warnant or Benetar chatted up a Belgian saxophone player named Fud Candrix, and, one day in 1952, convinced him to come to the studio.

In the 1920s, while still in his teens, Alfons 'Fud' Candrix had begun touring European night spots as a member of his brother Jeff's band. By 1929 he had his own jazz combo, The Carolina Stomp Chasers, and in 1937 formed a big swing band. Candrix played clarinet and violin, but his main instrument was tenor sax. In his mid-forties when he walked through the doors of Opika, his trim, well-dressed frame, graying mustache, and receding hairline gave him the look of a European aristocrat.

Candrix sat in on recording sessions over the next few days, improvising sax accompaniment to new songs by several artists, including Jhimmy and Kabasele. When the records appeared a few weeks later, Congolese music lovers snapped them up. 'Kale-Kato' (Kabasele and Katherine; the song is also known as 'Ambiance'), Kabasele's exaltation of his new wife, and 'Banga Jhimmy' (fear Jhimmy), Jhimmy's exaltation of himself, found special favor. The sax parts that Candrix contributed nicely complemented the rumba-based creations the Congolese favored. 'He revolutionized Congo music, because he played the sax so differently from the way Congolese played,' said Guy-Léon Fylla. 'He gave a jazz coloring to the music.' If not revolutionary, the Candrix stylings were at least evolutionary. Congolese horn players began to mimic them, and, more importantly, more recordings showed up using horns.

Although it can't be claimed with complete certainty, it appears that the European musicians who played the Guest House introduced the acoustic contrabass, or double bass, to the two Congos. Most of the visiting combos were trios or quartets with at least piano, bass, and drums. Nikiforos Cavvadias bought a bass for Ngoma in 1952. Benetar ordered one for Opika, where guitarist Albert Taumani took it up. Over at Loningisa, Honoré Liengo dropped his guitar in favor of the bass. Soon it became a standard ingredient in Congolese recordings. The black African rhythms that had helped give birth to American jazz were now returning by plane in the heads and hands of white Europeans.

In 1953 Bill Alexandre felt he had done all he could do with music in Belgium. Then in his early thirties, he had played guitar with the best, including Django Reinhardt and Fud Candrix, and had put together a band that performed in the finest clubs. He had started his professional career during the Nazi occupation in 1942 or 1943, and after the war had even played some bebop. By the early fifties, however, newly installed jukeboxes began to supplant live musicians in Belgian clubs, so when the two Greek owners of an import–export company called COMITURI offered him a chance to set up a recording studio in the Belgian Congo, Alexandre decided to take it.

Armed with his Gibson electric guitar, a small monophonic tape recorder, an expensive Electro-Voice microphone, and a big contrabass, Alexandre transformed the small room his bosses provided in their Léopoldville headquarters into the Compagnie d'Enregistrements Folkloriques Africains (CEFA) recording studio. Since the more seasoned Congolese musicians had contracts with Léopoldville's established studios, Alexandre set out to recruit younger artists who were looking for a place to start. 'I was lucky enough to meet a young boy, he was around sixteen or seventeen years old and was attracted to music,' Alexandre recalled. 'He more or less served as a watchdog for me. He was my secretary, he was my translator, he was, you know, my everything, and my good friend also. His name was Roger Izeidi.'

Izeidi had gotten into music by singing in a church choir just like his friend Joseph Kabasele. As Izeidi told it, Kabasele had heard about the new studio in progress, but since he was under contract to Opika, he asked Izeidi to go check it out. Izeidi was Alexandre's first hire.

Next on board came a young guitarist named Augustin Moniania whom Alexandre summoned off the street when he saw him carrying a guitar.

Moniania, better known as 'Roitelet' (little king), had learned to play from a couple of Ngoma's musicians. Roitelet had been working on the riverboats, but when offered the chance he signed on at CEFA full-time.

Izeidi brought others to Alexandre's attention: a tall, lanky office clerk named Victor 'Vicky' Longomba who sang with an appealing tenor; Antoine 'Brazzos' Armando, a fledgling guitarist who, like Roitelet, had worked the riverboats for a time; and Congo music's first 'Franco,' a singer named François Engbondu who used the nickname before its more famous possessor. These musicians – Roger, Roitelet, Vicky, Brazzos, and Franco – formed the core group at CEFA. Alexandre sat in on electric guitar, and another Belgian musician, Maurice Evans, then on an extended residence at the Guest House, played bass.

During auditions Alexandre asked singers to perform unaccompanied in order to determine their range. Then he adjusted the accompaniment to fit. 'My three or four guitar players, amateurs I had found, they couldn't play in these different tones,' Alexandre explained.

> So I had, first of all, to teach them to play in G and F, in A, B, and what have you, you know. And very soon they began to be stars there, because the other Congolese guitar players, they were astonished. 'Oh! He's playing there, he's playing there. He's playing with a pick.' Something very new to them.

'They brought the music, they composed the music, they composed the lyrics,' said Alexandre of his recruits. 'And while rehearsing we rearranged, you know, we squared, more or less, the thing, because sometimes there were too many measures to make a straight melody. That's the way it went, trial and error.' Since the Congolese didn't read music, 'we all played it by ear.' Izeidi remembered that 'we just had a small [tape] machine. It wasn't like today, thirty-two tracks. We only had one track.' Roitelet re-created the scene, pointing around an imaginary studio: 'We put the mike [in the middle]. Singers over there, maracas here. The amplifier for Bill's guitar there. Me, the contrabass, I get up on a table. I put the sheet music up there. When we play, it goes into one mike.'

After about three months of work, the group started to record. 'With my first tapes I went to Germany [to Deutsche Grammophon],' Alexandre explained. 'And these sound engineers, you know, they were so excited to hear that music. We started re-recording. We started adding reverberation, and making cuts and so forth. And so our first records came to the market.'

Among the initial CEFA recordings, released in July 1953, were 'Chérie

Three members of the CEFA crew (left to right) Antoine 'Brazzos' Armando, Augustin 'Roitelet' Moniania, and Roger Izeidi

Awa' (darling Awa), a rumba sung by Roger, Vicky, and Franco under the name Les 3 Caballeros, a name they lifted from a popular Disney movie; 'Congo ya Sika' (new Congo), by Vicky and Roger; and 'Pusana Moke' (come closer), featuring Marcelle Ebibi Fylla, the Cameroonian wife of guitarist Guy-Léon Fylla who joined the small group of women breaking into the business.

In contrast to other studios, CEFA musicians usually retained the rights to their compositions. Alexandre had his musicians register with SABAM, the Belgian performing rights society, so they could collect royalties. 'I've always been a musician at heart,' he said.

To promote his new label Alexandre opened a record shop, and he and his musicians toured the cité in a new 1953 Ford panel truck equipped with loudspeakers, playing their current creations. At night the group performed live in dancing bars around town. But the music played second fiddle to Alexandre's electric guitar, the like of which had never before been seen in central Africa. The shiny Gibson, the amplifier, and especially the pick were great curiosities and objects of much speculation, particularly among Congolese guitarists, who all plucked the strings with their fingers. 'We didn't understand,' said Antoine Nedule, better known as 'Papa Noël,' another guitarist who was coming of age at the time. 'How could his guitar resonate so well and make such beautiful melodies? What was he doing? So we tried to figure it out.... We would take up any old thing, a [crust] of bread, to make a pick.' People began to call the mild-mannered Alexandre 'Bill Indian' after the swashbuckling heroes of movies from India which found special favor among the youth of the cité. Within weeks of the new CEFA releases, orders for electric guitars from Léo and Brazza began to trickle into the offices of Europe's musical instrument dealers. By 1956, acoustic guitars had all but vanished from Congolese recordings.

Because of the close ties between Izeidi and Kabasele, a clandestine exchange began to develop between CEFA and Opika. Kabasele sold songs to CEFA that, in order to maintain cover, were recorded under Izeidi's name. Georges Doula sometimes sat in on guitar with Alexandre, although, because of his Opika contract, he could not be credited. But more importantly, Alexandre let his musicians take their instruments home. Unlike the other studio operators, who kept their instruments locked up, Alexandre believed in the educational and promotional value of his musicians performing in public.

Kabasele could also see the benefits. 'Kale-Kato' and 'Para-Fifi' had planted his name firmly in the public consciousness. It was time for them to know his face, and there was no better access to the public than playing in Léopoldville's rapidly multiplying bars. 'Opika, where Kabasele was, didn't give out instruments. If Kabasele wanted to hold a concert, he needed the two of us,' Izeidi said, referring to himself and Roitelet. 'If the two of us refused, we would take our instruments and no concert.' Money was the arrangement's key ingredient, Roitelet explained, 'If there was no money, I didn't have my bass.' In the clubs, Izeidi played maracas and sang behind Kabasele, while Roitelet, who had taken up the bass when Maurice Evans left town, slapped out the rhythm. And they borrowed CEFA's guitars for Kabasele's guitarists to play.

Kabasele was outgrowing the OTC group. When recording he relied more and more on younger musicians like the brothers Dechaud and Nico and another guitarist named Tino Baroza (said to be a cousin to Nico and Dechaud). These players, between 1953 and 1955, coalesced into a full-fledged band. 'It was Kabasele's idea that we had to pull something together,' Dechaud

Musicians from the CEFA studio playing for a radio broadcast (left to right) Roitelet on bass, André Scohy head of Radio Congo Belge-Emissions Africaines, Bill Alexandre, Marcelle Ebibi, Belgian pianist Alex Dumoulin, and Brazzos

declared. According to Nico, 'Opika's owner wanted it to be called Opika Jazz. Well, we changed it to African Jazz.' The word *jazz*, he remembered, attracted them. 'In the time of the gentlemen of American jazz ... Louis Armstrong and all those people, basically lots of American musicians talked about jazz, jazz. So we had this influence of jazz.' Because it evolved slowly from a pool of Opika session musicians, the band made no official debut. They recorded a song called 'African Jazz' that either conferred or confirmed the group's name. As early as 1953 the group was clearly discernible, and by 1955 it had become a bona fide band with an extraordinary following.

Who can explain fame's fickle nature? Its elements align with seeming randomness – for a poor black trumpet player blowing new music from New Orleans or a poor white truck driver belting the blues in a Memphis studio, for a shaggy-haired quartet from Liverpool or a dreadlocked Rastafarian in the Kingston slums. On the banks of the Congo River in the mid-1950s the elements fell into place for African Jazz. 'There was music in [Congo],' said saxophonist Isaac Musekiwa,

> Wendo, Adou Elenga, Bowane, there was music. Another kind of music. But when Kabasele started to sing, he changed everything. And when Nico and Tino Baroza started the solo for guitar, now it brought all the people to look for solo which was not there before. You see, that's how that music started.

African Jazz seemed to embody the aspirations of modern, urban Africans. Young, handsome, well educated for the time, and immensely talented, they floated their love songs on a river of guitars reinforced by the beat of the rumba. Congolese youth found the combination irresistible. People heaped affectionate nicknames on Kabasele: 'Le Grand Kalle,' 'Kalle Jeef,' and 'Kalle de l'Inspiration.' Nico became a teenage idol. Benetar sent a car to collect him after school, so he wouldn't miss rehearsals and recording. In what was perhaps a first, and certainly a rarity for the Belgian Congo, African Jazz began to play regular matinée dates in 1954 at a bar in the Sarma-Congo building located in the white ville. With concerts and records and tremendous personal appeal, the musicians of African Jazz dominated Congolese music in the middle fifties.

Nico, Dechaud, and Tino Baroza all made the switch to electric guitar. Albert Taumani or Joseph Mwena usually played bass, along with Baskis on percussion. Antoine Kaya, called 'Depuissant' (strong one), played locally made drums known by the generic name *tam-tam*, and with the brief but fruitful tenure of Fud Candrix in mind, Opika recruited saxophonist Isaac Musekiwa.

Musekiwa had migrated north to the Belgian Congo from his home in Salisbury, Southern Rhodesia (today's Harare, Zimbabwe), in search of better opportunities. Attracted to the saxophone, he had learned by watching a local Rhodesian band practice and then sneaking into the rehearsal room after hours to play the instruments left behind. In 1951 Musekiwa settled in Elisabethville in the Belgian Congo's copper mining region, where he worked as a driver by day and played sax at night in a small band run by a local bar owner. His music drifted to the ears of the Benetar brothers, who had a branch in Elisabethville. They recorded his band there, and then signed him alone for their studio in Léopoldville, where he took his place among Kabasele and the others in 1954.

Under Musekiwa's influence, African Jazz cut several sides in English. Songs like 'Flowers of Luckyness' (sic) and 'While She's Away' reflected his upbringing in an English-speaking colony and perhaps contributed to the band's growing popularity outside the two Congos. 'We were very young, all of us,' Musekiwa recalled. 'We didn't know that some records, you can get some money from that. We just liked music. What was pleasing us was for people to know I'm playing music, and that's all. We came to know money after.'

If musicians were slow to grasp the economic ramifications of their creativity, the studio owners understood them clearly. Competition jumped to a new level. By 1952, all the studios had converted to recording on magnetic tape, a more flexible and inexpensive system than the direct-to-disc process. Each year's record sales topped the one before. One of the colony's propaganda organs, the *Belgian Congo Today*, reported that as of 1955 'the natives are buying discs at the rate of about 600,000 a year [at] an average cost of about one dollar.'

Ngoma struggled briefly at the end of 1951 when Nicolas Jeronimidis died unexpectedly from an intestinal disorder. Jeronimidis's brother-in-law, Nikiforos Cavvadias, left his job at the Banque du Congo Belge to join Alexandros Jeronimidis in managing the studio. They hired a Belgian pianist named Pilaeis as A&R man and kept Ngoma alive on the strength of Wendo and the other musicians.

Before Nicolas's death, the Jeronimidis brothers had begun to augment their recording business with a variety of associated products. They sold gramophones, replacement springs, and needles under the Ngoma brand. To maximize exposure, they gave their records to radio stations, then started to sell radios and batteries. Cavvadias traveled around Africa to set up a network of distributors. When it proved difficult to conduct business in the French colonies from the Belgian Congo, Alex Jeronimidis went to France to open a pressing factory called Disco France. The factory shipped directly to French Africa, thus avoiding the obstacles presented by duties and currency exchange.

The Dutch company Philips sent equipment to the Belgian Congo around 1954 to record music at its headquarters in Léopoldville and Stanleyville. Records were subsequently pressed at the Philips factory in Holland. Opika lost at least two of its artists, Paul Mwanga and Georges Doula, to the new venture.

Basile Papadimitriou sometimes brought several Loningisa musicians downtown to play at his shop, especially when a new pattern of cloth was to be introduced. Their music turned the arrival of merchandise into a full-fledged event, luring customers in off the street to check out the fresh designs and the latest songs.

Bill Alexandre roamed the *cité* touting his young CEFA crew over the loudspeakers of the studio's Ford panel truck. Opika's Gabriel Benetar toured with his own mobile public address system. 'Benetar,' said Roitelet,

> when he had a new song, he would go out at four in the morning driving around the *cité*, 'Hello! Listen! New songs! All of Léopoldville, it's Jhimmy!' So Ngoma comes out with his truck too, 'Wendo! Wendo! He has brought a newborn into the world. Come listen to this record.' ... It was a big deal then. Benetar came with his car, the police didn't like it, and he left his car there playing music. He disrupted traffic. He said, 'Listen to Opika. O-P-Kaaaaah! Jhimmy!' The police would come and [Benetar] would say, 'Get out of my way. You don't know who I am. Benetar. Millionaire.' He would take money like this, and he would throw it [out the window].

In spite of the hype and the hustle, buyers bought what they liked. Jhimmy and his successor, Kabasele, humbled their competitors. But in 1956 Loningisa's own collection of young prodigies began to mount a challenge.

4
In need of a name

Essous, Franco, and O.K. Jazz, 1955–1956

Brazzaville's Chez Faignond was central Africa's Cotton Club. When darkness fell on the Poto-Poto district in the 1950s, Rue Mbakas bustled outside Faignond like the corner of Harlem's Lenox Avenue and 142nd Street in the early thirties. Tables filled an open area in front of the building right out to the street. Just inside, a bar lined one wall which pointed patrons to the main club, a huge room with a stage for performers and plenty of space for dancing. Chez Faignond even housed a separate movie theater.

The place was run by a half-Congolese, half-French businessman named Faignond who had fought with the French army in Indochina and then returned home to Brazzaville to create his entertainment palace. On nights when the great stars like Wendo or Jhimmy would play, Rue Mbakas choked with traffic. Patrons even crossed the river from Léopoldville to take in the action. 'For us,' said Jean Serge Essous, 'Brazzaville began and ended here.'

Early in 1955, Essous and some friends landed a steady gig at Chez Faignond for their new band, Negro Jazz. Essous played clarinet beside saxophonist Nino Malapet, with lead guitarist Joseph Kaba, singers Edouard 'Edo' Ganga and Célestin Kouka, plus rhythm guitar, tam-tams, and bass. About a month into their contract, Faignond announced he had booked African Jazz to play an upcoming weekend with them. Joseph Kabasele and his African Jazz were a band without peer in this era. 'These were all our idols,' Essous said.

The night African Jazz showed up, the club bulged beyond capacity. Even Europeans turned out. Negro Jazz asked to play first. If they had to follow the great Kabasele, they would suffer terminal embarrassment. But the star had his way. African Jazz played first, a twenty-minute instrumental set. Then the emcee announced 'Le Grand Kalle,' and the place went wild. 'Kabasele sang like a god,' Essous declared. 'People danced like crazy. There was a break. Then they called for us. We were under the table.'

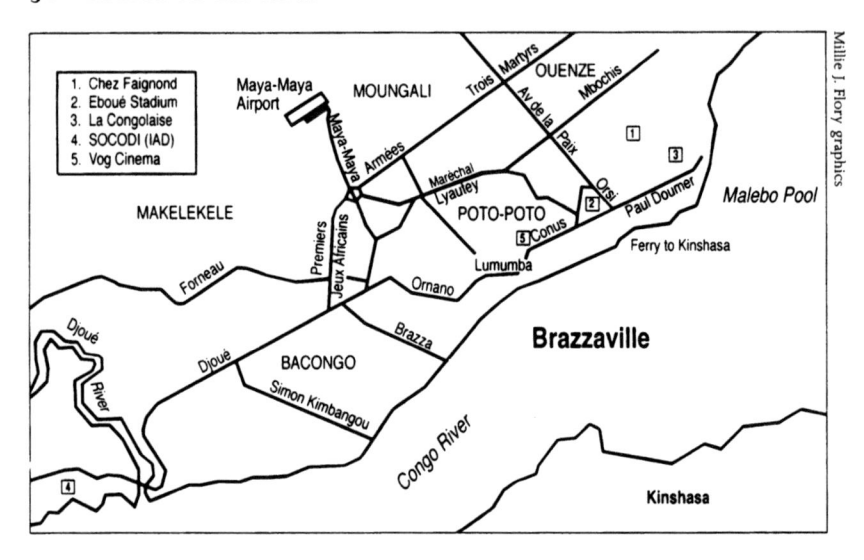

Joseph Kaba rallied his Negro Jazz troops. Their slow opening number pulled the Europeans onto the dance floor. They got a little applause. Then it was time to play their ace. Chez Faignond served as headquarters for a mutual assistance association of women called Violette, an elegantly dressed group who, at their most benign level, functioned as animators to get the crowd dancing. Violette and its counterparts, The Rose, Lolita, Elegance, and others, were also known to provide more personal services should a patron have the inclination and the wherewithal to back it up. Negro Jazz had been working up a new song that mentioned all these women's associations. They played it next, and people rushed to the dance floor. 'We were covered in glory,' Essous said. 'Even Kabasele congratulated us.' Negro Jazz had climbed a notch in the musical standings.

•

Jean Serge Essous was a short, wiry youth powered by lungs and legs strengthened during long hours on the football (soccer) field. Already twenty when he played at Chez Faignond, his boyish good looks, attenuated slightly by a smattering of hair on his upper lip and chin, rendered him a perpetual teenager.

As a child, Essous had moved to Brazzaville from Mossendjo, his home town in the Niari region of western French Congo, when his father found employment as a health worker in the capital. He got into music in the Boy Scouts, where he learned to play a small reed pipe known by the French *pipeau*. When his father bought a gramophone around 1947, Essous started listening to Louis Armstrong and Tino Rossi and the GV series of Latin American records. Around 1952, his father took up with a woman in Bangui, where he had gone on a vaccination campaign, so Essous quit school to begin work as an electrician in order to help his mother. But music was never far from his mind.

Together with a friend, Isidore Diaboua, known as 'Lièvre' (the hare), Essous helped form a group of seven pipeau players accompanied by guitar and percussion. Groupe Diaboua, as they came to be known, soon transformed itself with support and encouragement from the colonial government into Ballet Diaboua, which included dancers from the territory's various ethnic groups. Ballet Diaboua made a grand world tour in 1954 which included stops in France and China.

Back in Brazzaville the group's musicians began to perform occasionally with a French accordionist named Charly Yvorra, who played regularly at a local hotel. Loningisa's Basile Papadimitriou, something of an accordionist himself, heard the group one day and invited them to Léopoldville to record. The event proved propitious despite the record's poor public reception, because Essous and his friends met the great Henri Bowane. Short-lived for the moment, this acquaintance would soon be renewed to the greater glory of all.

The Diaboua dancers continued to perform, but the failure of their record and the loss of Charly Yvorra, who went home to France toward the end of 1954, caused the musicians of Diaboua to separate. One of the drummers, Saturnin 'Ben' Pandi, got a contract at Loningisa. Essous took a job at the Brazzaville office of IBM, began to learn clarinet from an Antillean co-worker, and practiced his other passion, football.

On the football field Essous met Jean Dieudonné Malapet, better known as 'Nino,' who had just returned home from studies in France. Nino Malapet was a nephew to Emmanuel Dadet, the prominent intellectual who led Brazzaville's pioneering band Melo-Congo. Malapet hung out at his uncle's rehearsals, where he started to pick up the saxophone. Essous and Malapet practiced clarinet and sax together, and with other football buddies, Edo Ganga and Célestin Kouka, formed the Negro Jazz group that, early in 1955, met Joseph Kabasele and his African Jazz at Chez Faignond.

Holding their own against Le Grand Kalle produced immediate benefits, because Henri Bowane had been in the audience that night. In addition to recording and recruiting for Loningisa, Bowane owned a night club in Léopoldville called the Quist. As Essous told it, 'If you went to Bowane's club, you were in. It was the height of all heights.' Bowane came through with an offer, so in the middle of 1955 Negro Jazz steamed across the river to play the Quist.

The center of Léopoldville's night life could still be found astride Avenue Prince Baudouin just a few streets south of the ville. The Quist opened its doors onto Avenue de l'Itaga. Another popular spot, the Air France, was just down the street on the corner of Avenue Baudouin, and across it, still on Avenue de l'Itaga, sat Chez Cassien, also known as the O.K. Bar. After a couple of good weeks at the Quist, Negro Jazz settled in for three months at the Air France, where Essous again met Basile Papadimitriou.

Papadimitriou wanted reed players for his studio. Loningisa was loaded with guitarists and singers but lacked the punch that Isaac Musekiwa's saxophone provided their competitors at Opika. Some of his musicians were already rehearsing two new songs by the gifted young guitarist François Luambo. Papadimitriou asked Essous and Malapet to work with them.

•

François Luambo was called Franco by his friends, a sobriquet said to have been conferred by Henri Bowane. It was the name that CEFA singer François Engbondu first brought to the musical world but relinquished when he fell ill and left the business. The new Franco played beside his mentor, Paul 'Dewayon' Ebengo, from whom he had learned the basics of acoustic guitar.

Dewayon had come to Léo from Bolobo, his home town up the Congo River halfway to Coquilhatville. He had worked briefly as a greaser on the riverboats but quickly succumbed to the lure of the capital. Dewayon remembered meeting Franco when he helped Franco's mother find living quarters for her family in a house his father owned in the Ngiri-Ngiri district of Léopoldville's new cité.

Franco was already a boy of the city with only distant roots in Sona Bata, his birthplace some fifty miles south of Léopoldville on the road to Matadi. He was 'a good-looking boy, tall and sociable,' Basile Papadimitriou remembered. His dark, gentle eyes sat wide apart, each underscored by a puffy welt pushing out from the bridge of his broad nose. The effect was to make him look older than his years, as though certain aspects of his face had been held over from a previous life. His skin stretched taut from bone to bone revealing a slender frame bereft of the padding an extra slab or two of manioc a day might have provided.

Franco's railroad worker father had been a good provider, but his sudden death in 1949 left ten-year-old Franco, his mother, and a brother and sister in near penury. From that point on school was out of the question. Everyone needed to work to ensure the family's survival.

In later years Franco's contemporaries, apparently wishing to avoid embarrassing their friend, rarely spoke on the record about his lack of education. But this particular shortcoming did not seem to bother Franco. He once told an interviewer that, 'I had enormous difficulties completing my education. As was symptomatic in my youth, I felt a lot of admiration for those who make music. Little by little I began to develop a real taste for the music.' Like the poor health that plagued his early years, the lack of education, far from being an embarrassment, was merely another obstacle over which he would eventually triumph. The lessons of everyday life, it seems, laid a better foundation for success in the treacherous world of the music business. And for Franco and other under-educated youth, the music business offered a way out of poverty.

Franco plucked his homemade guitar in the busy *wenze ya Bayaka* (market of the Yaka people) near his home, exhorting buyers to sample his mother's hot-from-the-kettle fried cakes. At home in the evenings he 'borrowed' Dewayon's guitar while Dewayon toiled nights in a textile factory. 'I gained mastery of my guitar with Dewayon,' Franco recalled. 'I also benefited from lessons with Citizen [Albert] Luampasi, a composer at the time for Ngoma.' As Franco's skills improved, he and Dewayon began to play together, eventually forming a group in 1950 with the two of them accompanied by assorted other novices. They called themselves Watam. Franco was just twelve years old, Dewayon a seasoned sixteen.

Watam played sporadic dates for nearly three years, with the members collecting small rewards for their efforts. Dewayon recalled, 'Our pleasure was when they called us to play a funeral. After that we got our case of beer, and that was it.' According to Dewayon, the band even recorded a couple of songs at Ngoma with the help of Albert Luampasi. Franco picked up some extra cash by cleaning the studio after hours.

Loningisa musicians of the early fifties (left to right) Jeef Mingiedi, a guitarist called Athos, Daniel 'De La Lune' Lubelo (nearly obscured by Athos), François 'Franco' Luambo (facing camera), Paul 'Dewayon' Ebengo, Eugene 'Gogene' Ngoy, and at the microphone Philippe 'Rossignol' Lando, Anna Ako, and Henri Bowane

In 1953, Dewayon and Franco auditioned for Henri Bowane. 'I realized those kids had a future, and I wanted to put them to work at Loningisa,' Bowane told an interviewer. The two young guitarists settled in alongside Loningisa's other session players, rehearsing and recording whatever songs survived the studio's screening process.

The original Loningisa in Foncobel had not worked out. The Papadimitrious moved it temporarily near their headquarters in the ville while they constructed a far more luxurious studio. The site they chose was Limete, yet another new area of town, immediately south of the airport. Limete was divided by Boulevard Leopold III (named for the successor to Belgium's Albert I) with an industrial area on the Boulevard's east side and housing for European employees of the industrial concerns on the west. The Papadimitrious had built a bakery in the industrial zone and, in 1954, erected the new Loningisa across the street.

The studio's main room, a twenty-foot by thirty-foot space with ten-foot-high ceilings, dwarfed the original. Velvety fabric covered the walls to suppress echo. At one end of the room a large glass pane looked into the control room, where a technician operated the microphone mixing board and single-track tape recorder. Musicians rehearsed in a smaller room adjacent to the main studio. The new building even housed toilets and showers for the musicians' use, and air conditioning tempered the tropical heat.

Basile Papadimitriou ran a tight ship. He had constructed the best studio in Léopoldville, signed the best musicians he could find, and even provided company housing for them in an area known as Yolo, on the western fringe of Limete. He valued creativity and provided the atmosphere to encourage it. But all songs were not created equal, so Papadimitriou set up a selection committee composed of Africans and Europeans to evaluate his artists' compositions. 'The members of the committee sold wrap-skirt cloth for women, with whom we dealt everyday in the store,' Papadimitriou explained. 'All day long the music played, the songs of our label Loningisa. Thus they had experience with the kind of music the [Congolese] men and women liked while they made their purchases.'

Papadimitriou, who spoke Lingala like a Congolese, sat in on the committee along with Loningisa's Belgian recording engineer, Carlos Monsieur, and various staff members from the Papadimitriou enterprises. Committee members convened in the evenings to listen to tapes. They accepted and rejected songs and made suggestions for improvements. 'We did good work in that way,' declared Edo Ganga, who would join Loningisa soon after Franco and Dewayon, 'because the songs we made are still loved today.'

Loningisa functioned like a combination factory, sports franchise, and think tank. Quality of production, astute talent acquisition, and conditions conducive to creativity began to show results in the marketplace. With songs like Franco's 'Bolingo na Ngai na Beatrice' (my love for Beatrice) and 'Dewayon Makila Mabe' (unlucky Dewayon) by Dewayon, Loningisa made gains against its rivals.

Loningisa's rise coincided with the fall of CEFA, whose demise would benefit Loningisa still further. Bill Alexandre's studio had gotten off to a promising start, but now the original owners, who had expected quick profits, lost interest and sold it. By most accounts, the new owner was a playboy who squandered the studio's money. In 1955, less than three years after it had started, CEFA was nearly bankrupt. 'During that short period of time we recorded something like 110 or 120 discs, double sides,' Alexandre said. But he had had enough of the business side of music. He went to work as a Volkswagen mechanic in a Léopoldville garage, then moved on to become a photographer for the Congolese newspaper *L'Avenir*. He sated his diminishing musical appetite by jamming with visiting jazzmen. After returning to Brussels in 1959, he never played music again.

With CEFA in decline its musicians scattered. Roger Izeidi hung in with yet another new owner, the Belgian company Fonior, which stepped in at the last minute to save the studio and gain a foothold in the promising Congolese music market. Roitelet freelanced for the other studios and wound up with a contract at Loningisa. Vicky Longomba went to work in a factory, but after much persistence on his part, he too signed with Loningisa. By late 1955 when Papadimitriou recruited the reed players of Negro Jazz, Jean Serge Essous and Nino Malapet, his studio was brimming with talent.

•

Bana Loningisa (children of Loningisa), as the studio musicians came to be known, was already rehearsing two of Franco's songs when Essous and Malapet sat in. 'Ngala ba Petit Mbongo' warned Congolese men to be careful of the *cité*'s young prostitutes; they are always asking for this and that. 'Anna Mabele ya Ngoya' declared, Anna you're my world. The two reed men from Negro Jazz were impressed. They found themselves among Henri Bowane, Franco and Dewayon, Roitelet, Vicky Longomba, their old friend Pandi from Groupe Diaboua, another Brazzavillean named Daniel Lubelo who called himself 'De La Lune' (of the moon), and Philippe Lando, better known as 'Rossignol' (nightingale). Essous and Malapet played on the two songs and were offered contracts when the records sold well. In the meantime Malapet accepted a contract offer from Ngoma, but in January of 1956, Essous signed on with Loningisa for double what he was making at IBM.

Like the early African Jazz, Bana Loningisa was an amorphous conglomeration of session players which, in one configuration or another, accompanied all the singers who passed through the studio. Some evenings several of the group would play for free at Bowane's Quist, because they felt Bowane to be their 'spiritual father' to whom most owed thanks for their employment. Down Avenue de l'Itaga, within earshot of the Quist, sat the O.K. Bar, owned by a half-Belgian, half-Congolese named Oscar Kashama. As Essous told it, one day in early 1956 Kashama proposed that the musicians come to play at his place for money. The group's six core members, Franco on electric guitar, singers Vicky and Rossignol, Essous on clarinet, Pandi on conga drums (which were gradually replacing the local tam-tams in the music's array of instruments), and contrabassist De La Lune, all agreed to the switch and began a fruitful stand at the O.K. Bar.

A few weeks later Kashama booked the group to play at the cultural center for an association of people of mixed origins called Home des Mulâtres (mulattos' home), situated appropriately on the border between black and white Léopoldville. During the course of the afternoon, Kashama introduced the musicians to a man who wanted the band to play for a railroad workers' party. To draw up a contract, the group needed a name. They recorded at Loningisa, but the musicians wanted to use something more their own. According to Essous, they thought of a name on the spur of the moment. 'We said, "We're playing at the O.K. Bar; our name's going to be O.K. Jazz."'

It was a name worthy of Madison Avenue. In addition to the obvious – the initials of Oscar Kashama or, as some liked to think of it, Orchestre Kinois (band of Kinshasa district) – the expression O.K. evoked the swagger and panache of the American Westerns that delighted youthful audiences at the cité's open-air cinemas. *Jazz*, on the other hand, suggested the hip sophistication of black America, Louis Armstrong and Duke Ellington. Kabasele had used it, and the Loningisa group aspired to be his equal. A show at the O.K. Bar on June 6, 1956, officially baptised the band, but it was a mere formality. O.K. Jazz was already a going concern.

Living together in Loningisa housing fostered personal and professional fellowship among the musicians. Closeness nurtured friendship, respect, and, above all, creativity. Essous, the band's first *chef d'orchestre* (bandmaster), remembered that Franco

> was always a boy who liked to work.... At that time he had a notebook, several notebooks, in which he had over a hundred songs. So he was a kind of genius.... Franco went in search of inspiration in public places, at the market, at the stadium. He went where women were doing hair, where women were sewing, and naturally he went to the bars.

He wrote down the words to his songs, but the music remained in his head. The others, while not as prolific, composed their own songs too.

To arrange the music its composer first taught his new work to the singers. High-voiced Rossignol took the soprano parts. Vicky sang tenor. When Franco had a song he really cared about, he would sing lead with the others backing him up. Sometimes they sang in unison; at others they used harmony. After the singers got the idea, the guitar part would be added. Unlike their rival

African Jazz, which used two and sometimes three interweaving guitars, O.K. Jazz usually used only Franco's. Essous's clarinet, added next to the mix, took the place of a second guitar. For the clarinet and guitar duo, Essous explained, 'We picked up the melody directly, arranging and harmonizing with it.... Or, when that wasn't the case, we looked for an arrangement which was different from the [melody], but respected the chords and tempos.' The addition of rhythmic underpinnings, bass and percussion, completed the process. On some occasions, De La Lune shifted to rhythm guitar and Roitelet sat in on bass.

As 1956 wore on, the members of O.K. Jazz performed with increasing confidence. Weekdays were spent in the studio. Saturday nights they played the O.K. Bar from eight until around midnight. After a few hours of sleep, they returned for a Sunday matinée, broke for late afternoon football matches, then came back to the bar for an evening set. Every so often the players entertained in Brazzaville or ventured up-river to places like Coquilhatville. 'So there we were, going along,' Essous said. 'It was good. It was very, very good. I think it was one of our finest periods.' Young and full of ambition, they started to give Kabasele a bit of a challenge. 'Put yourself in my place. From where we came from, to get that far, it was extraordinary.... We just wanted to burn through all the stages.'

Despite the band's auspicious launch, which seemed to bode well for the studio, the growing popularity of O.K. Jazz extracted a price from Loningisa. The great Henri Bowane, accustomed to his lofty status as the studio's top star, began to feel neglected in the band's wake. Bowane enjoyed the perquisites of stardom. He is said to have lived in a house in the ville – an extraordinary situation in light of the city's *de facto* racial segregation – and to have cruised around town like royalty in a big white Cadillac convertible. But Bowane's music was becoming passé. His was the sound of a fading era. The studio that owed its existence to him now nurtured his successors. The affront, it seems, was too much; Bowane decided to leave Loningisa.

Trouble brewed on another front as well. The matter of royalty payments for compositions had begun to play a prominent role in studio matters ever since Bill Alexandre introduced the concept three years earlier. When a musician presented a new composition, most of the studios paid a one-time fee to purchase all the rights to it. The fee was certainly good for the era, many times over the daily wage of an average worker. But it meant that whatever royalties accrued from sales went to the studio's owner.

According to Basile Papadimitriou, this was not the case at Loningisa: in addition to a salary, 'each composer received a percentage on the number of records received or sold.' Nevertheless there was at least a current of dissatisfaction at the studio, forced to the surface by Roitelet and Pandi. In talks among the musicians, it came out that Franco, the studio's most prolific composer, earned less per composition than his brethren. Rather than go directly to Papadimitriou with demands for rectification of what they saw as an injustice, the musicians decided to stage a one-day work stoppage. According to Roitelet (who later became a professional union organizer), they chose a day when Franco was supposed to present some new songs and stayed away from the studio. When they reappeared the following day, Papadimitriou packed them off for an audience with the territorial administrator, who warned them sternly about honoring their contracts.

It is unclear whether or not Franco ever benefited from this rather bold show of unity. What is certain is that two of his supporters lost their jobs. As Roitelet told it, Loningisa's recording engineer, Carlos Monsieur, overheard their scheme on an open studio mike and fingered the ringleaders. In December of 1956, Papadimitriou wrote the territorial administrator to inform him that the contracts of Roitelet and Pandi had been terminated.

Pandi admits he was fired. Roitelet says he quit. Whatever the case, the two no longer worked for Loningisa. The five remaining members of O.K. Jazz selected a fledgling guitarist named Nicolas Bosuma, whom everyone called 'Dessoin' (from *de soin*, connoting care and orderliness in French), to replace their stellar drummer Pandi. Dessoin had already worked with Pandi a bit, so he seemed a logical choice. Later in the month the group recorded a song to announce their new lineup. 'On Entre O.K. On Sort K.O.,' a clever play on words in French and American slang, proclaimed that one enters their show O.K., and one leaves it K.O. – kayoed, the boxing term for knocked out. The energetic, Franco-penned rumba introduced the band's altered lineup: Essous, Franco, Vicky, Rossignol, De La Lune, and Dessoin. But the new configuration would last barely a month. More changes lay just ahead, for the band, for the music industry, and for the entire continent of Africa.

5
A change in mentality

Kasavubu, Lumumba, Rock'a Mambo, O.K. Jazz, and Orchestre Bantou, 1957–1959

The bold but brief job action at Loningisa reflected a pervasive dissatisfaction that festered beneath the surface of French- and Belgian-imposed order. The gods of colonialism favored their European worshipers. Pandi and Roitelet were only the latest to give voice to that truth. But a rising chorus of protest was being heard across Africa, and its prayers were about to be answered.

If Winston Churchill did 'not become the King's First Minister in order to preside over the liquidation of the British Empire,' then an occasional riot, a well-timed strike, and the political skills of leaders like Nigeria's Nnamdi Azikiwe and Ghana's Kwame Nkrumah forced his successors to do exactly that. Asia led the way when India won its independence from Britain in 1947 through masterful use of the non-violent tactics of Mohandas Gandhi. The Dutch relinquished Indonesia in 1949, and in Southeast Asia the Viet Minh defeated France in 1954 with a bloody finale at Dien Bien Phu.

In central Africa, resistance to foreign occupation had sometimes surfaced as the resister's subtle expropriation of the foreigner's own doctrine. Christian proselytizing took a surprising turn, much to the alarm of Belgian colonial officials, with the advent of an African prophet. Simon Kimbangu heeded the call to serve God revealed to him in a series of dreams in 1921. Resistant at first, feeling himself neither preacher nor teacher, he was at last persuaded when his mother dreamed that a stranger had summoned her son to heal a sick child in a nearby village. Kimbangu went to the village of his mother's dream to pray for the child, and it was made well.

A change in mentality 61

Word of the miracle quickly spread. Despite arbitrary colonial boundaries, Kimbangu's village of Nkamba, near Matadi on the lower Congo River, was soon overrun by the sick and afflicted from both Congos and from Angola. Kimbangu opposed traditional beliefs, preaching instead the standard gospel, but delivered, to the accompaniment of music and dancing, with a fervor and trembling that emulated the spiritual possession of traditional healers. This synthesis of African and European spiritual elements attracted many followers. Africans too could have their prophets.

Kimbangu's rise recalled a similar event some 200 years earlier in the Portuguese-controlled ruins of the old Kongo Kingdom. Around 1704, a young African woman named Kimpa Vita was called by an apparition of Saint Anthony to attack the evil that beset her land. She changed her name to Dona Beatriz and preached a synthesis of traditional beliefs and Portuguese Christianity to powerful effect. Her assertion that 'Congo was the true Holy Land and that the founders of Christianity were black' directly challenged the area's Capuchin missionaries.

Followers of Dona Beatriz (the movement was called Antonianism from Saint Anthony) and of Simon Kimbangu (Ngunzism, from the Kikongo word *ngunza* or prophet) posed a threat to established authority. If broadly interpreted – and foreign rulers, not taking any chances, did just that – the message they preached had all the characteristics of a call for nationalism, if not revolution. In 1706, under pressure from the Capuchins, the Mani-Kongo had Dona Beatriz burned to death. Two centuries later, in 1921, Simon Kimbangu was arrested by Belgian authorities, tried for crimes against the state, and sentenced to death by hanging, a sentence later commuted to life in prison. He died in prison in 1950.

More overtly political was the movement of André Matsoua, called the Société Amicale des Originaires de l'Afrique Equatoriale Française. Matsoua, a Congolese from Brazzaville living in Paris, organized several expatriate Congolese into this mutual aid group in 1926. Two years later, some of the members went home to establish a branch of the Amicale. It quickly grew to become a breeding ground of resistance to French colonial authority. Like Kimbangu before him, Matsoua paid for his efforts with a lengthy stay in prison. He died in 1942 during a second term of imprisonment. More movements, some religious, others labor-related, followed on the heels of Kimbangu and Matsoua. Nearly all bore an anti-European current that bubbled just below the surface.

For Africa south of the Sahara, the first bloom of liberation came in 1957

62 Rumba on the River

when the British colony of the Gold Coast became the independent nation of Ghana. Many Congolese on both sides of the river hoped the event foretold something of their own future. Aspirations were particularly high among the growing Congolese upper class, known as *évolués*, 'evolved ones.' These were the better-educated, French-speaking priests, clerks, railway workers, medical assistants, and the like, who, although still far below the station of their European counterparts, earned good salaries and lived a Europeanized lifestyle, albeit separate from the Europeans.

In her book *The Belgian Congo* Ruth Slade described the frustration of the *évolués*:

> They became aware that while the whites had taken seriously their task as 'tutors' ... there was a point at which they seemed determined that the process should stop.... The limit was reached ... when Africans began to want to be treated on terms of equality, as adults, to be regarded as brothers rather than as sons, and when small but increasingly vocal groups of *évolués* began to criticize white paternalism and to demand that a completely new relationship should replace the old.

In an effort to appease this increasingly disgruntled segment of the population, colonial governments in Brazzaville and Léopoldville began to make changes. France's overseas territories were incorporated along with France itself into the French Union in 1946. The Congolese of French Equatorial Africa were granted French citizenship, allowed to form political parties, and permitted to participate in a complex electoral system that chose members of local advisory councils and representatives to the French parliament. Colonial policy, however, continued to be dictated from Paris. France opened centers of higher learning in Brazzaville to train Africans for service in the colonial administration, and, with somewhat less trepidation than the Belgians, allowed some of its Congolese subjects to attend universities in Europe.

Colonial officials in the Belgian Congo grudgingly allowed a few *évolués* to depart for study abroad and set about constructing the Belgian Congo's first university, Lovanium, which opened in 1954. Congolese were appointed to various government advisory councils, but the authorities viewed political emancipation, if it was to come at all, in the much longer term. One Belgian professor, A.A.J. Van Bilsen, drafted a plan in 1955 which envisioned it happening thirty years down the road.

Belgium's modest alterations failed to placate Léopoldville's disaffected *évolués*. The bold among them began to organize. Abbé Joseph Malula, Joseph Kaba-

A change in mentality 63

sele's uncle, formed a loose-knit discussion group in 1951 that occasionally issued its observations in a journal edited by Joseph Ileo called *Conscience Africaine*. In July of 1956, shortly after O.K. Jazz had staged its official coming out, *Conscience Africaine* published the first Congolese political declaration. The extremely moderate document called for gradual emancipation roughly along the lines that Professor Van Bilsen had suggested. But in politically repressed Léopoldville its publication caused an uproar. Even those who couldn't read reportedly bought copies. 'The excitement was engendered,' anthropologist Alan Merriam wrote, 'not so much by what the Manifesto said as by the fact that a group of Congolese dared to say it at all.'

Strongest reaction to the *Conscience Africaine* declaration came not from the Belgians, but from a rival, much more politicized group of Congolese known as ABAKO. The Association pour la Sauvegarde de la Culture et des Intérêts des Bakongo, as ABAKO was officially known, had formed in 1950 as an organization to preserve and defend the ways of the Kongo people, descendants of the ancient Kongo kingdom centered at Mbanza (São Salvador). It was headed by Joseph Kasavubu, a short, avuncular man whose surfeit of reserve seemed ill suited to a budding politician. In August of 1956, ABAKO members issued a statement offering polite praise for *Conscience Africaine* while upping the stakes with a far more urgent call for reform. 'Our patience is already exhausted,' they declared. 'Emancipation should be granted us this very day rather than delayed for another thirty years.' The sudden temerity of the évolués rippled through the cité, emboldening other activists.

Wittingly or not, Pandi and Roitelet contributed to this new spirit of agitation with their short-lived strike at Loningisa. In the early months of 1957, the evolutionary pace of politics and music began to quicken.

•

Despite intense competition from Ngoma and Loningisa, Opika, first with Jhimmy and then with Kabasele's African Jazz, had dominated Congolese music for much of the 1950s. But as the decade began to wane, for reasons that remain unclear, Opika unexpectedly closed its doors. Its closing seemed especially mysterious since the Benetars had recently announced a deal with Puerto Rican musicians in New York to record Congolese songs, and a licensing agreement with the French office of His Master's Voice (La Voix de Son Maître) to distribute Opika's catalog in Europe. Some speculated that the Benetars had made their fortune and simply decided to leave the Congo while they were ahead. Whatever the case, when African Jazz returned to

Jean Serge Essous (left) and Rossignol in 1957

Léopoldville from a tour of the provinces in early 1957, they found themselves without a record company.

Henri Bowane found himself in a quandary as well. Relegated to the shadows of O.K. Jazz, he left Loningisa with his ego bruised more than a little. What to do next to boost his flagging career? He turned once again to Léopoldville's community of Greek businessmen, where he found a willing collaborator in a general merchant named Constantin Antonopoulos.

Antonopoulos, better known to friends as Dino, was a dynamic and likeable young entrepreneur with a fondness for a good game of volleyball. He had built a prosperous business selling fabric and bicycles, *nouveautés aux prix imbattables* (fancy goods at unbeatable prices), to a predominantly African

Esengo label

clientele. At the end of 1956 Bowane convinced him to open a recording studio. They gave it a Lingala name, the word for happiness or joy, Esengo.

Bowane recruited Esengo's musicians, many of whom he had previously brought to Loningisa, including guitarist Eugène Ngoy, better known as 'Gogene,' along with Pandi and Roitelet. His biggest coup, however, was his raid on O.K. Jazz. With one quick strike in January of 1957 he managed to purloin a third of the band, Essous and Rossignol.

While O.K. Jazz regrouped, the new Esengo ensemble rushed to record its first songs. But the hasty release of two new 78s failed to impress Congolese record buyers. The poor technical quality of the discs obliterated whatever merit the songs may have had. A disappointed Antonopoulos upgraded the technical side with the purchase of Opika's equipment from Benetar. Bowane deepened the talent pool by persuading Kabasele that the studio-less African Jazz should join Esengo. A mix of musicians from African Jazz and the original

Esengo ensemble then went back to the newly equipped studio to try again. Dipping into their Cuban bag, this time for the fashionably new *chachachá*, they recorded an Essous-penned song called 'Baila' (dance, in Spanish).

'Baila's snappy cha-cha rhythm buoyed a melody concentrated within the range of only a few notes. Kabasele and Rossignol sang Spanish lines like, 'Oh Baila, la música bella Mexicana Santa Maria' in a *joie de vivre* song encouraging people to dance. Nino Malapet, who had extricated himself from his Ngoma contract, played saxophone accompaniment alongside Essous's clarinet, with Nico Kasanda and Tino Baroza on guitar and bassist Roitelet. 'Baila' turned out to be a smash, just the medicine needed to keep the nervous Antonopoulos in the business. He rewarded Essous with a brand new motor-scooter.

Although the label made no mention of it, with the line 'ritmo rock'a mambo, música africana' 'Baila' introduced a newly evolving Esengo band called Rock'a Mambo. The name was a marvelous play on a Ki-Kongo expression, *rocamambu*, which loosely translates as 'one who looks for problems.' It comes from an old folk tale, similar to the biblical prodigal son, about a man driven from home because he was thought to be a do-nothing. He works hard and returns home rich. Kongo people called him 'Rocamambu.' (Some had affectionately applied the name to Brazza on his third expedition to the Congo in the 1880s.) The musicians of Esengo, most of whom fit the rocamambu mold, gave it a well-turned musical update.

With two fervent Latinophiles, Kabasele and Essous, leading the way, Esengo kept the music in a Latin American groove. Essous began calling himself 'Jerry Lopez,' and the rumbas and cha-chas came thick and fast. Musicians from African Jazz and Rock'a Mambo seamlessly merged and separated according to the material at hand. Recordings by combinations of the two groups were sometimes issued under the name African Rock, while others bore the name of one of the singers and whichever band did the backing.

One studio's closing, the opening of another, and a raid on a third dramatically redrew the musical battle lines. Musicians who had been competitors at Opika and Loningisa became collaborators at Esengo. The studio's two main groups shook out like this: Rock'a Mambo featured the voice of Rossignol, guitarists Gogene and Antoine 'Papa Noël' Nedule, Essous and his clarinet, Malapet on saxophone, Honoré Liengo on contrabass, and Pandi playing congas. Singer and maracas player Roger Izeidi, although still employed by the moribund CEFA, joined African Jazz, headed by Kabasele, with Nico, Dechaud, and Tino Baroza playing guitar, saxophonist André Menga, trumpet player Dominique 'Willy' Kuntima (a.k.a. Willy Mbembe), Albert Taumani on contrabass, and Baskis and Depuissant on percussion. Most of Opika's other musicians came over to Esengo with African Jazz, including the Belgian Congo's most famous woman entertainer, Lucie Eyenga.

•

Women in Congo, the singer Abeti Masikini once remarked, 'cook and have babies. That's it. For women especially, music is a disaster, because it's [considered] a bad life.' In the village, music was everyone's province. Like work and food and sleep it was part of the rhythm of life. Citified popular music, on the other hand, was a product to be sold for profit. And worse than that, it abetted the evil of the bars. Even for men the job of professional musician was, in general, thought poorly of, particularly by parents whose sons might choose to pursue it. Nevertheless, the urban popular music of the two Congos was developing as a domain of males.

Throughout the colonial period, men recruited for their labor in various European enterprises led the movement from rural areas to the cities. In the 1920s, men in Léopoldville outnumbered women by more than three to one. At the end of World War II the imbalance was still two to one. Although Brazzaville's population was much smaller, a similar pattern of disparity between the sexes developed there.

For women left behind in the depopulated villages, the burdens grew, and soon they too began to move to the cities to join husbands, lovers, or other relatives. For most women, however, city life failed to live up to expectations. Until the 1950s, colonial era wages were rarely sufficient to support a family, and employment opportunities for women were scarce.

Given those conditions and the preponderance of men, many women organized themselves into the associations like Violette, The Rose, and Elegance, which Negro Jazz immortalized in song at Chez Faignond. These women's associations, Georges Balandier observed, 'curiously mingle mutual aid with amusement and with prostitution.' Their members were often the *ndumbas* of popular song, 'free women' who quickened the night (and day) life of Léopoldville and Brazzaville as much as the (male) musicians who alternately praised and lectured them.

Other women turned to more conventional means of support. They engaged in petty trading, gardened in small plots, or, like Franco's mother, cooked food to sell from their houses or in the local market. Some who came to town with savings opened small kiosks or *salons de coiffure*. A few who had managed to get some formal education landed jobs in male sectors as secretaries, postal workers, and the like. Fewer still attempted to break into the entertainment business.

Radio Congo Belge-Emissions Africaines, 'The Broadcasting Service for Natives' inaugurated in 1949, employed a Congolese woman announcer, Pauline Lisanga, in order 'to convince the indigenous community that women have also a part to play in the social and cultural advancement of the people.' The versatile Lisanga recorded several songs at Loningisa, where a few other women singers, Josephine Amba, Marie Kitoto, and Les Trois Amies, had also managed to gain a foothold. CEFA introduced Cameroonian singer Marcelle Ebibi Fylla, while over at Ngoma, Martha Madibala and Henriette Balako recorded a few sides.

Lucie Eyenga had begun to record at Opika in 1954. The twenty-year-old daughter of the capital made her debut in celebrated company – Kabasele, Nico, Dechaud, Tino Baroza – most of whom played on her sessions. Songs like 'Ohé Suka ya Rumba' (above all, the rumba) and 'Mokili Makalamba' (all the colors of the world) endeared her to a generation. When Opika closed, Esengo welcomed her.

•

One important exception to the mass movement from Opika to Esengo was Isaac Musekiwa. Noting the presence of a clarinetist and three saxophone players at Esengo, Musekiwa decided to try his luck at Loningisa, where O.K. Jazz was scrambling to regroup. With handsome Vicky Longomba at the mike and Franco, the 'guitarist who makes the hearts of women spin,' scribbling out hit after hit, O.K. Jazz held too much promise to be scuttled by personnel defections.

The remaining members of O.K. Jazz looked again to the old Negro Jazz for replacements. Singer Edo Ganga came in to sing with Vicky, while Célestin Kouka augmented the rhythm section on maracas. This was the group that Musekiwa joined when he came over from Opika. Soon after he arrived, the final piece fit into place when Brazzos, one of Vicky's cohorts from CEFA, signed on to play second guitar. They recorded a song, 'Babomi Mboka' (literally 'village killers,' in the sense that their music knocked people dead), to reintroduce themselves. 'Franco, Vicky, Edo, [Cé]lestin, De La [Lune], Dessoin ... Brazzos, Isaac, na bana O.K. Jazz.' They included their girlfriends in a second refrain, 'Franco na Majos-a, Vicky Victorine-a, Edo Josephine-a,' as if to say Franco loves Marie-José, and so on down the line. The addition of

The classic formation of O.K. Jazz from the late fifties (left to right) Nicolas 'Dessoin' Bosuma, Isaac Musekiwa, Brazzos (seated), Célestin Kouka, Victor 'Vicky' Longomba, Edouard 'Edo' Ganga, De La Lune on the electric upright bass, and Franco

Musekiwa and the others completed the classic O.K. Jazz lineup of the period. The musicians stayed together for the better part of two years.

The new personnel fostered an evolution of the group's sound. With Essous gone, Musekiwa's saxophone replaced clarinet in the duo with Franco's guitar. But more often than not, Franco and Brazzos fashioned their own version of the interweaving guitars made popular by African Jazz, freeing Musekiwa to back and fill and take a solo on the sebene.

Where African Jazz relied primarily on Kabasele's vocals, O.K. Jazz offered the duo of Vicky and Edo. 'We copied Patrice and Mario a little,' Edo said. The Italian-born, France-resident twosome of Patrizio Paganessi and Mario Moro had won popularity as Patrice and Mario by crooning sentimental songs in European music halls and on records during the forties and fifties. Edo continued:

They were very popular because, you see, they had come here [to Brazzaville]. They came here, and they also performed in Léopoldville. So they came and the musicians were very interested in their style, and they began to sing in that style. Sometimes in unison, sometimes we separated the voices out, first, second.

Léopoldville's musical realignment placed old friends in competing camps. Among them developed a contest of extraordinary intensity, but one of comity rather than bitterness. Musicians of each studio strained to create the next hit that would humble their rivals, then hung out with them later in the neighborhood. Edo Ganga recalled that if

> Esengo came out with something really hot, our boss would say, 'Did you hear that record that came out over there? Do something!' We do something. We do something. When our record comes out, the guys over there would say, 'Aaaaah! Did you hear that? Those guys over there – ' It was like that every time. Even with Kabasele it was like that.... So we started teasing each other like that. And then at a certain point, all of us had Vespas, eh! On the other side they had Lambrettas. We had Vespas. So when we would all meet up, everyone would be there, varoom, varoom. It was fabulous, fabulous competition.

While the contest between Loningisa and Esengo produced the hottest action, Ngoma carried on. The death of Nicolas Jeronimidis had left the studio in the hands of his brother-in-law Nikiforos Cavvadias, while changing trends had transformed it into the studio of the older generation. Most new talent signed contracts elsewhere. Like Bowane at Loningisa, Ngoma's older stars, Feruzi, Wendo, and D'Oliveira, found themselves out-paced by younger, larger bands. Wendo had responded in 1953 by electrifying his guitar and his fans with 'Bakosi Liwa ya Wendo,' which condemned premature talk of his musical death.

Around 1954, the studio embarked on a grand promotional tour of the provinces. Packed into two vehicles, equipment, musicians, drivers, technicians, and Cavvadias traveled to Stanleyville, Elisabethville, Luluabourg, and dozens of smaller towns in between. 'The drums had already told everyone that Ngoma with Wendo was coming,' Cavvadias said. 'We came with three of our big stars of the era, who were Bukasa, D'Oliveira, Wendo, whom I named at the time the Trio BOW.' The troupe would set up, often outdoors in a forest clearing or village common, to entertain vast audiences, most of whom knew the musicians from radio or records.

A change in mentality   71

courtesy of Alexandros Jeronimidis

Léon Bukasa promotes Vidor batteries and Bush radios for Ngoma

Ngoma built a new, more spacious and better-equipped studio during this period in an area known as Gombe in Léopoldville's west end. The musicians, however, felt it was too far away from the cité, so most recording continued to take place at the original outpost behind the Jeronimidis building. A new artist, Antoine Mundanda of Brazzaville, brought his likembe troupe to Ngoma in 1954, recording several songs that seemed to confirm the link between traditional likembe and modern guitar picking. Guitarist Adou Elenga struck a chord in this era of political awakening with a song called 'Ata Ndele (mokili ekobaluka)' (sooner or later the world will change). While not overtly political, the title alone sparked much rumor and debate about its meaning. The authorities condemned the song, and it was quickly deleted from the Ngoma catalog. Following that episode, Elenga's career began to fade. Of all the greats in the Ngoma stable only singer-guitarist Léon Bukasa, a former apprentice lathe operator from the far-off mining town of Elisabethville, seemed able to keep up with the public's changing musical tastes.

When he first came to Ngoma in 1950, Bukasa called his backing band, whoever it might include, Watoto wa Katanga, 'the children of Katanga,' his home province. Towards the latter part of the decade, in response to the prevailing fixation on the word *jazz*, he dubbed his backers Jazz Mango. Bukasa hired Antoine Nedule, a young guitarist of similar age and potential as Nico and Franco, who, because of his birth on Christmas Day, became known as 'Papa Noël.' In 1957 they recorded a rumba about a woman named 'Clara Badimuene' and began to tour the country in a quartet with saxophonist Albino Kalombo and bass player Joseph Mwena.

Bukasa's crisp, distinct baritone contrasted sharply with the higher pitched voices of Kabasele and the day's other singers. He kept his band small to leave space for its individual elements to be heard. Long instrumental openings create a distinct ambiance for each song before Bukasa begins to sing about his subject. On 'Louise Mungambule' Bukasa tells how Louise carried him – on the dance floor in this case – with the rumba that is sweeping the Congo. Papa Noël's successor Raymond Braynck (Braink) chimes in the background, picking his guitar like the palm wine players of West Africa. 'Kobeta Mwasi Te' features a jaunty guitar and clarinet duo in support of Bukasa's warning, 'don't strike a woman.' Bukasa successfully joined the cha-cha challenge with 'Bukasa Aleli,' Bukasa weeps (over a broken heart). Towards the end of 1958, Léon Bukasa seemed to carry the Ngoma banner almost by himself. But reinforcements were on the way.

Over at Esengo, Roitelet was stirring up trouble. Just as he had done at Loningisa, he rallied his colleagues to demand more money from the studio owner. When talk failed to produce a raise, Roitelet, who dreamed of a musicians' union, organized the others to stay away from work. But, as before, the tactic fell short. The colonial law of contracts prevailed. Roitelet lost his job once again, along with Tino Baroza.

Ngoma's Cavvadias, weighing the bounty of talent over the baggage of disputation, sent his driver to fetch Roitelet and Baroza. He signed up the two Esengo outcasts to begin working with Camille Feruzi and the A&R man, Pilaeis, on new material. Cavvadias had been recruiting other young artists too, singers Jean-Marie Assumani who called himself 'Franc Lassan,' André 'Depiano' João from Angola, and a third called 'Tchadé,' along with the more seasoned guitarist Pierre Bazetta, known as 'De La France.' These four plus bassist Roitelet, guitarist Baroza, Albino Kalombo on saxophone, trumpeter Henri Etari, and a drummer called Pierrot, fashioned a new formation they called the Beguen Band (named, according to Cavvadias, after the *beguine*).

The Beguen Band (left to right) Tino Baroza, Henri Etari, André 'Depiano' João, Albino Kalombo, a singer called Tchadé (holding drums), drummer Pierrot, Franc Lassan, Roitelet, and Pierre 'De La France' Bazetta

With these new arrivals, Ngoma presented a more balanced mix of old-line stars and youthful challengers. As if to consecrate the studio's rejuvenation, Wendo and the Beguen Band gave the celebrated 'Marie-Louise' a facelift, as a cha-cha.

•

In the late 1950s studios began to resemble professional sports franchises in the period of free agency. Their rosters frequently changed as old contracts expired and new ones grew shorter. Despite numerous comings and goings and the births of several new bands, the battle for musical supremacy was largely fought between African Jazz and O.K. Jazz, with Rock'a Mambo, Beguen Band, and the others sniping from close range. 'It was so fine, it was so good,' Edo Ganga effused.

> If you could go back to that period, I think it was better making music at that time. Because at least, whether it was the music lover, the man in the street, they knew how important this cultural moment was. It was fantastic. It was a passionately engaging time.

In less than a decade the handful of local studios had turned a doubtful avocation into a well-paid profession. From the sanctuary of the studios Congolese musicians had created works of such inspiration that the demand for records exceeded supply on both sides of the Congo River.

Even as sales increased, however, expensive record players and the fragile 78 r.p.m. discs remained out of financial reach for the majority of Congolese. Radio Congo Belge-Emissions Africaines filled some of the void with a variety of music and *disques demandés* (record request) programs. Radio Brazzaville did the same. But radios, like record players, were largely the toys of better paid laborers and the *evolués*. For the average resident of Brazza and Léo the likeliest place to hear the hottest new records was in one of the two cities' many bars.

Brazzaville boasted the prestigious Chez Faignond, Léopoldville its O.K. Bar, Air France, and Quist. But for each of the more famous watering holes, scores of lesser known spots catered to the common people. Like the populations of both cities, their numbers had exploded to meet the demand for entertainment. One estimate had it that Léopoldville's old *cité*, Kinshasa and Kintambo districts, plus the new one southwest of the airport – the districts Dendale, Kalamu, and Ngiri-Ngiri – contained 330 bars.

Some, like the one Belgian journalist Jean Welle discovered in the 1950s, were rather commodious,

> a spacious enclosure surrounded by white walls, no roof, decorated with garlands and Chinese lanterns. Loaded with glasses and bottles of beer, the tables are encircled with many patrons. In the center, the dance floor, and on a platform, the band.

Others were no more than an ordinary house parlor with a record player for the dancers, and a few tables and chairs scattered about.

Bar patrons could unwind from the day's travail with food, conversation, and companionship accompanied by the latest Congolese music and pints of lukewarm beer. The food would likely be mounds of *nkwanga*, manioc, a thick paste made from cassava root, or *mosaka*, a dish of rice, chicken, cassava leaves, and palm oil. The beer was 'super bon' Polar or its staunch competitor, Primus, 'la bonne humeur en bouteille,' the standard-bearers of Léo's two main breweries. And conversation in this era of political awakening probably gravitated to the declarations of *Conscience Africaine* and ABAKO. What better place for a stranger from the hinterland to cultivate connections and sharpen his political skills?

•

Patrice Lumumba came to Léopoldville in 1957 in much the same way as he would leave it a few years later, in the custody of the authorities. He had worked in the colonial postal service in Stanleyville but earned much of his high visibility as a member of various associations of *évolués*. Although the truth is difficult to discern, it appears that Stanleyville authorities feared the political ramifications of Lumumba's increasing popularity. They turned his occasional borrowing from postal funds – money which, according to Lumumba's biographer Robin McKown, he accounted for openly with signed notes and repaid in full – into a charge of embezzling postal funds. A Stanleyville court sentenced him to two years in prison. Six months later he was brought to the capital for his appeal to be heard. According to Thomas Kanza, who covered the hearing for *Congo*, the Belgian Congo's first independent Congolese-run newspaper, colonial authorities in Brussels intervened at this stage to prevent 'a political or racial scandal.' The court responded by reducing Lumumba's sentence to the six months he had already served.

Upon his release, Lumumba went to work as sales manager for Bracongo, brewers of Polar, Léopoldville's number two beer behind Primus. Tabu Ley Rochereau, at the time still a schoolboy and not yet professionally involved in music, remembered that Lumumba chartered an airplane to drop leaflets across the *cité* touting the pleasures of Polar. Lumumba hired Rock'a Mambo as part of his advertising scheme, a partnership that dissolved some months later when members of the band were caught drinking Primus.

Lumumba cut an imposing figure. His slender frame stretched a full head above most Congolese as if his bloodline flowed in part from the elegantly tall Tutsi people of eastern Africa. Brush strokes of goatee and mustache dotted his angular face under a serif of close-cropped hair neatly parted on the left. His piercing eyes, slightly magnified by the lenses of dark-framed spectacles, riveted onto whatever came within their purview.

Lumumba's greatest asset and his most successful tool, for both Polar and himself, was his considerable power of persuasion. He spent hours each day touring the bars, chatting up consumers of his chief competitor's product. By the beginning of 1958, these contacts had pushed Polar beer into the number one position, but more importantly, they had increased Lumumba's own personal following. Soon politics would replace beer at the top of his agenda. Like the maturing music of the bars, the movement for Congolese self-determination was coming of age.

•

The maturing of Congolese pop music had been spectacularly swift. Like other notable offspring of encounters between African and European music – the Cuban *son*, American jazz, and the soon-to-emerge reggae of Jamaica – Congo music had made the leap from traditional to modern in roughly the span of a single generation. Sheltered by Léopoldville's recording studios, part-time minstrels had quickly grown into full-time professionals. Elements mingled in a musical salad, to use Guy-Léon Fylla's metaphor. Conga drums, maracas, and the big contrabass refashioned village rhythms and their cousins from Cuba. Trilling guitars playing in rhythm-and-solo duos, like the left and right hands on a piano keyboard, echoed likembe players of old. Singers, sometimes in the falsetto voice common to traditional music, soloed in the emotive spirit of Tino Rossi or harmonized with each other in the manner they had learned in mission school choirs or by listening to Patrice and Mario. They reached out to the village again for call and response flourishes with each other or one of the instrumentalists, and they plumbed the depths of life in the city for the stories they put into song.

While composers wrote out the words to their songs, almost none knew how to write musical notation. The Congolese rumba was music of the head, emerging first from the composer's imagination then arranged by the group and memorized. Each composition consisted of a series of verses, often interrupted after the first one or two by a brief instrumental passage, the section Henri Bowane had called the sebene on 'Marie-Louise.' More verses, sometimes alternating with a refrain, followed before a longer sebene and perhaps another verse or two (occasionally repeats of earlier verses) closed out the song. Little vocables, an 'eh' or an 'o' and often 'mama,' Congo music's equivalent of 'baby' (on some songs 'mama' meant the more respectful 'mother'), were sometimes added to lengthen a line or make it rhyme.

Many bands punctuated their rumbas with a dum dum dum – da da da sequence from the instrumentalists, often followed by a one-beat rest or a note held for two beats, that appears to be a Congolese refinement of a similar feature of the Cuban *son*. The figure creates a beguiling little pause, then the music takes off again. Lead guitar or saxophone, and occasionally trumpet, would solo on the sebenes, but rarely would such privilege extend to the rhythm guitar and never to the bass or the congas. If the guitar supplied the sebene's underpinning, one of the horns would improvise on top. Likewise if a horn laid the foundation, the lead guitarist was free to improvise on that.

Gone were the days when Congolese musicians simply mimicked the latest songs from abroad. They had fused the foreign with the familiar to produce their own Congolese sound. Lucie Eyenga said it with 'Ohé Suka ya Rumba':

> Singers sing
> So let those who dance, dance,
> And those who watch, watch,
> And those who listen, listen.
> But for us, in the end,
> It all comes down to rumba –
> our rumba.

As the Congolese rumba matured, its language began to change. A song or two in Spanish still came out from time to time, but singers of Ki-kongo, Tshiluba, and Swahili turned increasingly to the emerging vernacular, Lingala. Lingala is thought to have developed early in the twentieth century as a pidgin to facilitate trade among the various peoples along the Congo River. Each group, having its own language, needed a way to communicate with the others. Although linguists have yet to fully agree on its origins, Congo (Kinshasa) linguist Tshimpaka Yanga argues persuasively that Libinza speakers coined the name Lingala. The Bobangi people who came to dominate the river trade contributed much of Lingala's vocabulary. Missionaries in need of more words to translate the Scriptures borrowed from other local languages to expand its vocabulary and usage still further. The Force Publique, a collection of men from various ethnic groups, gradually adopted Lingala as its official language in the late twenties and early thirties. And in the urban melting pots of Brazza and Léo, Lingala bridged the barriers between African workers of varying background.

Musicians composed more and more songs in Lingala, contributing their own additions, often slang expressions or changes in connotation, to the growing lexicon. Franco, for example, through his repeated use of ndumba – Lingala for unmarried woman – to suggest a woman of loose moral character or a prostitute, all but rendered the word's original meaning obsolete. The music's popularity spread Lingala to the farthest reaches of the two Congos. Its use had the effect of eliminating the ethnic baggage that songs in, say, Kikongo or Tshiluba would carry, giving them more universal appeal. Lingala 'de-tribalized' the music as well as the Force Publique, Léopoldville, and, to a lesser extent, Brazzaville.

Towards the end of the fifties a hip new dialect emerged among Léopoldville's alienated youth, a hodgepodge of slang derived from French and Lingala called Hindoubill. The colonial system educated young Congolese through primary school but offered them few opportunities for employment. Secondary schools had space for only a fraction of primary graduates, and in any case jobs requiring higher education were largely reserved for Europeans. As a result the ranks of under-educated, unemployed Congolese youth steadily grew. Many amused themselves with *diamba* (marijuana) and attendance at American cowboy movies. They called themselves 'Bills' from Pecos Bill and Buffalo Bill of the big screen. *Ngandas* were their hideouts and bicycles their horses. They favored jeans and checkered shirts, preferably purchased at a *prix yankee* (Yankee price, or bargain), and adopted names like Wayne and Tex.

Hindoubill became their idiom, named in part for the Hindu of Indian movies, which competed for favor with the Westerns. *Ko pedalé*, from French for pedaling a bicycle, evoked 'death' in Hindoubill much like 'bought the farm' in the jargon of America. For the English slang 'bread' or 'scratch' the Bills were said to have at least twenty money metaphors. Hooligans were *balados*, the clever were *yankés* (Yankees), and they called their neighborhoods Texas, Dallas, and Santa Fe.

Hindoubill enriched the repertoires of Congolese bands. Composers injected their songs with slang expressions, and, as musicologist Damien Pwono reports, Hindoubill sometimes helped fit a line of verse to a troublesome melody where the use of standard Lingala would not work. The Bills' swaggering speech and smoldering discontent spiced the urban stew. Their anger seethed in tandem with that of the *évolués*, albeit from the opposite end of the social spectrum.

•

The Belgians seemed unmoved by the growing unrest among 'their' Congolese. In a speech to the Belgian parliament towards the end of 1957, the minister of overseas territories, Auguste Buissert, declared, 'This country has firmly decided to continue its African task and not to abandon any of its sovereign rights, which guarantee that the job will be finished.' But across the river in Brazzaville, deliverance looked less like a pipe dream.

On an August afternoon in 1958, a plane carrying Charles de Gaulle touched down at Brazzaville's Maya-Maya Airport. De Gaulle had acceded to power in France the previous June in the midst of a political crisis – precipitated by the war for independence being waged in the French colony of Algeria – which ended the Fourth Republic. He was touring France's overseas territories in a campaign to sell his new constitution for the budding Fifth Republic. The document proposed a French community of autonomous republics, one of which would be the French Congo. A *yes* vote in a referendum to be held at the end of September would seal this new relationship. Independence, de Gaulle told the crowd assembled at Eboué Stadium, could follow if the Congolese wanted it. Although France would clearly be the senior partner under the new arrangement – keeping control over defense and foreign policy along with finances and raw materials – limited autonomy and the promise of eventual independence produced overwhelming approval in all the French African territories except Guinea. On November 28, 1958, the old Moyen-Congo became the Republic of Congo (République du Congo), a member of the new French Community.

These events were closely watched across the river in Léopoldville. In October, Patrice Lumumba, along with Joseph Ileo and others from *Conscience Africaine*, formed a new organization called the Mouvement National Congolais (MNC). Where ABAKO advocated an independence based on regional and ethnic separatism – ideally a Bakongo state, or, barring that, a kind of loose federation – the MNC favored a unified nation-state to encompass the entire territory of the Belgian Congo. In December Lumumba attended the All-African Peoples Conference in Accra, where he met other nationalist leaders like Ghana's Nkrumah and Tom Mboya of Kenya. On his return to Léopoldville Lumumba spoke openly for independence.

For the Belgian colonials, the rudest awakening came on January 4, 1959. An ABAKO meeting planned for that day at a Y.M.C.A. in the Kalamu district of the new *cité* had been banned by the mayor of Léopoldville. According to Ruth Slade, ABAKO supporters gathered anyway and

> talked wildly of independence; M. Kasavubu who was also present, failed to calm them. The police arrived and resorted to the use of firearms; anger spread throughout the native city, and the cry of independence was taken up; the pent-up fury of many months was unloosed; Europeans were attacked and churches, schools, hospitals, and social centres destroyed. The Europeans gave way to panic, the Army was called in, and the repression was violent.

More than forty Africans died, and hundreds on both sides suffered injuries.
While attacks on whites and cries for independence made headlines in the West, the social conditions that caused them did not. 'The overpopulation and the poverty of parts of the native city were appalling,' Slade wrote. 'The salaries of certain categories of workers were too low to pay for adequate food and lodging for a family.... In addition, there was a very large number of unemployed – estimates vary between fifteen and forty thousand.' Many of these were young adolescents like the Bills who hung out in the markets and on street corners with little to hope for and less to do.

In the wake of the riots, Africans and Europeans began to take stock. Belgium's King Baudouin (successor to his father, Leopold III), echoing General de Gaulle, spoke for the first time of independence for his Congo. Recommendations for reform that had long been under study were announced by the government, among them freedom of speech, an end to racial discrimination, and new institutions for self-government of the colony whose members would be elected on the basis of universal suffrage. Congolese leaders organized more political parties and held a congress in Luluabourg for members of the various groups to meet and discuss strategy.

Congolese musicians began to examine their own positions. Freedom of speech opened a whole new range of possibilities for composers. No longer would they be consigned to sing platitudes of love or mask convictions under a veil of innuendo. Evocative yearnings like 'Ata Ndele' (sooner or later) or 'Congo ya Sika' (new Congo) could be much bolder now. Roitelet's dream of a musicians' union might even have a chance to be realized.

The changing situation on both banks of the river caused the Brazzaville musicians who worked in Léo to think of new possibilities. 'Independence for the Belgian Congo is coming,' Nino Malapet recalled telling his compatriots. 'There is going to be a change in mentality. Are we going to continue to live in a foreign country? There are enough of us good Congolese musicians from Brazzaville to form a band and return home.' Malapet, Essous, and Pandi were already together in Rock'a Mambo. They talked to Edo Ganga, Célestin Kouka, and De La Lune, the Brazzavilleans in O.K. Jazz. All agreed on the project. Lacking guitarists, the Brazzaville six recruited two from the Belgian side, a lead player called Dicky and an accompanist, Jean Dinos. Each carried on with his respective band, but when circumstances permitted, the musicians stole away to Kinsuka along the Congo River cataracts on the western outskirts of Léopoldville to rehearse their new ensemble. A name for the group had already surfaced, a name based on the word, common to many central and southern African languages, meaning people. They would call themselves Orchestre Bantou. In June of 1959, after six months of secret rehearsals, all but Malapet – who again had contractual problems – quit their studios and moved back across the river.

The Brazzaville they returned to was vastly different from the one they had left a few years earlier. Instead of headquarters for the Federation of French Equatorial Africa, Brazzaville had become the capital of a Congolese republic. Although still in the domain of the French Community, Congo Brazzaville was now ostensibly governed by Africans elected by Africans. Their leader was Prime Minister Fulbert Youlou, a defrocked Catholic priest and former mayor of Brazzaville, who had taken up the mantle of the fallen André Matsoua, the man who had started the mutual aid Amicale movement. Since 1956, Youlou had gradually built his UDDIA (Union Démocratique de Défense des Intérêts Africains) from its base among the Lari people, many of whom were Matsouanists, into a political party of standing equal to that of the more established MSA (Mouvement Socialist Africain). Elections for the old Moyen-Congo territorial assembly in 1957 had seen the MSA led by Jacques Opangault edge Youlou's UDDIA by only one seat. An MSA defector gave the UDDIA a one-seat majority the following year, and Youlou used it to consolidate his power through approval of a new constitution and a redistricting of assembly seats that would favor his party. As the musicians of Orchestre Bantou returned home in June of 1959, new elections gave Youlou an overwhelming majority.

Homecoming was sweet for Essous and his friends. They had departed as neophytes in the old Negro Jazz and returned as well-seasoned veterans. Back at Chez Faignond, their original *patron* agreed to help them once again. For two months the group rehearsed intensely with instruments provided by Faignond. Then on August 15, 1959, Orchestre Bantou played its first public concert. Rue Mbakas crackled with excitement as Brazzavilleans flocked to Chez Faignond. The night was 'extraordinary,' Essous remembered. 'When people came in, they were happy. Happy and proud. Because at least for once they had a band in their home town, a worthy one.'

In fact, a group of newcomers led by saxophonist Rigobert 'Max' Massengo had gotten nearly a year's head start on Orchestre Bantou. Calling themselves the Negro Band, this Brazzaville-bred ensemble of beginners had also played at Chez Faignond. But the musicians of Negro Band lacked the stature Essous, Pandi, Edo, and the others had gained through their work with O.K. Jazz and Rock'a Mambo. When Orchestre Bantou mounted the stage at Chez Faignond that August evening, Brazzavillean music lovers surrendered unconditionally.

Orchestre Bantou sounded very much like Rock'a Mambo, with Essous's clarinet hovering prominently behind the singers or playing off the lead guitar. Edo and Célestin contributed a taste of O.K. Jazz on vocals, sometimes in the company of Essous, who loved to sing. Célestin and De La Lune were the group's original dandies. They wore baggy, pleated trousers up around the lower chest just like those worn in Paris. Célestin groomed his hair meticulously, combing each lock with a great sweeping motion, parting them on one side, then securing his handiwork with the touch of a hot iron. On some nights the musicians took the stage dressed like pirates in ruffled shirts, bandanas on their heads, sporting an earring like Errol Flynn at the height of swashbuckling extravagance. Women dissolved in spasms of giddy delight. Men simmered with admiration and jealousy.

While Brazzaville celebrated, Léopoldville mourned. The defectors had riven the ranks of O.K. Jazz and Rock'a Mambo. Both bands struggled to plug the gaps. Difficulties within O.K. Jazz were compounded by Franco's untimely incarceration for traffic offenses incurred on his Vespa. The band carried on in the hands of Vicky Longomba, but within a few months he too would be gone. The tumultuous end of the fifties foretold uncertain sixties.

6
Celebrations and sorrows

Kasavubu, Lumumba, African Jazz, and O.K. Jazz, 1960–1961

A call for musicians came at the end of 1959 from Thomas Kanza, an employee of the European Economic Community and the Belgian Congo's first African to attend the distinguished Louvain University near Brussels. Events had overtaken Belgium's policy of gradual self-government for its colony. On December 15 the Belgian government announced that a 'Round Table' conference of Congolese and Belgian leaders would be held early in the new year in Brussels to sort things out. Kanza, the son of a prominent ABAKO leader, Daniel Kanza, was acting as a liaison between the various conference participants. He wanted some musicians to come to Belgium to entertain Congolese delegates. Negotiating independence was like bringing in the crops: both required music to lighten the load.

Joseph Kabasele, the Belgian Congo's greatest star, was an obvious choice to go, as was Franco of O.K. Jazz. 'During his last visit to Léo, Mr. Thomas Kanza contacted Kabasele and me to form a select band which would perform in Belgium in the days to come,' explained Vicky Longomba, then the leader of O.K. Jazz. 'I then submitted the question to Franco. He declined the proposal claiming that he couldn't take on such a mission since O.K. Jazz had already accepted [another] engagement.' But Vicky himself and O.K. Jazz guitarist Brazzos agreed to join with Kabasele. The group would number seven: Kabasele, Nico, Dechaud, and Roger Izeidi of African Jazz; Brazzos, who would play bass, and Vicky from O.K. Jazz; and a conga drummer named Pierre 'Petit Pierre' Yantula. They would perform together as African Jazz.

Several of the remaining musicians of African Jazz, many of whom had day jobs and couldn't travel anyway, regrouped in Kabasele's absence under the name Jazz African, while O.K. Jazz scrambled to replace its two key members.

The hastily re-formed African Jazz gave a farewell concert at the Lisala Bar in Léopoldville at the end of January 1960 and then boarded a flight for Europe. Delegates to the Round Table conference had been in session for nearly two weeks when the band arrived in Brussels. African Jazz brought them a little taste of home. At Kanza's request, Charles Hénault, a Belgian jazz drummer who had played the Guest House in Léopoldville a couple of years before, rented equipment and purchased matching tuxedos for the musicians to wear. Two nights a week the group played the posh Plaza Hotel, headquarters of Joseph Kasavubu and the ABAKO delegation. At other times they worked smaller clubs and private parties around Brussels. On off nights they hung out at the Anges Noirs (black angels), a night club which catered to a mixed crowd of Africans and hipper Europeans. There they met the leader of the house band, a saxophone-playing Cameroonian named Manu Dibango.

The band also encountered Gilles Sala, a singer from Guadeloupe who also worked as a radio broadcaster and print journalist and was covering the cultural side of the Round Table for RTF French radio. 'Personally I was very impressed by African Jazz, this style of playing, this way of doing things,' Sala said. 'These famous guitarists, these marvelous singers who really had a sense for popular music. Tunes that stayed with you. A sense for commercial music. That was extremely important.'

For the ordinary Belgian it was as if a contingent of Martians had landed its flying saucers at the Palais de Congrès. South African journalist Colin Legum observed at the time, 'The sight of two hundred black faces in the streets and squares and hotels of Brussels made the *presence* of the Congo a reality for the majority of the Belgians for the first time in their lives. People stood unashamedly and stared.' Roger Izeidi remembered that 'people came, women especially, to see if [my color] came off.... They picked up the instruments to see if they were real. People thought we had put a tape on.' Nico Kasanda said, 'It was the first time they had seen an African guitarist, more specifically Congolese.' According to Nico, a Belgian radio announcer was so taken with his playing she called him a doctor of his craft. Nico Kasanda picked up his Ph.D. His fans would call him Docteur Nico for the rest of his life.

The Round Table conference held its first session on January 20 without Patrice Lumumba. The MNC leader had been arrested after rioting broke out

African Jazz at the Plaza Hotel in Brussels 1960 (left to right around the microphone) Vicky Longomba, guest Gilles Sala, Joseph Kabasele, and Roger Iziedi. Behind them, Charles 'Dechaud' Mwamba, Pierre Yantula, Brazzos on the bass, Nicolas 'Docteur Nico' Kasanda, and Charles Hénault. An unidentified admirer dances on the right following one of his speeches in Stanleyville the previous October. But the Belgian authorities were obliged to release him when the Congolese delegates already in Brussels threatened to stay away from the meetings. Lumumba landed in Brussels six days after the conference opened and went on to dominate the proceedings. The day after his arrival the Africans of the Belgian Congo heard the announcement they had hoped for: their country would gain its independence on June 30, 1960. Thomas Kanza later observed, 'The Belgians, having done nothing to promote among the Congolese any exercise of national responsibility, suddenly found that they had to achieve in four months what they had refused to do for the past fifty years.' It was a tall order.

In the heady atmosphere of the Round Table, where Congolese leaders for the first time met their Belgian masters on seemingly equal footing, Kabasele introduced the song for which he will always be remembered, 'Indépendance Cha Cha.' Its simple but eloquent words saluted Congolese leaders and their parties by name set to music of almost uncontrolled exuberance. 'Indépendance cha cha tozwí eh,' independence, we've won it!

While the Round Table delegates thrashed out the sixteen points of their provisional constitution, the musicians of African Jazz busied themselves in a recording studio associated with Gramophone (HMV). They recorded several songs, including 'Indépendance Cha Cha,' another Kabasele song 'Table Ronde,' and a composition by Vicky Longomba entitled 'Vive Lumumba Patrice.' As Izeidi told it, Gramophone wasn't interested in the recordings, so Kabasele shopped the masters around to other companies, eventually making a deal with Fonior. The records were released on the African Jazz label bearing the Brussels address of Thomas Kanza's *Congo* newspaper. These new recordings, Gilles Sala declared, 'sent a musical shock wave. It was pretty extraordinary, this spontaneous, natural music.' As colonial dominoes began to topple, Africans across the continent celebrated their freedom to the tune of 'Indépendance Cha Cha.'

Back home in the Congo little time and less will remained for Congolese and Belgian leaders to develop plans for an independent state. Political parties – some based on ethnicity, others regional, and fewer of national outlook – campaigned furiously to elect their candidates to six provincial assemblies and a national chamber of deputies. Once constituted, the provincial assemblies were to elect representatives to sit in a senate which, together with the chamber of deputies, would comprise the country's bicameral parliament. The parliament would then draft a constitution and select the first president and prime minister of the Congo. For the country's Europeans, the thought

African Jazz label

of being governed by their former subjects was unsettling to say the least. Hundreds began to transfer financial assets out of the country, and hundreds more transferred themselves.

While the political drama played on, the musicians of African Jazz returned home in May, following concerts in Holland and France, to find themselves at the absolute pinnacle of success. They brought a new recruit with them, the Belgian jazz drummer Charles Hénault, who had helped to facilitate their European sojourn. Hénault was amazed at the band's homecoming welcome: 'We crossed the river' from Brazzaville, where the flight from Paris had landed,

> and cars were waiting for us. And we rode around all of [Léopoldville], oh la la!, the modern city and the old city. People were screaming, they threw flowers at us. It was crazy. It was crazy. It was almost like a president's motorcade. It was incredible. And the horns, and the noise. The noise as though there were some big wedding going on.

'Indépendance Cha Cha' seemed to flow in overlapping waves from every record player and sound system in the cité.

Kabasele summed up the trip for the newspaper *Présence Congolaise*:

> During our first concert in Europe, the foreign press present interviewed me. All could well believe that we were from the Congo, but not that we were capable of making such beautiful, such impressive music. I assure you that, to some degree, we confirmed for the other nations that the Congo was old enough to enjoy its independence.

Some of the musicians who had stayed behind in Léo working as Jazz African rejoined Kabasele and the others. Depuissant reclaimed his conga drums from Pierre Yantula, while Charles Hénault moved in beside Depuissant with his traps. It wasn't the first use of a jazz-style drum set in Congolese music — Cavvadias had purchased a set for Ngoma around 1958 — but with a white drummer handling the sticks, it was surely the most extraordinary. African Jazz towered above its competitors like a boxer, arms upraised, rejoicing over a sprawling opponent.

For lovers of Congolese music, zeal in support of their favorite band was no vice. Like the athletes and spectators at a Saturday afternoon football match, musicians and their fans formed allegiances of great passion. As younger players emerged and new bands formed, music lovers appraised them with reference to their more established competitors. Nearly everyone *was* a critic, and the continual debate gave rise to the notion of stylistic schools. A new group might be said to follow the African Jazz school or the O.K. Jazz school.

These distinctions were drawn, for the most part, on comparisons between each group's singers and guitarists. Among the singers, Joseph Kabasele reigned without peer. He was a *chanteur de charme*, a charm singer in the fashion of Tino Rossi. Kabasele's voice evoked feelings of passion and sentimentality that Congolese music lovers found irresistible. Congolese singers followed the Kabasele school even if they wanted to sing in O.K. Jazz.

Where guitarists were concerned, the debate proved more contentious. Nico and Franco emerged as great stars, each with a different approach. Nico favored a relaxed manner picking his way through a piece one crystal-clear note at a time. He loved to improvise and claimed he rarely played a song the same way twice. Franco too could pick, but he often preferred to pluck his electric guitar like his old acoustic model, playing chords using thumb and forefinger. Whereas Nico's playing echoed the likembe, Franco's style resembled the traditional lute players. One Congolese music critic observed that 'African Jazz (which no longer has anything African for that matter) leans toward an Americo-European modernism at which it clearly excels, while O.K. Jazz intends to remain typically African.'

When Antoine 'Papa Noël' Nedule later joined Orchestre Bantou of Brazzaville, a third school of guitar began to develop. Jazz-lover Papa Noël preferred a more fluid style of picking that blended notes and chords less starkly. He and especially Nico were considered more outward looking, while Franco came to be seen as a link to tradition. Yet the classification of musicians into disparate camps overlooked their similarities. Both Nico and Franco claimed to draw inspiration from traditional sources, and there is no reason to doubt them. But both were also committed modernists who pushed the musical boundaries. Indeed, as the ensuing years would show, Franco the supposed traditionalist, not Nico or Noël, would demonstrate the temperament, managerial skills, and musical vision to shape the future of the Congolese rumba.

Among Léopoldville's burgeoning crop of young singers, the next star would come from the school of African Jazz. His name was Pascal Tabou, but he became known by his answer to a question from a primary school history lesson, 'Who is the French colonel who defended Belfort during the Franco-Prussian war?' As Tabou related the story, only he knew the correct answer, Colonel Pierre Denfert-Rochereau. His merciless classmates never let him forget it. From that point on Tabou, not Pierre, was the Rochereau.

Although born in Bagata along the Kwilu River, Rochereau was a city boy, raised and schooled in the capital. His slender frame and lean features, common among Léopoldville's children, made him appear taller than the five-and-a-half feet he measured. He grew up to the tunes of Wendo and Kabasele, Tino Rossi and Gilbert Bécaud, and the religious hymns he sang in church. The fathers in the local parish hoped he would train for the priesthood, but his mother objected since he was her only son. His first brush with notoriety (beyond his knowledge of French history) came as a fifteen-year-old contestant in a singing competition held to select those who would fill out a program in honor of King Baudouin's 1955 visit to the Congo.

Emboldened by his good reception and being a fan of Kabasele, Rochereau began to send his compositions to the leader of African Jazz. He edged his way closer to the band's inner circle until the musicians allowed him to sit in on rehearsals. In this way he learned the group's entire repertoire. One day in 1958, with Kabasele out of town, Rochereau made his first recording at Esengo singing on a song by Nino Malapet and Rock'a Mambo called 'Micky Me Quiero' (Micky loves me, in Spanish). A year later, again in Kabasele's absence, he sang with African Jazz before a live audience at the most fashionable of the new cité's clubs, the Vis-à-Vis (face to face). Rochereau gave the date as June 6, 1959: 'That was the great beginning.' Kabasele loaned the young singer to O.K. Jazz to cover for Vicky's departure, but when the musicians of African Jazz returned from the Round Table, Rochereau took his place among them.

•

In the volatile year of 1960, music and politics could hardly remain separate. Kabasele supported Lumumba and, according to Rochereau, often took him around town in his big white convertible with young Rochereau himself at the wheel. In song, however, Kabasele and the other Congolese musicians supported independence and unity but refrained from taking sides in the elections. Léon Bukasa, for example, wrote his own independence cha-cha, 'Kongo Dipanda' (Congo independence), recorded by the Beguen Band.

With time evaporating rapidly, Lumumba had precious little for socializing. As leader of the MNC, one of the few parties to cultivate a country-wide following, he spent the months between the Round Table and May's elections campaigning for the party's candidates for the new Chamber of Deputies. His principal opposition came from the Parti National du Progrès (PNP), a coalition of more than twenty local parties from around the country. Belgium viewed the PNP, led by Paul Bolya, as a moderate party which might be more amenable to the soon-to-be-former ruler's interests than Lumumba's MNC. With the PNP, the Belgians placed their hopes and considerable money. Other parties were ethnic or regional, like Joseph Kasavubu's ABAKO of the Kongo people and the Confédération des Associations Ethniques du Katanga (CONAKAT) of Moïse Tshombe. Based in Katanga, where the Belgian company Union Minière was heavily invested in mining the Congo's copper, CONAKAT was Belgium's wildcard should the PNP fail to win power.

Elections went off remarkably well given the country's lack of experience with the exercise. Results showed that Lumumba's MNC had picked up the most seats, thirty-six, with the PNP in second place at fourteen. Lumumba's party had won seats in five of the six provinces, with support in the sixth ensured by its ally, BALUBAKAT (Baluba in Katanga), winners of six seats in Katanga. But in the 137-seat Chamber of Deputies no one had a majority. Whoever was to govern would have to bargain with his opponents.

Following a couple of false starts, Lumumba managed to deal and cajole his way into the position of prime minister of the first government of an independent Congo. One compromise gave the ceremonial post of president to Joseph Kasavubu, while ministerial portfolios were distributed among other parties who joined in coalition with the MNC. The group formed an unlikely

Celebrations and sorrows 91

alliance of rivals whose good will was far from assured. Thomas Kanza, soon to be Congo's ambassador to the United Nations, later wrote,

> Each time the Council of Ministers met I was amazed at how people so different, so opposed in their ideas, with such complex personalities and such diverse and divergent ambitions could hope to form a homogeneous group for effective and coherent administration.

At 11:00 a.m. on Thursday, June 30, 1960, the ceremony to transfer power to the Congolese began at the Parliament building in Léopoldville. Belgium's King Baudouin spoke unapologetically of his distant relative King Leopold II and what the Belgians had 'accomplished' in their colony. President Kasavubu replied with appropriate diplomatic niceties. Prime Minister Lumumba, however, would have no part of diplomacy. Although he was not scheduled to address the gathering, he had secretly arranged to do so just the same. Lumumba spoke from the heart about the suffering of the people he now would try to lead.

> This struggle of tears, fire, and blood makes us profoundly proud because it was a noble and just struggle, an indispensable struggle to put an end to the humiliating bondage imposed on us by force. Our lot was eighty years of colonial rule; our wounds are still too fresh and painful to be driven from our memory.

With Baudouin and Kasavubu looking increasingly uneasy, Lumumba went into overdrive, reciting a litany of wrongs committed by the Belgians. He then called upon his people to put aside differences for the sake of unity. 'Together, my brothers, we are going to begin a new struggle, a sublime struggle which is going to lead our country to peace, prosperity, and grandeur.'

When Lumumba finished, to strong applause, officials of both countries signed the independence proclamation, and the new Republic of the Congo embarked on a long weekend of celebration. Joseph Kabasele and African Jazz recounted the occasion with a new song, 'Bilombe ba Gagne' (the courageous have won), as searing as Lumumba's speech.

> Such was the state of things yesterday
> The black man knew poverty
> Forced labor, the whip
> Whatever he said, his words met with a poor reception:
> 'Monkey shut up!'

Freedom had surely come.

The thrill of emancipation lasted a scant three days. Belgium had hoped for the kind of flag-and-anthem independence France had engineered in many of its African colonies, where the appearance of self-rule masked continued control by Paris. To that end the Belgians had backed the moderate PNP. Patrice Lumumba's electoral success and his ability to pull together a government from diverse parliamentary factions foiled that prospect. But Belgium had hedged its position in three important areas: it had courted the politicians of Katanga, where its most important economic interests lay; additional Belgian troops were flown in to augment the existing garrisons; and Belgian officers still commanded the Congolese Force Publique.

On July 4, the first back-to-work Monday in the new independent Republic of the Congo, Congolese soldiers began to wonder why, with Lumumba, Kasavubu, and an entirely African council of ministers in charge, they still took orders from Belgian officers. After all, the Force Publique had ceased to exist; they now belonged to the Congolese National Army. Their Belgian commander-in-chief, Lieutenant-General Emile Janssens, posed the answer in the plainest of terms: 'after independence = before independence.'

Congolese soldiers in Léopoldville would have none of this effrontery. They began to openly disobey orders. By Friday, a week after independence, a revolt among Congolese army troops had spread throughout the Congo. Foot soldiers arrested their white officers, and trouble spread to the civilian population. Verified reports of violence against Europeans and unsubstantiated rumors of every description began to filter back to the capital. Lumumba fired General Janssens, who promptly fled the country along with thousands of panic-stricken Europeans. Belgian troops left their bases to occupy the capital and other major areas of unrest.

Lumumba and his ministers moved quickly to Africanize the army's officer corps by directing the soldiers in each unit to elect their own officers. The Lumumba government selected two men with past service in the Force Publique to lead the reorganized army. Victor Lundula, mayor of one of the districts in Jadotville, was appointed general and commander-in-chief to replace Janssens. A secretary of state to the presidency, Joseph Mobutu, became the army chief of staff with the rank of colonel.

Two days later, on July 10, Belgian paratroopers descended on Elisabethville to protect the mining interests of Belgian companies that extracted Katanga's riches. The next evening Katangan leader Moïse Tshombe announced the province's secession. Lumumba's government reacted by breaking diplomatic relations with Belgium and requesting military assistance first from Ghana and then from the United Nations.

The expanding crisis throttled the music business. With curfews becoming routine, bands would have to survive on record sales and whatever daytime gigs they could find. 'There was a short time to play,' said Isaac Musekiwa. 'Wherever there is war or something ... they must [have] music to make the people happy.' Some of the more educated musicians were pressed into service to staff essential positions left vacant by fleeing Europeans. Docteur Nico, for one, taught classes in a technical school until replacements from friendly countries such as Haiti could be brought in to take over.

The music business also began to see a shift in power as primacy passed from the expatriate-owned studios to the Congolese bands themselves. The success of African Jazz and O.K. Jazz produced a flowering of imitators, Beguen Band and the like. These groups, not the studios, gradually became the focus of allegiance among musicians. On his return from Europe Kabasele defined the new relationship: 'We are becoming independent, but Esengo will have the monopoly on sales of all our music.' In fact, Kabasele was already making plans to return to Brussels to do more recording. But in the turmoil of the moment, plans would be fluid at best. The country seemed to be disintegrating even more rapidly than it had rushed to independence.

Patrice Lumumba's vision of a strong, unified Congo as the linchpin of pan-African solidarity seemed not to include the messy details of how to make it happen. In all likelihood the task was beyond the abilities of any leader who intended to work within the hastily constructed and unfamiliar framework of Western democracy, even one as brilliant and charismatic as Lumumba. King Leopold's misbegotten colossus bore forces too strong to contain. Ethnic and regional differences, long smothered under the boot of colonialism, suddenly breathed cranky new life. The Congo's political leaders lacked experience, and most shared little of Lumumba's vision. Political intrigue infected alliances even within his own council of ministers. Belgium continued its intervention and convinced other Western nations that Lumumba was a communist. The Soviet Union, inexperienced in supporting democracy, came to his aid. The United States, well practiced in its subversion (Guatemala and Iran being its most recent 'successes'), plotted his assassination. Out of irrational fear and unforgivable ignorance the big powers pursued their rivalries safely removed from their own territory. It began to look like the scramble for Africa all over again, this time in the context of the cold war.

President Kasavubu moved in September to dismiss Lumumba as prime minister. Lumumba countered by sacking Kasavubu. Parliament voted to reinstate both men, but Colonel Mobutu had Lumumba placed under house arrest and installed an interim 'college of general commissioners' composed of university students and recent graduates to run the country. Government dissolved in confusion as Congolese leaders maneuvered for advantage over one another.

At the periphery of the chaos, a momentous event took place in Brazzaville. The Republic of Congo gained its independence from France on August 15, 1960, although ties with Paris remained close. President Fulbert Youlou, a strong ally of his neighbor's president, Joseph Kasavubu, also publicly supported Moïse Tshombe's Katanga secession. Brazzaville overflowed with refugees from the turmoil across the river.

With the stalemate in Léopoldville showing no sign of resolution, Lumumbist leaders began to regroup in Stanleyville, the seat of their support. At the end of November, Lumumba slipped away from his guards, setting out by car for Stanleyville to join his loyalists. But according to his colleague, Thomas Kanza, Lumumba seemed to court disaster. His campaign-style procession squandered the surprise of his escape. An alarm went out from the capital as Lumumba greeted well-wishers along the way. Soldiers who opposed him began the hunt. At a river crossing in Kasai they caught him. Lumumba was beaten and taken to prison in Thysville, southwest of the capital. At the beginning of the new year his captors, agents of Kasavubu and Mobutu, transferred him into the hands of Katangese secessionists at Elisabethville, where he was murdered.

Lumumba's death ended all hope that the government duly constituted at independence would be restored. As troops from the United Nations tried to maintain order, power devolved to three main centers: Lumumbists in Stanleyville under the leadership of Lumumba's deputy Antoine Gizenga; Moïse Tshombe and his Katangese secessionists; and President Kasavubu and his newly appointed prime minister, Joseph Ileo, in Léopoldville. All the main factions and several minor ones commanded their own armies, a grim array which included the Congolese National Army of the Kasavubu–Ileo central government led by Colonel Mobutu.

•

As the dispute among the country's political leaders moved from parliament to the battlefield, the capital's musicians carried on as best they could. A self-inflicted wound hampered African Jazz when, in September of 1960, Docteur Nico and his brother Dechaud deserted the band, charging that Kabasele had mishandled its money. Kabasele rebutted the charges of fiscal impropriety and accused Nico and Dechaud of poisoning the band with the ethnic and ideological venom of the politicians. The two former members of O.K. Jazz, Vicky and Brazzos, also left African Jazz, but the rest of the musicians stuck with Kabasele. The dispute dragged on until the end of the following May when Kabasele and Nico agreed to reconcile.

While the dispute with Nico percolated, Kabasele had been arranging for the group's return to Europe to record more songs. This time he wanted Manu Dibango, the Cameroonian saxophonist African Jazz had met at the Anges Noirs in Brussels, to sit in. In early June of 1961 the reunited African Jazz boarded a plane bound for Brussels at the invitation of the Fonior company, Belgium's licensee for Decca Records.

•

The Fonior company had a profound effect on the spread of Congo music beyond central Africa. Founded in 1929 by Eugene Willy Pelgrims de Bigard, a Belgian baron who saw promise in the incipient recording industry, Fonior became the flagship of the International Pelgrims Group. The company's evolution paralleled the explosion of recording technology and the burgeoning sales of popular music. It grew to encompass SOFRASON (Société Française du Son), Decca's French licensee; record pressing plants in Belgium and France; a rack-jobbing operation (suppliers to record racks in food, drug, and convenience stores) called Centrale Maison Bleue; and DURECO studios and pressing in the Netherlands. Brussels being his headquarters, it seemed logical for Willy Pelgrims to look towards Belgium's central African colonies for further opportunities.

Pelgrims purchased Bill Alexandre's old CEFA operations in 1955, and soon afterward he began construction of a new studio, record pressing plant, and sales outlet. The pressing plant called MACODIS (Manufacture Congolaise du Disque) was located in Limete and had a capacity of two million records a year, Africa's second largest record production facility after South Africa. In addition to servicing its own CEFA label, the plant pressed records for Loningisa, Esengo, and the other local studios – a service that spared them the cumbersome process of importing their records from European pressing plants for sale in the Congo.

Fonior's Congolese sales and publishing arm was called ECODIS (Editions

Congolaise du Disque). For distribution of Congolese records in Europe and the rest of Africa, the company created the Fiesta and African labels. With its SOFRASON subsidiary in Paris, Fonior was particularly well positioned to penetrate markets in France's African colonies.

Roger Izeidi had learned the business from Bill Alexandre at CEFA, and he stayed on with the company to work with Fonior's manager in Léopoldville, Fernand Mission. With Izeidi's help, Kabasele negotiated the deal for African Jazz to return to Brussels, where the studios were technically superior. There, each musician had his own microphone. The sound engineer could set audio levels, shade tones, and otherwise mix the music in a far more sophisticated fashion than was possible in Léopoldville. Recording in Brussels raised the quality of the music to a new level. A pilgrimage to the Fonior studios would become a rite of passage for Congolese bands in the sixties.

A typical contract for a Fonior session called for the recording of forty or fifty songs within the space of about two weeks. That meant three or four completed songs each day. 'They used to come with ten songs already ready,' Manu Dibango recalled. 'And the other ones, they used to find right in the studio. Like going twenty minutes, like that, composing something.' After a song was recorded, Rochereau explained,

> I again take up my piece of paper – compose again, quick, quick, quick. I take my piece of paper [makes scribbling noises]. Okay, come here a minute [starts to sing a song as if demonstrating it to others]. Okay, uh huh, we go. Every single one done in the middle of recording just like that.

The others composed in a similar fashion. With an idea in mind, a singer would call a guitarist, or a guitarist a singer, to begin working out the arrangement. Next came the bass, and then the full band rehearsed.

Such work required an extraordinary level of mental and physical stamina. The musicians recorded all together 'live,' so a mistake by one meant the entire group had to begin again. Reels of tape wound relentlessly while each player rallied his powers of concentration. 'When we would go to the studio, before we went in, there was someone there who made breakfast for us, coffee,' Dechaud remembered.

> We had our coffee, and then we went into the studio. We'd record and record and record, ten, fifteenth, twentieth song. So one day I said I wasn't feeling very well. Right in the middle of a recording session I fall right down on the ground with my instrument. Plop! The technician comes running, and he says, 'He's sick! He's sick!' And I say, 'No. I'm starving.'

The band received a flat sum for their work along with transportation, food, and lodging. Rochereau recalled that in addition, Fonior paid a royalty on record sales. According to Dibango, Kabasele bought the songs his musicians composed and therefore presumably controlled the rights and collected the royalties. Dibango said he was well paid, but Nico remembered the group receiving only about $200 a session to share among its members. The music industry bears a reputation for dishonesty to which African musicians heartily attest. Rare is the artist who believes the word of a record company or producer. As music historian Christopher Small has observed, 'If an artist or group makes a lot of money [from recording] it is only after a lot of other people have made a lot more money first.' The musicians of African Jazz and those who followed them to Brussels likely never received adequate payment for their work. Instead, their recordings brought them fame and lifted Congo music to unequaled heights of popularity across Africa.

The personnel of African Jazz changed from session to session, but during June of 1961 and in another Brussels session the next year – which included Tino Baroza, who had split with Ngoma – the band recorded some of its most memorable works, with Manu Dibango sitting in. Dechaud's classic 'African Jazz Mokili Mobimba' (African Jazz all over the world, often referred to today as 'Africa Mokili Mobimba') managed to squeeze in the musicians' names along with a number of Congolese cities and African countries and capitals – a device from traditional praise singing regularly copied by African pop artists. The song's abundant five-minute length heralded the African debut of the vinyl 45 r.p.m. record, which more than doubled the capacity of the old three-minute 78s. Rochereau's 'Bonbon Sucré' (sweet candy), a Lingala song with a French title (not uncommon in Congo music), featured Dibango on piano (very uncommon) and a rare trumpet solo by the Satchmo of Congo music, Willy Kuntima. The duo of Dibango on sax and clarinetist Edouard 'Edo Clari' Lutula jammed prominently on many songs, including Baroza's 'Mayele Mabe' (evil mind). And throughout each piece the delicious guitar accompaniment of Nico, Dechaud, and Baroza came rippling to the fore.

With his eye on the ferment back home, Kabasele contributed two songs in a more serious vein.* 'Matata Masila na Congo' pleaded for an end to trouble in the Congo:

---

* Some of Kabasele's songs, perhaps those with political overtones, were said to have been written by his uncle Abbé (later Cardinal) Joseph Malula.

> All of us who live in the Congo
> Place our confidence in you
> Oh you, all of Congo's parliamentarians
> Save our country!
> Get along and live in harmony
> Put an end to your fratricidal wars!

He pursued the same theme in 'Toyokana Tolimbisana na Congo' (let's understand and forgive in the Congo).

> In this world where even the whites are divided
> Let's hold each other's hand
> We are all brothers from the same country.

During its first trip to Brussels for the Round Table Conference, the band had recorded and released songs on the African Jazz label with help from Fonior. This time Kabasele renamed the label Surboum African Jazz (African Jazz party) and with that became the Congo's first African music publisher. The deal's intricacies remain unclear, but Kabasele marketed his label exclusively in Congo (Léopoldville) while Fonior received the distribution rights for Europe and the rest of Africa.

At the end of their grueling two weeks in June 1961, the members of African Jazz flew home with a set of master discs to be pressed into records at MACODIS. A month later, at Kabasele's invitation, Manu Dibango joined them in Léopoldville to begin what was scheduled to be one month of concerts around the country. Congolese music fans were curious to see this piano playing saxophonist from Cameroon. His jazzy licks didn't sound like Isaac Musekiwa, the Congo's unchallenged sultan of sax. And with Musekiwa recently returned to O.K. Jazz after a brief stint with Ngoma's band Vedette Jazz, and a new singer Jean 'Kwamy' Munsi at the O.K. Jazz microphone, the arch-competitor of African Jazz was regaining its footing.

The neophyte Dibango received a quick introduction to the intensity of the two groups' rivalry. 'It was like Duke Ellington and Count Basie,' he said. 'There was a contest. Each of them had his own fan club. When Kabasele was playing, there were spies coming from O.K. Jazz to see what's happening, the new equipment.'

Kabasele had opened the doors to Europe. To maintain his own group's stature, Franco knew he would have to follow. So despite their intense artistic competition, Franco turned to Kabasele for help in arranging a recording trip to Brussels. The two great stars struck a deal. In return for Kabasele's help,

New additions to African Jazz, Charles Hénault (left) and Manu Dibango

Franco's records would be released on Kabasele's label. So, barely rested from his own recent trip, Kabasele returned to the Fonior studios with Franco and O.K. Jazz. 'Many people don't know it,' Franco remarked, 'but I owe him my first musical equipment. Kalle decided on this purchase with the money brought in by sales of my first records which came out on the label Surboum African Jazz. And I will tell you that for me it meant a lot.' Among the songs that ultimately paid for the new equipment were Franco's 'Liwa ya Wechi' (the death of Wechi), a lament for a childhood friend; 'Lopango ya Bana na Ngai' (the parcel of land of my children), another Franco-penned song which appeared to be addressing tensions within the Congolese extended family; and Kwamy's 'Liwa ya Champagne' (the death of champagne), a none-too-subtle dig at the departed Belgians. But each song appeared on the label of Franco's competitor.

While Franco and Kabasele danced their peculiar rumba of competition and cooperation, Vicky Longomba stood ready to cut in. Both Vicky and Brazzos had left African Jazz shortly after the band returned from the Round Table. Brazzos went back to O.K. Jazz, but hard feelings continued to fester between Vicky and Franco. Thus estranged, Vicky decided to mount his own band. Amid the comings and goings of African Jazz and O.K. Jazz to Brussels, Vicky staged a raid on both his former groups. He took two musicians he had brought into O.K. Jazz during his tenure as its leader, guitarist Léon 'Bholen' Bombolo and singer Hubert 'Djeskin' Dihunga. From African Jazz he hired the venerable saxophonist André Menga. Singer Gaspard 'Gaspy' Luwowo took the mike beside Vicky. Bassist Alphonse 'Le Brun' Epayo, drummer Samuel 'Samy' Kiadaka, and guitar accompanist Jean Dinos, a defector from Orchestre Bantou, rounded out the new ensemble. They called themselves Négro Succès.

Vicky's aggregation was only the most famous of a number of new bands that formed to accommodate the expanding supply of young musicians and to profit from Congo music's heightened popularity. Despite the continuing crisis in Congolese politics, Congo music thrived. Money and fame followed success along with its shadowy offspring, egotism and distrust. In the coming years they would help to sow the seeds of disarray and brilliance.

7
Congo music

Orchestre Bantou and Ry-Co Jazz, 1960–1963

Compared to the clamor of Léopoldville, Brazzaville felt like an enclave of serenity. The twenty-minute ferry ride furnished an interval of inactivity for acclimation and reflection, a riverine refuge in which to make the transition. As the confusion in Congo-Léo wore on, more and more of its residents made the trip. It became the outing of choice, for those who could afford it, to escape from curfews and the effects of Léopoldville's withering economy. Brazzaville's shops evinced a little touch of Paris. Luxuries abounded, along with more mundane necessities like cloth and spare auto parts that were often in short supply in Léo. African Jazz and the other groups also made the crossing to join their Brazzavillean counterparts Orchestre Bantou and Negro Band in nightlife unfettered by the tumult of civil strife.

Still, the natural buffer of the Congo River failed to completely insulate Brazzaville from the ebb and flow of its neighbor's conflict. President Youlou's support for Tshombe and the Katanga secession strained relations with the government in Léopoldville. The bickering led to a general climate of mistrust and periodic halts in river traffic between the two Congos. Franco added to the controversy with a song which many thought demeaned Youlou. Although the song was apparently never recorded, word of its inclusion in the O.K. Jazz night club repertoire reached across the river, where the government promptly forbade reproduction or performance of any work by Franco and O.K. Jazz anywhere in Congo-Brazza. Franco's words won supporters on the Congo-Léo side, but many felt political matters were better left to the politicians.

Of greater importance for President Youlou, however, was the increasing dissatisfaction among his own supporters. Youlou had co-opted his political opponents by awarding them posts in his government. In 1962 he dissolved the opposition parties with the aim of creating a single party to 'unify' the country. But his apparent acumen in the political sphere was unmatched when it came to dealing with his country's economic difficulties. Inflation, stagnating wages, and chronically high unemployment – exacerbated by the steady movement of rural people to the cities – undermined his credibility in the street.

Labor unions began to pressure Youlou for reform. When, in August of 1963, he had failed to meet their demands, the unions called for a general strike. On August 13 they launched *les trois glorieuses*, three 'glorious' days of demonstrations and civil disobedience. On the afternoon of the 15th, with angry crowds surrounding the presidential residence, army officers persuaded Youlou to resign. Power shifted to a Conseil National de la Révolution led by Alphonse Massamba-Debat, a former president of the legislature and leading Youlou opponent.

•

While Brazzaville's political theater played out, the members of Orchestre Bantou began to thrive in their home town. Essous, Pandi, and company played often at the prestigious Chez Faignond. Lacking a studio in Brazzaville, they occasionally crossed over to Léo to record at Esengo, where Antonopoulos created the Ndombe (black or Negro) label for recordings by the Brazzaville bands.

More than any other group of the period, however, Orchestre Bantou earned its keep and its fine reputation by touring. Starting with Togo's independence celebrations in April of 1960, Orchestre Bantou spent several months a year on the road. 'No African country could organize its independence celebration without Orchestre Bantou,' Guy-Léon Fylla declared, and in this era there were a lot of them. Nino Malapet rejoined his old companions when Rock'a Mambo broke up in the middle of 1960. Papa Noël came on board around the same time.

The band still chafed under one major constraint. Faignond owned the equipment they performed with, so he ultimately exercised control over their affairs. 'But we had already laid our plans,' Pandi explained. 'We had this white guy who had signed a contract with us who said [for] every concert you play, you get an amp. A concert, a bass. A concert, an instrument.... So

Nino Malapet of
Orchestre Bantou

we got all the instruments. We had everything.' Thus equipped, the group severed its relations with Faignond and began to tour in earnest.

Bangui in the newly independent Central African Republic (formerly Oubangui-Chari), some 650 miles up-river, became a frequent stop on Orchestre Bantou's expanding African circuit. Although their travels took them as far west as Dakar, Senegal, the Lomé Cotonou Lagos corridor proved to be the most lucrative area. There lay three major cities plus the smaller Dahoman capital, Porto Novo, all linked by 180 miles of good road. Orchestre Bantou assumed the role of Congolese music's ambassador, playing most of the major night clubs along the way, including Nigerian highlife star Bobby Benson's famous Caban Bamboo in Lagos.

At Benson's club in 1961, Orchestre Bantou met a Nigerian saxophonist named Dele Pedro and invited him to work alongside fellow sax man Nino Malapet and clarinetist Essous. Back in Brazzaville the group's fans got used to the twin saxophones, so when Dele Pedro returned to Lagos upon the death of his father a few months later, Essous took up the instrument. 'The first time I played the sax people left,' he laughed. But after that his clarinet made only an occasional appearance.

In August of 1962, Orchestre Bantou suffered the malady that afflicted other bands. Edo Ganga and De La Lune, wooed by O.K. Jazz with promises of free housing and more opportunities to record, deserted. When Congo-Brazzaville's minister for youth heard what was happening he tried to block their departure, but the two musicians slipped away by motorboat in the middle of the night to return to O.K. Jazz. Essous replaced them with singer Joseph 'Jojo' Bukassa and bass player Francis Bitshoumanou.

In 1963, Essous hired a teenaged singer named Yves André M'Bemba, who called himself 'Pablito.' The Brazzaville-born Pablito, who would go on to fame as Pamelo Mounk'a, had acquired his passion for music by hanging around outside Léopoldville's Kongo Bar when he would cross the river to visit relatives. He had an ear for Spanish and the beat of Latin America, which for Pablito made the music of Joseph Kabasele and African Jazz particularly attractive. With his idols Kalle, Nico, and Rochereau in mind, he wrote songs instead of studying his school lessons.

Through an older brother who attended business school with Rochereau, Pablito got to meet the rising star of African Jazz. 'Rochereau listened to my songs in Spanish. He kept three songs which he sang, which he later recorded,' Pablito recalled during his incarnation as Pamelo Mounk'a. 'I did "Paquita",' he said, referring to a song which became a big hit under Rochereau's name. 'At the time I didn't even know what [author's rights] meant. And then for me it was a pleasure to be sung by such a great singer.' According to Pablito, Rochereau wanted him to join African Jazz, but Kabasele said he was too young. It was left to Essous as leader of Orchestre Bantou to give Pablito his professional start.

Towards the end of 1962, just before Pablito hired on, the musicians of Orchestre Bantou (sometimes referred to during this period as Bantous Jazz) made their first pilgrimage to the Fonior studios in Brussels, thanks to help from Roger Izeidi. Izeidi's visibility in the Pelgrims empire had begun to

Saturnin Pandi in Brussels, 1962

increase with the advent of Congolese independence. Pelgrims sold him the CEFA label, Izeidi explained,

> but he sold it without the back catalog. When he sold it, I sent Les Bantous, with Essous, to Belgium. There, [Pelgrims] helped me pay Les Bantous money and record. So their songs came out on my label, CEFA. Franco also recorded there, on that label.

In return for organizing recording trips to Brussels, Izeidi got exclusive rights to distribute the resulting records within Congo-Léo. As usual, Fonior, through its African and Fiesta labels, sold to the rest of the world.

Orchestre Bantou recorded fifty songs in two and a half weeks. Among their new records which trickled out over the next year, several gems outshined the rest. 'Tokumisa Congo' (we congratulate Congo), composed by Essous, praised Congo-Brazza's progress since independence with a snappy call-and-response dialogue between the singers and Essous's clarinet. Papa Noël's jazzy guitar solo fortified 'Tu Silencio' (your silence), a Malapet cha-cha sung in Spanish; 'If you love me or you don't love me, tell me.' Noël excelled again on a rumba, 'Camarade Mabe' (bad friend), penned by Essous.

> That's how we do it, my friend
> If you make money, you pay and we drink
> In all friendship
> If I make money, I pay and we drink
> That's how we do it
> But it's not good to count only
> On the pocket of one's companion.

Each song pushed well beyond the three-minute mark to take advantage of the new 45 r.p.m. format. 'Les Bantous de la Capitale,' a Célestin Kouka song, touted the group with a deft exchange among the singers and Malapet's saxophone. The song became the band's theme, and in later years the players adopted its title as their official name.

Without the Fonior connection, Congolese bands would have been increasingly hard-pressed to get their music on disc. Congo-Léo's political turmoil precipitated economic decline and a crisis of confidence among members of the European business community that doomed the local recording studios. Opika had closed in 1957 for reasons that remain unclear. With the coming of independence, Olympia's owner, Fernand Janssens, closed the company's Léopoldville office but kept the label going in Belgium. Although no certain date has been established for Esengo's demise, it appears the studio folded in 1961. Philips withdrew its Congolese recording operations around the same time. Basile Papadimitriou, whose property had been damaged during the 1959 riots, shut down Loningisa in 1962. Only Ngoma continued to hold out against the trend, although conditions in the studio deteriorated badly. Manu Dibango remembered the building being used for chemical storage. 'It was difficult to stay ten minutes in the studio because of the chemicals,' he said.

The outlook for recording improved briefly in 1963 with the arrival in Brazzaville of a certain French clothing salesman named Stein. Stein came to town in the employ of Angel de Paris to expand the central African market for the company's line of men's wear. As the story goes, Stein was good at his work. He sold so many suits that the market approached saturation. Faced with declining sales he proceeded to open a dry-cleaning establishment to care for the clothes he had sold. Stein also tasted Brazzaville's nightlife. His fondness for Congolese music moved him to open his own bar, called Super Jazz, and to convert a corner of his house into a recording studio.

Stein concluded a deal with Essous to record some songs by Orchestre Bantou. Pressing and marketing outside of central Africa would be done by the French company, Pathé Marconi, while locally the records would be released on Stein's STENCO label. Other groups in Brazzaville, including Negro Band, followed Orchestre Bantou to the tiny Maison STENCO. Stein, a talented jack-of-all-trades, engineered the recordings, photographed the musicians for record jackets, and marketed the discs as vigorously as he had Angel clothes. His enterprise held much promise for the future of the Brazzaville groups, until he somehow ran afoul of Congo-Brazzaville's authorities. No one seems to recall his transgression, but Stein was forced to close up shop and leave the country after less than two years in business. By the mid-1960s Willy Pelgrims, with his MACODIS and ECODIS operations, would have the market for recording and production of Congolese records pretty much to himself.

•

As ambassador of Congo music, Orchestre Bantou had a rival in Ry-Co Jazz. The six-member Ry-Co Jazz (the name stood for Rythme Congolais) had been created by Henri Bowane in 1958. After helping to get the Esengo studio into operation, Bowane decided to abandon performing to become a full-time impresario. He recruited the half-dozen newcomers who would form his new group and packed them on board a riverboat heading for Bangui in Oubangui-Chari. The musicians rehearsed on the boat for what would grow into nearly two years of shows around Oubangui-Chari, Chad, and Cameroon.

In 1960, the musicians split from Bowane and regrouped into a lean four-piece touring group. Led by singer Freddy Nkounkou, better known as 'Freddy Mars,' with jocular Jerry Malekani on guitar, bassist Panda Gracia, and Casimir 'Casino' Mbilia on congas, Ry-Co Jazz played its way across West Africa as far as Senegal. With Dakar as base camp, the musicians made repeated forays into Guinea, Sierra Leone, Liberia, and Côte d'Ivoire, where they dazzled crowds with enthusiastic renditions of hits by Franco and Kabasele along with their own compositions. On more than one occasion along the way, the quartet reinforced itself with a local musician or two, a practice that transformed the band into a school for West African musicians to learn the Congolese method of playing.

Every few months Ry-Co Jazz recorded songs in a small Dakar studio run by a French businessman. Master tapes were sent to Paris to be turned into records by the French label Disques Vogue. Distributed back in Africa, the new 45s kindled the band's popularity even more. Ry-Co Jazz songs ran the gamut of the musical influences astir in early sixties' West Africa. 'Caramba da ma Vida,' sung in a mixture of Spanish and Lingala, shuffles along to the cha-cha rhythm. 'Twist with the Docteur' sounds like it came from Memphis with Scotty Moore backing a French-speaking, African Elvis. 'Give Me Bombolo' incorporates a *double entendre* from the Krio language of Sierra Leone. 'Bana Ry-Co' (the children of Ry-Co Jazz) echoes the music of Kabasele's African Jazz.

•

Apart from sales directly to individual music buyers, the records of Ry-Co Jazz, Orchestre Bantou, and other Congolese bands helped to spread the music over the radio. With its powerful 50,000-watt transmitter and links to other French stations in Douala, Dakar, and Abidjan, Radio Brazzaville introduced Congolese music to West Africa and the Americas in much the same way that radio had brought the Cuban *son* back home to Africa in the thirties and forties. Programs on the Voice of America (VOA) and the British Broadcasting Corporation (BBC) also played Congo music along with other genres of African pop.

In print, *Bingo*, a kind of *People* magazine for French-speaking Africa, championed the music of the two Congos – Rochereau and Franco were favorites – especially in the columns of Gilles Sala, the man who had covered the arrival of African Jazz in Brussels for the Round Table conference. The combination of *Bingo* and other publications; touring bands like Ry-Co Jazz and Orchestre Bantou; records from the Pelgrims distribution network and its smaller competitors, Ngoma and Disques Vogue; and the powerful transmitters of Radio Brazzaville, the VOA, and the BBC became a formidable force in the music's propagation.

Everywhere it was heard in Africa, and that was nearly everywhere, the music found an audience. People called it Congo music. It was foreign and perhaps more sophisticated than local styles, but it was still palpably African. It transcended geographical and ethnic boundaries but had a familiar ring. The predominantly Lingala lyrics, although rarely understood, had a marvelously melodious quality that blended into the mix like another instrument. Words like *motema* (heart) and *bolingo* (love) rolled off the tongues of music

Ry-Co Jazz record jacket from the early sixties. Musicians pictured are (left to right) Justin 'Jerry' Malekani, Casimir 'Casino' Mbilia, and Freddy 'Freddy Mars' Nkounkou

lovers in West and East Africa as if they belonged to the local dialect. Many a fan could sing Congolese songs from memory without understanding a word. And the stunning inter-weaving guitars were the music's centerpiece. Musicians across the continent scrambled to incorporate Congolese guitar arrangements into their own styles.

In the space of little more than a decade, Congo music had advanced from parochial curiosity to continent-wide phenomenon. The troubles in Congo-Léo still constrained the musicians at home, but on the road they were royalty, expanding the empire as they went.

8
Money changes everything

African Jazz, African Fiesta, Moïse Tshombe,
O.K. Jazz, and Orchestre Bantou, 1963–1965

Storm clouds hung heavy over Joseph Kabasele's wedding, but on this bright Saturday in May of 1963 they had little to do with the weather. The heavy rains that lash the southern tropics early each year had begun to abate, leaving a well-scrubbed Léopoldville green and refreshed in their wake. Honored guests had gathered to witness the official marriage of Kabasele to one Antoinette France Cédal, who had replaced the unofficial Katherine of 'Kale-Kato' fame in the heart of Le Grand Kalle. Kabasele's uncle, Joseph Malula, who had risen to the rank of monsignor in the hierarchy of the Roman Catholic Church, presided over what should have been a celebration of personal and professional fulfillment.

Only three months earlier Kabasele and his musicians had returned from a resoundingly successful ten-week tour of West Africa. Beginning in Mali, where they entertained President Modibo Keïta and a packed Bamako stadium, African Jazz went on to play for enthusiastic crowds in Upper Volta (today's Burkina Faso), Senegal, Liberia, Côte d'Ivoire, and Nigeria. As one correspondent summed up the trip, 'When African Jazz heated up, [dancers] literally assaulted the floor.' Back on Congolese soil in early February, they reunited with their fans for a rousing Saturday night at the Petit Bois club. Later in the month African Jazz lit the night in Brazzaville with a much praised concert at the Tam Tam Bantou.

Now, before a gathering of 1,500 friends and relatives at Léopoldville's Eglise St. Pierre, Monsignor Malula led Joseph and Antoinette through their

Joseph Kabasele,
'Le Grand Kalle'

marriage vows. The wedding party followed mass with a reception at a nearby hotel. In the evening guests crowded into the Restaurant of the Zoo for a grand wedding-night ball. But up on the bandstand something was wrong. Familiar faces took their places, but they belonged to Orchestre Bantou of Brazzaville. No Nico or Roger or Rochereau appeared. Where was African Jazz?

Preparing to leave for Brussels was the answer. The following Tuesday the band returned to the Fonior studio to record new songs on their leader's account without his presence or permission. In essence the musicians had fired Kabasele. Unlike the previous dust-up, which isolated Nico and Dechaud, this time the musicians stood together. Critics fingered Roger Izeidi as the ringleader because of his connections to Fonior. 'We were always fighting with Kabasele over money,' Izeidi recalled.

> He got money from a concert and didn't pay us.... So we came to ask, 'Are you giving us the money or are you not giving us the money?' And he said, 'I'm not giving you the money.' I was still a director at Pelgrims's. I said, 'Okay, he doesn't want to pay us, we'll go to Europe.' We went to Europe, and we left him by himself.

Kabasele told a reporter for *Présence Congolaise* that the group had arranged for each player to be paid a monthly salary. Formerly he had advanced them money from his own pocket, but, he said, Nico and Rochereau hadn't seen the use in that. He paid his musicians once each month by their own agreement. They had no grounds to complain. And so it happened that the greatest band in Congo music's short history cast its celebrated leader adrift at a very embarrassing moment.

Joseph Kabasele was the most popular personality of his time, the archetype of a modern Congolese star. He had been in the music almost from its birth. Some even called him its father. 'Kabasele was, I can say, an African dandy, African hip man,' said Manu Dibango, who had left African Jazz near the end of 1961 to run a Léopoldville night club.

> He had a big Cadillac in that time, a big white Cadillac, I'm telling you.... So when I came [to Léopoldville] he took me to the Cadillac with the driver, and it was like a president. Everywhere we went Kabasele was passing, sitting [waves his hands]. 'Kalle! Kalle!' They were very glad to have him as their own star.

Rochereau likened Kabasele to Spanish singer Julio Iglesias, 'because women would swarm around him. He was a good-looking man.'

Ties between Kabasele and Izeidi went back to the late forties and their old neighborhood in the Kinshasa district of Léopoldville. 'If he got mad [at me], I got mad too,' Izeidi said.

> But the same day we would meet up ... then we'd have a drink together, and then it would be over.... Kabasele would go where there was great ambiance. Wherever there was dancing and drinking, that was home to Kabasele. He wasn't obsessed with getting ahead. If he had the money, he would come in and buy everyone a drink. And when it was gone, it was gone.

Kabasele's work habits reflected his necessity-is-the-mother-of-invention approach typified by the bouts of pressure-driven composing in the midst of recording at Fonior. 'When Kabasele didn't have money, he would come up with an idea,' Rochereau said.

> 'Here's what we can do.' He puts it down on paper, and the next day we would start working on it, for the next two weeks or a month. And [claps] the money would be there. But when the money came in, it was over. Work finished. When the money ran out, we started again.

While endearing to some, Kabasele's methods drew increasing fire from the other members of African Jazz. 'They split every two or three months for money problem or for girls problem, as usual in the musical sphere,' Dibango said. 'And then reconciliation. This one's come back again, or they have a project to do a record. Well, normal.'

Kabasele was the product of an earlier era, when music, not money, compelled the players. In the beginning they were naïve, Isaac Musekiwa once said when trying to explain the changes that had come over the business.

> In that time the music was very nice, more than now. But now when everybody's playing, you think of money straight away. [The musician] knows I start at this time, I've got to finish that time, they must pay so much. See, there's a mistake. Now it's spoiling everything, money. If I get less than what I think, I won't play all right next time. Because now there's money first, music after. First there was music first, money after.

The early makers of Congo music held jobs in government or commerce. Music was a pastime to be pursued in off-hours. But as Léopoldville's recording industry expanded and matured, the studios offered comfortable salaries and a chance for artists to make music full-time. Their taste of fame and relatively good money allayed suspicions that the studio owners might be exploiting them unfairly – although Roitelet's short-lived strikes had demonstrated a streak of discontent. With the coming of independence and the studios' decline, musicians shifted their feelings of mistrust to their particular group's leader, who, as a peer, was more easily criticized.

Kabasele, the star and proprietor of Surboum African Jazz, became the first casualty of these changes. He had made the transition from a maker of music to a maker of money, and his musicians began to feel cheated. Rochereau says their concerns stemmed from a lack of accountability within African Jazz.

> At that time we didn't know if we were going to be paid. We didn't know if we had a salary. If poor Kabasele were alive today, he couldn't take a piece of

paper and say, 'Here, in such and such a month I paid these people this much and that much.' It doesn't exist. But that doesn't mean that Kabasele was wrong, because at that time the bands were not established as legal entities. They had no administrative structure.

This time there would be no question of reconciliation. The band had humiliated Kabasele by ignoring his wedding and flying off to Brussels. He owned the group's name and their label. No way would he allow them to use it without him. Such was the labor that gave birth to Orchestre African Fiesta.

'Bilombe ya Africa' (champions of Africa), a Nico composition from the latest Brussels sessions, naïvely used the name African Jazz in the lyrics as if Kabasele would accept his overthrow without a fight. 'We made records, but they were still on the Surboum African Jazz label,' Izeidi explained. 'When [Kabasele] heard about it he took us to court. We said okay, we did it on his behalf, he's taking us to court, so let's change. So that's how we created African Fiesta.' On the business side, Izeidi established the Vita label to issue African Fiesta's new recordings.

Along with 'Bilombe ya Africa,' the musicians recorded several other songs in the African Jazz tradition. In his lovely intro to Rochereau's 'Mwasi Abandaka' (it is the woman who starts), Nico hints at the Hawaiian licks he would later employ with such flair. Willy Kuntima and Jeef Mingiedi sound like a mariachi brass section on another Rochereau composition, 'Pesa le Tout' (give everything), whose chief chorus, 'Léopoldville, c'est la capitale,' repeats in answer to the fluid call of the horns. 'Ngonga Ebeti' (the bell is ringing), a relentless rumba from the under-recognized Depuissant, features Nico's crisp picking and cascading call-and-response vocals that flow as smooth and forcefully as the Congo River. In Izeidi's 'Mobembo Eleki Tata' (it's a long journey father), Nico veers back and forth from his clean, one-note attack through a muddy swamp of reverb and distortion, an experiment with rock elements that seems to have fascinated him throughout the session.

Reaction to African Fiesta and its music quickly erupted into a war of words on the street and in the press. Léopoldville's *Actualités Africaines* expressed approval with a flowery verbosity unequaled in translation:

> African Fiesta's songs maintain a harmonization and range of emotion clearly noticeable to well-informed connoisseurs who have maintained some auditory discernment insofar as the melodic systems established on the various principles of music are concerned.

Présence Congolaise, however, offended by the insult to Kabasele, rebutted such pompous praise with a biting critique:

> It is generally known by everybody that African Fiesta is in obvious decline in the musical domain. Its latest songs are indisputably cacophonous. Nico's guitar lately shines only by the monotony of its immutable onomatopoeia, 'tôtôtôtôtô-tô,' which has become disgusting.

Polemics aside, in record shops and night clubs African Fiesta was winning where it counted.

Songs from the Brussels session trickled out every few weeks, and new ones extolling the African Fiesta name were recorded in Léo and during a second trip to Brussels in 1964. Izeidi, Nico, and Rochereau arrived at an arrangement for sharing responsibility that seemed, for the moment at least, to restrain the restless impulses of egotism and paranoia. The musicians – tarnished in the eyes of many by their treatment of Kabasele – worked hard to refurbish their reputations, even stooping to an appearance on the same bill as O.K. Jazz.

Administrative tranquility, the need to regain status, and a dose of personal maturity elevated the group's individual and collective output. Rochereau, once outside of Kabasele's prodigious shadow, acceded to his mentor's lofty position. Possessed of a clear, elegant tenor which he often pushed even higher, Rochereau coaxed the maximum emotion from nearly every word. Writing in the early seventies, one observer called him 'a constant pleasure' and 'full of [Congolese] soul.... His voice is a spring of pure water, sensual and nostalgic. It seems so natural and relaxed that we forget the intense work given to it by the singer.'

Rochereau's compositions, long a source of strength to African Jazz, brought the same quality of melody and sentiment to African Fiesta. The recording of his 'N'daya Paradis' embodies the essence of African Fiesta's blend of experimentation and convention: Nico's startling intro on Hawaiian steel guitar; Rochereau's solo voice rising in a crescendo of passion for N'daya, his love; and the exhilarating accompaniment of Nico and Dechaud, toying with the beat, at once frugal and abundant.

Nico's innovative solos and tasteful vamping rarely found their equals in the other Congolese bands. Dechaud, stringing his guitar like Jhimmy's in the style of the *mi-composé*, created a rhythmic canvas to receive Nico's dabs of color. The two brothers formed the music's ultimate guitar duo.

The band fortified itself with the addition of Joseph Mwena, a veteran of years at Ngoma, as full-time bassist. As time went on, others came on board, including Roger Izeidi's younger brother Faugus playing third guitar, singer Paul Mizele, and a young woman singer named Photas Myosotis (Photas forget-me-not).

One other element distinguished African Fiesta from its closest rivals. Where O.K. Jazz and Orchestre Bantou championed the saxophone, African Fiesta countered with the trumpet of Dominique 'Willy' Kuntima. The oldest of the group, Willy had gotten his start in the late forties with orchestre Odéon Kinois. He went on to record at Ngoma and briefly joined the Loningisa stable, where he worked with the nascent O.K. Jazz. But it was at Esengo, in the company of Kabasele and Dechaud, that Willy found his niche. Intense and 'full of fire,' as one Congolese journalist put it, Willy 'would attack his trumpet with an incredible ferocity. Standing on both feet, his elbows bent, dancing and contorting himself while sweat trickled down his nose, chin, and neck, he seemed to want to force the trumpet to submit.' With clamorous Latin flourishes and an occasional jazzy solo, Willy distinguished the compositions of his comrades.

•

As African Fiesta took off, Joseph Kabasele tried to rebuild his African Jazz. First he lured Papa Noël away from Orchestre Bantou. The two then traveled to Kampala, Uganda, in 1963, where another Congolese group, Vox Africa, had fallen on hard times. Singer Jean Bombenga, a Kalle protégé and former member of Jazz African, had formed Vox Africa around the time of Congo-Léo's independence. Now he and Kabasele struck a deal to join forces. Their merger gave birth to a new African Jazz which included the musical double triple of Kabasele, Bombenga, and Mathieu Kouka sharing vocals and Papa Noël, André 'Damoiseau' Kambite, and Casimir 'Casino' Mutshipule on guitar. Papa Noël dropped out a few months later, but even with him in the lineup the new African Jazz was a lesser outfit than the original.

•

Over at O.K. Jazz, Franco fared better than his friendly rival Kabasele. Franco's renown as a musician had grown to the point where people called him 'sorcerer of the guitar.' His boyish charm earned him the additional sobriquet 'Franco de mi amor' (Franco of my love, in Spanish), which he had inscribed on his guitar. Jean 'Kwamy' Munsi (a.k.a. Kwamy Mossi) had joined

Dominique 'Willy' Kuntima

Franco's corps of singers in 1961 before the band left to record at Fonior in Brussels. Guitar accompanist Simon 'Simaro' Lutumba hired on within weeks of Kwamy, just in time to make the trip. In 1962, Franco reconciled with Vicky Longomba, who returned after two years in exile with Négro Succès, and Edo Ganga and De La Lune returned to the fold from Orchestre Bantou. O.K. Jazz found itself bulging with talent and flush with bookings.

During one curfew-less week in the middle of 1962, the musicians announced they would take the stage from 8:00 p.m. to midnight, Tuesday at the Vis-à-Vis, Wednesday at the Petit Bois, Thursday Chez La-Bas, and Friday back at the Vis-à-Vis. On Saturday they would play from 8:00 p.m. to midnight at the Restaurant of the Zoo then move on to the Kongo Bar from 1:00 to 4:30 a.m. Sunday they scheduled a matinée at the Dithéo Bar and an evening gig at the Petit Bois.

In 1963 the group added saxophonist Georges 'Verckys' Kiamuangana and trumpet player Christophe Djali. O.K. Jazz also became the first of the top bands to employ a woman, when singer Henriette Borauzima joined for a brief four months at the mike. Late in the year, on a tour of Nigeria, the band hired Dele Pedro, the saxophonist who had briefly belonged to Orchestre Bantou.

During this period O.K. Jazz recorded one of its most memorable songs, 'Ngai Marie Nzoto Ebeba' (I, Marie, whose body is wearing out). 'Ngai Marie' fused the elements of Congo music to near perfection – smoothly flowing lyrics, stunning guitar licks, saxophones responding to the call of the vocals, and two mini-sebenes. Franco appeared at the peak of his art, laying a glorious ribbon of single notes behind the singers and delivering a lovely, inspired solo at the first break. A saxophone (unidentified but probably Verckys) gives and takes with the singers before rocketing into a solo. Vicky and Edo, polished and eloquent, sing of Marie, who earns a living with her body only to be condemned by the women whose husbands solicit her.

> Your husbands are yours
> They come to call on me
> I see that I am single
> With no money to dress myself
> The man is handsome, generous
> How can I not like him.

'Ngai Marie' was one of Franco's more incisive commentaries on morality and the plight of women in the urban society colonialism had wrought.

The following February, 1964, O.K. Jazz officially registered as a company. A certain Joseph Emany became the group's administrator; De La Lune served as *chef d'orchestre*; Vicky Longomba, president; Edo Ganga, secretary general; and Franco, founder. They negotiated a deal with Paris-based Pathé Marconi to record and distribute their records. For the home market the musicians created their own publishing house, Epanza Makita (literally, the rain that disperses gatherings, the implication being that O.K. Jazz would scatter the competition) and added a second one, Boma Bango (kill them, i.e. the competition), later in the year. Another company, Lulonga (from Luambo, Longomba, and Ganga), was set up in Brazzaville to handle the band's business there.

•

While Congolese musicians sorted themselves out, the more serious problems of consummating independence continued their disruptive drumfire. Following Patrice Lumumba's murder in January 1961, a succession of governments in Léopoldville attempted to cope with the crisis. In the breakaway province of Katanga, sporadic fighting and exasperating negotiations dragged on through 1962 while the UN gradually built up its forces. When UN troops took Jadotville north of Elisabethville, Katanga's leader, Moïse Tshombe, folded his hand. On January 14, 1963, he announced that Katanga's secession had ended. Shortly thereafter, Tshombe flew off to exile in Spain.

The country's then prime minister, Cyrille Adoula, struggled to restore a semblance of order and national unity, but his fractious constituents refused to reconcile. Several opposition parliamentarians crossed the river, where they organized a Conseil National de Libération (CNL) under the protective wing of Brazzaville's new Massamba-Debat regime. From there and sanctuaries in Burundi to the east, CNL fighters began to launch a series of raids back across the border. For the first time fighting broke out in Léopoldville, which until then had suffered only the relatively minor disruptions of curfews, border closings, and lack of consumer goods.

In the early months of 1964, Edo Ganga and O.K. Jazz came face to face with urban guerrillas. 'We were playing in the Parc de Bock,' Ganga recalled.

> I had written a song, a twist. 'Aie! J'ai mal aux pieds! Ah! Qu'est-ce que c'est?' [Oh! My feet hurt! Ah! What's going on?] Well, people really liked that. So we were playing, and people were dancing on the dance floor. Suddenly we hear over there, pow! pow! pow! Plastic explosives. So then I, like an idiot, said, 'What is it? It's nothing, let's go, keep going. Everybody twist!' And people kept twisting. Until the bombs reached the dance floor.... And there were wounded people on the dance floor.... The next morning I was called in by the army. They took me, and I was incarcerated. At the army they asked me, 'Why did you say it's nothing?' ... I said, 'No, that's part of the song. 'Qu'est-ce que c'est? Ce n'est rien.' [What's going on? It's nothing.] So Franco and the others did everything they could to get me out with the contacts they had.... In all that tumult we continued to play. People needed to have fun, but they had to be careful too.

The Congolese central government weathered the raids on Léopoldville, albeit with greatly reduced credibility. As confidence in Adoula and the national army evaporated and UN troops withdrew following the surrender of Katanga, Moïse Tshombe returned home from exile at the end of June. A few days later President Kasavubu invited him to form a new government. In early August, less than a month after the Tshombe regime was installed, Stanleyville fell to the CNL rebels.

Prime Minister Tshombe reacted on three fronts. He pushed through a new constitution, ordered the expulsion of all African aliens, the majority of whom were from Congo-Brazza, and reinforced the national army with white mercenaries and the remnants of his Katanga army. The expulsion order looked like retaliation against Massamba-Debat for overthrowing Tshombe's ally, Youlou, and giving sanctuary to CNL rebels. Musicians, football players, no alien gained exemption. People left with only what belongings they could carry. Tshombe's rejuvenated national army was on the move too. In a final push at the end of November, aided by an American airlift of Belgian paratroops, the central government's forces retook Stanleyville.

The focus of events then shifted back to the political arena. In March of 1965 a Tshombe-led alliance of political parties won a parliamentary majority in elections under the new constitution. But in November, in a move seen as a bid to eliminate his chief rival in presidential elections to be held the following year, President Kasavubu dismissed Tshombe as prime minister and invited Evariste Kimba, an anti-Tshombe member of parliament, to form a government. Tshombe's majority coalition refused to acquiesce to this rerun of the Kasavubu–Lumumba affair.

Once again Joseph Mobutu, by this time a general, moved to break the stalemate. In the middle of the night of November 24, 1965, and into the following day, the army seized control of the government, installing General Mobutu as head of state. Mobutu had learned from his previous intervention. This time he moved swiftly to consolidate his power. He ordered his soldiers into battle against the remaining pockets of rebellion, purged the army's leadership of potential rivals, and sent the politicians packing. They had ruined the country, he said. He pledged that he would do better.

•

Prime Minister Tshombe's expulsion of aliens in 1964 caused O.K. Jazz to lose two key members, Edo Ganga and De La Lune. Expelled with them was a third Brazzavillean named Michel 'Michaux' Boybanda, who had only joined O.K. Jazz a couple of months before. The band's strong organization, relative stability, and wealth of talent helped to cushion the shock.

Loss to O.K. Jazz produced gain across the river. After helping De La Lune start up a new band called Orchestre Tembo, Edo Ganga moved back beside his former colleagues in Orchestre Bantou. There he found a familiar face from Léopoldville, Joseph 'Mujos' Mulamba. Mujos had been busy doing what he would do throughout his career, writing great songs and moving compulsively from group to group. The singer had gotten his start at Esengo in 1958 when he joined Rock'a Mambo. Soon afterward he began an odyssey that would take him to nearly every one of Congo music's prominent bands.

'I often leave bands because I don't want to be taken advantage of,' he once remarked. His business card bore a list of his former employers – 'ancien musicien de Rock'a Mambo, O.K. Jazz, African Jazz, African Fiesta, Orchestre Bantou' – the equivalent of notches on a gunslinger's pistol.

Another stint with O.K. Jazz would soon follow, but not before Mujos wrote the song that helped launch the dance craze of 1965. 'Danse des Bouchers' (dance of the butchers) was made to order for the men who sold meat in the local markets. 'They have just sold meat, they have money. They came to dance.' Essous explained. One of the butchers choreographed movements which mimicked his work. 'And then everyone began to follow that. And we called it the dance of the butchers.' It begins with the hands making a series of jerky chopping motions, then 'everything ends up with your backside.' Mujos's 'Bouchers' chopped on dance floors on both sides of the Congo River.

Despite the strong challenge from Orchestre Bantou, African Fiesta emerged as chief rival to O.K. Jazz in the battle for Congo music supremacy. Joseph Kabasele had been overthrown just like the era's principal politicians. New leaders – Franco, Nico, and Rochereau – would begin to shape the music's future.

9
Revolution

Mobutu, Franco, Bavon Marie Marie, Kwamy,
Docteur Nico, Rochereau, and Essous, 1965–1967

'Léo-la-Belle' the Belgians had called their transplanted tendril of Europe which wound itself along the Congo River. But the Africans who streamed in from the countryside following independence found a city left tattered and tense by the intractable political crisis. Still it was far from the 'Léo-la-Hell' that some expatriates groused about, for the capital remained a refuge largely untouched by the violence that afflicted other areas of the country.

In the first seven years of independence Léopoldville's population leaped from some 400,000 to more than 900,000. Adding to these numbers came thousands more new arrivals who squatted just outside the city's official boundaries on land once restricted by the Belgians. One estimate claimed a tenfold increase in this so-called 'Zone Annexe' in just two years, from 31,458 in 1959 to 358,308 in 1961. Under the Belgians the old *cité* of Kintambo and Kinshasa districts had been joined by a new one containing the districts Dendale, Kalamu, and Ngiri-Ngiri. To the east lay Limete, the industrial zone; to the south a new airport at Ndjili, some fifteen miles from downtown; and in between, more and more housing for new arrivals.

Léopoldville's rapid expansion brought with it new demand for services, not the least of which was entertainment. In 1966 Congolese writer Michel Lonoh counted thirty first-rate bands in Léo and Brazza, and many lesser groups aimed to join them. 'Nightlife was very powerful,' Manu Dibango remembered, despite the occasional curfew and sporadic guerrilla attacks. Music, dance, and the ambiance of the bars lessened the pain of rough times.

Dibango's presence had enlivened the capital. Before his return to Cameroon in 1963, he ran two nightclubs in Léo, the Afro-Négro and later the Tam-Tam, where he played piano, vibes, and sax – 'dance music from jazz to Congo music' – with a variety of Congolese musicians, including Brazzos, Faugus Izeidi, Franc Lassan, and the Belgian drummer Charles Hénault. Dibango's 1962 hit, 'Twist à Léo,' recorded with musicians from Léopoldville under the name African Soul, brought the international dance craze to the Congo in the most personal of ways. 'My song was about their turf and became their twist,' he said.

Singer Philippe 'Rossignol' Lando took advantage of Léopoldville's new opportunities by resurrecting his old group, Rock'a Mambo. With help from Henri Bowane, who had returned from West Africa, following his split with Ry-Co Jazz, Rossignol put his new group through a shakedown tour of Cameroon, Nigeria, and Dahomey (Benin) at the end of 1963 and into 1964 before presenting it to the home folks. (Bowane this time remained in West Africa, where he would spend the next nineteen years.) Lacking the stature of Rock'a Mambo's first incarnation, Rossignol's new version became a showcase for young talent. Singers Henriette Borauzima and Camille Lola – the latter known by his sobriquet 'Checain' – both nudged their careers along with a stint beside the old master.

Franco's former mentor, Paul 'Dewayon' Ebengo, was also on the move. Dewayon had left Loningisa with Henri Bowane in 1957 to join the new Esengo studio. There he formed his own band called Conga Jazz. When Conga Jazz dissolved in 1960, Dewayon joined Orchestre Conga Succès, a band his younger brother, guitarist Jean 'Johnny' Bokelo, had started in 1958. Stylistically, the group leaned toward the Franco school. Dewayon played a mellow accompaniment while Bokelo favored a harsher attack on the strings. Their songs followed the usual themes of love and death, but stood out musically as harder-edged, at times raucous.

Sometime in 1962 Bokelo and Dewayon concluded an amicable split. Bokelo continued to lead the musicians of Conga Succès, but with a self-restraint that smoothed out the sound and brought it even closer to Franco's. Bokelo's series of recordings entitled 'Mwambe' (No 1, No. 2, etc.) voiced his concern with the direction society was taking.

> You know yourself that we have won independence
> At the store *pagnes* [wrap-skirt cloth] are expensive
> One costs 10,000 francs
> *Pagnes* at 'Papa[dimitriou]'s' cost 10,000 francs

> Nigerian *pagnes* cost 10,000 francs
> *Pagnes* from Brazza cost 10,000 francs
> Senegalese *pagnes* cost 10,000 francs.

Apart from Bokelo, Dewayon regrouped with new musicians in a formation he called Cobantou (Congo-Bantou). His new lineup included the guitar-playing cousins Raymond Braynck and Papa Noël, both of whom had previously accompanied Léon Bukasa. Cobantou followed Conga Succès into the Franco school but with more subtlety and less obvious imitation.

Another musical brother enhanced the prospects of the fading Négro Succès. Bholen, Djeskin, and the others carried on when Vicky Longomba returned to O.K. Jazz in 1962, but it was hard to replace the character and charisma of their former leader. Then along came Franco's little brother, Bavon Siongo, or 'Bavon Marie Marie' as he liked to be called. Nearly six years younger than his famous brother, Bavon dreamed of joining him in the limelight.

Ignoring his mother's disapproval — and Franco's too, it was said — Bavon learned to play the guitar, and in 1961, at age seventeen, ran away to Boma on the lower Congo to join a band called Les Cousins Bleus. He returned to Léopoldville, having made his point with his family, to play in Orchestre Jamel, a group of young musicians on the way to bigger things. After a brief stop beside Dewayon in Cobantou, Bavon settled in with Négro Succès in 1964. Through the force of his great personal charm, Bavon gradually emerged as the band's main attraction.

Bavon joined the growing list of younger musicians — Pablito of Orchestre Bantou, Rock'a Mambo's Checain, Samuel 'Samy' Bumba (later Bumba Massa) of Conga Succès — playing the music of the day with a youthful vigor that set them apart from the musicians whose fame dated from colonial times. Older artists like Gaspy and Bholen kept Négro Succès rooted firmly in Congo music's orthodox school, while Bavon, singer Leon 'Zozo' Amba, and sax player Michel 'Deyesse' Empompo attracted a younger crowd looking for something new. As it turned out, Bavon gained such a following it probably didn't matter much what Négro Succès did musically.

Bavon's flowering prompted *Etoile du Congo* to write that 'already one speaks of him as the future flag-bearer of Congolese music.' Personally he seemed preoccupied, if not obsessed, by his appearance. His assiduous use of eye liner and skin-lightening creams recast his face in a ghostly mask akin to that of today's Michael Jackson. Professionally his songs gave voice, through the singers of Négro Succès, to the rapture and heartache of young love and its tangled corollaries. He favored a girl named Lucie and in a series of songs spoke to her of his adoration and infidelity. With 'Lucie Tozongana' (Lucie let's reconcile) from 1966 he confesses:

> Love made me something like crazy
> I took another woman
> That woman is your younger sister
> I became ashamed and broke up with her.

While Bavon's addition boosted Négro Succès, big brother Franco created a controversy with a song about local morals. The song, 'Quatre Boutons' (four buttons), concerned a certain Marie, a woman of modest means who had managed to acquire a wig and a motorbike. 'It certainly is Kapinga's husband who bought them for me,' she admits, 'but not without having opened certain buttons.' Seeing a clear implication, many Congolese were quick to call the song scandalous and immoral, and some suggested it was time to censor such records. Franco responded to critics with a lame rebuttal. 'I wanted to be a moralist in my songs,' he said. 'Of course I use scenes from daily life. I've come close to impropriety in the past without going all the way. Must one see in this a predisposition to immorality? I don't think so, I really don't.'

Music lovers and the newspapers dissected Franco's words, but his rivalry with African Fiesta looked like a larger problem. At the beginning of 1965 African Fiesta enticed the singer Kwamy Munsi away from O.K. Jazz. Later in the year Franco discovered that African Fiesta had contacted Georges Kiamuangana, the saxophonist known as 'Verckys,' about playing for them. Fed up with such tampering, Franco placed an open letter in a newspaper. He accused African Fiesta of going beyond a mere search for musicians and instead trying to sabotage O.K. Jazz. 'We hereby inform you that starting tomorrow, on the 3rd of the present month [July 3, 1965],' Franco wrote sarcastically, 'all the musicians of O.K. Jazz, beginning with Franco and Vicky, are at your band's disposal.'

Verckys stayed with O.K. Jazz, but the matter didn't rest there. One of Kwamy's first compositions for African Fiesta was a satirical piece entitled 'Faux Millionnaire' (false millionaire). At first listen it sounds like a straightforward commentary on the predicament of those who, for the sake of status, live beyond their means. 'Matondo, lend me money,' Kwamy sings with Nico's laconic guitar chiming in behind him.

> I have a problem with my rivals:
> I'd like to show them,

> That I too am someone.
> That way they'll respect me.

But later in the song comes this passage:

> If you learn I've been arrested,
> Don't be surprised, I'm riddled with debt.
> I have nothing left in the bank.

Radio trottoir (street talk) had it that with this latter verse Kwamy was accusing O.K. Jazz of withholding his money, and that the title, 'Faux Millionnaire,' was an allusion to Franco himself.

This was all too much for Franco. Towards the end of the year he issued his response in a song called 'Chicotte,' the hippopotamus-hide whip of King Leopold's day, which he no doubt wished to apply to the backs of Kwamy and his bosses at African Fiesta. 'Chicotte' is a work of delicious contrasts, a sweet melody with Franco's lilting guitar punctuating each line from the singers, a hooting sax cutting in at the break like a wagging finger in the face, and trenchant lyrics with the sting of a police dog's bite. 'I saved you from a certain death/ Who's forgotten the story?' a bitter Franco asks, all but naming Kwamy in the process.

> Then, you were rotting and stinking like a corpse.
> You drooled.
> Your burial would have been a burden on the State!
> And to think that I stood for this filthiness.
> And that today you consider me, Franco, as your enemy,
> Liar that you are!
> You came to find me in O.K. Jazz,
> I made you what you are today.

In case the Lingala doesn't make the point, he sums up with a line in French, 'Oh que le monde est méchant!' (Oh the world is so wicked).

Franco's outburst nearly capped a convulsive year that had seen everything from a battle of the bands to a *coup d'état* by General Mobutu; but 1965 held one more surprise. Roger Izeidi had gone to the United States in October to investigate business opportunities for himself and African Fiesta. There he enjoyed a visit to New Orleans, the cradle of jazz, and spoke to a number of music critics, teachers, and other musicians during a tour spanning two months and eight cities. Once back in Léopoldville, however, the effervescent Izeidi ran smack into a deflating barrage of charges from his partner Docteur Nico. Chief among them was Nico's assertion that Izeidi illegally pressed records on an 'anonymous' label, ASL (Associated Sound Limited, an actual Kenyan company), that were then sold in other countries. As chef d'orchestre of African Fiesta, Nico took it upon himself to fire Izeidi. Rochereau, Nico hinted, was also involved and would be dealt with soon.

At a press conference just before Christmas, Izeidi explained that according to their company charter, Nico, Izeidi, and Rochereau, the three leaders of African Fiesta, had granted the Fonior company the right to sell the group's records outside of the Congo. Fonior was therefore the source of the records in question, and, said Izeidi, Nico knew all about the arrangement. Furthermore, since Nico was only one-third of the three-member management team, he was out-voted.

From Brussels, where he had gone to buy new instruments, Nico dispatched a telex that restated his charges against Izeidi and imposed a 'ban for life' on Rochereau for 'complicity.' Rochereau, at his press conference, hoped for a reconciliation but blamed Nico for the current dissension, calling him a 'véritable sécessioniste.' 'Let Nico,' he said, 'not claim to speak in African Fiesta's name.'

By the middle of January it became clear there would be no reconciliation. Nico announced a new lineup for the band that exposed the extent of the split. Brother Dechaud, singers Kwamy, Paul Mizele, and Lambert 'Vigny' Kolamoy and trumpeter Jeef Mingiedi joined Nico's faction. He filled out the group with guitarist Pierre 'De La France' Bazetta, a veteran of Ngoma and the Beguen Band, and bassist André 'Zorro' Lumingu, among others. They called themselves African Fiesta Sukisa, sukisa meaning cease or stop, as if to say, 'we can't be challenged.'

On the other side, Rochereau and Izeidi held the allegiance of Joseph Mwena, Willy Kuntima, Izeidi's brother Faugus, and a saxophonist named Armand-Louis Samu, who had only been with the group a few months. Depuissant refused to join either faction. The two leaders, casting about to replace Nico and the others, lured guitarist Jean Paul 'Guvano' Vangu away from a band called Diamant Bleu (blue diamond) and picked up itinerant guitar accompanist John Bokasa. Two young singers, René 'Karé' Kassanda and Sam Mangwana, joined up to back Rochereau on vocals. Henriette Borauzima also joined to secure a female presence among the major groups. Rochereau called her 'Miss Bora' and himself maréchal (marshal); his faction became known as African Fiesta 66.

Both African Fiestas went into the studio to get fresh songs recorded and ready to market under their new names. Each launched a new label – Sukisa for Nico, Flash for Izeidi and Rochereau – and presented their first records in the early months of 1966. Sukisa adopted President Mobutu's slogan with 'Retroussons les Manches' (let's roll up our sleeves), exhorting themselves and the country to work hard.

With that said, they fired off another volley in the Kwamy–Franco feud, although the song could just as easily be construed as a shot at the band's ex-members Rochereau and Izeidi. In his composition called 'Cimetière' (cemetery), Kwamy takes an allegorical walk through a forest.

> I meet a monkey wading in the mud.
> I clean its face and its hands.
> Instead of thanking me, it bites my hand.

He attacks those 'who no longer recognize their commitments, provoke quarrels, arguments, etc.' Echoing Sartre ('Hell is – other people!'), he concludes that 'hell does not exist. If there is one it is found in this world full of wickedness and hatred. For that, each will be judged here on earth and by the people.'

Rochereau and Izeidi, on the other hand, appeared to have little thirst for battle, preferring instead to return to the less controversial themes of personal relationships, 'Zando ya Malonga' (beautiful Zando), and mortality, 'Mokolo Nakokufa' (the day I die). The latter was a philosophic discourse from several perspectives – the poor, the rich, the dissolute – the kind of song that so endeared Rochereau to his audience.

> The day I die, I the pauper,
> I will think of Ida, the woman I married.
> I will think of the children I have fathered.
> I will be happy because I'm leaving the suffering of this world,
> The day I die.
>
> The day I die, I the rich man,
> I will think of all the money I have left behind.
> I will think of my property and my trucks,
> I will think of my children whom I have sent to Europe,
> Ah, the day die.
>
> The day I die, I the drunkard,
> I will think of my glass of wine.
> What else would I think about but those times at the end of the month,
> When I drank with my friends,
> Ah mama, the day I die.

With Guvano's guitar mimicking Nico in the background, Rochereau displays the full range of his gifts for composition and singing.

Although both African Fiestas flooded the market with new records, Fiesta 66 had the advantage of Roger Izeidi's connections to Fonior. Until Nico could cultivate his own channels, the works of Fiesta 66 would get wider distribution outside of the two Congos.

•

As the two Fiestas sorted themselves out, the question of who would represent Congo-Léo at the rapidly approaching World Festival of Black Arts in Dakar began to overshadow the back-stabbing among Congolese bands. A mid-January announcement from the government that African Fiesta had been selected raised the additional question, which one? The press thought it was Nico's faction.

A month later the Cultural Affairs Department reversed the decision and awarded the honor to O.K. Jazz. 'I am proud,' Franco told Agence Congolaise de Presse. 'All the more because the president of the republic himself designated us.' To make certain there would be no tampering with his musicians during the course of preparations, he announced he would move the band across the river to Congo-Brazza.

At the end of March, on the eve of departure for Dakar, a confident Franco described his lineup:

> We have three singers in brilliant form: Vicky, Mujos, and Michaux [Michel Boybanda]. We have three saxophonists: Isaac Musekiwa, Dele Pedro, and Verckys.... All these three musicians also play trumpet, clarinet, trombone, etc. We have Brazzos who is a soloist, a bassist, and an accompanist, at the same time. Simaro and Picollo fulfill the same functions as Brazzos. Myself, I am the soloist, and we have two young drummers of much promise for Dakar: Nestor [Diangani] and Dessoin.

Equally proud and confident was Franco's counterpart Jean Serge Essous, leader of Congo-Brazza's musical entry at Dakar, Orchestre Bantou. Essous's band had grown and strengthened with Pablito at the mike, and the arrival of singer Côme 'Kosmos' Moutouari. The 21-year old Kosmos (originally Cosmos) worked for the government as an apprentice statistician. But, he said, 'I had a wild desire to do music. When I was young I had a sense of composition. I wrote lots of songs.' Kosmos contacted Célestin Kouka, who in turn introduced the young singer to his colleagues. Soon Kosmos was sitting in on the band's rehearsals. 'The first song I gave them [was] entitled

Côme 'Kosmos' Moutouari

"Ebandeli ya Mosala" ... the start of work,' he recalled. 'I presented the difficulties of beginning a job ... because every beginning is difficult.' Kosmos was nervous at his own debut, but he and his song became extraordinarily popular with the followers of Orchestre Bantou.

Pablito and Kosmos, along with veterans Edo Ganga and Célestin Kouka, made for a dynamite front line. 'Gerry' Gérard Biyela, Joseph Samba 'Mascott,' and Alphonse Mpassy 'Mermans' traded guitar licks backed by a rhythm section of Pandi and Henri Wateto on congas and bassist Alphonse Taloulou. And the saxophone duo of Essous and Nino Malapet, Congo music's Parker and Coltrane, applied color and texture as if icing a cake. They too were ready for Dakar.

The Dakar festival of April 1966 provided a chance for the descendants of Africa to come together and celebrate their contributions to the world's music, dance, drama, literature, and fine arts. Masters from the motherland like Essous and Franco mingled with stars of the African diaspora like Katherine Dunham and Duke Ellington. It was a welcome break from the struggles for civil rights and political independence, a chance to take a deep breath, reflect, and re-energize for the difficult times that lay ahead.

•

The personal dissonance that first splintered African Jazz and then African Fiesta appeared to be highly contagious; O.K. Jazz had no immunity, as Franco discovered on his return from Dakar. The first sign of trouble surfaced in June of 1966 when Brazzos failed to appear with the band. In an interview at the end of July he declared, 'I have, in fact, left O.K. Jazz without any hope of returning this time.... The reason certainly won't escape you, since it's become a classic with we musicians: poor money management.' Others were rumored to be leaving as well, perhaps as many as nine. As it turned out, the breach was only marginally less serious. Brazzos, Mujos, Isaac Musekiwa, Dessoin, bassist Jean 'Picollo' Tshamala, and trumpet player Christophe Djali all deserted. The six joined Kwamy, who quit Fiesta Sukisa, guitarist Wela Kingana, called 'John Payne' after the American cowboy actor, and a quartet of lesser-known musicians to begin rehearsing a new band. The rest of O.K. Jazz remained loyal to Franco. 'O.K. Jazz est toujours là,' he told a reporter, O.K. Jazz is still here. Nevertheless he took a swipe at Kwamy in one of his next releases, 'Course au Pouvoir' (race to power).

> You have become a wanderer
> Like a poor orphan
> And all you say about me
> Is only the result of a frantic race to power.

Kwamy and his band of renegades made their debut in April of 1967. They called themselves Orchestre Révolution. Many Congolese saw this as a slur against Franco, but Kwamy, Mujos, and the others were more likely attuning themselves to the country's changing political culture, where another revolution of sorts was afoot.

In the early stages of his regime, President Mobutu consolidated political power in the office of the president while using his control of the military to put down the remaining pockets of insurrection. He began to remove the superficial vestiges of colonialism with the announcement that, as of July 1, 1966, the sixth anniversary of independence, European names for cities would be replaced by names of Congolese origin. Stanleyville would become Kisangani, Elisabethville would now be Lubumbashi, and Léopoldville, the capital, would be called Kinshasa.

The following year, Mobutu introduced the zaïre, a new unit of currency valued at two U.S. dollars, with his picture on the bills. In April, the same month that Orchestre Révolution gave its first public performances, he began to reshape what remained of the country's political structure. He announced the formation of the Mouvement Populaire de la Révolution (MPR) with himself, its 'founder-president,' at the top. Despite several attempts, no other party was able to gain official recognition. In June, Mobutu forced acceptance of a new constitution for the country which 'legitimized' his presidential system.

Mobutu and Kwamy had more in common than their use of the word *révolution*. Kwamy's band had been recruited and financed by an association of Kinshasa *hommes d'affaires*, wealthy or connected (usually both) individuals who could make things happen. They had formed a company called Société des Editions de Disques Boboto, whose most noteworthy presence was a military man, one Denis Ilosono, private secretary to President Mobutu. Whether Mobutu's initiative or money was behind the new venture is unclear, but the debut of the MPR and Orchestre Révolution in the same month of 1967 seems unlikely to have been a coincidence.

If Mobutu was the unseen hand behind Orchestre Révolution, his minions had selected two notoriously unstable characters, Kwamy and Mujos, to lead the group. Stylistically the band was tight, very much from the school of O.K. Jazz. The musicians recorded a song, 'M.P.R.,' to commemorate the new party but, for the most part, stayed with the less controversial themes of everyday life. Michel Boybanda left O.K. Jazz to join Révolution a few months after its debut. By December he had become the group's leader as Kwamy and Mujos disappeared in Brussels. The erratic duo returned from time to time, although they appeared to be terminally dissatisfied. They were treated as mere employees of Editions Boboto, the same unhappy status they had suffered in previous groups. Brazzos, the other founder, also disliked the arrangement. Despite Boybanda's efforts, the undercurrent of discontent made it nearly impossible for the musicians to work effectively. Orchestre Révolution disbanded in August of 1968.

•

Revolution was the word in Brazzaville, too, where President Massamba-Debat had installed his Mouvement National de la Révolution as the country's sole political party. His government tried to walk the fine line of neutrality by courting France and the West along with countries of the eastern bloc. 'The revolutionary Congo,' a French journalist wrote, 'with its Chinese matches lighting Cuban cigars smoked by Russian advisers and French cooperators.' The Congolese called it scientific socialism, but as the government imposed controls on business and labor, it became an ever more cumbersome presence in people's lives.

One who resented the intrusion was Jean Serge Essous, leader of Orchestre Bantou. Government restrictions affected his music. By 1964 permission to travel, even across the river, had become a matter for negotiation with the government. Censorship of newspapers and song content imposed limits on expression and creativity that Essous accepted only grudgingly.

Following their appearance at the Dakar festival, Orchestre Bantous de la Capitale, as the musicians had begun to call themselves, stayed on in Senegal to try to earn some money. Three months later they moved to Abidjan to begin what promised to be a lucrative one-year engagement. But, Essous said, 'the Congolese minister of foreign affairs came and took the bread out of our mouths.' He annulled the contract and ordered the band to return home to play for independence day celebrations in mid-August. For Essous, that was the final straw. He packed his troops on a flight to Brazzaville, but he took another to Paris.

News of Essous's departure shocked music lovers on both sides of the river. Les Bantous had been cruising at their audience-pleasing peak. The youthful duo of Pablito and Kosmos, whose evocative compositions and striking good looks transcended generational barriers, had brought stability to the band's vocal corps and made them every bit the equal of the competition. 'We were so happy with the two of them,' Essous said. 'It was a period where we had extraordinary successes, songs. We did it all. Ah! At that time everything that came out was a hit. Every record that came out was a hit, played in Kinshasa, played everywhere.' The hits didn't stop when Essous left. The band continued to thrive under Nino Malapet's direction. Nevertheless, 'it was a sad case,' Pandi remembered. 'It's like when someone dies, kills himself. We stayed really sad. There was a big hole, a big hole. And now we had to try to round out, to fill in a little, not even a lot but a little, even if part of it stayed empty.' Pablito could have been thinking of Essous when he wrote 'Masuwa' (the boat), his classic exchange between lovers Pati and Evie.

> The boat has left
> Taking you to another country
> Above all don't forget you left me on the bank
> I'm waiting for you

> The boat is far away now
> I have tears in my eyes, Pati.

In Paris, Essous went looking for Manu Dibango. The two had met years earlier when Dibango played with African Jazz and again in Cameroon on one of Orchestre Bantou's tours. Dibango was in touch with Joseph Kabasele, who also happened to be in town, so the three got together to cook up a recording project. The spur-of-the-moment session produced the first of a series of Afro-Latin-jazz fusion records released under the name African Team.

Essous's stay in Paris yielded longer-term benefits as well. He found Ry-Co Jazz, now making its home base in the French capital. Jerry Malekani, Freddy Nkounkou, and Casino Mbilia, the three remaining original members, had reinforced their lineup with a fresh mixture of Parisian Africans and Frenchmen. Essous joined them for a year of gigs around France.

Toward the end of 1967, Ry-Co Jazz signed a contract to play some Christmas dates in far-off Martinique in the French Antilles. That first contract led Ry-Co Jazz to five years of concerts and recording in the Caribbean. So began another spin on the great musical circuit that had started with the sale of Africans into slavery in the Americas and continued with the commerce of radio and records. 'For the Antilleans,' Nkounkou told an interviewer, 'our music was a discovery, so we started our rhythms going over there. The same for us, we learned many things.' Ry-Co Jazz helped wean the region from the musical dominance of Haitian bands and contributed to the swirl of crosscurrents which eventually produced zouk.

North America also received its first live dose of Congo music with the appearance of Rochereau's band, now called African Fiesta National, at the 1967 World's Fair in Montreal. After long debate and some embarrassing confusion that saw one government ministry select Nico's African Fiesta Sukisa and another choose Kabasele's African Jazz as the country's representative, Rochereau had emerged victorious on the strength of Fiesta National's first-place finish in a song competition. Still, it would take more than a visit by Rochereau to open minds clogged with the traffic of rock and roll. In the late 1960s, North America seemed oblivious to the allure of the Congolese rumba. Meanwhile, back home along the banks of the Congo River the rumba was getting a new look.

10
Dances and disorder

Docteur Nico, Rochereau, Sam Mangwana, and Franco, 1968–1969

John F. Kennedy once observed that 'victory has a hundred fathers and defeat is an orphan.' Soukous, the dance craze of the late sixties, is in league with victory when it comes to counting its sires. Bavon and Bholen's Négro Succès is 'le premier au marathon du soucous,' *Etoile du Congo* announced in 1968. Some thought the band had originated the style. Rochereau claimed to have done just that during a West African tour the same year. Orchestre Bantous de la Capitale, which spread the soukous much as it had the boucher, is often credited with its invention.

Soukous the word evolved from the French verb *secouer*, to shake. It was originally written as the noun form *secousse*; one who moved *par secousses* moved jerkily. *Secousse* became *soucousses* and then *soucous* on the street and in the press until the c fell into disfavor and gave way to a k.

Soukous the dance began in Brazzaville with a newly formed group of novice musicians. The players came together in 1964 as the Super Band, the creation of budding guitarist Jacques Kimbembe. Soon afterward they changed their name to Sinza, which essentially means 'root stock.' Orchestre Sinza introduced the soukous to Brazzaville bar patrons in 1966 but lacked the connections to convert its popularity into greater success for themselves. Other bands soon picked up the steps, and the soukous sent the boucher into retirement.

Boucher and soukous were among the first of a number of variations on the basic rumba that enlivened the waning years of the 1960s. Like their counterparts in the West who were 'twisting,' 'strolling,' and 'doing the chicken,' Congolese musicians in search of a competitive edge deployed a progression of new dance styles. Orchestre Sinza updated the soukous in 1968 with a new wrinkle called *mossaka*. The ensuing popularity plus the addition of singer Pierre Moutouari, the brother of Kosmos, finally earned the band a trip to Paris and a recording contract with Pathé Marconi.

Later that year Docteur Nico introduced the kiri-kiri based in part on the 'jerk' from Western rock. Kiri-kiri numbers began in the normal fashion but came to a slight retard after the second verse. A brief guitar flourish signaled a slowed-down sebene where dancers showed off the new steps. 'Kiri-Kiri Mabina ya Sika' (kiri-kiri the new dance), a Nico composition about a man searching the streets of Kinshasa for his girlfriend so they could go to the night club to dance the kiri-kiri of Fiesta Sukisa, was the genre's defining piece. For added pizazz Nico imported equipment to stage light shows like those of the French pop singer Johnny Hallyday.

Around the same time, Les Bantous de la Capitale developed a hybrid with Pablito's song 'Masuwa,' billed as a *soucous-kiri-kiri*. Rochereau jumped in with the *jobs*, a dance that he claimed borrowed from both the jerk and the rumba, but was less of an imitation of foreign styles. His song 'Martin Luther King,' dedicated to the assassinated civil rights leader, was, he said, a typical jobs.

The King piece was curious for a number of reasons, not the least of which was Rochereau's improbable linking of King, Johnny Hallyday, and Mao Tse Tung, among others. The song stretched on for more than eight minutes to cover both sides of a 45 r.p.m. disc, a device more and more bands had begun to use. And it employed a Western-style drum kit. Rochereau's heavy-handed traps, which until then had been used only sparingly in Congo music, hinted at the approaching obsolescence of the standard percussion set-up, especially the maracas.

Other dances followed: Jean Bombenga's *mambenga*, Kabasele's *yéké yéké*, the 'eighth phase of the rumba,' the *Apollo 11*, and many more. 'We invent a new dance style every day,' Nico would later boast. But the rumba remained the base.

•

In the late sixties, O.K. Jazz, the two African Fiestas, and Orchestre Bantous de la Capitale still ranked at the top of Congo music's hierarchy, followed closely by Négro Succès, Conga Succès, and Cobantou. For Nicolas Kasanda, the leader of African Fiesta Sukisa, it was an especially good time. Freed from

Docteur Nico

the constraints of other leaders, the Docteur could operate on his own terms. Nico was a diminutive man with a towering talent. Barely an inch or two over five feet and as thin as a sapling, he could easily be mistaken for just another hanger-on if you didn't know him by sight. Even on stage one's ears found him first, then eyes darted in search of the source. And there he stood nearly motionless, save for a soft flicker of fingers caressing the strings of his guitar.

By the end of 1967 Nico had assembled perhaps the strongest lineup of his career. He installed two unproven teenagers at the microphone, Valentin Sangana and Etienne 'Chantal' Kazadi, who would more than reward his judgement. These two joined Dominique 'Apôtre' (apostle) Dionga, Paul Mizele, Lambert 'Vigny' Kolamoy, and newcomer Victor 'Bovic' Bondo, to form one of the period's strongest aggregations of singers. André 'Zorro' Lumingu played bass alongside a drummer called Adjos, trumpeters Jeef Mingiedi and Pedro 'Cailloux' Matandu, and Michel Ngwalali on flute and saxophone. Dechaud and De La France accompanied Nico on guitar.

The use of three guitars had evolved over the years to become a Congo music standard of which Nico and company were but one illustrious example. Les Bantous featured Gerry Gérard, Samba Mascott, and Mpassy Mermans, while Franco soloed in the company of Simaro and Brazzos and a number of Brazzos's successors. Rochereau employed Jean Paul 'Guvano' Vangu, Faugus Izeidi, and Johnny Bokasa in his Fiesta; Dewayon played with Ray Braynck and Henri Bowole in Cobantou. This practice gave rise to the term mi-solo to identify the third guitar which played between the solo (lead) guitar and the (rhythm) accompaniment.

Docteur Nico and his brother Dechaud set the standard for solo and accompaniment in Congolese music. Fans called Nico 'dieu de la guitare' (god of the guitar), Dechaud the guitarist 'who made Lucifer and his 500,000 devils dance.' With De La France playing mi-solo between them, African Fiesta Sukisa featured what may have been the finest guitar threesome ever to grace the company of a single band, anywhere.

Nico was the virtuoso, his notes, in the words of Essous, 'separate from one to the other like pearls of rain.' Years later Nico tried to explain his gift in an interview with the Voice of America.

> The most characteristic thing about the way I play guitar is my conception of what is abstract in the melody sung by the singers. I synthesize [it] in a linear way which allows me to express, to create, in accordance with the harmony and rhythm of the band. What you must also understand about my style is the source of my inspiration. Most of the melodic themes I create have their source in my traditional past. When I'm in the process of creating on stage, I am no longer with my band, I'm spiritually in my village, Mikalayi.

Nico loved experimentation and innovation, his introduction of Hawaiian steel guitar being one of the more spectacular examples. During his days at Esengo in the late fifties, before the advent of electronic effects pedals and multi-track recording, he discovered a way to create reverberation where each note shimmered into the next one. It sounded faintly like he might be playing a keyboard, a harpsichord perhaps, but it was all done on his guitar. Nico called the style merengue – his 'Merengue Scoubidou' and 'Merengue President' being two of the style's better known examples – because it echoed the stuttering accordions of Dominican merengue. 'I wanted to create one of the great bands of Africa,' he said on another occasion,

> but for lack of means I couldn't do it, because all that stuff costs money. You have to pay for instruments. For lack of means, my means were limited, I

Dances and disorder 139

couldn't buy instruments. But if that hadn't been the case I could have gone much farther.

Nico, like nearly all other Congolese musicians, did not read or write music in the Western manner with staffs and notes. Still, when composing he liked to jot his ideas down on paper to the point of sketching out each player's part. He would then go over the material with the musicians, taking suggestions for improvements. More changes followed during rehearsals until the final arrangement emerged.

African Fiesta Sukisa toured extensively within the country and outside to East and West Africa. Travel inspired songs like Nico's 'Aruna,' about a girl from Tanzania, Chantal's 'Nakeyi Abidjan' (I am going to Abidjan), and 'Echantillon ya Pamba' (useless example) by Lessa Lassan who joined the band in 1969, inspired by a visit to Sierra Leone. The latter backfired in Sierra Leone when a passage in the local vernacular meant as a self-deprecating joke on the band offended some listeners for whom the musicians were gods.

Back home in Lingala, on the themes of life and love, the band worked in safer territory. But for Fiesta Sukisa words seemed like mere baubles to adorn the body of a richly varied music. Nico's 'Suavilo' (from *suave* [smooth] in Spanish with a Lingala twist) builds a seductive Cuban *guajira* around the nimble flute of Michel Ngwalali. On 'Ozali Suka ya Mobali' (you are the ideal of a man) Nico takes the sebene, playing variations on the hook without ever repeating himself. 'Limbisa Ngai' (forgive me) puts the Hawaiian guitar up front, and 'Pauline' mixes it with Mingeidi's splendid trumpet. Mysterious clicks from Nico's guitar introduce 'Bougie ya Motema' (light of my heart). 'Marie Pauline' showcases the guitars as likembes of traditional music. If anyone ever doubted it, Docteur Nico in the late sixties confirmed himself as a master, Congo music's most consistent producer of high-quality material. Nearly every song of this period emerged from his nurture, fresh and original.

In May of 1968, as Fiesta Sukisa opened for Johnny Hallyday in a concert at the Kinshasa Zoo, Joseph Kabasele walked on stage to sing beside Nico for the first time since their acrimonious split. In that brief, electric moment, five years of controversy and bitterness dissolved in a flood of nostalgia. But seven months later, as if to dramatize that the old days would never return, news came that their colleague from Opika and Esengo, Tino Baroza, had been killed in an automobile accident in Yaounde, Cameroon.

More grief followed as Nico's own leadership deficiencies began to surface. Musical brilliance failed to translate into the skillful handling of other areas,

Dechaud

personal relations in particular. A scant year after his reunion with Kabasele, Nico's entire band, except for Dechaud, walked out on him. 'We've had enough of the inhuman treatment that Nico inflicted on us,' Paul Mizele told *Etoile du Congo*.

> We're his collaborators, but he treated us like servants. We don't see clearly the financial plan or one for pressing records. And since he refused dialogue, we preferred to tell him good-bye, because he probably had no need for us, and he always declared that it was his guitar that attracted the clientele.

In that, Nico was probably right. He and Dechaud could have carried almost any band regardless of who was in it. But to lose the quantity and quality of musicians who left him still came as a serious blow. The two brothers couldn't play by themselves. Nico found a young singer of the caliber of Chantal and Sangana in Lessa Landu who called himself 'Lessa Lassan.' With a pick-up drummer and bassist and Nico himself singing second voice behind Lassan's strong tenor, Fiesta Sukisa was back in the clubs within a month. As 1969 proceeded, singer Josky Kiambukuta hired on to sing with Lassan while William 'Serpent' Kabamba moved in to play mi-solo between Nico and Dechaud.

Near the end of the year Fiesta Sukisa left Kinshasa for an extended tour of West Africa, but Nico's management style seemed not to improve. 'He didn't want to rub shoulders, because we were the younger generation,' said guitarist Bopol Mansiamina, who played with the band briefly in 1970. 'He didn't rehearse with us, that was the problem. He had his ideas which were very firmly set. We were forced to follow what he wanted.' Little space remained for individual expression, so Nico concocted his magic with a constantly changing array of discontented sidemen.

•

Rochereau's wing of African Fiesta splintered even sooner than Nico's. After 1966 Rochereau and Roger Izeidi had begun to call their group African Fiesta National or sometimes Le Peuple (the people) to reflect the rhetoric of President Mobutu's new political party the MPR. Like Docteur Nico, their collaborator-turned-competitor, Rochereau and Izeidi had put together an impressive band. Sam Mangwana sang with Rochereau, Izeidi, Karé Kassanda, and Miss Bora. Guvano, Faugus, and Johnny Bokasa handled the guitars. Joseph Mwena held steady on the bass beside drummer Henri 'Fredos' Dongala, saxophonist Armand-Louis Samu, and the twin trumpets of Willy Kuntima and Jean Pierre 'Jean Trompette' Nzenze. Even the great Wendo, who had been remembered more than seen since Ngoma finally closed its Kinshasa studio in 1966, returned to open shows for Fiesta National during a European tour. But one day Rochereau le maréchal slighted Mobutu le président, and that led to his undoing.

On New Year's Eve 1967, Congolese authorities staged a gala celebration under the patronage of President and Madame Mobutu. The affair began at 6:00 p.m. highlighted by the appearance of traditional dancers and magicians, comedians, a beauty contest, and fashion show. The evening's consummate moment was to be a performance by African Fiesta National, but Rochereau and his band showed up late. By the time they took the stage, after eleven o'clock, the head of state and his wife had departed. Despite the New Year's Day holiday a ministerial decree issued on January 1, 1968, ordered Rochereau and his band suspended from all activities for a period of three months for 'attempted sabotage of the artistic and cultural evening.'

Rochereau and Roger Izeidi reportedly served most of the suspension out of the country. Guvano fell ill and felt abandoned, while Sam Mangwana and the others grew restless and insolvent. Before the suspension was up, Mangwana, Guvano, Johnny Bokasa, Jean Trompette, and Rochereau's newest recruit, guitarist Michel 'Michelino' Mavatiku, decided to seek work on their own. Together with Depuissant, the conga drummer from African Jazz and African Fiesta, and defectors from Vox Africa who included singer Daniel 'Dalienst' Ntesa, they formed a new band, Festival des Maquisards.

They were mostly young musicians who fancied themselves as rebels. A *maquisard* was a man of the *maquis*, underground forces of the French resistance to the Nazi occupation. Although the tyranny of their elders was scarcely comparable to the Nazis', the new maquisards opposed the old order. Businesswise there would be no boss. They would make decisions together so each member understood what was happening. Festival des Maquisards signed with Editions Boboto, the same company that sponsored Kwamy's Orchestre Révolution.

Rochereau and Izeidi, back in Kinshasa after their suspensions expired, tried unsuccessfully to block the new band with an appeal to the minister of culture. But Rochereau sabotaged his own case by luring solo guitarist Pierre 'Attel' Mbumba away from the band African Kings. Karé, Faugus, Willy, Fredos, Samu, and Mwena all remained loyal to Rochereau. Newcomer Denis Lokassa, the future Lokassa ya Mbongo, who played, like Dechaud, using the mi-*composé*, took over as accompanist; Paul 'Pepe' Ndombe from Orchestre Super Fiesta of Kikwit and Simon 'Diana' Nsimba signed on to bolster the vocal corps.

Rochereau and Izeidi had rebuilt in the space of a few months. Even before all the pieces were in place they took the stage at the Vis-à-Vis, one of the clubs in the Renkin neighborhood of the new *cité*, to defend their turf against the renegade Maquisards who were making their debut appearance nearby at Chez Engels. Then, with their new members safely on board, they went into the studio to record songs that would address the recent troubles. 'Today I return to you/ My whole heart [my only wish] is for the joy of you, my people,' Rochereau sings in 'Peuple.' 'I thought I would be pardoned,' he says at one point, tacitly admitting his New Year's Eve error. He addressed his departed musicians less directly in 'Libala ya 8 Heures du Temps' (eight-hour marriage). There Rochereau tells the story of a woman who marries at an advanced age. She admonishes her detractors by saying that 'even though my marriage might only last eight hours, the important thing is that everyone knows I am married.' With that, African Fiesta National took off on a tour of West Africa.

Rochereau was to lyrics what Nico was to music. His words cut to the quick of modern life and reflected its quirks back to his listeners. Near the end of 1968 he released a wry commentary on acquisitiveness as represented by Kinshasa's latest status marker, the Toyota automobile. 'Toyota' tells the story of two women friends. The first falls for a wealthy lover, Fely, 'a Congolese Aga Kahn,' who promises to buy her a Toyota, a luxurious house in a fancy neighborhood, and a Vespa for her servant to run errands on. When Fely makes good on his promise the woman becomes a fervent Christian who prays for her man's continued fidelity so she won't lose her access to his inexhaustible wealth. 'Ah wealth, wealth,' goes the refrain. 'Ah pleasures, pleasures/ I looked for money/ Today fortune knocks on my door.' The second woman, envious of her friend, resorts to occult forces and succeeds in acquiring similar possessions. Rochereau leaves the moral of the story up to the listener, but by drawing attention to the 'Toyota life' he made sure the subject would be debated.

'Toyota' made up part of an eight-song, 33⅓ r.p.m. album released on the Ngoma label, which, despite the closing of its Kinshasa studios, remained in business in France under the direction of Alexandros Jeronimidis and Nikiforos Cavvadias. The album was Rochereau's first and among the first by any African artist to be sold in Congo-Kinshasa. (Albums of Congo music that appeared in Europe were usually compilations of 45 r.p.m. releases.) The standard format had been the 45 r.p.m. disc which was relatively cheap at 50 makuta ($1) compared to 6 zaïres ($12) for an LP. Release in the album format posed an economic risk for the artist as the higher price threatened to depress sales. Rochereau thought of it as a necessary innovation in the market.

The new disc came out under the name 'Seigneur Rochereau.' Following his suspension, Rochereau had dropped the military title *maréchal* for the more distinguished *seigneur* (lord). The new title seemed to befit a figure of Rochereau's age, experience, and stature.

Le Seigneur then set out to consolidate his position. In October of 1969, he removed his long-time partner, Roger Izeidi, from the band. 'Equal work for equal pay' was his terse explanation to the press, as if to imply that Izeidi was somehow deficient. 'I heard on my car radio that Rochereau didn't want to work with me any more,' Izeidi said. The abrupt split brought an end to nearly a decade of fruitful collaboration. Only the partnership of brothers Nico and Dechaud remained from the glory days of African Jazz. Rochereau carried on as sole head of African Fiesta National, while Izeidi retired from performing to attend to his interests on the business side of music.

Sam Mangwana, meanwhile, took up Rochereau's discarded title *maréchal* in the Festival des Maquisards. A short, wiry man whose inner spring appeared to be perpetually wound, Mangwana jumped from project to project in great bursts of energy and enthusiasm. But once a certain success had developed, boredom seemed to set in. He lived as a fighter who enjoyed the battle but never lingered to savor the victory. Kinshasa wags dubbed him *le pigeon voyageur*.

Mangwana was born in Kinshasa to parents who had fled the oppressive Portuguese colony of Angola. At least the Belgians had schools for Africans, Mangwana said, even though one could only become a low-level office worker. Growing up he listened to the music of Rock'a Mambo, O.K. Jazz, African Jazz, watched touring groups from Latin America, Louis Armstrong from the United States, and did his own singing in school choirs.

Shortly after his eighteenth birthday in 1963, Mangwana approached Rochereau, who encouraged him to sing something. Impressed with the youngster's voice, he called Nico in to listen. Both leaders of African Fiesta thought he sounded a lot like Mujos, who had just quit the band. Mangwana remembered that they told him, 'Small boy, if you want to catch your chance it's better to join us.... This is a big chance for you. This is a short cut in life for you.' The opportunity and the money both sounded good, Mangwana thought, so in spite of his parents' disapproval he joined his idols on stage in October 1963.

Mangwana's move into music caused a rift in his family which forced him to move out. After six months with African Fiesta he left the pressure of Léopoldville altogether. Across the river in Brazzaville, Mangwana, calling himself 'Sam Moreno,' and Tino Baroza's brother Dicky Baroza put together a short-lived band called Los Batchichas. Mangwana also sang briefly with the Negro Band and De La Lune's fledgling Orchestre Tembo before returning to Léopoldville to join Rochereau's African Fiesta 66.

Mangwana's new Festival des Maquisards was strong at first, reinforcing its ranks with guitarist Dizzy Mandjeku; a new singer, Camille Lokombe; Miss Bora, emerging from more than a year of inactivity; and Diana Nsimba, who left Rochereau after only a few months of service. Musically the Maquisards remained close to their mentors. Songs about women like 'Georgine' and 'Colette' were the group's standards. 'Yambi Chérie' (welcome my darling), a continent-wide hit composed by Michelino, wrapped around both sides of a 45 to accommodate Guvano and Michelino's sparkling sebene. Mangwana's

'Zela Ngai Nasala' (wait while I work) addresses the more serious predicament of a working man whose wife holds him to the standards of the rich.

By the middle of 1969 the egalitarian *maquisards* faced the same personnel problems that plagued their dictatorial elders. 'My colleagues,' Mangwana said, 'they were working for money and for the beautiful girls. They were not working for the future.' Dalienst called it a personal 'misunderstanding' between himself and Mangwana. 'He [Mangwana] wanted me to leave the band. The group said, "No, no, no. If you want to, you can go."' And so Mangwana did, along with Guvano, to re-form a new, philosophically compatible but short-lived version of the group. Dalienst, Dizzy, and Diana eventually reworked the remaining faction into Les Grands Maquisards.

•

Disagreements and defections had already devastated O.K. Jazz when many of the band's musicians left in 1966 to form Orchestre Révolution. Franco and Vicky could take some measure of satisfaction from Révolution's collapse less than a year and a half later, but the period in between had been difficult. At the beginning of 1966 the ban on Franco and his music was lifted in Congo-Brazzaville, allowing O.K. Jazz to resume accepting invitations to play across the river. When Franco's musicians deserted him later in the year, he looked to Brazzaville for replacements. There he hired a teenager named Gilbert Youlou to shore up his vocal corps and picked up a new rhythm section in bassist Francis Bitshoumanou and conga player Jean Félix Pouéla, who went by the stage name 'Du Pool.'

Despite the new infusion of talent, the defection of so many of its stars hobbled O.K. Jazz through most of 1967 and into the following year. The band's recording output dropped off and the number of club appearances dwindled to the point where it was news when the band finally stepped up its schedule in the middle of 1968. 'Missing for long months from the musical scene, master Franco's T.P.O.K. Jazz has just regained its public, both in the dancing bars of the capital and on the record market,' *Etoile du Congo* wrote. Perhaps as a morale boost Franco and Vicky had added the initials T.P. for *tout puissant* (all-powerful) to the band's name in the manner of a local football team, T.P. Engelbert. The ploy seemed to help as T.P.O.K. Jazz gradually emerged from the doldrums.

Franco's troubles hadn't ended, however. In 1966, based in part on the criticism of 'Quatre Boutons' and a general wringing of hands on the part of 'music authorities' about the state of the music, the Mobutu government installed a censorship commission within the justice ministry. Now, in 1968, three new O.K. Jazz records failed to meet the commission's arbitrary and often narrow test for social appropriateness. Franco's 'Mobali na Ngai' (my husband) and an unnamed song by Verckys were banned outright. The fate of the third, Franco's 'La Vérité de Franco' (Franco's truth), in which he tells of his 'secret' affair with a married woman, was left in suspension until more information could be gathered. It is unclear what finally happened, but since both of Franco's records were already in the shops, whatever action the commission took could only have limited further sales.

•

The troubles in O.K. Jazz and the two African Fiestas resulted from some of the more notorious episodes of division within Congolese bands. These in turn spawned increasing numbers of new formations among Kinshasa's musicians. Docteur Nico's former singer, François 'Franchard' Landu, helped to start Baby National in the middle of 1968. Most of those who left Nico in 1969, Mizele, Apôtre, Lumingu, Ngwalali, went on to form African Soul. Papa Noël, who ran a close second to Mujos when it came to heeding wanderlust, gathered a group of fresh, young recruits – including future stars Paul 'Bopol' Mansiamina and Blaise Pasco Mayanda, known later as Wuta Mayi – into Orchestre Bamboula in November of 1968.

Dewayon and his Orchestre Cobantou suffered through a round of dislocations in May of 1969. Dewayon dismissed four musicians for 'very serious lapses,' and his soloist, Etienne 'Diamant' Makengela, quit to form a new band called Kin-Bantous. Dewayon's brother, Johnny Bokelo, found himself in a troubling dispute over royalties. Bokelo had renamed his Conga Succès as Conga 68 and created his own label, Landa Bango, but the band members threatened to quit claiming they had received no money from the new venture.

'Congolese musicians strongly resemble loose women who live at the expense of those who listen to them,' complained Jean Bombenga, whose Vox Africa strongly resembled a revolving door. 'I consider Congolese musicians in general and Kinshasan musicians in particular like loose women, the "ndumba",' agreed Franco. For Docteur Nico, the epidemic of defections was 'a simple question of caprice and lack of seriousness' on the part of musicians. An alarmed minister of culture directed Roitelet of the nascent musicians' union to examine each band in an effort to discover the causes of the departures.

The root of the trend, however, could be reduced to three basic elements unlikely to be altered by anyone's intervention: creative differences about the music, lack of trust in matters of money, and the tendency to put oneself before the interests of the group. Each separation and new alliance energized individuals and renewed creative impulses, giving birth in turn to some great new music. Troubling though it was to some, the rate of turnover among musicians in Congolese bands seemed to be an inevitable progression along the music's developmental path.

In June of 1969, at Kinshasa's Premier Festival de la Chanson (the first of what promised to be an annual song festival), the judges awarded first prize to a phenomenal fourteen-year-old singer named Emile Soki. He won a trip to Europe and five cases of Heineken beer with his terrific performance. The second prize of 400 zaïres and four cases of Heineken went to Antoinette Etisomba, a young woman who was just nineteen. The event capped a decade of music that had belonged to the mostly male offspring of the colonial-era recording studios. If the festival's winners offered a clue to the future, the seventies would look more kindly on women and the young.

11
Rhythm of the time

Franco, Verckys, Bella Bella, Zaïko Langa Langa,
Bavon Marie Marie, Franklin Boukaka, and Rochereau,
1969–1970

Ten years had passed since rioting in the streets of Léopoldville sent the Belgian Congo careening down a fast track to independence. The Congo crisis had become a dreadful but increasingly hazy memory, and the idealism of Lumumba had given way to pragmatic Mobutuism. In the four years since his seizure of power, President Mobutu had forcibly united the country, installed his Mouvement Populaire de la Révolution as the sole political party, and, through deft manipulation or physical elimination of possible challengers, carved out an apparently invulnerable place for himself as ruler. A couple of short-lived rebellions in Katanga; the 1968 execution of Pierre Mulele, the Kwilu rebellion leader who had been lured back to the country from Brazzaville with a promise of amnesty; and 1969's protest demonstration by Lovanium University students, which cost the lives of at least thirty at the hands of Mobutu's soldiers, produced only minor blips on the radar screen of tranquility. Joseph Kasavubu, the last surviving link to the first republic's legitimacy, died in April of 1969. Slightly over a year later, Joseph Mobutu, sole candidate for president, won 99 percent of the vote for a new seven-year term.

Life in the Congo was better since he had come to power, Mobutu declared during his campaign. Few could deny that it was true. Yet, largely because of the civil war, the Congo's urban residents were poorer. In the ten years of independence Kinshasa's wage index had increased sevenfold, but the index of prices had risen at twice the rate of wages, leaving workers with only half the spending power. Moreover, expatriates 'continued to hold over one-half of managerial posts and well over one-third of supervisory positions,' according to a government survey. These developments, coupled with the decade-long tripling of the capital's population to 1.3 million and the phasing out of United Nations technical assistance, made Mobutu's 'let's roll up our sleeves' admonition all the more relevant. Still, government reforms had managed to correct some of the problems. Inflation fell to a modest 2.5 percent, the new zaïre remained stable at a value of $2 (U.S.), wages began to rise, and the economy as a whole responded with a robust 8 percent expansion.

Kinshasa's bars and bands appeared to multiply in direct relation to its exploding population. People's desire for entertainment and Congo music's tremendous appeal seemed to insulate music-related businesses from whatever ills might befall the rest of the economy. According to Professor Michael Schatzberg, beer consumption rose steadily from a yearly 1.7 liters per capita in 1946 to 10.07 at the time of independence to 23.62 in 1974. 'At the official government price of 20k per bottle [.72 liter], this works out to an expenditure of Z6.60 per year for beer. The average per capita income for Zaïre is, at most, Z50 ($100).'

The focus of nightlife had shifted over the years as if in search of the growing city's center. The new cité had supplanted the old, yet the broad avenue that once provided most white residents with their only view of the African quarter served as the backbone for both. Formerly named for Belgium's Prince Baudouin, Avenue President Kasavubu connected Kinshasa and especially its night life in a most fundamental way. Starting downtown near the river, the avenue ran south past the park and the zoo, scenes of many a memorable concert, across Avenue de l'Itaga, home of the O.K. Bar, Air France, and Quist. At the edge of the new cité it leaned slightly, like a tipsy reveler, to meet Avenue de la Victoire in the heart of Renkin, home of the increasingly prestigious Vis-à-Vis and dozens of other bars, before curving sharply, like a camel's hump, westward to Bandalungwa, Kintambo, and back to the river.

Renkin, soon to be renamed Matonge, trembled to the tenor of music. 'Nganda Renkin' (Renkin the hideout, in the language of the Bills) Michelino and the Maquisards had called it in song. When the sun went down, people turned out to feast on the sounds and the smells and the profusion of sights which the quarter rarely failed to deliver. A sea of vendors of every sort engulfed entrances to the bars and clubs, and if a band were playing, the ngembo, swarms of curious children, clung like bats to the walls outside. Record shops, loudspeakers at full throttle, grappled with the bars for attention. A record shop was

> often a shaky little shack with four cases covered with records, a counter and a book of blank bar tabs for a receipt book, the walls decorated with giant photos of Johnny Hallyday, Verckys posters, etc. And a pretty female citizen to finish off the decor.

The record business approached its zenith as the seventies began. Willy Pelgrims carried on with his recording, pressing, distribution, and sales operations, MACODIS and ECODIS in Kinshasa and Fonior and SOFRASON abroad. Although he looked close to achieving a monopoly, room still remained for other entrepreneurs. His recording studio in Kinshasa had never been first-rate. It had filled the gap when the Greeks closed up shop, but there was a clear need for better facilities. STAR (Service Technique Africain de Radiodiffusion), a small, two-track studio run by the Catholic Scheut Fathers to prepare religious programs for the country's assorted radio stations, opened its doors to a few pop groups. Other bands waited until they could make connections for a recording trip to Europe. Obvious opportunity and the return of stability in the country caused businessmen to take a new look at music.

Philips, the Dutch record company that grew into an electronics multinational, had maintained its Philips-Congo sales branch in Kinshasa throughout the civil conflict. Phonogram, the Philips record division, had made recordings in the Congo in the fifties but, like Loningisa and the others, it halted operations shortly after independence. Towards the end of 1969, Phonogram announced it was ready to try again with the opening of a modern new studio and record pressing plant. Société Phonographique et Industrielle du Congo (SOPHINCO) set up shop in a building in the Kingabwa industrial area near the river that Philips had used for assembling radios. 'Africans are very gifted in music, but until now lack of technical and artistic assistance put them at a disadvantage,' a company official declared. 'I think that combining these essential elements, African records will be able to conquer the world market.'

Congolese entrepreneurs also stood ready to become more than mere consumers of their own music. Back in 1961, Joseph Kabasele had become the first Congolese label owner with his Surboum African Jazz. Under the auspices of Fonior, Roger Izeidi had purchased the CEFA label and launched others, including Vita, Flash, and Tcheza; Franco, Vicky, Nico, and Rochereau all had their own labels. As the sixties wound down, however, a new class of Congolese label owners emerged. Called *patron* in French, the English equivalent of boss, they were usually businessmen, not musicians, who played the role of producer. A *patron* had the money to outfit a group, buy instruments, book concerts and studio time, and see to the pressing and distribution of records. The Société des Editions Boboto (SOCEDIBO), a small company with a lofty name, owned in part by Denis Ilosono, a military man with more cash on his hands than his meager government salary could account for, had been among the first of such outfits. SOCEDIBO had footed the bill for Kwamy's Orchestre Révolution and the Festival des Maquisards before Ilosono ran afoul of Mobutu and the company's creditors seized its assets to settle outstanding bills.

As the seventies began, more Congolese *patrons* got into the business; some even created their own bands rather than sign an existing one. Jean Kindoki, owner of Editions Keje (K.J., his initials) and Orchestre Symba, described his operation for *Zaïre* magazine.

> I created Orchestre Symba-Keje because I love music. I've organized my band so that everyone is happy with his work. Most of my musicians are students. They make music because they love music. I bought the musical instruments, and I earn next to nothing from an evening's receipts. Nonetheless my band gets fifty percent and Editions Keje forty percent. I put the remaining ten percent in what we call a social fund. The account is managed by a committee. With me, all of Symba's musicians are indirectly shareholders.

Other businessmen would join the list of *patrons* in the early seventies, most notably Charles Pierre Loukelo with his Editions La Musette and Mfumu Muntu Bambi of Editions Parions ou Mondenge.

•

The *patron* who created the broadest impact on the music industry during this period embodied a combination of talents and personal quirks that scarcely any of his competitors could match. A musician and composer with a gift for business — audacious, flamboyant, covetous, and possessing a sense of self that excluded the notion of failure — Georges Kiamuangana, the man known as Verckys, was the quintessential wheeler-dealer. He had grown up in Léopoldville, where he attended school through three years of post-primary before dropping out to pursue his interests in music. Already proficient with flute and clarinet, he joined a small group that performed at services in a church run by believers in the Congolese prophet Simon Kimbangu. Within this group he eventually graduated to saxophone. In 1961, while still in his teens, Verckys played his first professional gigs on sax with Dewayon's Conga Jazz. Franco hired him for O.K. Jazz in 1963, a move said to have met an icy reception from Isaac Musekiwa, who was less than thrilled to find a new competitor at his side.

Franco and Verckys were an unusual pair. Six years apart in age – Verckys was two months younger than Franco's little brother, Bavon Marie Marie – each had arrived in O.K. Jazz from a vastly different route. Franco had been a shy boy who grew up poor and unschooled to become a leader of one of Africa's best bands. The confident Verckys was a relatively well-educated son of a successful businessman and viewed the band as a stepping-stone to bigger things. The two men complemented each other's immense musical talent and shared a robust dose of ambition and resolve.

Their mutual obstinacy had led to a falling out in 1967 when Franco took Verckys to court for failing to participate in a recording session. Verckys countered that he was acting in protest at Franco's insinuation that he had been involved in the theft of some instruments in Brazzaville for which Nestor, the drummer, had been jailed. Their differences were smoothed over at the time, but scarcely a year later new difficulties arose.

In September of 1968 Verckys announced that he and singer Gilbert Youlou had created a new label called Véve. Six records were released under the new mark which Verckys insisted had nothing to do with O.K. Jazz. He and Youlou were still members of the band. The new label was simply a side-project, the realization of a dream.

In December, with Verckys in Brussels on business, the story behind the six Véve records began to leak out. They had been recorded illegally by *nzonzing* (moonlighting) musicians under exclusive contract to O.K. Jazz. A furious Franco fired his wayward saxophonist, but on reflection agreed to take him back in return for 40 percent of the profits from the illicit discs. That arrangement lasted little more than a month. Verckys quit O.K. Jazz in February of 1969 and severed ties with Youlou, who chose to stay with Franco.

Once independent, Verckys moved swiftly to organize a band, so swiftly in fact that it looked like he had been at it while still in Franco's employ. At the beginning of April 1969, scarcely two months after leaving O.K. Jazz, Verckys introduced his brand-new Orchestre Véve at the Vis-à-Vis. Alongside Verckys, the group included a former lead guitarist from Vox Africa known as Danyla; Maproco Munange, a veteran of the Esengo studio, on second sax;

A Verckys record jacket
from the early seventies

a trio of new singers, Matadidi Mabele, Marcel Loko, and Bonghat Tshekabu, who called themselves 'Mario,' 'Djeskain,' and 'Max Sinatra'; and 'Mister Fantastic' Bovic Bondo, a singer from Docteur Nico's band. In their first year together the musicians of Vévé would go on to make thirty-five records. 'In a very short span of time, Orchestre Vévé of Verckys, the man with lungs of steel, has made people talk and earned the esteem of music lovers,' *Etoile du Congo* told its readers near the end of the group's first year. 'Verckys plays guitar well, sings marvelously, and handles the organ enigmatically [sic] making him a complete show-business artist.'

Early in 1970 Verckys signed the Dalienst faction of the Festival des Maquisards to record with Editions Vévé under the name Les Grands Maquisards. In the manner of a full-fledged *patron*, he provided instruments and made arrangements for recording the band. He was on a roll now and soon began mapping plans for his own recording studio.

How Verckys managed to move so far so fast remains something of a mystery. He made frequent trips to Brussels, and some people, without offering evidence, speculated that he engaged in the smuggling of mercury, a central ingredient in the skin-lightening creams favored by Kinshasan youth. Verckys flatly denied the charge. 'In O.K. Jazz I had to work pretty hard to survive,' he explained.

> Well, I am a born worker. So instead of waiting for the end of the month to receive my salary, which was 30,000 francs, I would make [O.K. Jazz] badges in red and black (the favorite color of the boss of O.K. Jazz), and I would cross [Stanley] Pool to sell them over there. Sometimes I bought oil which I went to sell in [Brazzaville].

With these extracurricular earnings and profits from the first Véyé records, he was able to procure instruments through Roger Izeidi and ECODIS. Whatever the truth of his finances, Verckys proved to be a bold and clever businessman as well as an excellent musician. In the years to come many would question his ethics, but no one could ignore his contributions to Congo music.

•

While more Congolese entered the commercial side of the business, the number of artists making the music continued to increase apace. In the early years the best new groups – Orchestre Bantou, African Fiesta, Négro Succès – had started as offshoots of the two great bands established during colonial times, African Jazz and O.K. Jazz. By the mid-sixties, however, groups like Orchestre Sinza of soukous fame that lacked such an illustrious pedigree appeared with increasing frequency.

In 1965 Orchestre Los Angel [sic] made its debut led by guitarist Albert Missia who played under the sobriquet 'Robin Mopepe.' While Los Angel fixed itself in the school of O.K. Jazz, many of the bands that followed were less bound by the constructs of their elders. These were dubbed *groupes yé-yé*, ensembles of young, inexperienced musicians who were just as likely to borrow elements from Johnny Hallyday and James Brown as from Franco and Rochereau.

Yé-yé – French for pop musician, a term inspired by the 'yeah! yeah!' exclamations of rock and roll – evolved as the latest fad within the culture of Léopoldville's students and young workers. Having more to do with 'cool' and 'style' and less with juvenile delinquency, yé-yés were regarded as benign versions of the 'Bills.' Girls wore miniskirts or pants and perhaps a wig or extra hairpieces. 'They wear funny make-up and take on a slightly shabby look. They wear long necklaces, the longest around. Earrings are always of unusual color, length and size.' Men grew their hair long and often wore make-up. 'Hats, wild glasses and masks are also the yé-yé's mark. They prefer motorcycles to cars.... They drive fast. They often take on a snooty air.' Men liked beautiful women. Women 'adore the "jazzers" – guys with light skin.' And their speech was littered with foreign phrases like 'pop music,' 'rhythm and blues,' 'hippies,' and, thanks to the Jackson Five's bubble-gum soul, 'blues au chewing gum.'

The yé-yé band Cinq Punaises (five bugs) appeared in 1966 followed by Les Etoiles (later renamed Minzoto Wella Wella) in 1967 and a legion of like-minded brethren in 1968 which included Les Ecureuils (the squirrels), Thu Zaina (or Thu Zahina), Les Mustangs, Les Vipères Noirs (black vipers, led by Robin Mopepe, who had left Los Angel), the Stukas Boys, and the Yss (or Iss) Boys. Several musicians called themselves Otis, as in Otis Redding. One went so far as to become Otis Yé-yé.

The outpouring of new talent continued the following year with the appearance of Les Chaussettes Noires (the black socks), Panthères, The Famous, and the Eagles. These yé-yé groups, while never much of a threat to main-stream Congolese bands, nevertheless played to the swelling ranks of enthusiastic young fans and provided a proving ground for talent and innovation from which Nico, Franco, and the others could draw.

One example of the yé-yés' impact could be seen in the music's changing rhythm section. Although Ngoma had tried an upright electric bass at the end of the fifties, it had failed to dislodge the old acoustic standby. But the yé-yé groups, with their fondness for rock and soul, rejected the stodgy contrabass in favor of the solid-body electric bass guitars used by their heroes in the West. Congas and maracas were also seen as passé; yé-yés preferred Western-style traps. In order to keep pace, older Congolese bands started to use the new instruments too. By the end of the sixties congas and maracas, if they appeared at all, played in the umbra of the drum kit, and the contra-bass too was nearly extinct.

Youth bands (*groupes des jeunes*), as the yé-yé groups came to be known, sprang up to satisfy wants that the established bands – despite their addition of 'chanteurs yé-yé' and a few 'jerk' numbers could not. 'Young Congolese of today feel ill at ease in our fast-changing society,' one observer wrote. 'Whence their burning need to catch hold of something and identify with a model that makes them feel bigger, validates them, and at the same time gives them a chance to express themselves vicariously.' Paul Bakunde Ilondjoko of the Stukas Boys, known to his fans as 'Pablo Redding,' explained that when we were born, young bands were rare. The few groups that existed developed, for the most part, in the central city in very narrow [social] circles. It was hard for us to go to have fun too far from our neighborhoods, or to go to evening dances organized by the big bands. Almost spontaneously we started our own.

Despite its distance from the neighborhoods, a hip new club just off Avenue Kasavubu in the former whites-only ville established itself as youth central. 'The Perruche Bleue [Blue Parakeet] has become the temple, the meeting-place for all the gals and guys of the capital,' Etoile du Congo told its readers. They meet there 'to dance the jerk ... to James Brown's latest creations which the Mustangs interpret sensationally and with fantastic excitement.'

'Over a book, a glass, or a guitar, the son of a bourgeois and the son of a laborer can make contact with less difficulty than before,' wrote a Kinshasa 'hippie' in response to older critics.

> Finished with arbitrary classifications, all of youth is living to the rhythm of its time.... At the Perruche, at the Show Boat, the Saint Hilaire, a jerk bursts out over the humming of conversations. They all go to it without distinctions of creed or color.

They weren't dropouts, the writer insisted, merely serious students and workers relaxing on a Saturday night or Sunday afternoon. 'The main thing for them is to do each thing in its own time.'

Kinshasa's most enduring youth bands incorporated scattered influences from the West but rooted themselves in the rumba of their elders and even borrowed a few licks from the music of the village. The singing brothers Soki were more of this bent. Emile Soki, the fourteen-year-old winner of 1969's Premier Festival de la Chanson, sold one-half of his prize, the plane ticket to Europe (there's no record of what happened to the five cases of Heineken), and joined with other students to form a group called Les Myosotis (the botanical name for the forget-me-not).

Meanwhile young Soki's older brother Maxime Soki, a university student in Lubumbashi (Elisabethville), had left his studies at the beginning of 1969 to join Négro Succès at the urging of some of the group's members whom he'd met on the band's recent tour of Katanga province. In April, several musicians quit Négro Succès, effectively grounding the band for a time and leaving the elder Soki adrift in Kinshasa. He caught on briefly with another band that was trying to form, but by the early part of 1970 it seemed clear the group would go nowhere. The younger Soki's Myosotis split around the same time, leaving brothers Max and Emile in roughly similar predicaments. From this apparent dead end, Orchestre Bella Bella was born.

Max Soki began to rehearse with a new, more cohesive group of musicians. At the same time he made the acquaintance of Charles Loukelo of Editions La Musette, who agreed to provide rehearsal space. Max recruited Emile to share vocals, and under Loukelo's direction the group recorded several songs at the new Phonogram studios. With their first records ready for market, Orchestre Bella Bella made its debut in August of 1970 with a series of club gigs around Kinshasa.

One of the band's first hit records, 'Lisolo' (negotiations), told of a confrontation between two lovers: 'Let's agree once and for all, because our friends have had enough of our quarrels and reconciliations.' It could have made a perfect theme song for Bella Bella, because trouble plagued the band almost from the start with one or the other Soki usually at the root. Emile caused the first fracture when he allowed Loukelo to convince him to record some of his songs with another band, Concierto National, composed of a faction of the old Myosotis. When the same songs appeared on record by two different bands, the scandal broke into the open. Some of Bella Bella's musicians quit, brother mistrusted brother, and all decried Loukelo's duplicity. Such were the shaky beginnings of Orchestre Bella Bella.

As the ingredients for Bella Bella began to fall into place, another significant band was beginning to come together. 'Our dream is one of greatness, as a band to become standard-bearers for the youth,' the group's founder, Vital 'D.V.' Moanda, would later tell an interviewer. 'We hope through our advice and our songs to influence, little by little, the morale and life of young people.' Moanda had been rehearsing a small group he called Belguide, but the musicians he assembled hadn't seemed to click. In 1969, he recalled,

> my friend [Henri] Mongombe and I assumed responsibilities as advisers and publicity agents for Orchestre Thu Zaina, which at the time was one of the rare youth groups. We realized that for tormented, abandoned, anxious youths, music was a preferred escape and entertainment. So we took off in a new direction

A new band of teenaged students from the Renkin neighborhood gave life to their idea. They called it Orchestre Zaïko, a combination of Zaïre and Kongo. Moanda built the group around a nucleus of holdovers from Belguide: singer Nyoka Longo 'Jehrsy Jossart' and guitarist Félix Manuaku 'Pepe Felly.' New recruits included singer Jules 'Jules Presley' Shungu, who would go on to greater fame as Papa Wemba; bass player 'Bapuis' Muaka Mbeka; guitarists Matima Mpioso Kinuani and 'Enock' Zamuangana; and two additional singers, Siméon Mavuela and Michel Anto who called himself 'Evoloko.' Moanda himself played congas. All were in their teens or early twenties.

Orchestre Zaïko made its official debut near the end of March 1970 at the Hawaii Bar not far from the Renkin neighborhood. 'In the beginning Zaïko wasn't impressive,' Manuwaku recalled, but as time went on it got better. While basing their music on the rumba, Zaïko's musicians served up a version quite different from the older groups. 'We eliminated the wind instruments,' Shungu said of a departure with particular significance for the sebene. In the older groups, the lead guitar would often improvise a solo during the sebene then yield to the saxophone or trumpet. On other songs the guitar and horn might engage in a bout of call and response, the guitar laying down a couple of bars and the saxophone answering back. But the horn-less Zaïko had no such flexibility. Of necessity, the guitar assumed the dominant role in the sebene. The guitarists played the sebene in riffs, finding a hook and repeating it over and over. While this practice may have been used to cover for inexperience – most of the guitarists were teenagers who lacked the skills of a Nico or Franco – it may also have been a conscious borrowing from traditional music, where the use of repeating figures is common. For the sake of variety and ambiance, the singers gave little shouts called 'animation' to lure people to the dance floor.

Many of the musicians insist dropping the horns was a decision taken to differentiate themselves from their elders. After all, their counterparts in Western pop music, to whom they were closely attuned, tended to employ horns less and less frequently. But the decision may have had as much to do with economics and availability as it did with artistic innovation. Forming a band was expensive; horns were non-essential items that could be cut to save money. Young horn players were also in short supply. Most younger musicians either sang, which required no expenditure, or chose to learn the more glamorous guitar.

Soon after it had formed, Zaïko added Meridjo Belobi on traps, another important change from the older groups who had employed the Western-style drum kit only sparingly. And in the clubs Zaïko staged a dynamic visual show. Where their elders merely stood and played, Zaïko's musicians choreographed their performances with steps picked up from film clips of James Brown. One of Zaïko's earliest creations was a catchy little dance which Shungu named the *langa-langa*, from the Lingala word *langa*, 'to get drunk.' Almost immediately people began to refer to the band as Zaïko Langa Langa, and the musicians followed their lead.

A year after Zaïko Langa Langa's debut, the group's first recordings were issued on Phonogram's Polydor, the same youth-oriented label that was about to sign 'soul brother number one' James Brown. 'We rocketed up the charts starting from our first series with "Mosinzo Nganga," and "Pauline",' Moanda declared. 'The second series confirmed our determination with "La Tout Neige" [sic], "Francine Keller." That's the fruit of our assiduous and continuous work.' In fact an August 1971 issue of Zaïre ranked 'La Tout Neige' and 'Mosinzo' at numbers one and two on its 'Hit Parade.' By then the band had added yet another guitarist, Teddy Sukami, and singer André Bimi.

The Congolese press offered mixed assessments of the younger generation's creations. While generally approving of Bella Bella's 'Lisolo,' *Etoile du Congo* called it

> a schoolboy's song. It's all there: naïveté, a certain clumsiness in the story line, a slightly careless orchestration that makes you sometimes think the singers didn't get together before they crossed the recording studio's threshold.

Zaïre gave an equally equivocal blessing to 'Bolingo ya Bomwana,' a new Thu Zaina release.

> Childhood love: a poor theme, knocked off quick without working too hard. But one is struck by the sweetness that emerges from the melody and the piece's orchestration. This atmosphere is rare among the 'Black Pals' [i.e. the younger generation of Congolese musicians].

What mattered most, however, was that the youth bands succeeded in the marketplace. A few weeks after Zaïko's 'La Tout Neige' peaked out, Bella Bella took the *Zaïre* hit-parade's number one position with an Emile Soki love song called 'Lina.' In the latter half of 1971, Kinshasa's youth bands consistently held down five of the hit-parade's top ten spots. During one week in August they owned numbers one through six. Polydor reported combined sales of its youth bands had reached nearly 206,000 records for 1971, approximately one-fifth of the country's annual one million or so output. While small by Western standards, the numbers represented a sizeable expenditure in a country whose annual per capita income was the rough equivalent of $100. 'Young people will no longer obey the big stars' rules,' a Polydor executive told the press. 'Since 1970 they have issued a cry of revolt and no longer need their elders.'

One could forgive the youths if they felt the tingle of invincibility. They had demonstrated in no small way that the established groups were vulnerable. The passions of a new generation that had begun to stir with the ascent of Bavon Marie Marie had come to full flower. At the Perruche Bleue and dozens of other clubs, all of youth was living to the rhythm of its time.

•

As Orchestre Bella Bella and Zaïko Langa Langa struggled through their formative stages, guitarist Bavon Marie Marie still enjoyed the adulation of the young. The year 1970 began with his band Négro Succès in fine form. Three of the group's members, Bavon, Bholen, and 'Didi' Kalombo, each had a sizeable hit record. Bavon's 'Libanga na Libumu' (a stone in the stomach) held the number one spot on Zaïre's hit-parade for nearly two months before yielding to Didi's 'Munga Josephine' (a woman's name).

'Libanga' is a curious collage that sounds as if all of Congo music's competing forces had suddenly collided in the middle of Négro Succès. It begins with a wistful sounding rumba in support of gloomy lyrics:

> I cry ye ye ye o
> Because it is too late, I will have no child
> I have the old women's stone in my stomach.

Then the band shifts into a funky sebene replete with James Brown-like horn charts and grunts of encouragement for dancers. The sebene wraps around to the B side of the 45 where funk gives way to a passage of repeating guitar figures. A final barrage of Congolized funk brings the song to a close.

By the end of March a second Bavon record, 'Maseke ya Meme' (sheep's horn), broke onto the charts. Grounded firmly in Congo music's orthodox school of rumba, 'Maseke' deals with greed, death, and sorcery.

> This family is bad
> Witchcraft has become a profession
> ...
> They better kill me and I will die.
> I am tired of it.
> What fortune do I have?
> I am not tired of living,
> Yet they want me dead.

In the days to come Bavon's words would elevate him to the rank of prophet. For in the early morning hours of Wednesday, August 5, 1970, he died in a wrenching auto crash.

Beyond the basic fact of Bavon's death at the age of twenty-six, the precise how and why of it remain something of a mystery. 'Siongo Bavon, alias Bavon Marie Marie, former soloist of orchestre Négro Succès was killed yesterday at about one o'clock in the morning in a serious auto accident on Avenue Kasavubu in the vicinity of Cosbaki in the commune of Bandalungwa,' *Etoile du Congo* reported in its August 6 edition. Follow-up pieces later in the month made no further mention of the circumstances of his death, no hint of investigation. Years later Sylvain Bemba wrote that Bavon had been 'coming home in the wee hours after a dance where his band Négro Succès had played.' His Volkswagen, said Bemba, had run into a tree. British authors Chris Stapleton and Chris May say Bavon was with his girlfriend, Lucy. 'He pulled out from behind a lorry and smashed into an oncoming car. Bavon was killed; Lucy had both legs amputated.'

Franco's biographer, Graeme Ewens, reports that the accident was the culmination of a disagreement between Franco and Bavon that had simmered for some time. On the night of his death, with Franco, Lucy, and members of O.K. Jazz present, Bavon accused Franco of sleeping with Lucy. She fled the scene in a taxi with Bavon in hot pursuit. He forced the taxi to stop along Avenue Kasavubu. 'Angry, shouting and evidently distracted, Bavon packed the girl into his car, did a fast U-turn and, in the darkness, he drove head-on into a parked military truck which had broken down at the roadside.'

Several years after Bavon's death, one of his friends appeared to confirm much of the Ewens version, although he referred to the woman in question as 'M.J.' and added that Bavon had been drinking. Rumors about the accident ran wild at the time, including some that held Franco responsible. Bavon's last records fed talk of premonitions and sorcery. With the passage of time, hearsay gained credence. But regardless of whatever else happened that night, death had pierced the shield of youthful invincibility, and young Congolese had lost one of their earliest heroes.

In early September, Kinshasa's music community came together at the Eglise Christ-Roi for a mass of thanksgiving in Bavon's memory. The mourners included some of Congo music's biggest names, Franco, Vicky Longomba, Docteur Nico, Rochereau, Jean Bombenga. Following the ceremony, Franco received mourners at the Vis-à-Vis. According to Ewens, Franco was devastated by the loss of his brother.

After Bavon's death, he withdrew from the limelight for several months, retreating with his private grief into a long period of mourning. One month after the burial, the musicians resumed work but the band was virtually ignored by Franco.

A day after the memorial mass, Bavon's colleagues in Négro Succès gave a concert in his honor. In mid-December they emerged from mourning with a gig at the Vis-à-Vis featuring guitarist Paul 'Dercy' Mandiangu in the unenviable position of replacing Bavon. Less than a year later, however, the entire band deserted Bholen to start a new group they called Négro National. The newspaper *Salongo* would later provide a suitable epitaph: 'Négro-Succès died with [Bavon] Siongo.'

•

Through sheer numbers of people and an infrastructure that survived the civil conflicts, Congo-Kinshasa dominated the production of Congo music. The musicians of Brazzaville had contributed greatly to its early development, but recurring disputes, based on each Congo government's support for opponents of the other, tended to isolate them from their brethren in Kinshasa. Les Bantous de la Capitale continued to prosper despite Essous's residence in the Caribbean. New groups – Mando Négro Kwala Kwa with Fidèle Zizi and Didi Siscala, Orchestre Super Boboto (made up of insurgents from Orchestre Tembo and led by singer Ange Linaud), and Freddy Kebano's Les Fantômes – took off. Orchestre Sinza, with Pierre Moutouari on board, kept a full schedule of live shows around central Africa with an occasional trip to record in Paris. The Negro Band enjoyed a brief revival when Michel Boybanda joined the group. But the impulsive energy that incited the youth bands of Kinshasa seemed, in Brazzaville, to channel itself more toward politics.

Brazzaville had its share of clotheshorses and hippies, to be sure, yet it also fostered a number of serious youth organizations like the Jeunesse Mouvement National de la Révolution (JMNR), the youth arm of President Massamba-Debat's ruling MNR. Although much of the leadership was in its late twenties or early thirties, the JMNR counted college and high-school students among its most radical members. Demonstrations in 1968, inspired in part by dissatisfied students within the JMNR, helped trigger Massamba-Debat's removal as president in a leisurely coup that began at the end of July and ended in December with army captain Marien Ngouabi assuming the mantle of chief of state. Ngouabi proceeded to rework the MNR into a new

Rhythm of the time 163

single political party, the Parti Congolais du Travail (PCT), pushed through a new constitution with expanded powers for the presidency, had himself promoted to the rank of major, and proclaimed his country the People's Republic of the Congo (République Populaire du Congo), to be guided by the principles of Marx and Lenin.

As part of a program to bring true self-sufficiency and independence to his people's republic, Ngouabi set out to establish state industries in sectors he deemed critical to national development. Often this meant simply nationalizing an existing, foreign-owned business. Less frequently he created industries from scratch like the Société Congolaise du Disque. SOCODI, he hoped, would relieve the country's musicians of their dependence on facilities in Kinshasa and Europe and perhaps generate a little revenue in the process. The new enterprise, complete with a modern recording studio and record pressing plant capable of turning out 33⅓ r.p.m discs as well as the standard 45s, opened its doors in the middle of 1970. One of its first productions was a 12-inch LP by Les Bantous de la Capitale, *De Brazzaville à la Havane*, that reflected the country's historic musical and current ideological ties to Cuba.

Nowhere in central Africa did music and ideology combine more forcefully than in the works of Brazzaville's Franklin Boukaka. Namesake of the U.S. president who had struggled to lift his country out of the Great Depression, Boukaka was possessed of similar qualities – a can-do spirit and a breadth of vision – to go along with his exceptional musical talent.

According to Boukaka's friend Michel Boybanda, the two of them began their careers together in a group called Sympathique Jazz. In 1958 they helped to form Negro Band before Boukaka left for Léopoldville. Across the river he joined the group of teenagers who hung out with Kabasele's African Jazz at the close of the fifties. When Kabasele went to Brussels for the Round Table conference, Boukaka, Jean Bombenga, Rochereau, Edo Lutula, and Casino Mutshipule, among others, performed together briefly as Jazz African. In 1960 Bombenga, Boukaka, and Casino moved on to launch the first formation of Vox Africa.

A year or two later, Boukaka returned to Brazzaville and joined Cercul Jazz, the band of a youth organization, the Cercle Culturel de Bacongo, that had been established by the French in the early fifties. The band played every Sunday afternoon at a bar west of town near the Djoué River. There Boukaka began to develop a following with his appealing stage presence, mellow baritone, and increasingly incisive compositions. Soon, recalled Guy-Léon Fylla, 'he was no longer satisfied to just sing about love. He was no longer satisfied to observe what was going on on the street. Instead he sought to analyze and criticize the human soul. And thus he targeted political men.'

In 1967 Cercul Jazz recorded Boukaka's 'Pont Sur le Congo' (bridge on the Congo) for Franco's Editions Epanza Makita. Employing a lean arrangement that recalled Congo music's early days – solo guitar, saxophone, bass, congas, maracas, and claves – Boukaka and a second singer delivered his mildly worded suggestion that with the white man gone perhaps the two Congos could be put back together.

> Accept this day my prayer
> For a united Congo.
> If we follow the teachings of Lumumba
> Kinshasa and Brazza will get on well together.
> Brothers and sisters of the two banks,
> Let's join hands and forge the glory
> Of our Congo.

Needless to say, with political power and national prestige on the line, Congolese leaders were unlikely to entertain the suggestion.

Later the same year, Boukaka put together a sanza (likembe or thumb piano) ensemble as part of a Congolese folklore troupe that traveled to Paris for an exhibition sponsored by OCORA, the French Office de Cooperation Radiophonique. Boukaka played acoustic guitar and sang with backing from the sanzas of Pierre Badinga and Albert Mampouya. His pairing of the sanzas like lead and accompanying guitar may have reflected the origins of the style that made modern Congolese music so distinctive.

While in Paris, the group recorded six songs for Gilles Sala Productions with Jean Serge Essous – apart from Les Bantous but not yet Caribbean-bound – sitting in on saxophone. 'I liked Franklin Boukaka's voice enormously,' Sala remembered. 'He had a beautiful timbre, a very pleasing voice. And then as a composer ... just like Joseph Kabasele, and like Nico, like Franco, they had a very developed sense of popular music.'

Back home in Brazzaville, Boukaka and his sanzas played concerts for the home folks. He worked 'Pont Sur le Congo' into the group's repertoire along with a new song he had been working on called 'Les Immortels.' At one point in 'Les Immortels' Boukaka relates a story: 'An old man, whom I always consider young, said to me one day, "Young man, every man must die one day, but not all deaths have the same meaning."' And then Boukaka recites his honor roll of martyrs: Lumumba, Ché Guevara, Malcolm X, Félix Eboué,

Franklin Boukaka

André Matsoua, Simon Kimbangu, and more. One could not help but hear in the words an implied criticism of the current crop of Congolese leaders which failed to measure up to the standards of his fallen heroes. Boukaka's performance of 'Les Immortels' at the 1969 Pan-African Cultural Festival in Algiers was said to have been one of the event's most stirring moments.

Boukaka reached his artistic zenith in 1970 with the release of an extraordinary twelve-song album. While not Congo music in the classic sense, it is a work of such power and beauty that it cannot pass unremarked. Reinforced by Manu Dibango's superb arrangements and accompaniment, *Franklin Boukaka à Paris* presents a passionate and eloquent portrait of modern Africa where urbanization erodes traditional mores and mendacious leaders fail to deliver on the promise of liberation. 'Oh Africa, where is your independence? ... where is your liberty?,' he asks on 'Le Bûcheron' (the woodcutter) accompanied by a pair of tearful violins and Dibango's measured piano in tap-for-tap tandem with a snare drum and high-hat.

> Cutting firewood is hard work,
> When I've cut some, selling it is difficult.
> Such suffering,
> My children and I in poverty,
> I cannot bear it!
> Some I have elected
> Fight over power,
> And cars.
> When election time comes,
> Then I become an important personage
> To them.
> I ask myself: now that the white man has gone,
> Independence, for whom have we gained it Africa?

As if suddenly unburdened of a great heartache, the song rides smartly out with Dibango's overdubbed sax poking and prodding the denuded emperors.

On the stylish rumba 'Likambo Oyo' (this problem) Boukaka sings,

> Now my wife's body is as yellow as a palm nut
> She has lost her head
> She thinks only of putting on ointments
> That eat her skin.

A remake of 'Pont Sur le Congo' puts piano and sax in place of guitar in a spare, more melancholy setting. A violinist plucks the strings like a likembe player while Boukaka recites his prayer of unity.

The album closes with a hauntingly beautiful version of 'Les Immortels.' Supported by acoustic guitar and piano, Boukaka leads his simple requiem for the martyrs with the even-tempered earnestness of one who has chosen a similar path. With 'Les Immortels' and much of the rest of the album, Boukaka accomplished the peculiar blend of fervent word and delicate melody that Bob Marley would deliver in Jamaica. Soon, however, Boukaka's convictions would push him beyond the musical realm into a far more dangerous arena. But no matter what happened in the future, *Franklin Boukaka à Paris* made certain that his musical brilliance would survive.

•

Shortly after Boukaka wrapped up his Paris sessions, one of his colleagues moved to break new ground in the French capital. Word that something was afoot had leaked in early January of 1970 when *Etoile du Congo* reported that 'from a reliable source we learn that Rochereau, who is indisputably one of the best singers and composers in the Congo, will soon play at the Olympia,' the renowned Right Bank concert hall. If true, it would be a stunning achievement for the leader of African Fiesta National and an important first for Congolese music.

Rochereau, it seems, had been writing for several months to the Olympia's venerable impresario, Bruno Coquatrix, trying to get a booking. 'After all, why not me?' he asked. Coquatrix would later tell a radio interviewer,

> I ended up being moved by the enthusiasm and the will of this man. After a year, I let him know that I was willing to spend three days in Congo-Kinshasa. I went there last June. I was beguiled by Africa and carried away with Seigneur Rochereau.

Rochereau's bubble nearly burst in early June when the papers reported that 'Papa Kalle,' Joseph Kabasele, had just played the Olympia. Kabasele had been spending more and more time in Paris since the defection of three singers in late 1969 put an end to what was left of the fabled African Jazz. Kabasele was currently playing with his off-again-on-again Afro-Latin-jazz group, African Team. But this time the papers were wrong. The African Team had actually performed at the Odéon, a Left Bank theater. Kabasele did not intend 'to cut the ground from under Rochereau's foot.' With a sigh of relief, Rochereau moved ahead with preparations. 'I'm anxious,' he said, 'because the Olympia is the only door by which you can break into Europe.'

For two nights in mid-December of 1970 the Olympia's 2,000 seats filled with the knowledgeable and the curious, come to see Rochereau and his twenty-strong African Fiesta National. Together with his dancers, the Rocherettes and the Rocherets, Rochereau led his audiences from the village kebo through Kinshasa's dancing bars to the cabarets of Europe. The months of anxiety evaporated in the breeze of warm applause. 'I can never forget it,' guitarist Lokassa ya Mbongo recalled. 'For me, it was an event!' Coquatrix himself was nearly as enthusiastic. 'The Congolese troupe's success has been considerable,' he told Agence Congolaise de Presse. 'I am always afraid when a country presents a troupe I like, because you don't know how Parisians may react. With Rochereau, this fear disappeared after the first minute.'

Despite some setbacks in 1971, Rochereau's performance at the Olympia provided a tremendous boost to his career. More importantly, however, it marked a change in outlook for Congolese music itself. While still firmly planted in the soil of Kinshasa and Brazzaville, Congo music of the seventies would increasingly strive to reach outward.

12
The name game

Vévé, Trio Madjesi, Afrisa, O.K. Jazz, Fiesta Sukisa, and Bantous de la Capitale, 1971–1973

One day in the early eighties, so the story goes, Fidèle Babindamana walked into the Paris office of SACEM, the French performing-rights society. Babindamana, a musician from Congo-Brazzaville, asked to see the boss so he could collect money owed him for song royalties.

'Your name, monsieur?' asked the receptionist.

'Zizi,' Babindamana replied, using his stage name, 'Fidèle Zizi.'

The receptionist flashed a glare of disapproval that almost masked the curl of a smirk that crept into the corners of her mouth. 'Monsieur!' she exclaimed. 'This is a serious office. We do not have time for foolishness. Your name, s'il vous plaît!'

'Madame, this is no joke. I am Fidèle Zizi. I want to see the boss.'

With that the entire secretarial staff broke into open laughter. Babindamana had unknowingly chosen a stage name that was the equivalent in French slang of 'faithful wee-wee,' a considerable asset, it can be safely said, but one perhaps better left unannounced.

Stage aliases have been a Congo music tradition as far back as anyone can remember. Most have translated to French less embarrassingly than Babindamana's, although Essous is careful to say his real name last-name-first, Essous Jean Serge, since the other way around turns him into a drunk ('Jean Serge est soûl'). Essous also discovered that a poorly chosen sobriquet can cost money. When, early in his career, he began to call himself 'Jerry Lopez,' SACEM informed him that an established Latin American musician of that name would likely collect his royalties. Essous eventually settled on the less risky 'Trois S' (Three S's).

SACEM at times misspelled a name in their books, which had the effect of permanence, because to overturn a bureaucratic mistake was more trouble than it was worth. In this way Cosmos of Les Bantous became Kosmos. He was just as happy, he said, 'because now you can tell the difference between me and [Brazzaville's] Hotel Cosmos.' To SACEM, Léon Bombolo was Bholen, and to the Congolese press often Bohlen or Bolhen. Raymond Kalonji invented his stage name, 'Ray Braynck,' cleverly embedding his first name into his last, only to have SACEM or Ngoma spoil it by changing the spelling to Ray Braink.

Some of the most indelible aliases came from shortening the artist's real name, like 'Franco' for François or 'Edo' for Edouard. Others mirrored a personal attribute – 'Rossignol' (nightingale) for Philippe Lando's sweet singing voice, 'Jerry' for Justin Malekani's penchant for making people laugh like Jerry Lewis – or an experience from childhood – Pascal Tabou's 'Rochereau' or Augustin Moniania's 'Roitelet.' Stage names often became so well known that the artists' given names were largely forgotten.

A stage name could link the players in a group like the Trio BOW of Bukasa, d'Oliveira, and Wendo, or subtly insult with double-entendre as when Samuel Nzungu, leader of the colonial-era dance band Tip Top Jazz, called himself 'Colon Gentil,' nice colonial. For the family of Daniel Lubelo, the famed bassist of O.K. Jazz, nicknames transcended earthly origins. Lubelo became 'De La Lune' (of the moon), his brother André Kinzonzi was 'Du Soleil' (of the sun), and they were said to have a sister called 'Des Etoiles' (of the stars). Over the years the ranks of Congolese musicians swelled to include a doctor, an apostle (*apôtre*), a great priest (*grand prêtre*), and a number of poets.

The president of Congo-Kinshasa himself had once employed an alias when, as a sergeant in the Force Publique, he began to write newspaper articles under the name José de Banzy, as in Joseph of Banzyville, his father's home town (today's Mobayi near Gbadolite). But as president of an independent republic, Mobutu saw names as more than personal identifiers or self-promotional catch-phrases. More often than not they reflected a European culture that had been imposed on the Congolese people against their will. Ever since 1966 he had been at the task of eliminating colonial references, renaming scores of cities and towns in the process. Now, in 1971, he announced that as of October 27, the Democratic Republic of the Congo would be called the Republic of Zaïre. The Congo River would be the Zaïre River. The following January, whatever European names remained on streets or places were replaced by those of Zaïrean origin. 'At the same time,' the New York Times later reported, 'there was a joyous uprooting of statues, generally honoring colonial administrators. Stanley disappeared from his watch over the Zaïre River and King Leopold II of the Belgians from in front of the National Assembly.'

And Mobutu hadn't finished. A few days after the new year of 1972 began, he shocked nearly everyone by proclaiming a law that compelled people with foreign-sounding names to change them to ones more authentically Zaïrean. In the middle of the month he followed his own directive and changed his name to Mobutu Sese Seko Kuku Ngbendu Wa Za Banga. The bomb thus dropped, he flew off to Switzerland for a month of rest and relaxation while the dust from his pronouncements swirled in Kinshasa. 'When I used to tell my children that my first name was Joseph-Désiré, it meant strictly nothing to them,' he explained years later. 'On the other hand, telling them that their father is called Mobutu Sese Seko Kuku Ngbendu Wa Za Banga, fixes them firmly in a line of succession and marks their membership in a warrior Ngbandi tribe.'

Not surprisingly the Catholic Church, which had probably baptized more than half the population, including Mobutu, with Christian names, vehemently protested this new directive. The Church's Joseph Malula, by this time a cardinal, led the opposition with such fervor that the government closed his official residence and forced him to leave the country. In general, however, Zaïreans embraced the changes, often with great enthusiasm. As the initial uproar subsided, even Cardinal Malula resigned himself to the new order and returned home.

Authenticity, as the new philosophy came to be known, charted a course that meandered between a left bank of Western influences and a right bank of cultural values from traditional Africa. What looked applicable to the construction of a modern African state was to be brought on board, the rest would be left at the dock. It was the kind of fusion that had occurred naturally with the rise of the Congolese prophet Simon Kimbangu, and with the development of modern Congolese music.

Under authenticity Zaïrean men and women, regardless of rank, were to be addressed by the egalitarian title citizen (*citoyen* or *citoyenne*). Men were instructed to abandon the European coat and tie in favor of a collarless shirt-jacket that buttoned up to the neck called an *abacost*, short for the phrase *à bas le costume* (down with the suit).

For Zaïre's musicians, a change of name was not to be considered lightly. Careers were built and fame sustained on the foundation of superior musicianship and name recognition. But names like Franco, Vicky, Nico, Rochereau, all looked and sounded European. How would their fans follow them into the murky reaches of authenticity? 'I had to start over again,' Rochereau explained,

> with a new name to launch the new artist I was to become. I mean Tabu Ley and no longer Rochereau.... I had to create a new image, and get my fans used to my new name. It wasn't easy, and some of our friends and colleagues never recovered from it. Who knows what's become of them today.

Like most Zaïreans, Rochereau kept his African last name, Tabou (de-Frenchified to Tabu), shifted it to first position and added a second, Ley, a name from one of his grandfathers. He had already – following the Olympia concerts – changed the name of his band to Afrisa, a combination of Africa and Isa, the name of his record label. Thus the metamorphosis of Rochereau and African Fiesta National into Tabu Ley and Orchestre Afrisa International.

One account of the period reported that 'special announcements were made every few minutes over Radio Zaïre of the new "authentic" names adopted by this or that noted personality.' Docteur Nico became Kasanda wa Mikalayi, that is, Kasanda of Mikalayi, his home village. Franco kept his Luambo and added others, most prominently Makiadi, a name given him by his mother. Verckys went from Georges Kiamuangana to a succession of new names before settling on Kiamuangana Mateta. Musicians from Brazzaville working in Kinshasa followed their Zaïrean brothers into the province of authenticity. Gilbert Youlou became Youlou Mabiala, Michel Boybanda was now Boybanda Baba, and Marcel Loko turned into Loko Massengo. The group African Soul changed its name to Le Géant Orchestre Malebo, Malebo being the new name for Stanley Pool. Zaïko Langa Langa's leaders revised the story of the band's name; it was no longer a combination of Zaïre and Kongo but rather short for *Zaïre ya bankoko*, Zaïre of our ancestors. The Congo in company names was replaced by Zaïre. MACODIS became MAZADIS; SOPHINCO became SOPHINZA.

As the initial confusion abated, the government took a relaxed attitude toward musicians' stage names. Nicolas and François had to go, but 'Docteur Nico,' 'Franco,' 'Rochereau,' and most of the others too, eventually resurfaced on record labels and in the press, especially for music distributed outside Zaïre.

Authenticity also turned the music on a new tack as artists bent with the prevailing winds. As 1971 drew to a close, Franco recorded several sides with one of the music's pioneers, Camille Feruzi (recorded before European names were banned), producing a mellow blend of acoustic guitar, accordion, bass, and indigenous persussion. 'Recours na authenticité,' recourse to authenticity, Franco intones at one point, mixing French and Lingala.

Tabu Ley went to number one on the *Zaïre* charts in April of 1972 with a lovely throwback to the days of Bowane and Wendo called 'Mongali.' A duet of acoustic guitars, bass, and tam-tam accompany Ley's story of a *mongali*, the male equivalent in street parlance of the female *ndumba*, in this story a younger man living with an older woman. Ley sings from the woman's point of view, 'So he will love me I prepare him delicious dishes.... I have no more savings from giving him money.... Congratulate me for I love you Mongali Yena.' Ley manages to work his *nom d'authenticité*, Tabu Ley, into the lyrics so there will be no mistaking who 'Rochereau' has become.

A few weeks later, Verckys followed Ley to the top of the charts with another song inspired by the new Zaïrean consciousness. 'Nakomitunaka' (I ask myself) directly answered the Catholic Church's objections to authenticity with a beautifully constructed meditation on the nature of Western-style Christianity and its appropriateness for Africa. The whispers of a lone guitar lead the listener into Verckys's thoughts. A saxophone's plain song gently draws the singer out; his words overflow in tones of measured bitterness.

> I ask myself,
> My God, I ask myself,
> Black skin, where does it come from?
> Our ancestor, who was he?
> Jesus, Son of God, was a white man.
> Adam and Eve were whites.
> All the saints were whites.
> Why then, oh my God?
> ...
> In God's books we see,
> All the angels: their images are only white,
> All the saints: their images are only white,
> But the Devil, his image is black.
> This injustice, where does it come from, oh mama?
> ...
> Black skin, where does it come from?
> The uncles [colonizers] keep us from understanding,
> The statues of our ancestors, they refuse them,

> The fetishes of our ancestors, they do not accept them.
> But in church as we can see,
> We pray with rosary in hand,
> We pray to images filling the church.
> But these images are only of whites.
> My God, why is that?
> ...
> The prophets of the whites, we accept them,
> But those of the blacks, they do not accept them.
> My God, why have you made us this way?
> Where is the ancestor of we blacks?
> Africa has opened its eyes.
> Africa, we will not go back, ah mama.

This was Verckys's masterpiece, in word and melody the indisputable equal of the best of Nico, Franco, or Rochereau – that is Kasanda, Luambo, or Ley – and a worthy cousin of the provocative works of Franklin Boukaka. Accompanied by songs like 'Nakomitunaka' and 'Mongali,' authenticity seeped into the collective consciousness.

•

In the midst of Zaïrean society's transformation, a none-too-subtle reminder of the hegemony of Western culture arrived in June in the person of the godfather of soul himself, James Brown. Friday, June 2, 1972, *le jour J* (D-day) the press called it, Brown's plane landed at Kinshasa's Ndjili Airport just before midnight. The next day, the city's 'pop-boys' and 'pop-girls' packed into Le Théâtre de Verdure at Mount Ngaliema (Stanley) for a matinée performance of the James Brown Show. 'People couldn't believe their eyes,' *Zaïre* reported. 'James Brown in Kinshasa, and above all in front of them, made them crazy.' Back in the evening for a second show, Brown received a nearly identical reception from 'the serious public.' Sunday and Monday he rocked the sold-out Stadium 20 May, then took off for additional performances in Lubumbashi.

James Brown's visit to Zaïre certainly reinforced the stature of the youth bands, particularly those that specialized in covering his songs. It also provided graphic evidence to support the budding concept of the 'show' or *spectacle* that Tabu Ley had been pursuing since 1969. 'I will marry the African experience with the European experience,' he had said back then, a pledge that came to fruition at the Paris Olympia. The idea was to play less in night clubs, where one ran the risk of overexposure, and recoup lost revenue by staging occasional grand concerts with dancers, special effects, and all the trappings at a large hall. It was a strategy that some bands would employ with greater frequency in the years to come.

The group that seemed most inspired by James Brown's visit, and the one that would take the 'show' concept to a new level, didn't technically exist when the American soul brother came to Kinshasa. They had come together in 1969 to form the front-line trio of singers in Verckys's new Orchestre Véve. Matadidi 'Mario' Mabele, whose family had come to the Belgian Congo from Angola, had gotten hooked on music by hanging around the original African Jazz. He began singing with a group called O.D. Jazz, then passed through several years and several bands in the provinces before catching on with Verckys. Loko 'Djeskain' Massengo, born in Kinshasa but a citizen of Congo-Brazzaville, had sung his way through Orchestre Jamel, Négro Succès, and Vox Africa on his way to Orchestre Véve. Zaïrean Bonghat 'Max Sinatra' Tshekabu (a.k.a. Saak Saakul) worked for a time in Vedette Jazz until opportunity called at Véve. But as James Brown gyrated across Zaïre, the trio was under suspension for what Verckys called 'indiscipline.'

In reality, according to Matadidi, 'we were dismissed' for financial reasons. He claimed that, contractually, Verckys was entitled to half of the author's rights for his, Matadidi's, compositions. Under that arrangement, he said, 'I did not have sufficient means to live like everyone else.' To ease the hardship he and his two companions wanted to record some of their songs elsewhere in order to receive their full rights but still remain a part of Orchestre Véve. Verckys's conditions for such an arrangement were so stringent that the parties came to no agreement. It turned out, however, that the trio had made some unauthorized recordings anyhow. When they refused to hand over the tapes to Verckys, he fired them.

The trio's surreptitious records came on the market in late July and immediately climbed the charts. By the first week in August they claimed four of the top ten positions, including numbers one and two. They called their backing band and their record label Sosoliso after one of Matadidi's compositions that had been a hit for Orchestre Véve. The name, literally 'chicken eye,' signified resistance, tenacity, and determination, Djeskain explained. By joining their stage names, Mario, Djeskain, and Sinatra, the three singers became known as the Trio Madjesi.

In four months the trio's new records sold over 65,000 copies, nearly one-fourth as many as the leading producer for all of 1972, Verckys's Editions Véve. With money from record sales they bought instruments for the band

and prepared to go before the public with their new act. At the end of October a poster in the heart of Matonge (Renkin) announced the group's debut: 'Ce soir, le trio Madjesi de l'attaque bazooka et l'orchestre SOSOLISO se produit à la grande place Vis-à-Vis.'

As show time arrived, the streets were thick with tension around the jam-packed Vis-à-Vis. Policemen fought to maintain order among the disappointed latecomers for whom there was no more room. 'Quite naturally the music of the Madjesi is in the image of the men themselves: direct, lively, joyous,' one observer wrote. 'Mario with his sly manner ... is the [Wilson] Pickett of the band. Djeskain, easy-going, outrageous in his blue jeans.... As for Saakul, alias Sinatra, he is the James Brown of Sosoliso.' Five hours and twenty-four songs later the Trio Madjesi had become Kinshasa's new sensation.

'The Trio Madjesi may not currently be the best band of all time,' the same observer noted, but 'in any case it is the one most talked about. The young men enjoy incomparable celebrity.' Orchestre Sosoliso – which boasted four guitarists, including Mandiangu, Bavon Marie Marie's replacement in Négro Succès; sax player and chef d'orchestre, Mbole Tambwe; along with a second saxophonist, two trumpet players, bass, traps, and congas – sounded a lot like a slightly immature version of Orchestre Vévé. But their musical deficiencies mattered very little, because, as with James Brown himself, the music was only half of the story.

Dressed in matching outfits of sartorial whimsicality marked by the vogue for bell bottoms, the three rarely relinquished center stage. They played the sound of classic Congo music but put a little James Brown into everything they did, including an obvious takeoff from Brown's 'Sex Machine' called 'Sex Madjesi' (a.k.a. 'Sosoliso na Sosoliso'). Strong of voice and deft of step the Trio Madjesi's sinuous harmonies and scintillating choreography left audiences gasping. 'Du soul à la sauce moamba,' soul with palm oil sauce, Zaïre called them. When it was announced that the group would perform in Brazzaville in March of 1973, there was talk of le jour J all over again as excitement mounted in the Congolese capital.

During one busy week in November the trio held a Saturday press conference followed by a film festival. On Sunday they hosted a bicycle race, 'Grand Prix Sosoliso,' in the morning and an afternoon football match for the 'Madjesi Cup.' Monday and Tuesday were spent rehearsing for a Wednesday show at the downtown Palladium Theater; Thursday they held a reception for members of the musicians' union; and Friday they played a dance at the Vis-à-Vis along with four other bands. James Brown had left his mark on central Africa in the early seventies, but the Trio Madjesi rendered the foreigner's magic into an intensely Zaïrean conjuration. It must have made the gods of authenticity smile.

•

Despite the loss of the Trio Madjesi, Verckys's own Orchestre Véve continued down its successful path with little apparent difficulty. Verckys alone was more than enough attraction, singing, playing guitar, sax, and keyboards, resplendent in a Jheri-Curl wig. He replaced his departed trio with new recruits Makiadi 'Kelly,' Bébé Kisatu, and 'Juslain' Makanga. At the same time his own James Brown takeoff, 'Sex Vévé,' hit the market along with the more memorable 'Nakomitunaka.' In the early part of June 1972, Verckys's Editions Vévé owned seven of the top ten positions on *Zaïre's* hit-parade, three with his own band and four by Orchestre Bella Bella, which he had signed the previous year.

The current Bella Bella was a one-Soki formation led by elder brother Max, who now called himself Soki Vangu. The erratic *tout petit* Soki, Emile, now Soki Dianzenza, had left for reasons that remain largely unexplained except perhaps by a flash of sibling rivalry. ' "Soki against Soki": a duel between Abel and Cain?' *Zaïre* asked rhetorically. While the elder Soki and Bella Bella steamrollered onto the charts, Soki Dianzenza attempted to form a new band he called Super Bella Bella. The group made a few recordings and fewer public performances before organizational problems ended it. On his next try, toward the end of 1972, Dianzenza launched Orchestre Bella Mambo, anchored by lead guitarist Dino Vangu, with better success. 'Now that I've succeeded in getting my own band on its feet,' he announced, 'I'm going to work much more seriously.'

Meanwhile, Verckys's long-dreamed-of recording studio had opened in early 1972 and, like Ngoma and Opika in the old days, it rapidly became a wellspring of new talent. Much to Verckys's good fortune, Tabu Ley's drummer, Seskain Molenga, wanted to record some songs apart from Ley's Afrisa. He recruited a group of neighborhood youths who called themselves African Choc to work with him at Editions Vévé. Using Verckys's instruments they recorded a number of songs under the name Les Bakuba. In May of 1972 Molenga managed to reach the top ten with songs for two different bands at the same time, Les Bakuba (using the name Seskain) and Afrisa (as Molenga). For Verckys, in the midst of his difficulties with Soki Dianzenza and the soon-to-be Trio Madjesi, the presence of a new group of musicians gave him room to maneuver.

Chief among the newcomers was a twenty-year-old singer who dwarfed his cohorts, though not through talent alone. At nearly six feet two inches tall, Kabasele Yampanya, alias 'Pepe Kalle,' stood literally head and shoulders above most Zaïreans, who probably averaged a good eight to ten inches less. He already weighed two hundred pounds and appeared still to be growing. He claimed to have lived for a time in the household of Joseph Kabasele (no relation), where he received coaching from Le Grand Kalle himself. At Editions Vévé he sang with Bella Bella and added backing vocals on several of Verckys's songs, including 'Nakomitunaka,' but Les Bakuba was his hope for the future. 'I like that name a lot,' he said, 'because the king of the Bakuba is as big as I am.'

Another young singer, new to the Vévé studio, lent his formidable voice to Bella Bella alongside Soki Vangu and Pepe Kalle. Nyboma Mwan Dido had learned to sing in his church choir in Nioki, 200 miles northeast of the capital. While still in primary school, he moved with his family to Kinshasa, where he continued his singing in the school chorus. He won his first professional job at age eighteen with Baby National, graduated to Négro Succès, until the death of Bavon Marie Marie, then signed at Vévé to sing with Bella Bella. The *attaque-chant* of orchestre Bella Bella – 'a menacing Soki Vangu, an incisive Nyboma Mwan Dido, and a matchless Kabasele Yampanya' – compelled the band's followers to overlook Soki Dianzenza's absence.

The studio environment at Editions Vévé which encouraged development of new musical groupings was unable to provide immunity from the problems of personal rivalry and financial chicanery. Bella Bella's *attaque-chant* soon succumbed to both. The eldest and best established, Soki Vangu, was the first to bolt from the Vévé stable in March of 1973. 'I've worked enough for others,' he said. He had reconciled with his brother, and the two of them wanted control of their band and, implicitly, their money. Verckys at first disputed the brothers' claim to the name Bella Bella, but he later relented, saying that instead he would launch a new group aptly named Lipua Lipua (also Lipwa Lipwa), meaning confusion or disorder.

With Bella Bella gone, the instruments they had used courtesy of Verckys now went to his new formation, Lipua Lipua, fronted by Nyboma and Pepe Kalle along with two other singers, Assosa Tshimanga and Tagar Mulembu. By April the group was on the charts with a composition by Nyboma called 'Kamalé.'

Nyboma Mwan Dido

Pepe Kalle did not stick with the group for long. His Bakuba had led a phantom life, existing mainly on records since the group had no instruments of its own. Verckys had promised to supply them but had never followed through. Tiring of second-class status, Kalle and his musicians, including singers 'Dilu' Dilumona and 'Papy Tex' Matolu Dode, left Editions Véve a few months after Bella Bella. 'I don't have a grudge against my former publisher [Verckys],' Kalle told Zaïre. 'I have to admit, however, that for a long time I've wanted to fly on my own.' With help from the Trio Madjesi's Editions Sosoliso, his Orchestre Empire Bakuba became a reality.

In the space of about four years, six robust bands had bloomed in the gardens of Véve: Verckys's Orchestre Véve, Les Grands Maquisards, Bella Bella, the Trio Madjesi, Lipua Lipua, and Empire Bakuba. While most removed themselves to grounds they hoped would be more fertile, their flowering spoke volumes for Verckys's abilities as a cultivator of talent.

Seed from the old guard continued to bear musical fruit as well. Tabu Ley and his band had hurried home following his Paris concerts at the Olympia in time to play for President Mobutu on New Year's Eve. In January of 1971 the band took off on a government-sponsored tour of the provinces, then flew to Dakar for a week of performances in February. Back home in March the band recorded some new songs and introduced a variation on the rumba that Ley dubbed the *soum djoum*. By the middle of the year, however, trouble began to surface. Bassist Joseph Mwena, guitarist Faugus Izeidi, and several of the dancers quit. Ley admitted that he hadn't paid his musicians for nine months, and his solvency appeared in doubt. In September he was jailed briefly in a dispute with a creditor. Following those setbacks, Ley decided to lie low for a while. 'For me 1971 was a failure,' he said.

The departure of Faugus signaled the birth of yet another new band, Fiesta Populaire, put together with the help of Faugus's brother, Roger Izeidi, who was now a full-time manager and impresario. This would have been a minor blow to Ley but for what followed early the next year. It seems that a certain unnamed entrepreneur made overtures to others of Ley's disgruntled musicians in an attempt, successful it turned out, to lure them away. Chief among the targets was Attel, the guitar soloist, who was reported to have been paid 5,000 zaïres ($10,000) to leave Afrisa. Singer Paul 'Pepe' Ndombe, now Ndombe Opetun, and saxophonist 'Deyesse' Empompo Loway went along and together with Beya Maduma (a.k.a. 'Moro Maurice'), a saxophonist from Négro Succès, they formed a group called Afrizam.

At the end of January, while Afrizam was taking shape, the great trumpet player Willy Kuntima died in a traffic accident. Kuntima had been with Ley since the days of African Jazz, and his loss must have been far more devastating to the leader of Afrisa than the current series of defections. For Tabu Ley, 1972 was shaping up to be as bad as its predecessor.

Many of Ley's musicians remained faithful, however. The guitarist Michelino, now Mavatiku Visi under authenticity, had joined Ley to play *mi-solo* after a stint with the Festival des Maquisards. Ley promoted him to soloist beside the loyal (Denis) Lokassa 'ya Mbongo' Kasia, who stayed on to play accompaniment. By the end of March, Afrisa had four records in Zaïre's top ten, including Mavatiku's 'Demayo' at number one. Early the following month Ley's 'Mongali,' the piece that seemed inspired by authenticity, went to the top. By October, with Empompo back in the fold, the band was sound enough for another European tour. In January of 1973 Afrisa nailed down five of the top ten spots on the hit-parade, including numbers one, two, and three. For the moment at least, Ley's troubles appeared to be behind him.

•

The spasms that caused Afrisa to deliver Fiesta Populaire and Afrizam developed in O.K. Jazz as well. There, the last of Congo music's great alliances, that of Franco and Vicky, came to an end. Franco had spent the last months of 1970 in mourning for his brother Bavon, but as the new year dawned he started to emerge from his depression. Vicky, on the other hand, fell ill and flew off to Europe for treatment. In his absence, O.K. Jazz came back strong with a series of new recordings which were released in the latter half of the year. 'Infidélité Mado' (Madeleine's infidelity), a composition by Francis Bitshoumanou, and 'Ma Hele' (my Helen) by Simaro Lutumba, two songs in the soon-to-be-discarded classic O.K. Jazz style, clung to the charts for several weeks. With Vicky out of the lineup, Franco's strengthening baritone could be heard backing the lead voice of Lola 'Checain' or Michel Boybanda, who had returned to the group from his wanderings. Short, crisp verses, guitars picked swift and nimble with a little garnish of trumpet and sax could still produce hit records.

There are several versions of what happened next. The most frequently heard has it that with Vicky, still ostensibly co-leader of the group, away in Europe, Franco purchased a dozen cars for certain members of the band. When Vicky returned from his convalescence and found out what had happened, he was quick to disapprove. A short while later he resigned from O.K. Jazz and announced his intention to mount a new band.

Vicky himself explained his departure in less dramatic terms. 'The decision to leave O.K. Jazz was taken by mutual agreement with my friend Luambo Makiadi,' he said. 'As you know, there can't be two captains of one boat.... You can't read continual conflict into our separation, as some scandalmongers would lead you to believe. There has never existed such a conflict between the two of us.' Apart from Franco toward the end of 1971, Vicky gathered a new group which he called Lovy du Zaïre.

Franco, now free to run O.K. Jazz as he pleased, began to change the band's direction. He flirted with the 'show' concept that had seemed to work for Tabu Ley and the Trio Madjesi, and began to spend lavishly on new personnel and equipment, including a mobile recording unit. In mid-1972 he boasted that he had spent 47,000 zaïres (nearly $100,000) to outfit O.K. Jazz. 'I have five guitarists on stage,' he said,

> two bassists, three saxophonists, three trumpeters, two [trap] drummers, three singers – four including Franco. We have more than twenty-four spotlights on stage and two psychedelic lights which transform the movements of dancers, twenty or so mikes with a control board and some twenty loud-speakers, echo chambers, closed-circuit television.

Including a number of women dancers called the Francolettes and two conga players whom he neglected to mention, O.K. Jazz had grown to nearly thirty members.

Over the course of the band's sixteen years, Franco himself had grown from a slim, handsome teenager into a decidedly stout 34-year-old. Biographer Graeme Ewens repeats an observation by one O.K. Jazz musician that 'Franco could eat 25 *kwanga* (slabs of cassava dough) at a sitting, with a whole chicken for himself, plus sausages, *kamundele* (kebabs) and *pondu* (green vegetable) [cassava leaves].' And it showed.

Franco owned a fancy house in Limete surrounded by a posse of vehicles, a Volkswagen van, Volkswagen pick-up, two Mercedes Benzes, a Jeep, and a dump truck. He had at least one wife and admitted to being the father of six children. Rumor had it that the number of each was far higher. He even found time to preside over the affairs of a soccer team, the Vita Club (formerly Victoria).

It is difficult to say with certainty that Vicky's presence had been a restraining influence, but with Vicky gone, Franco began to exhibit professionally the same excesses he indulged in apart from O.K. Jazz. In addition to the size of the band, Franco's songs grew longer. The pithy poetry of old gave way to chatty prose. Words and music often seemed to labor to find each other. 'I know my public particularly well, especially its whims,' he said at the time. 'My repertoire is thus composed in a way to satisfy both [young and old] generations.' Despite his declaration, Franco appeared to be increasingly distracted by the non-music aspects of his life. Consciously or not, he was making the transition from *chef d'orchestre* to *président directeur général*.

•

The third member of Congo music's ranking big three also found himself in a state of transition. Despite the massive defections of 1969, Docteur Nico had managed to keep his African Fiesta Sukisa in business with a patchwork of additions. When in Kinshasa, the band usually played two or three nights a week at the Zaïre Club in Matonge. Since the birth of Fiesta Sukisa, Nico had never played the prestigious Vis-à-Vis. He was, perhaps, better appreciated by music lovers outside of Zaïre. The ceaseless accolades he received in East and West Africa kept the band on the road for several months of each year.

In April of 1971, on the eve of a two-month, seven-country tour of West Africa, Fiesta Sukisa again began to fracture. This time singer Josky Kiambukuta and bassist 'Serpent' Kabamba decided to leave. Whether it was Nico's prickly demeanor or a simple matter of younger musicians wanting to strike out on their own, the resignations dropped Sukisa back a notch and set another band in motion. Josky and Serpent joined another Sukisa-ex, Bopol Mansiamina, and together with singers Blaise Pasco Mayanda, Tino Mwinkwa, and Sita 'Thamar' Malukisa they formed the band Continental.

Following his West Africa tour, Docteur Nico reached out in desperation to Congo music's equivalent of a desert mirage. Mujos was back in Kinshasa after working with Joseph Kabasele in Europe, and he answered Nico's call. 'For me, Mujos is a brother,' Nico told the press. 'We are going to do our best to show modern Congolese music to advantage.' The two announced plans for a grand six-month tour of more than thirty African countries and set about recording new songs.

The presence of Mujos gave the band a noticeable lift. He and Lessa Lassan joined Valentin Sangana, who had signed on for a second turn with the band, to give Fiesta Sukisa a first-rate trio of singers. The grand tour of Africa never happened, but several of the band's new records made it into Zaïre's top ten. Stability had returned for the moment.

One night in March of 1972, while the band played at the Zaïre Club, someone loosened the lug nuts on Nico's car in an apparent effort to steal the tires. Early the next morning two wheels came off as Nico drove home from the gig. Fortunately, he was traveling slow enough to suffer nothing more than the indignity, but the event seemed to serve as an omen. Soon afterward, Lassan and Sangana quit, and when Franco called early the next year, Mujos also jumped ship. This time there would be no quick fix.

Nico somehow managed to keep his weekly engagements at the Zaïre Club and even toured again in 1973. But, whether out of frustration or boredom, his sound began to change. He called himself Dokta Kasanda and peppered his music with traditional village sounds in a much too generous embrace of authenticity to suit Kinshasa's music lovers. A cartoon in the music magazine Likembe starkly portrayed his decline. The first panel, titled '1964–1969: la gloire,' shows a crowd cheering wildly as Docteur Nico plays his guitar. In the second panel, '1973,' a few disgruntled patrons file out of the Zaïre Club as Nico beats on a log drum. An angry Dechaud gives him a kick in the seat of the pants and asks, 'Kasanda, what are you doing? What's going on?' Nico answers irritably, 'It's folklore! What's your problem, grrrrrr!!!'

•

Despite his instability, Mujos seemed to have a salutary effect everywhere he went. Since no one expected him to stay long, musicians of whatever band simply enjoyed his presence, absorbed the benefits of his excellent songwriting and steady voice, and prepared for his departure. Before he came to assist Docteur Nico, Mujos had been working in Paris with Joseph Kabasele and the African Team. Toward the end of 1970 the group recorded a touching little song Mujos had written called 'Essous Spiritou,' arranged Latin-style with punchy horns and a small string section. 'Essous Jean-Serge-eh/ Called Trois S-eh,' Kabasele and Mujos sang. 'I was with Nino in Brazzaville/ Edo, Célio, Pamelo, Pandi, they say hello.' Across the Atlantic in the French Antilles, the song crackled through the speaker of Essous's short-wave radio. 'I was just so proud the day I heard that song,' he recalled. 'In my hotel room, I cried. Because when you're 12,000 kilometers from home, and you hear Mujos's voice...' A flood of homesickness came rushing out. Inside of a month, at the end of January 1971, Essous was back among his friends in Congo-Brazzaville.

The repressive conditions that moved Essous to exile himself with Ry-Co Jazz had abated by 1971. Marien Ngouabi now ruled the country, and artists were relatively free to practice their professions unimpeded, unless, of course, they were foolish enough to attack his regime. A conservative strain within some youth organizations, especially the Union de la Jeunesse Socialiste Congolaise, which seemed possessed 'by a puritanical reflex against dancing, prostitution, alcoholic beverages, and foreign films,' appeared to have little effect on nightlife. Essous resumed his place in Les Bantous de la Capitale – although Nino Malapet remained chef d'orchestre – and took on added responsibility as artistic adviser at Brazzaville's new recording studio and pressing plant, SOCODI.

Although they had enjoyed many fine moments in his absence, Essous's return supplied an unexpected morale boost for the musicians of Les Bantous. Essous was their founding father, and his contagious enthusiasm and considerable musical and administrative talents had been missed. Now the band was whole again.

Joseph 'Mujos' Mulamba

Another important handicap had also been removed. In 1968 Ngouabi had severed diplomatic relations with Mobutu's government in a show of outrage at the execution of rebel leader Pierre Mulele, who had returned to Kinshasa on the promise of amnesty. A month before Essous reached home, however, diplomatic ties were restored, and Brazzaville's musicians regained access to the enormous Kinshasa market.

Congo-Brazzaville's domestic politics were as turbulent as its relations with Kinshasa. Leftist members of Ngouabi's Parti Congolais du Travail constantly pressured him to institute socialist policies with more speed and less deliberation. The undercurrent of discontent surfaced abruptly on the morning of February 22, 1972, when a group of them attempted to seize control of the government. Led by army lieutenant Ange Diawara, the revolt – 'poorly planned, badly timed, and based on a grave miscalculation of local support' – fell apart within a few hours in the face of stiff opposition from the army, most of which remained loyal to Ngouabi. Diawara escaped, but a number of people were arrested, and three were reported killed, including singer Franklin Boukaka. The circumstances of his death 'have not been explained,'

La Semaine reported. 'It seems that it was due to irresponsible people acting without authorization.' Further details never came out, although many Congolese suspect he was executed – all the more so because his name had originally turned up on a list of those who had been arrested. In truth, no explanation could ease the loss of one of Brazzaville's most principled and creative figures. Diawara, the coup plot's leader, was himself hunted down and killed after a year on the run.

Later in 1972, as two of its songs entered Zaïre's top ten, disharmony jarred the ranks of Les Bantous. The model of solidarity for eight productive years split over 'administrative problems,' which, in the parlance of Congo music, usually involved money. Three bands regrouped from the ruins, the Trio CEPAKOS, Célestin, Pablito now calling himself Pamelo, and Kosmos; Les Nzoi (the bees, because they stung) of Edo Ganga, Ange Linaud, Théo Bitsikou, and Mpassy Mermans; and the 'original' Bantous de la Capitale with stalwarts Nino Malapet, Essous, Pandi, Gerry Gérard, Alphonse Taloulou, and the others.

It must have been a bittersweet period for fans of Les Bantous. The parts could never equal the whole, yet three relatively solid bands emerged. Les Nzoi, through Edo's connections, turned to Franco for technical and financial assistance. The band recorded in Kinshasa with Franco's new mobile unit, and the records were released on Franco's Editions Populaires.

The vocal Trio CEPAKOS needed musicians to back them. With seed money from the ruling PCT they formed a new band called Le Peuple (the people). (Jean) Kindoki Ndoki of Editions Keje agreed to distribute the group's records in Zaïre on the label Editions Peuple.

Les Bantous original, on the other hand, needed singers, so they hired an alumnus of Negro Band named Joseph 'José' Missamou. He was joined by Pambou 'Tchico' Tchicaya and Théo Blaise Kounkou to give Les Bantous a promising, if much less experienced, front line.

As Les Bantous and its offshoots repaired the damage, SOCODI, the state-owned company that operated Brazzaville's recording studio and pressing plant, collapsed under a pile of debt brought on by poor management. Lots of recording took place, but the company had apparently failed to develop a marketing strategy. 'Promotion, zero!' Edo Ganga declared.

> They forced Orchestre Bantou to record every night 'till really late. They told us, 'You're going to become big shots. They're going to sell like hot cakes.' They said it so much. It didn't work out that way.... They left piles and piles of 45s with no promotion.

To ensure that SOCODI would have something to do when it started, Congo-Brazza's government had forced Congolese musicians to sever their recording and distribution contracts with European firms like Pathé Marconi and Fonior. SOCODI's failure meant those foreign ties would have to be re-established, a painstaking and in some cases impossible task.

In spite of the obstacles, music in the early seventies continued to flourish on both sides of the Congo/Zaïre River. The whims of governments and the wants of individuals produced astonishing changes and extraordinary growth. 'Each month, each week, and perhaps every three days, a band is born in the capital,' *Zaïre* opined. Near the end of 1973, the magazine counted 104 of them in Kinshasa. Although the number was much smaller, Brazzaville experienced a similar proliferation among its musical groups. For the most part Zaïrean and Congolese musicians had weathered the vicissitudes of authenticity and socialism. Now in its third decade, Congo music seemed stronger than ever, and it was about to receive a boost from an unexpected quarter.

13
The guys have it

Abeti, Franco, and Mobutu, 1973–1974

Henriette Borauzima of Stanleyville became the first woman to integrate one of the great bands. With help from Vicky Longomba, Borauzima joined O.K. Jazz in 1963 for a brief four-month engagement before unspecified differences ended the collaboration. Late the same year she caught on with Rossignol's resurrected version of Rock'a Mambo for the band's turn-of-the-year tour of Cameroon and Nigeria. Back home in Léopoldville at the end of 1964, Borauzima got her biggest break. Sitting in with Orchestre City Five at the Afro Mogambo club, she came to the notice of Tabu Rochereau.

Rochereau used woman dancers, the Rocherettes, for his Olympia shows, a novelty the other bands copied with their Francolettes, Zaïkorettes, and Madjesiennes. But he had also opened the door for women to play more substantive roles in the bands. While still with the original African Fiesta, Rochereau had employed a woman singer named Photas Myosotis. He liked the musical possibilities a soprano created and the relief a female delivered to the group's persistently all-male lineup. After his split with Docteur Nico at the end of 1965, Rochereau hired Borauzima to play a similar role in his Fiesta 66. He billed her as 'Miss Bora,' and the two worked on and off together throughout the rest of the sixties.

In spite of the pressure these pioneering women brought to bear on the barriers of sexism, as the decade of authenticity dawned none had become a major star. A new aspirant, Antoinette Etisomba, had rallied to a second-place finish behind fourteen-year-old Emile Soki in the 1969 Festival de la Chanson in Kinshasa. Etisomba, only nineteen herself, had grown up in

Antoinette Etisomba

Kinshasa and worked as a secretary while she pursued a career in the entertainment business. Her impressive performance at the festival led Congolese cultural authorities to select her to accompany Papa Noël and his Orchestre Bamboula at the Pan-African Cultural Festival in Algiers later the same year. In 1970, she recorded some songs for Philips, but just as happened with her predecessors, Etisomba's breakthrough to the level of men like Franco and Nico never quite developed.

Perhaps the most startling event in the women's chronicle occurred at the end of 1971. On a November evening in the hall of the MPR, an all-woman band called Orchestre Emancipation took the stage. For the first time in memory women played electric guitars, bass, drums, even a saxophone, together and in public. Fronted by its most famous member, singer Sophie Laila, the group, it seems, played well. Created and controlled by men, however, it failed to live up to its name. After a hopeful but unsteady first few months the group quietly dissolved. A woman's road to stardom, it turned out, would be a more singular journey.

Two strangers met in Kinshasa towards the end of 1970. She was an impish bundle of unconventionality with music in her soul. He was twelve years her senior, a Togolese come to Kinshasa by way of Paris, where he had seasoned himself in the entertainment business. Together they would make her a star.

Abeti Masikini had come to Léopoldville from Stanleyville around the time of independence, when political violence engulfed her hometown and eventually killed her father. As a young girl in the provinces she had learned songs at school and in church and taught herself to play them on a church organ. She felt, she later recalled, that she had music in her from the time she was a little girl. 'My parents were worried. They thought I might not be normal. Because a little kid who played like that with no help, it's not normal.'

Once in the capital, Abeti continued to sing at boarding school, where her mother had sent her, a brother, and four sisters for protection against any further attacks on the family. Despite her mother's disapproval, Abeti tried to enter singing competitions, although she was often barred for being too young, or a girl.

Shortly before Abeti moved to Léopoldville, Gérard Akueson made his way to Paris from his home in Togo. He worked on the periphery of the French entertainment industry singing his compositions as a solo performer and together with friends as the Trio Los Makueson's. As his familiarity with the ways of Paris grew, he began to produce concerts for other African artists, including Ry-Co Jazz and Cameroon's Francis Bebey. Akueson expanded his activities still further in 1968 with the launch of his own record label, International-Disques-Akué. Africa possesses young talents, he explained at the time, 'but the big record companies offer them only small chances to assert themselves.'

Among the label's first releases were Akueson's own works and those of a vocal group from Congo-Brazzaville called Les Echos Noirs. The next year he recorded a new young singer from his own country named Bella Bellow. Soon afterward he became Bellow's manager and returned home to Togo to promote her career full-time. There he organized a troupe of young artists with Bella Bellow as the headliner to tour in West and central Africa. At one of the troupe's performances in Kinshasa in 1970, Akueson met Abeti.

'Abeti came to ask if she could sing on the program,' Akueson recalled. 'She was very young, seventeen or so. I said no.... You have a nice voice, but right now the program is set. You can't sing on it. But if you're lucky, maybe one day, you never know.' The day arrived in less than a year. Around the middle of 1971 Bella Bellow, tired of her frenetic schedule, decided to take time off to get married and have a child, a move that left Akueson without his main attraction. At that point he remembered Abeti. Back in Kinshasa he asked around, but no one knew who she was. As a last resort he aired an announcement over the radio, which Abeti answered.

Abeti remembered Akueson observing her in a singing competition and arguing with the judges, who had placed her third instead of the first he felt she deserved. He asked her to go with him to Togo, where he was well established. 'I left with him, because I absolutely wanted to sing,' she explained. 'I could see I was never going to be able to do it, because no one wanted to give me my chance, and I had to leave with him.' In spite of her family's opposition and the hurdles of Zaïrean bureaucracy, they managed to get out of the country.

For the better part of the next two years Abeti worked to refine her talent. Akueson asked her to listen to other singers to understand what they were doing. He urged her to search for a song's emotional content. 'I didn't know how to put life into the words,' she acknowledged. 'I sang everything in the same tone.' After months of intensive rehearsal Akueson took Abeti and his troupe on the road again to Senegal, Côte d'Ivoire, and the rest of French-speaking West Africa. Abeti even played a few exploratory gigs in Zaïre with Pepe Ndombe's Afrizam, but her greatest successes came on the road outside her homeland. By the middle of 1972 Abeti had reached a level of popularity among West Africans that she could only have dreamed about at home. 'When you leave your own country you become a star,' she later observed. And indeed it had happened to her.

Never one to be lulled by past accomplishments, Akueson had already been thinking of bigger things. Abeti had charmed West Africa; why not Paris? Back in the French capital he renewed the contacts he had made during his long residence there. He had met Bruno Coquatrix in the sixties; now he called on him to book Abeti into the Olympia. 'It was very, very, very difficult,' Akueson recalled, but after a period of intensive negotiation Coquatrix was persuaded. In Togo, meanwhile, at the beginning of 1973, Abeti rehearsed with Les Ecureuils, a band from Kinshasa that featured her brother, Abumba, on lead guitar.

On a wintry Monday night in February at the Paris Olympia, Abeti faced a European audience for the first time. Akueson's publicity apparatus had turned out a good crowd, but the people were mostly French, not the Africans he had expected. In the wings as she prepared to go on stage, Abeti felt sick. 'I was afraid to face that audience. I said to myself they will never accept me. They won't think I'm good ... I trembled so much I dropped the mike on the stage.'

As she walked before them, 'not very big, plump and dimpled, gilded like an appetizing fruit, ... ravishing in her traditional gowns,' the crowd greeted her with applause. Les Ecureuils had warmed them up, now Abeti took over. 'The musicians in the background are hidden by lighting effects and a sheer curtain. They play discreetly. Abeti moves forward singing and dancing, alone on that vast stage.' In Swahili, Lingala, and French, her repertoire ranged from traditional to modern, with an Edith Piaf song for good measure. Word on the performance was upbeat. Akueson remembered that one newspaper called her 'Abeti the tigress, idol of Zaïre.' But back home in Kinshasa scarcely anyone knew who she was.

Before returning to Zaïre, where the ultimate judgement on her progress would be delivered, Abeti made her first recordings, fourteen songs for French fashion designer Pierre Cardin, who had recently started a record label. Abeti had been composing most of her own material since her late teens, and she pulled a couple of staples from her show for the Cardin sessions. 'Bibilé' sets to music a folk tale about a river guarded by evil spirits who had to be calmed before people could cross it and enter the forest to hunt. 'Fulani' tells the more citified story of two young girls gossiping about future husbands. With Abumba and Les Ecureuils backing her up, Abeti cut the tracks and then joined (Antoinette) Etisomba Lokindji for concerts in Brussels, at a conference on Zaïrean authenticity. Then it was time to take the show home.

In Kinshasa, Akueson cranked up the promotion for her end-of-June homecoming. 'When they found out that I was from Zaïre and that I had been at the Olympia, it was a real surprise to the public,' she recalled. 'They said, "But where did she come from?"' They learned the answers at the Palladium Theater, where Abeti unveiled her *spectacle* before a capacity crowd of old friends, knowledgeable fans, and the more plentiful ranks of the curious. At concert's end nearly all were impressed. 'It became almost a kind of family thing,' she said. '"That's our daughter who went to the Olympia." And that's when my career took off at home.'

Zaïre gushed about everything from her clothes to her pose to her erotic allure, 'A true queen amid her dancers.' *Salongo* viewed subsequent performances with a bit more reserve but conceded that she achieved 'appreciable success with regard to her song themes,' even if the instrumentation and

Abeti (right) in Paris, 1982, with Colette LaCoste and Charles Maniatakis of Safari Ambiance

dancing needed a little work. 'In the meantime, the critics are unanimous in recognizing that Abeti has really won a Kinshasan audience.'

What to do for an encore? 'When I was young, I was really sharp,' Akueson chortled.

> When I wanted something, I got it. I just took the plane, and I went [to New York] to present the press book to introduce Abeti over there. We hoped she would play Carnegie Hall. Well they showed me, they got out [photos of] the great jazz men, the big stars who played there and everything. Well, with my usual persuasiveness I convinced them that Abeti was a big star at home, she had just played the Olympia, and why not Carnegie Hall?

And again he got what he wanted.

With help from American producer Norman Seaman, who knew the intricacies of staging a show in New York, Abeti brought her act to the home of Louis Armstrong, Benny Goodman, and Ella Fitzgerald on Saturday night, March 9, 1974. 'I sang with all my heart for that audience, and I am delighted,' she said afterward. So, apparently, were those who came to see her. They applauded her performance lustily and besieged her afterwards for autographs. 'It's the same thing in Zaïre,' she told a reporter. 'Everyone loves our dancers and our singers, the old as well as the young and the Europeans just like the Africans. The theme of my songs is life, their life.'

Apart from the angelic voice and impassioned dance, Abeti's performance marked one of the first uses of a synthesizer in Congo music. To keep expenses down she traveled with just four dancers and six musicians. The synth filled in for absent African drums and other traditional instruments that would normally have played live. For better or worse it was an innovation that would gain increasing acceptance in the music over the next few years.

The Carnegie Hall concert was to be the opener of an introduce-Abeti-to-America tour of downtown theaters and campus auditoriums. All the arrangements were in place when Zaïre's minister of culture called to say that Abeti was requested to perform at a conference in France where President Mobutu would be speaking. Abeti and Akueson felt a threat of unspecified consequences should they choose to refuse the 'invitation.' They decided to cancel the tour. A day or two later the discouraged musicians filed onto a Paris-bound airliner only to learn that Mobutu's speech had been called off and their presence was no longer required. With one inept stroke Zaïrean authorities had turned Abeti's Carnegie Hall success into a disaster of broken bookings that American promoters would not soon forget. The road to a wider audience for Zaïrean music had become a more uncertain passage.

In Zaïre, newspapers hailed Abeti's success; her setback passed unmentioned. She had zoomed to a level approaching that of Franco and Rochereau, even surpassing them outside of Africa. Reporters recounted her professional routine and spiced it with personal gossip. Equally important, Abeti's achievements seemed to help her showbusiness sisters. Etisomba began to get more ink, and Miss Bora, now the authentically correct Bora Uzima Kote, reappeared in Kinshasa after more than two years of travels in the Central African Republic and eastern Zaïre. Under the reign of Abeti and the renewal of Etisomba and Bora Uzima, 1974 was the closest thing to a year of the woman that Zaïre's male-ordered music business was likely to see. Near the end of May, Abeti came home for the first time since her adventures in the United States. Led by Franco, their president, the entire leadership of UMUZA, the musicians' union, drove to the airport to welcome her.

•

If Abeti's airport reception vouched for her lofty stature, it also affirmed the accumulation of power of the welcoming delegation's leader, Luambo Makiadi 'Franco.' Franco had come a long way from his days as Dewayon's protégé at Loningisa. As *président directeur général* of the O.K. Jazz empire he supervised the band, his Editions Populaires label (the seventies' successor to Epanza Makita and Boma Bango), various real-estate investments, and the impressive Un-Deux-Trois night club which opened early in 1974.

Franco had acquired the old Chez Engels night club on Avenue Gambela at the northern edge of Matonge around the end of 1972. The transaction, unorthodox to say the least, served as a barometer of Franco's upward mobility within Zaïre's ruling class. The Engels parcel had been owned by, or was at least under the control of, Denis Ilosono, the former *patron* of Orchestre Révolution and one-time secretary to the president. Having fallen into disfavor, Ilosono forfeited the parcel, which then passed, via Madame Mobutu it is said, into Franco's hands. The deal appeared to be compensation for the 1966 raid on O.K. Jazz that provided musicians for Orchestre Révolution, an operation that may well have originated with Mobutu himself. Franco then began construction of his new Un-Deux-Trois night club on the site.

Much more than the average club, the Un-Deux-Trois contained three main dance floors, four bars, and plenty of office space. The primary club occupied a courtyard formed by an L-shaped building, five stories on one wing and four on the other, and a corresponding L-shaped wall. The first two floors of the lower wing opened, like the decks of a stadium, onto the courtyard for seating. The bandstand where O.K. Jazz held forth stretched along the tall wing. In the middle of the yard sat a circular dance floor, its roof doubling in the dry season as a dance floor for customers seated on the second level. The Mama Kulutu, a smaller club, was located inside the tall wing. A chic watering hole called the Onyx overlooked the courtyard from one of the upper floors, a spot where the well-heeled could sequester themselves from the main action. The top floors also housed the offices of Franco and his assistants. As president of UMUZA, the Union des Musiciens Zaïrois, Franco established its headquarters at the Un-Deux-Trois.

UMUZA was the latest in a series of musicians' organizations whose noble purposes had eluded practical implementation. By royal decree the Belgian Congo had joined the Berne Copyright Convention in 1948. The convention's basic principle holds that 'the creator of a work of music or a text is entitled to some kind of remuneration when the work is performed in any country that has ratified the convention,' but at the time of the royal decree few Congolese knew about it.

Bill Alexandre had raised the first widespread awareness among Congolese when he registered the CEFA musicians with SABAM, the Belgian performing rights society. Roitelet's agitations at Loningisa and Esengo brought the issue of musicians' rights into sharper focus. When independence arrived, SABAM withdrew from Léopoldville, and a short-lived, ill-managed cooperative called the Société des Artistes et Compositeurs Congolais (SACCO) sprang up to take its place. After SACCO failed, the government helped to establish ONDA, the Office National des Droits d'Auteur (national office of author's rights), another musicians' cooperative under a rotating directorship that included, at different times, Dewayon and Roitelet. But, like its predecessor, ONDA seemed to have difficulty depositing money into the proper pockets. On top of that, money collected for foreign artists whose records sold in the Congo was not being paid to their nations' authors' rights societies. In retaliation, foreign rights societies began to withhold payment from Congolese musicians for their works sold abroad, an especially hurtful move since most Congolese musicians used their foreign royalties to purchase new equipment in Europe.

In 1969, in an effort aimed at reform, President Mobutu ordered that ONDA be replaced by a new government-controlled Société Nationale des Editeurs, Compositeurs et Auteurs (SONECA) and appropriated 35,000 zaïres ($70,000) to get it started. A board of directors selected from the membership and presided over by one of Mobutu's cabinet ministers was to constitute its governing body. Heading up the working staff was Franco's old friend and former administrator of O.K. Jazz, Joseph Emany.

Meanwhile Roitelet's vision of a union to represent musicians' interests in disputes with employers had finally been realized. The Fédération Nationale des Artistes Musiciens came to life as an affiliated member of the Union National des Travailleurs Congolais (UNTC), an amalgamation of independent unions forced on the labor movement by President Mobutu in 1967. (The UNTC, Mobutu's effort to control a possible source of opposition to his regime, was set up with assistance from the American AFL–CIO and, it is alleged, the CIA.) In the directive that created SONECA, however, Mobutu ordered that all other musicians' associations be dissolved, an action that appeared to finish off Roitelet's federation.

Mindful of the potential for corruption, the musicians reorganized themselves within SONECA as the Syndicat des Artistes Membres de la SONECA under the leadership of the former Colon Gentil, Samuel Nzungu. The syndicate, it was thought, could better protect the interests of musicians by monitoring SONECA's activities from inside. Beyond its initial stages, little was heard from the Syndicat, perhaps because SONECA seemed to function more or less as planned for its first couple of years. By 1973, however, Zaïrean

The guys have it 197

musicians began to grumble openly about not receiving prompt and full royalty payments.

> The musicians complain that SONECA does not take care of them – but on the other hand, a certain minority of the big heads of modern Zaïrean song benefit enormously from the national society's services. When it comes to paying author's rights, for example, those big heads are always served first.

One of the unnamed 'big heads' was presumably SONECA's current president, (Joseph) Kabasele Tshamala. The mounting dissatisfaction moved President Mobutu to 'invite' the musicians to organize themselves outside the SONECA bureaucracy. And so a new union, UMUZA, appeared in 1973 with Franco – at this point unquestionably a 'big head' – as its president.

A few months after UMUZA's creation, Mobutu and his National Executive Council gave Franco unprecedented control over the country's musicians. On May 3, they decreed that bands wishing to travel abroad were 'required to have prior authorization by the National Executive Council.' Requests for such authorization were to be made through the channels of UMUZA. In practice this meant that any musician who wanted to leave the country had to clear it with Franco and the union's executive board, which included (Gérard) Madiata Madia, (Franc Lassan) Fariala ya Yembo, (Armand-Louis) Samu Bakula, Dewayon, Verckys, and Zozo Amba, along with the union's secretary-general, Roitelet.

Having barely assimilated that mandate, Franco and his board moved to expand their authority by declaring that UMUZA had decided to suspend the creation of new bands and record producing companies. They claimed to have counted 371 bands in Kinshasa the previous year, a situation which they deemed detrimental to the music business. Although they said their action was meant 'to preserve the profession's honest, noble, and respectable character,' other observers saw it as a reaction to youthful competition. *Salongo* editorialized that apart from a few older stars, Zaïrean music was the creation of young people.

> It seems unjust to bar the path to young people, and UMUZA's action (whose members, as competent as they may be, represent neither collectively, and even less so individually, the true trends of our current music) would seem in the eyes of the young to be a simple asphyxiation measure.

Beyond the controversy over UMUZA's declaration it seemed doubtful that the union possessed the means of enforcement. On the other hand,

UMUZA's power to regulate travel by musicians had the full force of government behind it.

A pronouncement by President Mobutu later in the year would, in its consequence, further endow the leader of O.K. Jazz. In a speech before the National Legislative Council on November 30, Mobutu signaled his intention to end foreign control of Zaïre's business sector. 'Zaïre is the country which, up to now, has been the most heavily exploited in the world,' he declared. 'That is why farms, ranches, plantations, concessions, commerce, and real estate agencies will be turned over to sons of the country.'

Mobutu was at the height of his power. The MPR had become synonymous with the state, and Mobutu stood as the unchallenged leader of both. He fancied himself as 'Le Guide,' a term which people quickly found it wise to adopt. Shuffling his ministers from post to post, Mobutu punished them for lapses, rewarded them for loyalty, and in the process created a cadre of unquestioning sycophants who would do almost anything to maintain their privileged positions. The parceling out of a billion-zaïre pot of foreign-owned goodies could, it seemed, only enhance their subservience. Politicians salivated as the general public looked on with increasing anxiety.

While Mobutu paid lip service to the honorable concepts of economic independence and the public good, with 'equitable compensation' to the foreigners, he had apparently given little thought to the new policy's implementation. 'What then transpired,' as professors Crawford Young and Thomas Turner describe it, 'was a tumultuous, disorderly, and profoundly demeaning scramble for the loot.' Zaïreans who received a portion became known as *acquéreurs* (acquirers). Foreigners who had their property confiscated received, in most cases, nothing in return, despite the president's assurances to the contrary.

Chief among the *acquéreurs* was President Mobutu himself, who took control of what Young and Turner have called 'a vast agricultural empire' consisting of 'fourteen major enterprises ... grouped into a conglomerate entitled Cultures et Elevages du Zaïre (CELZA) incorporated on 1 July 1974.' Mobutu's ministers and other well-placed officials grappled for the rest of the booty. A few months later and farther down the list of *acquéreurs* another name appeared, as familiar to Zaïreans as that of their president. Luambo Makiadi 'Franco' had the good fortune to be awarded the Zaïrean corner of Willy Pelgrims's recording empire.

MAZADIS, as the operation was now called under authenticity, consisted primarily of an aging record pressing plant on 13ème Rue in Limete. Most

Franco in the early seventies

of the country's recording and publishing functions had already been assumed by Zaïrean entrepreneurs without Mobutu's help, but manufacturing in Zaïre and distribution abroad had remained in the hands of the foreign firms MAZADIS-Fonior and SOPHINZA-Philips. With Franco now in charge at MAZADIS, the last foreign monopoly was broken, but the deal immediately provoked gossip about the guide of the republic and the sorcerer of the guitar.

Franco's ties to Mobutu went back as far as the late sixties. Like most of Zaïre's musicians, Franco had written songs in praise of the *president-fondateur* and his MPR, but his efforts appeared to go beyond the ritual recitation of puffery necessary to avoid suspicion. He performed songs in support of

Mobutu's 1970 election and, two years later, toured the country with O.K. Jazz to promote the doctrine of authenticity. In the latter period Franco acquired the parcel where he built the Un-Deux-Trois. When the announcement came in September of 1974 that MAZADIS too was his, more than a few Zaïreans saw it as further evidence of the pair's cozy relationship.

Unlike many *acquéreurs*, who had little or no knowledge of the businesses they now controlled, Franco knew a lot about MAZADIS. 'I've come to tell you,' he said on his first day at the office, 'that sixteen or seventeen years ago I worked in this shop.' He had also recorded at the company's studio and released many songs on its affiliated label CEFA. His more recent exploits at the factory, however, had been welcomed with less enthusiasm.

Before the takeover, many of Kinshasa's smaller producers had accused Franco of intimidating MAZADIS workers, forcing them to press his records while their orders sat unattended. Operations were already too slow on the factory's manually controlled machinery. 'This, especially,' noted *Salongo*, 'when the worker running the machine grants himself the pleasure of a glass of beer between the pressing of two records.' Mfumu Muntu Bambi of Editions Parions complained in June of 1974 that since the previous November,

> I have placed an order for at least 195,700 records! I haven't received more than 34,000! As an immediate consequence, I've proceeded to close all my agencies in the interior. Having no merchandise, I couldn't continue to maintain personnel who had nothing to do.

The small producers alleged that through their interference Franco and other unnamed stars were trying to sabotage them.

One particularly nasty incident pitted Franco against a Mr. Dema, owner of a small label called La Hutte.

> Come to MAZADIS to press his records, Luambo found the presses occupied with Dema's masters. Without saying a word, he set himself to freeing up the machines to use them. Absolutely incensed, Dema fought Luambo's action with unheard of violence. Luambo, noticing that he was dealing with someone stronger and more determined than he, beat a retreat declaring, 'Ozali miso makasi!' [you're stronger than I thought].

Other small producers were not as successful as Dema. 'The situation,' said *Salongo*, 'is so anarchic that no one knows which saint to pray to anymore.' With its decision to hand over the factory, however, the government made certain that everyone knew who to pray to at MAZADIS. Saint Franco appealed to his fellow artists and producers for cooperation:

I swear to you that I have made a clean slate of the past.... Although I've already proven in the eyes of the world that I was the best organized musician in Zaïre, I do not authorize myself to do this work alone. It is with everyone's collaboration that we will, all of us, create the new MAZADIS factory!

With that he acknowledged the person they all had to please.

The best way to thank the president-founder of the party for the confidence he has shown in me by giving me this unit is to do everything to make it prosper.

With more of Franco's time and energy occupied by business affairs, it is little wonder that people noticed his music slipping. His pen grew increasingly idle. The once nimble and resourceful guitar developed a repetitive clang. 'In effect,' wrote *Salongo*, 'many music lovers claim lately that the master player of O.K. Jazz makes no more effort to improve! And that, in almost all his songs, you find the same guitar notes. As if he had reached the end of the line.' An indignant Franco denied he was losing his touch.

Those rumors are empty and unfounded! ... I would also like to point out to the music lovers who think they find my solos monotonous that from 1956 until today, I have changed my solos many times! You can't tell me that the notes I play today are the same as the ones I played four years ago!

One Franco composition, 'Nakobala na Ngai ata Mbwa' (I will even marry a dog), a humorous recital of desperation in which none of the protagonist's human relationships seems to work out, was banned by the censorship commission. 'Scandalous, obscene,' *Salongo* called it, '[Franco] dog-paddled – to public clamor – in the vilest baseness.' Another, entitled 'Ye' (which could mean *he* or *she*), a tale of sexual licentiousness released at the end of 1973, passed muster somehow with the censors but earned general disapproval from the press. 'Not only does it debase women to the level of an object, but it also celebrates the debauchery of men.' None of Franco's songs appeared on Zaïre's hit-parade during the entire next year.

If Franco's performance had fallen off a bit, it was more than offset by the band. The OK Jazz of the middle seventies was awash in talent, beginning with the front line of singers, Sam Mangwana (temporarily Mangwana Mayimona for the sake of authenticity), Boybanda Baba, Lola Checain, Josky Kiambukuta, Youlou Mabiala, and Wuta Mayi (newly arrived from Continental). Brazzos had returned to the guitar corps to join Franco, Simaro, and more recent additions 'Deca' Mpudi and (Alphonse) Epayo, both of whom could play bass. Isaac Musekiwa headed the seven-man horn section with himself, Dele Pedro, 'Rondot' Kasongo, and Kongi Aska on sax, along with 'Baramy' Milanda, Adamo Kadimoke, and Kapitena Kasongo on trumpet. Ngiandu Kanza played traps, (Simon) Moke maracas, and, although they briefly fell out with Franco in 1974, Dessoin and Du Pool were usually found behind their accustomed congas.

Picking up the slack in the composition department, (Simon) Lutumba Ndomanueno Massiya, the man called 'Simaro,' almost single-handedly kept O.K. Jazz on the charts. Simaro was the antithesis of the pop musician stereotype. A tall, austere-looking man with a pair of spectacles perched on the end of his nose, he resembled a university professor who had absent-mindedly wandered on stage. Just eight months younger than Franco, Simaro had begun his career around 1959 under the tutelage of Raymond 'Ray Braynck' Kalonji in a band called Micra Jazz. Simaro and Kalonji left Micra to join Gérard Madiata's Congo Jazz (a short-lived remnant of Dewayon's Conga Jazz), but when Franco called in 1961, Simaro left his friends for O.K. Jazz in time for the band's first trip to Brussels to record. Through talent and long service, he had grown second only to Franco in stature within the group.

Simaro had managed to come up with at least one hit song, often with a spiritual theme, nearly every year, but beginning in 1973 he penned a succession of best-sellers that rivaled Franco's former output. 'Ebale ya Zaïre' (River Zaïre), a poignant poem sung by Sam Mangwana, evokes the sadness of the loss of a loved one carried away on a riverboat. Very much in the band's new style of lengthy discourse, the song's placid rumba gathers its current from Simaro's words.

> Today I thought about you a lot, Jeannie,
> In a haze of alcohol, I began to dream:
> You were resting your head on my shoulder,
> And you were telling me things in a little whisper.
> Jeannie my friend, it was just a drunken dream, ah, what great misfortune.
> The boat is taking my love away, oh my God.

Simaro followed 'Ebale' with the even more successful 'Cedou,' a fable about relationships and the course of human existence. Mangwana repeats on lead vocals with Franco singing several lines of the refrain.

'We have ideas and words that [non-Lingala speakers] don't understand,' Simaro declared. '[They're] only listening for the music.' But, he asserted, Zaïrean and Congolese musicians are often talking about serious matters in their songs.

In the middle of 1974, O.K. Jazz released one of the great songs of the seventies, Simaro's meditation on the nature of life and death, 'Mabele' (the earth). Also released under its Kikongo name 'Ntotu,' this rumba seems faster, more insistent than the others. A flourish of horns arouses the brain, the rhythm seduces the feet. Mangwana, again, restless and intent, gives voice to Simaro's words.

> In his youth, man thinks of thrift.
> He plans for his old age.
> But, once old, he changes his mind,
> He decides to squander all his savings,
> Fearing that after his death, they will go to those who didn't have difficulty,
> And who will profit from them; Oh earth, I lament for you.

The sebene cuts an engaging groove; guitar and cymbal play the rumba, as a sax swoops in to scatter the cerebral daze. This 'Mabele' spins on an axis of exquisite polarity. The band sustains the music's muscle while Mangwana delivers the summation.

> Evening arrives, the day disappears,
> Night falls; it is the hour of sorcerers and fetishists.
> The child remains the souvenir of our union.
> The boat perishes, but the port remains.
> Lola's mother has named the child for his father Massiya.
> The world will disappear because there are too many sins,
> But God's name will live eternally.
> The white man has made cannons to destroy the world,
> But to destroy the truth,
> The white man has not been able.
> Oh the earth.

The pairing of Mangwana's voice with Simaro's words was a calculated move by the band's executives, Franco, Simaro, and Brazzos. The leaders of O.K. Jazz wanted someone from a different school of Zaïrean song to jolt the band from its doldrums. As a graduate of African Fiesta National, in the line of succession from Joseph Kabasele, Mangwana looked like a good choice. None of the players likely imagined immediate success. *Zaïre* noted that 'people wonder whether Mangwana will be able to marry his voice to the style of this musical group. As you can observe, the marriage between Mangwana and Makiadi is difficult.' Mangwana himself confessed to having had doubts. But the success of 'Ebale' sanctioned the match, and 'Mabele' confirmed its wisdom. *Salongo*, without attempting to restrain its enthusiasm, wrote that in 'Mabele,' the voice of Mangwana expresses practically every intensity of feeling, every sentiment: happiness, romantic impulses, religious fervor, eroticism, frustration, disappointment, liberty, hope, pride, all the nuances of human emotional and spiritual life.

The public clearly agreed. From its debut in the middle of July, 'Mabele' stayed on Zaïre's top ten until the end of November. In the land of the brief, when it came to a song's shelf-life, 'Mabele' must have set some kind of a record. For a week in September, as a new batch of releases hit the market, Simaro's discs held the top three spots – 'Mabele' at number three, 'Monzo' (a person's name) number two, and 'Bakozila Trop' (they're going to wait a long time) in the top spot. In a poll of *Salongo* readers, 'Mabele' was chosen as the best song of 1974; Simaro was voted best composer for the second year in a row. An artist, he once said, needs to be close to his public. 'The public gives us things to reflect on – "What did they say? What did they say? Ah, good. Ah, good." And we gain our inspiration.' Simaro 'the poet' had few peers when it came to making that connection.

Others in O.K. Jazz, Checain and Mangwana in particular, also contributed hits, which, together with Simaro's streak, produced one of the band's most successful periods. Franco, however, at least as Michel Boybanda told it, was not about to let his composers get fat heads.

> Now it was always at five o'clock in the morning that I would see [Franco's] car come to get me. He sent the car to get Lutumba. He sent the car to get Sam Mangwana, at the time he was with us. He sent the car to get Josky. He sent the car to get Checain.... He sat us down. He said, 'Okay. Look at yourselves for a minute. You are the important people in O.K. Jazz. You are what makes O.K. Jazz great. But I've called you together this morning to ask you to let me give the songs to the band for the next eight months. So now I want it to be that only Franco feeds songs to O.K. Jazz.... Let me work, manage, give the songs for eight months and if the band doesn't reap success, we would still be together, and I would ask you to come back and you'll give songs, and we'll continue to work.' So that was because [Simaro] Lutumba created the song 'Mabele.'

Simaro may have been a great composer, but there was only one boss in O.K. Jazz. And yet, in spite of this apparent flash of jealousy, Franco continued to surround himself with the best musicians he could find. 'Among us, discipline is the golden rule,' Franco told a reporter.

> Each person's salary is respected. Fines are also provided for, especially for latecomers and for absentees, because most are transported. All of the older

members have received 'VW 1500' cars ... A [van] and two buses transport the staff and some new musicians.

Talent and discipline nurtured prosperity, but felicitous connections didn't hurt. 'Since O.K. Jazz did extraordinary things, in other words helped the politicians,' Boybanda declared, 'we didn't lack for anything.'

With a great band under his direction, control of MAZADIS and UMUZA now in hand, and the patronage of the country's president, Franco edged closer to concluding in the music world what Mobutu had achieved in statecraft. But the disorderly business of music attracted more than the quorum of independent spirits necessary to maintain competition. Now women could make it as entertainers; Abeti bore witness to that. Others would soon follow her example. Despite UMUZA's ban on the creation of new groups, Kinshasa's restless youth clamored to get into the act.

14
What goes up...

Mobutu, George Foreman, Muhammad Ali, Tabu Ley, Bella Bella, and Zaïko Langa Langa, 1974–1976

Mobutu 'Le Guide' aimed for greatness. His domain, the third largest country in Africa, short of first-place Sudan by only a few thousand square miles, lay at the continent's center. Its wealth of people, plants, and minerals seemed boundless. The government had controlled the mining industry, its largest earner of foreign exchange, since the 1967 nationalization of Belgian-owned Union Minière. That same year Mobutu's MPR had 'revolutionized' the political structure; now authenticity rallied the people. The new Inga dam on the lower Zaïre River was being built to power the country's industrialization. A steel mill was already under construction.

Mobutu also promoted Zaïre, and especially himself, in the diplomatic sphere. He vied for leadership among his African neighbors, nine of which shared a common border with Zaïre. Once Israel's friend, he courted the Arabs by announcing a break with the Jewish state in 1973. He played the cold war for all it was worth, winning credits and loans for grandiose schemes from Europe and America, China and Japan, although not the Soviet Union.

A few leaks in the country's propulsion system seemed at first not to matter. Prices in the copper market where Zaïre earned much of its income began to fall in 1974, but they had declined before and always recovered. Zaïreanization worried some, but it was just in the initial stages. Problems could be worked out. Mobutu and Zaïre would not be stopped by a few minor difficulties. In August of 1974 Mobutu pushed through a new constitution that affirmed what was already apparent. The MPR was the country's supreme institution and Mobutu its paramount chief. Henceforth, all Zaïreans belonged to the party and were obliged to support the revolution. Inspired and directed by Le Guide, the party would lift Zaïre into an orbit of greatness. A celebration was in order to trumpet this Zaïrean version of Manifest Destiny, and for help with that, Mobutu turned to American boxing promoter Don King. King, a former numbers banker from Cleveland, had managed to rebound from a murder conviction into professional boxing's morass of shady operators and gullible athletes. King was tight with the current heavyweight champion, George Foreman, and getting closer to former champ Muhammad Ali, who had been stripped of his title in 1967 when he refused induction into the U.S. Army on religious grounds. Ali had fought his draft case through the legal system and won a unanimous decision from the U.S. Supreme Court in 1971 which cleared the way for him to resume boxing. By 1974 he was ready for a title shot against Foreman. With $9.6 million of Zaïre's money supplied by Mobutu, King brought the fight to Kinshasa.

As an adjunct to what Ali called the 'rumble in the jungle' – Zaïreans preferred the more refined but inflated *super-combat du siècle* – King and his friend, singer Lloyd Price, planned to stage a preliminary event, a three-day musical extravaganza called 'Zaïre 74.' As it turned out, the fight had to be postponed for five weeks when Foreman received a cut over his right eye during a sparring session, but the music festival went ahead, almost as scheduled. Set to begin on Friday, September 20, the assemblage of artists from Africa and the Americas kicked off a day late at the completely renovated Stadium 20 May. Attendance was sparse the first two nights. Tickets were overpriced for the locals, and all the foreign highrollers had gone home to wait out the fight's postponement. Only on the final night, when the government gave away tickets, did the stadium fill to its 70,000-person capacity.

Each evening, in a succession of stunning sets that spanned the hours from nightfall to dawn, the festival presented a most incredible gathering of musicians from Africa and the African diaspora. Celia Cruz, Ray Barretto, Johnny Pacheco, and the Fania All Stars came from Latin America. Manu Dibango and Miriam Makeba augmented an African contingent dominated by Zaïrean artists O.K. Jazz, Afrisa, Zaïko Langa Langa, the Stukas Boys, Abeti, Verckys, the Trio Madjesi, Wendo Kolosoyi, and several groups of traditional musicians. In the U.S., Price had recruited a musicians' who's who to rival the Zaïreans: B.B. King, Bill Withers, the Pointer Sisters, the Spinners, Sister Sledge, Etta James, and, making a return engagement, the incomparable James Brown.

Zaïre called the festival 'une victoire totale.' 'For the first time in the world, the Zaïre of Mobutu and of its people, energized by the flame of its revolution, has succeeded in assembling, in a gigantic festival, the superstars of the black world of song.' A month later, at the end of October, Muhammad Ali sprang from his 'rope-a-dope' defensive posture to knock out George Foreman in the eighth round and regain the heavyweight title. The bout was televised around the world. Now nearly everyone knew of Mobutu's Zaïre.

•

One of Zaïre 74's better moments was the superb performance of Tabu Ley Rochereau. Recalling his pre-Olympia days, Ley and his Afrisa International won the crowd with a solid set of the group's standards and some magnificent footwork from the dancers. The current band, slightly smaller than in its glory days as African Fiesta National, built on the voices of Ley and his backups, Augustin 'Hennecy' Malao from the Central African Republic and Karé Kassanda. They were supported by guitarists Mavatiku Visi, Lokassa ya Mbongo, and Bopol Mansiamina (fresh from the collapse of Orchestre Continental), bassist 'Philo' Kola Ntalulu, veteran trumpet players (Alphonse) Biolo and (Jean Trompette) Nzenze, and saxophonist Mekanisi Modero. Traps, congas, an occasional appearance on sax by Empompo Loway, and a couple of dancers rounded out the band's current version.

Whether or not Afrisa's downsizing or Ley's own personal renewal – following his 'lost year' of 1971 and a 1973 brush with the law for alleged involvement in a coffee exporting scam – had anything to do with it, the group had recently been producing some of its best work of the decade. 'All the musicians who worked with Rochereau got a good lesson,' Lokassa declared. 'He really knew how to work. He really knew how to lead things.'

'My band,' said Ley, 'has assigned itself the duty of presenting the public with one hit per quarter of the batch of songs it puts out.' Near the end of 1974 Afrisa managed a feat that had lately been rare. With a heartrending song called 'Kaful Mayay,' it wrested the top spot on *Zaïre's* hit-parade away from Simaro and O.K. Jazz.

Like 'Mongali' before it, 'Kaful Mayay' caught the tenor of authenticity by combining rhythms and a theme from Ley's Yansi ancestors with an arrangement for modern instruments. Peals of electric guitar pierce the silence as Mavatiku introduces the piece. Lokassa chimes in with a palm wine rhythm while a snare drum dances around the beat like a village percussionist shaking a stone-filled gourd. Snatches of saxophone embellish the words as Ley,

Tabu Ley 'Rochereau' (front row left) and his Orchestre Afrisa International around the time of Zaïre 74

his voice raised in anguish, sings from Mayay the wife's point of view the disturbing story of an arranged marriage gone bad.

> I am going to return to my relatives' village because my husband mistreats me.
> I'm running away from the shame.
> Look at the wrong that has been done to me,
> Me, my mother's child.
> At night, I can't sleep, mama, my husband keeps beating me,
> Let me leave today,
> I hurt too much.
> If I remain, I'll die from it.
> May I not allow myself to be chained by the so-called joys of marriage.

Ley's words tail off into a closing sebene of male voices chanting 'kaful Mayay' (go ask Mayay, about the tradition of arranged marriage) to the beat of guitars plucked like likembes and the wails of a mournful sax. It is a wonderful synthesis of old and new with a timeless story which, like so many Congo music songs, leaves much to the listener to interpret. Is it simply a tale of forced marriage and abuse? A commentary on the ills of modern life? Or perhaps a critique of conditions in Zaïre under the rule of the MPR? 'Kaful Mayay' offers something for everyone, and as 1974 drew to a close, it looked like nearly everyone was buying it. The song stayed at number one on Zaïre's hit parade from November to January until another of Ley's songs, 'Karibou ya Bintou' (welcome to Bintou, in Swahili), rose to replace it.

•

Congo music's old guard staunchly defended its positions with songs like Ley's 'Kaful Mayay' and Simaro's 'Mabele,' but beyond that its ranks were thinning rapidly. Léon Bukasa, one of the early pioneers, died at the beginning of 1974. Outside of his role as SONECA's president, (Joseph) Kabasele Tshamala was largely inactive except for an occasional appearance with the Géant Orchestre Malebo of Samu Bakula and several of Docteur Nico's former sidemen. Nico himself outlined plans for a comeback, although little of substance developed. (Vicky) Longomba Besange Lokuli struggled with health problems, and his Lovy du Zaïre reflected the uncertainty. (Jean) Bombenga Wewando revived Vox Africa by reuniting with Papa Noël, but the collaboration went no further than a few initial recordings. Dewayon's Cobantou had disbanded; his brother, (Johnny) Bokelo Isenge, spent most of the time running his recording studio.

Of the bands that seemed to span the generations, the Trio Madjesi and Orchestre Vévé maintained their strong positions. Abeti built on her international exposure to earn respect at home. But Les Grands Maquisards of Dalienst Ntesa, which had been successful earlier in the decade, came apart in 1974. Nearly all of its musicians, led by Dizzy Mandjeku and (Camille) Lokombe Nkalulu, quit the band, leaving Dalienst and fellow singer Kiesse Diambu to fend for themselves. Mandjeku and the others went on to form the house band at the Suzanella Maison Blanche, where they called themselves Kossa Kossa and specialized in performing note-for-note covers of the hits of Kinshasa's other bands.

Despite the tenacity of the remaining older groups, the musical agenda of the mid-seventies was being set by younger bands like Bella Bella and Zaïko Langa Langa. These two jockeyed for position, covering the charts with hits and topping each other in assorted polls. Close behind came Lipua Lipua and the upstart Stukas Boys led by 'showman' Lita Bembo.

The Stukas Boys had gotten their start as a neighborhood band doing James Brown covers in 1968, nearly two years before their more successful competitors Bella Bella and Zaïko came along. In 1970 the group had improved to the point that it was able to secure a booking at the prestigious Para Fifi night club (named for Joseph Kabasele's hit song from the fifties), and the next year it cut some records. By then a fairly stable core had evolved that included singers Lita Bembo, Lomingo Alida, Kisola Nzita, and Suke Bola, guitarists Samunga Tediangaye and Bongo Wende, and drummer Bakunde Ilondjoko.

Like the Trio Madjesi, the Stukas Boys were known less for their music than for their great live performances. And Zaïre's developing show system was made to order for their front man, the incredible Lita Bembo. Young and athletic, Lita (formerly Gaby Lita) had a workmanlike voice but the instinctive moves of a premier dancer. Once on stage, he alone commanded the audience's attention.

Samunga, barely into his twenties, anchored the band with a flashy lead guitar which he sometimes plucked with his teeth à la Jimi Hendrix. But when the 'showman' Lita Bembo appeared, no one else had a chance. 'The young man will literally dominate the scene,' *Salongo* reported. 'He will make the mike "suffer." Dropping to his knees like a voodoo man in a trance, exhibiting his sacred dance.... Lita Bembo proves his skill by showing off impossible postures.' After his stellar performance at Zaïre 74, *Salongo* declared he 'set the tone for the evening. And the concert he presented to the public brilliantly confirmed his rank as a great star of Zaïrean music.' The paper's readers voiced agreement by voting Lita Bembo best musician of 1974.

The same readers' poll selected Bella Bella as best band to replace Zaïko, which had won the previous year. Given Bella Bella's shaky beginnings, the honor must have felt like vindication for big brother Soki Vangu, who kept the band together in spite of his younger brother's erratic behavior and an uneasy relationship with the group's *patron*, Verckys. The split with Verckys in 1973 and Soki Dianzenza's return to the fold led to the band's most productive period. Scarcely a week went by in 1974 without a Bella Bella song on the charts; often there were two or three.

The brothers Soki fronted the group, taking turns on lead vocals. Bass player and composer Shaba Kahamba anchored a band of lesser lights which included a horn section and the usual complement of guitars and percussion. Although Bella Bella was considered a youth band, its music remained rooted in the sound of the older groups. The musicians lacked the polish of a Nico or a Franco and the composers fell short of Simaro's lyricism and Tabu Ley's sophistication, but together they energized the music with a youthful exuberance that their elders rarely matched.

By dint of age and experience, Soki Vangu led the band. He lacked Dianzenza's seductive charm, but shared his gift for composition. 'Zamba,' one of his most popular songs, invoked the metaphor of the forest to illuminate the human, or, perhaps more to the point, the Zaïrean, condition.

> Forest, kingdom of the animals.
> And you, elders,
> Help us a little.
> All work here below [on earth] has an aim,
> All work here below deserves pay.
> ...
> Give to each one his chance.

Soki Dianzenza, young (only nineteen in 1974), handsome, and single, attracted crowds of women to Bella Bella's gigs, and crowds of men would follow. People called him 'the prince' and gossiped about his social life. Who was he seeing? When would he choose a wife? 'Soki Dianzenza': one headline announced, 'a hundred titles on the market before I marry.' By then he had thirty-eight.

One of his more popular tunes, 'Kamavasthy,' tells the ironical story of a husband and wife who produce three daughters, Kathy, Mathy, and Vasthy. The wife, suspecting the birth of a succession of females is due to her husband's infidelity, leaves the bewildered man to return to her less than enthusiastic parents. Another song, 'Nganga,' links unemployment to prostitution:

> I Nganga, what do you want me to do
> My work is my livelihood
> You find me money, my brothers
> I will help you

Life with the younger Soki verged on precariousness. From his appendicitis in Abidjan to his zest for independence, the prince's instability always posed a threat to the band's cohesiveness. The brothers had become *patrons* in their prosperity, forming their own Bella Bella label and helping new bands get started. In 1974 they created a second label just for Dianzenza called Allez-y Frères Soki (Go! Brothers Soki). 'It is only to give him a chance to prove his abilities as the manager of a business,' Vangu declared. But the new venture's effect was to institutionalize the natural competitiveness that existed between the brothers. A year later Dianzenza resurrected Orchestre Bella Mambo. He worked for a time with both bands before leaving Bella Bella altogether at the end of 1975. The two Sokis and their groups were weakened in the process, and although they each spoke optimistically of the future, their best days were already behind them.

Bella Bella record jacket from the early seventies featuring Soki Dianzenza (left) and Soki Vangu

Of all the youth bands, Zaïko Langa Langa appeared to be the strongest. Since its humble debut at the Hawaii Bar in 1970 the group had fixed its personnel and developed a boisterous style that attracted considerable attention. Six singers packed Zaïko's front line: (Michel) 'Evoloko' Anto, (Jules) Shungu Wembadio, (Siméon) Mavuela Somo, Efonge Isekofeta, (André) Bimi Ombale, and Nyoka Longo. Evoloko, Shungu, and Mavuela nicknamed themselves Isifi, short for the French il suffit, it's enough. The others comprised the vocal attaque choc (shock attack). (Félix) Manuaku Waku and Matima Kinuani played lead guitar; 'Enock' Zamuangana and 'Teddy' Sukami handled the accompaniment. Drummer Meridjo Belobi and bassist Muaka Mbeka, better known as 'Bapuis,' formed the rhythm section with the group's founder and manager, D.V. Moanda, on congas. The band also carried a couple of yé-yé singers, who performed covers of Western hits. In 1974, with drummer Meridjo Belobi beginning a 21-month prison sentence for some unpublicized transgression, Zaïko hired the former Stukas Boys drummer, 'Pablo' Bakunde Ilondjoko, as a replacement. A singer from the group Minzoto Kulutu, Mbenzuana Ngamboni, who called himself 'Bozi Boziana,' joined around the same time.

The Zaïko Langa Langa of 1973–74 was an impressive collection of young, talented performers, each of whom would excel in the business for many years to come. They appeared to possess the kind of intelligence and rapport that had distinguished the best formations of African Jazz, African Fiesta, and O.K. Jazz. Although Zaïko lacked a formidable leader like Franco or Kabasele, the group's egalitarian, ensemble approach worked on stage and dampened the internal fuses of egotism and jealousy. Most of the musicians were students when the group had formed. Some still claimed to be. But, for better or worse, Zaïko Langa Langa became the center of their lives.

Each musician had his own fanatical following, but there was surely a first among equals in the personage of Evoloko. The flamboyant teenager was a magnet for attention. Short and skinny with his hair parted on the right, he wore dark glasses and hung amulets around his neck. Like a Harlem hepster of the 1930s dressed in the garb of the motherland, his look mirrored the confluence of cultures that engulfed Kinshasa. He was brash and cocky, the king of aliases, with 'Lay Lay,' 'Atshuamano,' and 'Anto Nickel' among his favorites.

In 1973 Evoloko created a new dance that swept the capital. Shungu Wembadio gave it a name, *cavacha*. There are many stories of how the cavacha evolved, one of which Evoloko told himself. It seems a *papa bouffon*, a street character, amused Evoloko's neighborhood with a dance of exaggerated hip movements that resembled a football player's feints. The dance, he said, came from the Sakata people along the Kasai River. He had simply modernized it. 'In the beginning I couldn't get my legs and shoulders synchronized. But by rehearsing I managed to come close to the tradition.' The cavacha rendered all the current dances passé.

As Zaïko's most conspicuous personality, Evoloko became a lightning rod for criticism. *Zaïre* panned his song 'Mbeya-Mbeya':

> The text is inaudible. The voices are lost in a hodgepodge of trivial words, and don't harmonize. We hear nothing, barely some 'yelele yelele' [cries of animation]. But what does that mean? And as though to make us dizzy, the recording is defective. The public deserves better than this!

Salongo was only slightly more reserved in its assessment of the entire band. Conceding that the musical arrangements were good and with praise for Manuaku's guitar, the writer went after the singers.

> Bizarre voices! ... Discordant voices ... in bad form.... Was Zaïko's vocal objective to create an original? To sing in a style that has no elders here? By

turning the old concept of refined, clear and limpid voices upside down? If that was its aim, then Zaïko has succeeded. Brilliantly!

Zaïko's fans, most of whom were teenagers, could not have disagreed more. 'For me,' wrote one, 'the best band of the year is Zaïko Langa Langa. For having launched many songs and because it is the favorite band of all hip young people.' This clash of tastes recalled the 1950s in the United States when Chuck Berry and Bill Haley assaulted the ears of Frank Sinatra listeners. But for all the liberties Zaïko took with the music, it was still the Congolese rumba, just rougher around the edges, as if it had endured a back-alley mugging. Kabasele had crooned like Tino Rossi. Vicky and Edo blended their voices in seamless harmony. Evoloko and company sounded strident in comparison. Where Nico evolved a freely flowing solo, Zaïko's guitarists locked themselves onto a riff. Although Zaïko's musicians had once auditioned a saxophonist, no horns would color their music. 'In our band,' Evoloko declared, 'our soloist plays trumpet with his guitar.'

If some had trouble understanding their words, it wasn't because they had nothing to say. Evoloko's 'Onassis ya Zaïre' (Onassis of Zaïre) tells the story of a rich older man's pursuit of a younger girl.

> You get into the house since [you're] a friend of papa's
> When I go to school you follow me with your Toyota
> Another day you wait for me with your Mazda
> ...
> I'm going to denounce you to my family and to papa.

Teddy Sukami addressed the evils of money in 'Vie ya Mosolo' (life of money).

> You are only proud with your father's money
> When you're short of it you will steal
> All that, friend, to gain popularity.

With 'Liwa ya Somo' (fearful death) Shungu Wembadio gave voice to the plight of the ordinary citizen.

> if I had been a sorcerer
> I would have been rich
> To help my family
> Survive difficult days.

On stage the musicians exuded a swaggering self-confidence. Dancing the cavacha and the other steps of the day, Zaïko's Isifi front line resembled a machine of perpetual motion. Songs often began as slow-paced rumbas then subtly shifted in the space between verses to a faster, more relentless tempo. Cries of animation marked the sebene as guitars and traps stoked the embers of excitement. *Beau désordre* someone called it, beautiful disorder. No wonder they billed themselves as 'Tout Choc' (total shock) Zaïko Langa Langa. Every performance was a bacchanal celebration of youth.

Although Zaïko's musicians thought they were different, that their free-form 'organization' and equality of rank could somehow protect them from discord, they were mistaken. Founder and manager, D.V. Moanda, appeared to exert little control over his headstrong charges. *Chef d'orchestre* Teddy Sukami seemed equally ineffectual at instilling a sense of discipline. As *Salongo* put it, 'Everyone made the rules. Especially, of course, the people who had gotten a certain renown thanks to their works recorded on disc.'

Each of Zaïko's composers made his own deal with a record label. Thus Evoloko's songs were released by Parions, Efonge's by Véve, Nyoka's by Cover, and so forth. The composers pocketed their royalties while the rest of the band only shared a small session fee and the proceeds from live performances. By the end of 1973, the equal partners had become grossly unequal. Moanda and his co-founders decreed that individual musicians from the group, while they had the right to work on outside projects, could no longer use the Zaïko name on them. Manuaku, who replaced Sukami as *chef d'orchestre* in mid-1974, tried to rein in the composers by proposing that the band establish its own label. By issuing their works on their own label, everyone in the group would benefit. Outside deals would no longer be acceptable.

Evoloko, it seems, became the focus at this point. His work habits had been less than exemplary. He showed up late for concerts and often refused to rehearse. When he balked at Manuaku's attempted reform, he drew a suspension. Moanda and most of the rest of the band backed Manuaku. When negotiations with Evoloko failed to produce an accord by the end of November, Manuaku and Moanda fired him.

Like African Jazz and O.K. Jazz before it, Zaïko Langa Langa had completed the cycle of birth, growth, and maturity. It now began to spin off its own progeny. In the midst of the turmoil, Efonge defected to Véve, where he attempted to launch a new band called Maika. The balance of the Isifi crew, Shungu, Mavuela, and Bozi, quit in solidarity with their brother Evoloko. 'It's that way in every group where there are many more stars, there's always an explosion,' Shungu said years later in his incarnation as Papa Wemba. This explosion set in motion a new band, headed by the quartet of singers, called

Lokole Isifi. *Lokole* (a type of drum), Shungu explained, was their replacement for the French word *orchestre*. They joined forces with singer Vadio Mabenga, whose crippled legs failed to diminish his enthusiasm for performing, and recruited instrumentalists to back them. In January of 1975, Lokole Isifi had its first records on the market.

Zaïko began to replace the departed singers by hiring Likinga 'Redo' Mangenza away from Empire Bakuba and adding an untested newcomer named Nsumbu 'Lengi' Lenga. With their instrumental lineup still intact, the players worked up a new repertoire and reintroduced themselves to the public. Zaïko Langa Langa had survived its first major crisis.

•

The president of the republic did not fare as well as the country's leading youth band. Zaïreanization had become a nightmare. The *acquéreurs* (acquirers of foreign-owned businesses), most of whom were politicians or politically well connected, were rapidly turning the economy into a shambles. Many were ill equipped to run the businesses they now controlled. Ordering goods, meeting a payroll, and otherwise managing an enterprise seemed incomprehensible to these instant entrepreneurs, most of whom had only lived from the sweat of others. Some simply sold off their firm's assets, laid off the employees, and pocketed the money. Others fired experienced workers in order to give jobs to their relatives. In the words of Crawford Young and Thomas Turner, 'The mismanagement and incompetence of the *acquéreur* class as a whole was widely conceded by August 1974, and by 1975 had become official orthodoxy.'

Shortages of food and other essential goods became apparent. Shortages produced inflation. Inflation prompted hoarding, which fueled increased inflation. Suppliers refused credit to new, unfamiliar owners. Industries found it difficult to purchase raw materials and spare parts. MAZADIS, now in Franco's hands, suddenly had to come up with cash if it wanted to continue operating. Gaps began to appear on record store shelves. To make matters worse, world copper prices remained depressed, further robbing the country of income.

Disorder in the economy and intense press criticism of the *acquéreurs* prompted Mobutu to declare war on the bourgeoisie. 'It is unthinkable that I, who have battled relentlessly against 300 Belgian families who have exploited our country, could tolerate having 300 Zairian families substitute themselves for the Belgians.' The solution to the problem, he said, would be a 'radicalization' of the revolution. But, as with so much of the president's reformist rhetoric, little of substance followed. Most of those who had acquired businesses were allowed to keep them, and Zaïre's economy declined still further.

With disaster looming large toward the end of 1975, Mobutu had no choice but to retreat. In concert with the International Monetary Fund and Zaïre's other creditors, he took the first steps to undo Zaïreanization. In most cases 40 percent of each Zaïreanized business was offered to its former owners if they would return to Zaïre to help run it. Few of the foreigners accepted, however, so the figure was increased to 60 percent the following year. In this way Fonior became Franco's majority partner in MAZADIS. By 1976, many of the other foreign businessmen had what was left of their enterprises returned to them completely. But the damage had been done. Most of the firms had been looted to the point that it made little sense to begin again. There would be no return to the relative prosperity the country had enjoyed at the start of the decade.

Zaïreanization left the record industry badly wounded. Supplies of raw materials and spare parts that fueled the pressing plants dwindled. 'In the capital's music publishing circles, conversations mainly turn to the shortage of records on the market,' *Zaïre* reported in September of 1975. 'Kiosks everywhere display shelves either empty or filled only with old creations.'

Inflation pushed the price of records beyond the means of increasing numbers of consumers. The official devaluation of the once-mighty zaïre in 1976 exacerbated the industry's troubles. The imported materials of production would cost more in local currency, a cost to be passed on to music buyers already strapped for cash.

Sagging record sales deprived the artists of a ready source of income. From this point on, Zaïre's musicians needed to look beyond the home market. Zaïre could no longer guarantee them their musical livelihoods.

15
...Must come down

Abeti, M'Pongo Love, Papa Wemba, Franco, and Tabu Ley, 1975–1978

Like a boulder dislodged from the base of a cliff, Zaïreanization stripped the underpinnings from a body of enormous potential. The body in this case, Zaïre's economy, collapsed in an avalanche of miscalculation, incompetence, and greed. A fledgling nation lay smothering in the rubble, but it would suffer a lingering death. Cold war antagonists and agents of international finance administered intermittent resuscitation. Meanwhile, the life of the people continued. As they had done during the crisis following independence, Kinshasans looked to their entertainers for relief from trying times.

While the economy's predicament stifled the industrial side of the music business, its artisans continued to flower. Recording income declined sharply, but live audiences could still provide a band with a healthy payday. Matonge's clubs bloomed with nightlife; auditoriums catered to devotees of le show.

Abeti Masikini seemed particularly well positioned to weather the current difficulties. Her status as Zaïre's only major female star and her attachment to the limited-edition, show-style concept of performance gave every Abeti appearance a special cachet. Gérard Akueson, her manager, maintained his ties to West Africa and Paris. If conditions became unbearable in Kinshasa, Abeti could play concerts abroad for a while.

After Carnegie Hall, Abeti had brought her act to Kinshasa's Palladium Theater, wowed the crowd at Zaïre 74 before the Ali–Foreman fight, and closed out the year on the road with concerts at major towns in Zaïre's interior. 'For a young star especially, tours are of capital importance,' she told a reporter.

They allow her to expand her horizons and to make herself known. Me, I'm ambitious. I'm anxious to become international. That's the reason why I play in foreign countries, and I release a lot of records in foreign markets. I'm already known here in Zaïre. I'm not worried about this side. I need to conquer the rest of the world.

The new year of 1975 took her to France for an April tour of the country and a two-night return engagement at the Paris Olympia. Of all the other musicians from Congo and Zaïre, only Tabu Ley had played the famed concert hall, but now the upstart Abeti had done it twice. Back in Kinshasa at the end of May she replayed her Olympia show in a weekend stand at the Palladium before tapering off to accommodate the effects of an advancing pregnancy.

As far back as May of 1974 the Kinshasa press had printed rumors of Abeti's marriage to Akueson. Although they denied it at the time, the two, if not married, had at least become a couple, and their union produced a daughter near the end of 1975. They later affirmed their marriage, but wished to keep the knowledge from spreading for fear of damaging Abeti's popularity.

In late March of 1976, a scant three months after giving birth, Abeti took the Palladium stage to resume her career. The show reunited Abeti with the talented Brazzavillean keyboard player Freddy Kebano – he had worked on her initial outings in West Africa – who had recently joined the band. With Kebano on board, brother Abumba Masikini leading the band, now called Les Redoutables, and her dancing Tigresses in top form, Abeti showed no sign of relinquishing her mastery of *le show*.

•

Unbeknown to Abeti, she and her sister entertainers had inspired a young woman from Boma on the lower Zaïre. M'Pongo Landu came to Kinshasa fresh from secondary school, where she had sung in the choir while completing her studies. She had loved to sing from childhood, she said, and she wanted a career in music. As a woman the odds were against her, in spite of Abeti's breakthrough. And she had an additional impediment to overcome. At four years of age, the reaction to a medical injection had paralyzed her lower legs. In time she had learned to walk again, but the pirouettes of Abeti and Etisomba would always be beyond her.

Once in Kinshasa M'Pongo enrolled in a shorthand typing course, then worked as a secretary while pursuing showbusiness contacts in her off hours. She introduced herself as M'Pongo Love, a name she said her parents had called her since childhood. In December of 1975, at age nineteen, she met

M'Pongo Love

saxophonist Empompo Loway, then ostensibly in the employ of O.K. Jazz. Empompo adopted the development of her career as his personal project.

A false start with a first *patron* led the two musicians to the door of Editions Toulmonde (a play on the French *tout le monde*, meaning everybody) and its owner Ngwango Isionoma, better known as 'Seli-Ja.' Seli-Ja had earned his reputation and his bankroll as the manager of Afrisa, but after falling out with Tabu Ley he had gone into business for himself. Seli-Ja put up the money to get Empompo and his protégée started.

Despite the shortage of raw materials that had forced the MAZADIS and SOPHINZA pressing operations to a near standstill, Empompo and Seli-Ja prepared to record some songs with M'Pongo to introduce her to the market. A pop band that had started out in Lubumbashi called The Black Devils backed her on her first four sides around May of 1976. A less productive session with Minzoto Wella Wella, born of the 'Bills' phenomenon, followed.

Later in the year a third session was held with a group called Ya Tupas, named, its members said, after the Tupamaros guerrillas of Uruguay whose exploits had been in the news. Bopol Mansiamina, having recently separated from Afrisa, was at the core of the band, along with Manuaku moonlighting from Zaïko, and a keyboard player named (Ray) Lema-a-Nsi. As artistic director, Empompo produced all of M'Pongo's recordings and delivered the sax parts as well.

The two most fruitful sessions, those with The Black Devils and the Ya Tupas, could scarcely have been more different. The Black Devils delivered their derivative sound with lead guitar up front and the backing rhythms of American R&B. The best track, an M'Pongo composition called 'Pas Possible Maty,' tells of a secretary who pursues a romantic infatuation while she is supposed to be working and loses her job and the object of her desire as a result.

The Ya Tupas, on the other hand, restored the rumba but buried the guitar in favor of Lema's electronic piano. The best song to emerge from their work was written by Mayaula Mayoni, who was something of an oddity in the business, an independent. Mayaula preferred to compose his songs and then offer them to whichever artist he felt they fit. Many of his more memorable efforts found their way to O.K. Jazz, but his latest, 'Ndaya,' was meant for M'Pongo. The story tells of a woman happy in her marriage and confident of keeping her husband, despite the overtures of other women. 'Tcheke tcheke,' M'Pongo chirps at the sebene, a call that would become her trademark. It means joy and laughter in Swahili, she explained. Lema's piano hones a riff, then Empompo cuts in with a withering solo. If further evidence of Empompo's ability was needed, he furnished it with his work for M'Pongo. Here was an artist every bit the equal of the music's best saxophonists and arrangers.

Even though they had suspended their music charts in response to the Zaïreanization-induced record famine, *Zaïre* selected 'Pas Possible Maty' as one of the best songs of 1976. When the crisis eased and the pressing plants cranked up in the middle of the following year, 'Ndaya' rode the charts for several weeks.

In the meantime M'Pongo sat for press interviews, sang on a television show, and began rehearsing with Orchestre Jambo Jambo, the house band at the former Perruche Bleue, now called Club Kamalondo (later, the Jambo Jambo). On April 30 she headlined a show at the Palladium. The following night she played a May Day dance at the hall of the MPR, then returned to the Palladium the next weekend. Her extraordinary beauty and the sexy squeak of her voice took Kinshasa by surprise. 'This little unknown of twenty literally fell from the clouds,' said *Zaïre*. A new star had been born almost overnight.

•

While Abeti and M'Pongo expanded the orbit of female musicians, fragments from the Zaïko Langa Langa big bang hurtled along forming new constellations in its wake. Rumblings were heard within less than a year from Lokole Isifi, where too many stars inhabited too little space. News surfaced in September of 1975 that Evoloko had been organizing a new band. By December, however, it became clear that Shungu Wembadio, Mavuela Somo, and Bozi Boziana were the ones who would be bailing out. Lokole Isifi would be left to Evoloko and Vadio Mabenga.

Shungu, now using the sobriquet 'Papa Wemba,' Mavuela, Bozi, and a former yé-yé singer from Zaïko, Mbuta Mashakado, formed Yoka Lokole. This new band seemed star-crossed almost from the start. The musicians recorded and released their first songs for Parions early in 1976, but by April a dispute over money ended the relationship between band and label. At the same time Bozi went back to Isifi for a short stop on the way home to Zaïko.

Wemba and the remaining musicians nicknamed themselves the Fania All Stars of Zaïre. Everyone in Yoka Lokole was a star, they boasted, but as it turned out, there were still too many for comfort. By the end of the year another divorce began to play itself out with Mavuela and Papa Wemba vying for custody of the band. Mavuela won this round, keeping Yoka Lokole for himself. But Papa Wemba regrouped with apparent ease, launching another band, Viva La Musica, at the end of February 1977.

Within the space of about two years, Zaïko Langa Langa had spun off three new groups, each with a star of the Isifi crew at its head: Evoloko fronted Lokole Isifi, eventually changing its name to Ba Isifi Baye; Mavuela controlled Yoka Lokole; and Wemba his Viva La Musica. In addition, Efonge, calling himself 'Gina wa Gina,' reappeared after a period of inactivity with a new band he called Libanko, and Vadio Mabenga split with Evoloko to form Orchestre Muchacha. Zaïko now ranked with African Jazz and O.K. Jazz when it came to propagation of the musical species.

Of all the groups to evolve from Zaïko's gene pool, Viva La Musica appeared to be the fittest. Viva was led by the energetic Papa Wemba, a short, trim man of nearly twenty-seven years with a well-developed sense of style. He called his Matonge home Village Molokai after the Hawaiian island he had seen on film. He was its *chef coutumier*, the customary chief. Taking a page from the Trio Madjesi's book, Wemba also indulged his fondness for fashion. Sartorial savvy enhanced his public persona while providing the band's performances with an extra draw. 'I had to set myself apart from the others,' Wemba explained. 'I couldn't always look the same. I had to have a look.... I have to go on stage looking really sharp.'

In Zaïko and the other bands, Papa Wemba had had to share the spotlight. Now, as Viva's sole proprietor, primary composer, and lead singer, he was freed from that constraint. 'That was my own group,' he later said with satisfaction. Now he could exert the full force of his considerable talent and personality.

Wemba staffed his new ensemble with an impressive collection of largely unknown musicians, many of whom would go on to become stars in their own right. Rigobert 'Rigo Star' Bamundele played solo guitar, while Kisangani Djenga, alias 'Prince Espérant,' Jadot Sombele, who called himself 'le Cambodgien' (the Cambodian), and Paulino de Guimarães, of Angolan ancestry, known as 'Pepe Bipoli,' backed Wemba on vocals.

Wemba by himself sounded a lot like his idol Tabu Ley, but he often boosted his voice into a singsong falsetto that speared the listener's consciousness like the cries of a wounded animal. His group's sound naturally derived from the Zaïko school of raucous vocals and repeating guitars with nary a peep from a horn. Typical of Viva's early recordings was the cacophonous and somewhat forced 'Mère Supérieure' (mother superior), an indictment of women's purported hypocrisy in affairs of the heart couched in an ironic title. Writers for the Kinshasa daily *Elima* selected Viva as best band of 1977, 'Mère Supérieure' best song, and Papa Wemba revelation of the year. 'This artist was incontestably the one who attracted the most attention from the population.'

Within less than a year Viva La Musica suffered its first setback when Jadot, Espérant, and Bipoli left to form Karawa Musica. But, despite the loss, Viva proved to be durable. Zaïko had survived its deserters, and Viva would do the same. The spin-off bands Isifi, Yoka, Libanko, Muchacha, and Karawa would all eventually fold. Only Zaïko and Viva could muster the strength to endure.

Whatever the lifespan of Kinshasa's younger bands, durability in the world of Zaïrean music was defined by Franco and Tabu Ley. By 1975, Franco had been a professional musician for more than twenty years, nineteen of them with O.K. Jazz. The slightly younger Ley could boast of fifteen years in the business. Each had risen to head one of Congo music's two original strains. Franco led the school of O.K. Jazz, music for the common people. Ley inherited the mantle of Joseph Kabasele and African Jazz, the school of the intellectuals.

The lines between them had blurred over the years as the bands evolved stylistically and increased levels of education and economic opportunity opened new vistas for their fans. Nevertheless, many differences remained. In spite of O.K. Jazz's growing size and wealth of equipment, Franco preferred playing in the clubs, especially his Un-Deux-Trois, where the crowd could join the action. Ley, on the other hand, had pioneered le show, and he appeared to prefer it. Franco plucked his guitar with thumb and forefinger where Ley's guitarists picked in the style of Docteur Nico. Ley's voice soared in the grand tradition of Kabasele; the singers of O.K. Jazz blended into an ensemble.

Although the two were nominal colleagues and spoke of each other with respect, competition, at times, grew heated. If rival musicians crossed paths, Isaac Musekiwa recalled, cordiality often masked contempt.

> He cannot like me, but when he sees me he must show me that he likes me.... Just like a detective, you know? When a [policeman] wants to arrest somebody, he's laughing, but you are arrested, but he's laughing with you.... That's how musicians are.

When it came to throwing his considerable weight around, Franco showed little reticence. His political connections, partial ownership of MAZADIS, and presidency of UMUZA added up to a great deal of power. As part of Mobutu's radicalization of Zaïreanization, Franco convened an April 1975 meeting of UMUZA attended by representatives of some 360 bands. There he passed along the government's request that they help to educate the masses by playing revolutionary songs at the beginning and end of each performance. In addition, he advised the musicians to censor their own songs before recording them. Records had to be approved by the censorship commission before they could be released. Old records at the Voice of Zaïre would also be censored. Finally, regulations for musicians traveling abroad required that they show proof of funds to cover their stay. The latter two points, censorship and travel, would soon test the power of the president of UMUZA himself.

Zaïre's original censorship commission, set up in 1967, had, over the years, allowed its decisions to be influenced by certain gifts from musicians whose work might otherwise have been deemed unsuitable for release. Franco seemed particularly adept at avoiding the commission's sanctions, but he couldn't escape the scrutiny of the press. Several of his songs from 1975 and a Mayaula Mayoni composition for O.K. Jazz called 'Chérie Bondowe' created a public furor. Unlike Manuel D'Oliveira's 'Chérie Bondowe' from the fifties, who was the object of the singer's affection, Mayaula's song presented the life of a prostitute from her point of view, 'that song which defends prostitution,' as Zaïre bluntly put it. Along with 'Chérie Bondowe' the band had recorded several other numbers, 'Nakoma Mbanda na Mama ya Mobali Ngai' (I've become my mother-in-law's rival), 'Bimaka,' 'Liberté,' 'Salima,' and 'Falansua.' Zaïre called 'the songs, taken together, an interminable magnificence of vice.'

'Chérie Bondowe,' for one, was first released in Belgium and rapidly found its way back to Kinshasa. O.K. Jazz performed all the songs in public and even on television. 'Bootleg' tapes of their performances appeared for sale in the street, although some in the press accused Franco of putting them out himself. He and the band's manager, Manzenza Sala Musala, both denied the charge. All the songs were eventually released on record in Kinshasa. 'Nakoma Mbanda...' was even selected as best song of 1976 by the readers of *Salongo*; Franco was voted best musician. He had neatly evaded the censors.

Following this incident, Zaïre's attorney general, Kengo wa Dondo, presided over the commission's reorganization. A new thirteen-member body was created which included six representatives from the government, three each from the clergy and the music industry, and one from the International Union for the Protection of Childhood. Motivated by the rhetoric of radicalization, the commission took its work seriously. By early 1977, dozens of songs by various groups had been interdicted by the authorities.

On the question of musicians' travel abroad, Franco *was* the authority. The government had decreed that all requests for permission to travel be submitted to UMUZA. As the union's president Franco had the power to decide who had fulfilled the requirements. The case of the Trio Madjesi served to illustrate how that worked in practice.

In May of 1975, after the Trio Madjesi announced that it had a contract to play at the Olympia in Paris the following year, UMUZA slapped the band with a twelve-month suspension, the equivalent of a death sentence. The reason given for this action was an allegation that the trio had traded zaïres for foreign currency on the black market in order to finance their planned trip to Paris. UMUZA claimed the decision had come from the department of culture, but all communications concerning the affair issued from UMUZA. The government took no official action in the matter, which alleged a crime punishable by law. Many, including the trio themselves, thought the order had come from a jealous Franco. 'UMUZA, a union or a court?' asked *Zaïre*. 'Someone wants to suffocate the rising music in order to maintain things that are beginning to get tired and out of date at the podium!'

While behind the scenes negotiations dragged on, the musicians of Sosoliso, the trio's backing band, began to look elsewhere for work. By August, however, the discussions and some mediative words from Tabu Ley got the suspension lifted. The *explosif* and *sportif* Trio Madjesi returned to the Palladium's stage in October. Despite Sosoliso's loss of personnel, the group appeared to be back on track. Arrangements proceeded for their date in Paris the next December.

As the new year dawned, however, less and less was heard from the Trio Madjesi. Although Saak Saakul, the 'Sinatra' of the group, had gone to Paris to sign the Olympia contract, it was learned by mid-1976 that Matadidi 'Mario' had gone to his ancestral home in Angola and Loko 'Djeskain' to his in Brazzaville. When December's Olympia date passed without the trio, it seemed clear the group was dead.

In a 1977 postmortem Saakul indirectly blamed UMUZA. 'Sadly, the necessary authorizations, requested in good time, I didn't get them. Administrative slowness or bad faith? I don't know. The fact remains that I didn't have the necessary authorization [from UMUZA] to make the trip, despite an authorization to leave dated 12 May 76 signed by the commissioner of state for culture. Once again I saw myself caught in the trap of sabotage.'

From the safety of his home in Brazzaville, Loko Massengo spoke more bluntly. 'I can't forget the bad faith of Luambo Makiadi, who put up the gallows and won the bet by mocking Sosoliso.... The Trio Madjesi was assassinated by Luambo Makiadi.'

While the case of the Trio Madjesi unfolded, Franco and O.K. Jazz celebrated the twentieth anniversary of the band's founding. Of the six musicians who played the first official date at the O.K. Bar on June 6, 1956, only Franco remained. He had helped to build the band with collaborators like Essous, Vicky, and Edo, then gradually assumed control as each of the partners drifted away. There had been some low points – the defectors of Orchestre Révolution, the death of Franco's brother – but mostly the times had been good. The band's records caught the mood of the day and its shows enlivened the night. Nearly every Kinshasan could relate at least one experience in their own lives to the existence of O.K. Jazz.

Franco's knack for business had bred an organization strong enough to accommodate its changing cast. As Isaac Musekiwa put it, 'Some are dead. Some went away. Some they go and come back. You can go again and come back again. We will still carry on.' Franco could be ruthless with his rivals, but those who worked for him say he honored his commitments and treated his employees fairly. 'When I had the opportunity to work with him for the first time, I requested a condition which was to sign a contract with him,' Malambu ma Kizola, one of Franco's counselors, recalled.

> But he said to me, 'Listen, there's no point signing a contract. We can sign a contract, but a contract can be observed or not observed the same way. A contract is the trust you place in me, and that I place in you. As long as we understand each other the contract is observed.'

Everyone knew where they stood with Franco. Those who returned his trust found job security in O.K. Jazz.

As part of the twentieth anniversary celebrations, Franco was made an officer in the National Order of the Leopard, one of Zaïre's highest honors. It was a measure of his importance to the country's cultural life and the esteem accorded by the Zaïrean people and their president. 'As I have just received this distinction, I will try to change my behavior,' he said. 'I must now be worthy. One does not trifle with work.'

With the exception of coverage of the twentieth anniversary of O.K. Jazz, Franco had lately been getting bad press. Kinshasa's scribes were especially harsh in their coverage of the censored songs and the Trio Madjesi's undoing. Whether this motivated Franco's next venture is difficult to say, but in 1977 he launched his own music magazine, called Ye! The weekly publication featured the musicians of O.K. Jazz prominently, although the other bands received attention too. More importantly it provided Franco with a voice in the press unfettered by editorial whim.

Tabu Ley also made some strategic moves. Back in 1969, long before Franco built his entertainment palace, Ley had gotten into the saloon-keeping business with a dancing bar called Le Sebene. In 1976, in keeping with his status as one of the music's two enduring masters, he opened a more distinguished night spot called the Type K (pronounced *teep ka*). 'Type K means in slang,

Kinshasan guy,' he said. 'I dedicate this temple to all lovers of music and culture.' Not far from the runway of Ndolo Airport (the former Sabena Aerodrome), the new club sparkled with all the latest amenities: dressing rooms for the artists, a stage with a curtain, a large dance floor, and state-of-the-art lights and sound. Over the next few years, the Type K would play host to an abundance of memorable events, including the debut performance of Papa Wemba's Viva La Musica.

When it came to power and influence Ley's upward movement in SONECA gave him some clout to go with his reputation. SONECA, the body charged with collecting monies due from the performance of musical works and paying royalties to their authors, made Tabu Ley its president in 1977. The organization's performance had been less than stellar. Charges against it ran the gamut from slow or no pay to outright corruption. As SONECA's president, Ley would be in a position to affect the livelihood of every musician in Zaïre, including Franco. And with Franco already in charge of UMUZA and MAZADIS, the two stars together had something – often a lot – to say about almost every aspect of the business. In the milieu of intrigue and competition that prevailed, it was probably inevitable that *les grands manitou*, the big shots, would clash.

Ever since Kwamy's defection from O.K. Jazz to African Fiesta and Fiesta's alleged tampering with Verckys, the two camps had reached a tacit understanding that neither one would raid the other's talent. Sam Mangwana's move to O.K. Jazz raised questions of stylistic integration, but since Mangwana had left Ley's employ years before, there could be no claim of sabotage. At the end of 1974, however, Mangwana's contract with O.K. Jazz expired. Although he could have stayed with the band, Mangwana was approached by Tabu Ley, who wooed him back to Afrisa.

From the outside it looked like a raid, but Mangwana claimed he had Franco's blessing.

> We made a press communication to say, okay, Sam Mangwana with Franco, no problem, but the contract is finished. Sam Mangwana wants to renew with Tabu Ley. And then again the press said, oh, Sam Mangwana is a rebel, he's a mercenary.

Perhaps the switch was amicable, but Mangwana's behavior seemed curious. He disappeared to Angola, his ancestral home, for several months before making his debut in Afrisa in October of 1975.

In a move that smacked of Franco's revenge, Afrisa's lead guitarist, Mavatiku Visi, changed sides in August of 1975. O.K. Jazz manager Manzenza denied doing anything wrong. 'We hired an unemployed man, Mavatiku, who was fired by his former employer.' To compensate for Mavatiku's departure, Ley hired Dizzy Mandjeku from the faltering Kossa Kossa. Singer Diana Nsimba returned to the fold a few months later, and guitarist Dino Vangu moved in to play alongside Mandjeku at the end of 1976. Ley's reunion with Sam Mangwana, on the other hand, lasted less than a year. A squabble over money separated the stars once again.

In 1975, around the same time that Mavatiku was changing sides, Afrisa alumnus Ndombe Opetun joined the O.K. Jazz singers. After leaving Tabu Ley in 1972, Ndombe had enjoyed moderate success with his new group, Afrizam, but when several musicians quit, he accepted Franco's offer to join O.K. Jazz. The following year Franco added the leader of the defunct Grands Maquisards, singer Ntesa Dalienst, and guitarist 'Thierry' Mantuika Kobi, who had played for Thu Zaina.

Franco's appetite for acquiring talent rivaled his mealtime gluttony. In October of 1976 *Salongo* counted thirty-six musicians in O.K. Jazz, including nine singers, eleven guitarists, six saxophone players, four trumpeters, two trombonists, two conga players, and two drummers. Early the next year the former solo guitarist of Les Grands Maquisards, Gerry Dialungana, joined the band, to be followed in 1978 by Papa Noël. Many of these musicians had developed stylistically outside the school of O.K. Jazz. Dialungana patterned himself after Docteur Nico. Thierry Mantuika came out of the youth band Thu Zaina. Papa Noël was a school unto himself. Ndombe, Dalienst, and Wuta Mayi, like Sam Mangwana before them, were steeped in the tradition of African Jazz and Afrisa. By accumulating artists from across the musical spectrum, Franco seemed intent on developing a band that could synthesize all of Congo music's varieties.

Inevitably, talent flowed in the other direction too. Early in 1977 Michel Boybanda quit. Youlou Mabiala followed him at the end of the year. In 1978, Franco fired Ndombe Opetun and Mavatiku Visi for allegedly planning to start a new band. Mavatiku, in fact, formed his own Orchestre Makfé, while Ndombe turned up beside Tabu Ley at a concert in Brazzaville.

Ndombe's case looked suspiciously like tampering, and one journalist lumped it together with a number of other grievances in two unflattering articles about Ley in *Ye!*, Franco's music magazine. Ley heatedly denied the accusations. The two leaders had had a verbal agreement since 1967 not to steal each other's musicians, he said. The articles defamed him. 'Luambo, who remains for me a genius and a legend for Zaïrean music, is in the wrong.' A few months later Ndombe quietly resumed his place in O.K. Jazz. The incident provided added confirmation of Franco's ability to intimidate his colleagues. *Ye!* gave him a voice in the press. He had the money to hire almost any musician he wanted. He could control his competitors' travel and, to some degree, the pressing of their records. As his friend President Mobutu had done in the political realm, Franco had amassed the instruments of power in the music industry. Within its confines he would answer to no one. Or so it seemed.

At the beginning of September 1978, Franco talked about his music to a reporter from the newspaper *Elima*.

> Listening to my music, it's dreams and reality. Because you live the dream, and it controls your reality.... For me, music is the accompaniment to mental imagery, but the listener has to interpret it correctly. That is to say that the song is only half-composed, and the listener himself has to take responsibility for the rest of the composition to reap the impact. The listener has to add the meaning.

Later in the month, when new releases from O.K. Jazz hit the streets, listeners could scarcely believe their ears. Three of Franco's songs, 'Hélène,' 'Jacky,' and 'Sous-Alimentation Sexuelle' (sexual malnourishment), left little room for interpretation. The three were part of a salacious four-song recording released on cassette tape in an effort to avoid the censors.

It didn't work. The press had huffed about Franco's songs in the past, but this time the headlines exploded. 'Luambo at the height of stupidity,' cried *Salongo* from the top of its music page. Calling Franco an 'inveterate recidivist,' the paper launched a blistering attack on the songs

> where no sentence can be transcribed in French [the language of the paper] at the risk of glorifying the baseness or of shocking. Woman, for whom the [MPR] party has done so much, is presented as an object. An object of pleasure and denigration, the model used for inspiration to deliver such a litany of insanities as to award its author the Oscar for mediocrity and baseness. Foolish stupidity, the backdrop to these songs, is herein crowned.

Elima joined the drumfire. 'Luambo: please! Stop your stupidity,' ran the headline on a front-page story. The writer expressed shock at the explicit sexual content of the songs and pointed out that the titles, two of which were foreign names, 'undermined authenticity.'

> For some time now, the owner of O.K. Jazz has made himself famous for his villainies. But today things have gotten far more serious for, he has come – after veiled words here, lecherous and pernicious allusions there – to openly defy public order by composing hors-d'œuvres of insanity that should logically have been vigorously suppressed from their first distribution. Alas! These songs spiced with the lucubrations of a delinquent's brain fill our bars and even our residences. That is called moral complicity with the composer.

The article went on to dispute claims from O.K. Jazz that tapes of its works were bootlegs.

> The tapes in circulation now ... are the fruit of standard recording and a professional piece of work.... It is, in fact, Luambo himself who is proceeding to record and distribute these songs.

Stylistically the songs followed Franco's evolving inclination towards long, chatty pieces, built around a simple riff. The biggest offenders, 'Jacky' and 'Hélène,' wind on for more than fifteen minutes while Franco delivers his screed in a series of singsong verses alternating with a refrain. 'Jacky' takes the brunt of Franco's rage for her liaison with another man. 'Jacky, why did you do this to me?' he asks, in one of the few quotable passages. The song rapidly degenerates into a graphic discussion of who did what to whom and what Franco would like to do again. 'Hélène' continues in a similar vein with Franco's description of a woman who has stood him up once too often. She's overweight, lacks even a modicum of personal hygiene, and asks for money in advance because she doesn't know what to do in bed, he complains. Perhaps such sentiments were uttered in private conversation among friends, but never had they been expressed so publicly.

The censorship commission answered the outcry at the end of September. It banned the recordings, suspended O.K. Jazz for two months, and ordered the Un-Deux-Trois and Editions Populaires closed for the same period. Six other clubs and a shop that had publicly played the recordings were shut down for one month. President Mobutu went on the record with an official order that anyone possessing a copy of the recordings should surrender it to the proper authorities within forty-eight hours. Anyone caught after that would be punished with a year in jail and a 1,000 zaïre fine.

It is unclear whether Mobutu's heart was in it or his hand had been forced by the uproar in the press. Nevertheless, his next action fit the pattern of his dealings with the politicians. What Le Guide giveth, Le Guide taketh away. Just below the text of the president's order a bold headline announced, 'Luambo Makiadi arrested.'

Following a weekend to reflect in his cell, Franco appeared at a Kinshasa court on October 2, where he was sentenced to a fine of 2,500 zaïres and six months in prison. Most members of the band received either two- or four-month sentences. Dalienst, Ndombe, and Empompo escaped more or less unscathed. Dalienst established that he had not participated in the public performance of the songs, Ndombe had been in the middle of his short-lived exile, and Empompo was on the road with M'Pongo Love.

Shortly after the court pronounced judgement, one commentator claimed, erroneously it appears, that the president had dismissed Franco from the National Order of the Leopard. Another called for his ouster as president of the musicians' union. 'Luambo Makiadi is no longer entitled to preside over the destiny of UMUZA. For the simple reason that his presence at the head of that union freezes its activities, discredits its reputation, and compromises its existence.' And with that, the uproar subsided.

A week into his sentence, Franco was transferred from Luzumu Prison, in the province of Bas-Zaïre south of the capital, to a Kinshasa clinic. He was said to be suffering from a bad case of nerves. Near the end of October, about three weeks after they had been arrested, Franco and his musicians were all released from custody. This turn of events followed Mobutu's pattern of inflicting harsh penalties on wayward subordinates and then pardoning them in a grand gesture of magnanimity. 'It will be necessary now, and for the future, to be prudent,' Franco said from the comfort of his home, where he was reported to be recovering from the ordeal.

Prison had apparently triggered an introspective turn in the leader of O.K. Jazz. If he enjoyed a spiritual life it was an aspect of himself that he had previously chosen to keep private. His musical trifling with the public morals doubtless convinced many Zaïreans that he communed with the devil. Perhaps the outcry and detention resulting from the three banned songs sincerely moved him. He seemed, at least, to see the need to change his image. To accomplish that he publicly embraced teachings that sharply contrasted with his own immoderation. At a Friday service in mid-November, Franco joined his colleague, Verckys Kiamuangana, in converting to Islam. The two musicians adopted second names as part of the ritual: Franco would be called Abubacar Sidick; Verckys took the name Ali Omar.

Like the president of the republic, Franco had reached the peak of his power. Now it would slowly slip from his grasp. In a letter dated October 29, a month after his arrest, he resigned the presidency of UMUZA. Already he had lost 60 percent of MAZADIS with the undoing of Zaïreanization. Even his magazine *Ye!* folded for lack of newsprint. In December Franco publicly reconciled with Tabu Ley, putting the last of the year's unpleasantness behind him. He retained his wealth and his remarkable talent. They would be the keys to his future.

16
Exodus

Bantous de la Capitale, Mobutu, African All Stars,
Verckys, Koffi Olomide, and Docteur Nico, 1977–1980

Like the splendid guitar whose timbre imbued the rumba, Joseph Mulamba, the wandering 'Mujos,' inspired the music with his voice. Mulamba Pania, as he was known under authenticity, transcended the various schools, African Jazz, O.K. Jazz, and Les Bantous de la Capitale. He sang with all the great bands, bending each in his direction and stretching himself in the process. Like Franklin Boukaka's hypothetical 'Pont Sur le Congo,' Mujos bridged the chasms between countries and styles. Perhaps it's not true that he ran out of bands, but on December 26, 1977, Mujos ran out of time.

Death, thus far, had dealt a lenient hand. Approaching the end of only its third decade, the popular music of Congo and Zaïre still enjoyed the company of most of its creators. In September of 1977, Stukas Boys' lead guitarist Samunga Tediangaye died suddenly, just short of his twenty-fourth birthday. Hepatitis was said to be the cause. Like Bavon Marie Marie before him, Samunga had departed before he reached his prime. But the death of Mujos three months later took one of the music's best-known stars and contributed to the sense that the guard was indeed changing.

Little had been heard from Mujos since his final turn with O.K. Jazz in 1973. Rumors surfaced occasionally about a rebirth of African Jazz with Kabasele, Mujos, and perhaps Tabu Ley, but nothing ever happened. Toward the end of 1976 he worked briefly with Sam Mangwana and a band of older musicians called Bakolo Miziki (music masters). He ignored an invitation from Franco to return to O.K. Jazz and instead began to record new songs for Verckys's ZADIS label.

As his final year wore on, Mujos sank further into indigence and ill health. He was reported to be suffering from diabetes and heart problems. The Mobutu Sese Seko Fund had been set up within the department of culture to assist in such cases, but the president's personal contribution of 100,000 zaïres had disappeared into the bureaucracy. Tabu Ley told the press that UMUZA and SONECA had purchased an air ticket for Mujos to fly to Europe for treatment, but he died before he could use it. Despite his status as one of the music's elders, he was only thirty-six.

•

Death also stalked political men. On March 18, 1977, assassins killed the president of the People's Republic of the Congo, Major Marien Ngouabi. The murder ended eight years of revolutionary rhetoric and less radical action that had earned the president increasing criticism. He had countered his opponents with a variety of policy shifts, government shake-ups, and purges of the ruling Parti Congolais du Travail but ultimately lost the struggle.

Brigadier General Joachim Yhombi Opango emerged as the Congo's new president, ruling from an eleven-member military committee of the PCT. Although Opango had once been close to Ngouabi – he had put down the Diawara coup in which Franklin Boukaka was killed – he had been eased into political obscurity by the late president. His assumption of power appeared to be a transitional maneuver by the military committee, all the more so when the committee removed him two years later and selected the more politically astute Denis Sassou Nguesso as president.

•

In the musical realm, Brazzaville's Bantous de la Capitale still ranked among the top bands on either side of the Congo River. *Bakolo mboka*, Congolese called them, owners of the village. President Ngouabi had honored the musicians as Chevaliers (Knights) of the Order of Devoted Service to Congo (*dévouement congolais*) in 1974, and most people regarded the band as a national treasure. Les Bantous had survived the defection of some of its biggest stars, Pamelo (Pablito), Kosmos, Edo Ganga, and the others. Their departures made room for a new generation of singers, Lambert Kabako, Tchico Tchicaya, Théo Blaise Kounkou, while pushing the veterans, Essous, Malapet, Gerry Gérard, to a new level of performance. Although they toured less regularly than they had at the beginning, the musicians of Les Bantous still played as far afield as Zanzibar and Cuba.

Edouard 'Edo' Ganga

Havana in 1978 furnished the setting for the World Festival of Youth, the eleventh in a series that had begun in Moscow in 1957. An expanded version of Les Bantous was organized to be Congo's representative at the festival. As Pamelo told it, no less a fan than President Yhombi Opango asked him to rejoin his former colleagues. Edo Ganga, whose splinter group Les Nzoi had come apart, was also persuaded to go. Ganga recalled that during the course of preparations the old camaraderie began to develop once again. At the end of June 1978 the musicians flew to Oran in Algeria to board a ship bound for Cuba and July's festival. 'We rehearsed so much and got along so well that when we returned on the boat we decided to re-form Les Bantous.' Edo and Pamelo both went back to work with their former collaborators. One year short of its twentieth anniversary, Les Bantous was nearly whole again.

Pamelo's return to Les Bantous reduced the Trio CEPAKOS to a duo of Célestin and Kosmos and their backing band, Le Peuple. The latest desertions fit the pattern of setbacks the group had been forced to overcome since it began in 1972. A traffic accident in 1975 destroyed much of the band's equipment, although it provided inspiration for Kosmos's subsequent hit, 'Accident ya Peuple.' Later, several of the band left to form Orchestre Télé-Music. Nevertheless, Le Peuple with the Trio CEPAKOS gradually established itself as one of Brazzaville's better bands, built as it was around a core of newer musicians including guitarists Michel Moumpala and Denis Loubassou, and veterans like trumpet player Samy Malonga. The band made its headquarters at a Brazzaville night club called the Lumi-Congo, where it played a regular schedule of Thursday, Saturday, and Sunday gigs. By 1978, however, the band encountered financial problems. And when Pamelo returned to Les Bantous, the days of Le Peuple were numbered.

The plague of instability, as Le Peuple and Les Bantous could attest, flourished in Brazzaville as it did in Kinshasa. Music and musicians on both banks of the Congo River seemed closely attuned, despite the erection of national boundaries. Although the two governments aligned themselves on opposite sides in the cold war – Congo followed the Eastern bloc and Zaïre the West – the stormy relations of the sixties yielded to tranquil cooperation in the seventies.

With the collapse of SOCODI, Congo's state-run recording studio and pressing plant, Brazzaville's bands crossed the river to take advantage of Kinshasa's shaky but still functioning recording industry. O.K. Jazz, M'Pongo Love, Abeti, and Afrisa toured clubs and stadiums in Congo, while Les Bantous, Le Peuple, and other Brazzaville bands played Kinshasa's Type K and the Un-Deux-Trois.

Many of Brazzaville's musicians worked with bands in Kinshasa, but a few Zaïreans trekked in the opposite direction. Guitarist Dercy Mandiangu of Négro Succès and Sosoliso moved to Brazzaville in 1976, where he joined Le Peuple. Singer Tino Mwinkwa of Continental and Vévé also caught on with Le Peuple. Kwamy and Mujos both did time with Les Bantous.

The smaller Congolese capital must have seemed like an oasis of serenity after life in frenetic Kinshasa. Both cities had grown rapidly since independence, but Brazzaville contained a manageable one-third of a million residents in 1977, while Kinshasa had ballooned to nearly two million. The Congo suffered its share of economic woes but nothing of the magnitude that befell Zaïre. When all was said and done, the French still backed the CFA franc, the currency of most of France's former African colonies. The fading zaïre enjoyed no such guarantee. Still, in spite of Congo's apparent advantages, the fate of its musicians was linked to conditions in Zaïre.

'We are the victims of a lack of a studio and a [pressing] factory in the country,' Nino Malapet complained. 'To bring out records you have to go to France or Zaïre. And to be successful you need money. It's not an easy thing.' Zaïre's large population also provided a broader market for Congolese bands.

Les Bantous, Trio CEPAKOS, and the others all sold their records in Zaïre and occasionally broke onto the best-seller lists. When Zaïre's economy began to unravel, Congo's musicians suffered along with their Zaïrean brothers and sisters. Live performances could still generate a decent payday, but musicians from both sides of the river needed to look no farther than the morning's newspaper to know that they were in trouble.

•

'S.O.S. pour le disque zaïrois!' cried a headline at the end of 1978. The distress call had been heard before, but it usually signaled one critic or another's displeasure with the music's quality or the instability of the bands, an intellectual discourse on propriety. This time the alarm struck an ominous tone.

Zaïre's crumbling economy had hobbled the music business as far back as 1975 at the height of Zaïreanization. Pressing plants had slashed production for want of raw materials. Music lovers met empty shelves when they went to their favorite record shop. While Zaïreanization's undoing produced a fleeting renaissance, the music industry had been fundamentally damaged. The slowdown in record production had opened the door for an insidious new invention.

Philips, the Dutch multinational corporation that owned Kinshasa's SOPHINZA pressing plant, introduced the audio tape cassette in 1963 to battle for a share of the market with various other tape formats. A dozen years later the cassette had vanquished its principal competitor, the eight-track cartridge, and threatened the dominance of vinyl records, at least in developed countries. At first, Congo and Zaïre seemed impervious to the cassette's allure. When times were good, Kinshasa's pressing factories could supply enough records to satisfy demand on both banks of the river. Consumers with the means to do so had invested in record players. Recording studios, distributors, and retail shops all survived on vinyl.

Zaïre's censorship commission caused the first major breach of vinyl's supremacy, although it did so unwittingly. The banning of songs created immediate interest, much more than a routine release. Franco's recording of 'Chérie Bondowe' seemed to establish a precedent. Foreign pressings and bootleg cassettes of the song evaded the censors and eventually forced its acceptance. Forbidden songs from other groups circulated in the same manner.

Compared to the complexity of making a record, cassette technology was simple. Vinyl required a factory with sophisticated machines and skilled labor. Cassettes could be recorded in someone's living room as long as blank tapes were available. When Kinshasa's pressing plants slowed to a crawl in the throes of Zaïreanization, vinyl's hold on the market was broken. People wanted their music, and they would get it any way they could.

By 1976 the word 'pirate' had entered the language of the music business. *Salongo* reported on a shop operating in downtown Kinshasa that sold compilations of scarce 45 r.p.m. records from many different bands. 'The recording made is of clarity and incredible precision.' At ten zaïres ($20) a cassette of 'Chérie Bondowe' and six other banned songs from O.K. Jazz sold for slightly more than the usual eight zaïres charged for a collection of approved songs from the likes of Afrisa or Zaïko Langa Langa.

Pirating in vinyl, although technologically more difficult, also occurred, especially outside the country. Nairobi was notorious for its traffic in Zaïrean music, much of it stolen. Phonogram-Kenya, in conjunction with its sister company, Phonogram-Zaïre, and acting as Fonior's agent in East Africa, was responsible for the legal sale of most Zaïrean records. But at least one rogue pressing factory would purchase clean, single copies of legal records and remaster them for illegal manufacture. The records were released on the company's own labels without benefit to the bands or composers.

When lack of raw materials strangled production at Kinshasa's pressing plants, Zaïrean producers looked to Nairobi for help. Verckys, Bokelo Isenge, Soki Vangu, and several others began carrying master tapes to the Kenyan capital to get their music pressed onto records for import back into Zaïre. Apart from this relatively straightforward transaction, however, several Zaïrean producers engaged in a bit of piracy of their own.

The practice involved licensing of Zaïrean recordings to Kenyan middlemen for sale in East Africa. Such licenses were usually illegal because most Zaïrean producers had signed contracts with Fonior under which the Belgian firm held the exclusive right to distribute the producers' records outside of Zaïre. After collecting a large advance against future sales from the first Kenyan middleman, the Zaïrean producer would approach a second, and perhaps even a third, sell him the same music, often with a different title, and collect another advance. The Zaïrean producer would return home with the money, leaving Phonogram-Kenya, Fonior's agent, to battle the Kenyan pirates in court.

Some Zaïrean producers also listed themselves as authors of the music they were selling. On the outside chance that royalties were collected on the illegal discs, these would accrue to the producers' accounts instead of those of the legitimate composers. The victims of this nefarious business included Zaïre's treasury, because the currency involved in the pirates' transactions was usually traded on the black market; SONECA, which collected no royalties from the pirated discs; and the creators of the music, who received nothing in return for its sale.

'The problem lies in the fact that our production at home is not sufficient,' Verckys told a reporter.

> The day we succeed in flooding the Zaïrean market and selling the surplus abroad, there will be no more talk of pirate records. But as long as production is insufficient to satisfy our whole national clientele, we must expect that others will jump at the opportunity to plunder our works.

Others specifically blamed Fonior for the problem. The MAZADIS factory was old and decrepit, they charged. The few records that came out were of inferior quality. Fonior was making a lot of money from African music, why not put some back in to upgrade the factory? Bokelo Isenge insisted that 'we must re-examine the contracts binding us with Fonior which, in my opinion, are colonial-style. Because Fonior only looks after us when we are producing.'

Fonior came in for more heated criticism in October of 1978 when it announced its intention to close MAZADIS. 'More than ten thousand families live from records, and MAZADIS is the most important [record] factory in Zaïre,' stated one commentary.

> Until this point, it has operated regularly to great and general satisfaction. Thus we do not understand how, just when our country has resolutely entered the most important phase of the battle undertaken for its economic recovery, this company can be thinking about closing its doors. That Fonior chose this period to give MAZADIS the order to close its doors resembles economic sabotage.

It was not so much that they wanted to, according to company statements, but the factory could not obtain licenses to import raw materials and spare parts to keep the factory running. The zaïre was unacceptable as payment for imported items. Stable foreign currency – dollars, pounds, francs – had to be purchased from the Bank of Zaïre to complete such transactions. Without the necessary licenses, foreign currency could not be obtained. Franco, a 40 percent owner of MAZADIS, was at this point serving his time in jail for distributing obscene songs, so he was in no position to comment on his factory's closing. Lopes Neves, the factory manager, spoke for the company. 'We always had the intention of modernizing our factory by installing full stereo disc mastering lathes ... but it was put in black and white on the licenses, denial of visa and validation.'

Zaïre's record producers pointed to Fonior's earnings from Zaïrean music sold abroad. Why couldn't they use those profits to pay for operations at MAZADIS? Fonior countered that they had been doing that for the past two years and were owed nearly ten million Belgian francs. They would not continue to subsidize the factory.

SOPHINZA, the Philips-Phonogram pressing plant, experienced similar difficulties but attempted to carry on (the company's original agreement with the government had prevented its Zaïreanization). A few months into 1979, however, SOPHINZA ceased operations. Dr. Z. van Wulfften Palthe, SOPHINZA's director for many years, recalled that the crisis was largely a matter of choice on the part of the government. 'Of course there was no shortage of foreign exchange. All kinds of luxury goods were available in the shops but not one penny for raw materials and spare parts.' Nevertheless, when Franco got out of jail he kept MAZADIS going, albeit sporadically. He purchased SOPHINZA's equipment, imported raw materials when he could, and when they ran out, he melted down old records to be pressed into new ones.

Although he chose to stay out of the dispute, the president of the republic deserved much of the blame for its occurrence. Zaïreanization had been an economic disaster that could never be satisfactorily reversed. Falling prices for exports of Zaïre's copper and rising prices for its imports of foreign oil fueled the crisis further. Mobutu's government kept prices paid to rural farmers artificially low in an effort to stem the rise in urban wages. The result was a decrease in agricultural output and an increase in food imports to compensate. Debt to foreign banks that financed Mobutu's grandiose development schemes grew at an alarming rate. The government expanded the money supply to cover its budget deficits and thereby unleashed a wave of inflation that rose above 60 percent a year.

The economy was further disrupted in 1977 and again in 1978 when Zaïrean exiles living in Angola 'invaded' the former Katanga province, now known as Shaba. On both occasions Mobutu's ineffectual army had to be rescued by foreign soldiers – in the first instance Moroccans and French, and in the second French, Belgian, and American. Mobutu's help to the United States and apartheid South Africa in exacerbating civil war in Angola earned him continued assistance from Washington and the undying enmity of his neighbors.

To top it off, by nearly every reputable account the president himself was a thief. As the unchallenged leader of the party and the government, Mobutu treated the national treasury as an extension of his own bank account.

Exodus 243

According to *Wall Street Journal* reporter Jonathan Kwitny, records that 'turned up' in Belgium showed that 'Mobutu himself withdrew 364.3 million Belgian francs from the Zaïrean national bank in 1979, the equivalent of more than $13 million.' From 1977 to 1979, Mobutu and members of his family withdrew '$2.8 million in U.S. cash, $132.1 million in Belgian francs, $6.4 million in French francs, and $268,000 in Swiss francs, worth altogether some $141.6 million.' More than one observer was moved to label the Zaïrean state a 'kleptocracy.' Although he cultivated the image of father of his country, Mobutu functioned as its owner. He had become an African King Leopold II, turning Zaïre into his own personal plantation.

The dimensions of the plunder are difficult to trace and harder still to prove. Mobutu always denied the allegations. 'The legend was taken up in chorus by the organs of the press every time they needed to have a dig at me,' he told journalist Jean-Louis Remilleux.

> Everyone has finally understood the calumnious nature of the fictitious fortune which they have always attributed to me. They add together a few villas – and why not my leopard-skin hats and my canes? – to credit me with greater riches than the GNP of Zaïre. Where could I have got it from?

Nevertheless it is safe to say that as production at MAZADIS and SOPHINZA dwindled, the Mobutu fortune grew.

Like Zaïre as a whole, the performing rights society SONECA continued to suffer from institutional corruption and the economy's decline. Payment of royalties to artists ranged from slow to non-existent. In addition, SACEM, the French performing rights society, halted its payments to SONECA for the performance of Zaïrean music under its jurisdiction because SONECA hadn't paid SACEM for the performance of French music in Zaïre. This further reduced SONECA's ability to pay its member musicians. In the music industry's battle for survival, Zaïrean musicians languished at the bottom of the food chain. Only tycoons like Franco, Verckys, and Tabu Ley could muster the wherewithal to mitigate the effects of Zaïre's decline.

•

Late in 1977 Tabu Ley and Afrisa embarked on a lengthy tour of Europe and West Africa (with a brief interruption to campaign for candidates in elections back home). Concerts and recording were among the planned activities, but the trip also revealed the human side of the crisis in Congolese–Zaïrean music. In Paris the members of Afrisa encountered a budding community of

Zaïrean musicians. No less a personage than Le Grand Kalle, Kabasele Tshamala, in Paris to undergo treatment for chronic hypertension, headed the ranks of the expatriates. Although they were often on the road with Manu Dibango, Jerry Malekani and Freddy Nkounkou had called Paris home ever since the breakup of Ry-Co Jazz in 1972. Former Thu Zaina guitarist 'Jack' Pela Nsimba and Zozo Amba from Négro Succès also lived in the French capital.

Before Afrisa could get out of town, three of its players joined the ranks of Zaïrean expatriates. Bondo Gala, the bassist known as 'Bovic,' conga player Armando Ama, and drummer Seskain Molenga all disappeared in Paris. A furious Tabu Ley called them 'fugitives' in an open letter to the management of SOFRASON-Fonior aimed at keeping the trio unemployed. The following year Abeti's drummer, Boffi Banengola, deserted her band during one of its trips to Paris for recording.

For those who lacked the means to go to Europe directly, East Africa extended a hand of welcome. Ikomo 'Djo Djo' Ingange of the group Bana Modja and former O.K. Jazz guitarist Mose 'Fan Fan' Se Sengo were among the more notable Zaïreans to try their luck there. Nearer still, Brazzaville embraced returning sons like Michel Boybanda and Youlou Mabiala along with a few of their Zaïrean colleagues.

None of the émigrés made more of his new surroundings than the 'pigeon voyageur' Sam Mangwana. Mangwana's final separation from Tabu Ley had been laced with acrimony. The usual squabble over money and broken promises played itself out during the early months of 1976. Mangwana hung around long enough to fuel rumors that he would soon rejoin O.K. Jazz. He played a May date with the pop group The Black Devils and an August reconciliation concert with Dalienst, from whom he had split in the Festival des Maquisards, but he continued to take hits in the press. 'They wrote bad things about me saying I'm a stranger, I'm not really Zaïrean, I'm stupid, I'm a mercenary,' Mangwana recalled. 'And I said okay, I must show these people that Africa is big. And I left Zaïre to go to Ivory Coast [Côte d'Ivoire].'

Mangwana headed up-river for Bangui in the Central African Republic and then set out by road to Cameroon and Nigeria. Early in 1977 he arrived in Abidjan, the capital of Côte d'Ivoire, a politically stable and relatively affluent (as long as coffee and cocoa prices held up) former French colony near the center of coastal West Africa. Informed that Ivoireans would avoid records sung in Lingala, Mangwana began to tune his ear to the street French of Treichville, a residential quarter for the common people across a lagoon from Abidjan's posh downtown. He worked with a handful of local musicians,

photo by Leni Sinclair

Sam Mangwana

revving up the rumba to the speed of local tastes, and recorded an album called *Maria, Maria* which went over reasonably well. After a year, however, no great breakthrough had been won.

Meanwhile Tabu Ley and company, still unsettled from the defections of three of the band in Paris, launched a six-week tour of West Africa early in 1978. Should problems crop up again, the band had formed a committee to deal with them composed of guitarists Dizzy Mandjeku and Lokassa ya Mbongo, saxophonist Modero Mekanisi, and bass player Philo Kola. But when Afrisa reached Abidjan at the beginning of March, the committee, Modero excepted, deserted the band along with drummer 'Ringo' Moya Lotula.

'When a child grows up ... he says to himself, well now I'm grown, and now I have to do for myself, in a way, to see what will come of it,' Lokassa said, explaining why he quit. By then he had served ten years in Afrisa. Mandjeku cited different reasons.

> I noticed that Zaïrean songs that came from Kinshasa, nobody was buying them any longer.... First of all the quality was bad. These were records that had been

melted down, 45s that had been pressed again, that people sent back to the boilers. And the style, the style was very slow compared to the evolution [of pop music]. Disco and funk had started to come out, so people wanted something livelier. But we kept playing real slowly in the style we used to play in. People didn't like that music any more.

A fresh start in Abidjan looked attractive.

The four deserters assembled a new group they called Amida. At the same time they could hardly overlook the presence of Sam Mangwana in Abidjan nor could he fail to notice them. Mangwana had also seen the decline of Zaïrean music's popularity. It was the time of Nigeria's Prince Nico Mbarga and his smash hit 'Sweet Mother' with its Zaïrean-style guitars in a highlife setting recorded on modern, multi-track equipment. Both Mandjeku and Mangwana felt Zaïrean musicians needed to do something to counter this threat to their supremacy. Mangwana contacted his compatriots in Amida and began to discuss a collaboration.

Philo Kola decided to go in a separate direction, but the three others agreed with Mangwana that they should join together. The new quartet recruited another singer, Théo Blaise Kounkou, a former member of Les Bantous de la Capitale who had come to Abidjan. To round out the group, the musicians added a Cameroonian bass player named Roland M'vogo. They gave themselves an English name, the African All Stars.

The name sounded like a bit of hyperbole; still it wasn't far off the mark. All the musicians were first-rate players, and Mangwana had the name recognition from his vocal triumphs with O.K. Jazz. They enlisted the help of a Nigerian producer in Abidjan named Badmos and set about developing new material. As Dizzy Mandjeku recalled it,

> I started ... to suggest to the others that we cut out the [slow] rumba side of the beginning. Because I had noticed in clubs, because these were 45s, they only played the B side where it started with the sebene. But when they played the A side, well, there was the whole story we were telling [with the lyrics in Lingala]. People didn't understand it.

Adjusting to their perception of the marketplace, the All Stars worked out an innovative synthesis that set the polished harmonies and jazzy improvisations of the older school to the faster-paced beat of the youth bands. 'The solo guitar plays a kind of leitmotif with phrases that recur, for example three loops that repeat over and over,' Mandjeku explained. 'Our style was a little different because the figures, the harmonies that I played were not the same

Dizzy Mandjeku

as in Zaïko's style.... I took my personal style from a little of Nico's style. It was a little jazzy. I improvised.' Lokassa by this time had altered the mi-composé by leaving the standard E (mi) string alone and instead replacing the second and fourth strings, the standard B and D strings, with D strings tuned to C. The bass lightened up a bit and the drummer moved off his snare and up to the cymbals to give the rhythm section a freer, more lively feel. It was, as Mandjeku has termed it, a 'sort of new beat,' familiar, yet unusual.

With an assist from producer Badmos, the group traveled to Nigeria – where recording studios were superior to those in Abidjan – arriving in Lagos around the middle of 1978. At nine in the morning on the appointed day, the African All Stars entered EMI's studio in Apapa, across the harbor from Lagos, under the auspices of a local Badmos connection, Adios Records. Working until three the next afternoon with a short break to allow another band to use the studio, the All Stars recorded enough material for three albums – one of Mangwana's compositions, a second of Théo Blaise's work, and the third, a mixture of songs from four of the musicians.

Mangwana's songs hit the market first, released as an album entitled *Sam Mangwana et l'African All Stars*. But for all the talk of a new beat, it was an easygoing rumba that became the disc's runaway hit, 'Georgette Eckins.' According to Mandjeku, it was the last song recorded that session. The name was that of a young girl who sold the musicians fish and other food in

Abidjan. 'When we went into the studio, we didn't even have a refrain. There were only the verses. Right in the studio we came up with "I planted coco." He was very inspired, Sam was.' 'Georgette' told a simple tale of unrequited love with a tongue-in-cheek delivery that couldn't help but trigger a smile. Singing mostly in French, Mangwana resignedly recounts each attempt to win favor, and the band responds with a chronicle of defeat.

> As for me, I planted coco
>   But coco couldn't grow
> I planted yams
>   But yams couldn't grow
> I planted love
>   I harvested treason
> I planted confidence
>   I harvested disappointment
> Georgette muana mama
> You have made me very ill
> Georgette muana mama
> You are breaking my heart.

One can almost see Georgette walking past, her nose pointed toward the heavens. In the background Ringo Moya rides the high-hat in the company of Roland's insistent bass, while Dizzy and Lokassa set their guitars to shimmering like the old merengues of Docteur Nico. A small horn section colors the infectious groove, which the band sustains for nearly ten minutes. Hinting at things to come, 'Georgette' closes with a riff from the old days of Congo music that had been running around in Mangwana's head, Manuel D'Oliveira's 'Maria Tchebo.'

'Georgette Eckins,' the undisputed hit of the session, even won acceptance back home in Zaïre in spite of its *inauthentique* title. Over the long haul, however, the rest of the songs driven by the faster 'new beat' created a more lasting effect. 'Georgette's sister songs leaped to full throttle from the first crack of the cymbal. The All Stars' remake of Mangwana's 'Zela Ngai Nasala' (wait while I work), for example, sounds like it came right out of a late 1980s Paris soukous session. The other albums from the EMI session, *Les Champions* and Théo Blaise's *Zenaba*, keep up the faster pace.

The music was made more widely accessible by the frequent use of lyrics in French with a smattering of English thrown in for good measure. Following the example of Dechaud's classic 'African Jazz Mokili Mobimba,' which recited the names of places around the world, the title track from *Les Champions* named people from various walks of life, including Badmos the producer, Nigerian pop stars Sonny Okosuns, Fela, and Nico Mbarga, and even radio personality Georges Collinet, whose popular program on the French service of the Voice of America was believed to influence record sales. As the music's center gradually shifted away from Kinshasa and Brazzaville over the next few years, more and more artists would adopt the All Stars' new beat.

With the wave of enthusiasm for the All Stars mounting, the band moved their headquarters to Togo's capital, Lomé, where the cost of living was lower. Under the patronage of businessman Alhadji Albarika from next-door Benin the group fortified itself with the latest equipment and began to stage a series of concerts along the same convenient corridor from Accra to Lagos that Les Bantous de la Capitale had covered many years before. While in Ghana around the beginning of 1979, they returned to the studio – Ambassador Records in Kumasi – to record some fresh material. This session produced the group's next big hit.

'Suzana Coulibaly' possessed all the pizazz of 'Georgette' plus the added kick of the new beat. It was another Mangwana song about a woman, this time his wife, the mother of his children, who spent his hard-earned money on her boyfriends. In a new twist, the All Stars stripped the sebene down to a race between Lokassa's rhythm guitar and Ringo Moya's wood block and high-hat combination. The duo produced a mesmerizing jam that must have burned up the dance floor. 'Soukous sophistiqué,' Mangwana cries at one point, suggesting a name for the new sound seducing Africa.

As the African All Stars were riding high with 'Georgette' near the end of 1978, more Zaïrean musicians left home for what looked – from downtrodden Kinshasa at least – like the more prosperous climate of West Africa. Bopol Mansiamina from the Ya Tupas ended up in Lomé along with former members of Vicky Longomba's Lovy du Zaïre and its successor Orchestre Kara, guitarists Syran M'Benza and Pablo Lubadika. Soon after they arrived, Mangwana invited them to become All Stars.

When 'Suzana Coulibaly' followed 'Georgette' up the charts in the middle of 1979, the All Stars proved they were no one hit wonders. They had tinkered with the music and had only success to show for it. Everything looked good on the surface, but in fact the band was coming apart. After recording a final album, *Matinda*, in Lagos, Mangwana, Syran, Bopol, and Pablo went west to Abidjan, leaving Dizzy, Lokassa, and Ringo Moya behind in Lomé. Roland had already departed. Théo Blaise struck out on his own. Mangwana explained his actions in an interview at the end of August.

> If I no longer collaborate with the African All Stars, who were in fact my backup band, it's because my friends had made commitments to a man who owns instruments whose work methods were not to my taste.... Currently I'm in the process of setting up my own ensemble.

Dizzy Mandjeku was less diplomatic in a letter to the editors of *Elima*.

> At the height of our glory we dispatched Sam Mangwana to Abidjan to negotiate [pressing and distribution] with publishers there for our two latest LPs. To this day we have not received a single sengi from these works. Curiously, Mangwana preferred to take certain members of the group to live in Abidjan rather than coming to give us an account.

According to one version, the dispute boiled down to a tussle over the band's new instruments. The contract with Albarika called for the All Stars to deliver four albums a year for four years, after which the instruments would become the property of the musicians. How this would work for Mangwana, since he played no instrument, became the insoluble issue. Mandjeku recalled that it was simply a matter of philosophical differences. Mangwana wanted an informal association to record and play an occasional gig but not the expense of lodging and salaries that went with maintaining a band. Mandjeku, on the other hand, wanted a permanent group.

The African All Stars had survived for barely a year. In the space of that brief existence they recorded enough music for eight albums, scored two incontestable hits and a number of lesser ones, and created a new strain of Congo music. Equally important, they proved that Zaïrean and Congolese musicians could prosper outside the unraveling cocoons of Kinshasa and Brazzaville. Each faction tried to carry on using the All Stars name for their live shows. Dizzy Mandjeku recruited singer Nyboma Mwan Dido and guitarist Ndala 'Dally' Kimoko from Orchestre Kamalé, successor band to Lipua Lipua, bringing them to Lomé to work with his group. Mangwana played with an ever-changing lineup, including singer Lea Lignanzi of the Central African Republic and Brazzaville guitarist Michel Moumpala. Although their records continued to sell into the early eighties, the original African All Stars was finished.

•

Worsening conditions in Zaïre had only managed to weaken the music business. The music's creators and disseminators were far too resourceful to allow governmental greed and incompetence to separate them from their livelihoods. Although many chose to leave the country, many more stayed home.

The new year 1978 witnessed the opening of a brand new entertainment complex just off Avenue de la Victoire in the heart of Matonge. Vévé Centre was Verckys Kiamuangana's six-story answer to Franco's Un-Deux-Trois and Tabu Ley's Type K. The building housed shops, restaurants, and the offices of empire Vévé. A large dancing bar that could convert to a cinema hall or theater opened on the ground floor. A more intimate club for select clientele nestled discreetly three floors up. Verckys's office and private movie theater took up the fifth floor along with apartments for invited guests. And above it all, an open-air dancing bar and restaurant served up food and song into the early morning.

The demands of business had diverted Verckys's attention from music-making even more drastically than they distracted Franco. Orchestre Vévé had scarcely been heard from for more than two years. A few other bands were still under contract at Vévé, and several more, including Zaïko Langa Langa, relied on the company for promotion. Vévé studio continued to thrive as one of Kinshasa's three main places to record. ZADIS, the company's distribution arm, functioned as well, despite the current shortage of products. Added to these responsibilities was Verckys's presidency of UMUZA (he had succeeded Franco), oversight of the construction of Vévé Centre, and his constant travel to Europe and East Africa to see to the pressing of records. He had little time left for his saxophone or his band.

New faces and names also burst on the scene, among them a 22-year-old singing college student named Agbepa Mumba, who called himself Koffi Olomide. Splitting time between studies in Europe and performing in Kinshasa, Olomide managed to place ahead of the great Tabu Ley, in Elima's judgement, as best composer for 1978.

As a teenager, Olomide had made friends with some of the members of Zaïko Langa Langa, Papa Wemba in particular. He followed them through their various breakups and eventually sat in on vocals beside Wemba and Viva La Musica. His own successful string of recordings began early in 1978 with help from promoter Mfumu Muntu Bambi of Editions Parions. Backed in the studio by Viva La Musica, Olomide sang of the love of a charming woman named 'Synza.' A series of other love songs followed, 'N'Djoli' and 'Fleur Rose' among them, with Olomide backed by assorted moonlighting musicians whom he called Ba La Joie (The Joys). Delivered with Olomide's supple baritone, each song was a great success, especially among women. 'I compose all my songs relaxed, in good spirits,' he said at the time. 'The idea comes from the heart, and I improvise the rhythm and the arrangement to myself. I don't rush to release it. That's why my works don't have that slapdash feeling you find elsewhere.'

The end of the decade also produced some surprising collaborations, none more so than the alliance of Tabu Ley and Papa Wemba. Critics voiced skepticism and the public shock. Two generations and two different styles, how could they possibly mesh? On the surface the union appeared to be an artistic inspiration: the young Papa Wemba, leader of Viva La Musica, would perform beside his idol Tabu Ley in Ley's Orchestre Afrisa. But behind the scenes Wemba was said to have money problems, and his hero had agreed to help. Whatever its origins, the duo of Wemba and Ley, backed by Afrisa, played concerts around Kinshasa in June of 1979 that were generally well regarded. Dates in West Berlin, Bonn, and Brussels followed. Back in Kinshasa again, Afrisa and Viva La Musica – the latter had continued to perform without Wemba during this period – made a joint appearance. When Ley's contract with Wemba expired early the next year, the parting was less than amicable. Nevertheless, the pairing had been an artistic success, and, more importantly, Papa Wemba was once again solvent.

In another unexpected turn Tabu Ley reunited with his old friend, and sometime adversary, Docteur Nico. The road had been long and difficult for Nico since his African Fiesta Sukisa disintegrated in 1973. For the past six or seven years he had been mostly the subject of rumor and speculation, a man in his house instead of on stage. Talk of family problems and drinking made the rounds while Nico struggled to rebuild his life. From time to time a reporter would appear on his doorstep to check on the Docteur's health. Inevitably he'd be told that things were improving and that Fiesta Sukisa would soon return to some semblance of its former glory.

In 1977 Nico appeared with his former singer, Sangana, and a revamped Fiesta Sukisa for a weekly gig at a new Kinshasa club called Les Jardins Fleuris. The band cut several records at the beginning of 1978, then Nico fell ill and remained out of sight for most of the year. During an interview in November, he declared that his life as a recluse was over.

> Next year will be a year of work for me. Getting a record out is fine, but it's absolutely necessary to get on the stage. In order to do that I'm waiting for new equipment, because a great band should have instruments worthy of it, not something approximating. When they get here, I will begin to give free concerts for African Fiesta fans at my compound.

Despite the optimistic pronouncement, little more was heard from Docteur Nico until, on the last day of May 1980, he walked on stage at the Type K to accompany Tabu Ley in a reprise of their first collaboration in African Jazz. They would work together again, they announced, beginning with a grand soirée in August at President Mobutu's latest extravagance, the new $34 million Chinese-built Palais du Peuple. There, in the glittering banquet room on August 16, Docteur Nico put the rumors to rest. 'Kasanda equal to himself,' *Elima* proclaimed. He had not forgotten his old hits. His extraordinary skills survived, barely dimmed by the years of inactivity.

Docteur Nico wasn't alone in finding new life with Afrisa. For a brief period in 1980 and 1981 the band resembled a team of oldtimers retaking the field. Kwamy Munsi and Bombenga Wewando sang beside Tabu Ley and the former Maquisard Kiesse Diambu. Nico shared the solo guitar with Dino Vangu; Shaba Kahamba of Bella Bella played bass; and Empompo Loway returned to take up his sax. Afrisa's hall-of-fame lineup reaped a bonanza of free publicity.

•

Beginning with Zaïko Langa Langa's birth and the flowering of the youth bands, the seventies had orchestrated a decade of ill-fated optimism. Congo and Zaïre – especially Zaïre – seemed ready to reap the benefits of independence and stability. The euphoria generated by Zaïre 74 and the Ali–Foreman fight turned to apprehension amid the disaster of Zaïreanization. African Fiesta Sukisa reached the summit only to hit rock bottom. African Fiesta National played the Olympia and grew into Afrisa. Strong, talented women sang and danced their way into the spotlight. Franco grabbed for power and ended up in prison. As once productive pressing plants grew gradually silent, pirates appeared on the scene. Discouraged musicians took their acts on the road and adapted to new surroundings. For many artists from both sides of the river, 'the road' would lead to their renewal.

17
Paris

Franco, Pamelo Mounk'a, Bopol, Pablo,
M'Pongo Love, Kosmos, Kanda Bongo Man,
and Les Quatre Etoiles, 1979–1982

Franco, the sorcerer of the guitar, was also a business wizard. Melodies that flowed from his right brain vied with artful schemes from his left. O.K. Jazz was the channel that conducted his thoughts to fruition. At the end of June 1980, Franco's left brain was largely in charge as he and one of his senior counselors, Malambu ma Kizola, packed their bags for Brussels.

Their trip was hastened by dramatic news from the Belgian capital. The International Pelgrims Group, an industry fixture and Congo music's strongest link to the rest of the world, had collapsed. Economic recession coupled with rising prices and falling demand for records at the end of the seventies had vastly reduced profits among giants like Polygram, CBS, and Warner Elektra Atlantic. Smaller concerns like the Pelgrims Group racked up losses they couldn't sustain.

By almost any standard, outside of the record business at least, Willy Pelgrims had assembled an impressive fleet. During the best of times in the mid-seventies the Pelgrims Group comprised 2,400 employees and twenty-seven companies. The first ranks included Fonior, the flagship, and the FABELDIS pressing plant in Belgium, SOFRASON and the AREACEM pressing plant in France, and DURECO studios and pressing plant in Holland. But one by one when hard times turned up Pelgrims's companies began to go under.

Looking back, Fonior's refusal to subsidize operations at MAZADIS in 1978 may have been an indication of the company's deeper troubles. In any case there was no mistaking the situation when the Pelgrims Group announced at the end of 1979 that it was placing SOFRASON in receivership and slashing the workforce at AREACEM. Early the next year AREACEM folded, followed quickly by FABELDIS, and then in March, Fonior itself. It was unclear for the moment what would happen to the treasury of Congo music that Fonior had stashed in its vaults. But it was all too obvious that the musicians had lost an important production and distribution channel, while they gained an opportunity to forge new alliances that might better serve their interests. Franco, for one, saw the possibilities, and he and Malambu took off to Europe to set up a new company called VISA 1980.

VISA, Franco joked in English, stood for 'very important singer of Africa.' 'We founded Visa '80 in order to remain master of the distribution of our works outside the country. Because the whites who were doing it until '80 broke faith with us.' The venture got off to a rocky start when the Belgian government expelled the two Zaïreans after five days on the job for entering the country with improper travel documents. They moved on to set up shop in Paris, leaving one Madame Tingaut, a Frenchwoman with experience in the business, to run the Brussels office.

Franco signed other bands to his new label, including Viva La Musica, Empire Bakuba, and Zaïko Langa Langa, promising them new equipment and showcase tours of Europe in return for their recordings. Such collaborations met with mixed success. Belgian authorities gave Viva the boot after alleging that some of its members were trafficking in drugs. Zaïko recorded eight songs for VISA 1980, but when several of the musicians recorded songs for another producer too, Franco refused to give the promised new equipment to the band. Seeing what had happened, Empire Bakuba flatly refused to enter the studio.

Despite these initial setbacks, VISA 1980 issued the first of several 12-inch, 33⅓ r.p.m. albums – the preferred format in Europe – by O.K. Jazz, Zaïko, Viva, and a few by other artists under the banner 'Franco Présente.' The following year Franco launched a successor to VISA 1980 called Edipop (a contraction of his Kinshasa-based Editions Populaires), which became the primary label for O.K. Jazz releases over the next few years. In addition, he created two other labels in concert with the French publisher Nana Music, Le Passeport and Choc Choc Choc, and eventually established a music publishing arm in Brussels called African Sun Music. When Malambu ventured to ask why so many labels, Franco simply answered, 'Let me do it. I know what I'm doing.' Franco's two main rivals, Tabu Ley and Verckys Kiamuangana, also moved to take advantage of Fonior's demise, Ley with his Genidia label and Verckys with Evvi.

The perpetual lure of Paris drew personalities of every stripe. Its budding community of Zaïreans joined a clutch of would-be Steins and Hemingways and hosts of habitués from France's former colonies. By the time Franco and Malambu showed up, Eddy Gustave was a regular. Gustave had left his home on Guadeloupe in the French Antilles in 1960 and gone to Paris to study chemistry. He loved listening to jazz, especially Charlie Parker, and had learned to play the saxophone. He played his horn to pay his school fees, but music soon consumed him.

Gustave started a band that performed in Paris and made occasional tours of neighboring countries. Around 1976 he opened a record shop near the Père Lachaise Cemetery to sell the music that he liked, much of it Caribbean and African. By 1978 he had moved into the production side of the business with his Société Eddy'Son Consortium Mondial. Eddy'Son, literally Eddy sound or Eddy's sound, also produced a pun in the form of Edison, the inventor of the phonograph. Consortium mondial, worldwide consortium, reflected aspirations rather than reality. The logo for his label, Disques Sonics, featured an astronaut in orbit with an arm load of records, hurling them frisbee-like toward the earth. Record jackets bore the slogan, 'Une bonne musique/ Un bon son/ C'est l'affaire d'Eddy'Son.'

Gustave smelled a market for African music and set out on a search for talent. 'At the beginning in Paris, there were very few [African] musicians,' he explained. 'If you wanted to find a group that was really functioning well, you had to go to Africa.' Nevertheless, he landed one of his earliest successes with a phone call. Gustave had been impressed by what he'd heard of the African All Stars on records that had shown up in Paris. In 1979, just after the All Stars split, he placed a call to Abidjan to arrange for Sam Mangwana, Syran M'Benza, Bopol Mansiamina, and Pablo Lubadika to fly north at his expense for a recording session.

In Paris in September the quartet went into the studio with a Gustave-led horn section and a session drummer to remake 'Georgette Eckins' and 'Suzana Coulibaly' along with six other Mangwana compositions from the All Stars repertoire, enough material for two albums. The new 'Georgette' captured much of the feel of the original, albeit with slightly altered horn charts and no mention of the African All Stars. 'From Zaïre to the Antilles with a stop in Abidjan and Paris,' Mangwana says at one point in the sebene, effectively tracing the route Congo music was presently taking. 'Suzana' fared less well

Eddy Gustave

in the remake, from the title's altered spelling ('Souzana Koulibali') to the overall sluggishness of the performance. The sebene in particular fails to generate the spark Lokassa and Ringo Moya had produced. Still the Eddy'Son versions picked up a sizeable share of the European and American market that the West African-released originals had missed. And more Zaïrean musicians had found a way to Paris.

'Almost all the musicians I went and got from Africa were working there,' Gustave said,

> but their salaries there were very low. They didn't make much money. But when they came to Paris, the sessions were pretty well paid. Not one of them wanted to go back. Almost all of them stayed in Paris.... Ultimately, I didn't have to go get a whole group. I could bring over one good singer, one good guitarist, and I could have the ones who were already here play [with them].

Gustave and his like-minded competitors usually provided air fare and expenses for artists coming from Africa. Each musician would be paid per recording session, with the star of the work, Sam Mangwana for example, receiving royalties based on record sales. Each composer was also supposed to be paid royalties for the performance of his songs.

Gustave signed Théo Blaise Kounkou, another of the African All Stars, to re-record his compositions from the band's *Zenaba* album plus two additional albums of new music. But his biggest catch was another Congolese singer, the former Pablito now Pamelo M'Bemba. Pamelo's three-year reunion with Les Bantous de la Capitale had begun to go sour. Upon hearing of the success of Mangwana and Kounkou, Pamelo decided to fly to Paris to see what he could do. He had met Gustave during one of Gustave's talent scouting visits to Brazzaville; Eddy'Son had packaged and distributed a compilation of his hits with Les Bantous. So when Pamelo arrived in Paris in 1981, he went straight to the offices of Eddy'Son.

By the time Pamelo arrived, Gustave's little black book bulged with the names of African musicians looking for a gig. He hooked Pamelo up with another Congolese, Ignace Nkounkou, better known as 'Master Mwana Congo,' a former lead guitarist with Orchestre Mando Négro Kwala Kwa who had been in Paris since 1977. The two friends from Brazzaville began to rehearse Pamelo's newest compositions in the company of Pablo Lubadika, who played rhythm guitar, drummer Domingo Salsero from the Central African Republic, and a number of other session musicians. After a couple of weeks of preparation, the musicians went into the studio to record the tracks for Pamelo's Paris debut album.

During the course of their discussions in Brazzaville and Paris, Gustave had urged Pamelo to adopt a more distinctive name. 'He said Pamelo is fine, but something needs to be added,' Pamelo recalled. 'I spent a couple of days thinking about it, and I came up with Mounk'a. Mounk'a is a Bateke name ... that is to say, glory.' It was a word he had previously used in a song, 'Alléluia Mounk'a,' with the Trio CEPAKOS.

Around the middle of the year Eddy'Son released *L'Argent Appelle L'Argent* by Pamelo Mounk'a. The four-song album sprang from the Bantous school of rumba, nothing flashy, just solidly professional music that caught the ear and set feet to shuffling toward the dance floor. The title track alone made the album a runaway hit. 'Money attracts money,' Pamelo complains in French and Lingala, singing a truth most of his audience knew all too well.

> I go to the bank
> Where I am a client
> To ask for credit
> From that to become rich
> But they complicate things
> Because I have no money
> Oh, if I were rich
> There would be no problem.

Borrowing touches of disco and zouk, Domingo paces the tune with the sizzle of cymbals and a bass drum's steady thump thump. Master Mwana Congo swaps licks with a chorus of horns as the sebene simmers and stews. In the case of 'L'Argent Appelle L'Argent,' music attracted money, and it set the stage for a sequel.

Samantha came out at the end of the year, a brilliant green double-fold package that pictured Pamelo waving from the driver's seat of a fancy car and proclaimed him 'No. 1.' The music seconded the notion. Pamelo had returned with a head full of gentle melodies, and he voiced them with unwavering aplomb. 'She's only my secretary' ('Ce N'est Que Ma Secretaire'), he pleads in the face of rumors of another woman in his life. 'Don't be jealous/ You are my love.'

'Buala Yayi Mambu' (this place has a lot of problems), a largely instrumental piece, included brief passages sung in Kikongo that discuss how the country (presumably he meant Congo) revolves around money. On the title track Pamelo sings of love:

> Samantha,
> Pretty Samantha, Hindu treasure
> ...
> Your name comes from historic Asia
> You conquered me child of Africa.

Pablo and Master Mwana Congo play a return engagement on guitars with Lea Lignanzi of the Central African Republic backing Pamelo on vocals. The group is joined by a Cameroonian duo, saxophonist Jimmy N'vondo and his trumpet-playing partner Fredo Ngando, better known as 'Tete Fredo.' These two would grace nearly every Paris session of note in the years to come.

Samantha took off in pursuit of the sales that *L'Argent* had already racked up. Figures of any sort are difficult to come by; reliable ones have never appeared. Those who have ventured an educated estimate say that sales in the range of 5,000 copies were the era's break-even point. For an African record, sales above 20,000 would have been considered an unqualified hit. Judging from the reaction to *L'Argent* and *Samantha*, both were hits many times over. On the strength of their two hot records Pamelo Mounk'a and Eddy Gustave became leading figures of the rapidly developing Paris scene.

•

Bopol Mansiamina

Eddy Gustave's importation of remnants of the African All Stars helped another producer taking the plunge in Paris, (Charles Pierre) Loukelo Menayame of Kinshasa's Editions La Musette, who introduced himself to Europe as Loukelo Samba. Loukelo signed Bopol Mansiamina to his Star Musique label early in 1980 for an album called *The Original Innovation* (actually recorded in Togo), also known by its lead track, 'Déception Motema.' The work sold well enough to warrant another try. Next time out Loukelo teamed Bopol with a little-known singer named Baba Ley Assaka for the second of what was to become a series of albums featuring different artists entitled *Innovation*. The second album, called volume one, contained a single gem, 'Pitié, Je Veux La Reconciliation' (take pity on me, I want reconciliation). 'Pitié' was enough to send the album streaking up the sales charts.

For subsequent volumes Loukelo optimistically dubbed his session musicians Orchestre Mode Succès and developed stronger material. Volume 2/5, known by its opening song 'Chérie Makwanza,' featured an obscure guitarist named Julios Lukau and six solid tracks that packed the cumulative wallop of a Jane Fonda workout. Bopol and Assaka returned to the series in 1981 with volume three, known for the hot '(Tu m'as déçu) Marie-Jeanne' (you have deceived me Marie-Jeanne), and volume four, 'Elisa Kina Kimbwa,' more songs on the vicissitudes of love from the male perspective.

These early *Innovation* releases were marked by extraordinarily accomplished drumming – the African All Stars' Ringo Moya on *The Original Innovation* and an uncredited series of session drummers on the others. In Bopol's case the rhythm guitar rises to solo status and he and the drummers re-create some of the same fire that Lokassa and Moya set on the African All Stars' 'Suzana Coulibaly.' Nearly every song – many written by Loukelo under the pseudonym L.M. Kiland – fashions a relentlessly uptempo dance groove, another legacy of the All Stars' success. Less laudable is the incursion of a squeaky synthesizer onto a couple of tracks, an ominous harbinger. On the whole, however, Loukelo's *Innovation* series was an artistic and commercial success.

•

The African All Stars connection extended further still, to another new production company called International Salsa Musique. The venture's founder, Richard Dick, came to Paris from his native Togo in the late seventies and began to produce records soon after his arrival. Like Eddy Gustave, Richard Dick relied on Paris-resident African musicians to back his featured artists. Noting the success of *L'Argent Appelle L'Argent*, Dick had tried unsuccessfully to lure Pamelo away from Eddy'Son. His luck was better with the bassist from Sam Mangwana's troupe, Pablo 'Porthos' Lubadika.

Early in 1981, through the magic of multi-track recording, Pablo laid down the bass and three guitar parts – alongside additional guitar licks from Master Mwana Congo, Lea Lignanzi's vocals, the drums of Domingo Salsero, and a couple of horns – for a four-song album of his own compositions called *Ma Coco*. Pablo's new work delivered the latest increment in the music's evolution, a *ménage à trois* of old-school musicianship, the African All Stars' faster-paced new beat, and the repetitive guitar phrasing of Kinshasa's youth bands. The music aimed below the waist, and it succeeded famously.

As *Ma Coco* emptied record racks and exhausted dancers, the International Salsa Musique stable, which included artists from both West and central Africa, came to the attention of Chris Blackwell, owner of Island Records, the label with the lock on Jamaican reggae. Island's executives, with an eye to expanding their label's reach, struck a deal with Richard Dick to license some of his African music productions. Their first release was a 12-inch single of Pablo's 'Bo Mbanda' (rivalry), one of the hottest tracks from *Ma Coco*. Congolese and

Zaïrean musicians and their fans were ecstatic. After nearly a quarter-century reign as the king of African pop, Congo music would get the worldwide exposure that only a major label could provide. And not just any label but the label of Bob Marley, Jimmy Cliff, and Toots and the Maytals. The outlook for mainstream acceptance looked more hopeful than ever.

As 1981 wound to a close, Island released 'Madeleina,' a second 12-inch single from *Ma Coco*, and an album compilation of International Salsa Musique artists entitled *Sound D'Afrique*. The following year a second compilation of songs from Pablo and Richard Dick's other artists appeared. Fishing for a title, the album's producers hit upon the same name that had occurred to Sam Mangwana as he sang of 'Suzana Coulibaly.' Soukous.

'I sat with Richard Dick in the foyer of Island Records before the release of *Sound D'Afrique II* trying to find a title for the thing,' recalled Ben Mandelson, a consulting producer on the project. 'We discussed *bobina* [dance] and other such Lingala possibilities. Going nowhere. I asked Richard what was the local name for this stuff, and he said "soukous." There was the title.' It was a bit of a stretch. *Sound D'Afrique II 'Soukous'* included music from Mali and Cameroon alongside that of Congo and Zaïre. Nevertheless, in his liner notes Mandelson redefined the term to be more inclusive.

> Soukous is a dance music. Soukous is the body movement which goes with the dance music. Soukous is a word understood throughout French-speaking Africa (the source of this album). It simply means: going out, checking the music, dancing and, cool or passionate, having the Best Time.

Meanwhile Island's executives, apparently ignorant of Congo music's broad popularity, signed their first African artist, Sunny Ade, a practitioner of a style known as juju which had scarcely been heard of outside its country of origin, Nigeria. Unlike Congo music, which carried no ethnic baggage, juju was closely identified with the Yoruba people among whom it developed. With Island's heavy promotion, juju would make temporary inroads among Westerners looking for relief from Top Forty rock, but it lacked the enormous following in Africa and among Africans in the West that routinely produced hits for Congolese and Zaïrean artists. Congo music's proven appeal could have provided Island with solid core support from which to gradually expand sales into other markets just as it had done with reggae from its base of Jamaican fans. Nevertheless, all the benefits of major label affiliation that Congolese and Zaïrean musicians hoped would come their way fell instead to the obscure Sunny Ade. While the *Sound D'Afrique* albums garnered good reviews and rang up sales in spite of a lack of promotion, Island abandoned the music leaving only the name soukous as the legacy of its dalliance.

•

Despite the rebuff from Island, Congo music – or soukous as it was rapidly becoming known in the West – continued to attract Paris-resident entrepreneurs who believed in the music's artistic merit and its potential for producing profits. None were more enthusiastic boosters than the French actress and her Greek suitor who entered the music business as proprietors of Safari Ambiance. Colette LaCoste modeled for magazines and sang and acted in French films and theater. Charles Maniatakis loved to sing but earned a living in his family's tradition of dealing in antiques. The two met as teenagers while performing in a theater in Paris, and their mutual attraction eventually led to marriage.

During a visit to friends in West Africa in the early seventies, LaCoste and Maniatakis were captivated by the music they heard. Several more visits only enhanced its allure, so they decided to put out a record of their favorite pieces. With that initial offering, *Safari Ambiance* volume one, containing six African tracks plus two by LaCoste herself, their production and distribution company was born. Safari Ambiance, as the new enterprise was called, built slowly on the work of early signees like Cameroonian keyboard player Eko Roosevelt and Boncana Maiga, a Malian flute player with a hankering for Cuban music. Label names, Dragon Phénix and Safari Sound, were introduced.

Word of mouth spread the news to the point that by 1978 Safari Ambiance had become well known among African musicians. One of the company's first artists to come from the banks of the Congo River was Brazzaville guitarist Fidèle 'Sammy' Massamba. A fan of the music of black America, Massamba had come to Europe in the early seventies as a member of a touring Congolese gospel group, Les Cheveux Crépus (literally, the woolly hairs). Once in Paris, Massamba decided to stay. He played with a number of bands, eventually winding up in the company of Eko Roosevelt in a group called Dikalo. The two found their way to Safari Ambiance, where Massamba became the house arranger.

With the talented Massamba and a variety of other artists on board, Safari Ambiance was well positioned to catch the wave of enthusiasm for African music that was building in the West in the early eighties. All the more so because Zaïrean singer M'Pongo Love knocked on the door looking for a contract. M'Pongo's career had been one of steady improvement since her debut in 1976. Avoiding the bars in favor of the show style of presentation, she performed periodically at Kinshasa's larger venues and toured within and outside of Zaïre with her Orchestre Tcheke Tcheke Love. But as conditions worsened in Kinshasa, M'Pongo followed her colleagues to Paris. 'Having begun in Zaïre and been celebrated throughout Africa, it was to be expected that I would come to Paris for an international career,' she explained diplomatically.

M'Pongo made her first recording for Safari Ambiance at the end of 1979, a seven-song album released early the next year entitled *La Voix du Zaïre*. The record did reasonably well, especially in Zaïre, but the 'international career' M'Pongo sought would not materialize for another year. Meanwhile she resumed her schedule of live performances back home in Africa.

In mid-1980 she broke with Empompo Loway, her mentor and artistic director, who had taken on a new protégée, singer Vonga Aye. Four years into a successful career, M'Pongo seemed able to take care of herself. 'I owe my success to my talent, my work, and to the organization that I have surrounded myself with,' she said. 'Add to that Lady Luck, who continues to help me, and the unconditional support I enjoy from my fans. Still, I don't feel I have totally succeeded. I will only be satisfied when I reach certain goals I have set for myself.'

In the spring of 1981, following a number of appearances in Sweden, M'Pongo returned to Paris and Safari Ambiance with the makings of a new album. 'Her voice was much better on the second record,' LaCoste said. 'I had a friend who sang, who was an opera singer, who gave her [lessons], who made her work a little bit. And she was a quick study. And on the second record her voice really blossomed.' Sammy Massamba arranged the music and directed a band composed of studio musicians and members of Orchestre Tcheke Tcheke Love as M'Pongo recorded the tracks for *Femme Commerçante* (businesswoman). This was to be her breakthrough. The album's striking cover said simply 'M'Pongo Love,' M'Pongo in pink and Love in white, next to an alluring close-up of her face radiating from a black background. The cover by itself must have sold thousands, but when the record hit turntables there was no stopping it.

The six-song album mixes gentle rumbas and faster-paced soukous as M'Pongo's voice, singing mostly in Lingala with a few lines of French, more than lives up to LaCoste's accolades. The title track, an uptempo homage to Zaïrean women, features a rousing sax-driven sebene by a talented but uncredited substitute for Empompo. 'Déception d'Amour,' with its slippery guitar runs and bold brass charts, and 'Trahison' (betrayal) begin as rumba ruminations on love and duplicity before shifting into high-gear dance jams.

The sparkling 'Mbele-Mbele' (perhaps, perhaps) offers a beautiful guitar refrain. Reaction to the album was overwhelmingly positive both at home and in Europe and America. It had to have been one of Safari Ambiance's best-sellers. But sales or no sales, the album was a masterpiece.

Shortly after M'Pongo Love signed on, another singer from the opposite side of the Congo River came calling at Safari Ambiance. Côme 'Kosmos' Moutouari had resigned as leader of Brazzaville's Orchestre Le Peuple in early 1980 as the group continued to struggle following Pamelo's return to Les Bantous two years earlier. Later in the year Kosmos flew to Paris at the suggestion of his brother, Pierre Moutouari, who had already cut a record at Safari Ambiance. LaCoste and Maniatakis liked his voice and charming demeanor, and they agreed to record him.

The first effort by Kosmos ranked with the best of the early crop of Paris productions. Known by its lead track, 'Kamani Mado,' the six-song album was a product of collaboration between Kosmos and Sammy Massamba. The two co-wrote most of the songs; Massamba arranged the music, played guitar, and directed the session band.

The album offers four love songs, but apart from the standard-fare lyrics it was more varied musically than most recordings of the period. From *Kamani Mado*'s bubbly intro on the title track the rumba gives way to Kosmos's ballad-style lead into 'Edith' backed by piano and synthesizer. 'Melia' features a brief percussion jam and snatches of rock guitar. Kosmos purrs on 'Ata Ndele' (not Adou Elenga's song of the same name), his ample tenor at its warm, sexy best. 'Ebandeli ya Mossala' (sic) (the start of work) presents a surprising reworking of one of his earliest and most famous compositions into a fresh reggae version. Someone, Massamba perhaps, slides into the sebene scat singing in unison with his guitar, and then the song vaporizes into an ethereal conjunction of keyboards and rhythm section. 'Music is a job of constant research,' Kosmos told *Bingo* magazine.

> In creating this album I wanted to interest an international audience. I think I've succeeded, because the reggae version of 'Ebandeli ya Mossala' achieved enormous success abroad. On the other hand, the Congolese were shocked. They had never imagined such a change.

●

Change and experimentation with an international outlook defined the Paris scene in the early eighties. Along with Congolese and Zaïreans, musicians from other French-speaking former colonies began to show up. Antillean guitarist Jacob Desvarieux had already come to the French capital by way of Senegal. Cameroonian hornsmen Fredo Ngando and Jimmy N'vondo were becoming fixtures in the recording studios, while their countryman Manu Dibango was in and out of town, often in the company of members of the old Ry-Co Jazz who had spent time in the Caribbean. Musicians from Senegal, Côte d'Ivoire, Mali, and Togo began to arrive, all in search of better means of production and promotion and the break that would make them international stars.

Still, the major record companies failed to take notice. For the moment at least they ceded the Paris scene to the expanding circle of independent producers who eagerly offered financing and marketing, albeit on a limited scale. Just as Ngoma and Loningisa had done in Kinshasa at the music's beginning, Paris production houses like Eddy'Son and Safari Ambiance fostered a collaboration among musicians and a flowering of experimentation and creativity. Music that withered in Kinshasa and Brazzaville was reborn in Paris.

•

David Ouattara Moumouni, a bus conductor in his youth in Abidjan, came to Paris in 1969. He sold Renaults at a car dealership on the Champs Elysées and saved his money for the day he might devote himself to his first love, music. By the mid-seventies he had opened a record shop where he sold a mixture of French variety music, Jamaican reggae, and the funk and R&B of black America. Finding it difficult to procure African records, especially the popular works from Congo and Zaïre, Ouattara decided in 1981 to produce his own. A friend, hearing of Ouattara's search for suitable talent to record, introduced him to a young singer from Zaïre named Kanda Bongo.

Kanda, a dapper, gap-toothed dynamo, had been in Paris for nearly two years working odd jobs to support himself while trying to restart his singing career. Born in 1955 in Bandundu along the banks of the Kasai River 150 miles northeast of Kinshasa, he had gone to the capital shortly after Zaïre's independence. There he began to sing with school friends and in neighborhood groups. He won his first professional job around 1976 singing beside Soki Dianzenza in Dianzenza's resurrected Bella Mambo.

Another musician who turned up in Paris had also played in Bella Mambo. His name was Yancomba Dibala, known by his nickname, 'Diblo.' Like Kanda, Diblo had been born in the provinces – in his case Kisangani – and come to Kinshasa as a youth. He learned to play guitar while still a schoolboy from

Ouattara Moumouni

Les Grands Maquisards' soloist, Mageda Nsingi. Diblo began his professional career with a brief tour as a member of the 1973 version of Bombenga Wewando's Vox Africa. He worked next in a youth band called Ifanza before moving on to join Bella Mambo around the same time as Kanda Bongo.

Instability seemed to shadow Bella Mambo's leader, Soki Dianzenza. After less than a year, with the inevitable tensions mounting, Kanda, Diblo, and some of the other musicians broke away from the younger Soki to form Orchestre Bana Mambo (the children of Bella Mambo) at the end of 1976. With Kanda as its leader and backing from a Kinshasa businessman, Bana Mambo stayed together for two years. The group performed in Kinshasa's nightspots and recorded an occasional 45 before finally breaking up during a disastrous tour of Uganda near the end of Idi Amin's horrific reign.

Back in Kinshasa in the middle of 1979, Kanda and Diblo joined Bella Bella under the again reunited Soki brothers, but their time in the group was short. Before the year was out, Diblo sold his guitar and bought a plane ticket to Brussels. Soon afterward, Kanda flew to Paris.

By the time Kanda Bongo was introduced to Ouattara Moumouni in 1981, Diblo had also made his way to Paris. When Ouattara and Kanda struck a deal to make a record, Kanda turned to his old friend and a few other musicians, including session drummer Domingo Salsero, to back him. The resulting album, *Iyole*, released on Ouattara's new Afro Rythmes label, introduces Kanda as Kanda Bongo Man. It was the first production outside of Africa for all three principals, and their inexperience shows. Kanda's voice shines through, but the songs lack fire. Diblo has yet to perfect his talent for developing an engaging riff. Some pressings mislabel the album's tracks. In spite of the rough spots, *Iyole* is notable for its economical instrumentation and unrelenting speed. The stripped-down band – three guitars, bass, and drums – cranks the tempo up to the level Julios Lukau set with *Chérie Makwanza*. Only the polish is lacking.

A second effort in 1982 called *Djessy* shows strong improvement. Perhaps it was a function of experience or maybe the presence of veteran Bella Bella guitarist Shaba Kahamba, but this time the band sounds tight. Harmonizing voices enrich Kanda's luscious timbre. Diblo attacks with confidence, his lead meshing seamlessly with Shaba's steady accompaniment. As before, the tempo is quick, but the melodies seem more agreeable, the arrangements far more interesting. *Djessy* and its predecessor heralded better times for Kanda and Diblo. Both began to get calls to work on other projects. The Paris scene was expanding rapidly. Ouattara's Afro Rythmes had produced two new stars and secured its own presence in the process. And like his competitors Eddy Gustave, Loukelo Samba, and Richard Dick, Ouattara would go on to profit from the demise of the African All Stars.

Following their remake of All Stars' hits for Eddy'Son, the Sam Mangwana wing of the group – Mangwana, Bopol Mansiamina, Syran M'Benza, and Pablo Lubadika – shuttled back and forth between Paris and the Abidjan–Lomé corridor. They played concerts and recorded together as International Sam Mangwana for Mangwana's new production company, Système Art Musique (SAM). *Maria Tebbo*, the most successful of three albums produced by this formation, came out in the middle of 1980 featuring an update of Adou Elenga's recording of Manuel D'Oliveira's 'Maria Tchebo.' This is the song alluded to at the end of 'Georgette Eckins.' Mangwana changed the title's spelling, added some lyrics in English and French, and turned it into a fourteen-minute dance marathon.

Bopol sat out the session – probably because of work on his own projects with Loukelo – so Pablo doubled up on bass and rhythm guitar, and a moonlighting Sammy Massamba came in to play *mi-solo* guitar. Another notable presence was Denis Hekimian, a Frenchman of Armenian descent who

Diblo Dibala

pioneered the use of the drum machine and became a sought-after session drummer. In keeping with the 'international' in International Sam Mangwana, the album's B side contained 'Tchimurenga Zimbabwe,' in honor of the people of Zimbabwe who had just won their independence after a long civil war against white-minority rule, and 'Bana ba Cameroon,' children of Cameroon.

Maria Tebbo added to the already considerable body of hits bearing the name of Sam Mangwana. By 1981, however, after three albums, the group International Sam Mangwana began to fizzle out. All but Mangwana had decided to settle in Paris. Bopol was in the middle of recording volumes three and four of Loukelo's *Innovation* series, while Pablo put the finishing touches on *Ma Coco*. Syran busied himself with session work and developed solo projects.

Meanwhile down in the Togolese capital of Lomé, the Dizzy Mandjeku wing of the African All Stars followed a similar if less spectacular script. Dizzy, Ringo Moya, and Lokassa ya Mbongo played live dates and did session work at Lomé's state-run recording studio with replacements Nyboma Mwan Dido and Dally Kimoko. But as Nyboma himself put it, quoting a Lingala proverb, 'The fish go where there's water,' and the waters of Paris looked inviting. At the urging of Syran and Bopol, Nyboma moved north in the early months of 1982.

'Right away, right when we got here, we had a producer who knew us from Africa,' Nyboma recalled. 'That was Ouattara.' According to Syran, Ouattara called him.

> He said, 'Okay, I want you, Bopol, Nyboma, and you find someone else, I want you to make a record for me.' So we thought of Wuta Mayi, who was with Franco. We said Wuta Mayi can be the fourth.

Wuta Yundula Mayanda had been known as Blaise Pasco during his early career alongside Bopol in Papa Noël's Bamboula, Rossignol's revived Rock'a Mambo, and Orchestre Continental. When Continental broke up in 1974, Bopol had joined Tabu Ley's Afrisa, and Wuta caught on with Franco's ensemble of singers. Using the stage name Wuta Mayi, he sang with O.K. Jazz for eight years until health problems compelled him to come to France for medical treatment. When his three friends from Kinshasa invited him to record with them, Wuta Mayi decided to stay in Paris.

The quartet's 1982 debut on Ouattara's Afro Rythmes label introduced them as '4 Grandes Vedettes de la Musique Africaine' (four great stars of African music), only a minor exaggeration. Each was surely an accomplished musician with a distinguished pedigree. Nyboma's work in front of Bella Bella, Lipua Lipua, and Kamalé had made him a household name in Kinshasa. The *Innovation* releases had introduced Bopol to an international audience. If Syran and Wuta were less well known, it wasn't for lack of talent. Their contributions were simply less obvious, their names clustered in the supporting credits behind the likes of Vicky or Franco. With their Afro Rythmes debut, the four 'grandes vedettes' arrived at equal rank.

As a musical work the album broke no new ground. Its four songs, one composition by each member, were pleasing enough, with the beat accelerated in the manner of the African All Stars. The most engaging song, 'Mama-Iye-Ye,' is an exemplary remake of Nyboma's 'Mbuta,' originally recorded during his days with Bella Bella. With a new title, faster beat, altered lyrics, and smoother production, the song assimilates easily into the age of soukous. The album was Ouattara's best production to date. His use of horn solos and ensembles adds color and variety that his earlier recordings lack. The overall sound wears smooth and clean.

Beyond their ability to conceive pleasant melodies and appealing dance grooves, the four stars set a new standard for cooperation and partnership. Figuring that the prime source of conflict among musicians back home was a lack of freedom, the quartet fashioned a looser-knit relationship. Each would be free to pursue his own solo projects while owing allegiance and assigning priority to the group. 'That's freedom, that's democracy,' Bopol declared.

> We did it this way because before in Zaïre, you know, like for example in O.K. Jazz you couldn't accompany one of Rochereau's musicians. But we said to ourselves there's no point. Music is not a football team. It's for everyone. That's why you need the freedom to make it.

By removing one of the greatest sources of conflict – money being the other – the four hoped to foster a more enduring relationship. Each recorded his own solo albums, always in the company of one or more of the others. And each played on the sessions of other artists recording in Paris. Although they wouldn't officially adopt the name 'Les Quatre Etoiles' (the four stars) for another year and a half, the four musicians were laying the groundwork for a successful collaboration.

•

If freedom eased the stress of belonging to a group, it became a source of conflict between artists and producers. Paris producers, like their counterparts in Africa, wanted exclusive, long-term contracts with their most popular musicians. It they were going to invest money to record and promote someone, they wanted a degree of loyalty in return. Why, they reasoned, should they develop an artist only to have another producer reap the benefits on a later project? 'We created the look of the record jacket,' said Charles Maniatakis, 'because people weren't interested [in doing that] in Africa.... We were the first to make a real good recording with 24 tracks, big [record jacket], a poster and all that.' They sent materials touting the stars of Safari Ambiance all over the world, but Maniatakis and LaCoste felt the artists failed to appreciate their efforts.

'African musicians are not serious,' Ouattara complained.

> For example, when they're looking for work, for such a long time, and they don't find any work. You call him one day, you say, 'Come over. What do you want? Do you want some work? Okay then, come and work with me.' He

comes in, and he's happy right away. But when he starts to make it, it's all over. He forgets you right away. He's gone. He's off to do business on his name. But you're the one who gave him his name.

Eddy Gustave agreed with his colleagues. 'We don't have any structure in the [African] music world.' The musicians 'don't obey the same rules as a Westerner, as a French person. They play a little bit here, it's great. Then they'll go play the same thing on another record with another group. It's no big deal.'

Musicians, on the other hand, lob the 'unserious' charge back at the producers. Wuta Mayi outlined his gripe with an example of a fictitious producer.

> Say he sells 10,000 copies. Why not pay author's rights and mechanical rights on all 10,000 copies to SACEM [the French performing rights society]? He goes to SACEM, and he declares, for example, 6,000 copies were pressed. There's one bad thing. Sometimes a producer will tell you, 'Hey, your record is really selling well.' And then when it comes to figuring out how much he owes you, 'Ah, it didn't sell very well.' Sometimes the record comes out here in France, 'Oh, it didn't sell very well,' and the man has sold thousands and thousands of cassettes in Africa.... Those people are not serious.

Pamelo Mounk'a resolved some of his claims against Eddy'Son in a novel way.

> At one point I was even forced to go to a car dealer and buy a car in the name of Eddy'Son. Fortunately for me, where I bought the car, the marketing director had been a cabaret singer in France. He understood what was happening. He said, 'Give me the address of your producer.' As [proof] he asked me to bring in my records. When he saw the record jacket he said, 'Oh, well, it's true you're a singer.' And then I went to Eddy'Son, and I asked him to write me out a promissory note. That's where I had him. Two weeks later I had the car. It ended up that when they saw the bill at Eddy'Son, and Eddy'Son resisted, he was forced to pay. Because the car, in fact, when the car was ready, the marketing director sent it to Antwerp and the car came [by ship] to Brazzaville.

The accusations and recriminations recalled tensions of an earlier era when Léopoldville's recording studios launched the music's stars and deflected their claims of exploitation. And as it happened in those early days, African artists in Paris required the help of producers to get themselves established. The antagonists' bonds of need and antipathy would hold throughout the early eighties.

Provoked by problems at home and encouraged by the success of Sam Mangwana, M'Pongo Love, and the others, migration became a contagion in the early eighties. Many Congolese and Zaïrean musicians turned up in Abidjan following the path of the African All Stars. Others went directly to Paris. Nearly every Zaïrean or Congolese band that toured in Europe lost at least one member to the growing population of guests that stayed.

Back home in Africa, however, the music made in Paris was accepted only grudgingly. At first, said Bopol, 'they turned up their noses at it.' Some of his records sold all right while others were largely ignored. 'When you put in good words, even if it's a little fast, they buy it. Because in Zaïre, the issue in Zaïre when they listen to a song, words are the most important. What's important is what you're saying in a song.' Diblo observed a similar resistance to his music among the people at home. 'It's beginning to be accepted now. Before, you know, it was difficult. Now it's beginning to be accepted. And I'm sure that later, even those who are still in Zaïre will do as we do. They'll follow us.'

•

As more musicians settled in Paris, their old works returned to the news. The various courts presiding over the dissolution of the International Pelgrims Group approved the sale of a number of assets like the AREACEM pressing plant in France, which resumed operations under new ownership. Most important for the musicians of Congo and Zaïre, however, was the disposition of Fonior in Brussels. The Belgian courts had appointed a trustee to administer Fonior's bankruptcy, collect debts owed the company, and sell off company assets in order to pay its creditors. Among the assets up for sale was Fonior's extensive catalog of Congo music, a veritable history of the music dating back to the 1950s.

The French-owned company Sonodisc was a prominent bidder for the treasure. Sonodisc had formed in 1970 as a partnership between former Ngoma employees Marcel Perse and Michel David. Ngoma had continued to function in France under the direction of Alexandros Jeronimidis and Nikiforos Cavvadias following its suspension of operations in Léopoldville. Docteur Nico and Tabu Ley, among others, had recorded for the France-based version of the label. Disco France, Ngoma's manufacturing arm, continued to press records, and the company established the Centrale de Diffusion du Disque (CEDDI) to handle distribution. CEDDI also took on the catalogs of other labels, notably Cairophon, with the great Egyptian singer Umm Kulthum (Om Kalsoum), and several small Caribbean labels. According to Jeronimidis and Cavvadias, several Ngoma recordings and confidential lists of clients and label contacts mysteriously wound up in the possession of Perse and David, who used them to start up Sonodisc.

While Sonodisc occasionally produced a record from start to finish – *Franklin Boukaka à Paris* had been their first – the company's primary business was the distribution of records from Africa – including the Umm Kulthum catalog – and the Caribbean. The purchase of Fonior's African catalog would be a compatible addition and the closest thing to a cash cow one was likely to find outside the bailiwick of Western music.

Zaïrean and Congolese musicians, on the other hand, wished to regain control of their works. To this end, SONECA, through its director general, Zinga Botao, and one of his predecessors, (Joseph) Emany Mata Likambe, lobbied the bankruptcy trustee. Since the trustee's obligation was to raise money to pay Fonior's debts, he was unlikely to entertain anything other than a cash offer. None was apparently forthcoming on behalf of the musicians involved (although President Mobutu could certainly have afforded to make one). In November of 1981, the bankruptcy trustee notified SONECA of his decision to sell Fonior's African catalog to Sonodisc.

News of the sale created a storm of controversy. Franco, Tabu Ley, and Verckys, in a manifesto they called the 'Charter of Paris,' announced their resignations from SONECA, denounced the organization as corrupt and ineffectual, and pledged to seek an injunction to suspend the African catalog's sale to Sonodisc. Director General Botao countered that SONECA had never been a party to the contracts Zaïrean producers had signed with Fonior (the implication being that Zaïrean producers should have tried to work things out with the trustee themselves). Furthermore, he accused Franco, Ley, and Verckys of being among those who owed debts to Fonior and had failed to pay them. This, he surmised, led the trustee to favor Sonodisc.

Years later, anger over the sale of Fonior's African catalog still simmers near the surface. (Roger) Izeidi Mokoy, one of the music's pioneers, both as a producer and a performer, was perhaps the Zaïrean most closely connected to the Pelgrims empire. 'I wrote to [the bankruptcy trustee] that my labels and the others of my friends were not Pelgrims's property.' Pelgrims, Izeidi emphasized, was merely a sales agent.

> I even sent a photocopy of the contract that we signed. In the contract Pelgrims was sub-publisher, was only to sell throughout the world. He didn't own them. They [the trustee] didn't care. Since they wanted to make money, they sold [them].... I went to see Sonodisc. They don't care. Perse doesn't care. He signed a contract with me saying he would pay, [but] he's no longer willing to

pay. He said he bought [the catalog] on the market, and he said he's not going to pay any more. Whereas author's rights are never sold in the marketplace. Here [in Zaïre] I try to make it understood, but since the [government] ministers are constantly changing...*

As usual, the controversy receded with nothing resolved in the musicians' favor. Some allege that *patrons* like Franco, Tabu Ley, and Verckys cut their own deals with Sonodisc to receive royalties, but, they say, no money reaches the other artists who composed much of the music. According to Ley, 'Sonodisc does pay, but, but, but, there are a lot of buts.' Citing the case of Dechaud, whose 'African Jazz Mokili Mobimba' has become a classic that still sells today, Ley says, 'Sonodisc knows that Dechaud, until his death, will be powerless to get to them to ask [for his money] or to go to court or to come to Paris or to go anywhere. He has to go ask, and even then, and even then. He's owed things.'

To this day, no court or delegation of important persons has been able or willing to restore the musical heritage of Zaïre and Congo to its authors. Like the musicians themselves in growing numbers, their extraordinary legacy resides in Paris.

---

* During a brief talk with Sonodisc's Patrice Fichet (successor to Michel David) in July of 1993, Fichet, after excusing himself to confer with Perse, returned to say that Perse did not wish to be interviewed and that Perse had stated that he had never had any connection with Ngoma. Marcel Perse's office would not respond to requests for an interview in December of 1996. Perse has since sold Sonodisc.

18
Article 15

Kabasele, Sam Mangwana, Franco, Tabu Ley, Mbilia Bel, and Docteur Nico, 1980–1985

In May of 1980, just after Fonior's collapse, the 'committee of sages' of the Union des Musiciens Zaïrois assembled at Vévé Centre under the gavel of the union's current president, Verckys Kiamuangana. Before they tackled a sticky agenda of personal disputes and the Fonior problem, the committee voted to bestow upon two of its illustrious members, Kabasele Tshamala and Luambo Makiadi, the title *grand maître* (grand master) of Zaïrean song. For Franco, the honor recognized a work in progress, a brilliant career in search of its zenith. For Le Grand Kalle, it acknowledged the debt that musicians on both banks of the river owed to Congo music's most revered founding father.

Kabasele had returned home towards the end of 1978 after spending more than a year in Paris, where, with financial assistance from President Mobutu, he sought treatment for chronic hypertension. Following a year of convalescence in Kinshasa he was well enough to sing with the Géant Orchestre Malebo during a party in his honor at a night club called La Hutte. The party spurred talk of putting African Jazz back together, but rumors of the sort seemed to crop up as regularly as reports of a Beatles reunion. A near miss occurred in July of 1980 when Manu Dibango came to town. Dibango, Roger Izeidi, Docteur Nico, and Tabu Ley performed together on a nostalgia-filled telecast for the Voice of Zaïre, but there was no sign of their former boss. He had returned to Paris for further medical treatment. Little was heard from Grand Maître Kabasele for more than two years until, on Friday the 11th of February 1983, the Voice of Zaïre announced that he had died.

Former members of African Jazz together again in 1980 (left to right) Manu Dibango, Docteur Nico, Roger Izeidi, and Tabu Ley

The outpouring of sentiment was swift and overwhelming. Tributes flowed from the president and the common people and every stripe between. Gérard Akueson may have said it best: 'Kalle embodies Zaïrean music. He made all of Africa dance.'

Kabasele's death at age fifty-two was attributed to the effects of hypertension. On the final morning, *Elima* reported, his left leg became paralyzed. In the afternoon he lost his hearing and was taken to Kinshasa's Mama Yemo Hospital, but nothing could be done to save him. Kabasele's body lay in state at the home of his uncle, Cardinal Malula. An estimated half-million people filed past the casket to say farewell. Edo Ganga led a delegation of musicians from Brazzaville that crossed the river to pay their respects.

The following Monday a funeral cortège bearing Kabasele's body threaded slowly through the grieving crowds to Kinshasa's Notre Dame Cathedral, where Cardinal Malula conducted a funeral mass. From Notre Dame the crush of mourners made its way to Gombe Cemetery a few blocks from the river's edge. Slightly less than a year before, at another cemetery, Kabasele himself had spoken at the burial of his sometime collaborator, Kwamy Munsi, who had died from a prolonged bout of malaria. 'Every human is only passing through this world paradoxically intended for people,' Kabasele had said. Now, he too was gone. The politicians made their speeches on behalf of the government. Docteur Nico, Albert Taumani, Isaac Musekiwa, and a few others played a song in their former leader's honor. And then he was laid to rest.

•

Word of Kabasele's passing caught the remaining *grand maître*, Franco, in Paris, and he was unable to return to Kinshasa in time for the funeral. Since the launch of VISA 1980, Franco had been spending longer periods in Europe attending to his business affairs. Still, he managed to keep the vinyl flowing with frequent trips to the studio, both at home and in Europe, to record with O.K. Jazz.

After winning 1980's 'best band' award, Franco ran afoul of the censors again at the beginning of 1981 with a song called 'Locataire' (renter) that made veiled references to prostitution. Several months later 'Tailleur' (tailor) was widely regarded as Franco's retaliation against Kengo wa Dondo, the former chief prosecutor on whose watch in 1978 Franco had been jailed. Although it seems doubtful that Franco's incarceration could have happened without the approval of President Mobutu, only those who harbored a death wish dared to criticize Le Guide. Kengo, having temporarily fallen from favor, provided safer prey for Le Grand Maître's venom. 'They have taken the needle away from you.... We are equal now,' he chided. (Kengo rebounded a year later to become Zaïre's prime minister.)

Also in 1981, during a trip to Abidjan to finalize plans for an O.K. Jazz tour, Franco ran into his former singer Sam Mangwana. According to Mangwana, Franco complimented him on his work and suggested the two of them make a record together the next time they met back home. That contact led to an album entitled *Coopération*, recorded in Kinshasa around March of 1982.

As the two old comrades rehearsed and recorded the tracks for *Coopération*, the jury of the Maracas d'Or in Paris announced it would award Franco a special trophy in honor of the body of his work. Gilles Sala and another Antillean journalist, Claude Labbé, had founded the Maracas d'Or (gold maracas), the francophone version of the Grammy, which awarded yearly trophies for the best traditional, popular, and experimental (*recherche*) recordings from French-speaking Africa and the French Caribbean. Franco was the third African musician to receive the lifetime achievement award, following in the footsteps of Miriam Makeba and Manu Dibango. Too busy to go to Paris for the presentation, Franco sent one of his daughters to accept on his behalf. The trophy was presented to Franco himself at a ceremony in Kinshasa a few weeks later, after *Coopération* had been recorded.

•

Sam Mangwana had written 'Coopération,' the new album's lead-off track, a lively dialogue between himself and Franco about people working together. Franco also contributed a song, but the best work took place after he and most of the band left the studio. A smaller group that included – according to Danish musicologist Flemming Harrev – the O.K. Jazz rhythm guitarist and composer Simaro Lutumba, Afrisa's guitarist Dino Vangu, freelance saxophonist Empompo Loway, parts of the O.K. Jazz horn section, and an unidentified drummer from the group Bobongo Stars backed Mangwana on his finest work of the period.

Harrev traced two songs to the session. The first, a composition by Simaro called 'Faute ya Commerçant' (the shopkeeper's fault), relates the story of a man who inadvertently gives identical dresses to his wife and his mistress. But the story is overshadowed by the song's extraordinary music. Simaro and the rhythm section set the framework, a lovely riff for Vangu and Empompo to embellish. Mangwana, rich of voice, overlays the melody, and the O.K. Jazz horns, including a trombone, drop in to buttress the mix.

The second song, a Mangwana composition called 'Liwa ya Niekesse' (the death of Niekesse), follows much the same pattern, only this time without the horns. Mangwana carries the melody as the solo guitar plays variations on the rhythm section's basic theme. It is a matchless display of the fundamentals of the Congolese rumba. 'Faute ya Commerçant' made it onto the *Coopération* album; both songs were included on an album entitled *Consommez Local* released in Abidjan under Mangwana's name.

Following the *Coopération* sessions, Mangwana took off for West Africa, where he triggered another reunion. In the latter half of 1982, Mangwana, Dizzy Mandjeku, Lokassa ya Mbongo, and Ringo Moya recorded together again as the African All Stars. The quartet regrouped in Côte d'Ivoire, recruited session musicians to replace original members Théo Blaise Kounkou and Roland M'vogo, and went into Abidjan's sparkling new JBZ studio to lay the tracks for three albums. Two featured mostly Mangwana compositions, while the third, dedicated to the coming New Year (1983), contained songs by Lokassa and was issued under his name.

If nothing else, the records served to illustrate how hard it was to recapture the original All Stars' freshness and vigor. Female voices and bursts of a flute add occasional dollops of color, but overall the recordings seem flat. Mangwana's 'Affaire Video' is perhaps the best of the lot, one of his patented tales of a hard-working man done wrong by a two-timing woman.

In mid-July 1983, half the remaining All Stars, Mangwana and Mandjeku, played a concert in Mozambique. In Maputo, the two Zaïreans sat in with local musicians to record an album called *Canta Moçambique*, two extended songs of encouragement for a country facing enormous economic and political troubles exacerbated by its dependence on white-ruled South Africa. After that, what was left of the African All Stars scattered for the last time. Dizzy Mandjeku went home to Kinshasa to begin work as artistic director for Verckys's expanding roster of bands.

Sam Mangwana also returned to Kinshasa – to start yet another group. Together with old friend Empompo Loway and singer Ndombe Opetun, who had recently left O.K. Jazz, Mangwana launched a band called Tiers Monde Coopération (third world cooperation). Two other defectors from O.K. Jazz, singers 'Djo' Mpoyi Kaninda and Diatho Lukoki, joined soon afterward, but Mangwana didn't even stay to the end of the year. As soon as the band got sufficiently organized he took off in pursuit of new projects. He would return some two and a half years later to join Empompo in temporarily re-forming the group as Tiers Monde Révolution.

•

For Sam Mangwana's former boss, Tabu Ley, the early eighties were a time of rejuvenation. Ley's attempt to resuscitate some of the older guard had wheezed to a conclusion when Docteur Nico and Bombenga Wewando resigned from Afrisa and Kwamy Munsi died. To replace them Ley looked next to youth and beauty.

Tabu Ley met Mbilia Mboyo near the end of 1981. She was a 22-year-old singer and dancer who had dropped out of school five years earlier after being inspired to pursue a show business career by the music of Togolese singer Bella Bellow. At the age of seventeen, Mbilia caught on as a back-up singer and dancer with Abeti's Tigresses, where she refined her talents over the next four years. She left the group to join Sam Mangwana for a brief series of concerts in Kinshasa and Zaïre's provinces. Following her work with Mangwana, some of Ley's musicians introduced her to their boss.

Ley had been looking for a woman to join his act. 'When we sing we take the woman's position,' he explained. 'I said this time I want to compose, but I'll give it to a woman to speak what a woman thinks.' He liked Mbilia's voice and manner and decided to give her the job, with one notable proviso: she should adopt the stage name Mbilia Bel.

The duo of Tabu Ley and Mbilia Bel was a hit from the very start. 'My first record was my biggest dream I had had for a long time,' Mbilia recalled. 'So when the first record came out, all the women of our country – [they] really [made] the success of this record.' Called 'Mpeve ya Longo' (essentially, 'holy spirit' in Kikongo) and written by Ley, it speaks directly about the domestic problems many women face. 'I talk about a woman who is complaining. Her husband has abandoned her with four kids. That's why women adore this song.'

> Full of worries, I think about entering a religious order
> I see my many children and ask myself where I can leave them
> It's a bad sign for the husband to repudiate you with the children

As the record took off in the early months of 1982, Ley and his band were on the road in Kenya and Angola sharpening the act that included their rising new star. In July they played Brazzaville's Vog Cinema before returning to Kinshasa to entertain the home folks. 'Mbilia Bel: a star in the firmament,' *Elima* crowed. Citing the great Egyptian singer Umm Kulthum and South Africa's Miriam Makeba, the writer declared that 'Mbilia certainly hasn't yet acquired that strong international dimension, but she has the talent.'

Late in the year, Afrisa took off again for five months of concerts and recording in Europe. If ever there had been doubts about the pairing of Ley and Mbilia Bel, the tour must have dispelled them. Enthusiastic crowds greeted the musicians at nearly every stop, and the recording sessions yielded one of the best albums of the eighties.

In March of 1983 Ley's company, Genidia, released two albums from the sessions, one featuring Ley himself and the other Mbilia Bel. Ley gave the best material to his protégée, and she rewarded his confidence. From the first notes of 'Eswi yo Wapi' (literally, where did it hurt you? i.e., getting a taste of one's own medicine), the opening number of Mbilia Bel's debut album, there is no denying Ley's ear for talent. Her voice rings strong and clear with a feel of innocence and the power of self-possession. Against the backdrop of Dino Vangu's fuzz-edged guitar, she sounds like chapel chimes. She and Ley recorded separate versions of his 'Lisanga Bambanda' (association of rivals), one for each of their albums, but a rootsy arrangement and that luminous voice gives hers the fresher touch. Her update of Ley's 'Kelhia' (originally 'Kelya') makes the song her own.

As good as they are, these plus the Dino Vangu composition 'Quelle Mechanceté' (what spitefulness) are only supporting pieces to the album's major hit. 'Eswi yo Wapi,' with writing credit to both Ley and Mbilia, dispatches the myth of male supremacy.

> Ask me to tell you
> What's the duty of a man
> God created Adam in this world
> So that he'd help Eve
> For the little you have given me you talked too much
> In what way are you a man
> Whether you buy me a house or cars
> You're only paying the debt of Adam and Eve

Afrisa struts in big band mode, propelling the rumba at a rapid clip. Male singers (probably Ley and Kiesse Diambu) deliver the choruses in sonorous contrast to Mbilia's limpid soprano. Dino Vangu takes charge of the sebene, his guitar shimmering under the influence of a fuzz tone. The hybrid cocktail attracted fans at home and abroad. 'Eswi yo Wapi' made Mbilia Bel an international star. Afrisa dominated Kinshasa's year-end awards for 1983, winning best band, best song for 'Eswi yo Wapi,' and revelation of the year, Mbilia Bel. *Elima*, rarely given to understatement, called her 'Queen Cleopatra, princess of the court, serene highness.'

•

While Tabu Ley and his 'queen' reigned in Kinshasa, Franco's business interests kept him in Europe much of the time. According to Franco's counselor, Malambu ma Kizola, himself a more or less permanent resident of Paris, Franco preferred Brussels for business but liked Paris for his family life. His second wife, Mpiso Mati, known as Annie, lived in a Paris suburb near Versailles, and most of his children attended French schools. Many members of O.K. Jazz spent long periods in Europe, accompanying their boss on live dates and in the studio, to the point that two discernible wings of the band developed. While movement between them was fluid, Franco, Dalienst, and Gerry Dialungana anchored the European group with Simaro, Checain, and

Papa Noël holding the fort in Kinshasa. Franco confirmed Simaro's authority over the Kinshasa wing by elevating him in 1982 to the post of vice-president of O.K. Jazz.

Franco's long absences and the return to political prominence of Kengo wa Dondo as prime minister fueled rumors that Le Grand Maître had been forced into exile. The talk was clearly off the mark since Franco did, in fact, return to Kinshasa from time to time. Nevertheless he was moved to address the question on several occasions. To *Elima* he explained that

> it's simple. First, the world of show-biz is in Europe. And the people who attended to us before, Fonior and the others, are no longer [operating] back home. So we had to attend to our works ourselves and promote them. That's what I'm doing. And beyond that, back home the infrastructure is lacking.

To *Bingo* he said there was no question of exile:

> It is rather my musical career that pushes me to work abroad. I am one of the prime movers in the musical life of my country, and more than that, I am a patriot.

Ever since their row in 1978, Franco and Tabu Ley had grown closer. They remained spirited competitors, but a cordial personal relationship appeared to take root between the two great stars. Near the end of 1982 they were jointly honored by a Senegalese producer based in Abidjan, Daniel Cuxac, and New York record dealer Roger Francis, two men who often collaborated in the production and distribution of African records. They presented each of the two stars with a gold record for accumulated sales over the course of their careers. The ceremony, carried on Zaïrean television, was followed by an audience for the two musicians with President Mobutu.

Ley and Franco shocked their fans the following year, by embarking on a joint recording project. That they had decided to record together was astonishing, but the recording itself, the initial release on Franco's new Choc (shock) label, provoked more comment and speculation. Entitled *Choc Choc Choc 1983*, the two-record album was recorded with a mixture of musicians from Afrisa and O.K. Jazz along with guest artist 'Michelino' Mavatiku Visi, who had done time in both bands back in the seventies. It contained one song per side, 'Lettre à Mr. le Directeur Général' and three others, all written by Franco.

Franco and Ley shared vocals on all but the third side, 'Suite Lettre No. 2.' There, Franco addressed the rumors about his long periods in Europe. He sings about growing up near the market 'wenze ya Bayaka, quartier Far West.'

'Can I really run away from Kinshasa?' he asks. 'Stop messing around with me.... We will meet again in Kinshasa.' The song also saw life as a 45 under the title 'Na Mokili Tour à Tour' (as the world turns).

'D.G.,' as 'Lettre à Mr. le Directeur Général' came to be known, was the album's set piece. It purported to attack the bureaucrats who ran Kinshasa's fading companies, but it wasn't much of a stretch to think that the Zaïrean regime itself might be the real target. The song's refrain sums up its message: 'You have always been good, D.G./ It's [your] entourage that does harm, why?' It was the kind of critique that could be heard on the streets of Kinshasa as recently as the early nineties. The president is good, but his ministers have destroyed the country.

The two maestros take turns airing the dirty linen. Ley observes:

> A lot of people let their Bics drop
> Everyone's become a businessman
> Markets in the city have become congested, why is this?

Franco lodges a more personal complaint:

> The entourage has compromised my work
> They've told the D.G. that I make fun of
> Him in private circles, why is this?

'D.G.' recalled a similar song of a couple of years before by Miyalu Kayonda and Orchestre Bana Odeon, a folk group as obscure as Franco was famous. Called 'Mwana Nsuka,' the last child, the song portrayed society's ills in the deaths of Miyalu's twelve children. One died from disease, a second from malnutrition. A daughter, turned prostitute, attracted many men and was poisoned by jealous friends. Robbers killed another who had no money. A road accident, suicide, Miyalu covered all the symptoms of the country's threatening demise. And somehow he got away with it.

•

The alarm that Miyalu, Franco, and Ley expressed was well founded. Kinshasa's population continued to swell – to an estimated 2.5 million in 1981 – with all the attendant problems of inadequate housing and nutrition, unemployment, poverty, and crime. The looting of Zaïre's treasury by the ruling elite and its international creditors pushed inflation and squeezed the people.

This was Mobutu's Zaïre in the early eighties, a time when it took six zaïres (1982), then thirty (1983), then forty (1984) to equal one U.S. dollar, and the purchasing power of the average wage earner sank to less than a quarter of what it had been at the time of independence. The price of a newspaper edged toward ten zaïres. People who wanted to attend the debut of a new band called Victoria Eleison on Christmas of 1982 had to come up with the hefty gate fee of fifty zaïres. A year later MAZADIS announced that the cost of a 45 r.p.m. record leaving the factory would rise from ten and a half zaïres to thirty-five. That would push the retail price up near fifty zaïres, depressing sales and opening the door still wider for the cheap cassettes of music pirates.

Except for the occasional *spectacle* by Abeti or Tabu Ley, the show style of performance all but vanished. People simply couldn't afford the price of a ticket. Instead they resorted to 'Article 15,' a bit of dark humor from the sixties that referred to a non-existent provision of the old South Kasai's fourteen-article constitution. Pepe Kalle explains it in his song 'Article 15 Beta Libanga' (Article 15, literally 'beat with a stone,' meaning 'work hard'):

> Whether you're young or old, we all face the same reality: the difficult life
> The daily nightmare
> What to do? If nothing else, refer to Article 15
> 'Do what you must to live'
> In Kinshasa.

Zaïre's economic crisis choked the flow of vinyl and spare parts to keep pressing plants and studios at the peak of operation. Franco's two aging factories, MAZADIS and SOPHINZA, continued to function at vastly reduced output. Verckys invested in a new, modern pressing plant known as IZASON (Industrie Zaïroise du Son) in 1984. But given the dearth of foreign exchange to finance imports of vinyl, it made little impact.

More significant help came from across the river. In 1983 the Congolese government inaugurated an improved version of the old SOCODI called Industrie Africaine du Disque (IAD). The new venture encompassed a 24-track recording studio, a pressing plant complete with mastering lathe, machines for cassette duplication, and printing facilities to produce four-color record jackets. Most Congolese musicians used the services of IAD. Many of their colleagues from Kinshasa, including Franco and Tabu Ley, crossed the river to do likewise.

In the middle of 1984, Zaïre's musicians paused to campaign for the man who had placed their livelihoods in jeopardy. Mobutu loved their music, had bought instruments for many, and funded medical treatment in Europe for a few. But these meager gestures paled in the face of the current calamity. Nevertheless, if you lived in Zaïre you supported Le Guide. Or else. Mobutu was the only candidate for another seven-year term at the helm. He won.

•

The songs that Franco had written for his joint recording with Tabu Ley refined his tendency to favor lengthy compositions built on a simple repeating guitar figure. Both tendencies, increasingly conspicuous as Franco's music evolved into its new format, were rooted in traditional music, where repetition is common and fatigue is often the primary motivation for a musician to stop. Playing live, Franco was free to follow a musical idea to its logical conclusion (and sometimes beyond). On record, however, his music was constrained by the limits of recording technology. Ever since the coming of the 45 r.p.m. record, pop songs in general had been getting longer. Where the old, 10-inch 78s could scarcely hold three minutes a side, 45s could double that, and then some. By the end of the sixties many songs faded out at the end of the A side only to resume play on side B. The 33⅓ r.p.m. album format solved that problem, allowing for more than twenty minutes a side. Franco relished the newly found license like the day's first plate of manioc.

Near the end of 1982 Franco had released a double album to celebrate his two recent honors, the Maracas d'Or and the gold record. The lead track, ironically entitled 'Très Fâché' (very angry), builds on a repeating guitar figure and covers the entire first side, winding on for fifteen minutes. The story alone takes twelve minutes to tell. *Elima* compared it to the works of the French poet Baudelaire, who explored the links between beauty and corruption, and to the function of Africa's own conservators of the people's oral history, wisdom, customs, and morals. 'Like a veritable *griot*, Luambo takes us through the twists and turns that show us the hidden face of the unfaithful woman.'

Rumor had it that 'Très Fâché' was aimed at a certain Paulina, a long-time lover (possibly legal wife) whom Franco had jilted in favor of his current wife Annie. 'No, no, no,' Franco exclaimed.

> I can't sing [about] that woman like some are hinting. In any case not in that way. That woman is the mother of my children, and I work to ensure the future of my children. I have always written my songs in the manner of 'Très Fâché.' That shouldn't be identified (and erroneously to boot) with her. To those who think I was singing about her, to hell with you!

But the gossip didn't end there. More rumors surfaced that Paulina had paid Tabu Ley to write a rebuttal to Franco for her, and that was the famous 'Eswi yo Wapi' sung by Mbilia Bel!

The subject of 'Très Fâché' was typical Franco, a distinguishing mark that moved him to deny on more than one occasion that he was a misogynist. 'Contrary to what they think, I am not against women,' he told *Afrique Elite*. 'But what I notice is that women are more wrong than men, which is why I give them advice in my songs.'

Franco continued in this vein with a song released near the end of 1983 called 'Non' (no), perhaps the most beautiful composition of his career. One can quarrel with its eighteen-minute length, and certainly with the subject matter, but the music itself floats a lovely, lazy rumba full of subtle twists and turns. Building on a simple guitar riff that encompasses just eleven notes, Franco arranges the supporting cast – a delicate saxophone chorus, his own authoritative bark, and the lyric tenor of Madilu Bialu – to near perfection. The words of Lingala tumble in graceful symphony, and when Franco and Madilu join their voices, the effect is positively thrilling.

It's almost better not to know the subject, for to Western ears, at least, it resounds with an embarrassing sexism. Translated, the mellifluous Lingala reveals a bitter, rambling satire on women's alleged misbehavior – refusing to be a man's second wife, divorcing their husbands, joining or abetting prostitution.

> Madilu I've always been surprised
> If a woman has just divorced her husband
> She'll take as her friend a prostitute of the worst kind
> One who knows all the workings of the trade
> She will lead her anywhere she pleases
> She will take her where men often meet
> ...
> What I have always wondered about
> Three women walking together is no fun
> They should walk in twos
> To get along well
> Even when they walk in threes
> Even when they walk in twos
> Scandalmongering is walking along too
> They spread lies everywhere
> They are disparaging everywhere
> They are hateful everywhere

> If you ask them why have you quarreled
> You'll hear tales with no real basis
> Ones that little children could evaluate
> You women, how did God create you?
> You cannot build a country.

The commentary on scandalmongering could have spoken equally to men since, in effect, Franco and Madilu were doing exactly what they accuse the women of. But men would have to wait for a taste of Le Grand Maître's tongue. Women were currently in the dock, and Franco rebuked them with a slanderous ode swathed in extraordinary beauty.

Franco had begun to sing in earnest back in the sixties when his corps of singers was thinner. As the years passed, his voice matured, and he recorded the vocals on more of his own compositions. By the eighties his gruff baritone could be heard on nearly all of them. What he lacked in range he more than made up with impeccable timing and delivery. His words, often spoken rather than sung, cascaded in stream-of-consciousness rants that assumed the character of improvisation, whether or not they actually were.

Franco's pairing of himself with Madilu turned out to be a master stroke. Were it not for the fact that Madilu had been around for a while, he would have given Mbilia Bel a run for 1983's revelation of the year award. He had made his debut as a nineteen-year-old in 1969 in a band called Symba. His early career included periods with Papa Noël's Bamboula, Les Etoiles, the Festival des Maquisards of Sam Mangwana, and Faugus Izeidi's Fiesta Populaire. In 1973, Madilu, guitarist Yossa Taluki, and a singer known as Pirès formed a band called Bakuba Mayopi (Mayopi came from the first two letters of each of their names). The group enjoyed moderate success, but never posed a threat to Kinshasa's first-tier bands.

After three years in Mayopi, Madilu quit to form his own group with an assist from Soki Vangu. He initially called it Orchestre Pamba-Pamba but soon changed the name to Madilu System. Although the band went nowhere, the name stuck to Madilu. In 1980, following two unhappy years with Tabu Ley's Afrisa, Madilu System joined O.K. Jazz. His inspired performance on 'Non' set his star ascending and assured his place at Franco's side.

With 'Non' and two other songs in the can for an album, *Chez Fabrice à Bruxelles*, Franco prepared the band for a hurried trip to the United States. It was the group's first crack at the U.S. market, and despite the short notice Franco was eager. 'O.K. Jazz was a rushed job, so we were only able to do Washington and New York,' producer Ibrahim Kanja Bah explained. Franco

Madilu System

kept adding to his entourage, which complicated the delicate process of obtaining visas and booking concert halls.

In late November 1983 the band took the stage before a packed house at George Washington University's Lisner Auditorium in Washington, D.C. Emcee Roger-Guy Folley of the Voice of America introduced a baker's dozen of the forty-odd troupe including the big three singers, Dalienst, Josky, and Madilu. Traditional dancers ushered Le Grand Maître on stage to enthusiastic applause.

A few days later, the scene repeated at New York City's Manhattan Center, where one thousand fans greeted the band. A critic for the *Village Voice* took issue with the program's lack of continuity, calling it 'a disconnected series of set-pieces.' Still, he found much to praise.

> The isolated high points – monumental bass lines and Franco's electrifying guitar work – were high indeed. When Franco climaxed the show with a

cutting contest pitting his guitar against the lead saxophone, he vindicated his 'Sorcerer of the Guitar' title with virtuoso rhythm chops.

A couple of gigs at smaller halls followed in early December, and then the brief fling ended. 'Our stay in the United States was fruitful,' Franco told television interviewers. 'We came as observers. We played, and we did a lot of looking. And we listened a lot. And we liked a lot. We're going to go home, and we're going to make an assessment.'

The diplomatic appraisal notwithstanding, Franco had to have felt a few pangs of disappointment. After twenty-five years as one of Africa's biggest stars, his truncated tour paled in comparison to the coast-to-coast spectacles Island Records helped to stage for the upstart Sunny Ade. The Top-Forty-fixated United States would be a tough sell. Without backing from a well-connected record label, chances for even a minor breakthrough looked remote.

Early the next year Tabu Ley gave the U.S. market his first shot. Unlike Franco, Ley allied himself with an American record company by licensing six of his latest Genidia recordings, including Mbilia Bel's 'Eswi yo Wapi,' to New Jersey-based Shanachie Records. Booking agent Paul Trautman, the man who brought Sunny Ade to the U.S., organized a seventeen-city, coast-to-coast tour that included four stops in Canada. Afrisa kicked off in Washington, D.C., the second week in February 1984. Although promotion was hampered by the new Shanachie album's late release, Trautman told *Billboard* that the tour was averaging about a thousand fans per performance. Tickets were so hot in Vancouver that a second show had to be added.

For all the careful planning, Ley appeared to lack confidence in his music's inherent appeal. He told the Kinshasa press he was going to the U.S. to carry the message of authenticity, but *Rolling Stone* called his stage show 'closer to Las Vegas.' *Village Voice* compared the show unfavorably to those of Sunny Ade.

> Afrisa warmed up with several long numbers, but never went for the communal play that Ade's African Beats project so successfully. Afrisa and Rochereau ... were consciously reaching west, covering 'Soul Serenade,' 'Let it Be,' and 'Sir Duke.' Now, juju from Nigeria is no more purely folkloric than 'Dark Star,' but King Sunny doesn't bend to such decadence as Rochereau crooning 'I love you/ Baby, touch me.'

The *New York Times* declared that 'by far the best part of the show was the infectious, purely Zaïrean dance music.' Ley had failed to understand that Western audiences were attracted by what he did best. He couldn't resist the compulsion to crossover.

Back home in Kinshasa Ley sounded equally confused. Following a grand welcome that included a delegation from O.K. Jazz, the Afrisa fan club, and a meandering parade through the streets of Kinshasa, Ley met the press. 'If I won in the United States,' he told reporters, 'it's because I played a lot of [the style of] Zaïko Langa Langa and Papa Wemba, and I danced like Lita Bembo.'
While Afrisa contemplated its identity crisis, O.K. Jazz carried on as before. Franco's European wing made its first appearance in London with a lively Easter Monday 1984 concert at the Hammersmith Palais. Except for the hype surrounding the show, *Melody Maker*, for one, approved. 'Soukous,' its reviewer wrote, adopting the new catchword, 'has played here in the shadows cast by the juju stars. Perhaps that's about to change.'

Soon afterward the next installment of the Franco–Madilu coffee klatch came out. As with 'Non,' the subject was women, but this time the tenor had lightened. Franco titled the much more obvious satire 'Tu Vois?' (you see?) as if to say, 'here's proof of what women are up to.' Record buyers called it 'Mamou,' the name of its female subject. Franco and Madilu take turns in the role of a woman friend whom Mamou uses to cover for her own extra-marital liaisons. Madilu sings, but Franco speaks his part like a busybody's back-fence prattle. In one hilarious verse bassist Deca Mpudi impersonates Mamou in a transparent falsetto. At that point in the story, she lives in Europe and schedules her philandering around her husband's twice-daily phone calls from Zaïre.

> Hello my children's father
> We're all doing very well
> But they're so unruly, your kids!
> Especially the youngest boy, who looks so much like you
> He surprises me
> He smashed to pieces the plate
> With your picture printed on it
> [The one] that allowed me to feel you near me
> That little boy is really unruly
> Just like you were in your childhood
> According to your mother
> My children's father
> I've no more to tell you
> Just send us some money to live on.

The Kinshasa wing of O.K. Jazz flourished during the boss's prolonged European trips. Apart from nights at the Un-Deux-Trois, the band played Sunday matinées at a Matonge club called the Faubourg. Without consulting Franco, the musicians did some recording too. Vice President Simaro Lutumba crossed the river to cut an album at IAD. The title track, 'Maya,' quickly rivaled Franco's 'Tu Vois?' in popularity. 'Maya's unfortunate timing and the fact that it didn't appear on one of Franco's labels strained relations between the two leaders. Papa Noël joined the mini-rebellion by following Simaro to IAD, where he recorded an album that included the song 'Bon Samaritan.' It too became a hit, and Papa Noël replaced Simaro in Franco's doghouse.

Both albums profited from the newest addition to the band's roster of singers, 23-year-old Lassa Ndombasi, known as 'Carlito.' Carlito had been discovered by former O.K. Jazz bassist Francis Bitshoumanou, who introduced him to Simaro. The new singer's performance on the two new albums confirmed Bitshoumanou's good judgement. When Franco returned to Kinshasa to rein in his troops, he found their wing, not his, had won many of 1984's year-end awards. 'Maya' and 'Bon Samaritan' finished one and two in the best song category. Simaro took the best composer award, and Carlito was chosen as the revelation of the year.

Some personnel shuffling unrelated to the competition between the band's two wings occurred in the waning days of 1984 and the beginning of 1985. Ntesa Dalienst, one of the three main singers of the European wing, decided to quit. A colleague of Dalienst's in Les Grands Maquisards, ex-Afrisa vocalist Kiesse Diambu, joined O.K. Jazz to fill the vacancy. Another former Maquisard, Dizzy Mandjeku, also joined the band, thus completing his circuit of the big three, Tabu Ley, Verckys, and now Franco.

Franco himself produced 1985's biggest story. After his relentless portrayal of women as stereotypes and the resulting accusations of misogyny, Franco next took aim at men. His victim was 'Mario,' a ne'er-do-well with 'five diplomas' who lives off a well-to-do woman. As usual Franco enlisted Madilu in the burlesque, the two taking turns as the aggrieved woman who's had enough of her live-in freeloader.

> Mario's parents believe
> That Mario gives me money
> But I'm the one who dresses him, feeds him, and lodges him
> Mario, I'm fed up
> Get out of my house, Mario
> Why ransom love?
> ...
> The gigolo found me in a state of prosperity
> He asked to rule me, I accepted
> The gigolo found me in a state of prosperity
> He asked to guide me, I accepted

Simaro Lutumba (right) with Papa Noël

> I began to go out with him
> And people started calling him 'Sir'
> Mario cheered up
> He believes all I own belongs to him
> Ah Mario! I am fed up!
> Go away Mario, I can't stand you anymore.

The band juggles a set of simple riffs, stringing them out one after the other then drawing them together in sumptuous union. A synthesizer whines where the horns would be, but the sturdy framework of crisscrossing patterns easily accommodates the change. The conga player (probably Dessoin) paces the performance with a virtuoso's flair and finesse. And Franco and Madilu, true to form, send 'Mario' up with gusto.

The melodrama stretched out over the A sides of two successive albums. Odd packaging – the two were distributed in identical record jackets at nearly the same time – created confusion, particularly among non-Lingala speakers, and probably diminished sales. Nevertheless, 'Mario' was a runaway hit, more so outside of Zaïre. Franco acknowledged that it was his biggest song, claiming sales of more than 200,000 records. Pirated copies undoubtedly pushed the figure much higher.

At home the reception was mixed. The people liked the song, but the press snubbed it. Kinshasa's music writers appeared to be giving Franco the same treatment they accorded the other Zaïrean musicians living in Europe. Their productions were foreign. In this case so was the *inauthentique* title. The writers preferred the home-grown product. When 1985's year-end awards were announced, 'Mario' failed to score. In a testy interview with *Elima* some months later a sarcastic Franco called the slight 'eloquent proof of the acumen of the press as far as its aptitude to judge without flaw.' His manager, Manzenza Sala Musala, paraphrased the Bible. 'No one is a prophet in his own land.'

•

Franco and Tabu Ley cruised at the top of their profession. Each had logged more than twenty years in the business and had enjoyed enormous success. For their erstwhile rival, Docteur Nico, life's path took a different turn. He too had been to the mountain top, but that was the early seventies. Since then, according to one who knew him well, Nico had struggled with personal problems. His first wife left him. To assuage the hurt he started drinking. Alcohol impaired his skills to the point where his hands shook when the took up the guitar. The result was a downward slide as extraordinary as his rivals' ascent.

By the time he returned to the stage as a member of Tabu Ley's Afrisa in 1980, Nico seemed to have fought his demons to a standstill. 'I dread dying poor when I have devoted a great part of my life to my long career,' he said then.

> Certainly it gives me reason for legitimate satisfaction on the artistic level, but on the financial level I don't see a rosy future. This is part of the reason that I was ready to abandon my musical career. Through the will of my fans and Tabu Ley, I will soon reconnect with the captivating ambience of the bars.

Early in 1981 Docteur Nico recorded several songs in Benin with Empompo Loway. One of them, 'Manzeta,' remade an old Nico composition with most of the lyrics sung this time in French. 'Oh Manzeta mama/ You've disappointed me in life.' In light of his troubles the declaration seemed apropos.

Nico appeared to gain confidence from his latest endeavors, so much so that in the middle of 1981 he quit Afrisa. He wanted to concentrate on making records, he said, even though he had to rent instruments to rehearse. Once he had acquired his own equipment he would return to the stage. 'People outside Zaïre think that I'm well off materially,' he complained, 'though in reality I live like a pauper and am left to my own devices.' Fortunately for Nico other benefactors appeared.

Saxophonist Empompo Loway worked on Nico's Benin sessions, but ever since his split with M'Pongo Love in the middle of 1980, he had concentrated on developing the career of newcomer Vonga Ndayimba, a young female singer who went by the stage name 'Vonga Aye.' Empompo put together a band called Elo Music to back her, and when Docteur Nico left Afrisa Empompo invited him to sit in on some of the group's projects.

At the end of 1981 Nico, Empompo, Vonga Aye, and three other musicians of Elo Music flew to Paris for a month of recording. In Zaïre, Empompo explained, 'we aren't equipped to turn out good work.... I've decided to try my luck elsewhere.' The group recorded enough material for six albums, he reported, two for each of the principals. Vonga Aye's four-song debut on the Bade Stars Music label made the biggest impression. The album included a song called 'Bonbon Kojack' – a tale of a young girl's attraction to a reluctant man – that registered the encroachment of American television into Zaïrean life.

A second album from the trip also appeared, this one produced by Richard Dick for his Africamania label. The record was released under Vonga Aye's name but featured two songs by each of the three artists. If there was indeed enough material for six albums, it is unclear what happened to the rest of it.

For Vonga Aye, her work with Empompo and Nico was an intermediate step on the path to a career of moderate success. She would never rise to the level of Abeti and M'Pongo Love, but she remained popular in Kinshasa throughout the early eighties. Docteur Nico, on the other hand, used the Paris trip to renew acquaintances with the owners of Bade Stars Music, Abeti and her husband-manager Gérard Akueson.

Abeti had been among the first of Zaïre's stars to voice alarm over the music industry's deterioration. As early as 1978 she had complained of out-of-date studios and poor-quality pressings. She began to record in Paris, where she and Akueson established a publishing house named for their son, Bade. Still Abeti considered Zaïre her home and continued to perform there regularly. In early 1981 she celebrated her tenth anniversary in showbusiness with nearly three months of special events in Kinshasa. Meanwhile, Akueson's friendship with Docteur Nico warmed up over the next several months, even as Nico continued to perform with Empompo and Vonga Aye.

The single disappointment of his career, Nico once confided, was that he had never received an official honor. 'That seems banal,' he said, 'but a decoration, for an artist of my worth, constitutes an extremely indispensable element of morale.' As his career resumed in earnest, however, officialdom finally noticed.

Across the river in Brazzaville, Congolese curators of culture selected Nico and two of his older colleagues, Wendo and Jhimmy, as honorees for Congo's inaugural National Music Festival to be staged in September of 1982. Jhimmy, a mentor to both Nico and his brother Dechaud in the days of Léopoldville's Opika studio, was flown in from the Central African Republic, where he had been living for the last several years. Dignitaries lauded the three legends in a ceremony at Brazzaville's Meridian Hotel. To cap the three-day event Nico performed several songs with Empompo and Vonga Aye during a gala at the Vog Cinema.

Akueson had had a hand in shaping the Brazzaville festival. Soon after it ended, he saw to it that Docteur Nico joined forces with Abeti's band, Les Redoutables. Nico produced his first album under the arrangement at the end of 1982. It included the song 'Bolingo na Brazza' (love in Brazzaville), inspired, no doubt, by his recent honor in Congo.

The death of Joseph Kabasele the following February moved Nico to reflect again on the condition of Zaïre's artists. 'Highly acclaimed by the public when their star shines, they almost always die poor,' he said during a tribute to his former boss. For all their quarrels over the affairs of African Jazz, there could be no denying the impact the two musicians' association had on both of their careers, and on Congo music itself. None would have been the same without African Jazz. 'I bet,' said Nico, 'that from now to the year 2000, few bands will attain the level of the performances of African Jazz.'

With Kabasele gone, Nico began composing new material for another round of recording with Abeti's Redoutables. The process consumed the rest of the year, since rehearsals with the band had to be arranged around Abeti's busy schedule. At the beginning of 1984 Akueson's entourage – Abeti, Docteur Nico, and Les Redoutables – crossed the River to Brazzaville for ten days of recording at IAD. The group included (Lucie) Eyenga Moseka, Zaïre's first woman singer of major stature, whose career, like Nico's, Abeti and Akueson hoped to resurrect.

Once in the studio, Nico felt Kabasele's presence. He had written a song for inclusion on the new album to honor his old boss. 'I found myself truly in another world, and I saw him giving me instructions,' Nico said. 'Because of that psychological state I dropped everything I'd created during rehearsals, and I resorted entirely to improvisation.' The creative juices that had nourished Nico's early years coursed again with passion.

With four albums – Nico's, one for Abeti, one for Eyenga, and another for the band itself – ready for pressing, the Bade Stars Music crew received a surprise itinerary. They would all be going to Lomé. Akueson had just been appointed by the Togolese government to revive the state-run Office Togolais du Disque (OTODI), a modern 24-track recording studio and pressing plant built by 3M France. Like their counterparts at the old SOCODI in Brazzaville, Togolese bureaucrats had failed to steer the studio along a proper course. Akueson, it was hoped, would do better. He and Abeti invited Nico and his brother Dechaud to join the effort.

Lucky Lomé witnessed the final stages of Docteur Nico's rebirth. When he performed in public, Togolese crowds cheered him on. In the studio, Akueson remembered, Nico's hands held steady. When he started to play, everyone stopped to look. He improvised with abandon. Retakes never copied originals. Nico and Dechaud clicked just like the old days. Together with Les Redoutables, they recorded four albums.

Each song pushed Nico's personal five-minute preference – beyond which the music 'gets monotonous' – to the day's standard of at least seven. In keeping with the more modern sound, traps replaced the congas and maracas. Sebenes became more repetitious. But riffing wasn't Nico's style, and he had a hard time repeating himself for very long. OTODI's twenty-four tracks allowed him the flexibility to record more than one part, to add a flourish of Hawaiian guitar or over-dub a solo. With modern technology and Abeti's Redoutables behind him, Nico's latest work bore all the polish of the Paris productions of Eddy'Son or Safari Ambiance.

Among the songs, 'Mikalayi' recalled Nico's home town. 'La Vie est un Combat' (life is a struggle) alluded to his own changes in fortune. 'Makiadi' told of a love from his youth, gone but still remembered. 'La Roue Qui Tourne' (the wheel that turns) pondered the nature of human existence. As a body they formed the recital of his life.

Later in the year, Nico joined Abeti and Les Redoutables on a three-country tour. August found them in Benin and Côte d'Ivoire. October took them to Burkina Faso. Everywhere he went Nico basked in the warmth of enthusiastic greetings. 'Docteur Nico, despite his age, has lost nothing of his mastery of the guitar and his vivacity,' the Cotonou newspaper Ehuzu reported. 'On the contrary it seems that wisdom has henceforth placed him in the ranks of the veritable masters who concoct sounds to perfection.' Following these encouraging events Nico announced that, like Franco and Tabu Ley, he would be going to the United States.

Nico traveled by himself, landing in Washington, D.C. in early March of 1985. 'There are two purposes for my trip here to the U.S.A.,' he told the Voice of America. 'In the first place I came with some material to be pressed [into records]. In addition I came to see this country and take advantage of the opportunity to get medical treatment.'

In light of the previous year's busy calendar, the need for medical attention came as a surprise. Nico had appeared to be healthy and well along the comeback road. His host in Washington, producer Ibrahim Kanja Bah, recalled that doctors spoke of a blood disorder and prescribed a course of treatment. Nico himself called it *intoxication* in French, a poisoning of the system, something he said he had lived with since the sixties. 'For that, they withdrew up to two bags of blood per day. I was ready to run away. But I held on.' Whatever the procedures were – blood transfusions or something else – they appeared to have a salutary effect. Nico looked well enough and even gained weight during his stay. He concluded an agreement with Bah for the release of an album and made preliminary plans for a full-fledged U.S. concert tour.

Back in Togo at the end of April, Nico briefed Akueson on his U.S. visit, and then he went on to Kinshasa. 'I was longing for home,' he said on arrival. 'I stayed one year outside my family circle. It was necessary at all costs that I rejoin it.' Things had gone well abroad, he said. 'I'm in shape. I've recovered, you might say, a second youth.' He would be returning to the United States soon.

Nico played a May date at La Crèche, a popular Kinshasa night spot, and plans were announced for the production of a video to introduce him to fans in Europe and America, most of whom had only heard his music. He would also perform in some of Zaïre's other major cities before embarking on his American tour. But neither project came to fruition. In July, Nico celebrated his forty-sixth birthday still intent on playing the States. Akueson stopped in Brazzaville in August on the way to East Africa, and Nico crossed the river to meet him. He looked terrible, Akueson remembered. Nico had lost all the weight he had gained in the U.S.

Whatever it was that ravaged his body it moved with incredible speed. In early September, with help from President Mobutu, Nico flew to Belgium to seek medical treatment. On Sunday, September 22, 1985, in the early morning hours, he died in a Brussels hospital.

Nico's body was returned to Kinshasa, to his home in Limete, where it lay in state on a grassy slope behind the house. Once again the makers and lovers of music gathered at Notre Dame Cathedral to hear a funeral mass for one of their heroes. Once again Edo Ganga led a delegation of Congolese musicians to pay tribute to a Zaïrean brother. 'Nico was not only Zaïrean,' he said, 'but African. So it is Africa that has lost.' The Zaïrean government decorated Nico with one of the nation's highest honors, elevation to the rank of Chevalier in the National Order of the Leopard. At Gombe Cemetery two of the greats of O.K. Jazz, Franco and Edo, eulogized their former rival.

Even in death Docteur Nico remained Africa's pre-eminent guitarist. His distinctive stylings live on in the works of generations of guitarists across the continent. Death deprived the world of his physical presence, but his musical spirit would never be silenced.

•

The deaths of Joseph Kabasele and Docteur Nico left Tabu Ley as sole standard-bearer of the African Jazz 'school' of music. But the fervent rivalry with O.K. Jazz had cooled to friendly competition. The unthinkable, collaboration, had even taken place. Franco and Tabu Ley acquired the status of elder statesmen. Once dueling denizens of Kinshasa, they now plied the currents of the world. And the music continued to move with them, ever so steadily outward.

19
You can't tell the players without a program

Empire Bakuba and Clan Langa Langa, 1979–1985

Anyone who cocked an ear towards Kinshasa's youth bands could hear that Nico lived. Almost to a man, the younger generation of guitarists had sharpened its picks to the sounds of the good Docteur. 'The style of guitar I play finds its origins in his school,' Zaïko's Manuaku Waku once remarked. Rigo Star of Viva La Musica, Thu Zaina's Roxy Tshimpaka, Zaïko's Matima Kinuani, and any number of others would have said the same. But in younger hands the Docteur's delicate accompaniment and fluid solos emerged rough and repetitious. Where Nico stood 'immobile as a Buddha,' the new generation danced. Looking west for an appropriate analogy, someone called it 'rumba rock.'

Among Kinshasa's rumba rockers, Empire Bakuba had matured by the end of the seventies into one of the country's most stable groups. Led by Kabasele Yampanya 'Pepe Kalle,' the 300-pound 'elephant of Zaïre,' the group muscled its way into the upper ranks of Kinshasa's bands on the strength of its talent and an evolved sense of loyalty and group purpose. Pepe Kalle and fellow singers Dilu Dilumona and 'Papy Tex' Matolu Dode, along with guitarists Ebuya 'Doris' Lange and Bwingi '737' Kinanga, formed a tight-knit core that seemed immune to the lure of fast talk and easy money.

Empire Bakuba rendered the music of Kinshasa's youth, smoother on the vocals than Zaïko Langa Langa, quicker of tempo than Orchestre Bella Bella, steady enough on guitar, with a smattering of horns like the older bands. 'I sing of love, of birth, of life, of death – of everything and nothing,' Kalle

Pepe Kalle

observed, summing up the band's repertoire. Songs from the late seventies included Kalle's 'Dadou,' which spoke of family problems engendered by an absent father. Matolu's 'Sango ya Mawa' (sad news) was said to have been inspired by his mother's death. Dilu's 'Kebo' based itself in part on the *kebo* village party of folklore. The band played regularly around Kinshasa with the amazingly agile giant, Pepe Kalle, always the focal point.

After a couple of second-place finishes in the year-end music awards, Empire Bakuba won the best band category for 1982. In addition to their tireless performances in the dancing bars of Kinshasa, the musicians spent months each year entertaining in the provinces and touring Europe and the rest of Africa. They rejoined the Vévé stable in the early eighties, where their ardent *patron* Verckys Kiamuangana provided the latest equipment and the city's most up-to-date recording studio.

Dilu's 1983 hit 'Kambile' (a man's name) told of a model couple whose love was tested by jealous neighbors and men's seemingly innate susceptibility to the charms of other women. Kalle's 'Mista John' from 1985 warns not to ridicule someone who has fallen on hard times, because that person might surprise you by mounting a comeback (as often happened in Zaïrean political life).

When in Kinshasa, the gigantic Pepe Kalle tooled around town in a Volkswagen Beetle. On a television program in 1980 he amazed the capital by introducing the group's newest member, Tumba Ayila, a dancing dwarf who went by the stage name 'Emoro.' 'I like contrast,' Kalle explained. 'When I come by with Emoro it really makes a flash. When I drive by in a small car, everybody looks and says, "No, it's not possible!"' Another striking comparison, this time between Empire Bakuba and most of Kinshasa's other bands, illustrated the Kalle group's basic strength. In 1982 its core members celebrated their tenth anniversary together. 'Without false modesty,' Kalle told a reporter,

> I must tell you that Empire Bakuba is the only band which has known no defections during or on return from its tours – quite simply because no one is cheating anyone…. The understanding and solidarity among our musicians is such that we are like family.

•

The flip side of the Empire Bakuba model of stability revealed itself in the volatile nature of Clan Langa Langa, the burgeoning number of spin-offs from Zaïko Langa Langa. The first phase of diffusion – the one that had produced Lokole Isifi, Yoka Lokole, Viva La Musica, Karawa Musica, Muchacha, and Libanko – eventually winnowed the clan down to two main families, Zaïko Langa Langa and Viva La Musica. Both would seed a second phase even more spectacular than the original.

Phase one's winnowing process had fostered a number of reunions, many of which appeared to be shaky. Zaïko's musicians cooly accepted Evoloko, their *enfant terrible* who now called himself 'Joker,' back into the fold in the middle of 1979, just in time for the band's tenth anniversary. His career had gone nowhere in the five years since he'd been asked to leave. Now he needed the work. 'For the moment,' he candidly observed, 'I'm in the position of a wife who abandoned her married home and returns to it after a long absence. It's quite normal that my husband sulks.'

The band had changed in Evoloko's absence. Singers Likinga 'Redo' Mangenza from Empire Bakuba and newcomer Nsumbu 'Lengi' Lenga had hired on, along with a second bassist, 'Djo Mali' Bolenge Boteku, from the old Lokole Isifi. Zaïko's musicians – by this time calling themselves Tout-Choc, L'Anti-Choc Zaïko Langa Langa (total shock, in their own performances; shock-proof, in the face of competitors) – kept to a busy schedule of live performances and recording. In March of 1980 they staged an impressive ten-day tenth anniversary celebration with the participation of Empire Bakuba, Viva La Musica, Afrisa, and O.K. Jazz.

Later in the year, as Zaïko auditioned former Thu Zaina and Orchestre Véve guitarist Roxy Tshimpaka and bade farewell to Mbuta Mashakado, who was returning to school, new stresses burst into the open. According to *Elima*'s account, singer Bimi Ombale had the temerity to suggest that the band's board of directors – founder D.V. Moanda, *chef d'orchestre* Manuaku Waku, his assistant Nyoka Longo, and two non-musician members who handled the group's business affairs – should be disbanded. Bimi received a two-month suspension for his insubordination. Manuaku took up the call by asking that so-called 'onlookers,' the non-musician members of the board, be cut loose so that the performers' salaries could be increased.

At the beginning of October the board of directors, including Nyoka Longo but without Manuaku, fired seven members of the band. Evoloko, Bozi Boziana, and Djo Mali got the ax, along with four lesser-known musicians. According to Zaïko's administrators, the band had become unwieldy. Discipline was lax and the old camaraderie missing.

Beyond the official line, however, Manuaku appeared to be the target. Dissatisfaction with his leadership had apparently been festering. He was said to be secretly rehearsing with the seven fired musicians and playing concerts with them on the side. Despite the fact that Manuaku had founded Les Ya Tupas, and other Zaïko members, including D.V. Moanda, played openly with a band called the Casques Bleus, Manuaku's latest *nzonzing* (moonlighting) was used as a pretext for dealing with problems in Zaïko itself. When Manuaku failed to gain support from other members of the band for the return of the sacked seven, he resigned. And that, according to one unidentified musician, was the point. 'We wanted to make him leave Zaïko honorably, and he found the best solution himself: to quit.'

Once the purge had succeeded, Evoloko, Bozi, and Djo Mali were accepted back into the group. Roxy Tshimpaka took Manuaku's place as guitar soloist. Manuaku and the four musicians still fired moved on to form Clan Langa Langa's newest offspring, Orchestre Grand Zaïko Wa Wa.

Zaïko Langa Langa appeared to emerge tighter and stronger from the shake-up. At its core the band counted singers Nyoka Longo, Bimi Ombale, and Lengi Lenga; guitarists Matima Mpioso Kinuani, Enoch Zamuangana, and Bapuis Muaka; and, although he had begun to suffer from increasingly frequent bouts of illness, founder D.V. Moanda on congas. Pablo Bakunde Ilondjoko played traps alone until Meridjo Belobi returned after serving his 21-month prison term. Both musicians decided to stay with the band to form the music's first and only kit drum tandem. Veteran member Teddy Sukami dropped out during a European tour in early 1981 to undergo surgery for the removal of a facial tumor (Sukami never fully recovered his health and died in February of 1986). Later in the year Likinga, *en route* to Zaïre from Europe, was jailed in Portugal for drug possession, effectively halting his career for the next five years.

Overall the departures did little to diminish the band's performance and may have indeed enhanced it. Fewer musicians produced a more coherent sound. Voices merged harmoniously when they didn't have to strain to be heard. Matima and Enoch (and Roxy until 1982) had room to play unencumbered by the clutter of others. Songs of the period seem more polished than those from earlier times. Stories unfolded to a slow rumba's gait before galloping into the sebene.

Nyoka's 'Crois-Moi' (believe me) from 1981 exemplified Zaïko's blend of maturing instrumentation and adolescent angst. It tells of a couple whose love has been frustrated by the great distance that the two must live one from the other. In the end the girl breaks off the affair, moving the boy to plead for reconciliation.

> I have begged you a lot
> It is true, my love, that you will end up killing me
> And when that happens, you will cry for me
> On hearing my name you will think of me
> But it will be too late.

Ever since it began, Zaïko had been a wellspring of inspired choreography. The *cavacha* of 1973 had helped to solidify the group's growing popularity. A decade later they replaced their reigning 'funky' with a new step, said to have been adapted from folklore, called the *zekete zekete*. One danced hands in pockets – preferably of designer clothes – leaning left, then right, crossing feet and acting cool. The music writers picked it as 1983's dance of the year.

•

Like the Zaïko family, Papa Wemba's Viva La Musica had grown in size and stature. Kinshasa's music chroniclers had voted Wemba the number one star of 1980. He took to calling himself 'Kuru Yaka,' essentially 'the great' in the

Papa Wemba

Lari language, and his musicians the Molokai Stars. Both appellations quickly caught on with the public. In a song called 'Analengo,' Wemba implored his fans: 'Dear mothers, dear fathers, dear friends, help me, support me so that I may reach the highest heights, so that I always climb higher.' The song borrowed heavily from traditional music, with lyrics in the language of the Tetela people of central Zaïre, and drum and guitar interplay that sounded like a middle-of-the-night village jam session. In spite of Wemba's deviation from the standard Lingala, his fans seemed to get the message. 'Analengo' became one of 1981's more popular songs.

At the same time, Wemba was reported to be grumbling that his twenty-plus-member band had grown too large. Some of the players had become unproductive. He wanted to cut the group down to a more manageable size. He should have known that the problem would take care of itself.

In September of 1981, less than a year after the Zaiko family had split, four of Viva La Musica's best-known musicians left the group. Deserting Papa Wemba were guitarist Popolipo Zanguila from the old Lokole Isifi days and three singers, Djuna Djanana, Dindo Yogo, and original Viva member 'Espérant'

Kisangani Djenga, who had returned following a previous defection to Karawa Musica. Not by chance, three members of Zaïko Langa Langa – the ones who had been temporarily fired at the time of Manuaku's departure, Evoloko, Bozi, and Djo Mali – also quit Zaïko. The seven defectors from their two respective families put together a new band they called Langa Langa Stars.

The hand of Verckys Kiamuangana was seen in the affair. Some accused him of fomenting the two simultaneous insurrections, but he denied the charges. The musicians, he claimed, had come to him asking for assistance. He only agreed to help when it was clear there would be no reconciliations.

In the middle of the following year, the last of the outsiders in Zaïko Langa Langa, Roxy Tshimpaka, left the band to join Langa Langa Stars. He and his new colleagues were joined by singer Mutombo 'Ben' Nyamabo, who had been making records on his own in Kinshasa after returning from a period in Italy.

For the family of Viva La Musica, the loss of three singers left the vocal ranks dangerously thin. Emeneya Mubiala, a singer who had joined Viva shortly after its founding, was now clearly the group's second most popular attraction behind Papa Wemba himself. Wemba quickly restocked with two new singers, Nzola Ndonga 'Petit Prince' and Sangua Mbaya 'Maray,' who joined Boloko Manzangi 'Safro,' a recruit from a few months earlier. Then, just before the new year of 1982 began, Wemba flew off to Europe to do some recording for VISA 1980, leaving the band in the hands of his manager.

After six months, during which rumors of his death or imprisonment made the rounds, Wemba returned home to a welcome worthy of a head of state. Large crowds greeted his motorcade as it wound through the streets of Kinshasa on the way to the Voice of Zaïre, where he was to give a homecoming interview. Soon afterward he took the band into the studio to record a new song to mark his return and address the rumors. He called it 'Evénement' (event).

> I went on a trip, that's all
> Behind me, people told a bunch of stories
> They spread false rumors
> Today, the truth is coming to light
> In the faraway place where I happened to be, I was dead in prison
> Today, here I am come to life again.

At the time of Wemba's homecoming, Jadot Sombele 'Le Cambodgien' rejoined the band after a long absence. His arrival reunited three of Viva's founding members, Wemba, Jadot, and Pepe Bipoli, who had returned to the group in 1978 following his involvement with Karawa Musica.

Unfortunately for Papa Wemba the reunion would be brief. A few months later, in October of 1982, ten of the nineteen members of Viva La Musica walked out. No one expressed much criticism of Wemba, but his extended trip to Europe without the band and his earlier collaboration with Tabu Ley appeared to have played a part. In both instances Viva's musicians had had to scrimp to keep the band together. Many said that they felt neglected, that their work had been under-appreciated. Emeneya, the ringleader, complained more openly of Wemba's egotism and arrogance. The ten deserters – Emeneya, his brother Joly Mubiala, Bipoli, Petit Prince, and Debaba Mbaki, all singers; guitarists Mongo Ley, Ntembo Pinos, 'Tofla' Tofolo Kitoko, and Nseka 'Huit Kilos' Bimuela (a.k.a. Fatima Lola); and drummer Mpasi Samba 'Patcho Star' – formed a new band called Victoria Eleison.

Theoretically the musicians were equal, but Emeneya Mubiala, 'Jo Kester' to his fans, was the new group's most prominent personality. Young, handsome, educated – he had attended university in Lubumbashi before dropping out to join Viva – Emeneya rivaled Papa Wemba when it came to style and flash. Victoria, he explained, stood for victory. Eleison came from 'Kyrie eleison,' a phrase of Greek origin used in Christian worship which means 'Lord, have mercy.' For devout Christian Emeneya, Victoria Eleison meant 'victory comes from God.' But the wherewithal to achieve it came from Verckys Kiamuangana, who provided instruments and a recording contract. In the early hours of Christmas morning during a grand dance at Vévé Centre, Victoria Eleison made its official debut. The religious overtones and Emeneya's long hair and beard led some of his fans to begin calling him 'Jésus.'

Emeneya's mentor Papa Wemba, whose band had been crippled by the desertions, was left to try casting the debacle in the best light possible.

> My group, it's more than a band. It's a school. I don't teach debauchery, delinquence.... I teach music to my students and also cleanliness, how to behave, good manners.... The majority have entered it unknown and left as big stars. I train accomplished stars. Once a separation has taken place I am always the object of harsh criticism. Each time I retain my composure, a calm I call Asiatic, Episcopalian.

Now he would have to do it again.

•

In the space of two years Clan Langa Langa had grown from two families to five – elders Zaïko Langa Langa and Viva La Musica and their new offspring Grand Zaïko Wa Wa, Langa Langa Stars, and Victoria Eleison. Each new offspring bore a stylistic resemblance to the clan's still relatively young patriarch, Zaïko Langa Langa. None of the bands added horns to their lineups. They tried instead to produce variety by varying the rhythms and shifting tempo within a song. The steady thump, thump of disco's bass drum intruded into the mix, diminishing the rumba's swing. Shouts of animation urged patrons onto the dance floor. 'The masses, the little people, as we say the "ngembo," adore animation,' one musician observed. 'Gentle music puts them to sleep.' Nevertheless, a certain sameness crept into the music of the youth bands that even the most vociferous animators failed to cover.

The proliferation of bands also diluted the base of talent. With each round of defections, new, untested recruits were rushed into action to fill the resulting vacancies. In the immortal words of the ball park vendor, you couldn't tell the players without a program.

•

As a result of Zaïre's failing economy and declining record sales, live performances took on greater importance. Stars' individual character and style could count for as much, perhaps more, than their music. The phenomenon of *la sape*, 'society of ambiancers and persons of elegance' (from the French *les sapes*, clothes or togs), appeared to spring in part from this development. Practitioners were called *sapeurs*. Nearly every young star – and soon many of their fans – joined in pursuing the fad. Sapeurs' predilection for European designer clothes flew in the face of authenticity, but Mobutu, with his seemingly insatiable thirst for European villas, must have understood.

Among Kinshasa's sapeurs Clan Langa Langa led the way, and Papa Wemba was *le pape de la sape* (the pope of sape). His manager, Sacré Marpeza, described Wemba's fondness for fashion as a good example for Kinshasa's youth.

> Papa Wemba knows how to show his body to advantage. He dresses himself expensively. Ungaro clothes, Weston shoes, hair close-cropped and parted, and several other creations see to it that the young take him for a model and adopt it 100%.

La sape gave rise to a dance known as *la griffe* (the label). 'When you dance you have to show off the [clothing] label,' Wemba explained. 'You can even take off your shoes to show the label on the shoes.' Wemba invented a dance called Firenze in honor of the fashion houses of Florence. One entrepreneur took the idea still further by opening a night club called La Griffe. Wemba's 1983 song 'Matebu' (a woman's name), a story about separated lovers, became one of the craze's anthems.

> My love, listen to me
> I await you, darling
> On that day, I want you to know
> On our wedding day, listen
> The label will be Torrente
> The label will be Giorgio Armani
> The label will be Daniel Hechter
> The label for shoes will be J.M. Weston.

One of *la sape*'s unintended consequences was that in order to emulate the stars, many of Kinshasa's increasingly poor young people would have to steal. 'All Wemba has to do is do his hair, dress, or walk this or that way for young people to do the same the next day,' one observer noted. Criticism from parents and older adults eventually grew to the point where Wemba was moved to deny that he was a delinquent. He recorded a song called 'Proclamation' in which he admonished sapeurs to behave themselves.

•

Apart from its two main families, Zaïko Langa Langa and Viva La Musica, Clan Langa Langa's new additions developed growing pains. Grand Zaïko Wa Wa got off to a wobbly start. Its lineup of musicians changed repeatedly as 'Pepe Felly' Manuaku searched for compatible collaborators. The band's singers became known as *parachutistes*, perhaps because they dropped in and out so often. Those who had come with Manuaku from Zaïko Langa Langa all left in the first few months. Through trial and error Manuaku slowly installed new players like Nzenze Mongengo, a pianist and organist who became the group's *chef d'orchestre*. Mumbata Mambu, a singer whose sexy good looks more than justified his nickname 'Joe Poster,' joined in 1981. Matumona Lulendo, known as 'Defao,' a twenty three-year-old with a hearty tenor, signed on early the next year, followed closely by a singer named Mbembe Mbilia, who called himself 'Joe Nickel,' and two more singers, Lukombo Mayemba 'Djeffard,' and Lukombo Nzambi 'Shimita.' In November of 1983, the band celebrated its third anniversary by opening its own bar in Matonge called Le Cosmique. A year later Kinshasa's music scribes selected Grand Zaïko as 1984's best band.

310   Rumba on the River

With Manuaku at the helm, Grand Zaïko sounded much like the Zaïko Langa Langa he had captained. But there were differences too, notably the presence of a synthesizer in the hands of chef d'orchestre Nzenze. Nzenze wrote one of the band's more memorable pieces, 'Pambu,' in honor of his wife. 'Using a style of imagery, I compared love to an egg,' he said. 'Everyone knows that an egg is very fragile. That is why you have to hold it in such a way that it won't fall and break.' In a series of 45s released at the end of 1983, Nzenze, apparently enthralled with the synth's capabilities, alternates among the sounds of a circus calliope, piano, and the Solovox organ of old. He returns periodically to the oscillating beep of a police siren, a kind of signature for the session. 'Zeke ya Pamba' (refers to a traditional procedure called *zeke* used to ascertain the truth of a matter), a song about infidelity, 'Mbongo' (money), and several others contributed heavily to the band's selection as best of 1984.

•

Langa Langa Stars, Clan Langa Langa's largest collection of veteran musicians, produced some of the best and some of the worst music that the new families had to offer. Songs like Djo Mali's 'Fleur Bakutu' featuring the quavering voice of Dindo Yogo could soar, while others, like Espérant's 'Mbongwana' (big change), fell flat. Djuna's 'Dalida' drops in a short rumba passage worthy of the older bands, but the frequency with which the tempo shifts disrupts the groove. 'Eliyo' by Evoloko injects ten seconds of gratuitous synthesizer that sounds more like wires have short-circuited in a distant corner of the studio. The band's inconsistency perhaps reflected the inability of so many established stars to work together effectively. Whatever the cause, the collaboration of the *sept patrons* (seven bosses), as they came to be called, was to last barely two years.

Trouble started in March of 1983 when guitarist Popolipo Zanguila left the band to join the Clan's patriarch, Zaïko Langa Langa. In September, Ben Nyamabo, Bozi Boziana, and Roxy Tshimpaka quit or were fired, depending on who tells the story. The separation took an unusual turn when the Zaïrean courts seized the band's instruments to settle a debt. Money was owed to Ben Nyamabo, suddenly an ex-member of the group. In addition to his music career, Nyamabo owned Scarpa Uomo (man's shoe, in Italian), a popular boutique that had outfitted the band for a television performance to the tune of 38,000 zaïres. Now he wanted his money. It looked like a clear-cut case until Verckys stepped in, contracts in hand, to claim the instruments for himself.

Somehow the dispute was settled, apparently to everyone's satisfaction, but the case exposed a dilemma young musicians faced. If they wanted to start a band and had no money of their own, they would need a *patron* like Verckys to provide instruments. The standard contract, in Verckys's case at least, bound the band to the *patron* for four years, during which time he retained title to the instruments. If the band stayed together and the instruments were still operable at the contract's expiration – in both instances an increasingly unlikely prospect – only then would the instruments belong to the band.

Once at liberty, Nyamabo, Bozi, and Roxy joined with Defao from Grand Zaïko and Bipoli from Victoria Eleison to form the Clan's newest member, the Choc Stars. Fortunately for them, Ben Nyamabo's boutique turned a profit. Nyamabo provided the band with the latest equipment, and he and the others recruited additional musicians. Choc Stars produced its initial waves on the dance floor with a new step called *roboti robota*. Created by Bozi Boziana, roboti took its inspiration from the American dance the smurf. By the end of the year, the Choc Stars' first records hit the market.

Part of the way through 1984 the ranks of the Langa Langa Stars experienced a further thinning. Dindo Yogo followed Popolipo to Zaïko Langa Langa, and Espérant dropped out to try his luck in Europe. Late in the year Djuna Djanana and Djo Mali were accused of violating Verckys's notorious contract by participating in a recording session outside the domain of Editions Vévé. After a lengthy public palaver, the two accused jumped to the Choc Stars. Following these latest events, Langa Langa Stars could be written in the singular. Of the seven bosses, only Evoloko Joker, 'the [J.R.] Ewing of Zaïrean music,' remained.

•

Over on the Clan's Viva La Musica wing, Emeneya Mubiala's Victoria Eleison experienced its share of difficulties. One of the singers, Debaba Mbaki, who called himself 'Debaba el Shabab,' left in October of 1983. He formed a band called Historia Musica, which stumbled into a precarious existence a short time later with a disastrous appearance on Zaïrean television.

Pepe Bipoli posed a more serious threat to Victoria Eleison. The erratic singer had left the group to help form Choc Stars, only to return a few months later. In March of 1984 he left again, taking with him guitarist Tofla Tofolo, drummer Patcho Star, and singer-guitarist Safro Manzangi, who had just joined Victoria after leaving Viva La Musica. The quartet formed yet another

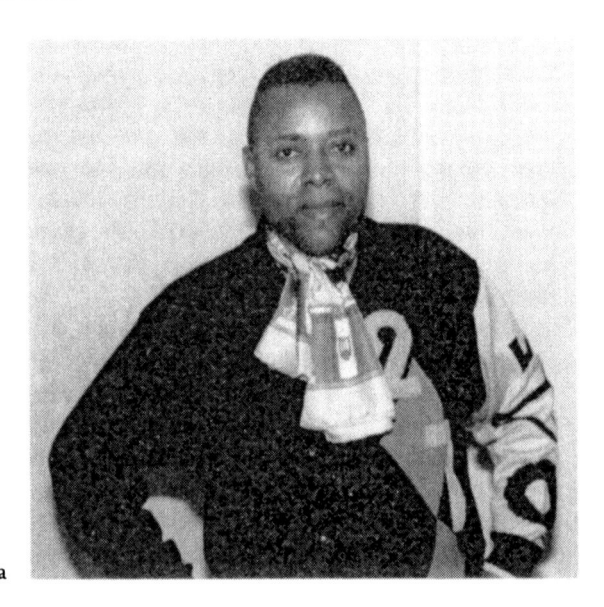

Emeneya Mubiala

new band, which they called Véritable Victoria (sometimes referred to, thanks to American television, as Victoria Principal).

In what appeared to be a response to the rebellion, Emeneya recorded a song called 'Sans Préavis' (without notice). On the surface it told of a woman who submitted to her husband's every demand only to be divorced after years of sacrifice. But in light of what was happening in the band, one could imagine the story's deeper implications. It opens with a snippet of the South African song 'Wimoweh' (a.k.a. 'Mbube' or 'The Lion Sleeps Tonight'), then slides into an easy rumba while Emeneya spins the yarn of treachery and double-cross. Guitarist Huit Kilos offers a swinging sebene accompanied by a disco-style bass drum. It was a polished performance by any standard and became one of Victoria Eleison's biggest hits.

A couple of months after 'Sans Préavis' came out, Huit Kilos joined the renegades. They cut a few records together, but the experiment looked less than promising. Before the year had ended, Tofolo and Huit Kilos returned to Victoria Eleison, and Véritable Victoria fell apart.

•

In the midst of the confusion over who belonged to which family, and, more important, which families remained viable, Clan Langa Langa's founding father, D.V. Moanda, passed away. Death came in the middle of the night of January 9, 1984. Moanda had started it all back in 1969 when he recruited the bunch of teenagers who were currently some of the music's biggest stars. He had battled poor health for almost as long as he guided the band. Now, at age thirty-six, his body succumbed to the siege. Zaïko Langa Langa's musicians canceled their engagements and entered a month-long period of mourning.

Following Moanda's death and the restoration of Victoria Eleison to near full strength, Clan Langa Langa settled down. Bipoli went back to Papa Wemba, who had rebuilt Viva La Musica with, among others, future singing stars Amisi Ngoy, known as 'Reddy Amisi,' and Pangu Nguisi 'Lidjo' Kwempa, a defector from Grand Zaïko. At times the Clan's families even cooperated. On several occasions in Kinshasa two of them played on the same bill. Papa Wemba and Evoloko performed together in Europe in 1985. That same year Emeneya, Dindo Yogo, and Manuaku joined forces to record an album.

As the longevity of Clan Langa Langa's principal families demonstrated, Kinshasa's youth bands were an enduring if somewhat unstable force. Their records and live shows enjoyed tremendous popularity and even triggered changes among the older groups. As a result, Congo music of the eighties became a colossus with three heads: the youthful Clan Langa Langa on the left, the older generation of Franco and Tabu Ley on the right, and in the center Pepe Kalle's Empire Bakuba and the growing numbers of Paris-resident Zaïreans and Congolese like Kanda Bongo Man and Les Quatre Etoiles who synthesized old and new.

20
Crossroads

Tshala Muana, Abeti, Rigo Star, Les Quatre Etoiles, Loketo, Kanda Bongo Man, Tabu Ley, and Mbilia Bel, 1985–1988

African skies waxed uneasy in the middle eighties. Rains as usual swelled the Congo River, but to the northeast, in the continent's fickle horn, crops and livestock languished under an unyielding sun. Cameras of Western news agencies captured desperate faces and thrust them into millions of comfortable living rooms. People who could do something to alleviate the suffering began to take notice.

In the spirit of Ravi Shankar and George Harrison – the organizers of a concert to raise money for refugees from the Bangladesh independence struggle over a dozen years before – artists of the world gathered in the name of famine relief for Africa. 'We Are the World,' 'Do They Know It's Christmas,' and the Live Aid concert enlisted Western musicians. Not invited to participate in those extravaganzas, African artists organized their own.

Manu Dibango's 'Tam-Tam Pour l'Ethiopie' (drum for Ethiopia) took shape in Paris at the beginning of 1985. From Gabon, where she was performing, M'Pongo Love telephoned her vocal track to be wedded to the 45 r.p.m. fund-raiser. Other Zaïreans, Souzy Kasseya and Ray Lema, added their parts in Paris.

Franco helped to launch a second benefit called Operation Africa, two concerts and a recording session held in Abidjan in August of the same year. Franco's friend, producer Daniel Cuxac, organized the events which brought musicians from several African countries together in the Ivoirean capital. Beya Maduma ('Moro Maurice'), the former Négro Succès saxophonist now living in Abidjan, wrote Operation Africa's main theme, a 'We Are the World' kind of mass participation recording called 'Africa.' Franco and several members of O.K. Jazz, Abeti, and Pamelo Mounk'a joined Beya Maduma to form the project's contingent from central Africa.

Apart from raising money for famine relief, Operation Africa cast a spotlight on what had been happening in Abidjan ever since the African All Stars formed there in 1978. The city, not noted for its own variety of popular music, had, nevertheless, become an important center for music production. The opening of the eight-track JBZ studio in the early eighties brought modern recording technology to local musicians and put it within a few days' reach of artists from neighboring Sierra Leone, Liberia, and Mali. For those farther afield in crumbling Kinshasa, Côte d'Ivoire was closer than France and provided opportunities to work while one laid plans for the inevitable move to Paris. Operation Africa's Beya Maduma was just one of a number of Congolese and Zaïrean musicians who followed the trail blazed by the African All Stars.

Few had more remarkable success than a dancer from the former Elisabethville, Lubumbashi. She too was called Elisabeth until the time of authenticity, but Zaïreans came to know her as Tshala Muana. Tshala left the unhappiness of an arranged marriage and the sorrow of her infant daughter's death and moved to Kinshasa, where she caught on as a dancer in M'Pongo Love's fledgling troupe Orchestre Tcheke Tcheke Love. Two years later, in 1978, she began her singing career by recording songs with Orchestre Minzoto Wella Wella. A short tour of Angola as one of Abeti's Tigresses followed, then she signed on with a bandleader from eastern Zaïre named Rachid King in hopes of furthering her singing career.

Tshala's brief collaboration with King ended abruptly at the beginning of 1980 when a manager she had fired threatened her with legal action for breach of contract. Tshala slipped across the river to Brazzaville and made her way slowly along the coast, arriving in Abidjan in 1981. At an audition soon afterward, she met a producer from Burkina Faso named Ram Ouedraogo. He in turn introduced her to Ivoirean band leader Jimmy Hyacinthe, who agreed to let her try out with his group.

With her straightened hair and evening gown, Tshala resembled one of the Supremes as she glided on stage at the cultural center of Abidjan's Treichville neighborhood. She sang her songs and danced the *mutuashi*, a traditional dance of the Baluba from Zaïre's Kasai province. 'Mutuashi,' she explained, was a Tshiluba word, a shout of encouragement for dancers that eventually became synonymous with the dance itself, and with Tshala Muana too. Subsequent appearances in Abidjan increased her nascent following.

In 1982, financed by money borrowed from a friend, she flew to Paris with Hyacinthe's band to cut a record. The A side, 'Amina' – a song given her by guitarist Souzy Kasseya, whom she'd met in M'Pongo Love's band – packs a funky West African feel and lots of brass in support of Tshala's tart commentary.

> Amina, shake my hand.
> Even if you're my opponent in this run-off,
> I can't hold it against you.
> The world is like that, today it's you, tomorrow it's me.
> Amina, I know what I think,
> I've known a long time:
> A man is like a hospital bed that takes in all the sick.
> When you're there it's you,
> When I'm there it's me.

Tshala sang 'Amina' in French to reach the widest possible audience, while the B side, 'Tshebele,' presented a more traditional piece with a percussion-driven sebene in the mutuashi style and lyrics in Tshiluba. Back in Abidjan, the finished disc was reported to have sold more than 11,000 copies in Côte d'Ivoire alone.

Ram Ouedraogo became Tshala's manager. He booked her with other artists in large, show-style spectacles where she honed the mutuashi, incorporating its rhythms into several of her songs to give them a different tilt from the standard rumba. Still, much of Tshala's music was an eclectic mix that reflected the cosmopolitan milieu of Abidjan. There her mutuashi bumped hip and shoulder with Caribbean salsa, makossa from Cameroon, West African highlife, and the familiar rumba of Congo music. During her stay of nearly four years she recorded songs like 'Baba Moussa' with Latin touches that recalled the work of Joseph Kabasele. Others followed the rhythm of the rumba or the mutuashi. She even recorded a ballad or two. Her songs, she explained, were about everyday life. 'I don't sing about love very often, no. In my songs in Tshiluba there are often proverbs, things that are a little different compared to the other [singers].'

Like her preference for the mutuashi rhythm, Tshala's use of Tshiluba, her first language, set her apart from most other Zaïrean musicians, who preferred Lingala. But that seemed to matter little. Her warm contralto embraces a song with a sensitivity that transcends language. With every concert tour

Tshala Muana

and each trip to Paris to record, Tshala's popularity strengthened. Her demure Motown image gave way to a more authentic look. The hair bristled naturally. The body bathed in fashions inspired by Africa.

What had begun as a professional relationship between Tshala and Ouedraogo developed an amorous side. By 1984, however, the mixture of business and personal affairs turned sour. Tshala and Ouedraogo split. 'When you're working, you have to content yourself with the work,' Tshala told the Ivoirean newspaper *Fraternité Matin*. 'Because when other things aren't going well, they come in and ruin the work too.' She flirted briefly with a marriage proposal from Ivoirean musician François Lougah, but in the end she turned him down.

Before 1984 had ended, Tshala moved to Paris. 'Here there is almost everything,' she declared. 'Paris is the capital of world music, of African music. It's a crossroads.' The move, she said, was the next logical progression in her career. After four years of preparation in Côte d'Ivoire, she arrived in Paris a seasoned and confident performer ready to compete on the international level.

With Cameroonian bassist and arranger Aladji Touré at the controls, Tshala produced her opening gambit, *Kami*, a cautiously generic album shrouded in a haze of electronics. Following that tepid beginning she turned to Safari Ambiance for help with her next two productions. *Mbanda Matière* (a matter of rivals), recorded in 1984 with arrangements by Souzy Kasseya, and *M'Pokolo* (*le petit ruisseau*) (small stream), recorded in 1985 and arranged by Touré, brought Tshala closer to her Zaïrean roots. *M'Pokolo* in particular, with Rigo Star's guitar pointing the way, won fans at home and abroad. In August of 1986 Tshala flew to Kinshasa for a pair of triumphal homecoming concerts. Like Abeti before her, she had left in obscurity and returned as an artist of international eminence.

•

Tshala Muana's arrival at Safari Ambiance roughly coincided with the departure of M'Pongo Love. Despite having achieved her greatest success in the hands of LaCoste and Maniatakis, M'Pongo tried to break her contract after recording *Basongeur* (gossipers), her follow-up to the acclaimed *Femme Commerçante*. The dispute wound up in the French courts, effectively preventing her from working in Paris for a time.

Rather than remain idle, M'Pongo moved to Gabon under the auspices of the Gabonese minister of labor and sometime musician, Alexandre Sambat. But her music suffered as a result. Her newest offerings lacked the superb quality of musical arrangements and production that she had enjoyed first with Empompo Loway and then at Safari Ambiance. The move reduced her visibility in the major markets of Europe and America. She focused instead on cultivating fans in West Africa, where she toured extensively in the latter half of the eighties.

•

The doyenne of Zaïre's women entertainers, Abeti Masikini, found herself on the move as well. A brief string of setbacks began when some of Abeti's Tigresses left to join Tshala Muana for promised engagements that never materialized. The incident triggered a round of unseemly public sniping as each star defended her position. Shortly after the squabble subsided, the Togolese government decided once again to shut down operations at the OTODI studios and pressing plant in Lomé. The move deprived Abeti and her husband-manager, Gérard Akueson, of their base of operations, sending them packing for Paris. Momentarily strapped for cash, the pair departed without the musicians of Abeti's band Les Redoutables.

Once in Paris around the middle of 1986, Abeti rebounded, but Les Redoutables remained alive in name only. In their stead the cream of the Paris session players graced her next album, *Je Suis Fâché* (I am angry). Boffi Banengola, Abeti's drummer in the seventies, headed the list along with three of the best guitarists in Paris, Lokassa ya Mbongo and Dally Kimoko, who had arrived from Lomé in 1984, and Rigo Star. Cameroon's Georges Seba wrote the title track and arranged it to capitalize on the current rage, zouk music from the French Antilles.

Zouk joined African rhythms retained from the days of slavery with more up-to-date stylings from popular music – including those of Ry-Co Jazz, the Congolese/Zaïrean band resident in the Antilles at the end of the sixties, and black America's seventies-style funk – and packaged the synthesis in the high-tech trappings of the Paris studios. The result, often characterized by monotonous, machine-produced rhythm tracks in the company of whining synthesizers, threatened to become the eighties' answer to disco. Abeti called her Zaïreanized version *le soukous parfumé*, flavored soukous. Others dubbed it *soukous-zouk* or, more succinctly, *zoukous*.

Abeti's rendering of Seba's 'Je Suis Fâché' must have pleased her, for it became the biggest record of her career. In the song her anger is directed at a runaway lover as she telephones around Africa to find him. But for Abeti it may have held broader implications. 'I just hate injustice,' she said. 'I don't like to see everything that oppresses women. I don't like it. When I see things like that, right away it puts me in the mind to compose, to defend myself.'

Finding themselves subordinate to a synthesizer, her talented trio of guitarists might have felt a little angry too. But Abeti defended the use of the new machines. 'I'm for this, this progress. It's good for us, because it brings in other sounds and doesn't destroy anything at all.' These are modern times, she said, 'We absolutely have to live this era right now.... They say authenticity, authenticity, and there we are driving cars, taking planes. We're in an electronic era ... but that doesn't take away our African soul.'

Maybe she was right. *Je Suis Fâché* rang up sales to the tune of more than 100,000 albums, a bona fide hit in the world of African music. At the end of the year Abeti collected her first gold record in recognition of the album's success.

•

The dissolution of her band, Les Redoutables, placed Abeti in the same circumstances as most other African musicians living in Paris. Unlike their counterparts in Brazzaville and Kinshasa who still belonged to bands, few in Paris worked as members of a group. Individual artists might be under contract to a producer like Richard Dick or Ouattara Moumouni, but when it came time to cut a record they would need to hire others to work the session. This had been the situation since the late seventies when the migration to France began in earnest. The African All Stars alone contributed mightily to the ranks of session players, with alumni like Ringo Moya, Bopol Mansiamina, Pablo Lubadika, and Syran M'Benza. For *Je Suis Fâché* Abeti used two players with All Stars connections, Lokassa ya Mbongo and Dally Kimoko. But one of the most highly recruited session men and the lead guitarist on *Je Suis Fâché* emerged from the ranks of the youth bands.

Rigobert Bamundele, better known as 'Rigo Star,' dropped out of Papa Wemba's Viva La Musica at the end of 1980 while the band was in Paris recording for Franco's VISA 1980 label. Rigo had begun to teach himself the guitar around the age of seven with encouragement from a cousin, the singer Tino Mwinkwa. He started to play seriously as a teenager in the mid-seventies with various groups from his neighborhood in Kinshasa. In 1977 he joined Papa Wemba's new band, Viva La Musica, where he quickly became a major force in shaping Viva's sound.

Like many of the early wave of migrants arriving in Paris, Rigo first went to work for producer Eddy Gustave. He played on a number of recordings including his own *Ringo Star* (sic), which featured Kanda Bongo Man on vocals and additional guitar licks from Diblo Dibala. But the multi-talented Rigo, who could even sing when pressed, found little time to pursue his own projects. His considerable skills as guitarist and arranger made him one of the most sought-after musicians in Paris. 'My telephone number doesn't change,' he said. 'They just call me.' His work for Abeti was merely the latest of an uncountable number of collaborations.

Rigo would soon assume the role of producer as well, following Abeti and many other artists away from affiliation with the main production companies. Abeti and Akueson had established their Bade Stars Music at the end of the seventies. Others took longer to gain their independence, but the chronic mistrust between artists and producers guaranteed that they would try. As early as 1982 Théo Blaise Kounkou, one of the African All Stars, parted with Eddy'Son to establish his own TBK label. After two outings for Ouattara's Afro Rythmes, Kanda Bongo Man declared his independence. 'I produce myself now,' he explained. 'African producers are not serious. They take all the money, they don't pay the musicians. After, you have a big problem. You go to court.' M'Pongo Love's latest moves followed the trend. 'My break with Safari Ambiance is a necessary evil,' she said. 'Now I feel more independent.'

In addition to record production and promotion, producers usually handled record distribution. As independents, African artists needed to develop their own distribution arrangements. On the strength of its acquisition of Fonior's back catalog of Congo music, Sonodisc was well positioned to meet this need. The company's distribution channels extended throughout Africa and Europe and into the Caribbean and North America.

A competitor to Sonodisc grew out of the rock label Celluloid. After several unsatisfactory attempts to distribute its records through the major record companies, Celluloid established its own distribution arm called Mélodie. The Mélodie catalog gradually expanded to include West African groups and then those from Congo, Zaïre, and southern Africa.

•

The musicians' independence movement was trouble enough for producers, but they faced a greater peril. Record piracy continued to rise, cutting sharply into sales and profits. Before piracy became widespread, business was relatively good, Colette LaCoste recalled. Record dealers from Africa would come to buy two or three hundred copies of a new release hoping to be the first to have it.

> When a record started out strong, there was a race for who would be the first client on our doorstep to buy the record. They would show up with money in their socks, CFAs in their socks.... And it put us in an awkward position, because they would say, 'You haven't seen Mr. so-and-so [their competitor] have you?' And we'd say, 'No,' but sometimes he'd be in the store. Then he would want to know if the competitor had bought a lot of records, because he'd say, 'If I buy some too, I'm not going to sell them.' It was nice. It was funny.

But instead of two or three hundred copies, unscrupulous entrepreneurs would buy one or two from which to make pirate cassette tapes. According to Michel David of Sonodisc, in the early days Africa 'made up forty percent of our sales, which is a very big part. Let us say that [today, 1991,] we can no longer calculate it, it's almost nothing, Africa ... not even five percent probably.' Mélodie's François Post said his company encountered similar difficulties. 'Kanda Bongo Man, for example, the record *Sai*, we think that over

300,000 or 400,000 copies were sold in Africa, but only pirate. Maybe he [Kanda] sold, himself, one percent of everything.'

Sonodisc tried an experiment to see if they could beat the pirates, Michel David explained.

> At one point we put out a series of cassettes on which we made no profit at all. All we did was give a tiny share to the producer, and we paid the author's rights plus production costs. And we sold it almost at cost. And that still wasn't enough to discourage the pirates. We can't go below the floor of profitability, because after that point it's not worth it.

Colette LaCoste recalled that

> once we were even pirated in a factory right here in Paris. We had a Gabonese record, it was Pierre Claver Zing's record. He was a big draw there. We were publishing his record, we were waiting for the record. We called the pressing plant, and the man at the plant said, 'Um, it's not done yet. It's not done.' And it turned out that the record had already left the factory for Gabon.... It was the factory that pirated us. We were never able to – we even sued them. We spent an insane amount of money.... It's a jungle!

Governments were slow to recognize the problem and slower still to take effective action. But even token measures yielded results. In 1987 three separate incidents at Brazzaville's Maya Maya Airport turned up 145,000 illicit cassettes of O.K. Jazz, Afrisa, Zaïko Langa Langa, the Antillean group Kassav', and several other bands. A more spectacular bust in Togo four years later netted 1.5 million cassettes. According to the London-based International Federation of the Phonographic Industry, it was the largest seizure ever of pirate cassettes. The IFPI fingered Singapore as the source and claimed that one plant in the Southeast Asian republic 'admitted to the manufacture of around 700,000 pirate cassettes for export to West Africa each month.'

Eddy Gustave estimated that for every record he sold in Africa pirates sold five cassettes. He and his colleagues in Paris simply couldn't compete. The cost of producing cassettes in France was more than the selling price of the illegal tapes. Wounded by the pirates and a downturn in the French economy, Gustave began to reduce the size of his company as early as 1983. LaCoste and Maniatakis started winding up operations at Safari Ambiance in 1987. Richard Dick went home to Togo. Ouattara scaled back from producing two or three records a month at Afro Rythmes to two or three a year.

Even as these main producers all but threw in the towel, others moved in to try their luck. Ibrahima Sylla had entered the business in West Africa around 1980. Born to wealthy parents, he indulged his interest in music as a youth in his native Senegal, where *griots*' traditional songs mingled with pop sounds from Dakar and the repatriated rhythms of Cuba and black America. Sylla lacked the talent to play music himself, so he moved into production, offering front money and artistic advice for the recording of local bands in Dakar. Using profits from these initial endeavors, Sylla set up for business in Paris in 1982.

Unlike his better-established competitors, Sylla avoided the entanglements of long-term contracts. If an artist came to him with an interesting project, Sylla would put up the money and arrange the details of recording, pressing, and distribution of the record. If artist and producer could agree on another project, fine. If not, no problem. Each was free to work with others. Thus Sylla was able to take advantage of the musicians' move toward independence. One of his earliest successes was the album *Soro* for Malian singer Salif Keïta, which gained major label release on Mango Records.

Sylla forged ties with Mélodie for distribution of his records in most of the world, but he kept Africa for himself. Determined to beat the pirates in African music's largest market, he duplicated cassettes and sold them in Africa before releasing the records in Europe. He told journalist Lois Darlington about his experience in Dakar with Ismael Lô's album *Diawar*: 'I sold 10,000 there in an hour. Wholesalers sell to smaller wholesalers who sell them out of town. Children take 20 cassettes and run around town selling them.'

Another who joined the profession was Jimmy Houetinou of the Republic of Benin. Houetinou had encountered Paris early in life when he attended school there in the early sixties while living with his father, who worked in the city. Back in France in 1975 to attend college, he decided to stay. His ear for music drew him to the soul of black America and the spirit of Jamaican reggae. He hung out with Jamaica's Errol Dunkley and Côte d'Ivoire's Alpha Blondy whenever they came to Paris. He befriended other musicians as well, and by getting to know them Houetinou gained an understanding of their problems. The best way to help, he concluded, was to produce their records.

Houetinou's first attempt came near the end of 1985 with an album for Congolese singer Aurlus Mabele. Mabele had been knocking around Paris since 1981, making jewelry and working odd jobs while trying to activate his lagging career. His first record died when the label, Totem Music, folded shortly after releasing the disc in 1983. He regrouped the next year with an album called *Nicoletta, Fille des Antilles* for Afro Rythmes that paired him with guitarist Diblo Dibala. Soon afterward Mabele met Jimmy Houetinou. Their

Aurlus Mabele

collaboration yielded *Africa Mousso* (woman of Africa, in the Bambara language) with Diblo arranging the music and playing lead guitar. The collection of four uptempo songs geared to the dance floor recalled Diblo's work with Kanda Bongo Man, although it lacked the melodic appeal of the Bongo Man's works. Nevertheless, the album was a club favorite and went on to win the 1986 Maracas d'Or as French Africa's best pop record. Jimmy's Productions had scored a hit on its very first try.

Houetinou's youthful enthusiasm, his knack for building rapport, and the success of *Africa Mousso* brought more musicians to his door. Like Ibrahima Sylla, Houetinou would do much of his producing outside the realm of Congo music. Yet both men would contribute substantially to the popularity of that genre, now being called soukous.

•

The move away from long-term ties between producers and artists roughly coincided with the development of tentative associations among some of the musicians themselves. The first of these had taken place at Afro Rythmes when Ouattara brought Syran M'Benza, Bopol Mansiamina, Wuta Mayi, and Nyboma

Mwan Dido together as the '4 Grandes Vedettes.' A year and a half after their initial recording, Ibrahima Sylla repackaged them as Les Quatre Etoiles (Four Stars) in a 1984 album known by its lead-off track, 'Enfant Bamileke.'

The song, written by Wuta Mayi, told of his infatuation with a beautiful Bamileke girl from the Cameroonian city of Bafoussam. Set to a sizzling groove by drummer Domingo Salsero, the four-song album features inspired guitar picking among Syran, Bopol, and guest artist Pablo Lubadika alongside the horns of the Cameroonian duo Fredo Ngando and Jimmy N'vondo. Bopol and Nyboma also recorded solo albums before the quartet parted company with Sylla.

Another group of the Quatre Etoiles type rose from the success of Aurlus Mabele's *Africa Mousso*. After working together on two straight productions, Mabele and Diblo Dibala decided to form their own loose-knit band that would back each other on solo projects and occasionally produce a group recording. Borrowing from a cry that recurs throughout the *Africa Mousso* album, they called themselves Loketo, the Lingala word for hip.

The name was well chosen. Loketo's music aimed strictly below the waist. Songs contained a minimal story-line with lots of cries of animation backed by Diblo's rapid-fire riffs. Two Jimmy Houetinou productions, *Super K* released on Diblo's name in 1987, and *Trouble*, a follow-up under the Loketo banner, were typical of the music's current trend. It was performed by a small group using spare instrumentation, and it moved at a breathtaking pace. Fans in Paris called it *TGV soukous* after *les trains grande vitesse*, France's high-speed trains. Despite an obvious tendency toward monotony, the overall sound was attractive, especially in nightclubs, where the first notes of a Loketo track would summon a crowd to the dance floor.

•

While Loketo cranked up the speed, the race itself went to Kanda Bongo Man. His early work with Diblo at Afro Rythmes had been part of the movement toward the fast-paced, stripped-down sound of soukous that followed from the work of the African All Stars and Loukelo Samba's *Innovation* series. By the latter half of the eighties Kanda had become its most successful practitioner.

His collaboration with Diblo had continued after the two departed from Afro Rythmes. Each successive production refined their sound, and by 1985, with the release of *Malinga*, Kanda Bongo Man was in a hit-making groove. *Malinga* was a solid five-song album that boasted the likes of Rigo Star, Domingo

Kanda Bongo Man

Salsero, Guadeloupean drummer Jean 'Ty-Jan' Arcon, and Angolan bassist Miguel Yamba, all sitting in with Kanda and Diblo.

The album's best moment is a song about a woman named 'J.T.' who appeared in one of Kanda's dreams. When he awoke, he knew he had to write about her. Rigo's rhythm guitar lives up to its name in a wicked workout with the drums and bass while Kanda sings of his encounter with the woman of his dream. Diblo sharpens the sebene with a succession of riffs that proves repetition need never be boring. Few who heard the song managed to keep control of their feet.

Kanda followed a year later with *Lela-Lela*, an uneven effort whose title track, nevertheless, turned a danceable phrase while paying lip service to the zouk craze sweeping Paris. In 1987 Kanda produced his finest work to date, one of the best albums to come out of Paris for the entire decade. The title combined the names of the lead tracks from either side, *Sai-Liza*. *Sai* means joy in Lingala, and in Kanda's music it becomes a celebration of just how far he has come. With Diblo sparkling once again on lead guitar, in the company this time of Lokassa ya Mbongo, Pablo Lubadika, and the incomparable Ty-Jan, nearly everything clicks. Kanda's voice displays more maturity and emotional range – born perhaps of age and confidence – as he sings of his love for 'Bedy' and admonishes a capricious 'Liza.' Even a synthesizer's screech on 'Cantique' (canticle) can't spoil Diblo's exquisite segue to the sebene. Ty-Jan fires the mix, enhancing his renown as a crack session drummer that no programmed machine could touch.

In addition to its splendid songs and virtuoso performances, *Sai-Liza* introduced the rest of the world to a new dance from the streets of Kinshasa. 'Kwassa-kwassa,' Kanda shouts on 'Sai,' echoing a play on the French, *C'est quoi ça?* (What's that?) The term was said to have been coined by a Zaïrean man called Jeannora in answer to a 'C'est quoi ça?' question about a new dance step he'd created: 'It's kwassa-kwassa,' he allegedly replied. But outside of Kinshasa, Kanda Bongo was the kwassa-kwassa man. Nearly everywhere he played shouts of 'kwassa-kwassa!' greeted his appearance.

The partnership of Kanda and Diblo had ripened over the span of six albums since the two had come to Paris. *Sai-Liza* marked the culmination of an extraordinary passage from obscurity to stardom. By this point both musicians had earned a worldwide following. Like many other songwriting teams, they worked as one to bring Kanda's compositions to life. 'You know Diblo is a good guitarist,' Kanda explained. 'He has many melodies when he plays the guitar. My melodies helped inspire him. I sing first. He listens to my melody. After that he plays the guitar as a function of the melody that I sing.'

Kanda took the basic rumba from Kinshasa, tinkered with it by varying the rhythm and speeding it up, but there was no mistaking him for a new-age noodler or wannabe rocker. He earned his popularity by sticking to what he knew best. And for Kanda fidelity to the distinctly Zaïrean style begot success. Joe Boyd, the owner of London-based Hannibal Records, caught one of Kanda's shows in London 'and was just knocked out.' He tracked the singer down in Paris and worked out a licensing agreement to release Kanda's music on Hannibal in the United Kingdom and the United States. Boyd repackaged *Malinga* and an earlier work, *Amour Fou*, by selecting tracks from each and issuing them as *Amour Fou/Crazy Love* in 1987. He repeated the process in 1989, combining *Lela-Lela* and *Sai-Liza* into a Hannibal release called *Kwassa Kwassa*.

Boyd's interest led to Kanda's successful North American tour in 1989, which included an appearance at the prestigious New Orleans Jazz and Heritage Festival. By then, however, Diblo had departed. His work with Aurlus Mabele had helped win a Maracas d'Or, and in Loketo he would be co-leader. Both Diblo and Kanda had prospered from their collaboration. But after recording *Sai-Liza* each went his own way.

•

Along with the kwassa-kwassa, the Kinshasa-bred phenomenon of *la sape* materialized in Paris. It seemed only appropriate since the sapeurs of Zaïre were moving in droves to Europe's perennial fashion capital. The creations of Pierre Cardin, Yves Saint Laurent, Jean-Paul Gaultier – scarce commodities in Kinshasa – could be bought off the racks of many a Paris boutique. And the home of Giorgio Armani and Gianni Versace was only an overnight train ride away.

Kanda Bongo Man, with his natty jumpsuits and trademark round-brimmed hat, certainly fit the mold. Several musicians took up clothing design themselves. Aurlus Mabele styled a spiffy leather ensemble to wear for a Loketo tour. The outrageous creations of singer-dancer Pierre Belkos received more attention than his music. The fad so fascinated the Western press that several artists, Papa Wemba the premier sapeur included, had to remind interviewers that they were indeed creators of music first. Fashion was only an adjunct. 'I'm much more a singer than a sapeur,' Wemba protested. 'I'm a singer, that's my profession. It was the journalists who put a lot of emphasis on that word. And everywhere I go now, people know me much more as a sapeur than as a singer. That doesn't make me feel good.'

•

Beyond the fads of fashion and dance the flow of musicians from the banks of the Congo River continued unabated. It was a perverse transfusion which seriously enfeebled the donor. By the second half of the eighties, Paris had supplanted Kinshasa as the recording capital of Congo music.

Tabu Ley's Orchestre Afrisa had surrendered some of its best musicians to the forces that compelled the change. Still, Ley always managed to muster a first-rate group in what seemed like an endless process of rebuilding. His latest stroke had been the hiring of guitarist Huit Kilos away from Victoria Eleison to replace Dino Vangu, who had departed. Aside from his own impressive gifts of voice and composition, Ley's greatest current asset was his 'Cleopatra of Zaïrean music,' Mbilia Bel. The two produced beautiful music together and a daughter named Melody too. Their lives appeared to be a glamorous whirlwind of rehearsals, recording, and spectacular concert tours.

Given the alarming state of the Zaïrean economy, Afrisa was about the only band left still staging concerts in Kinshasa's larger halls. The group kicked off 1986 with Music-Media '86, a February spectacular at the Palladium. Subsequent appearances in early March did much to discredit the bizarre rumor that Mbilia had attempted to kill herself. More rumors surfaced two months later when she flew off to Paris for a vacation. Ley inadvertently fueled the gossip by hiring a second woman, a singer named Itela Boketsu, known by the sobriquet 'Baniel,' to serve as Mbilia's understudy. When Baniel left later in the year he added nineteen-year-old Kishila Ngoyi, who would become known as 'Faya Tess.' In spite of the talk and the presence of a possible new rival, Mbilia took her place center-stage for the band's August–October tours of Rwanda, Burundi, and Kenya. Her place at Ley's side seemed secure.

A new album at the beginning of 1987 featured Mbilia Bel and Faya Tess, together on vinyl for the first time, in a duet about the bonds of family and spirituality called 'Nadina.' On stage in Tanzania in February and March, Mbilia was still the main attraction, but rumors of bad feeling between the two singers continued in spite of the outward signs of tranquility. Other talk had Mbilia coming under the influence of a producer from Gabon named Gustave Bongo, called 'Ngossanga' or 'Ngoss' for short, who was currently involved in the financial affairs of Zaïko Langa Langa. Mbilia denied there were problems between her and Faya. 'I was very happy when I learned of her official debut in Kinshasa,' she told Elima. 'I think the Kinshasan public should come to like Afrisa with a female star other than me.' As for the Gabonese producer Ngoss, he too was no problem. 'He is a great fan of Afrisa, of Tabu Ley, and of Mbilia Bel,' she said. 'People should get the idea that he's trying to divert me out of their heads.'

In October 1987 Afrisa staged a 'super show' before a standing-room-only crowd in the 3,500-seat Salle des Congrès of the Palais du Peuple in Kinshasa. The entire band was present – Tabu Ley, Faya Tess, and the recently returned Ndombe Opetun – but they merely formed the supporting cast. When she finally appeared, nearly an hour into the show, the spotlight belonged to Mbilia Bel. Dressed like the queen of ancient Egypt in a black toga trimmed

Rigo Star and
Mbilia Bel

with jewels, Mbilia enchanted the crowd with a performance of incredible range. She sang and danced her way through five costume changes and a repertoire that included her hits, a sampling of the works of her sister stars of Zaïrean music, songs from Kassav' and Nana Mouskouri, and the ritual duets with Ley and Faya Tess.

Elima called her 'stunning,' and compared her with the likes of international stars Sylvie Vartan, James Brown, and Johnny Hallyday. 'Every music lover present at this show might be tempted to assert that Mbilia Bel is the greatest female singer in Kinshasa.' Few could have imagined that she was bidding them farewell.

When Afrisa departed for Brazil in November, Mbilia Bel stayed home. A problem with one of her eyes was given as the reason, but that explanation failed to blunt a new crop of rumors. The year-end release of an album with Mbilia, Ley, and Faya Tess called *Contre Ma Volonté* (against my will) did little to quiet speculation. This time the rumors had substance. Before the new year arrived, Mbilia Bel left Kinshasa.

'I had the ambition to have a solo career,' she said when asked to explain. There were good times and bad in Afrisa. 'When I left, you know, if you want to leave the company, you're certain you're going to get something, you're certain you're going to achieve something more.' Ley had seen the split coming; still there was little he could do to prevent it. 'She became a success,' he said. 'I think she felt that she had arrived, that she could do good work alone. I couldn't use force to make her stay.'

After a brief stopover in Gabon that appeared to confirm Ngoss's hand in the affair, Mbilia flew to Paris early in 1988, where she began looking for someone to write songs with her and arrange her music. Friends steered her toward Rigo Star. 'I said, "No, no, no! He's very young, he can't do it",' she recalled in amusement. Despite her reservations she contacted the guitarist, and they began to develop a rapport. By April they had booked themselves into a Paris studio to record their new creations.

When the record came out in the middle of 1988 it was clear that the pairing had worked. The six-song album, entitled Phénomène, ranked with the best of the Paris productions. Mbilia and Rigo took pains not to deliver songs radically different from what Mbilia's public was used to. Instead of plunging into the realm of Paris soukous, Phénomène stuck close to the mellower Kinshasa sound. 'I owe my fame to Afrisa,' she told Manda Tchebwa of Zaïrean television. 'For now I am still working on the Afrisa model, because many people are used to listening to me in that style. An abrupt change would perhaps have shocked my fans.'

The music emerged appealing and fresh, a product of Parisian polish with Kinshasa clearly in mind. Rigo's masterful arrangements even included a horn section. The album's title track had the ring of autobiography. A woman who calls herself Phénomène leaves an abusive man to her rival. The rival, she warns, must be strong to endure what she went through. Mbilia sings with conviction as if the story is hers. She is the phenomenon. 'Manzil-Manzil' takes her back to the village for a citified version of a Bayanzi folk song. Rigo's guitar never sounded better, riffing with the rhythm like a likembe from the hinterland. Mbilia croons the romantic 'Cher Ami' (dear friend) with a genuine sweetness that's hard to resist. Rigo takes the sebene, his guitar leading the saxophone into a lovely counter-melody. Some of the flavor of 'Eswi yo Wapi,' Mbilia's biggest hit, permeates 'Tika-Bazuwa' (stop being jealous). The rhythm, the horns, and even male voices (Rigo's) on the chorus recall her heady days with Afrisa and point up the enormity of her decision to leave.

The change looked good at first glance. Phénomène was a hit from its first day on the street. Casting aside their dislike of foreign productions, Kinshasa's music writers voted Mbilia Bel best female singer of 1988 on the strength of the new album. The association of Mbilia and Rigo clearly appeared to have promise. On a broader plain, however, the record served as a marker for the decade. Mbilia may have been a phenomenon, but she was also part of a larger event. When a woman of the position she enjoyed with Afrisa gambled on giving it up, the move spoke volumes for the music's general predicament. Times were tough in Zaïre even in the best of bands. Like jazz without New Orleans, Congo music faced a future without Kinshasa.

21
Get out your program again

Clan Langa Langa, Koffi Olomide, and Empire Bakuba, 1985–1989

On the well-trodden road to Paris, bands of the younger generation followed in the footsteps of their elders. Papa Wemba's lengthy stay in 1982 had awakened him to the opportunities that lay beyond his Zaïrean home base. The upheavals that had followed his return to Kinshasa resulted in a 'new look' Viva La Musica that by 1986 included a formidable lineup of young singers: Reddy Amisi, Lidjo Kwempa, Litemo Luciana, Stino 'Stino As' (Ace) Mubi, and Ngizulu Kubiala, known as 'Fafa de Molokai.' On-again-off-again singer Pepe Bipoli was on again, along with Joe 'Joe Fat' Fataki, a singer from Wemba's old Yoka Lokole. A pedigreed newcomer, Vicky Longomba's son Awilo, joined them on drums. In all the band numbered around sixteen, including guitarist Bongo Wende.

The year 1986 would belong to Papa Wemba. Starting off in Europe he distanced himself from the usual paeans of love and self-promotion with an album called *L'Esclave*, the slave. Wemba unsheathes his tongue on the title track in a biting call for Africa's freedom. He reviews the history of the exploitation of Africans and their exportation as slaves to the New World. Then, invoking the names of Nelson and Winnie Mandela, he calls for freedom in South Africa. 'I wanted a change of look,' he explained. 'I decided from now on to denounce every injustice that oppresses humanity, like the slavery which is now disfiguring [the world] in the form of apartheid.'

In May Wemba pushed the boundaries further by taking his band on a five-show tour of Japan. Starting with three concerts in the Tokyo suburb of

Musashino, Viva La Musica moved south for a performance in Osaka, then returned for the finale in Tokyo. The tour was a first for a band from Zaïre and built on Japan's growing interest in African music whetted by previous visits from Sunny Ade and Senegal's Toure Kunda. Wemba and his band came home to a frenzied welcome in Kinshasa at the end of June.

While Viva La Musica worked abroad, Zaïrean film-maker Ngangura Mwenze was lining up financial and technical support to film a story that he had developed called *La Vie est Belle*, life is beautiful. The action revolved around a country boy who dreamed of becoming a city musician. Who better to play such a character than Papa Wemba?

Two months of shooting began in Kinshasa at the end of July with Ngangura and Belgian film-maker Benoît Lamy co-directing and producing. The film peeks at the nature of Mobutu's Zaïre – the common people who labor to survive, the acquisitive upper class, the enforcers of order, and the bribery, prostitution, sorcery, and street-wise cunning that oil the interaction among them – without lifting the shade so high as to offend Le Guide. There is even a glimpse of Kinshasa's modest women's movement, but it stands reproved in the end. The result of all of this is a humorous story of Kourou (Papa Wemba) and Kabibi (Bibi Krubwa), and their struggle with yearnings for each other and for success in life in the face of the slippery morality of the ruling order. Wemba seems like a natural, but then it was a part he had played in real life.

Music is a constant background to the film, with Wemba's compositions, including the title song, predominant. Pepe Kalle makes a cameo appearance, and his dwarf sidekick, Emoro, pops up continually as Kourou's personal harbinger of good luck. The story resolves in a grand finale at the fictional Bar Nvouandou, where the entire cast joins in a reprise of the song 'La Vie est Belle.' Based in part on 'Le Laboureur et Ses Enfants' (the laborer and his children) by French poet Jean de la Fontaine, 'La Vie est Belle' enunciates the average Zaïrean's approach to survival in an imploding social order.

> Work, for work pays – though the back bends:
> A resource that never fails
> ...
> Oh, Oh, Article 15
> Look out for yourself
> Look out for yourself.

The finished film came to Kinshasa in September of 1987 for a gala première at the Palais du Peuple. Film-makers Ngangura and Lamy and their star Papa

Wemba attended, along with an assortment of Zaïrean dignitaries. Reaction was generally positive. Sensitive subjects had been treated with sufficient tact. The film went on to win prizes in Belgium, Italy, and Brazil and received widespread distribution on video.

With the movie première out of the way, Wemba and Viva La Musica prepared for an October return to Japan. It turned out to be the band's final tour. In November Wemba announced that he had let most of his musicians go. He wanted to move in a different direction, and to that end he was starting to work with French producer Martin Meissonnier. In Kinshasa in December to help celebrate Zaïko Langa Langa's eighteenth anniversary, Wemba explained his actions to the press. He had been advised by Meissonnier's people that if he wanted to make it in France he needed to work with professionals, the implication being that Wemba's musicians weren't good enough.

> I've thus decided to collaborate only with the pros on a permanent basis. I have retained four of my singers, including Luciana, Reddy, and Stino. The others continue to collaborate with me only occasionally, and I pay them on a services-rendered basis.

Wemba's decision sparked controversy, as did the music he produced. Meissonnier had been involved in Sunny Ade's attempt to 'modernize' his juju music with Island Records, but disappointing sales had caused Island to drop the Nigerian's contract. Wemba's gamble with Meissonnier was no less fraught with danger.

The result of their collaboration, entitled simply *Papa Wemba*, came out in 1988. Its seven songs remade earlier Wemba recordings, each with a peculiar new flavor. Two whose original takes were most obviously based on folk rhythms suffered the most. One can recognize 'M'Fono Yami' from the album *L'Esclave* and the earlier work 'Analengo' by their distinctive introductions, but from there the new versions diverged widely from the originals. The plodding thump, thump of a straight-ahead drum and bass dilutes the complex crisscrossing rhythms nearly to the point of extinction. 'L'Esclave' fares better, retaining its essential character with the added touch of a saxophone, a first for Papa Wemba. Liberal helpings of keyboards on each of the album's seven songs fill nearly every available space to create the processed wall-of-sound so prevalent in Western pop. Songs were kept short in hopes of gaining radio air play in Europe and America. The entire album clocks in at around thirty-three minutes, the length of a normal four-song work.

Wemba's new music did not go well in Kinshasa nor among devotees of Congo music in the West. Whether or not his change of direction could attract a new base of fans superior to the one Viva La Musica had enjoyed remained to be seen. What was clear was that for all practical purposes Wemba had moved to Paris, and, like Abeti's Redoutables, Viva La Musica remained alive in name only. 'I give myself two years in Paris to succeed,' Wemba said. 'Otherwise I'll go to London, to New York.'

•

Before he moved to Paris, Papa Wemba's main rival for popularity among Kinshasa's youth had been his one-time collaborator Emeneya Mubiala. With the exception of 1984, when several musicians briefly defected, Emeneya's band, Victoria Eleison, had steadily improved since its birth in 1982 as a break-away faction of Wemba's Viva La Musica. Like Papa Wemba, Emeneya possessed an abundance of self-confidence and a wealth of talent to back it up. His tenor ascended into the upper register much like Tabu Ley's, but the sterling tones were tempered with a throaty edge that evinced passion. Cloaking brashness with humility, Emeneya mastered the art of gracious self-promotion. Papa Wemba was his mentor, he once said. 'It's thanks to him, thanks to his group, that I've become a great Zaïrean musician today.'

People seemed to agree with his self-assessment. Emeneya found it difficult to leave his house without drawing a crowd. His after-midnight concerts almost guaranteed a handsome income for all concerned. The band sounded tight and looked sharp. Stable for the moment, the mid-eighties version of Victoria Eleison rode the rhythms of Tofla Tofolo and Dju Dju Luvemba, known also as 'Dju Dju Chet,' on bass and drums. Huit Kilos and Safro Manzangi manned the guitars and new addition Makola 'Makolin' Dialuliba joined Joly Mubiala and Malembe 'El Chanto' in backing Emeneya on vocals. This core group was joined by assorted other players who drifted in and out of the lineup.

Kinshasa's music writers also sang Emeneya's praises. They awarded him the triple crown for 1985, best star, best band, and best song, 'Kimpiatu.' The sweep of the top prizes was all the more stunning because it had occurred in the year of 'Mario,' Franco's worldwide best-seller. 'It wasn't a surprise,' Emeneya told *Elima* with characteristic panache. 'I knew it from the work I was doing. Still, I was very happy. I'm going to celebrate this, and my band will press on forward this year [1986].'

'Kimpiatu,' the winning song, tells the story of a woman of high moral character who has pledged her love to a man named Tiayi Kimpiatu. The woman rejects another suitor only to have her relationship with Kimpiatu destroyed by false rumors of her infidelity. 'Kimpiatu' evoked a sense of agony and injustice that struck a chord with the public. The record sold briskly and, coming as it did toward the end of the year, nosed out the competition in the writers' poll.

As much as he enjoyed his current success, Emeneya spent 1986 rethinking his approach to music. The youth bands had made a conscious decision to play without horns in order to differentiate their music from the older generation. It had worked initially, Emeneya came to believe, simply because it was a young people's thing.

> There was no criticism, no critical spirit.... The neighborhood young people created an opinion that says that what I'm doing is good. Whereas those who were not into our music just weren't with it.... To be with it, you had to be into what the youth were doing.

But, he reasoned, recasting the music in a raucous style with less variety of instrumentation hurt the music in the long run.

In Europe near the end of 1986 Emeneya made several contacts with record companies, but, based on his concerts and a sampling of his past work, none agreed to sign him.

> So it was starting then that I told myself Zaïrean music is in decline, that it was true that Zaïrean music had lost the place it had had at one time internationally. Why? Because in the past the Rochereaus sold, the Nicos sold, the Kalles sold, they had gold records, they did shows, they were accepted. But now in Kinshasa from '82 to '85 I've been the best band in Zaïre. Here [in Europe] I do a concert, and they say it's no good. If I'm the model, and they don't accept me here, that proves there's something wrong with the music. So I started to look for what wasn't working.

In 1987, two albums developed from Emeneya's new thinking. The first included the entire band and aimed at the Kinshasa market. Entitled *Deux Temps* (literally 'two tenses,' present and future, about the phases of a relationship), the album was vintage Victoria with, courtesy of Franco, added punch from the O.K. Jazz horn section. The second work took an altogether different tack. This was Emeneya solo on his quest for a new sound. Backed by a variety of musicians from the U.S., Britain, Italy, and the Netherlands plus a Zaïrean trio of singers called Les Presets, Emeneya laid the tracks for *Nzinzi*, the fly.

The title cut opens in a swamp of beeping bugs and jungle creatures. A rhythm box unleashes a percussive pastiche. Synthesizers resound with a cornucopia of bells and whistles. Nary a guitar is heard. The electronic collage is a total departure from the classic rumba.

Zaïreans embraced *Deux Temps*, but felt betrayed by Emeneya's solo outing. 'When I came back home to Zaïre, they criticized me,' he recalled. '"What's he thinking? This is bad music. Here in Zaïre it's not going to go, because we're into authenticity. He's introduced a new sound, the synthesizer. Those are the white people's sounds."'

Despite the initial reaction many Zaïreans came to agree with fans outside the country who were enthusiastically buying *Nzinzi*. At the beginning of 1988, Kinshasa writers rewarded Emeneya with a special jury prize for the album. Emeneya accepted the award as further validation of his hard work and talent. He had turned a corner in 1987 with his new vision for the music. He had begun to see opportunity beyond the confines of Kinshasa.

Emeneya's conversion put him in philosophic agreement with Papa Wemba. The two families of Clan Langa Langa's Viva La Musica wing would pursue what their leaders perceived to be a more international sound. Like Papa Wemba, Emeneya went to Paris, at first to record and later, in 1991, to reside full-time.

•

Clan Langa Langa's hybrid, Langa Langa Stars, had itself split repeatedly. Formed originally by defectors from Zaïko Langa Langa and Viva La Musica, the 'sept patrons' (seven bosses) of Langa Langa Stars eventually reduced to one, Evoloko Joker. Evoloko managed to keep the band going with varying degrees of success, but after nearly four years at the helm he too began to frequent Paris. Although he continued to use the name Langa Langa Stars, by the end of the eighties Evoloko was essentially a solo artist producing his albums with session musicians.

Choc Stars, the splinter group of *patrons* from Langa Langa Stars, reaped greater success than its forebear. With Ben Nyamabo's bank roll, artistic direction by Bozi Boziana, and Roxy Tshimpaka's astute arrangements, the band controlled its own destiny. Roxy and bassist Djo Mali formed the group's instrumental core, with Nyamabo, Matumona Defao, Djuna Djanana, and Bozi on vocals.

At the end of 1985, Bozi was fired for recording outside the group, but by then the Choc Stars had acquired singer Nzola Ndonga 'Petit Prince' from

Victoria Eleison. Following Bozi's departure, Debaba el Shabab, leader of the ill-fated Historia Musica, added his voice to the Choc Stars along with Lassa 'Carlito' Ndombasi from O.K. Jazz, Nzaya Nzayadio of Mayopi and Lipua Lipua, and Zemanont Kanza, formerly with Zaïko Langa Langa. The eight singers formed Clan Langa Langa's best front line since the original Zaïko of the early seventies. When Djanana left the band for a short time in 1987 to return to Langa Langa Stars, his absence was scarcely noticed.

With animator Ditutala Kuama at the mike exhorting the crowd, the Choc Stars could blister a sebene, but on the whole their music had a softer edge than that of their cousins in Zaïko and Viva. The players developed a more coherent sound of consistent quality than they had been able to produce in Langa Langa Stars. Treading adroitly between the styles of their elders and the youth, between Kinshasa and Paris, the musicians of Choc Stars produced works of broad appeal. Kinshasa's music writers rewarded their efforts by selecting the Choc Stars as best band of 1986 and 1989.

Roxy's agile guitar drove the band. Known as 'Le Grand Niawu' (the big cat), Roxy had begun his career in the prototypal youth band, Orchestre Thu Zaina, before clan patriarch Zaïko Langa Langa was even born. But he was also accomplished in the older school, having played in Orchestre Véve and in Kossa Kossa, the band that specialized in performing covers of the hits of Kinshasa's other groups. By dint of his experience Roxy brought a certain historical linkage to the Choc Stars that the younger guitarists in other groups lacked. He sounded smart like Docteur Nico vamping behind the singers and swift like Diblo Dibala burning his way through a sebene. On a song called 'Farya' from the late eighties he mimicked the syncopated picking of Johnny Bokelo with a pumping rumba sebene.

The Choc Stars were prolific in the studio. They recorded four or more albums a year in the late eighties, numbers rivaled only by Zaïko Langa Langa and Empire Bakuba among the youth bands. 'Riana,' one of the songs that led to the group's 1986 best band award, was a typical Choc Stars chronicle of the vicissitudes of youth. Riana, a Kinshasan beauty, leaves her lover after a brief affair, too brief for the bewildered man, who cries, 'I haven't had enough of you yet/ Why are you leaving me like this?' With songs like 'Riana,' an upbeat but mellow delivery, and a rarely matched lineup of talent, the Choc Stars rose to become every bit the equal of the clan's head, Zaïko Langa Langa itself.

•

Meanwhile, the fired Bozi Boziana went on to form a new band of unknowns. Anti-Choc, the group's provocative name, succinctly summed up his feelings toward the musicians who had sacked him. Yet he claimed to be happy with the opportunity his dismissal presented. He still had to answer to Verckys Kiamuangana, who put up the money for equipment, but as long as he observed his contractual obligations Bozi was free to follow his muse.

Bozi assembled a collection of young, relatively inexperienced musicians whom he hoped to mold into stars. Givé Djonolo, a multi-instrumentalist with a pleasant voice, was one of the first to sign on. Djonolo had worked in some lower-tier bands but had never made it to the first ranks. Fifi Mofude, who had sung with Kossa Kossa, and singer Wally Ngonda from the Stukas Boys joined Djonolo alongside Bozi and a fourteen-year-old female vocalist named Afi Kiabelua. The backing band was built around another Stukas alumnus, solo guitarist Matou Dodoly, and assorted lesser-known players. Bozi, a ripe thirty-four-year-old, became known as *le grand-père* (grandfather) among his youthful recruits. 'Those I play with in Anti-Choc are students of those who were students of those I developed in Choc Stars,' he said.

Bozi's Anti-Choc followed the Choc Stars' school of clean, crisp production. Bozi's compositions were more consistently up-tempo and employed a heavier dose of synthesizer, but each song still relied on the solo guitarist, Dodoly, for its principal source of power. Anti-Choc added the attraction of at least one female voice, and usually two or more, to mitigate the music's male-dominated sound.

Afi Kiabelua's tenure was short; 'Jolie Detta' Kamenga Kayobote filled her position on a more permanent basis. Detta had tried out with the Choc Stars, but her presence, said Ben Nyamabo, had engendered 'indiscipline' in the group. She worked briefly for a band called Afro International and for O.K. Jazz before moving in beside Bozi. The principal source of the indiscipline Nyamabo referred to had been Bozi's infatuation with the winsome Detta. Now that he was the boss, there would presumably be no problem. Later, another talented woman, named Mukangi Déesse (goddess), a singer from Kisangani, joined the band. Bozi's duets with Detta and Déesse provided some of the freshest work to emerge from any of Clan Langa Langa's families.

Anti-Choc survived its biggest shock in the middle of 1987 when Djonolo quit, taking Dodoly with him, to form a short-lived offshoot called Choc Musica. Bozi shrugged off the defectors, hired Lidjo Kwempa away from Viva La Musica, signed bassist Ngouma Lokito, and took off for Europe to record new songs. *Coup de la Vie* (throes of life), an album with Master Mwana Congo

Bozi Boziana

sitting in on solo guitar in place of the departed Dodoly, answered those who thought the band was finished. A second album, *Mon Mari est Gabonais* (my husband is Gabonese), finds Rigo Star taking a turn on solo guitar. When Choc Musica folded a scant year later, Bozi welcomed Dodoly back to his old position. By 1988 the musicians of Anti Choc had reached the level of their Clan Langa Langa cousins. Kinshasa's writers selected them as the year's best band, Bozi as best star, Dodoly best guitarist, and Bozi's composition 'La Reine de Sabah' (the queen of Sheba), the story of a man's love for a beautiful woman and how it was destroyed by gossip and possibly betrayal, the year's best song.

•

Since his break with Zaïko Langa Langa in 1980, Manuaku Waku, one of the clan's founding fathers, had fashioned his Grand Zaïko Wa Wa into Kinshasa's best band of 1984. With himself on lead guitar; four solid singers, Joe Nickel, Joe Poster, Lukombo Djeffard, and Lukombo Shimita; and one of the music's few full-time keyboard players, *chef d'orchestre* Nzenze Mongengo, Grand Zaïko possessed a solid nucleus. Still, the band had difficulty maintaining its lofty status.

Grand Zaïko stayed alive playing clubs in Matonge and recording, on the average, one new album a year. A 1987 tour of French-speaking West Africa raised the group's profile outside its home base. *Menace de Divorce* (threat of divorce), an album released in 1988, received high praise. The same year, however, the group started to come apart when Djeffard left to join Tabu Ley's Afrisa. Shimita moved to Paris soon afterward, and Manuaku exiled himself to Switzerland at the start of the nineties.

•

In the contest with its offspring, Clan Langa Langa's first family, Zaïko Langa Langa, more than held its own. The defections that gave birth to the clan's other families appeared to have put the major disputes within Zaïko itself to rest. D.V. Moanda's death in 1984 had left the group in the hands of its senior member and president, Nyoka Longo. Several musicians from the group's earliest days remained, including Nyoka's fellow singer Bimi Ombale, guitar accompanist Enoch Zamuangana, solo guitarist Matima Mpioso Kinuani, Bapuis Muaka on bass, and the two drummers, Meridjo Belobi and Bakunde Ilo Pablo. Newer additions Lengi Lenga, Dindo Yogo, J.P. Buse, and a *chanteur pop* named (Gilbert) Benamayi rounded out the vocal corps. Matima shared solo guitar duty with Popolipo Zanguila and another guitarist named Avedila, who was better known as 'Petit Poisson' (little fish). An assortment of younger talent filled out the ranks, which usually numbered from sixteen to twenty. *Familia Dei, Eye Nkisi, Nkolo Mboka* they called themselves, family of God, this medicine (connotes magic and sorcery), village headman. The musicians of Zaïko covered all the bases.

The band appeared united, and its music sounded solid, yet its solvency was less than assured. Moanda and his board of directors had never run a particularly tight ship. Most of Zaïko's earnings paid salaries and expenses. Some money disappeared into the pockets of whoever currently wielded the checkbook. Little was left aside for emergencies and future projects. In the months following Moanda's death, Nyoka met Gustave Bongo, the businessman from Gabon who called himself 'Ngossanga,' or 'Ngoss' for short. This was the same Ngoss who would soon be rumored to be stealing Mbilia Bel from Tabu Ley. Ngoss was said to be related to Gabon's president, Omar Bongo, and a great fan of Zaïko Langa Langa. Perhaps he could be of service to the band's new administration.

When in Kinshasa, Zaïko usually played at the Ma-Elika, a modest club on Rue Kanda-Kanda in Matonge filled to capacity with Zaïko enthusiasts. In the middle of 1985, Ngoss bought the club with the aim of making it the band's headquarters. 'We're going to raze it in order to erect a modern building with a dancing bar on the ground floor, dance club on the second floor and offices on the third level,' Nyoka announced. But that would be in the longer term. For the time being, at least, the Ma-Elika was given a minor face-lift and renamed the Ngoss Club.

When not at the Ngoss Club, the band lived in the studio, or so it seemed. Only the venerable O.K. Jazz, Empire Bakuba, and the upstart Choc Stars rivaled Zaïko's recording output. A 1986 release entitled *Paiement Cash* is fairly typical of post-Manuaku, post-Moanda Zaïko. The four-song album explores the theme of love and separation with words of anguish set to tunes of joy. The guitars have mellowed with age, the voices blend with ease, yet the beat steps lively as before with a dose of synthesizer added in the name of progress. To repay Ngoss for his help, copies of *Paiement Cash* and other Zaïko albums went directly to Ngoss Productions in Libreville for distribution in Gabon. Zaïko distributed its own copies in Zaïre, while Safari Ambiance handled the pressing and European distribution.

When not in the studio or packing the Ngoss Club, Zaïko's musicians hit the road. They spent several months each year performing in Europe and taking advantage of the opportunity to record in the well-equipped studios of Brussels and Paris. East and West Africa played host to the band as well. In the middle of a series of Ngoss-produced concerts in Gabon near the end of 1985, Ngoss presented the musicians with new instruments. Unfortunately, so one report had it, they saw little of what were said to be considerable gate receipts. Nevertheless, Ngoss seemed to be a man who kept his promises, and the musicians rewarded their new *patron* by making him the band's honorary president. Zaïko's sebene vocabulary grew to include the cry 'eh Ngoss, eh Ngoss,' and an album with the phrase as its title soon came on the market. In October of 1986 Zaïko traveled to Japan for three shows at universities around Tokyo, as part of an African festival, and a farewell concert in Osaka.

The following year, the eighteenth of the band's existence, plans for an anniversary celebration unfolded. Unibra, the brewers of Skol beer and the event's sponsor, hosted a dinner and press conference in early December 1987 to announce that all of Zaïko's former stars would join the current band for a reunion concert at the end of the month. Although the band was in Europe at the time of the press conference, the musicians came home in mid-December to prepare for the spectacular. Kinshasa was awash with rumors that this star or that had returned to join the band for rehearsals at N'Sele, the presidential compound some thirty miles up-river.

The day-after-Christmas reunion concert lived up to its exalted billing. Papa Wemba, Mavuela Somo, Evoloko, Manuaku, all joined in the night of nostalgia. Among Zaïko's most noteworthy alumni only Bozi Boziana, Gina Efonge, Mbuta Mashakado, and Likinga Mangenza (who was still serving jail time in Portugal for drug possession) failed to show up. The more than 3,000 people who paid 1,500 zaïres to attend (about $12, a week or more's earnings for many Zaïreans) were treated to a reprise of the band's eighteen-year repertoire. Many in the crowd must have lamented the quarrels that split the family into competing camps. Still, what might have been had come to pass, if only for a couple of hours.

'Moanda create[d] an egalitarian society in which class disappears, where members don't live for themselves but for others, not for profit but for art,' Nyoka told the audience. That may have been true in the beginning, but as Zaïko grew and its musicians started families, money had assumed greater importance. That fact became clear once again as the glow of the reunion concert faded. Early in the new year of 1988 the guitarist Popolipo, citing a lack of satisfaction with his salary, announced that he was quitting.

Zaïko's involvement with Ngoss was also a source of contention among the musicians. He was, it seems, no philanthropist. Through his agreements to help the band, he had managed to gain control of a substantial portion of its income. As the divisions within Zaïko widened, it came out that he had indeed been involved in Mbilia Bel's split with Tabu Ley. Ngoss had offered to finance her own band and had recruited members of Zaïko – including, it was rumored, Pablo and Bimi Ombale – to be part of it. The wealthy stranger from Gabon suddenly stood accused of having the blood of two of Zaïre's most beloved institutions on his hands.

As Zaïko seethed with dissension through the early months of 1988, the

Nyoka Longo

battle lines drew into sharper focus. Bimi, Pablo, Popolipo, Petit Poisson, Lengi Lenga, and J.P. Buse lined up against the old guard, Nyoka, Matima, Enoch, Meridjo, and Bapuis. 'There are people who made Zaïko's name, and those whose names Zaïko made,' Nyoka acidly remarked. Tabu Ley, himself aggrieved in the affair, tried to mediate, as did representatives of the government's arts and culture ministry, but there would be no reconciliation. All that was left was to sort out the legalities, most troublesome of which was ownership of the name Zaïko Langa Langa. D.V. Moanda had registered the names Zaïko for music publishing and Zaïko Langa Langa for the band with Kinshasa city authorities but had apparently gone no further. The legality of such a registration was in question. Moanda's heirs claimed to have inherited the rights to the names, and they awarded them to Bimi's faction. A third party, one Moleka Nzoko, came forward claiming that Moanda had ceded the names to him in 1979 to use for promotion, production, and distribution of the band's works. Moanda's heirs had no right to the names, he argued. Whether or not the courts ever ruled on the matter is unclear, but ruling or no, two bands using the name Zaïko Langa Langa reappeared. Bimi's wing, calling itself Zaïko Langa Langa Familia Dei Loningisa (Loningisa was later dropped in favor of the more succinct Familia Dei, family of God) and in possession of the instruments Ngoss had purchased, made its debut first. Taking the stage at the Intercontinental Hotel on June 11, Familia Dei introduced Mbuta Mashakado – back on the scene after an eight-year absence to further his education – to the crowd as the group's newest member. The three-hour show included a selection of the musicians' past hits, introduction of new songs, the announcement of several generous donations to help the band get started, and a surprise guest appearance by Bozi Boziana.

Nyoka's wing took longer to get organized. The musicians who had left with Bimi and Pablo nearly constituted a full band. Nyoka's ranks were thinner. Dindo Yogo had decided to stay and became the group's *chef d'orchestre*. Matima, who suffered the effects of a nasty traffic accident in the midst of the breakup and was temporarily unable to play his guitar, became the group's artistic director. Manuaku was reported to be returning to Nyoka's side, but that never happened. Instead, two other musicians from Grand Zaïko Wa Wa, guitarist Bansimba Baroza and singer 'Adamo' Ekula, crossed over. Two more guitarists, 'Thylon' Muanda from The Best (the house band of the Intercontinental Hotel) and 'Chiro' Mvuemba of Minzoto Wella Wella, moved in alongside Matima, Enoch, and Baroza, while a singer known as Petit Aziza from the late seventies' version of Viva La Musica joined Nyoka, Dindo Yogo, newcomer Adamo, and holdover Benamayi on vocals. Several lesser-known players brought the group to full strength. They called themselves Zaïko Langa Langa Nkolo Mboka (village headman).

Following two months of intensive rehearsal at N'Sele, Nkolo Mboka returned to Kinshasa for a series of reintroductory concerts. They began in late July at FIKIN, Kinshasa's annual international trade fair, then moved on for August shows at the Intercontinental Hotel and the Palais du Peuple. The old guard was far from dead. With the Ngoss Club tied up in court proceedings over ownership, Nkolo Mboka settled in at the Kimpwanza, another Matonge club. Not far away, Familia Dei held forth at the Vis-à-Vis.

Each group strengthened itself in the ensuing months. Nkolo Mboka added drummer Patcho Star from Victoria Eleison, thus restoring its normal com-

Koffi Olomide

plement of two drummers. Likinga Mangenza returned to Bimi's side in Familia Dei after five years in a Portuguese jail. December of 1989 marked the twentieth anniversary of Zaïko Langa Langa's founding. Both factions bearing the illustrious name played to capacity crowds, but two Zaïko Langa Langas weren't necessarily better than one.

•

At a year-end spectacular in 1988, Zaïko Langa Langa Nkolo Mboka shared the bill at the Palais du Peuple with singer Koffi Olomide. Olomide, then riding a resurgent wave of popularity as leader of a band called Quartier Latin, was the perfect match for Zaïko. He had been a friend of the band from its earliest days, and Zaïko's musicians had helped him to launch his own career. Following his rapid rise to prominence in the late seventies, Olomide had found it difficult to sustain his success at the same level in the early years of the eighties. A bit of a maverick – he called himself the 'Rambo of Zaïre' and named his two sons Aristotle O'Neil and Elvis in defiance of authenticity – Olomide had preferred to remain solo in a musical culture dominated by bands. One result was that gigs were harder to come by, and as the infrastructure of the recording industry disintegrated, it became nearly impossible to make a living from records alone.

Olomide reacted on both fronts. He went to Paris in 1986 to record his first album, *Dieu Voit Tout* (God sees all), with a group of session musicians. A religious man in his personal life, Olomide prefers songs that address the nature of spirituality and the forces of life. His mother had told him he was born with one hand holding his chin as if in a contemplative mood. Emotion is the basis of the music, he said: 'I let my heart speak.' Upon his return to Kinshasa, Olomide formed Quartier Latin, anchored by bassist Massaka Djo Mass and guitar soloist Indianga Toussaint, to promote the new record.

Olomide reached the crest of his resurgence near the end of 1987 with an album known as *Rue d'Amour* (street of love) or *Tcha Tcho*, a phrase he invented to describe his music: 'all that is sweet, all that is good, all that is perhaps different, all that has a positive feeling.' Working with a small group of studio musicians, including the impeccable Rigo Star doubling on guitar and bass and the former African All Stars drummer Ringo Moya, Olomide produced a mellow marriage of Kinshasa rumba and Paris technology anointed with sentimentality. In the album's runaway hit, 'Myriam Immortelle,' Olomide plumbs the depths of his lower register for a melancholy ode to a lover. The rumba swings from Ringo Moya's hands embellished by guitar and calliope-inspired keyboards in a fluid arrangement of surprising elegance. 'Myriam' offered proof that innovations in electronics like the synthesizer and multi-track recorders need not be the music's enemy.

Tcha Tcho and its successor, *Elle et Moi* (she and I), won Olomide an international audience as Zaïre's equivalent to Jamaica's Gregory Isaacs, the king of lovers' reggae. Zaïre's commissioner of arts and culture presented him with an award for artistic merit for 1987, and Kinshasa's music writers made him their pick as 1988's best composer. He began to tour with Quartier Latin, splitting time among Europe, Zaïre, and a circuit around central Africa. His appearance at the Palais du Peuple in the company of Zaïko Langa Langa certified his revival.

•

No comeback was required of the elephant of Zaïre. Pepe Kalle and Empire Bakuba continued to be one of the country's most stable and popular bands in the 1980s. A focused agenda of recording and touring was the recipe for the group's success. Four or more albums a year bore the Empire Bakuba name, including a 1986 tribute to the late Docteur Nico and Matolu Dode's *Livre d'Or* (pound of gold). The latter's title track was an attack by the diminutive and soft-spoken 'Papy Tex' on what he saw as Kinshasa's declining moral standards. Businessman, barman, taximan, wife, no one escaped censure. 'Livre d'Or' helped Empire Bakuba win the best band award for 1987.

Tours took the musicians to French-speaking West Africa, where they had cultivated an ardent following. Côte d'Ivoire, Mali, Burkina Faso, Togo, and Benin comprised the usual circuit. The band hired Ram Ouedraogo, Tshala Muana's former manager and an Ivoirean national with roots in Burkina, to facilitate its trips. Europe beckoned too, especially for recording. 'We prefer to come to France, because France has a lot to offer, engineers who are specialized in [music],' Kalle explained. At the conclusion of its second period of association with Verckys in the early eighties, the band had again gone independent. 'If we've worked like this up to this point, it's because we're looking for a major label,' Kalle said. 'We need a major label which would take care of us. Really. Because working like this, going this way and that, it's not very good.... Working with just one label, one major distributor, that's our hope.'

Serendipity brought the band to Paris at the same time film-maker Thomas Gilou was in production for *Black Mic-Mac*, his cinematic look at Africans in Paris. Gilou recruited Empire Bakuba to appear in what turned out to be a precursor to the group's work back home in *La Vie est Belle*. Kalle stepped out from time to time to record without the band. A collaboration with Nyboma, his old friend from the days of Bella Bella, for producer Ibrahima Sylla yielded the zouk-influenced hit 'Zouké Zouké' in 1986. The two repeated their success on a second Sylla production in 1988 called *Moyibi* (thief). Kalle's work with Paris-based Zaïreans helped to make their other records more acceptable to the folks back home, who had, for the most part, shunned the light-on-content, up-tempo 'soukous.' Although they achieved success, such collaborative ventures were exceptional for Pepe Kalle. He preferred to nurture the 'empire' that he, Dilu, and Papy Tex had created.

Empire Bakuba, Quartier Latin, Choc Stars, Anti-Choc, Victoria Eleison, and the two Zaïkos survived at the end of the eighties. Although they verged on middle age, these groups seemed determined to carry the banner of youth into the nineties.

22
Matters of life and death

Bantous de la Capitale and O.K. Jazz, 1985–1989

The two jewels of the Congo River had undergone a metamorphosis in the nearly three decades since independence. Kinshasa's luster had dulled in proportion to the bloat in Mobutu's bank account. Brazzaville had done better in the relatively austere hands of Marien Ngouabi and Denis Sassou Nguesso. While it too was in hock to a plethora of creditors, Brazzaville showed no signs of the rot that undermined its sister capital. Oil off the coast of Pointe Noire paid the bulk of Congo's bills. And exports from Zaïre in search of hard currency transformed Brazzaville into a *de facto* brokerage for its faltering neighbor.

With the opening of the IAD studio and pressing plant, many of Kinshasa's musicians chose the economical ferry ride to Brazzaville over a costly flight to Paris in order to make new recordings. Pressing could be done at the Congolese factory or, if desired, the masters could be shipped to Europe for manufacture and release there on vinyl or the new compact disc format. Concerts in Brazzaville, Pointe Noire, and nearby Libreville, Gabon, were paid in CFA francs, a welcome alternative to the worthless zaïre.

Brazzaville's own bands took advantage of their fortunate circumstances, with varying degrees of success. Youlou Mabiala's Orchestre Kamikaze Loningisa enjoyed the highest profile of any of the groups in the early eighties. As a graduate of O.K. Jazz, Youlou remained faithful to its style, incorporating ensemble male voices, finger-plucked guitar, and a liberal dose of horns into the mellow rumba. At times he even matched his mentor in verbosity, if not in eloquence. People called him *le fils chéri de Franco*, Franco's favorite son.

Jean Serge Essous

Although not as large as O.K. Jazz, Kamikaze usually counted around twenty musicians, several of whom came from Zaïre. Lead guitarist Jacques Bazizila, known as 'Souza Vangou,' and singer N'Lemvo 'Serge' Kiambukuta, a brother of O.K. Jazz's Josky, were two of its more prominent members from the river's south bank. Kamikaze won a large following in Congo and in Kinshasa too, but the band's failure to tour outside its home base limited its popularity abroad. Not until 1986, in its sixth year of existence, did the band venture into Kinshasa to play a concert at the famed Vis-à-Vis.

No strangers to travel were the far more famous Bantous de la Capitale. During the early eighties, however, Kamikaze Loningisa had usurped some of Les Bantous' popularity among the Congolese. Les Bantous were down. The camaraderie that had sparked the partial reunion of 1978 had vanished by 1981. Pamelo Mounk'a went to Paris to record solo for Eddy'Son. Edo Ganga spent most of his time tending to his duties as president of the Union des Musiciens Congolais. The band's schedule of concerts and recording looked increasingly sparse. Equipment deteriorated, and salaries went unpaid.

Les Bantous looked better near the end of 1984 as they celebrated the band's twenty-fifth anniversary. The air hung heavy with nostalgia as Essous, Nino Malapet, Saturnin Pandi, Alphonse Taloulou, Gerry Gérard, and Mpassy Mermans took their accustomed places on stage at La Congolaise club. With Tino Mwinkwa and Lambert Kabako on vocals, the band ran through its considerable repertoire of hits for an enthusiastic crowd. Still, all was not well with *bakolo mboka*, the owners of the village. Nino Malapet summed up their current state: 'It's true that our endeavor is a frustration on the management level, but on the cultural level it's an unquestionable success.'

By 1986 equipment and morale had deteriorated to the point of alarm. Viewing Les Bantous as something of a national treasure, the deputy mayor of Brazzaville, Jean Jules Okabando, convened a conference of interested parties in an attempt to rejuvenate the band. Participants at the September meeting negotiated a structural adjustment of sorts. The mayor's office would provide the musicians with new instruments. Pamelo Mounk'a agreed to return as *chef d'orchestre*, replacing Nino Malapet, who was moved up to president of the band's board of directors. Edo Ganga would return to full-time duty along with Célestin Kouka and Théo Bitsikou. Kosmos wanted to continue his solo career but agreed to occasional appearances with the band. 'For people to talk about the Bantous again,' Pamelo declared, 'we must give birth anew to the team spirit that prevailed in the band in the years 1963 to 70.'

An album that had been in the works for some time came out soon after the official agreement was announced. Entitled *L'Amour et la Danse*, the new work contained two songs apiece from bassist Alphonse Taloulou and Pamelo, including the Samanthaesque 'Nora Mensah.' On the title track Pamelo revisits some of his old hits while appealing to his colleagues for peace. In January 1987 the united Bantous de la Capitale staged a grand soirée at Brazzaville's Palais de Congrès before an audience of dignitaries that included the country's prime minister and the deputy mayor who had engineered the reconciliation.

The next night the band played for its hard-core fans at a dance at La Congolaise. *Bakolo mboka* had returned to claim their turf.

•

If Les Bantous were the owners of Brazzaville, then Franco was Kinshasa's chief. As was the case with his Congolese brethren, few could imagine the music without him. And Franco showed no signs of leaving. 'Mario' had enjoyed astonishing popularity internationally, only slightly tarnished by its lack of recognition from Zaïre's music scribes. Upset by their slight and the press's general tendency to shoot from the hip, Franco had refused to talk to local reporters for most of 1986, despite its being the thirtieth anniversary year of O.K. Jazz. 'Your trade is linked to ours,' he admonished. 'Because we, we sing, you, you write about our work. So from now on, have the courage to contact us before writing, instead of coming out with any old thing for the sole purpose of creating a sensation.'

To the benefit of his fans, Franco was as loquacious in song as he was reticent with the press. His follow-up to 'Mario,' released as the June 6 anniversary date approached, finds Franco at his oratorical peak. A twenty-minute stemwinder, 'La Vie des Hommes' (the life of men), dissects men's behavior and the institution of marriage with the same incisive blade. Franco and Madilu System continue their fruitful partnership telling the gloomy story of Malélisa, a married woman with many children whose husband has deserted her.

> I weep for my stupidity, oh Mama
> I weep for my miseries, oh Mama
> It's the husband's bad character
> A husband who no longer thinks of his home
> He flees the house like a tenant
> Who is behind on the payment of rent
> The sufferings of marriage
> The famous marriages people often talk about
> Difficulties, children, I don't know how to get through it
> His friends, they are all brands of beer
> When I was still a girl
> I wondered whether I had to marry or not
> Something was telling me, get married? No, you mustn't
> What should I do? This can't be.

In what had become Franco's signature for the eighties, the band strikes a simple riff in support of the singers. The insistent repetition infuses Franco's conversational tone with a keen sense of urgency. Madilu delivers the emotional wallop, his voice racked with the pain of Malélisa's lament. The horn section and solo guitar alternate at the instrumental breaks, stretching and embellishing the basic theme before yielding again to Franco. So simple on the surface, 'La Vie des Hommes' requires multiple listenings to fully appreciate the complexity and beauty of what Franco had produced. The apparent confluence of careful arrangement and casual improvisation reveals his genius at every turn.

The sheer immensity of 'La Vie des Hommes' nearly overshadowed a fine composition on the album's flip side. Called 'Ida,' the song returned to one of Franco's favorite themes, women's alleged lack of judgement and propensity for infidelity. The sultry rumba features the voice of Franco's teenaged discovery, Malage de Lugendo. Malage's throaty baritone blends nicely with the boss's, and his solos evince the assuredness and dexterity of a more experienced singer. Franco beamed like a proud father whenever he introduced his young prodigy from the stage. 'Ida' presented him to a larger audience.

As far as Kinshasa was concerned, most of the celebrations for the band's thirtieth year took place on record. In addition to *La Vie des Hommes*, O.K. Jazz released four other albums in 1986, including one of the few to ever include a woman's voice. *Massu* introduced Jolie Detta for a fleeting stint in Le Grand Maître's ranks. June 6, the anniversary date, found the band in Kenya winding up a month-long tour. In Nairobi, Polygram Kenya presented Franco with a gold record for 'Mario.' Back in Kinshasa a reporter asked him about plans for a celebration. Franco, then in the midst of his one-sided feud with the press, replied sourly, 'As you well know, O.K. Jazz celebrated its thirty years of existence back on June 6th. The party is over.' Nevertheless he did agree to cooperate with a Zaïrean television documentary that recounts the band's three decades.

•

Franco's spat with Kinshasa's papers and his musical characterizations of assorted gold diggers and scoundrels soon gave way to a concern of more importance. Ever since its discovery in 1981, acquired immune deficiency syndrome (AIDS) – known in Congo and Zaïre by its French acronym, SIDA (*syndrome immunité déficient acquis*) – had been diagnosed in central Africa with growing frequency. Sensational reports and dubious statistics in the Western press often exaggerated the scope of the problem. Nevertheless, as the eighties wore on, verifiable infections and deaths from AIDS increased, more so in Zaïre than in Congo.

Franco joined the chorus of alarm shortly after the new year with a hastily recorded warning called 'Attention na SIDA.' 'When I composed that song in 1987, I was in Paris,' he explained. 'They were talking about it on TV, on radio. I had the sudden idea to record a piece to warn people.' The thought had come in the middle of a business trip without O.K. Jazz, so Franco contacted Emeneya Mubiala, whose band was on an extended European tour. Franco recorded the piece with Victoria Eleison in exchange for a promise to lend the O.K. Jazz horn section to Emeneya for some future project. (The promise was fulfilled on Victoria Eleison's *Deux Temps*.)

'Attention na SIDA' re-rendered 'Jacky,' replacing its orgiastic rant – the one that had landed Franco in jail – with a contrary warning about sexual promiscuity. Speaking alternately in French and Lingala to reach a wider audience, Franco recounts the now familiar specifics of AIDS' effects and methods of preventing its spread with all the fervor of an evangelist. 'I am afraid,' he told a reporter.

> You should know it. I protect myself. I shield myself, and I hold back. There you are. Like I say in the song, everyone is in danger, even babies, those who will be the life force of our nation and of Africa. If you contract this illness, you become a candidate for death. It is our duty to warn everyone.

Kinshasa wits had re-coined the SIDA acronym as *syndrome inventé pour décourager les amoureux*, syndrome invented to discourage lovers. Franco's 'Attention na SIDA' provided a powerful antidote to the indifference that implied.

•

The debasement of Zaïre's economy and innovations in the technology of music reproduction had altered the dynamics of Franco's organization, yet O.K. Jazz and associated subsidiaries still constituted a formidable enterprise. 'He was really constantly worried about O.K. Jazz continuing to make music,' said Malambu ma Kizola, Franco's senior counselor in Europe. 'He was a person who, as far as money was concerned, paid too little attention to his own personal concerns. His clothing, for example, that wasn't his concern. His concern was that his music succeed financially.'

Of the continued success of O.K. Jazz there appeared to be no doubt, but other areas of Franco's realm had begun to fail. His two record pressing factories, MAZADIS and SOPHINZA, remained shackled by shortages of imported raw materials and their growing obsolescence. Having established himself in Paris and Brussels, Franco was content to record and press his records there – and occasionally at IAD in Brazzaville – and then import them back into Zaïre for sale. From time to time he promised to modernize his factories, yet he no longer seemed genuinely concerned. In truth it made little sense for Franco to upgrade. By failing to meet the demand for records, vinyl had lost its hold on the market in Zaïre. Cassette tapes, many of them pirated, had become the dominant format. MAZADIS, SOPHINZA, and Verckys's IZASON could no longer be competitive. Most buyers of African vinyl records were now found in Europe and the United States.

The Un-Deux-Trois also fell victim to neglect. Once Franco's pride and joy, whose planning and construction he had meticulously overseen, the club looked worn and tattered by 1987. O.K. Jazz still played there, usually in Simaro's hands. However, Franco seemed to prefer conducting business from his home in Limete when he wasn't in Paris or Brussels. Musicians started to complain about delinquent salaries, especially when Franco was gone. Rumors of defections occasionally surfaced, but despite the missing pay checks, no other band could offer the security of O.K. Jazz.

Even Le Grand Maître himself looked different. 'I noticed, I observed a certain change in his physical state in '87,' said Malambu. 'I even, I permitted myself to ask him the question, I said, "Grand Maître, you no longer have your stoutness. You don't seem to look well anymore." He said to me, "Well, you know, a person can always get younger rather than older."' Indeed, Franco attacked his work with a youthful vigor, writing, recording, and planning for the future of O.K. Jazz.

After recording 'Attention na SIDA' with Victoria Eleison early in 1987, Franco returned home to work with his own band. His hiring of Jolie Detta had not worked out for the long term. In her place, he added two more women, 'Baniel' Itela Boketsu, who had been Mbilia Bel's understudy in Afrisa, and 'Nana' Akumu Wakutu, who had sung with Sam Mangwana's Tiers Monde Coopération. Franco took his new singers and the rest of the band across the river to Brazzaville to record fresh material that included an album featuring Nana and Baniel known by its lead track, 'Les On Dit' (gossip).

Tapes in hand, Franco flew to Paris in October to mix them and arrange for pressing and distribution. In an interview with a French journalist conducted at the offices of Celluloid – where, presumably, he had gone to discuss business – Franco sounded optimistic. 'Between now and 1990 I will have, I believe, a big recording studio. I want it at all costs, because I already have a record factory, and I will be able to work independently.' How may tracks, he was asked, thirty-two? 'A forty-eight-track studio, since I am big!'

Back in Kinshasa at the beginning of the new year 1988, the music writers voted Franco a special jury prize for 'Attention na SIDA.' Franco snubbed the writers. After assuring them that he would attend the awards ceremony, he sent Dizzy Mandjeku in his place to suggest that the prize be given instead to Victoria Eleison. Following that unpleasant incident – after which one writer referred to Franco as 'Gras Maître' (fat master) – the band took off for a tour of Rwanda and Burundi.

The nearly full complement of O.K. Jazz – including Simaro, Madilu, Josky, and the two women, Nana and Baniel – opened on January 28 in Gisenyi, a Rwandan border town opposite Goma, Zaïre. 'Dressed in red, in possession of all his artistic talents, he [Franco] proved that he hadn't stolen his title of Grand Maître,' wrote M'Biya Tshikala, reporting for *Elima* from Rwanda. 'Eminent singer doubling as a talented guitarist, he won over everyone with his languorous voice and the lively music that burst from his guitar.'

The tour was a mixed success. Two nights later in Kigali, the Rwandan capital, only a handful of fans showed up for a performance at the Meridien Hotel. The high cost of tickets, poor publicity, and the fact that promoters had previously advertised appearances by O.K. Jazz only to have the band not appear were given as the reasons. Franco stayed in his room, leaving the band to play a few numbers to a nearly empty hall. A second Kigali concert went better, with Franco again on stage playing to a sizeable crowd. The band went on for dates in Butare on the Rwandan side of the border with Burundi; in Bujumbura, Burundi's capital; and in Bukavu in eastern Zaïre. A final concert was to have been held on February 14 back at Goma across Lake Kivu. Unfortunately, the available plane could only safely carry the band's more than two tons of equipment plus Franco, Simaro, the tour manager, and a couple of technicians. The rest of the entourage traveled by road, arriving sixteen hours later, well after the concert's end. Franco and Simaro had held off the crowd by playing their songs in the company of a local band recruited to fill in at the last minute.

The drama continued when it came time to return to Kinshasa. The tour, it seems, had barely earned enough to cover expenses. There was no money left to buy tickets for a flight home. Franco, in full possession of his street smarts, managed to 'cooperate' with the pilot of a Zaïrean armed forces C-130 transport plane to ferry the band back to the capital. Some two hours into the flight, the C-130 lost power in two of its four engines. The plane limped along over the rainforest while the crew worked feverishly to find the cause of the problem. After many tense minutes, the engines kicked in again, and O.K. Jazz made it safely home.

Franco reached Kinshasa only to find that his friend and a co-founder of O.K. Jazz, Vicky Longomba, had fallen gravely ill. Although no longer a performer, Vicky had resumed active participation in the music business upon his election as president of UMUZA to succeed (Gérard) Madiata Madia in July of 1986. The road back had been long and difficult. Vicky's performing career had come to a halt in 1974 when doctors discovered what Vicky himself described as a cystic tumor on his head. Surgeons in Kinshasa successfully removed the growth. Worsening diabetes nearly cost him a leg two years later. In 1981 another tumor was found on his head. This time Franco intervened to pay for his friend's surgery in a Paris hospital. His elevation to the union's presidency was a triumph of resilience second only to a return to the stage.

As he lay in a Kinshasa clinic at the end of February 1988, death seemed a likelier prospect. But Vicky rallied again, recovering to the point where his doctors allowed him to go home. Several days later, however, he lapsed into unconsciousness and was rushed to another clinic. This time there would be no resurrection. Vicky died in the afternoon of March 12, 1988.

Franco, looking more fit than he had in years, joined the earliest stars of O.K. Jazz – Vicky's singing partner Edo Ganga, Jean Serge Essous, Lando Rossignol – and more recent members like Youlou Mabiala, along with Vicky's family and friends, for a vigil at the departed singer's house. At some point – it is unclear if before or after his death – Vicky was honored by President Mobutu with induction into the National Order of the Leopard at the rank of commander. A funeral mass was celebrated on Tuesday morning, March 15, at the Cathédrale Sainte Marie in Kinshasa's Lingwala district. The mourners then moved on to Gombe Cemetery, where Vicky was buried not far from Joseph Kabasele and Docteur Nico.

Apart from the void in the hearts of his family and friends, Vicky's death created an opening at the top of the musicians' union, one that Franco moved to fill. Three weeks of behind-the-scenes negotiations following Vicky's funeral ended on April 6 at the Intercontinental Hotel, where a general assembly of UMUZA members unanimously elected Franco to a five-year term as president. He humbly thanked the membership and promised to do his best on their behalf.

By the middle of the year, as Franco continued to shed his bulk, it became clear that something was wrong. Rumors began to circulate about the state

Matters of life and death   359

of his health. In Paris, Malambu heard directly from Franco's wife Annie and one of their daughters that indeed the boss was ill. 'He [Franco] would call me on the telephone,' Malambu remembered. 'Every time I asked him if he really was sick. He would say, "Of course not. I'm fine. There's no problem. Those people are just saying any old thing. I'm doing fine."' Ibrahim Bah, the producer who had booked Franco's concerts in the United States recalled hearing that Franco had died. He called Franco's home in Kinshasa only to have the man himself answer the phone. Rumors of possible defections also resurfaced, but if they ever contained a grain of truth, Franco managed to put things right before they could become reality. The band stayed together, and with Franco in attendance, recorded more songs at IAD in Brazzaville.

In October, Franco returned to Europe. Malambu met him at the plane in Brussels, and the two men took a car to Paris. 'As soon as I saw him I had a rush of strong feeling,' Malambu recalled. 'He no longer had the good build that he had.' Franco had asked Malambu to arrange for French doctors to examine him, but he arrived later than expected, and the appointments passed unkept. He was following a regimen prescribed by a doctor in Kinshasa and eventually did consult doctors in Europe as well.

After some days in Paris Franco decided to return to the studio in Brussels to add some final overdubs to the tracks recently recorded in Brazzaville and to record new songs he had written in answer to the swirl of rumors. Some members of the band flew up from Kinshasa to meet their leader in Brussels. 'We went into the studio, I think it was the beginning of November,' Malambu said.

> I think it took seven to ten days. And what astounded me was the incredible fire he [Franco] had in the studio. He went whole nights without stopping. At one point he said to me, 'Since I got sick, this is the first time that I've managed to stay standing up for such a long time.'

The session's set piece was Franco's twelve-minute jeremiad called 'Les Rumeurs (Baiser ya Juda),' the rumors (Judas kiss), delivered in an audibly weakened voice.

> Rumors are spreading in the country
> People are spreading rumors about me
> They say he's hospitalized
> They saw him in Ngaliema
> They say he went to Brussels
> They say they saw him in Antwerp

> He went to Paris
> They saw him in Geneva
> They say he went to America
> The party bought his ticket

They say that Franco has various sicknesses, he sings in Lingala. He has died three times in Kinshasa and three times in Europe. People are happy now that he's in pain. Then Franco slides into French in the middle of the piece to paraphrase the Bible.

> All my enemies are whispering
> Outside against me
> They think my misfortune
> Will cause my ruin
> He's dangerously sick
> See him lying down
> He won't get up again
> Even the people with whom I was at peace
> Who had my trust
> And who ate my bread
> Are lifting their heels against me
> Psalm 41, verses 6 to 10

Back in Lingala he grows increasingly bitter.

> People say that I already made my will
> I distributed my belongings to my children
> Who told them that in their dreams?
> Why is it that people laugh when someone is dying?
> When someone is sick?
> When someone is suffering?
> I have never seen this anywhere, only in Kinshasa
> There is not one compassionate person in Kinshasa
> What can I say?

Once the sessions were concluded, Franco released two albums of the songs largely recorded in Brazzaville, *Cherche une Maison à Louer pour Moi, Chéri* (find a house to rent for me, dear) featuring Nana and Baniel, and *La Réponse de Mario* (Mario's answer). He shelved the newest songs, including 'Les Rumeurs,' for the time being while he decided the proper time to release them. More recording followed early the next year for a two-album project that Sam Mangwana had cooked up. Mangwana recalled (in English) that 'when I saw Franco I said, "Okay, many people are saying that you have died and everything. But it is better to do something *heavy* to make a rectification to say that Franco is not dead."' The two arranged a deal that would see each man emerging from the project with his own record. 'You can't pay me,' Mangwana remembered telling Franco, 'and me also can't pay you. But you are going to sing inside of my record. I'm going to pay all expenses. And you also, you are going to pay for all expenses, and I am going to sing on your record.'

The recording sessions, held in Brussels in February of 1989, yielded Mangwana's four-song album For Ever, produced mainly with session musicians and a few members of O.K. Jazz. Franco sings and plays guitar on the lead-off track, the hopeful 'Toujours O.K.' (still/always O.K.), and contributes some guitar licks near the end of a second song, 'Chérie B.B.' He is equally in the background on his own album, Franco Joue avec Sam Mangwana, produced with musicians from O.K. Jazz. He belts out the words to 'Lukoki' (a song based in folklore that calls to mind the chimurenga music of Zimbabwe), which may indicate that the song actually came from an earlier recording session when he was still healthy. Only a few Franco or Franco-like flashes of guitar are discernible on the album's other three tracks. Rather than reassure, For Ever, at least, gave Franco's fans a scare. It was released bearing a photo of the once giant man, his body shrunken almost beyond recognition.*

Conscious of the need to conserve his strength, but still strong enough to work, Franco accepted an invitation to play a March date with Sam Mangwana at London's Hammersmith Palais. According to Mangwana, the show's promoter told the musicians to come to England, and he would have visas and work permits waiting for them. Mangwana and his musicians boarded a ferry at Boulogne in France for the trip across the English Channel while Franco and O.K. Jazz assembled at the port of Ostende in Belgium. When Mangwana's group reached the English port of Dover, no documents were to be found. 'They told us, "Okay, your promoter forgot to have your work permit for you. You must go back,"' Mangwana said. 'Disaster. It was a big disaster.' Soon after that embarrassment, a weary Franco flew home to Kinshasa.

The Un-Deux-Trois was closed now, ostensibly for renovation. Simaro, Papa Noël, and the other musicians of O.K. Jazz who remained in Kinshasa

---

* In 1994, more than five years after they had been recorded, 'Les Rumeurs (Baiser ya Juda)' and two other songs recorded in November of 1988 — 'Fabrice Akende Sanogo' and 'Mbanda Akana Ngai' — were packaged along with 'Batela Makila na Ngai' (protect my blood, i.e. my children or generations, a song released as 'Sadou' on the album La Réponse de Mario) and one song from the February 1989 sessions with Sam Mangwana — 'Laissez-Nous Tranquilles' (leave us alone) — and released on compact disc by Sonodisc under the title Les Rumeurs.

played at the Faubourg not far away. Work had begun on Franco's latest project in Kingabwa, an industrial zone on Kinshasa's eastern edge near the river. He envisioned it housing not only a studio but a modern record pressing plant, restaurant, and sleeping quarters for the musicians. The development's first phase, begun in the mid-eighties but not yet completed, was the construction of a modern health clinic.

Franco spent six weeks in Kinshasa tending to his affairs. 'When I saw him he had melted. He had lost a lot of weight. He had gotten thin, and he coughed a lot,' Papa Noël recalled. 'I asked him the question, I said, "Franco, what's wrong?" He said, "I was taking my bath, and I left the window open. Air came in."'

Franco went back to Europe at the end of April just in time to see the band off in May for its second tour of the United States, this time without him. 'When he got back from Kinshasa, let's say he had changed. He didn't look healthy any more,' Malambu said.

> Manzenza and I asked him what was wrong. So he told us, 'Look, I don't feel so good any more. Even though when I left I felt healthy, now that I'm back I feel like my health has gotten worse again. Things aren't going well.' We tried to console him.

Manzenza, the band's manager, led a seventeen-member contingent of O.K. Jazz on its American tour beginning in May. Dessoin Bosuma and Isaac Musekiwa, the group's longest serving members except for Franco, headed the list of musicians, which included Dizzy Mandjeku, Madilu System, Gerry Dialungana, Thierry Mantuika, and newcomer Lomingo Alida, who had recently joined the band from the Stukas Boys. O.K. Jazz played its own dates around the U.S. and Canada through May and June, and then in July joined a traveling variety show called Africa Oye! Rumors circulated that Franco would soon join the band to perform. Some promoters even advertised his presence as a sure thing. But Franco stayed in Europe, his condition improving a bit in time for his fifty-first birthday in July, then worsening in August just as the band returned to Brussels.

Throughout his months in Europe, Franco was besieged with requests for interviews. Most of them he ignored, preferring not to be seen in his current condition. He did, however, agree to a televised talk with an old friend, Zaïrean journalist Lukunku Sampu, to be conducted in Lingala. It was the language Franco felt most comfortable with, and he wanted to be able to express himself freely. The interview was taped on September 5, 1989, in the

Brussels studios of RTBF, Belgian television. Franco sat stiffly on a bright orange sofa, barely moving except for his head and an active right hand. A bluish-gray abacost, Zaïre's authentically correct male attire, hung loosely from his withered frame; thick glasses masked his eyes. Still, he appeared to be alert and in relatively good spirits, considering the precarious state of his health.

Franco sounded disconsolate about the gossip surrounding him. 'I can defend myself in any way, but people won't believe I don't have AIDS,' he said.

> If I have this illness, I'm going to die, and they'll do an autopsy to find out. If God exists and I don't have this illness and I feel better, I'm going to ask those people who are gossiping, one by one, 'You said I had AIDS, why am I still alive?'

References to God recurred throughout the fifty-five minutes of conversation. He had once believed in witchcraft, he said, and carried its protections. 'But now that I have been praying to God, I don't find the protections necessary, because God will always be with me. I didn't find those protections necessary, but now that I've thrown them away I have a big problem.' But later in the interview he was less contradictory. 'If it wasn't for God, I would not be here.... I'll be back in Kinshasa, and they're going to see me.'

He had started from nothing and worked hard to get where he was, he said. Why were people against him? 'I don't have a problem with anyone. My job is to do music, to make people laugh, and that's all.... For my enemies, I have left all to the Lord. If I did evil that I didn't know about, I apologize. I ask them to forgive me.'

It was thanks to women that he was a success, he declared, but they often acted badly, which was why he sang about them. As for the songs that landed him in jail, they weren't bad, he was only doing what Molière had done. He was simply ahead of his time.

Complaints against him by other musicians were unjustified. 'The most lying and the most evil people are musicians.' The president, on the other hand, could do no wrong. 'When the president makes a decision, the Zaïrean doesn't want to follow it, doesn't want to listen. When we start to listen, then we will start to help our chief.'

Franco ended by trying to console his family, imploring them to ignore all the rumors. 'I know you are suffering because of me. People are laughing at you because of me. Be patient. That's the way the world is. If someone is bothering you, don't respond. Leave everything to God.'

Sometime after the interview, Franco expressed a wish to pray at Lourdes, a small town in the Pyrenees where the Virgin Mary was said to have appeared in 1858, now a Catholic shrine. Like most Zaïreans, he had been raised a Catholic, but after his incarceration in 1978 he had converted to Islam. No one seems to recall him observing Islamic doctrine, so most attributed his conversion to some obscure ulterior motive. Perhaps it was a backhanded slap at his detractors' Catholicism or a deeper embrace of Mobutu's authenticity philosophy which viewed Islam as less alien than the religions of the West. Whatever the reason, Franco's Abubakar Sidick persona had vanished as quickly as it had arrived. Now, as the specter of death appeared, Franco sought solace in the religion of his youth.

Still pushing himself to the limit, Franco traveled to London in the third week of September to take care of formalities surrounding a scheduled end-of-the-month performance by O.K. Jazz to make up for the March fiasco. Several interviewers came to his hotel room, where he spoke from the comfort of his bed. It was a less than inspiring performance for anyone who hoped that Franco would be able to keep the September 30 date.

From London he returned to Brussels and, following a few days of rest, continued on to Amsterdam for the band's September 22 show at an entertainment complex called the Melkweg. Near the concert's conclusion a markedly enfeebled Franco was helped to a chair on the stage where he sang and played as well as he could. To see him in such a state bordered on impropriety, according to those who were there. Franco had insisted on trying to perform, but the sight was almost too painful to bear. 'I'm praying to God for this illness to go away as soon as possible,' he told an interviewer for the Dutch radio station VPRO after the show. 'I can't keep playing like this. I can only ask the public to excuse me for today. Maybe next year it will be different.'

Upon his return to Brussels on the morning of September 23, Franco met with Manzenza and Malambu. 'Manzenza was going to give him an accounting of the financial state, shall we say, of the concert,' Malambu recalled.

> Manzenza gave him all the proceeds that had been made at the concert. So he [Franco] began counting, counting, counting, counting. Finally he asked Manzenza, 'Are you sure what you gave me is right?' as always. Manzenza said, 'Yes, that's all we brought in.' So I said to Manzenza just as a little joke, 'Even sick this guy never forgets about money.' Well he heard us ... and he said, 'Oh! What do you mean forget? I can't forget. That's what rules the world.'

The following day, as the band prepared for a concert in Paris, Franco entered a Brussels hospital. Malambu and Manzenza attended the concert, then

Franco in a mid-eighties publicity photo

returned to Brussels to check on their boss. His condition was deteriorating rapidly, and he appeared to be in pain. His wife Annie had him transferred from the center of Brussels to Namur University Hospital several miles southeast of the city. Malambu and Manzenza went back to Paris the first week in October to attend to business matters. On Thursday, October 12, as they prepared for their return to Brussels the following day, they received a call from Annie. Franco had died that morning.

•

'On that day we were supposed to rehearse, because we rehearsed at Franco's, at his house in Limete,' Papa Noël remembered.

> That day when I got there I saw everybody was standing around. Everybody had this look, like they couldn't believe it. I came up, I said, 'What's

happening? Aren't we rehearsing?' We didn't know. We got there, and we found that something wasn't right. So for those who know Franco's house, in Limete, there's a girl's school right across the street. It was about noon or one o'clock. There were girls in the yard of the school there, and they were about to start afternoon classes. And I heard a great cry. It was wailing. The girls started crying. They came running to Franco's house. Then I saw Franco's sister come over crying. And that's how I understood that Franco was dead.

Not since the death of Bob Marley, nearly a decade before, had the world witnessed such a spectacle of emotion as that which followed the news of Franco's passing. Hundreds of mourners, friends and family, gathered on Sunday morning, October 15, to meet the Air Zaïre flight bringing his body home. Hundreds of thousands lined the fifteen-mile route from Ndjili Airport into the city. Many had waited for hours to get a final glimpse of Le Grand Maître. Verckys Kiamuangana could be seen at the head of a phalanx of musicians carrying the shiny black coffin to the car that would take Franco home to Limete. The coffin, surrounded by flowers with a large portrait of Franco at its head, rode atop a station wagon near the front of a massive cortège that stretched out for over a mile. In Limete, Franco lay in state in the courtyard of his home while assorted government dignitaries paid their respects. President Mobutu, currently out of the country, decreed a period of national mourning and sent the party's secretary-general to represent him. After the politicians left, family and friends maintained an all-night vigil that culminated in a private funeral service.

The following day Franco's body was transported to the Palais du Peuple, where it lay in state for the general public. Two lines of mourners filed past the bier throughout the day and into the night to pay homage to the man who had hectored and goaded them, poked fun at their foibles, and presented them with so much wonderful music. Tuesday morning, in a brief ceremony, Franco was promoted to the rank of commander in the National Order of the Leopard. Then, his coffin draped with the flag of Zaïre, he was taken to Notre Dame Cathedral for a solemn funeral mass.

Party officials and Franco's family lined the cathedral's front benches. Brazzaville's mayor led Congolese mourners, including Franco's one-time protégé Youlou Mabiala, O.K. Jazz founding member Saturnin Pandi, and Nino Malapet of Les Bantous de la Capitale. 'Franco was a prophet,' the officiating priest intoned.

> And while he was very often considered an upsetting force, it was precisely because his message, frank and direct, called his listeners to consciousness. He

was a missionary who understood his mission well. And he himself said that his mission was to provoke, to denounce, to say the truth.... He remained faithful to his mission until the end.

After mass the mourners proceeded slowly on foot to Gombe Cemetery a few blocks away. In the middle of the crowd one of Franco's sons carried his father's guitar. Verckys, Simaro, Franco's mother Mama Makiesse, and others offered a few words at the grave site. Then Franco's body was lowered into a concrete tomb lined with squares of white tile. The tomb's massive lid was slid into place, and mourners covered it with flowers as they said their final good-byes.

The barefoot boy who helped his mother in the market had been buried like a man of royalty. He had worked hard to distance himself from the poverty of his youth, and he had succeeded famously. 'Good memories for me,' he once remarked, 'are each time my band plays and money comes into the till. Because I've always considered that a man without money is dead wood.' The acquisition of wealth in Zaïre flowed from the country's political structure, to which Franco was well connected. Yet his politics never seemed to tarnish his image as a voice of the people. He didn't function so much as a spokesman for the downtrodden in the manner of Jamaica's Marley. He performed instead as a social critic who flayed society's stereotypes, often unjustly, sometimes bitterly, and almost always with an endearing humor.

His recorded output was prodigious, in the neighborhood of one hundred albums and an uncountable number of singles. Much of the material was uneven – O.K. Jazz had many composers to satisfy, many of whom did not share Franco's gifts – but he produced so many gems. Any record bearing Franco's name was sure to turn a profit. The endless stream of new releases fueled the behemoth that was O.K. Jazz.

Oddly enough, several of Franco's musicians decided not to return to Zaïre for his burial. They had all attended a memorial service in Brussels before Franco's body was sent home. Still, most Kinshasans felt a sense of outrage that some of Franco's men were not present at his funeral. 'It just wasn't right to let Franco's body leave and to stay in Europe. I think it's a condemnable attitude,' Malambu said. Madilu's absence was particularly glaring. 'If Madilu had gotten to the level he had, it was thanks to Franco. He was a product of Franco, and people really didn't accept that he behaved that way toward Franco.' The music's remaining elder statesman also failed to attend the funeral, but it was not for lack of trying. Tabu Ley, on tour in the United States, fought to obtain the necessary travel documents and alter his concert schedule, but he was unable to get back to Kinshasa until Le Grand Maître had been laid to rest. He immediately issued an apology and proceeded to the cemetery to visit the tomb of his fallen friend and rival.

Madilu and the others who had remained in Brussels arrived in Kinshasa a few days after the funeral. They had been abroad for nearly a year, and it was impossible, they said, to assemble their belongings and make travel arrangements at such short notice. They had meant no disrespect. Following a hostile reception, the delinquent musicians made peace with their fans. On December 8, O.K. Jazz returned to the stage at the Palais du Peuple under the leadership of Simaro Lutumba and a surprise new chef d'orchestre, Empompo Loway. Absent were the band's two doyens Dessoin Bosuma and Isaac Musekiwa, both said to be ailing. New member Boteku Bohomba sang Franco's parts with Madilu and played guitar in Le Grand Maître's style. But there could be no replacing Franco. For the first time in its 33-year history, O.K. Jazz contemplated a future without the boss.

23
The gray nineties

O.K. Jazz, Wenge Musica, Bantous de la Capitale, Soukous Stars, Abeti, Papa Wemba, and Tabu Ley, 1989 and after

After Franco came the flood. It seemed as if the legions of illness and insanity had at once been loosed by Le Grand Maître's death. In reality, of course, they had been afoot for years, relentlessly stalking among Zaïre's common people. The leader of O.K. Jazz was simply the weightiest personage to be consumed. The forces at work in Zaïre were too great for a sorcerer, even a sorcerer of the guitar, to hold at bay. With this particular passing, visited upon a great cultural figure and one of the country's privileged class, everyone suddenly looked vulnerable.

M'Pongo Love came home to Kinshasa in July of 1989, just before Franco died. 'I left Zaïre in '85,' she said. 'I should have come back in '86, but I was on tour all the time. And there was that damned case with Safari Ambiance which took too much time from my program to the detriment of my family and the promotion of my records.' Now home for the first time in five years and free of the court proceedings that followed from her breaking her Safari Ambiance contract, she presented to the public her third child, a seven-month-old daughter, and a brand new album. She hoped the new record, *Partager* (sharing), produced by Ibrahima Sylla with the participation of Bopol Mansiamina, would restore her waning popularity.

At home in suburban Binza, M'Pongo planned a new show to reintroduce herself to the Zaïrean public. Rumor had it that she might reunite with Empompo Loway, the man who had helped her to stardom, but little more was heard from the singer until shortly after Franco's death. M'Pongo, too, was sick. She was admitted to a Kinshasa clinic in December and was said to be slowly recovering. Her elder brother told the press that she had had a 'strong attack,' of what he wouldn't say. Hopes for her return to health went unfulfilled. M'Pongo Love had come home to die. The final moments of her brief thirty-three years passed on the morning of January 15, 1990.

Six days later, at another clinic, ill fortune struck again. M'Pongo's former mentor and the newest addition to O.K. Jazz, Empompo Loway, died. His ghostly appearance at the band's December concert had shocked many of his fans. He was reported to be suffering from a recurrence of tuberculosis, whose treatment he neglected in favor of work. There was a grim sort of poetry in the passings. Empompo and M'Pongo had made beautiful music together. Apart for more than ten years, they were reunited in their native soil.

Now death was stealing in pairs. The grand old men of O.K. Jazz – who were only in their mid-fifties – Isaac Musekiwa and Dessoin Bosuma both died in the following weeks. During the previous year's tour of the United States, Musekiwa showed the effects of accident or disease that hindered his use of one leg. Whatever it was apparently claimed his life. Dessoin suffered from throat cancer that refused to be contained. Many Zaïreans likened the passings to the often remarked phenomenon of the wife and husband who die around the same time. Perhaps Isaac and Dessoin had felt so close to Franco that once he died they simply lost the will to go on. The musicians of O.K. Jazz went back into mourning. It was something they would become accustomed to doing.

More bad news arrived in May. The child prodigy and fickle adult Soki Dianzenza died in Zaïre on the fourth. He was only thirty-five years old. Two weeks later, almost to the hour, his 42-year-old brother, Soki Vangu, passed away in a hospital in Germany. The brothers had been inactive in the music business in recent years. Orchestre Bella Bella had run its course by 1980. Soki Vangu had followed the path to Abidjan but failed to find the second wind that had boosted the likes of Sam Mangwana and Tshala Muana. Soki Dianzenza retreated in the opposite direction, traveling to Kisangani for a period of withdrawal from the scrutiny of Kinshasa. He resurfaced briefly in 1984 beside Emeneya in Victoria Eleison, then slipped again from view. The family's oldest son, Michel, speaking at Soki Vangu's funeral, addressed his remarks to his dead brother.

> Upon hearing from faraway Germany [where Michel and the brothers' mother had been visiting] of Soki Dianzenza's death, Mama and myself hoped that you would be out of danger, but you preferred to follow your brother Emile

[Dianzenza's Christian name] as if you two had made an appointment. What a sad fate for our family!

The extraordinary succession of deaths stunned Kinshasa's music community. The migration to Europe had been one thing; the musicians could always come back. But the deaths of so many established artists diminished people's links to the past while sowing seeds of doubt for the future. The often profligate nature of an entertainer's life fueled rumors of AIDS. None of the musicians spoke of having the disease; Franco had more or less denied it. Still, the rapid loss of weight and the deteriorating function of vital organs associated with several of the deaths mirrored the disease's classic symptoms. Regardless of the truth of the matter, the fact of the deaths and the gossip's believability spun a far more effective tale of caution than any song or public service announcement. AIDS or no, several of Zaïre's finest musicians had departed, and for that the world was the poorer.

•

Some news of the entertainment realm was good. Singer Ndombe Opetun returned to O.K. Jazz in the early months of 1990. After dropping out of Afrisa the previous year, he had cut a record with O.K. Jazz in Europe prior to Franco's death. Now he came back as a full-fledged member. The voice of Simaro's 'Maya' also returned to the band. Lassa Carlito had defected to the Choc Stars in 1986. He and Ndombe added to the depth of the O.K. Jazz vocal corps, which already included Madilu and Josky, along with their lesser-known brethren Lola Checain, Aime Kiwakana Kiala, and Lokombe Nkalulu. Although Dizzy Mandjeku, Thierry Mantuika, and Lomingo Alida had decided to remain in Brussels and Malage de Lugendo defected to Zaïko Nkolo Mboka, the post-Franco version of O.K. Jazz appeared to be solid and functioning well in Simaro's competent hands. The band took several of 1990's music awards, including best guitarist, Gerry Dialungana, and best singer, Madilu System.

New bands continued to emerge, although not as often as before. One such group was nearly a decade old before it came to prominence. Wenge Musica had started in 1981 as a vehicle for a group of students to play in during school vacations. Founded by guitarist Didier Masela and singer 'J.P.' Mpiana Mukulumpa, Wenge had evolved, by the end of the eighties, into a professional band that included guitarists Alain Makaba and Blaise Kombo and singer Ngiama Werason. The Wenge sound, although heavily synthesized, kept the guitars at the forefront along with ensemble vocals that were every bit the equal of many of the better-established groups. Kinshasa's music critics were impressed enough to pick Wenge Musica as 1988's 'revelation of the year.'

A traffic accident in 1990 claimed the life of Blaise Kombo, a tragic setback at a time when Wenge was threatening to break into the first ranks of Kinshasa's bands. Further difficulties ensued when a group of Zaïreans living in Paris led by a former Wenge bassist named Aime Buanga began to perform under the Wenge Musica name. Confusion abounded outside of Zaïre over which band was the real thing. Displeased but resolute, the musicians of Kinshasa's Wenge – 'Bon Chic, Bon Genre,' they bragged – went on to do their best work. *Kala-yi-Boeing*, a polished album recorded in Europe at the end of 1992, deftly blends the vigor of Kinshasa's youth bands with the slickness of Paris soukous. Although the existence of two bands with the same name continued to confound music buyers, Kinshasa's Wenge emerged as the stronger group.

The man whom many looked to as Congo music's guardian in the wake of Franco's death was strangely absent from the scene. The last of Zaïre's great band leaders, Tabu Ley Rochereau, now made his home in Paris and appeared to have little appetite for a return to wasting Kinshasa. All the members of Afrisa lived in Paris, he said in 1991. Faya Tess and sister singer Efomi Mondjoy, known as 'Beyou Ciel,' had replaced the departed Mbilia Bel. As *chef d'orchestre*, the bassist Shaba Kahamba conducted rehearsals of the current fifteen-or-so-member band that included regulars Huit Kilos on guitar and saxophonists Mekanisi Modero and Kongi Aska. Grand Zaïko's Lukombo Djeffard now sang behind Tabu Ley along with 'Wawali' Bonane Bungu and 'Dodo' Munoko Gisalu. The band maintained itself in expensive Paris by working regularly either in the studio or playing concerts in Europe, Africa, and North America. Kinshasa was rarely on the itinerary.

•

It scarcely made sense for Ley to go home, from a business standpoint at least. Conditions had reached such a state of decline that it was probably easier to make a go of things in Europe. Inflation continued to ravage the zaïre, putting even basic necessities out of reach of many Zaïreans. Only the wealthy could still afford to go out to a night club or buy the latest cassette. At one point in 1990 a dollar fetched 700 zaïres. A newspaper that sold for an exorbitant 200 zaïres at the beginning of the year cost 1,000 by year's end. The once tongue-in-cheek 'Article 15,' do what you must to survive, had become, for nearly everyone, a stark necessity.

As most Zaïreans could attest, the current economic bankruptcy stemmed from the dissolute nature of the country's political apparatus. 'When I assumed power, the nation lay in ruin, the victim of colonial exploitation, political unrest, economic collapse, and internal strife,' Mobutu told an interviewer in 1988, while failing to note that the country had almost come full circle. He asserted on several occasions that the MPR had served the nation well and would remain its sole legal party.

Despite the pronouncements of Mobutu and other like-minded leaders, the astonishing collapse of totalitarianism in eastern Europe gave hope to its opponents in Africa. In Togo, a national conference of political leaders threatened to unseat the country's long-standing dictator, Gnassingbe Eyadema. Neighboring Benin's president, Mathieu Kerekou, agreed to open the political process, a move that eventually cost him his job through a free election in 1991. Likewise in Zambia, Zaïre's southern neighbor, the only president the country had ever known, Kenneth Kaunda, yielded to pressure for reform. Multi-party elections in 1991 removed him from office.

The end of the cold war also brought pressure on Mobutu. He was thought to have been greatly affected by the sudden overthrow and execution of Romania's dictator, Nicolae Ceausescu, with whom he had a personal and professional affinity. The Western powers led by the United States, no longer in need of an 'anti-communist' ally, scampered out of Zaïre like rats deserting a ship whose hull they had gnawed to the point of rupture. It was time, they piously intoned, for Mobutu to give way to 'democracy.'

Still supremely confident of his standing among his own people, Mobutu called, at the beginning of 1990, for the citizens of Zaïre to voice their concerns. He had apparently given little thought to the consequences of this seemingly off-hand initiative, an idea that bore a striking resemblance to the blunder of Zaïreanization. What followed was an outpouring of comment on his regime, most of which Mobutu claimed to be favorable but which was, in fact, just the opposite. The most famous critique, suppressed in Zaïre, came from the Conference of Catholic Bishops, who called for a new constitution for the country and an end to the MPR's domination of political and economic life.

After mulling over the suggestions, the public statesman Mobutu declared on April 24, 1990 that, despite overwhelming praise for the MPR, he would now launch a new era of multi-party government. As chief of state, he would be above the fray, and was therefore resigning as leader of the MPR. The besieged dictator Mobutu responded rather differently. Several days after his magnanimous speech, as many as 100 students in Lubumbashi, a hotbed of opposition to the regime, were massacred by Zaïrean soldiers. Mobutu would continue to act in this vein – as he always had – the statesman proceeding as the wellspring of wisdom and moderation, the dictator loosing his soldiers on the opposition.

Once the opening of the system had begun, it was difficult to close back up. Newspapers, usually tools of the administration when it came to political matters, now bore headlines that editors could only have dreamed of a few short months before. 'Le MPR en Débandade!' The MPR in confusion. *Elima* paid the price in August of 1990 when employees were beaten and the offices sacked. 'A Commando [Unit] of MPR Killers Terrorizes Kinshasa,' screamed the paper's first edition following the raid. A year later its offices were bombed. By the beginning of 1991 more than 150 political parties had formed or surfaced from the underground. In August some 3,000 community, business, and religious leaders convened in Kinshasa for a national conference on the country's future. The conference would proceed sporadically over the next sixteen months, jockeying with Mobutu for control of the government.

Meanwhile, on September 23, 1991, Zaïrean soldiers whose meager salaries had gone unpaid for months staged a demonstration at their base near Ndjili Airport that turned to mutiny and then into full-scale riot. Bursting with anger at their betrayal by the government that they had helped to maintain in power, the soldiers swept into downtown Kinshasa, sacked the MPR headquarters, and set about looting shops, car dealerships, and the homes of the wealthy. Civilians and other soldiers quickly joined in the two-day pillage. France and Belgium sent in troops to evacuate their nationals, many of whom owned the looted homes and businesses. Mobutu, by this time back at the helm of the MPR, remained unshaken. Most of the army, especially the elite presidential guard, stayed loyal even as Mobutu's term as president officially expired on December 4, 1991. Later in December, the opposition to Mobutu presented a united front by electing the Episcopal archbishop of Kisangani, Monsignor Laurent Monsengwo Pasinya, as president of the national conference, but that too had little effect on Le Guide.

In August of 1992, the national conference completed work on the framework for a transitional government to lead the country to democracy in two years. The conference elected Etienne Tshisekedi wa Mulumba – a founding member of the MPR who had fallen out with Mobutu in the early seventies and subsequently became one of Mobutu's most public and persistent critics – as the 'first state commissioner' and directed him to form the transitional government. The conference then dissolved itself in favor of a Haut Conseil de la République led by Monsignor Monsengwo that would act as the country's transitional legislature. Mobutu refused to accept the actions of the national conference, and since he had an army to protect him, Zaïre wound up with two governments, neither of which had enough power to take effective action.

Given this background, only the most tenacious of musicians, and the poorest, remained in Kinshasa. A second episode of pillaging in January of 1993 left the city looking like the carcass of some prehistoric beast stripped clean by the ravages of time. All the city's banks had closed. If one were lucky enough to have a dollar, it would purchase four million crisp new zaïres from the stash of a well-connected businessman or an equal amount in tattered notes on 'Wall Street,' a makeshift market of money changers located in a park near the ambassador-less American Embassy. Wretched vehicles, years beyond junkyard condition, rattled through the streets belching instant emphysema. The wrecks were fueled by 'Qaddafis,' black market dealers who sold petrol by the bottle and never seemed short of supply.

Matonge, the center of Kinshasa's nightlife, was a shell of its former bustling self. The few record shops still holding on stocked only a smattering of cassettes imported from Brazzaville. Few dancing bars remained. The Vis-à-Vis sat empty; a pile of construction sand where revelers once had reveled hinted weakly at a possible rebirth in some unforeseen future of prosperity. Franco's Un-Deux-Trois was now home to an evangelical church. 'Cherchez l'eternel Dieu avant qu'il ne soit trop tard!' admonished a sign on an outer wall: seek God eternal before it's too late. The church was one of dozens of evangelical houses of worship to have sprung up throughout the city; a reflection, perhaps, of people's increasing desperation.

O.K. Jazz survived in the skeletal city along with Empire Bakuba, the two Zaïkos, and Wenge Musica. Koffi Olomide still made occasional appearances. A recording studio called Bobongo remained in operation. Verckys maintained his studio and the Véve Centre complex, but in the spirit of the new 'openness,' he had started two newspapers, Le Soir and News Stars, and begun to groom himself for a future in politics.

•

Across the river in Brazzaville, the Congolese navigated the transition to Western-style democracy with remarkable finesse, at least in the beginning.

President Denis Sassou Nguesso, in power for eleven years, began to come under pressure for reform in 1990. The Parti Congolais du Travail (Congolese Workers' Party) had controlled the rhetorically Marxist People's Republic of the Congo as its sole legal party since 1969. By financing the present through borrowing against future revenue from its offshore oilfields, Congo achieved a relatively high standard of living and stability, maintained in part by the government's willingness to hire graduates of its model school system into its increasingly bloated bureaucracy. Congolese referred to themselves as 'un pays de fonctionnaires,' a nation of civil servants.

Prosperity was less evident at the lower levels of society. With an eye on eastern Europe and their African neighbors, Congolese trade unionists, and some members of the ruling PCT itself, began to press for a more democratic form of government. To emphasize the point the unions staged a series of strikes. Near the end of 1990, after several ineffectual attempts to appease the reformists, Sassou Nguesso agreed to the formation of additional political parties and to the convocation of a national conference to plot the country's future course. Dozens of new parties formed, many led by former members of the PCT. The national conference, convened in May of 1991, quickly dismantled Sassou Nguesso's regime, rewrote the constitution, adopted a new national flag and anthem, dropped 'People's' from the country's name, and established the framework for a transitional legislature to lead the country until multi-party elections could be organized. Even more surprising was Sassou Nguesso's acceptance of the conference's actions.

Despite numerous problems, the nearly bloodless passage to democracy concluded with the election of a new Congolese president in August of 1992. Pascal Lissouba of the Union Panafricaine pour la Démocratie Sociale, a sixty-year-old scientist who had served in the government of Massamba-Debat and in the prison of Yhombi Opango, won a run-off election with the candidate of the Mouvement Congolais pour la Démocratie et le Développement Intégral, Bernard Kolelas. The two had placed first and second respectively in the initial round of voting. President Sassou Nguesso of the PCT, having finished third, threw his support to Lissouba in the run-off to provide the new president's margin of victory. 'The transition has come to an end as we have wished: without violence, without strife, in a calm atmosphere of dignity which reflects the maturity of our people,' Sassou Nguesso said at his successor's inauguration. 'Given today's African context, it is a beautiful victory for the Republic of Congo.'

With its peace, if not its prosperity, assured for the moment, Brazzaville looked like a good bet to supplant Kinshasa as Congo music's capital. IAD offered first-rate production facilities, favored, among others, by O.K. Jazz. Keyboard player and former member of Abeti's Redoutables Freddy Kebano operated an eight-track studio suited to the area's more experimental musicians. Another eight-track studio called Saturne opened in the early nineties not far from IAD. Brazzaville's La Congolaise was now the premier night club in central Africa. Chez Faignond had closed, although part of the building still housed a smaller, very popular, disco. Across the street, Bono Music bulged with the latest compact discs from Africa and the West along with a still substantial selection of vinyl records. A few doors away, a Senegalese named Amadou Ndaiye controlled the cassette trade.

The infrastructure had taken shape, but the marketplace had changed. Compared to its populous neighbor, Brazzaville was still a small city. The loss of the Kinshasa market to the destructive forces of Mobutuism had hurt Congolese musicians almost as much as their Zaïrean counterparts. Pirate cassettes ate into sales at home. And the lure of Paris with its access to more affluent European and American buyers was difficult to ignore.

Personnel problems among the bands also hindered progress. Jean Serge Essous of Les Bantous de la Capitale had fallen ill near the end of 1988. When he went to Paris for an extended stay to obtain medical treatment the band started to come apart. Health problems also slowed Pamelo Mounk'a, forcing him to relinquish his role as chef d'orchestre. Les Bantous played fewer dates, which made it difficult for the musicians to support themselves. Morale sank to such a low that the group split again in 1989. Nino Malapet kept the original Bantous alive, while core members Pamelo, Edo Ganga, Célestin Kouka, Mpassy Mermans, Gerry Gérard, and Alphonse Taloulou formed a new group called Bantous Monument. Youlou Mabiala's Orchestre Kamikaze also broke up around the same period.

Essous came home to Brazzaville at the beginning of 1993 after four years in Paris. He attempted to put Les Bantous back together again, but his efforts fell victim to an explosion of political unrest. The country's three main parties had formed along regional and ethnic lines, and the implicit tensions resurfaced. In a new round of voting for seats in the legislature conducted in May of 1993, the president's party and its coalition partners won a solid majority. The losers, claiming fraud, refused to accept the results. Supporters of both camps armed themselves to settle the dispute in the streets. Once again the institutions of Western democracy looked woefully ill-suited to the conditions that prevailed in post-colonial Africa. And any musician who continued to possess career aspirations would have to go elsewhere to pursue them.

•

If the location of the music's capital had been in doubt before, the early nineties settled the question. Paris had been the choice for recording for the better part of a decade, but now, if they didn't live there full-time, most musicians – including members of Empire Bakuba, Choc Stars, Anti-Choc, and Quartier Latin – spent much of their time in the French capital, or on tour in Europe. Several former members of O.K. Jazz – Dizzy Mandjeku, Ntesa Dalienst, Papa Noël, Lomingo Alida, and a few others – chose to settle in Brussels, and the Zaïkos made it their headquarters whenever they were in Europe.

In Africa, as Sam Mangwana once remarked, musicians live close to the people. The inspiration for songs springs from observations of daily life. 'We are reporters of the people. We are singing – inside of songs we are talking about problems inside our society.' Now, however, the musicians of both banks of the Congo River found themselves largely cut off from their roots. The high cost of living in Europe and, compared to Kinshasa, the limited opportunities to play live made it nearly impossible for bands to function as they had before. In most cases each musician was forced to make his or her own way. Of the permanent Paris residents, only Tabu Ley managed to hold a band together in the old style of Kinshasa, by hiring musicians and paying salaries. The others collaborated when necessary, working each other's recording sessions or forming temporary groups to play a club date or concert tour. Bands like Les Quatre Etoiles and Loketo – loose-knit collaborations of more or less the same personnel who maintained a group name as a marketing device – were formed by equal partners who decided their affairs collectively but retained the right to work on outside projects.

A new band of this type started to come together in Paris during an Ibrahima Sylla session for Congolese singer Ballou Canta. Ballou was Hyacinthe Ballou from Congo's Atlantic port city of Pointe Noire. He had begun singing seriously at school in Brazzaville, where his Spanish teacher used him as an example to illustrate the conjugation of the verb *cantar*, to sing, thus giving him his stage name. After college he sang professionally with Télé-Music, a band sponsored by the post office, before moving to Paris in the early eighties. Lokassa ya Mbongo played behind Ballou on the session for Sylla, and the two began talking about forming a group to support each other's projects.

Lokassa ya Mbongo

Shimita, the former Grand Zaïko singer who was recording for Sylla at the time, also expressed an interest. Lokassa contacted guitarist Dally Kimoko, whom he knew from the time of the African All Stars in Lomé, and singer-dancer Yondo Kusala, another former colleague from his days with Afrisa. A second singer from Congo, Neil Zitany, also joined the group. In 1989 the six musicians officially founded the Soukous Stars.

Several Soukous Stars albums, each under the name of a different 'star,' appeared almost simultaneously, but Lokassa's earned the greatest acclaim. Produced by Ibrahima Sylla, *Megamix Vol. 1* came out near the end of 1989. The album led off with 'Nairobi Night,' a fifteen-minute party piece compiled by Lokassa that sampled several East and South African songs (all uncredited) with a Zaïrean touch. While East Africans enjoyed 'Nairobi Night,' the rest of the world danced to the flip side, a medley of songs by Nigeria's Prince Nico Mbarga – including the extraordinary 'Sweet Mother' – sandwiched between two halves of a Lokassa composition called 'Lagos Night.' *Megamix* became an unmitigated hit, starting slowly then finding its legs in the early nineties.

The medley of African hits concept that Lokassa and Sylla inflated to 'megamix' had actually begun in the United States in the head of record producer Ibrahim Kanja Bah. Bah, who ran a Washington, D.C. record shop and spun African records on the radio, had grown up to the sounds of Congo music in his country of birth, Sierra Leone. Whenever a Zaïrean band came to Washington, Bah hired a few of its musicians and booked studio time to record a track or two. With the heart of the music laid down by the visitors, Bah then embellished it with the work of resident African musicians, many of them, like Fredo Ngando, veterans of the Paris scene.

Soul on Fire by Maloko, Bah's first medley released in 1988, put a novel spin on the way the music was evolving. Instead of adding Western elements to, perhaps, make Congo music more marketable in the States, he took seven American soul standards and produced them Zaïrean style. Ben E. King's 'Stand By Me' leads off the A side medley that ends in a rousing version of the Wilson Pickett classic 'In the Midnight Hour.' Otis Redding's 'Direct Me' keys the flip side. With Syran M'Benza of Les Quatre Etoiles on solo guitar and arrangements and instrumental support from Cameroon's Vincent Nguini, Bah's version of Zaïreanization vastly improves on the Mobutu original.

Soul on Fire and subsequent Bah-produced medleys triggered something of a mini-trend. Sylla used it with Manuaku Waku on Expérience 9, a reprise of Grand Zaïko hits, and, more successfully, with Lokassa's Megamix and a disc by Sam Mangwana under the same title. Before returning to Brazzaville, Jean Serge Essous organized a Paris reunion of Ry-Co Jazz for an album called Yo La! that utilized the medley style, and Ouattara Moumouni launched a medley series called Soukouss Vibration at Afro Rythmes.

Loose-knit groups like the Soukous Stars, particularly appropriate for Paris, where each musician had to scramble for his or her own living, still suffered the spasms of dislocation. Loketo's leaders, Aurlus Mabele and Diblo Dibala, divorced in 1990 when conflict over control of the group and a clash of nationalities – Aurlus's Congo versus Diblo's Zaïre – proved to be insurmountable. Mabele kept Loketo for himself. Diblo launched a new band called Matchatcha that hewed to the headlong TGV soukous style Loketo had helped engender.

•

Maturity failed to nurture stability as middle age set in among the youth bands. Ben Nyamabo's Choc Stars started to unravel in 1990 when Defao Matumona left to form Big Stars – perhaps named as much for the expanding waistlines of the musicians as for the quality of the group, which counted the now burly Defao and Joe Poster of Grand Zaïko as its only big stars. Djuna Djanana, Djo Mali, Debaba el Shabab, and even Roxy Tshimpaka also deserted Nyamabo. Choc Stars managed to stay afloat, however, in the rapidly diluting pool of talent.

Among the two Zaïkos, Nyoka Longo's Nkolo Mboka emerged as the dominant band. Continuing clashes between Bimi Ombale and Bakunde Ilo Pablo sapped the strength of Familia Dei. Pablo essentially ousted Bimi in the middle of 1990, forcing Bimi to attempt a solo career. Pablo kept Familia Dei together until 1996, when several of his musicians, including guitarists Petit Poisson and Jimmy Yaba, left to join Nkolo Mboka.

Death, not defections, haunted Nkolo Mboka. Two of its longest-serving guitarists died, Enoch Zamuangana in 1992 and Matima Mpioso Kinuani in 1996. Other bands suffered losses too. Anti-Choc lost singer Fifi Mofude and an alumnus gone solo, Wally Ngonda, both of whom died from illness in the middle nineties. Emoro, the dancing dwarf of Empire Bakuba, died in 1992 while on tour with the band in Botswana. He was reported to have suffered a heart attack. In the early hours of November 29, 1998, Empire Bakuba's leader Pepe Kalle was rushed to a Kinshasa clinic after collapsing at home. Efforts to revive him failed. Like his dwarf sidekick, the gentle giant was said to have been felled by a heart attack.

In Brazzaville, diabetes claimed the life of Pamelo Mounk'a at the start of 1996. Sporadic treatments in Paris had staved off the disease for a while. By 1993, however, his lower limbs had swollen to the point where he found it difficult to walk, let alone perform with his Bantous Monument. Afraid that Western doctors would want to amputate his feet, Pamelo chose to fight the disease at home with the help of traditional medicine.

The man who could rightfully be called the father of Congo music, Henri Bowane, also passed away, in 1992 at age sixty-three. Although he was never a member of O.K. Jazz, the band would likely not have existed without him. It was Bowane who persuaded the cousins Papadimitriou to open the Loningisa studio where the musicians who would form O.K. Jazz eventually met. Bowane became something of a mentor to the studio's young marvel, François Luambo, and, some say, coined his famous 'Franco' sobriquet. In 1958, after helping to create the Esengo studio, Bowane left the Belgian Congo with his new band Ry-Co Jazz. He returned briefly to an independent Congo, then spent the nineteen years from 1964 until 1983 in West Africa working as a musician, promoter, and occasional adviser to Zaïrean artists who followed the westward migratory route. He performed from time to time upon his return to Kinshasa, but for the most part enjoyed the well-deserved role of sage.

Death had become a familiar presence among the members of O.K. Jazz. The singer-guitarist who replaced Franco in the band's musical scheme, Boteku Bohomba, passed away in August of 1991, less than two years after joining the group. Three singers, Lola 'Checain' Djangi (1992), Aime Kiwakana (1992), and Djo Mpoyi (1993), all died during the next eighteen months. In Brussels, Rondot Kasongo, a former O.K. Jazz saxophone player and close confidant to Franco, died in 1994. Two years later, another O.K. Jazz alumnus, singer Ntesa 'Dalienst' Nzitani, passed away after battling a brain tumor.

O.K. Jazz encountered problems on the legal front as well. Franco's sister Marie-Louise Akangana had assumed control of her late brother's affairs in the name of the family. In conjunction with observances of the first anniversary of Franco's death, the family gathered at the house in Limete to announce the establishment of the Fondation Luambo Makiadi, whose task it was to administer Franco's labyrinthine heritage. Many of Franco's effects, they said, would be gathered for public display at a Musée Luambo to be located at the house in Limete. As a way to encourage local artists, an award called the Trophée Luambo would be established in Franco's memory. Little, however, was accomplished to bring the plans to fruition. By the middle of 1993, Marie-Louise found herself summoned to a Kinshasa court to answer charges, brought by Franco's children, of improperly conducting the estate's affairs. In another court, Denis Ilosono, the former private secretary to President Mobutu and failed impresario, sought legal recognition for his claim to the land occupied by the Un-Deux-Trois – residue from the mischief that saw the parcel into Franco's hands in the first place.

When it came to making music, O.K. Jazz prospered under Simaro's leadership in spite of the plague of deaths. Behind the scenes, however, conflict arose between the musicians and Franco's family, the owners of O.K. Jazz. Money lay at the heart of the matter: how much of the take should go to the family, and how much the musicians could keep. The dispute ended dramatically at midnight on December 31, 1993, when, in the midst of a show at a bar called the Mama Kusala, the members of the band, with the exception of Madilu System, announced that they were relinquishing the name O.K. Jazz. They would begin the New Year as Orchestre Bana O.K., the children of O.K. Jazz. After the show, they packed up their instruments and delivered them to the home of Franco's sister. Zaïre's minister of culture and arts appointed a commission, including Roitelet Moniania and Nyoka Longo, to mediate the dispute, but the two sides could not be reconciled. Madilu attempted to restart O.K. Jazz with new musicians only to quit after six months of rehearsals. At the end of its thirty-seventh year, the most durable and distinguished band that Africa ever produced had played its last notes.

•

The European haven to which most of Zaïre's musicians had fled harbored some of the afflictions of home. Former African All Stars drummer Ringo Moya had earned a reputation as one of the finest session drummers in Paris – an occupation imperiled by the drum machine – and became a producer of some note with an avid clientele that included Papa Wemba and Koffi Olomide. His experimental French and African group, Wassa, had been an early exponent of the budding 'world beat' phenomenon. But Moya's liver was not in the best of shape, and his lungs were weakening. The always slender drummer appeared especially gaunt in 1991 as he checked himself into a Paris hospital on the eve of a planned tour of Africa with Kanda Bongo Man. Medical treatment improved his condition. He even returned to work. In April of 1993, however, the failing organs gave out. Ringo Moya was barely forty.

A year and a half later, on September 29, 1994, Abeti Masikini succumbed to cancer, an event as improbable as Franco's passing. The sovereign of *le spectacle*, the queen of soukous, the *grande dame* of Congo music, cast a larger-than-life shadow that cruelly amplified the shock of her death. Abeti was an authentic international star who made the move to Paris seem as effortless as her stage performances. Having already conquered Carnegie Hall and the Paris Olympia, she stormed the latest venue of prestige, Le Zénith on the outskirts of Paris, with a September 1988 spectacular studded with guest stars including Pepe Kalle, Emeneya Mubiala, Aurlus Mabele, and François Lougah. In the middle of 1989 she embarked on a month-long tour of China, where she performed a dozen concerts seen by more than half a million people. 'Tina Turner gives me hope,' she said in 1991, referring to the aging American pop star's continuing popularity. Abeti was then approaching forty. Although she and her husband-manager, Gérard Akueson, owned their own production company, Abeti also worked for other producers. The album *La Reine du Soukous* (the queen of soukous) for Jimmy Houetinou in 1991 proved to be her last.

•

Abeti's career and her works exemplified the evolution of Congo music and reflected, in part, its three basic dichotomies: the contrasting sounds of

Abeti

Kinshasa and Paris, the young generation versus its elders, and well-to-do artists relative to their less affluent colleagues. During the course of her twenty years in showbusiness Abeti had moved, both rhythmically and instrumentally, from a careful blend of the traditional and modern to an all-out embrace of rapid-fire Paris soukous and the new technology being used to create it. 'I am always focusing on the international level,' she said. 'Because if I wanted to keep on doing things the way we do them at home, I never would have left.'

Paris soukous is, predominantly, the music of younger artists like Abeti, those who entered the business in the seventies and eighties. Their quest for a more 'international' sound – prompted in part by pop star fantasies that the Michael Jacksons and Madonnas of the world arouse – set them apart from the bands still rooted in Kinshasa. Several whose careers were made in Paris, like Kanda Bongo Man and Diblo Dibala, were scarcely known at home. 'The problem is the music [from] Paris is commercial music, it no longer has feeling,' Nyboma Mwan Dido explained.

> Music with feeling is much appreciated in Africa. Commercial music is appreciated here [in Paris]. Because here you don't put in a lot of words. You just put

in music that goes, Boom! Boom! Boom! Boom! Boom! To sell it, just to sell it. If you don't do that, you don't sell, so you won't eat.

The difference is a matter of language according to Bopol Mansiamina.

In Zaïre, to make a good song, a really popular song, it has to have really great lyrics. Everyone has to understand what you are trying to say. On the other hand, outside Zaïre people understand nothing of what we're saying. And that's why they like it when there's ambiance [animation]. That's why we get into it straight away.

New technology – drum machines and synthesizers, whose use often occurs in inverse proportion to a producer's financial health – abets commercialization. Drum machines put drummers out of work. Synthesizers have crowded the guitars and nearly eliminated the use of horns. The once-favored saxophone languishes all but unheard. Voices often struggle to emerge from an electronic blitzkrieg as if the singer were performing on the wrong side of the control room glass. Producer Jimmy Houetinou uses the new technology grudgingly. 'I don't like it at all,' he said, 'because I find it removes – how would you say it – it removes reality, because I mean really, a man hitting a drum gives you a different feeling.' Machines can only be justified for one reason, he said, and that reason is cost.

The best way to make records at a lower price is to computerize things. Before, to get the sound of the drum kit right in the studio, it might take all day to find the right sound. Whereas now, in thirty minutes, we program it, we find the drum sound.... So it's a matter of immediately making your money back, [but] the soul of the music is being killed.

Endless processing and multi-track recording have nearly eliminated the visceral edge a 'live' session could deliver. The raw immediacy of the days when African Fiesta and O.K. Jazz gathered around a single mike to knock out a song in one or two takes has succumbed to the quest for economy, convenience, and technical perfection. Musicians record their parts individually, often at different times to their colleagues. One person's inspiration or mistake no longer affects the other musicians as directly as in the past.

Multi-track recording machines also foster the one-man-band approach where music isn't so much created as it is constructed. For Mbilia Bel's *Désolé!!!* (sorry), the follow-up to the phenomenal *Phénomène*, Rigo Star conceived the music, arranged it, programmed the drums, percussion, and synthesizers, played all the guitar and bass parts, and sang backing vocals. Such an approach may keep production costs low, but even in the hands of a musician as talented as Rigo Star, the result, as in the case of *Désolé!!!*, is often disappointing.

Musicians tend to view the use of the new technology as a way of keeping pace with the times. 'In an artist's life you also have to try to follow [changing] conditions,' said Bopol.

> For example, I saw Michael Jackson's concert, there were no trumpets, there was nothing. Madonna, too, there was no trumpet, there was only a synth. And we are also trying to adapt. But on the other hand if I find a producer who really wants to put in the effort, I would need horns, real horns. And real drums. The problem is that it takes a lot of time, and that means you need money.... Synths and all that, that doesn't bother us. That's how things are changing. But on the other hand, I liked the way we worked before.

Diblo Dibala also sees the use of technology as a necessary evolution, but he embraces it more wholeheartedly.

> The world is changing, everybody has to change. I think [use of] the drum machine is going to diminish, because it sounds a little too much like a machine.... We'll still use it, but we'll also use a normal drummer, a person playing along with it. As for the synth, I think we'll always work with it. It's the instrument of the future.... For what we're doing there's no real room for the sax. The synth can play the same figuration as the sax, for example, can do what a saxophonist can do. We don't see why we should add in the sax again.

Diblo and like-minded colleagues have earned a loyal following, yet many other Congo music aficionados – attracted to the maturing combination of electric guitars, horns, and percussion all swinging to the rumba's beat – grimace at the sounds of electronic synthesizers and programmed rhythm tracks that often echo the beat of Western pop music. It's not that the synthesizer itself is inherently evil. After all, the Congolese rumba is a music born of encounters between traditional and modern styles. Over the years the music has continually absorbed new elements, including those very electric guitars, saxophones, and traps that synthesizers threaten to displace. What bothers lovers of the rumba's earlier incarnation is that use of the synthesizer seems gratuitous, as if injected into the mix for purely commercial purposes rather than in pursuit of artistic experimentation. Of the myriad sounds a synthesizer can produce, musicians nearly always choose the least pleasing, pseudo-accordion whine to embellish their works. This, coupled with the unflagging precision and monotony of the drum machine, tends to transform the swinging rumba into something less easily identifiable as Congo music.

The irony is difficult to ignore: the continent that gave the gift of rhythm to the world turns to the bingings and bonkings of a box of circuit boards to set its musical pulse.

Use of the new technology has become a generational marker in much the same way that Kinshasa's youth bands set themselves apart by eschewing a horn section. Papa Noël laments the current trend. 'What is a machine doing in all this? Because [music] is a matter of feelings. Music should be played within the soul. Does a machine have a soul?'

Jean Serge Essous worries less about the new technology than he does about where the next Willy Kuntima or Empompo Loway will come from.

> We've had a phenomenon for several years where we couldn't find any young saxophonists or trumpet players. Why? Because it takes a lot of time, and young people today don't have a lot of time to lose. They sing, they play guitar. They shout a little. As long as people are dancing, the band is good. And it's true. Why should they go to a lot of trouble since it's working?

Another problem facing Congolese and Zaïrean musicians is their freestyle method of doing business. Most are too quick to accept offers of money from inexperienced or dishonest promoters who often can't deliver on promises of a concert tour or recording session. Shows are routinely advertised on the basis of hope alone. Cancellations, results of bad faith or organizational incompetence, frequently occur, leaving legitimate promoters and music fans wary of bands from Africa. Part of Kanda Bongo Man's great success from the late eighties to the mid-nineties stemmed from his refusal to do business in a slipshod manner. 'If you don't have a manager, you don't have good organization,' he declared, touting the woman who handled his career. Kanda Bongo Man tours happened as advertised. While he continued to produce his own recordings, he left sales to the major distributors, Mélodie for Europe, CBS/Sony in East Africa, and Rykodisc for the United Kingdom and North America.

Poor organization is one aspect of what many artists feel is the lack of a broader structure. 'The problem we have is that our producers are still working in a closed circuit, a kind of ghetto,' Ballou Canta complained. 'And so we hope that big production houses will take an interest in our music without trying to denature the music.' Musicians like Ballou often cite the example of Island Records and its successful promotion of Jamaican reggae. Soukous, they say, needs the same sort of backing to break out of its second-tier status in the West.

Record executive Joe Boyd, whose company, Hannibal-Carthage (now part of Rykodisc), signed Kanda Bongo Man, thinks the Jamaican analogy apt for another reason. He feels that African musicians need to rethink their attempts to go 'international' by incorporating the rhythms of the West.

> In a way all those guys revere as a kind of hero, Bob Marley. But they don't seem to pay attention to the lessons that you can learn from his career. I mean if you analyze Bob Marley's tunes, they're like Dylan tunes, they're like folk songs, they're a grab bag of melodies. They're not particularly traditional Jamaican melodies, but the rhythm was always pure Jamaican – absolute, rock-solid, down-the-line reggae. And he conquered the world with it. And I think African musicians who ignore that lesson risk falling by the wayside. You know? I don't think that people in America, and in Britain and western Europe, they don't go listening to African musicians so they can hear mid-Atlantic [rock] rhythms.

•

Joe Boyd could have been thinking of Papa Wemba. If Abeti savored the new technology, her music still sounded palpably Zaïrean. Wemba's new direction went well beyond the use of technological innovation to an all-out change of musical style. Having laid off most of his musicians and marketed himself as a solo artist, Wemba devised a musical *mélange* – one that fit the category 'Euro-pop' or 'world beat' – a synthesis that leaned toward the musical equivalent of Calvin Trillin's culinary 'La Maison de la Casa House.' For one to whom the name Papa Wemba was unfamiliar, there was little to identify the music as a product of Zaïre.

Following his initial plunge with French producer Martin Meissonnier in 1988, Wemba signed on with a Japanese firm called Filament Music Publishers. That partnership yielded *Le Voyageur* in 1991, another world beat excursion produced with a heavy dose of synthesizers, programmed rhythm tracks, and pumped-up bass. Each song, short to accommodate European and American radio, is awash with computerized background fill and an occasional horn solo from the Kenny G school of syrupy sax. Wemba undoubtedly won new fans among the genre's adherents, but he was roundly condemned by followers at home and those outside who were attracted to Zaïrean music. For them, Wemba kept the name Viva La Musica alive with an occasional concert and recording using African musicians living in Europe. His head, however, if not his heart, stayed in the world beat arena.

Wemba's album *Foridoles*, recorded in 1994 with session musicians under the Viva La Musica name, made something of a concession to Afrophiles. The sound retains the highly processed flavor of world beat yet emerges as recognizably Zaïrean. The title track, a pleasant rumba designed as a play on words, 'for idols,' is sung in the name of reconciliation with those fans who felt Wemba had deserted them.

Wemba reverted to world beat for 1995's *Emotion* on Real World Records, then came all the way home towards the end of the year with *Pôle Position*, his finest work in nearly a decade. *Pôle Position* – conceived, as the title suggests, to put Wemba at the front of the pack – features a dozen songs in the classic style of Congo music. The rumba swings, the mix sounds fresh, and the musicians, including Manuaku Waku in a rare post-Grand Zaïko appearance, bear familiar names. There would be no mistaking *Pôle Position* for Euro-pop.

Another Papa, Papa Noël, confirmed that although he and his colleagues could no longer survive at home, they could still make great music. His *Haute Tension* (high tension), with vocals by Carlito Lassa and Wuta Mayi, ranked with Wemba's *Pôle Position* as one of the best of the mid-nineties. Divorced from its roots, the music had cause to wither, yet it continued to exhibit remarkable vigor. Sam Mangwana contributed *Rumba Music*, eight songs from earlier days rejuvenated with the help of Dizzy Mandjeku, Syran M'Benza, Miguel Yamba, and a handful of New York salsa musicians. Madilu System, fresh from his failed attempt to resuscitate O.K. Jazz, launched a solo career with *Sans Commentaire* (no comment), an Ibrahima Sylla production. Tshala Muana kept her streak of consistent, high-quality releases alive with a savory assortment of soukous, salsa, and mutuashi called *Mutuashi*. Zaïko Langa Langa Nkolo Mboka's 1996 compact disc entitled *Sans Issue* (no way out) confirmed its position as *the* Zaïko of the nineties.

The future looked less certain for Tabu Ley Rochereau. Now the music's doyen, Ley trod the path of self-imposed exile from Paris to the United States, where he attempted to break new ground. A stripped-down, dozen-member Afrisa – including old hands Huit Kilos, Mekanisi Modero, and Kongi Aska (but not Shaba Kahamba, Faya Tess, or Beyou Ciel) – began touring the U.S. in 1994 and signed a two-album deal with Rounder Records. In the beginning the outing went well. Bookings, including the Festival International de Louisiane in Lafayette, and the New Orleans Jazz and Heritage Festival, came easily.

Ley recorded the two Rounder albums in May 1994 at Dockside Studios in Maurice, Louisiana. *Muzina*, released later in the year, presents an agreeable collection of new material. The title track sets the pattern for what is billed as 'high definition soukous' when the band settles into a swinging rumba

Tabu Ley

groove about halfway through the piece with Huit Kilos's guitar taking the lead and a live drummer replacing the box. Ley introduces a new female protégée, Kizita Yal, backed by the male vocal trio of Djeffard Lukombo, Wawali Bonane, and Dodo Munoko.

The second album, *Africa Worldwide*, released in 1996 to coincide with Ley's thirty-fifth anniversary in showbusiness, remakes eleven of his better-known works like 'Marie Clara' and 'Mokitani ya Wendo' (successor to Wendo), and Dechaud's classic 'African Jazz Mokili Mobimba' (shortened to 'Africa Mokili Mobimba'). Ley gives the songs a nineties treatment with kit drums in place of congas and maracas but without the noticeable intrusion of electronic machinery. By 1996 the band had settled in Los Angeles, where, one by one, the members wandered off to participate in outside projects, an ominous symptom in the life of Afrisa.

Success or not in the United States, Tabu Ley had passed the point of having to prove himself. Thirty-five years in the business – thirty of them with the same band – hundreds of songs, and dozens of albums were markers enough for history. His extraordinary gift for translating the pulse of his people into sonnets of universal beauty earned a following far beyond the boundaries of central Africa. Towering above all was the marvelous voice, the voice against which all pretenders would be measured. Ley and his contemporaries followed the school of Kabasele, but subsequent generations took their lessons from Master Tabu Ley Rochereau. His star was fixed despite his own uncertain future.

•

On Muzina's closing track, a song called 'Requisitoire' (indictment), Ley pleads for reconciliation in Zaïre, a sentiment equally applicable to Congo.

> Look and see the great surprise
> White and black understanding
> In South Africa
> Why can't we people of the same skin
> Understand each other?

At the approach of the new millennium it looked like understanding would be reached at the point of a gun. Old animosities flared as Mobutu's control weakened. In eastern Zaïre, ethnic Tutsis, long the objects of hostility from other ethnic groups and from the Mobutu regime, who regarded them as foreigners, suffered escalating bouts of violence beginning in 1991. When ethnic tensions between Tutsis and Hutus erupted into full-scale war in neighboring Rwanda in 1994, the Hutu-dominated Rwanda army launched a pogrom that resulted in the killing of an estimated 800,000 Tutsis. Retaliation by Tutsi insurgents sent a flood of Hutu refugees into eastern Zaïre. Militant Hutus then used the refugee camps in Zaïre as staging grounds for reprisal attacks on Rwandan and Zaïrean Tutsis. The extreme disorder presented Mobutu's opponents with an opportunity to begin taking control of Zaïre piece by piece.

One opposition group, conveniently headquartered in the mountains of eastern Zaïre along the northern tip of Lake Tanganyika, was the People's Revolutionary Party, led by Laurent Kabila. Kabila had spent thirty years operating from exile in Uganda and Tanzania and from his more or less safe enclave inside Zaïre in an ineffective campaign to unseat the Zaïrean dictator. Now, however, Zaïre was in a state of collapse. Kinshasa could scarcely govern the people who lived in the capital. Several areas – the diamond center around Mbuji-Mayi, the Shaba copper belt – began to assume control of their own affairs with little regard for the central government. Mobutu had reached the most vulnerable stage in his thirty-one years in power, and he needed to go to Europe for treatment of a spreading prostate cancer.

Using troops from Zaïre's neighbors – notably Uganda and Rwanda, both Mobutu adversaries – and recruits from among the aggrieved Zaïrean Tutsis, Kabila's rebel army began to move against government forces in mid-October of 1996. With every thrust, small ones at first, the rebels gained control of new territory and added disaffected Zaïrean troops to their ranks. By early 1997 the rebel war had become a nearly bloodless march to the capital, impeded only by the rugged terrain and the ghastly condition of Mobutu's roads. Zaïrean soldiers fled without fighting, and province after province welcomed Kabila's men as saviors.

Mobutu Sese Seko fled from Zaïre on May 16. A day later, rebel troops entered Kinshasa to complete their seven-month, border-to-border dash. For better or worse Laurent Kabila would become the country's new leader. From his Lubumbashi headquarters, Kabila claimed the presidency for himself and announced that Zaïre would henceforth be known as the Democratic Republic of the Congo. Three days later he flew to the capital to take a tenuous hold of the government. (Mobutu himself died of cancer in Morocco on September 7, 1997.)

Less than a month after Kabila assumed power in Kinshasa, violence broke out again in Brazzaville in anticipation of presidential elections scheduled for the end of July. Congo-Brazzaville's president, Pascal Lissouba, who had managed to outmaneuver his opponents for nearly all of his five-year term, dispatched the Congolese army to disarm the 'Cobra Militia' of his chief rival for the presidency, former president Denis Sassou Nguesso. Lissouba's move proved to be a colossal miscalculation. With overt assistance from Angola and the covert blessing of France, Sassou Nguesso's militia more than held its own in nearly five months of fighting that sent Brazzaville's civilian population fleeing and reduced much of the city to ruins. On October 16, 1997, the Cobra Militia defeated Lissouba's forces and Sassou Nguesso once again took power in Brazzaville.

The destruction of Brazzaville and Laurent Kabila's shaky administration in Kinshasa made it unlikely that many of the cities' musicians would soon return. Congo music, it seemed, would continue to evolve in the far-flung metropolises of Europe and America, divorced from the roots of its inspiration. But while most of the music's current stars continued to toil abroad, new strains struggled to be heard at home. For all the diamonds, copper, and petroleum that endowed the land, joy in either Congo was still measured in the notes of a song. Perhaps a new generation of Congolese youth would repeat their elders' triumph.

Notes

Quotations not otherwise noted are taken from interviews with the author.

3   'It reflects strongly...': Gunther, p. 651.
3   'still an African city...': ibid., p. 691.
4   'Brazzaville a far prettier...': Greene, p. 65.
4   For more about Davidson's thesis on modernizing out of one's own traditions and history see Davidson, *Black Man's Burden*, passim.
5   'different but equal': Davidson, *Story of Africa*, p. 19.
6   Slave trade: Statistics on the slave trade are slippery at best. The figure of twenty million comes from Davidson, *Story of Africa*, p. 147; five million from the Congo area is from Davidson, *African Slave Trade*, p. 170. In the original edition of *African Slave Trade*, originally entitled *Black Mother*, Davidson estimated fifty million Africans had been landed alive, been killed in the hunt, or had died from the harsh conditions of captivity and shipment. His downward estimate is based on Curtin's exhaustive census of the slave trade. Curtin estimates that nine and one-half million slaves landed alive in the Americas (p. 268). According to Curtin (p. 276), 'The literature on the slave trade tends to put the mortality rate at sea somewhere between 13 per cent and 33 per cent.' There is no way to know how many died in Africa as a result of the slave trade. Davidson says (*African Slave Trade*, p. 98), 'It cannot have been less than several millions from first to last. It may have been many millions.'
6   10,000 captives ... 12,000 a year: Austen, p. 68. These figures may have been much higher. Davidson (*African Slave Trade*, p. 198) cites a British observer who, in 1839, 'reckoned that between 40,000 and 45,000 slaves were being sold there [Zanzibar] every year.'
6   '3Cs': quoted in Pakenham, p. xxii.
7   'and the cotton-spinners...': quoted in West, p. 101.
10   'When Leopold's ambition...': Mazrui, p. 232.

Notes

14 'there are native...': Starr, p. 14.
14 guitar and likembe picking: Roberts, *Black Music of Two Worlds*, p. 244.
14 Missionaries translated ... : Kazadi, pp. 270–71.
15 *popo*: Fyfe, *History of Sierra Leone*, p. 170.
16 'more openly Europeanized...': Pepper.
17 Population statistics from Pain, p. 19, and Morrison, p. 421.
18 'The growth is so rapid...': Balandier, *Ambiguous Africa*, p. 168.
18 'bear witness less...': ibid., p. 169.
20 'as a social chronicle...': Acosta, p. 54.
21 '"rhumba with an H"...': Gerard, p. 61.
21 rumba mis-labeled: Llerenas.
21 'The rumba...': Lonoh, p. 108.
22 'They gave me the taste...': *Elima*, Dec. 22, 1986.
26 Although Bowane told an interviewer (*Elima*, Dec. 22, 1986) that he went to Léopoldville on Dec. 25, 1949, it appears likely that he was off by a year. Other events, including his recording at Ngoma – some of the studio's earliest releases were Bowane records – and subsequent role in the opening of Loningisa in 1950, would seem to indicate that Bowane arrived in late 1948 or early 1949. Wendo remembered that he and Bowane recorded 'Marie-Louise' in late 1949, and that it was released in 1950.
26 'I went to knock...': *Elima*, Dec. 22, 1986.
27 'about women who...': the speaker was Roitelet Moniania.
28 Daily minimum wage statistics from Young, pp. 206–8.
28 'I don't know how many...': *Zaïre*, Jan. 29, 1973.
28 'Marie-Louise' transcription from booklet for compact disc *Ngoma: The Early Years, 1948–1960*, p. 17.
30 Population statistics from Pain, p. 19, and Morrison, p. 421.
35 'pyromaniac ... : Bemba, p. 96.
39 'Para-Fifi' transcription by Tshonga-Onyumbe, *Zaïre-Afrique*, No. 184 (April 1984), pp. 230–31. Tshonga's transcription comes from a later version of the song, but the words quoted here appear in the original.
39 The Solovox, an electronic instrument with three octaves of keys, was manufactured by the Hammond Instrument Company beginning in 1940 as a way to produce a wind instrument sound to accompany piano. Although it could be played alone, as was done in Léopoldville's recording studios, the keyboard was designed to attach to the front edge of a piano so the player could play both keyboards in the manner of an organist. Ngoma, Opika, and Loningisa all used the Solovox for a brief period in the early fifties.
42 The existence of two 'Francos' has created confusion in the release of their music on records. For example, the 'Franco' that appears on the African label album No. 360164, *Les Stars des Années 50*, from Sonodisc is François Engbondu, not the more famous François Luambo Makiadi.
47 'the natives are buying...': *The Belgian Congo Today*, Jan. 1956, p. 25.
53 'I had enormous difficulties...': *Zaïre*, July 24, 1972.
53 'I gained mastery...': ibid.
53 'Our pleasure was...': OZRT, 'A l'occasion des 20 ans...'

Notes 395

54 'I realized those kids...': ibid.
60 'not become the King's...': Gilbert, p. 254.
61 'Congo was the true...': Scholefield, p. 47.
62 'They became aware...': Slade, *Belgian Congo*, p. 11.
62 Van Bilsen plan of 1955: Anstey, p. 220.
63 'The excitement...': Merriam, p. 75.
63 'Our patience...': quoted in ibid., p. 333.
67 Population statistics from La Fontaine, p. 28.
67 'curiously mingle...': quoted in Davidson, *African Genius*, p. 300.
68 'The Broadcasting Service...': *Belgian Congo Today*, April 1953, p. 65.
68 'to convince the indigenous...': ibid., July 1952, p. 102.
74 Number of bars from ibid., Jan. 1956, p. 26.
74 'a spacious enclosure...': Welle, p. 42.
75 'a political...': Kanza, Thomas, p. 30.
77 'Ohé Suka ya Rumba' transcription from Tshiteya, p.23.
77 Much of the discussion on Lingala comes from Yanga, *passim*, but especially pp. 129–30 and 135.
78 Hindoubill discussion in part from Pwono, p. 149, Yanga, pp. 139–42, and *Zaïre*, March 7, 1977.
78 Hindoubill sometimes helped fit: Pwono, p. 76.
78 'This country has firmly...': *Belgian Congo Today*, Oct. 1957, p. 8.
79 'talked wildly of independence...': Slade, *Belgian Congo*, p. 49.
80 'The overpopulation...': ibid., p. 48.
83 'During his last visit...': *Présence Congolaise*, Jan. 30, 1960.
84 'The sight of two hundred...': Legum, p. 75.
86 'The Belgians...': Kanza, Thomas, p. 89.
88 'During our first concert...': *Présence Congolaise*, May 14, 1960.
88 'African Jazz (which...': ibid., Sept. 2, 1961.
91 'Each time the Council...': Kanza, Thomas, p. 120.
91 'This struggle of tears...': quoted in Merriam, p. 352.
91 'Together, my brothers...': ibid., p. 353.
91 'Bilombe ba Gagne' transcription from Bemba, p. 113.
92 'after independence...': Kanza, Thomas, p. 187. An alternative version with the same meaning is given in Hoskyns, p. 88.
93 'We are becoming...': *Présence Congolaise*, May 14, 1960.
93 For more on the American plot to assassinate Lumumba see Kalb, Kwitny, Mahoney, and Stockwell.
94 For Kanza's account of Lumumba's flight, see Kanza, Thomas, pp. 314–26.
97 'If an artist or group...': Small, p. 407.
98 'Matata Masila na Congo' transcription from *Hommage à Grand Kalle*, p. 96.
98 'Toyokana Tolimbisana na Congo' transcription from ibid., p. 95.
99 'Many people don't...': ibid., p. 45.
106 'Camarade Mabe' transcription from Bwantsa-Kafungu, p. 22.
110 'When African Jazz...': *Présence Congolaise*, Mar. 2, 1963.
112 The *Présence Congolaise* account of Kabasele's dealings with his musicians appeared May 18, 1963.

396 Notes

114 'African Fiesta's songs...': quoted in *Présence Congolaise*, Sept. 5, 1964.
115 'It is generally known...': ibid.
115 'a constant pleasure...': *Zaïre*, Aug. 12, 1974.
116 'full of fire...': ibid., Feb. 21, 1972.
118 'Ngai Marie Nzoto Ebeba' transcription by Tshonga-Onyumbe, *Zaïre-Afrique*, No. 205 (May 1986), p. 295.
119 Tshembe's new constitution included a change in the country's name from Republic of the Congo to Democratic Republic of the Congo.
121 'I often leave...': quoted in Lonoh, p. 158.
122 Population statistics come from Pain, p. 19, and La Fontaine, p. 31.
123 'My song was about...': Dibango, p. 46.
123 'Mwambe No. 1' transcription from Tshonga-Onyumbe, *Zaïre-Afrique*, No. 205 (May 1986), p. 295.
124 'already one speaks...': *Etoile du Congo*, April 2, 1966.
125 'Lucie Tozongana' transcription from Tshonga-Onyumbe, *Zaïre-Afrique*, No. 208 (Oct. 1986), p. 497.
125 'It certainly is Kapinga's...': *Etoile du Congo*, July 22, 1965.
125 'I wanted to be a moralist...': ibid.
125 'We hereby inform you...': ibid., July 3, 1965.
125 'Faux Millionnaire' transcription from Dzokanga, pp. 86-7.
126 'Chicotte' transcription from ibid., pp. 88-91.
127 Account of Izeidi's press conference from *Etoile du Congo*, Dec. 23, 1965.
127 Account of Nico's telex from ibid., Dec. 25, 1965.
127 Account of Rochereau's press conference from ibid., Dec. 31, 1965.
128 'Cimetière' transcription from ibid., June 2, 1966.
128 'who no longer recognize...': ibid.
128 'Mokolo Nakokufa' transcription from Dzokanga, pp. 92-5.
129 'I am proud...': *Etoile du Congo*, Mar. 3, 1966.
129 'We have three singers...': ibid., Mar. 24, 1966.
131 'I have, in fact, left...': ibid., July 30, 1966.
131 'O.K. Jazz est toujours là': ibid., June 18, 1966.
131 'Course au Pouvoir' transcription from *Franco and his T.P.O.K. Jazz in U.S.A.*
132 'The revolutionary Congo...': Honorin, p. 36.
133 'Masuwa' transcription from Bemba, p. 146.
134 'For the Antilleans...': *Bingo*, July 1972, p.58.
135 'le premier...': *Etoile du Congo*, Sept. 22, 1968.
139 Others have reported that Tino Baroza was murdered, but that claim appears to be based more on rumor than on reality. Newspapers of the day, *Etoile du Congo* (Dec. 5, 1968) and *La Press du Cameroun* (Dec. 12, 1968), both reported that Baroza's death was due to a traffic accident.
140 'We've had enough...': *Etoile du Congo*, May 10, 1969.
141 'attempted sabotage...': ibid., Oct. 18, 1968.
142 'Peuple' transcription from ibid.
142 'Libala ya 8 Heures du Temps' synopsis from ibid., Aug. 16, 1968.
143 'Toyota' synopsis from ibid., Jan. 24, 1969. 'Toyota' transcription from Tshonga-Onyumbe, *Zaïre-Afrique*, No. 205 (May 1986), p. 300.

Notes 397

143 'Equal work...': *Etoile du Congo*, Oct. 18, 1969.
145 'Missing for long months...': ibid., June 24, 1968.
146 'Congolese musicians...': ibid., Apr. 26, 1969.
146 'I consider Congolese...': ibid., July 26, 1969.
146 'a simple question...': ibid.
148 Wage and price statistics from Bobb, p. xxxii. Young and Turner (p. 132) present a different set of figures showing only a one-third decrease in purchasing power.
149 'continued to hold...': Kaplan, p. 185.
149 Population statistics from Bobb, p. xxviii.
149 Statistics on inflation, wages, and economic growth from Young and Turner, p. 280.
149 Beer consumption statistics from Schatzberg, p. 84.
149 'At the official...': ibid.
150 'often a shaky little shack...': *Zaïre*, July 31, 1972.
150 'Africans are very gifted...': *Etoile du Congo*, Oct. 18, 1969.
151 'I created Orchestre Symba-Keje...': *Zaïre*, Sept. 20, 1971.
153 'In a very short span...': *Etoile du Congo*, Jan. 24, 1970.
154 'In O.K. Jazz...': *Salongo*, Mar. 28, 1976.
154 'They wear funny make-up...': *Etoile du Congo*, Feb. 28, 1970.
155 'Young Congolese...': *Zaïre*, Sept. 20, 1971.
156 'when we were born...': ibid., Nov. 15, 1971.
156 'The Perruche Bleue...': *Etoile du Congo*, Feb. 7, 1969.
156 'Over a book...': ibid., July 19, 1969.
157 'Lisolo' transcription from *Etoile du Congo*, Nov. 10, 1970.
157 'Our dream is one...': *Zaïre* Nov. 8, 1971.
157 'my friend [Henri] Mongombe...': ibid.
158 'In the beginning Zaïko...': ibid., Mar. 24, 1975.
158 This account of the origin of the name *langa langa* comes from guitarist Gégé Mangaya, who, although not a member of Zaïko, was around the group at the beginning. Elima, June 13, 1988.
159 'We rocketed up...': *Zaïre*, Nov. 8, 1971.
159 'a schoolboy's song...': *Etoile du Congo*, Nov. 10, 1970.
159 'Childhood love:...': *Zaïre*, June 21, 1971.
159 'Young people will no longer...': ibid., Feb. 14, 1972.
160 'Libanga na Libumu' transcription from Bemba, p. 137.
161 'Maseke ya Meme' transcription from Pwono, pp. 170–71. Pwono attributes these lyrics to the wrong song title.
161 'Siongo Bavon.': *Etoile du Congo*, Aug. 6, 1970.
161 'coming home in the wee hours...': Bemba, p. 137.
161 'He pulled out...': Stapleton and May, p. 152.
161 'Angry, shouting...': Ewens, *Congo Colossus*, p. 124.
161 'M.J.' and Bavon, Elima, Mar. 5, 1979.
162 'After Bavon's death...': Ewens, *Congo Colossus*, p. 125.
162 'Negro-Succès died...': *Salongo*, May 22, 1974.
164 'Pont Sur le Congo' transcription by Honoré Mobonda from *La Semaine Africaine*, Nov. 8, 1984.

Notes

166 'Le Bûcheron' transcription from Dzokanga, p. 22.
166 'Likambo Oyo' transcription from Bemba, p. 122.
167 'from a reliable source...': *Etoile du Congo*, Jan. 17, 1970.
167 'After all...': *Bingo*, Dec. 1970.
167 'I ended up...': *La Semaine Africaine*, Dec. 20, 1970.
167 'to cut the ground...': *Etoile du Congo*, June 25, 1970.
167 'I'm anxious...': *Bingo*, Dec. 1970.
167 'The Congolese troupe's...': *Etoile du Congo*, Dec. 15, 1970.
171 'At the same time...': *New York Times*, June 23, 1972.
171 'When I used to tell...': Remilleux, p. 110.
171 Mobutu's name has been loosely translated to mean 'the all-conquering warrior who triumphs over all obstacles' (Young and Turner, p. 153). Mobutu himself said, 'I can tell you that Sese is a synonym for Mobutu, that Seko is the name of my grandfather, and that Kuku Ngbendu means "pili-pili ya mobescu," which means green pepper. What do you make of that?' (Remilleux, pp. 110–11).
172 'I had to start over...': *Bingo*, Dec. 1978.
172 'special announcements...': Du Bois, p. 7.
173 'Mongali' transcription from Tshonga-Onyumbe, *Zaïre-Afrique*, No. 208 (Oct. 1986), p. 494.
173 'Nakomitunaka' transcription from Dzokanga, pp. 14–17.
174 'People couldn't believe...': *Zaïre*, June 19, 1972.
174 'I will marry ... :' *Etoile du Congo*, Jan. 23, 1969.
175 'we were dismissed': *Zaïre*, Aug. 7, 1972.
175 'I did not have...': ibid.
175 Meaning of Sosoliso from ibid., Feb. 5, 1973.
175 Record sales figures from ibid., Jan. 29, 1973.
176 'Ce soir...': ibid., Feb. 5, 1973.
176 'Quite naturally...': ibid.
176 'The trio Madjesi may not...': ibid.
176 'Du soul à la sauce moamba': ibid., Sept. 30, 1974.
177 '"Soki against Soki..."': ibid., Nov. 8, 1971.
177 'Now that I've succeeded...': ibid., Oct. 2, 1972.
178 'I like that name...': ibid., July 17, 1972.
178 '*attaque-chant*...': *Salongo*, Nov. 3, 1973.
178 'I've worked enough...': *Zaïre*, Mar. 12, 1973.
179 'I don't have a grudge...': ibid., Oct. 8, 1973.
180 'For me 1971...': *Zaïre*, Jan. 31, 1972.
181 'The decision to leave...': ibid., Sept. 4, 1972.
182 'I have five guitarists...': ibid., July 24, 1972.
182 'Franco could eat...': Ewens, *Congo Colossus*, p. 30.
182 'I know my public...': *Zaïre*, July 24, 1972.
183 'For me, Mujos...': ibid., Sept. 27, 1971.
183 Cartoon about Docteur Nico appeared in *Likembe*, No. 21, 1973.
184 'by a puritanical reflex...': Gauze, p. 222.
185 'poorly planned...': ibid., p. 185.
185 'have not been explained...': *La Semaine*, Mar. 19, 1972.

Notes 399

187 'Each month, each week...': *Zaïre*, Oct. 11, 1971.
190 'but the big record companies...': *Bingo*, Oct. 1968.
192 'not very big...': ibid., May 1973.
192 'The musicians...': ibid.
192 'A true queen...': *Zaïre*, July 30, 1973.
192 'appreciable success...': *Salongo*, Aug. 27, 1973.
193 'I sang with all...': ibid., Mar. 16, 1974.
193 'It's the same thing...': ibid.
195 'the creator of a work...': Wallis and Malm, p. 47.
196 For more on Mobutu's UNTC and its connections to the American AFL–CIO and the CIA, see Kwitny pp. 45 and 343–6.
197 'The musicians complain...': *Zaïre*, Feb. 19, 1973.
197 'required to have...': ibid., June 3, 1974.
197 'to preserve the profession's...': *Salongo*, May 25, 1974.
197 'It seems unjust...': ibid.
198 'Zaïre is the country...': quoted in Young and Turner, p. 326.
198 'What then transpired...': ibid., 337.
198 'a vast agricultural empire...': ibid., p. 179.
200 'I've come to tell you...': *Salongo*, Sept. 30, 1974.
200 'This, especially...': ibid., June 19, 1974.
200 'I have placed...': ibid., June 15, 1974.
200 'Come to MAZADIS...': ibid., June 19, 1974.
200 'The situation...': ibid.
201 'I swear to you...': ibid., Sept. 30, 1974.
201 'In effect...': ibid., May 6, 1974.
201 'Those rumors are empty...': ibid.
201 'Scandalous, obscene...': ibid., Dec. 8, 1973.
201 'Not only does it debase...': ibid.
202 'Ebale ya Zaïre' transcription from Dzokanga, pp. 4–7.
203 'Mabele' transcription from ibid., pp. 8–13.
203 'people wonder whether...': *Zaïre*, Sept. 25, 1972.
204 'the voice of Mangwana...': *Salongo*, Oct. 13, 1974.
204 'Among us, discipline...': ibid., June 1, 1973.
208 'For the first time...': *Zaïre*, Sept. 30, 1974.
208 'My band...': *Salongo*, Oct. 27, 1974.
209 'Kaful Mayay' transcription from Dzokanga, pp. 66–7.
211 'The young man...': *Salongo*, Mar. 25, 1974.
211 'set the tone...': ibid., Sept. 24, 1974.
212 'Zamba' transcription from Dzokanga, pp. 24–5.
212 'Soki Dianzenza...': *Salongo*, Nov. 15, 1974.
212 'Nganga' transcription from Tshonga Onyumbe, *Zaïre-Afrique*, No. 205 (May 1986), p. 307.
212 'It is only...': *Salongo*, Oct. 27, 1974.
214 'In the beginning...': *Zaïre*, Oct. 1, 1973.
214 'The text is inaudible...': ibid., Feb. 4, 1974.
214 'Bizarre voices!...': *Salongo*, Jan. 5, 1974.

400 Notes

215 'For me...': ibid., Dec. 29, 1973.
215 'In our band...': ibid., Feb. 4, 1974.
215 'Onassis ya Zaïre' transcription from Tshonga-Onyumbe, *Zaïre-Afrique*, No. 162 (Feb. 1982), p. 86.
215 'Vie ya Mosolo' transcription from ibid., No. 172 (Feb. 1983), p. 109.
215 'Liwa ya Somo' transcription from ibid., No. 217 (Sept. 1987), p. 432.
216 'Everyone made the rules...': *Salongo*, Dec. 8, 1974.
217 'The mismanagement...': Young and Turner, p. 347.
217 'It is unthinkable...': quoted in ibid., p.351.
218 'In the capital's...': *Zaïre*, Sept. 8, 1975.
219 'For a young star...': *Salongo*, Oct. 20, 1974.
220 Many have attributed M'Pongo's paralysis to polio. She claimed it was the result of an injection (*Amina*, Oct. 1, 1985). She may have acquired the disease from an injection of polio vaccine.
223 'This little unknown...': *Zaïre*, Nov. 1, 1976.
224 'This artist was incontestably...': *Elima*, Jan. 1, 1978.
226 'that song...': *Zaïre*, Dec. 15, 1975.
226 'the songs, taken...': ibid., Feb. 16, 1976.
227 'UMUZA, a union...': ibid., June 2, 1975.
227 'Sadly, the necessary...': ibid., May 30, 1977.
227 'I can't forget...': *Likembe*, No. 39, 1978.
228 'As I have just...': *Salongo*, July 9, 1976.
230 'We hired an unemployed...': *Zaïre*, Feb. 16, 1976.
231 'Luambo, who remains...': *Salongo*, Aug. 10, 1978.
231 'Listening to my music...': *Elima*, Sept. 4, 1978.
231 'Luambo at the height...': *Salongo*, Sept. 17, 1978.
231 'Luambo: please!...': *Elima*, Sept. 25, 1978.
232 'Luambo Makiadi arrested': ibid., Sept. 30, 1978.
233 'Luambo Makiadi is no longer...': *Salongo*, Oct. 1, 1978.
233 'It will be necessary...': ibid., Nov. 2, 1978.
238 Population statistics from Morrison, p. 421, and Mbumba Ngimbi, p. 29.
238 'We are the victims...': *Elima*, Oct. 8, 1979.
239 'S.O.S. pour le disque zaïrois!': ibid., Dec. 4, 1978.
240 'The recording made...': *Salongo*, Feb. 2, 1976.
241 'The problem lies...': ibid., May 30, 1976.
241 'we must re-examine...': ibid., Oct. 5, 1978.
241 'More than ten thousand...': ibid., Dec. 4, 1978.
241 'We always had...': *Elima*, Dec. 11, 1978.
242 Inflation rate statistic from Young and Turner, p. 71. For readers interested in more information about Zaïre's economy and other aspects of life under Mobutu, Young and Turner's book is an excellent source.
243 'Mobutu himself withdrew...': Kwitny, p. 91.
243 'The legend was taken...': Remilleux, p. 182.
244 'fugitives': *Likembe*, No. 35, 1978.
248 'Georgette Eckins' transcription from *Elima*, Nov. 12, 1979.
250 'If I no longer collaborate...': ibid., Aug. 27, 1979.

Notes 401

250 'At the height...': ibid., Feb 25, 1980.
250 A sengi was Zaïre's smallest monetary unit during the Mobutu era. The zaïre was divided into one hundred makuta, one of which was a likuta equivalent to two U.S. cents. The likuta was further divided into one hundred sengi, one of which was equivalent to two hundredths of one U.S. cent.
251 'I compose all my songs...': Salongo, Jan. 17, 1979.
252 'Next year will be...': ibid., Nov. 28, 1978.
253 'Kasanda equal to himself...': Elima, Aug. 18, 1980.
255 'very important singer...': Elima, Dec. 23, 1980.
262 'Soukous is a dance...': from liner notes to Sound D'Afrique II 'Soukous', Mango Records MLPS 9754.
264 'Having begun in Zaïre...': Mbarga-Abega, p. 15.
264 'I owe my success...': Elima, Jan. 12, 1981.
265 'Music is a job...': Bingo, Dec. 1982.
277 'Kalle embodies...': Elima, Feb. 14, 1983.
278 'Every human...': Mweti, Mar. 9, 1982.
278 'They have taken...': Pwono, p. 190.
279 The account of the Coopération sessions comes from Harrev's liner notes to Canta Moçambique, Popular African Music, PAM05 (not to be confused with the original Canta Moçambique, SAM 4). Harrev, however, errs in his statement that Franco was awarded the Maracas d'Or for Coopération. That album was still being recorded when Franco's award for lifetime achievement was announced.
281 'Mpeve ya Longo' transcription from Tshonga-Onyumbe, Zaïre-Afrique, No. 205 (May 1986), p. 309.
281 'Mbilia Bel: a star...': Elima, July 12, 1982.
282 'Eswi yo Wapi' transcription from Tshonga-Onyumbe, Zaïre-Afrique, No. 205 (May 1986), pp. 294 and 306.
282 'Queen Cleopatra...': Elima, Feb. 6, 1984.
283 'it's simple...': ibid., June 18, 1984.
283 'It is rather ... :' Bingo, Feb. 1986.
283 A gold record in France – the standard Cuxac was presumably working under since there was none established in Senegal or Côte d'Ivoire – represents album sales of 100,000. A gold record in the United States represents album sales of 500,000. On the basis of accumulated sales (not a certifiable category for the awarding of gold records) both Franco and Ley would surely have qualified under either standard.
284 'Suite Lettre No. 2' transcription from Pwono, p. 192.
284 'D.G.' transcription from Mbamba Toko W., pp. 148–50.
284 Population statistic from Mbumba Ngimbi, p. 29.
284 Economic statistics from Young and Turner, p. 132 (purchasing power), and West Africa, Sept. 12, 1983, Sept. 19, 1983, and Dec. 24, 1984 (exchange rates).
285 'Article 15' transcription from Manda Tchebwa, p. 259.
286 'Like a veritable griot...': Elima, Jan. 31, 1983.
286 'No, no, no...': ibid., June 18, 1984.
287 'Contrary to what...': Denis, p. 22.
287 'Non' transcription from Mbamba Toko W., pp. 102–12.

402 Notes

289 'a disconnected series...': *Village Voice*, Dec. 13, 1983.
290 'Our stay...': from video tape interview conducted by Kazadi wa Mukuna and Jackie Peters.
290 'closer to Las Vegas...': *Rolling Stone*, Oct. 25, 1984.
290 'Afrisa warmed up...': *Village Voice*, Mar. 6, 1984.
290 'by far the best...': *New York Times*, Feb, 13, 1984.
291 'If I won...': *Elima*, May 7, 1984.
291 'Soukous...': *Melody Maker*, May 5, 1984.
291 'Tu Vois?' transcription from lyric sheet in the album *Très Impoli*, Edipop POP 028.
292 'Mario' transcription from Mbamba Toko W., pp. 118–30.
294 'eloquent proof...': *Elima*, Sept. 1, 1986.
294 'No one is a prophet...': ibid.
294 'I dread dying poor...': ibid., July 7, 1980.
294 'Oh Manzeta mama...': ibid., Mar. 16, 1981.
294 'People outside Zaïre...': ibid., Aug. 10, 1981.
295 'we aren't equipped...': ibid., Jan. 18, 1982.
295 'That seems banal...': ibid., July 7, 1980.
296 'Highly acclaimed...': *Hommage à Grand Kalle*, p. 34.
296 'I bet...': ibid.
296 'I found myself...': *Elima*, Jan. 23, 1984.
297 'Docteur Nico...': *Ehuzu* (Benin), Aug. 10, 1984.
298 'There are two...': Voice of America.
298 'For that, they withdrew...': *Elima*, Apr. 29, 1985.
298 'I was longing...': ibid.
299 'Nico was not only...': ibid., Sept. 30, 1985.
300 'The style of guitar...': *Elima*, Aug. 13, 1984.
300 'immobile as a Buddha': Bemba, p. 127.
302 'Without false modesty...': *Elima*, Mar. 25, 1985.
302 'For the moment...': ibid., Oct. 22, 1979.
303 'According to Elima's account...': ibid., Nov. 3, 1980.
303 'We wanted to make...': ibid., Oct. 13, 1980.
304 'Crois-Moi' transcription from ibid., Aug. 18, 1981.
305 'Dear mothers...': ibid., June 8, 1981.
306 'Evénement' transcription from ibid., Aug. 31, 1982.
307 'My group...': ibid., Feb. 28, 1983.
308 'The masses...': Mbembe Mbilya quoted in ibid., May 3, 1982.
308 'Papa Wemba knows...': ibid., Mar. 8, 1982.
309 'Matebu' transcription from Gandoulou, pp. 196–7.
309 'All Wemba has to do...': *Elima*, Aug. 26, 1985.
310 'Using a style...': ibid., Feb. 8, 1982.
311 'the [J.R.] Ewing...': ibid., June 27, 1983.
317 'When you're working...': *Fraternité Matin* (Abidjan), Feb. 12, 1984.
319 Album sales of 100,000 qualify for gold certification in France.
321 'My break with Safari...': *Elima*, July 24, 1989.
322 Michel David of Sonodisc was interviewed before the author learned of the controversies surrounding Sonodisc's origins and its acquisition of the African

Notes 403

       label catalog from Fonior. David has since died.
322 'admitted to the manufacture...': IFPI press release, Mar. 28, 1991.
323 'I sold 10,000...': Darlington, p. 32. Ismael Lô is a singer-guitarist born in Niger and raised in Senegal.
329 'I was very happy...': *Elima*, July 6, 1987.
330 'Every music lover...': ibid., Oct. 5, 1987.
331 'I owe my fame...': ibid., Oct. 17, 1988.
333 'I wanted a change...': *Elima*, July 7, 1986.
334 'Work, for work pays ... never fails': Moore, p. 109.
335 'I've thus decided...': *Elima*, Dec. 21, 1987.
336 'I give myself...': ibid.
336 'It wasn't a surprise...': ibid., Jan. 27, 1986.
340 'Those I play with...': ibid., Feb. 24, 1986.
343 'We're going to raze...': ibid., June 3, 1985.
344 'Moanda create[d]...': ibid., Dec. 28, 1987.
345 'There are people...': ibid., May 23, 1988.
348 'all that is sweet...': *Ivoir'Soir* (Abidjan), Oct. 1, 1989.
352 'It's true...': *La Semaine Africaine*, Dec. 13, 1984.
352 'For people to talk...': *Mweti*, Sept. 27, 1986.
353 'Your trade is linked...': Luya Laye Kelaka.
353 'La Vie des Hommes' transcription from Mbamba Toko W., pp. 132 and 140.
354 Album sales of 10,000 qualify for gold certification in Kenya.
354 'As you well know...': *Elima*, Sept. 1, 1986.
355 'When I composed...': Denis, p.22.
355 'I am afraid...': *Elima*, Aug. 3, 1987.
356 'Between now and 1990...': Denis, p. 22.
357 'Gras Maître': *Elima*, Feb. 1, 1988. The writer was Botowamungu Kalome Tokomusa.
357 'Dressed in red...': ibid., Feb. 8, 1988.
361 Sam Mangwana sings on two numbers, 'Aziza' and 'Decca,' from the B side of *Franco Joue avec Sam Mangwana* (the songs are listed in the wrong order on the record jacket and label).
363 'I can defend myself...': Lukunku Sampu.
364 'I'm praying to God...': from interview conducted by Dutch radio station VPRO, Sept. 22, 1989.
366 'Franco was a prophet...': OZRT, video tape of Franco's funeral.
367 'Good memories for me...': Luya Laye Kelaka.
369 'I left Zaïre...': *Elima*, July 24, 1989.
370 'Upon hearing...': ibid., May 31, 1990.
372 Bon Chic, Bon Genre or BCBG, loosely translates as 'a class act,' from the French slang for 'yuppie, clean-cut, upper middle class.'
373 'When I assumed power...': Elliot and Dymally, p. 42.
374 'Le MPR en Débandade!': *Elima*, Aug. 1, 1990.
374 'A Commando...': ibid., Aug. 30, 1990.
376 'The transition has come...': *West Africa*, Sept. 7, 1992.
388 'La Maison de la Casa House': Trillin, p. 3.
391 'Requisitoire' transcription from Tabu Ley Rochereau, Gaar, and Cheyney.

Bibliography

Acosta, Leonardo. 'The Rumba, the Guaguancó, and Tio Tom.' In *Essays on Cuban Music*, edited by Peter Manuel, 49–73. Lanham, Md.: University Press of America, 1991.
Adams, Lois. 'Women in Zaïre: Disparate Status and Roles.' In *Comparative Perspectives of Third World Women: The Impact of Race, Sex, and Class*, edited by Beverly Lindsay, 55–77. New York: Praeger, 1980.
L'As des As (Kinshasa), October 1990.'Une année après sa mort, Luambo Makiadi honoré...' Special issue on the one-year anniversary of Franco's death.
Andersson, Efraim. *Messianic Popular Movements in the Lower Congo*, Studia Ethnographica Upsaliensia, XIV. Uppsala, 1958.
Anstey, Roger. *King Leopold's Legacy*. London: Oxford University Press, 1966.
Austen, Ralph A. 'The Trans-Saharan Slave Trade: A Tentative Census.' In *The Uncommon Market: Essays in the Economic History of the Atlantic Slave Trade*, edited by Henry A. Gemery and Jan S. Hogendorn, 23–76. New York: Academic Press, 1979.
Axelson, Eric. *Congo to Cape: Early Portuguese Explorers*. London: Faber & Faber, 1973.
Balandier, Georges. *Ambiguous Africa: Cultures in Collision*, translated by Helen Weaver. London: Chatto & Windus, 1966.
———. *The Sociology of Black Africa: Social Dynamics in Central Africa*. Translated by Douglas Garman. London: Andre Deutsch, 1970.
———. *Sociologie des Brazzavilles noires*. 1955. Reprint. Paris: Presses de la Fondation Nationale des Sciences Politiques, 1985.
Baruti, Barly. *Papa Wemba: Viva La Musica!* Kinshasa: Afrique Editions, 1987.
Belgian Congo Today (Brussels: Inforcongo), 1952–1960.
Bemba, Sylvain. *50 ans de musique du Congo–Zaïre*. Paris: Présence Africaine, 1984.
Bingo (Dakar and Paris), 1963–1985.
Bobb, F. Scott. *Historical Dictionary of Zaïre*. Metuchen, N.J.: Scarecrow Press, 1988.
Bwantsa-Kafungu, S. Pierre. *Congo en musique*. Léopoldville: Lovanium University, 1965.

Capelle, Emmanuel. *La Cité indigène de Léopoldville*. Elisabethville: Le Centre d'Etude des Problèmes Sociaux Indigènes, 1947.
Chanan, Michael. *Repeated Takes: A Short History of Recording and its Effects on Music*. London: Verso, 1995.
Clark, John F. 'Congo: Transition and the Struggle to Consolidate.' In *Political Reform in Francophone Africa*, edited by John F. Clark and David E. Gardinier, 62–85. Boulder, Colo.: Westview Press, 1997.
Comhaire-Sylvain, Suzanne. *Food and Leisure among the African Youth of Léopoldville*. Cape Town: University of Cape Town, 1950.
———. *Femmes de Kinshasa: hier et aujourd'hui*. Paris: Mouton, 1968.
Congo Belge 1944, edited by Information and Propaganda Service of the Belgian Congo. Léopoldville, 1944.
Coquery-Vidrovitch, Catherine. *African Women: A Modern History*. Translated by Beth Gillian Raps. Boulder, Colo.: Westview Press, 1997.
Cowley, John H. 'uBungca (Oxford Bags): Recordings in London of African and West Indian Music in the 1920s & 1930s.' *Musical Traditions* 12 (summer 1994): 13–26.
C.R.I.S.P. *Congo 1959*. Brussels: Centre de Recherche et d'Information Socio-Politiques, 1962.
———. *Congo 1960* 2 vols. and annexes and biographies. Brussels: Centre de Recherche et d'Information Socio-Politiques, n.d.
———. *Congo 1962*. Brussels: Centre de Recherche et d'Information Socio-Politiques, 1963.
Curtin, Philip D. *The African Slave Trade: A Census*. Madison: University of Wisconsin Press, 1969.
Darlington, Lois. 'A Blind Date with Sylla.' *World Beat*, June 1991: 30–32.
Davidson, Basil. *The African Genius: An Introduction to African Social and Cultural History*. Boston: Little, Brown, 1969.
———. *The African Slave Trade* (originally titled *Black Mother*, 1961). Boston: Little, Brown, 1980.
———. *The Story of Africa*. London: Mitchell Beazley, 1984.
———. *The Black Man's Burden*. New York: Times Books, 1992.
Decalo, Samuel. *Coups and Army Rule in Africa: Studies in Military Style*. New Haven: Yale University Press, 1976.
Denis, Jean-Michel. 'Le Grand Maître a-t-il joué Franco?' *Afrique Elite* 21 (December 1987): 21–2.
Dibango, Manu with Danielle Rouard. *Three Kilos of Coffee*. Translated by Beth G. Raps. Chicago: University of Chicago Press, 1994.
Du Bois, Victor D. 'Zaïre Under President Sese Seko Mobutu, Part I: The Return to Authenticity.' American Universities Field Staff, *Fieldstaff Reports, Central & Southern Africa Series* 17, no. 1 (1973).
Dzokanga, A. with Anne Behaghel (Conseil International de la Langue Française). *Chansons et proverbes Lingala*. Paris: EDICEF, 1978.
Elima (Kinshasa), 1978–92 (formerly *Le Courrier d'Afrique*).
Elliot, Jeffrey M. and Mervyn M. Dymally. *Voices of Zaïre: Rhetoric or Reality?* Washington, D.C.: Washington Institute Press, 1990.
Etoile du Congo (Léopoldville/Kinshasa), 1963–70.

Bibliography

Ewens, Graeme. *Luambo Franco and 30 Years of O.K. Jazz*. London: Off The Record Press, 1986.

———. *Congo Colossus: The Life and Legacy of Franco & OK Jazz*. North Walsham: Buku Press, 1994.

Eyre, Banning. 'Soukous: Zaïre's Six-Stringed Wizards.' *Guitar Player*, February 1996: 75–84.

Franco and his T.P.O.K. Jazz in U.S.A. Tour program. N.p., November–December 1983.

Fyfe, Christopher. *A History of Sierra Leone*. London: Oxford University Press, 1962.

Gandoulou, Justin Daniel. *Entre Paris et Bacongo*. Paris: Centre Georges Pompidou, 1984.

Gauze, René. *The Politics of Congo-Brazzaville*. Translated, edited, and with a supplement by Virginia Thompson and Richard Adloff. Stanford: Hoover Institution Press, 1973.

George, Susan. *A Fate Worse Than Debt*. New York: Grove Press, 1988.

Gerard, Charley. *Salsa! The Rhythm of Latin Music*. Crown Point: White Cliffs Media, 1989.

Gilbert, Martin. *Road to Victory: Winston S. Churchill, 1941–1945*. London: Heinemann, 1986.

Graham, Ronnie. *The Da Capo Guide to Contemporary African Music* (originally published in England as *Stern's Guide to Contemporary African Music*). New York: Da Capo Press, 1988.

———. *The World of African Music: Stern's Guide to Contemporary African Music* volume 2. Chicago: Research Associates, 1992.

Greene, Graham. *In Search of a Character*. New York: Viking, 1962.

Gunther, John. *Inside Africa*. New York: Harper & Brothers, 1953.

Guthrie, Malcolm. 'The Lingua Franca of the Middle Congo.' In *Africa: Journal of the International Institute of African Languages and Cultures* 14, no. 3 (July 1943): 118–23.

Hall, Richard. *Stanley: An Adventurer Explored*. Boston: Houghton Mifflin, 1975.

Harrev, Flemming. Liner notes for Sam Mangwana, *Canta Moçambique*. Frankfurt: Popular African Music PAM 05, 1989.

———. 'Sam Mangwana: A discography.' Photocopy.

Hommage à Grand Kalle. Kinshasa: Editions Lokole, 1985.

Honorin, M. 'Au Congo-Brazzaville, la révolution n'est pas Chinoise elle est ... Congolaise.' *Croissance des Jeunes Nations* 50 (December 1965): 36–8.

Hoskyns, Catherine. *The Congo Since Independence: January 1960–December 1961*. London: Oxford University Press, 1965.

Jahn, Janheinz. *Muntu: The New African Culture*. New York: Grove Press, 1961.

Kalb, Madeleine G. *The Congo Cables*. New York: Macmillan, 1982.

Kanza Matondo ne Mansangaza. *Musique zaïroise moderne*. Kinshasa: Conservatoire National de Musique & d'Art Dramatique, 1972.

Kanza, Thomas. *The Rise and Fall of Patrice Lumumba: Conflict in the Congo*. Rochester, Vt.: Schenkman Books, 1994.

Kaplan, Irving, ed. *Zaïre: A Country Study*. Washington, D.C.: American University Press, 1979.

Kazadi, Pierre Cary. 'Trends of Nineteenth and Twentieth Century Music in the Congo-Zaïre.' In *Musikkulturen Asiens, Afrikas und Ozeaniens im 19. Jahrhundert*, edited by Robert Gunther, 267–83. Regensburg: Gustav Bosse Verlag, 1973.

Kazadi wa Mukuna. 'The Origin of Zaïrean Modern Music: A Socio-Economic Aspect.' *African Urban Studies* 6 (Winter 1979–80): 31–9.

Kazadi wa Mukuna and Jackie Peters. Video tape interview with Luambo Makiadi Franco [Washington, D.C., December 1983]. N.p.

Keller, Edmund. 'Urbanisation and the Emergence of the Politics of Independence: Belgian Congo (Zaïre).' *Mawazo*, the Makerere Journal of the Arts and Social Sciences (Uganda) 4, no. 2 (1974): 37–51.
Kelly, Sean. *America's Tyrant: The CIA and Mobutu of Zaïre*. Washington, D.C.: American University Press, 1993.
Knappert, Jan. 'Origin and Development of Lingala.' In *Readings in Creole Studies*, edited by Ian F. Hancock, 153–64. Ghent, Belgium: Story-Scientia P.V.B.A., 1979.
Kwitny, Jonathan. *Endless Enemies: The Making of an Unfriendly World*. New York: Congdon & Weed, 1984.
La Fontaine, J.S. *City Politics: A Study of Léopoldville, 1962–63*. London: Cambridge University Press, 1970.
Legum, Colin. *Congo Disaster*. Baltimore: Penguin Books, 1961.
Likembe (Kinshasa), 1972–78.
Llerenas, Eduardo. Brochure notes for *Real Rumba from Cuba*. Corason COCD110, 1994.
Lonoh, Michel. *Essai de commentaire sur la musique congolaise moderne*. Kinshasa: S.E.I./A.N.C., 1969.
Lukunku Sampu. Video tape interview with Luambo Makiadi Franco. [Brussels, September 5, 1989]. Zaïre: L.S. Production, 1989.
Lumumba, Patrice. *Congo My Country*. New York: Praeger, 1962.
Luya Laye Kelaka. 'A bâton rompus avec Luambo Makiadi.' *Lokolé* (Kinshasa) 29 (January 1987): 33.
McDonald, Gordon C. *Area Handbook for People's Republic of the Congo*. Washington, D.C.: American University Press, 1971.
McKown, Robin. *Lumumba: A Biography*. Garden City, N.Y.: Doubleday, 1969.
Mahoney, Richard D. *JFK: Ordeal in Africa*. New York: Oxford University Press, 1983.
Mailer, Norman. *The Fight*. Boston: Little, Brown, 1975.
Manda Tchebwa. *Terre de la chanson: la musique zaïroise: hier et aujourd'hui*. Louvain-la-Neuve, Belgium: Duculot, 1996.
Manuel, Peter with Kenneth Bilby and Michael Largey. *Caribbean Currents: Caribbean Music from Rumba to Reggae*. Philadelphia: Temple University Press, 1995.
Maquet, J.-N. 'Note sur les instruments de musique Congolais.' Académie royale des sciences coloniales. Classe des sciences morales et politiques. Mémoires in-8°. Nouvelle Série. Tome VI, fasc. 4, 1956.
Mazrui, Ali. *The Africans: A Triple Heritage*. Boston: Little, Brown, 1986.
Mbamba Toko W. *Autopsie de la chanson de Luambo Makiadi Franco*. Paris: UHURU/Universal Connection, 1992.
Mbarga-Abega, Mathieu. 'Le dernier tube de M'Pongo Love.' *Amina* (Paris) 195 (October 15, 1986): 14–15.
Mbumba Ngimbi. *Kinshasa 1881–1981: 100 ans après Stanley: problemes et avenir d'une ville*. Kinshasa: Centre de Recherches Pédagogiques, 1982.
Meditz, Sandra W. and Tim Merrill, eds. *Zaïre: A Country Study*. Washington, D.C.: American University, 1994.
M.E.N./I.N.R.A.P. *La Chanson congolaise*. Brazzaville: O.N.L.P., 1984 (also Paris: Fernand Nathan, 1984).
Merriam, Alan P. *Congo: Background of Conflict*. Evanston, Ill.: Northwestern University Press, 1961.

408 Bibliography

Moore, Marianne, trans. *The Fables of La Fontaine*. New York: Viking, 1954.
Morel, E.D. *History of the Congo Reform Movement*, edited by William Roger Louis and Jean Stengers. London: Oxford University Press, 1968.
Morrison, Donald George. *Black Africa: A Comparative Handbook*. New York: Paragon House, 1989.
Mweti (Brazzaville), 1980–1988.
Newfield, Jack. *Only in America: The Life and Crimes of Don King*. New York: William Morrow, 1995.
O'Brien, Conor Cruise. *To Katanga and Back: A U.N. Case History*. London: Hutchinson, 1962.
Olema, Debhonvapi. 'Société Zaïroise dans le miroir de la chanson populaire.' *Canadian Journal of African Studies* 18, no. 1 (1984): 122–30.
OZRT (Zaïrean television). 'A l'occasion des 20 ans de Télé Zaïre et des 30 ans de L'OK Jazz.' Kinshasa: OZRT [1986].
———. Video tape of the funeral of Luambo Makiadi Franco [October 17, 1989]. Kinshasa: OZRT [1989].
Pain, Marc. *Kinshasa: la ville et la cité*. Paris: Editions de l'ORSTOM, 1984.
Pakenham, Thomas. *The Scramble for Africa*. New York: Random House, 1991.
Pauwels-Boon, Greta. *L'Origine, l'évolution et le fonctionnement de la radiodiffusion au Zaïre de 1937 à 1960*. Sciences Historiques Serie IN-8°, no. 5. Tervuren, Belgium: Musée Royal de l'Afrique Centrale, 1979.
Pepper, Herbert. Brochure notes for *Anthologie de la vie africaine*. Disques Ducretet-Thompson, nos. 320C126, 320C127, 320C128.
Presence Congolaise (Léopoldville), 1958–65.
Prince, Rob. 'Le Grand Maître.' *Folk Roots* 79/80 (January/February 1990): 13–16.
Le Progrès (Kinshasa) 1967–72 (became *Salongo* after authenticity).
Pwono, Damien Mandondo. 'Institutionalization of Popular Music in Zaïre.' Ph.D. diss., University of Pittsburgh, 1992.
Radu, Michael S. and Keith Somerville. 'People's Republic of Congo.' In *Benin, The Congo, Burkina Faso*, by Chris Allen, Michael S. Radu, Keith Somerville, and Joan Baxter, 147–236. London: Pinter, 1989.
Read, Oliver. *The Recording and Reproduction of Sound*. Indianapolis: Howard W. Sams, 1952.
Remilleux, Jean-Louis. *Mobutu: Dignity for Africa*. Paris: Albin Michel, 1989.
Revue Noire: African Contemporary Art 21 (June, July, August 1996). 'Kinshasa, Zaïre.' Issue devoted to artists and musicians of Kinshasa. Paris: Revue Noire.
Roberts, John Storm. *Black Music of Two Worlds*. New York: William Morrow, 1974.
———. *The Latin Tinge*. New York: Oxford University Press, 1979. Reprint. Tivoli, N.Y.: Original Music, 1985.
Salongo (Kinshasa) 1973–92 (formerly *Le Progrès*).
Santos, John. Introduction and notes for recordings by Verna Gillis, *Music of Cuba*. Folkways Records FE 4064, 1985.
Schatzberg, Michael G. *Politics and Class in Zaïre: Bureaucracy, Business, and Beer in Lisala*. New York: Africana, 1980.
———. *The Dialectics of Oppression in Zaïre*. Bloomington: Indiana University Press, 1988.
Scholefield, Alan. *The Dark Kingdoms: The Impact of White Civilization on Three Great African Monarchies*. New York: William Morrow, 1975.
La Semaine Africaine (Brazzaville), 1963–70.
Slade, Ruth. *The Belgian Congo*. London: Oxford University Press, 1961.

———. *King Leopold's Congo*. London: Oxford University Press, 1962.
Small, Christopher. *Music of the Common Tongue: Survival and Celebration in Afro-American Music*. London: John Calder, 1987.
Stapleton, Chris and Chris May. *African All-Stars: The Pop Music of a Continent*. London: Quartet Books, 1987.
Starr, Frederick. *The Truth About the Congo, the Chicago Tribune Articles*. Chicago: Forbes & Company, 1907.
Stewart, Gary. 'Docteur Nico: A Legend of African Music.' *The Beat* 5, no. 5/6 (1986): 43–5.
———. 'Motown Meets Matonge.' *West Africa*, Dec. 12, 1988, 2334–5.
———. 'Soukous: Birth of the Beat.' *The Beat* 8, no. 6 (1989): 18–21.
———. *Breakout: Profiles in African Rhythm*. Chicago: University of Chicago Press, 1992.
Stockwell, John. *In Search of Enemies: A CIA Story*. New York: W.W. Norton, 1978.
Tabu Ley Rochereau, David Gaar, and Tom Cheyney. Song lyrics in brochure notes for *Tabu Ley, Muzina*. Rounder Records CD5059, 1994.
Tati, Gabriel. 'Congo.' In *Urbanization in Africa: A Handbook*, edited by James D. Tarver, 125–40. Westport, Conn.: Greenwood Press, 1994.
Thompson, Virginia and Richard Adloff. *The Emerging States of French Equatorial Africa*. Stanford: Stanford University Press, 1960.
———. *Historical Dictionary of the People's Republic of the Congo*. Metuchen, N.J.: Scarecrow Press, 1984.
Trillin, Calvin. *The Tummy Trilogy*. Reprint of *American Fried*. New York: Noonday Press, 1994.
Tshiteya M'Biye. Brochure notes for *Rumba cha-cha: musiques des deux Congos (1950–1960)*. Paris: Services Coopération et Production Musicale de RFI, 1992.
Tshonga-Onyumbe. Series of articles on content of Zaïrean popular songs appearing in *Zaïre-Afrique*, nos. 162, 169, 172, 177, 180, 181, 184, 186, 205, 208, 217 (1982–1986). Kinshasa: Centre d'Etudes pour l'Action Sociale.
Turnbull, Colin M. *The Lonely African*. New York: Simon & Schuster, 1962.
Turner, Thomas. 'Zaïre: Flying High Above the Toads: Mobutu and Stalemated Democracy.' In *Political Reform in Francophone Africa*, edited by John F. Clark and David E. Gardinier, 246–64. Boulder, Colo.: Westview Press, 1997.
Voice of America. 'Interview avec le Docteur Nico à la Voix d'Amerique.' [Washington, D.C., March 1985.] Photocopy.
Wallis, Roger and Krister Malm. *Big Sounds from Small Peoples: The Music Industry in Small Countries*. London: Constable, 1984.
Welle, Jean. 'Rumbas congolaises et jazz americain.' In *The African Music Society Newsletter* 1, no. 5 (June 1952): 42–43.
West Africa (London), 1950–97.
West, Richard. *Congo* (originally published in England as *Brazza of the Congo*). New York: Holt, Rinehart & Winston, 1972.
Yanga, Tshimpaka. 'A Sociolinguistic Identification of Lingala (Republic of Zaïre).' Ph.D. diss., University of Texas at Austin, 1980.
Young, Crawford. *Politics in the Congo*. Princeton: Princeton University Press, 1965.
Young, Crawford and Thomas Turner. *The Rise and Decline of the Zairian State*. Madison: University of Wisconsin Press, 1985.
Zaïre (Kinshasa), 1969–79.

Select discography

Congolese music has been issued over the years in a jumble of new releases and re-releases, some of the same material on competing labels, often of questionable legality, and usually with minimal, misleading, or no documentation regarding personnel, recording dates, and studios. What follows is a sampling of the works mentioned in the text from the most readily available sources. The selection has been limited to the music that was in print at the time of writing. Songs and albums are listed by performer, not composer, and refer to releases on compact disc unless otherwise indicated.

Abeti
'Bibilé' and 'Je Suis Fâché' on *Souvenirs, Souvenirs: Compilation 1*. Déclic Communication, 50567–2.

African All Stars
'Affaire Video' on *Sam Mangwana et l'African All Stars*. Ngoyarto, SM010.
'Les Champions,' 'Georgette Eckins,' and 'Zela Ngai Nasala' (original versions) on *Sam Mangwana: Georgette Eckins*. Sonodisc, CDS7002.

African Fiesta
'Bilombe ya Africa,' 'Merengue President,' 'Mobembo Eleki Tata,' 'Mwasi Abandaka,' 'Ngonga Ebeti,' and 'Pesa le Tout' on *L'African Fiesta: Nico, Rochereau, Roger*, volume 1. Sonodisc, CD36509.
'Faux Millionnaire' on *Nico, Kwamy, Rochereau et l'African Fiesta*. Sonodisc, CD36512.
'Ndaya Paradis' on *Ndaya Paradis*. Sonodisc, CD36580.
'Paquita' on *African Fiesta*. Sonodisc, CD36574.

African Fiesta National
'Martin Luther King' and 'Peuple' on *Rochereau & l'African Fiesta National*. Sonodisc, CD36525.

Select discography 411

'Mokolo Nakokufa' and 'Zando ya Malonga' on *Le Seigneur Rochereau*. Sonodisc, CD36515.
'Toyota' on *Rochereau & l'African Fiesta*. Sonodisc, CD36549.

African Fiesta Sukisa

'Bougie ya Motema,' 'Echantillon ya Pamba,' 'Marie Pauline,' and 'Pauline' on *Nico et l'African Fiesta Sukisa*. Sonodisc, CD36524.
'Kiri-Kiri Mabina ya Sika,' 'Limbisa Ngai,' 'Ozali Suka ya Mobali,' and 'Suavilo' on *Merveilles du Passé: Eternel Docteur Nico*. Sonodisc, CD36516.

African Jazz

'African Jazz Mokili Mobimba' and 'Indépendance Cha Cha' on *Grand Kalle & African Jazz: Succès des Années 50/60*, volume 1. Sonodisc, CD36579.
'Bonbon Sucré,' 'Mayele Mabe,' 'Merengue Scoubidou,' and 'Table Ronde' on *Merveilles du Passé: Grand Kalle & African Jazz*, volume 1. Sonodisc, CD36503.

African Team

'Essous Spiritou' on *Grand Kalle & l'African Team*. Sonodisc, CD36543.

Afrisa International

Africa Worldwide. Rounder, CD5039.
Muzina. Rounder, CD5059.
'Kaful Mayay' on *Rochereau: l'Afrisa International*. Sonodisc, CD36544.
'Mongali' on *Tabu Ley 'Rochereau'*. Sonodisc, CD36552.

Anti-Choc

'La Reine de Sabah' on *Bozi Boziana*, volume 1. Ngoyarto, NG020.

Les Bantous de la Capitale

'Bantous de la Capitale,' 'Camarade Mabe,' and 'Tokumisa Congo' on *Les Bantous de la Capitale*. Sonodisc, CD36527.
'Ebandeli ya Mosala' (original version) on *Kosmos & les Bantous de la Capitale*, volume 1. Glenn Music, GM324007.
'Masuwa' (spelled Maswa on the CD) on *La Belle Epoque*, volume 1. Glenn Music, GM324001.

Beguen Band

'Marie-Louise' (chachachá) on *Ngoma: The Early Years, 1948–1960*. Popular African Music, pamap 101.

Bella Bella

'Kamavasthy' on *Les Plus Grands Succès de l'Orchestre Bella Bella*, volume 4. Ngoyarto, NG032.
'Zamba' on *Soki Vangu et L'Orchestre Bella Bella*, volume 3. Ngoyarto, NG031. (Written 'Zamba Zamba' on the CD. This is a sanitized version of the original – likely the result of Mobutu's censors – that lacks the lines quoted in the text.)

Franklin Boukaka

Franklin Boukaka: ses Sanzas et son Orchestre Congolais (LP record). Gilles Sala, GS8403.
'Le Bûcheron,' 'Les Immortels,' and 'Likambo Oyo' on *Frankin Boukaka à Paris*. Sonodisc, CD50048.

412 Select discography

Henri Bowane
'Kotiya Zolo Te' on *Roots of Rumba Rock: Zaïre Classics 1953–1954*. Crammed Discs, CRAW 4.
'Liwa' on *Roots of Rumba Rock 2: Zaïre Classics 1954–1955*. Crammed Discs, CRAW 10.

Léon Bukasa
The works mentioned in the text are out of print, but several others are available. Look for *Ngoma: The Early Years, 1948–1960*, Popular African Music, pamap 101.

Choc Stars
'Farya' on *Les Merveilles du Passé: Defao et Choc Stars*, volume 2. Flash Diffusion Business, FDB300002.
'Riana' on *Zikonda/Riana*. Flash Diffusion Business, FDB300018.

Cobantou
Several works not mentioned in the text appear on *Dewayon & Cobantou: Niama ya Zamba*. Sonodisc, CD36590.

Conga Succès
Several works not mentioned in the text appear on *Merveilles du Passé: Musique Congolo-Zaïroise Compilations*, volume 1. Sonodisc, CD36504.

Emeneya Mubiala
Nzinzi. Kaluila, F170.

Empire Bakuba
'Livre d'Or' on *Pepe Kalle and Papy Tex, 8,000 KM*. Plus de Paris, EPP01.

Festival des Maquisards
'Zela Ngai Nasala' on *Festival des Maquisards: Zela Ngai Nasala*. Sonodisc, CD36573.

Franco and Sam Mangwana
For Ever. Mélodie, 38775-2.

Franco and Rochereau
Lettre à Mr. le Directeur Général. Sonodisc, CDS6857.

Marcelle Fylla
'Pusana Moke' on *Les Merveilles du Passé*. Sonodisc, CD36501.

Grands Maquisards
Several works not mentioned in the text appear on *The Very Best of Ntesa Dalienst & les Grands Maquisards*. Ngoyarto, NG012.

Pepe Kalle and Nyboma
Moyibi. Syllart/Mélodie, 38752-2.

Kanda Bongo Man
'J.T.' on *Amour Fou/Crazy Love*. Rykodisc, HNCD1337.
'Sai,' 'Liza,' 'Bedy,' and 'Cantique' on *Kwassa-Kwassa*. Rykodisc, HNCD1343.

Langa Langa Stars
'Dalida' and 'Fleur Bakutu' on *Les Meilleurs Succès de Langa Langa Stars*, volume 1. Flash Diffusion Business, FDB300096.

Lipua Lipua (Lipwa Lipwa)
'Kamale' on *Kamale & Lipwa Lipwa*. Sonodisc, CD36567.

Loketo (with Aurlus Mabele and Diblo Dibala)
Extra Ball. Shanachie, 64028.
Soukous Trouble. Shanachie, 64025.

Los Angel
Several works not mentioned in the text appear on *Compilation Musique Congolaise: Bantous Zembe Zembe*. Sonodisc, CD36591.

Pablo Lubadika
'Bo Mbanda' on *Sound d'Afrique*. Mango 162539697-2.
'Madeleina' on *Sound d'Afrique II 'Soukous'*. Mango, 162539754-2.

Aurlus Mabele
'Africa Mousso' on *Trente Ans de Musique Africaine, 1960-1990*. Sonodisc, MC52910. (Cassette only; CD version does not contain this song.)

Madilu System
Sans Commentaire. Stern's Africa, STCD1055.

Maloko
Soul on Fire. African Music Gallery, AMG006.

Sam Mangwana
Rumba Music. Stern's Africa, STCD9003.
'Maria Tebbo' on *Sam Mangwana*. Stern's Africa, STCD3011.

Mbilia Bel
Désolé!!! Mélodie, 66917-2.
Phénomène. Flash Diffusion Business, FDB300016.

Pamelo Mounk'a
'L'Argent Appelle L'Argent' and 'Samantha, Tresor Hindou' on *Volume 1 des Plus Grands Succès de Pamelo Mounk'a*. Karac, 44430.

M'Pongo Love
'Ndaya' and 'Pas Possible Maty' on *Compilation Musique Congolo-Zaïroise*. Sonodisc, 36531.

Négro Succès
'Libanga na Libumu' on *Siongo Bavon Marie Marie & l'Orchestre Négro-Succès*. Ngoyarto, NG023.
'Lucie Tozongana' on *Le Négro Succès de Bholen & Bavon Marie-Marie*. Sonodisc, CD36583.
'Maseke ya Meme' on *Compilations Orchestres Congolo-Zaïrois*. Sonodisc, CD36537.

Select discography

Papa Noël
Haute Tension. Les Mampoko's, MPK001.

O.K. Jazz
As this book went to press, Stern's Music was about to issue a retrospective of Franco's work. The four-CD boxed set was slated to include several of the songs mentioned in this book, accompanied by an illustrated booklet about the life and works of this great musician. Look for: *Francophonic: The Essential Recordings of Franco Luambo Makiadi, King of Congo Music, and his O.K. Jazz, 1953–1988*. Stern's Music, STCD 3015.

Attention na SIDA. Sonodisc, CDS6856.
Les Rumeurs. Sonodisc, CDS6981.
'Babomi Mboka' on *Franco et l'O.K. Jazz*, volume 1. Sonodisc, CD36502.
'Chérie Bondowe' on *Mayaula Mayoni: The Best Of*, volume 1. Sonodisc, CDS6850.
'Chicotte' and 'Quatre Boutons' on *Franco et l'OK Jazz*. Sonodisc, CD36522.
'Course au Pouvoir' on *Franco, Vicky, Edo & L'OK Jazz: la Belle Epoque*. Sonodisc, CD36553.
'Ebale ya Zaïre' on *Franco, Simaro et le TP OK Jazz*. Sonodisc, CD36520.
'Faute ya Commerçant' on *Franco, Simaro, Sam Mangwana & le T.P.O.K. Jazz*. Sonodisc, CDS6854.
'Ida,' 'Mario' (parts 1 & 2), and 'La Vie des Hommes' on *Franco et le Tout Puissant O.K. Jazz*. Sonodisc, CD8461.
'Infidélité Mado' and 'Ma Hele' on *Franco et l'OK Jazz*. Sonodisc, CD36529.
'Mabele' (ntotu) on *Franco & le T.P.O.K. Jazz*. Sonodisc, CD36538.
'Nakoma Mbanda na Mama ya Mobali na Ngai' on *Franco: Nakoma Mbanda na Ngai*. Sonodisc, CD36571.
'Ngai Marie Nzoto Ebaba' on *Franco, Vicky et L'OK Jazz*. Sonodisc, CD36521.
'Non' on *3ème Anniversaire de la Mort du Grand-Maître Yorgho*. Kaluila, KL068.
'On Entre O.K. On Sort K.O.' on *Originalité*. RetroAfric, RETRO2CD.
'Tailleur' on *Franco & le T.P. OK Jazz*. Sonodisc, CDS6859.
'Tu Vois?' (Mamou) on *Franco Chante 'Mamou' (Tu Vois?)*. Sonodisc, CDS6853.
'La Vérité de Franco' on *Franco et TP OK Jazz*. Sonodisc, CD36518.

Koffi Olomide
'Elle et Moi' on *Tcha Tcho*. Stern's Africa, STCD1031. (This is not the same *Tcha Tcho* referred to in the text, which contained the hit 'Myriam Imortelle.' As of this writing, 'Myriam Imortelle' is out of print.)
'Fleur Rose' and 'N'Djoli' on *Koffi Olomide: Ba La Joie*. Ngoyarto, NG028.

Les Quatre Etoiles
'Enfant Bamileke' on *Sangonini*. Stern's Africa, STCD1049.

John Storm Roberts
Afro-Cuban Comes Home: The Birth and Growth of Congo Music. Original Music (cassette), OMWP01. (Narration with examples of the music being discussed.)

Ry-Co Jazz
Yo La! Hibiscus Records, 92001–2.
'Bana Ry-Co,' 'Caramba da ma Vida,' 'Give Me Bombolo,' and 'Twist with the Docteur' on *Rumba 'Round Africa: Congo/Latin Action from the 1960s*. RetroAfric, RETRO10CD.

Soukous Stars
Megamix. Syllart/Stern's, SYLCD83100.

Thu Zaina (Thu Zahina)
Several works not mentioned in the text appear on *Coup de Chapeau*. RetroAfric, RETRO14CD.

Trio Madjesi
The works mentioned in the text are out of print, but several others are available. Look for *Trio Madjesi: Butteur*. Sonodisc, CD36587.

Tshala Muana
Mutuashi. Stern's Africa, STCD1069.

Verckys
'Nakomitunaka' on *Les Merveilles du Passé*. Sonodisc, CD36501.

Victoria Eleison
'Kimpiatu' on *Les Meilleurs Succès de Victoria Eleison*, volume 2. Flash Diffusion Business, FDB300093.
'Sans Préavis' on *Les Meilleurs Succès de Victoria Eleison*, volume 1. Flash Diffusion Business, FDB300092.

Viva La Musica
Foridoles. Sonodisc, CD72424.
Pôle Position. Sonodisc, CDS8815.
'Analengo' and 'Matebu' on *Papa Wemba & l'Orchestre Viva La Musica*. Glenn Music, GM312001.
'Mère Supérieure' on *La Naissance de l'Orchestre Viva La Musica de Papa Wemba*, volume 1. Ngoyarto, NG026.

Papa Wemba
Papa Wemba. Stern's Africa, STCD1026.

Wendo and Bowane
'Marie-Louise' on *Ngoma: The Early Years, 1948–1960*. Popular African Music, pamap 101.

Wenge Musica
Kala-yi-Boeing. Wibe, WIBE001CD.

Zaïko Langa Langa
Sans Issue. Sun, JWS616.
Zaïko Langa Langa. Hits Inoubliables, volume 4. Plus de Paris, EPP07. (Contains the songs from *Paiement Cash*.)
'Crois-Moi' on *Zaïko Langa Langa: Hits Inoubliables*, volume 7. Plus de Paris, EPP017.
'Liwa ya Somo' on *Les Eveilleurs de l'Orchestre Zaïko Langa Langa*, volume 2. Ngoyarto, NG014.
'Mbeya-Mbeya' on *Jeunes Orchestres du Congo/Zaïre des Années 70*. Sonodisc, CD36539.
'Onassis ya Zaïre' on *Zaïko Langa Langa*. Flash Diffusion Business, FDB300241.
'Vie ya Mosolo' on *Compilation Musique Congolo-Zaïroise*. Sonodisc, CD36531.

Acknowledgments

The idea for this book originated over a dozen years ago when the late Docteur Nico visited Washington, D.C. My friend Ibrahim Kanja Bah of the African Music Gallery, who played host to Nico, called me at my (then) home in Berkeley, California, and urged me to come to Washington to meet the legendary guitarist. I went almost immediately and recorded one of the last interviews Nico ever gave. I am grateful to Ibrahim for introducing me to Nico and Tabu Ley Rochereau, and for interpreting my interviews with these two great artists. During the course of my writing this book, Ibrahim has continued to supply insights and information from his wealth of knowledge about African music.

When I began my research in earnest in the early nineties Jean Serge Essous showed me the way. Essous provided the book's outline with his oral history of the music during several hours of conversation in Paris. Later he acted as my host in Brazzaville, setting up interviews with other musicians and introducing me to Saturnin Pandi, who in turn allowed me access to his 'Orchestre Bantou Museum.' Across the river in Kinshasa, Moniania Roitelet took me in and arranged my interviews with musicians there. I am forever thankful to these three pioneers of Congolese music.

In the Netherlands, Peter Toll graciously made his extensive library of African music available to me and spent many hours of his own time gathering helpful bits of information. Also in the Netherlands, Stefan Werdekker agreed to allow me access to his incredible treasure of Congolese music and videos, even though he had no idea who I was and had reservations about anyone attempting a project as vast as the telling of the history of Congolese popular music. Stefan's and Peter's assistance has made this a much better book than it would otherwise have been.

Additional help with music and videos came from Vincent Luttman in London;

Acknowledgments 417

Ken Braun at Stern's Music in New York; C.C. Smith, editor of *The Beat* magazine; Leo Sarkisian, the Voice of America's 'music man for Africa'; Jaspar Chantal and Claude Dogon in Brussels; Marina Bernelle of Radio-Télévision Belge de la Communauté Française; Tony Ziselberger at the House of Musical Traditions in Takoma Park, Maryland; and from (Maurice) Makaya Dianuaku, Richard Henderson, Banister Koroma, and Terry Mahoney.

Belgian jazz historian Robert Pernet not only came to my aid with music from his pristine collection of Congolese 78 r.p.m. records, but he opened his archive of printed material from the days of the Belgian Congo. Pernet also introduced me to Charles Hénault, whose recollections, photos, and documents from his days with African Jazz were immensely helpful. Also in Belgium thanks must go to Dizzy Mandjeku, whose assistance went far beyond the ordinary interview; to Jean Darlier, Nicole Dethier, and Georges Martens, for their help in piecing together the story of Olympia; and to the staff of the Musée Royal de l'Afrique Centrale at Tervuren.

In Paris, several members of the staff of Radio France Internationale provided me with significant assistance. Maïc Chomel introduced me to her colleagues, thus paving the way for my access to RFI materials. Georges Mettra provided hours of listening to RFI's collection of Congolese 78s. Anne Khédir allowed me to photograph record labels and jackets from the collection at the RFI Discothèque. And Claude Nahmias opened her RFI documents archive to me. Additional thanks to Gilles Sala, whose links to Congolese music go back to the days when he covered the Round Table conference in 1960; to Michel de Breteuil of *Amina* and *Bingo* magazines for photos from the *Bingo* archives; and to Jean Bergé of Disco France for help with the story of Ngoma.

In London, Dr. Janet Topp Fargion of the British Library's National Sound Archive and Suzanne Lewis of the EMI Music Archives provided information about HMV's famous GV series of Latin American 78s; Martin Sinnock 'Muana Machete' contributed photographs.

And in the United States, C.C. Smith, my editor at *The Beat*, read and commented on the manuscript and otherwise urged me on to complete the work. Ken Braun also commented on the manuscript. Ken and his wife Bosondo, along with Veronique Lala, Aimée Kanyankogote, Betty Sekimongo, and Ricardo Lemvo, helped with Lingala translations. Kenneth Bilby arranged for and interpreted our joint interview with Raymond 'Ray Braynck' Kalonji. Maria Foscarinis – with an assist from Madame Krissoula and Monsieur Mimis of the Greek Community Center in Kinshasa – helped to track down Basile Papadimitriou. Leon Gast gave me a look through his camera lens at Zaïre 74. Leni Sinclair provided wonderful photos from her collection. Millie J. Flory created original maps and made valuable suggestions for the cover design. Helen Winternitz loaned me books from her collection of works on the two Congos. The great staff of the Library of Congress facilitated my research there.

Acknowledgments

Finally, thanks to the Congolese journalists who diligently covered the music scene and to the hundreds of musicians and bands whose names – for the sake of what I hope is a coherent narrative – I omitted but who, nevertheless, contributed to the music's development and to the joyful ambiance of Brazzaville and Kinshasa.

I am extremely grateful to the following artists and music business people who were kind enough to allow me to interview them:

Abeti Masikini
Gérard Akueson
Bill Alexandre
Ibrahim Kanja Bah
Ballou Canta
Bopol Mansiamina
Michel Boybanda
Joe Boyd (by phone)
Nikiforos Cavvadias
Dalienst Ntesa
Michel David
Dechaud Mwamba
Dessoin Bosuma
Gerry Dialungana
Diblo Dibala
Manu Dibango
Emeneya Mubiala
Jean Serge Essous
Guy-Léon Fylla
Fylla Saint-Eudes
Edo Ganga
Eddy Gustave
Charles Hénault
Jimmy Houetinou
Roger Izeidi
Alexandros Jeronimidis
Pepe Kalle
Raymond Kalonji
Kanda Bongo Man
Colette LaCoste
Lokassa ya Mbongo
Lukombo Shimita
Lutumba Simaro
Aurlus Mabele
Malambu ma Kizola

Nino Malapet
Jerry Malekani
Ben Mandelson (by letter)
Dizzy Mandjeku
Sam Mangwana
Charles Maniatakis
Kosmos Moutouari
Manzenza Sala Munsala
Mbilia Bel
Moniania Roitelet
Pamelo Mounk'a
Isaac Musekiwa
Papa Noël Nedule
Fredo Ngando
Docteur Nico
Nyboma Mwan Dido
Koffi Olomide
Ouattara Moumouni
Z. van Wulfften Palthe
Saturnin Pandi
Basile Papadimitriou (by letter)
Xavier Pelgrims de Bigard
François Post
Gilles Sala
Rikky Siméon
Rigo Star
Syran M'Benza
Tabu Ley Rochereau
Faya Tess
Tshala Muana
Papa Wemba
Wendo Kolosoyi
Wuta Mayi
Yondo Kusala

Index

a/c = author/composer

Abeti Masikini, 67, 207, 280, 295–7, 315, 318, 319; American tour spoiled by Mobutu, 194; awarded gold record, 319; background of, 190–91; Bade Stars Music and, 295, 320, 383; children of, 220, 295; dancers (Tigresses) of, 220, 280, 315, 318; death of, 383; Les Redoutables and, 220, 296–7, 319, 320, 377; moves to Paris, 318–19; plays Carnegie Hall, 193–4; plays the Olympia, 191–2, 220; relationship with Akueson, 220; returns home a star, 192–3, 210, 219; tours of, 191, 238, 383. Works written or recorded by: 192, 319, 383
Abidjan, 244, 246, 248, 250, 256, 268, 273, 278, 279, 283, 314–15, 370. *See also* Côte d'Ivoire
Abumba Masikini, 191, 192, 220
'Accident ya Peuple' (a/c Kosmos), 237
Acquired immune deficiency syndrome (AIDS), 354–5, 363, 371
Adé, Sunny, 262, 290, 334, 335
Adios Records, 247
Adjos (musician), 137
Adoula, Cyrille, 119
'Affaire Video' (a/c Mangwana), 280

AFL–CIO, 196
'Africa' (a/c Beya Maduma), 315
Africa Mousso (Aurlus Mabele), 324, 325
Africa Worldwide (Afrisa), 390
Africamania label, 295
African All Stars: breakup of, 249–50; connections to Paris groups, 256–7, 260–61, 268–70, 320; formation of, 245–6, 315; musicians of, 245–6, 249, 320, 348, 383; reunion of, 279–80; style of, 246–9, 270, 325. Works recorded by: 247–9, 256–7, 261, 262, 268, 280
African Fiesta, 111–16, 125–7, 138, 141, 144, 188, 229
African Fiesta National. *See* Afrisa International
African Fiesta 66. *See* Afrisa International
African Fiesta Sukisa, 127–8, 131, 134, 137–41, 146, 183–4, 252. *See also* Kasanda wa Mikalayi
'African Jazz' (author unknown), 45
African Jazz, 95, 110, 134, 235, 276; breakup of, 111–14, 167; Eschgo and, 65–7, formation of, 44–6; meets Negro Jazz at Chez Faignond, 49–50; musical arrangements of, 69, 96; musicians of, 44, 46, 66–7, 87–8, 89–90, 100, 104, 142, 143, 163, 252–3, 296; O.K. Jazz and, 98–9; rebuilds with new musicians, 116; records in Brussels, 86, 95–8; Round Table conference and, 83–8; stylistic school of, 88–9, 225, 230, 299. Works recorded by: 45–6, 86, 91, 97–8, 104, 138, 248, 275. *See also* Kabasele Tshamala
African Jazz label, 86, 98. *See also* Surboum African Jazz
'African Jazz Mokili Mobimba' (a/c Dechaud), 97, 248, 275, 390
African Kings (band), 142
African label. *See* Fonior
African Rock (band), 66
African Soul-Dibango, 123
African Soul-Mizele et al. *See* Géant Orchestre Malebo
African Sun Music, 255
African Team, 134, 167, 184
Afrisa International (includes African Fiesta National and African Fiesta 66), 188, 221, 252, 303, 322; becomes African Fiesta National, 141; becomes Afrisa International, 172; dancers (Rocherett[e]s) of, 167, 180, 188; formed as African Fiesta 66, 127–9; musicians defect, 244–5; musicians of, 127, 141, 142, 144, 177, 180, 203, 208,

229–31, 253, 270, 279, 280, 288, 292, 294–5, 329, 342, 356, 371, 372, 379, 389–90; plays at Montreal World's Fair, 134; plays the Olympia, 167; Rochereau and Izeidi split, 143; stages super show, 329–30; suspended for slighting Mobutu, 141; tours of, 142, 238, 243–4, 245, 252, 281, 290, 329, 330, 372, 389; at Zaïre 74 festival, 207–8. See also Afrisa's works listed by title
Afrizam (band), 180, 191, 230
Afro International (band), 340
Afro Mogambo (night club), 188
Afro Rythmes label, 268, 270, 320, 322, 323, 324, 325, 380
Afro-Negro (night club), 123
Agbaya, 15
Agbepa Mumba 'Koffi Olomide,' 251, 347–8, 375, 378, 383
Air France (night club), 52, 149
Akangana, Marie-Louise, 382
Akueson, Gérard, 190–94, 220, 277, 295–8, 318–20, 383
Akumu Wakutu 'Nana,' 356, 357, 360
Albarika, Alhadji, 249, 250
Albertum Cinema, 18
Alexandre, Bill, 41–4, 48, 55–6, 58, 96, 195
Ali, Muhammad, 207, 208, 219
'Alléluia Mounk'a' (a/c Pamelo), 258
Allez-y Frères Soki label, 212
Ama, Armando, 244
Amba, Josephine, 68
Amba, Leon 'Zozo,' 124, 197, 244
Ambassador Records, 249
Americain, Orchestre, 21
Amida (band), 246
'Amina' (a/c Souzy Kasseya), 316
Amisi Ngoy 'Reddy,' 313, 333, 335
L'Amour et la Danse (Bantous de la Capitale), 352
Amour Fou/Crazy Love (Kanda Bongo Man), 327–8
'Analengo' (a/c Papa Wemba), 305, 335
Anges Noirs (night club), 84, 95
Angola, 5, 144, 227, 229, 242, 315, 326, 392
'Anna Mabele ya Ngoya' (a/c Franco), 56
Anti-Choc, 340–41, 378, 381
Anto (Michel) 'Evoloko,' 158, 213–17, 223, 302–3, 306, 310–11, 313, 338, 344

Antonopoulos, Constantin 'Dino,' 64–66, 102
Apollo 11 (dance), 136
Arcon, Jean 'Ty-Jan,' 326, 327
L'Argent Appelle l'Argent (Pamelo Mounk'a), 258–9, 261
Armando, Antoine 'Brazzos,' 42, 68–9, 83, 95, 100, 123, 129, 131–2, 138, 201
Article 15 (expression), 285, 334, 373
'Article 15 Beta Libanga' (Pepe Kalle), 285
'Aruna' (a/c Nico), 139
Assaka, Baba Ley, 260
Associated Sound Limited, 127
Association pour la Sauvegarde de la Culture et des Intérêts des Bakongo (ABAKO), 63, 79, 83–4, 90
Astra Cinema, 38
'Ata Ndele' (a/c Kosmos), 265
'Ata Ndele (mokili ekobaluka)' (a/c Adou Elenga), 71
'Attention na SIDA' (a/c Franco), 355, 356, 357
Authenticity, 171–4, 200, 206, 208, 294, 308, 347
Avedila 'Petit Poisson,' 342, 345, 381
Aziza 'Petit,' 346
Azpiazu, Don, 13

Ba Isifi Baye (band), 223
Ba La Joie (band), 251
'Baba Moussa' (a/c Tidiane Coulibaly), 316
Babindamana, Fidèle 'Zizi,' 162, 169
'Babomi Mboka' (a/c Franco), 68
Baby National (band), 146, 178
Bade Stars Music, 295, 297, 320
Badinga, Pierre, 164
Badmos (producer), 246–7, 249
Bah, Ibrahim Kanja, 288, 298, 359, 380
'Baila' (a/c Essous), 66
Bakolo Miziki (band), 235
'Bakosi Liwa ya Wendo' (a/c Wendo), 70
'Bakozila Trop' (a/c Simaro), 204
Bakuba Mayopi (band), 288, 339
Bakunde Ilondjoko (Paul) 'Pablo,' 155–6, 211, 213, 304, 342, 344–6, 381
Balako, Henriette, 68
Ballou, Hyacinthe 'Ballou Canta,' 378, 387
BALUBAKAT, 90
Bamanabio, François, 20

Bamboula (band), 146, 189, 270, 288
Bamundele, Rigobert 'Rigo Star,' 224, 300, 318, 319, 320, 325–6, 331–2, 341, 348, 385–6
'Bana ba Cameroon' (a/c Mangwana), 269
Bana Mambo (band), 267
Bana Modja (band), 244
Bana Odeon (band), 284
Bana O.K. (band), 382
'Bana Ry-Co' (a/c Malekani), 108
Banengola 'Boffi,' 244, 319
'Banga Jhimmy' (a/c Jhimmy), 40
Baniel. See Itela Boketsu
Bansimba Baroza, 346
Bantous de la Capitale (Orchestre Bantou, Bantous Jazz), 111, 135, 162; decline of, 352, 377; Essous leaves, 133, 184; formation of, 80–82; government honors awarded to, 82, 116; musical arrangements of, 82, 116; musicians of, 80, 82, 100, 102–4, 116, 118, 120, 124, 129–30, 184, 186, 236–7, 246, 258, 352, 366, 377; plays at Dakar festival, 129–30, 133; records at Fonior, 105–6; records at STENCO, 107; reunification of, 237, 352–3; split within, 186, 377; tours of, 102–4, 236–7, 238, 249; twenty-fifth anniversary of, 352; Works recorded by: 105–6, 121, 130, 133–4, 136, 163, 352
'Les Bantous de la Capitale' (a/c Kouka), 106
Bantous Monument (band), 377, 381
Baroza, Dicky, 144
Baroza, Tino, 44, 46, 66, 72, 97, 139, 396
Basongeur (M'Pongo Love), 318
'Batela Makila na Ngai' (a.k.a. 'Sadou') (a/c Franco), 361n
Baudouin, King of Belgium, 80, 89, 91
Bavon Siongo 'Bavon Marie Marie,' 124–5, 160–62
Bazetta, Pierre 'De La France,' 72, 127, 137, 138
Bazizila, Jacques 'Souza Vangou,' 351
Bebey, Francis, 190
'Bedy' (a/c Kanda Bongo Man), 327

Index 421

Beguen Band, 72–3, 90, 127
Bel, Mbilia. *See* Mbilia Mboyo
Belgian Congo. *See* Congo,
 Democratic Republic of the
 Belgium: annexes Congo Free
 State, 10–11; early history of,
 7; grants independence to
 Congo, 83, 86, 91; intervenes
 in independent Congo, 92–3,
 120, 242; resistance to colonial
 policies of, 60–63, 78–80. *See
 also* Brussels
Belguide (band), 157
Belkos, Pierre, 328
Bella Bella: 156–7, 159, 177–8,
 210–12, 253, 267, 268, 270,
 349. *See also* Soki Dianzenza;
 Soki Vangu
Bella Bella label, 212
Bella Mambo, 177, 212, 266–7.
 See also Soki Dianzenza
Bellow, Bella, 190–91, 280
Benamayi, Gilbert, 342, 346
Benetar, Gabriel Moussa, 33, 34,
 36, 38, 40, 41, 45, 46, 48, 63,
 65
Benetar, Joseph, 33, 34, 46, 63
Benin (Dahomey), 15–16, 103,
 123, 249, 294–5, 297, 323,
 349, 373
Benson, Bobby, 104
Berlin West Africa Conference,
 9–10
Berne Copyright Convention,
 195
The Best (band), 346
Beya Maduma 'Moro Maurice,'
 180, 314–15
Beyou Ciel. *See* Efomi Mondjoy
Bholen. *See* Bombolo wa Lokole
'Bibilé' (a/c Abeti), 192
Big Stars (band), 380–81
Bills, 78, 80, 149, 154, 222
'Bilombe ba Gagne' (a/c
 Kabasele), 91
'Bilombe ya Africa' (a/c Nico),
 114
'Bimaka' (O.K. Jazz), 226
Bimi Ombale (André), 159, 213,
 303, 342, 345–7, 381
Bingo magazine, 108
Biolo, Alphonse, 208
Bipoli. *See* Guimarães, Paulino de
Bismarck, Otto von, 9
Bitshoumanou, Francis 'Celi
 Bitshou,' 104, 145, 181, 292
Bitsikou, Théo, 186, 352
Biyela, Gérard 'Gerry,' 130, 138,
 186, 236, 352, 377
The Black Devils (band), 222,
 244

Black Mic-Mac (film), 349
'Bo Mbanda' (a/c Pablo
 Lubadika), 261
Bobongo (studio), 375
Bobongo Stars (band), 279
Bokasa, John 'Johnny,' 127, 138,
 141, 142
Bokelo Isenge (Jean) 'Johnny,'
 123–4, 146, 210, 240, 241,
 339
Bolenge Boteku 'Djo Mali,' 302,
 303, 306, 310, 311, 338, 381
'Bolingo na Brazza' (a/c Nico),
 296
'Bolingo na Ngai na Beatrice'
 (a/c Franco), 55
'Bolingo ya Bomwana' (Thu
 Zaina), 159
Boloko Manzangi 'Safro,' 306,
 311, 336
Bolya, Paul, 90
Boma Bango label, 118, 195
Bombenga Wewando (Jean), 116,
 136, 146, 161, 163, 210, 253,
 267, 280
Bombolo wa Lokole (Léon)
 'Bholen,' 100, 124, 160, 162,
 170
'Bon Samaritan' (a/c Papa Noel),
 292
Bonane Bungu 'Wawali,' 372,
 390
'Bonbon Kojack' (a/c Mawatu
 Moke), 295
'Bonbon Sucré' (a/c Rochereau),
 97
Bondo Gala (Victor) 'Bovic,' 137,
 153, 244
Bonghat Tshekabu (a.k.a. Saak
 Saakul) 'Max Sinatra,' 153,
 175–7, 227
Bongo, Gustave 'Ngoss,' 329,
 331, 343–4, 346
Bongo Wende, 211, 333
Bonne Espérance, 19
Bono Music, 377
Bopol. *See* Mansiamina Mfoko
Bora Uzima Kote (Henriette)
 'Miss Bora,' 117–18, 123, 127,
 141, 144, 188, 194
Bosuma (Nicolas) 'Dessoin,' 59,
 129, 131, 202, 295, 362, 368,
 370
Boteku Bohomba, 368, 382
Boucher (dance), 121, 135
'Bougie ya Motema' (a/c Nico),
 139
Boukaka, Franklin, 163–6,
 185–6, 236, 274
Bowane, Henri, 4–5, 11–13, 22,
 26, 52, 56, 76, 107, 123,

381–2; Esengo and, 64–5;
 Loningisa and, 30–32, 54, 56,
 58, 123; Ngoma and, 28–30
Bowole, Henri, 138
Boybanda, Michel (Boybanda
 Baba) 'Michaux,' 120, 129,
 132, 162, 163, 172, 181, 201,
 204–5, 230, 244
Boyd, Joe, 327–8, 388
Boyimbo, François 'Gobi,' 35, 36
Boziana, Bozi. *See* Mbenzuana
 Ngamboni
Brazza, Pierre Savorgnan de,
 6–9, 10, 14, 66
Brazzaville: Bacongo district of,
 20; bars of, 74; conditions in,
 350, 377; description of, 3–4,
 20, 49, 101, 162; destruction
 of, 392; founding of, 7–9;
 Lingala usage in, 77–8; map
 of, 50; as market for Kinshasa
 bands, 238–9; political culture
 of, 162–3; population of, 17,
 30, 238; Poto-Poto district of,
 20, 49; racial segregation in,
 20; rural people move to, 4,
 17–18, 30, 67; women of, 67.
 See also Congo, Republic of
Brazzos. *See* Armando, Antoine
Britain, 9. *See also* London
British Broadcasting Corporation
 (BBC), 108
Brown, James, 159, 174, 207,
 210
Brussels, 83–6, 252, 282, 359,
 364–5. *See also* Belgium
'Buala Yayi Mambu' (a/c
 Pamelo), 259
Buanga, Aime, 372
'Le Bûcheron' (a/c Boukaka),
 166
Buissert, Auguste, 78
Bukasa, Léon, 30, 71–2, 90, 124,
 170, 210
'Bukasa Aleli' (a/c Bukasa), 72
Bukassa, Joseph 'Jojo,' 104
Bumba Massa (Samuel) 'Samy,'
 124
Burkina Faso (Upper Volta), 110,
 297, 315, 349
Burundi, 119, 329, 357
Buse, J.P., 342, 345
Bwingi Kinanga '737,' 300

Cairophon label, 273
'Camarade Mabe' (a/c Essous),
 106
Cameroon, 98, 107, 108, 123,
 139, 188, 190, 244, 246, 259,
 262, 263, 318, 319, 325, 380
Canada, 134, 290, 362

422 Index

Candrix, Alfons 'Fud,' 40, 41, 46
Canta Moçambique (Mangwana), 280
'Cantique' (a/c Kanda Bongo Man), 327
Cão, Diogo, 5, 11
'Caramba da ma Vida' (a/c Casino), 108
Cardin, Pierre, 192
Carnegie Hall, 193–4, 219, 383
Carthage label, 388
Casques Bleus (band), 303
Catholic Church, 171, 173
Cavacha (dance), 214, 304
Cavvadias, Nikiforos, 28, 41, 47, 70, 72, 88, 143, 273
CBS/Sony, 387
'Ce N'est que Ma Secretaire' (a/c Pamelo), 259
'Cedou' (a/c Simaro), 202
Celluloid label, 321, 356
Central African Republic (Oubangui-Chari), 11, 103, 107, 194, 208, 244, 250, 258, 259, 296
Cercul Jazz, 163–4
CFA franc, 238, 350
Chachachá, 66, 72, 73, 108
Chad, 11, 107
Les Champions, (African All Stars), 248–9
Chantal. See Kazadi, Etienne
Chaussettes Noires (band), 155
Checain. See Lola Djangi
'Cher Ami' (a/c Mbilia Bel), 331
Cherche une Maison à Louer pour Moi, Chéri (O.K. Jazz), 360
'Chérie Awa' (Les 3 Caballeros), 42–3
'Chérie B.B.' (a/c Mangwana), 361
'Chérie Bondowe' (a/c D'Oliveira), 226
'Chérie Bondowe' (a/c Mayaula), 226, 239, 240
'Chérie Makwanza' (a/c Lukau), 260, 268
Les Cheveux Crépus (band), 263
Chez Engels (night club), 142, 195
Chez Fabrice à Bruxelles (O.K. Jazz), 288
Chez Faignond (night club), 49, 81, 102–3, 377
Chez La-Bas (night club), 117
'Chicotte' (a/c Franco), 126
China, 206, 383
Choc Choc Choc label, 255, 283
Choc Choc Choc 1983 (Franco and Tabu Ley), 283–4
Choc Musica (band), 340
Choc Stars, 311, 338–9, 340, 343, 371, 378, 381
'Cimetière' (a/c Kwamy), 128
Cinq Punaises (band), 155
City Five (band), 188
'Clara Badimuene' (a/c Bukasa), 72
Coastmen, 15, 19, 28–9
Cobantou (band), 124, 146, 210
Cold war, 93, 206, 219, 238, 373
'Colette' (a/c Mangwana), 144
Colonialism, 7–11, 60–63, 78–80
Comité d'Etudes du Haut Congo, 7
Compagnie d'Enregistrements Folkloriques Africains (CEFA), 41–4, 48, 52, 55–6, 66, 68, 95, 105, 150, 195, 200
Compagnie Minière du Congo Français, 17
Concierto National (band), 157
Confédération des Associations Ethniques du Katanga (CONAKAT), 90
Conference of Catholic Bishops, 373
Conga Jazz (band), 123, 152, 202
Conga 68 (band), 146. See also Conga Succès
Conga Succès (band), 123–4, 146
Congo (newspaper), 75, 86
Congo, Democratic Republic of the (Kinshasa) (includes Congo Free State, Belgian Congo, and Zaïre): becomes Democratic Republic of the Congo, 392, 396; becomes Zaïre, 170–71; beer consumption in, 75, 149; college of general commissioners installed in, 94; conditions under Mobutu regime in, 148–9, 206–7, 375; early history of, 5–11; economic decline of, 217–18, 219, 238–9, 242–3, 284–5, 308, 350, 372–3, 375; elections in, 90, 148, 286; foreign policy of, 206, 238, 242; Greeks in, 23; independence of, 83–7, 90–91; map of, 8; Mobutu driven from power in, 1, 391–2; movement toward political reform in, 373–5; name changes in, 131, 170–72; political parties form, 79–80, 374; post-independence crisis in, 92–4, 106, 118–20; relations with Congo-Brazzaville, 101, 119–20, 185; resistance to colonialism in, 60–63, 78–80; students killed in, 148, 374; world wars and, 17–18, 19. See also Authenticity; Mobutu Sese Seko; Zaïreanization
Congo Jazz (band), 202
Congo music, 4, 108
Congo, Republic of (Brazzaville) (includes Moyen-Congo and People's Republic of Congo): becomes People's Republic, 163; early history of, 5–11; economy of, 101, 350; foreign policy of, 94, 101, 119–20, 238; independence of, 79, 81, 94; leadership changes in, 102, 162, 185, 236, 376, 392; map of, 8; political reform in, 375–6; relations with Congo-Kinshasa, 94, 101, 119–20, 185; resistance to colonialism in, 61, 79; world wars and, 17–18
Congo-Moderne (night club), 11
Congo (Zaïre) River, 3, 5, 101, 171
Congo Rumba (band), 19
'Congo ya Sika' (Vicky and Roger), 43
La Congolaise (night club), 352, 353, 377
Congolia, 18–19, 25, 27
Conscience Africaine, 62–3, 79
Conseil National de Liberation (CNL), 119, 120
Consommé Local (Sam Mangwana), 279
Continental (band), 183, 201, 208, 238, 270
Contre ma Volonté (Afrisa), 330
Coopération (Franco and Sam Mangwana), 278–9
Coquilhatville. See Mbandaka
Le Cosmique (night club), 309
Côte d'Ivoire, 107, 110, 191, 244, 266, 297, 315, 317, 349. See also Abidjan
Coup de la Vie (Anti-Choc), 340
'Course au Pouvoir' (a/c Franco), 131
Les Cousins Bleus (band), 124
Cover label, 216
La Crèche (night club), 298
'Crois-Moi' (a/c Nyoka Longo), 304
Cuba, 20–21, 163, 237
Cuxac, Daniel, 283, 314

Dadet, Emmanuel, 22, 51
'Dadou' (a/c Pepe Kalle), 301
Dahomey. *See* Benin
Dakar, 103, 107–8, 129–31, 133, 180, 323. *See also* Senegal
'Dalida' (a/c Djuna Djanana), 310
Dalienst. *See* Ntesa Nzitani
'Danse des Bouchers' (a/c Mujos), 121
Danyla (musician), 152
David, Michel, 273, 321, 322
De Brazzaville à la Havane (Bantous de la Capitale), 163
De Gaulle, Charles, 79
De La France. *See* Bazetta, Pierre
De La Lune. *See* Lubelo, Daniel
De Saio, Manoka, 30
Debaba Mbaki 'Debaba el Shabab,' 307, 311, 339, 381
Decca Records, 95
'Déception d'Amour' (a/c M'Pongo Love/Dino Vangu), 264
'Déception Motema' (a/c Bopol), 260
Dechaud, *zee* Mwamba Mongala
Defao. *See* Matumona Lulendo
Dele Pedro, 104, 118, 129, 202
Dema (producer), 200
'Demayo' (a/c Mavatiku), 180
Depuissant. *See* Kaya, Antoine
Désolé!!! (Mbilia Bel), 385–6
Desvarieux, Jacob, 266
Detta, Jolie. *See* Kamenga Kayobote
Deutsche Grammophon, 42
Deux Temps (Victoria Eleison), 337–8, 355
Dewayon. *See* Ebengo Isenge
'Dewayon Makila Mabe' (a/c Dewayon), 55
Diaboua, Isidore 'Lièvre,' 51
Diaboua, Groupe, 51, 56
Dialungana Kasia 'Gerry,' 230, 282, 362, 371
Diamant Bleu (band), 127
Diana. *See* Nsimba, Simon
Diangani, Nestor, 129, 152
Diatho Lukoki, 280
Diawar (Ismael Lô), 323
Diawara, Ange, 185–6, 236
Dibango, Manu, 122–3, 207, 244, 266, 279, 314; African Jazz and, 84, 95, 96–8, 112, 113, 276; African Team and, 134; records with Franklin Boukaka, 165–6
Diblo Dibala. *See* Yancomba Dibala
Dick, Richard, 261–2, 295, 322

Dicky (musician), 80
Dieu Voit Tout (Koffi Olomide), 348
Dihunga, Hubert 'Djeskin,' 100, 124
Dikalo (band), 263
Dilumona (Joseph) 'Dilu,' 179, 300, 301, 349
Diluvila, Etienne 'Baskis,' 35–6, 46, 67
Dindo Yogo, 305, 310, 311, 313, 342, 346
Dinos, Jean, 80, 100
Dionga li Djembo (Dominique) 'Apôtre,' 137, 146
'Direct Me' (a/c Redding/Cropper), 380
Disques Sonics, 256
Disques Vogue, 108
Dithéo Bar, 117
Ditutala Kuama, 339
Djali, Christophe, 117, 131
Djeffard. *See* Lukombo Mayemba
Djessy (Kanda Bongo Man), 268
Djo Mali. *See* Bolenge Boteku
Djonolo, Givé, 340
Djuna Djanana, 305, 310, 311, 338–9, 381
Docteur Nico. *See* Kasanda wa Mikalayi
Dodoly, Matou, 340–41
D'Oliveira, Manuel, 30, 70, 170, 226, 248, 268
Dona Beatriz, 61
Dongala, Henri 'Fredos,' 141, 142
Doula, Georges, 35, 38, 44, 47
Dragon Phénix label, 263

Eagles (band), 155
'Ebale ya Zaïre' (a/c Simaro), 202
'Ebandeli ya Mosala' (a/c Kosmos), 130, 265
Ebengo Isenge (Paul) 'Dewayon,' 52–4, 55, 56, 123–4, 138, 146, 196, 197, 210
Ebibi, Marcelle (a.k.a. Marcelle Fylla), 43, 68
Ebuya Lange 'Doris,' 300
'Echantillon ya Pamba' (a/c Lessa Lassan), 139
Les Echos Noirs (band), 190
Les Ecureuils (band), 155, 191, 192
Eddy'Son, 256–9, 266, 272, 320, 352. *See also* Gustave, Eddy
Edipop label, 255
'Edith' (a/c Kosmos/Massamba), 265
Editions Congolaise du Disque (ECODIS). *See* Fonior

Edouard, Georges, 30, 36
Efomi Mondjoy 'Beyou Ciel,' 372, 389
Efonge Isekofeta 'Gina wa Gina,' 213, 216, 223, 344
Ekula 'Adamo,' 346
'El Manicero' (a/c M. Simóns), 15, 21
Elenga, Adou, 30, 71, 268
Elenga, Zacharie 'Jhimmy,' 34–6, 38, 39, 40, 115, 296
Elima (newspaper), 374
'Elisa Kina Kimbwa' (a/c L.M. Kiland), 261
Elisabethville. *See* Lubumbashi
'Eliyo' (a/c Evoloko), 310
Elle et Moi (Koffi Olomide), 348
Elo Music (band), 295
Emancipation (band), 189
Emany Mata Likambe (Joseph), 118, 196, 274
Emeneya. *See* Mubiala Emeneya
EMI studio (Lagos), 247, 248
Emoro. *See* Tumba Ayila
Emotion (Papa Wemba), 389
Empire Bakuba (includes African Choc and Les Bakuba), 177–9, 217, 255, 285, 300–302, 303, 313, 339, 343, 348–9, 375, 378, 381
Empompo Loway (Michel) 'Deyesse,' 124, 180, 208, 221–2, 233, 253, 264, 279, 280, 294–6, 318, 368, 369–70
'Enfant Bamileke' (a/c Wuta Mayi), 325
Engbondu, François 'Franco,' 42, 43, 52
Epanza Makita, 118, 164, 195
Epayo, Alphonse 'Le Brun,' 100, 201
L'Esclave (Viva La Musica), 333, 335
Esengo: 70, 72, 93, 102, 106, 196; founding of, 64–7, 107, 381; musicians of, 64–7, 68, 89, 116, 120, 123, 138, 152
Essous, Jean Serge 'Trois S' (a.k.a. Jerry Lopez), 121, 164, 169–70, 358, 387; African Team and, 134; background of, 35, 50–52; Bantous de la Capitale and, 80–82, 102–7, 129–30, 133, 162, 184, 186, 236, 352, 377; Fsengo and, 65–6; Loningisa and, 52, 56; Negro Jazz and, 49–50, 52; O.K. Jazz and, 56–8, 59, 227; Ry-Co Jazz and, 134, 184, 380
'Essous Spiritou' (a/c Mujos), 184

424 Index

'Eswi yo Wapi' (a/c Tabu Ley/ Mbilia Bel), 281–2, 287, 290, 331
Etari, Henri, 72
Etisomba Lokindji (Antoinette), 147, 188–9, 192, 194
Les Etoiles (band), 155, 288. *See also* Minzoto Wella Wella
Euro-pop, 388
Evans, Maurice, 42, 44
'Evénement' (a/c Papa Wemba), 306
Evoloko. *See* Anto
Evolués, 62–3, 78
Evvi label, 255
Excelsior, Orchestre, 19
Expérience 9 (Grand Zaïko), 380
Eyenga Moseka (Lucie), 67, 68, 77, 296–7

'Fabrice Akende Sanogo' (a/c Franco), 361n
'Falansua' (a/c Franco), 226
The Famous (band), 155
Fania All Stars, 207
Les Fantômes (band), 162
Fariala ya Yembo (Jean-Marie Assumani) 'Franc Lassan,' 72, 123, 197
'Farya' (Choc Stars), 339
Fataki, Joe 'Joe Fat,' 333
Faubourg (night club), 291, 362
Faugus. *See* Izeidi, Augustin
'Faute ya Commerçant' (a/c Simaro), 279
'Faux Millionnaire' (a/c Kwamy), 125–6
Faya Tess. *See* Kishila Ngoyi
Fédération Nationale des Artistes Musiciens, 196
Femme Commerçante (Mpongo Love), 264–5, 318
Feruzi, Camille, 20–21, 24, 30, 70, 72, 173
Festival de la Chanson (Kinshasa), 147, 156, 188
Festival des Maquisards, 142, 144–5, 149, 151, 153, 180, 244, 288
Fiesta label. *See* Fonior
Fiesta Populaire (band), 180, 288
Filament Music Publishers, 388
Firenze (dance), 309
Flash label, 128, 150
'Fleur Bakutu' (a/c Djo Mali), 310
'Fleur Rose' (a/c Olomide), 251
'Flowers of Luckyness' (a/c Musekiwa), 46
Fonior: CEFA subsidiary of, 56, 95, 150, 200; collapse of, 254–5, 273; creation of, 95–6; disposition of Congolese music catalog of, 255, 273–5; distributes Congolese records, 86, 95–6, 98, 105, 108, 127, 240; Editions Congolaise du Disque (ECODIS) subsidiary of, 95, 107, 150, 154; employs Izeidi, 56, 96, 104–5, 112, 129; labels of, 96, 105; other subsidiaries of, 95, 254–5, 273; Phonogram-Kenya and, 240; recording at, 96–9, 104–6, 111–12; Société Française du Son (SOFRASON) subsidiary of, 95, 150, 244, 254. *See also* MAZADIS
For Ever (Sam Mangwana and Franco), 361
Force Publique, 24, 77–8, 92
Foreman, George, 207–8, 219
Foridoles (Papa Wemba), 388–9
France: at Berlin conference, 9–10; claims African territories, 7–10; French Community and, 79, 81; French Equatorial Africa and, 11, 81; resistance to colonial policies of, 61, 62, 79; Sassou Nguesso and, 392; sends troops to Zaïre, 242; transfers power to independent Congo, 94. *See also* Paris
'Francine Keller' (Zaïko Langa Langa), 159
Francis, Roger, 283
Franco (François Engbondu). *See* Engbondu, François
Franco (Luambo Makiadi). *See* Luambo Makiadi
Franco Joue avec Sam Mangwana, 361
Franklin Boukaka à Paris, 165–6, 274
French Equatorial Africa, Federation of, 11, 81
'Fulani' (a/c Abeti), 192
Funky (dance), 304
Fylla, Guy-Léon, 13, 15, 20, 30, 40, 43, 76, 102, 163

Gabon, 11, 314, 318, 322, 329, 331, 343, 350
Ganga, Edouard 'Edo,' 186, 277, 299, 352, 358; Bantous de la Capitale and, 80, 82, 120, 130, 236–7, 352; discusses competition among studios, 70, 73–4; forms Bantous Monument, 377; Les Nzoi and, 186; Loningisa and, 55; Negro Jazz and, 49, 52; O.K. Jazz and, 68–70, 104, 117, 118, 119, 120, 227; vocal style of, 69–70, 215
Géant Orchestre Malebo (African Soul), 146, 172, 210, 276
Genidia label, 255, 281, 290
'Georgette Eckins' (a/c Mangwana), 247–8, 256, 268
'Georgine wa M.T.' (a/c Dalienst), 144
Germany, 9–10, 42, 252, 370
Ghana (Gold Coast), 15, 19, 62, 93, 249
Gilou, Thomas, 349
'Give Me Bombolo' (Ry-Co Jazz), 108
Gizenga, Antoine, 94
Gombe Cemetery, 277, 299, 358, 367
Gramophone (HMV), 86
Gramophone Company, 13
Gramophones, 25
Grand Zaïko Wa Wa, 303, 308, 309–10, 311, 313, 342, 346, 372, 379, 380, 381, 389
Les Grands Maquisards, 145, 153, 179, 210, 230, 267, 292
La griffe (dance), 308
La Griffe (night club), 309
Guadeloupe, 20, 84, 256, 326
Guaguancó, 20–21
Guest House, 40, 84
Guimarães, Paulino de 'Pepe Bipoli,' 224, 307, 311, 313, 333
Guinea, 107
Gustave, Eddy, 256–60, 272, 320, 322
GV series records, 13, 15, 18, 21
Guvano. *See* Vangu, Jean Paul

Haiti, 93, 134
Hallyday, Johnny, 136, 139
Hammersmith Palais, 291, 361
Hannibal Records, 327, 388
Haute Tension (Papa Noël), 389
Hawaii Bar, 158, 213
Hekimian, Denis, 268
'Hélène' (a/c Franco), 231–2
Hénault, Charles, 84, 87–8, 123
'Henriette' (a/c Jhimmy), 34
Hindoubill, 78. *See also* Bills
His Master's Voice (HMV), 13, 63, 86
Historia Musica (band), 311, 339
Home des Mulâtres, 57
Houetinou, Jimmy, 323–4, 325, 383, 385
Hourdebise, Jean, 18–19, 26
Huit Kilos. *See* Nseka Bimwela
La Hutte (night club), 276

Index 425

La Hutte label, 200
Hutu people, 391
Hyacinthe, Jimmy, 315–16

'Ida' (a/c Franco), 354
Ifanza (band), 267
Ikomo Ingange 'Djo Djo,' 244
Ileo, Joseph, 63, 79, 94
Ilosono, Denis, 132, 151, 195, 382
'Les Immortels' (a/c Boukaka), 164–5, 166
'In the Midnight Hour' (a/c Pickett/Cropper), 380
'Indépendance Cha Cha' (a/c Kabasele), 86
Indianga Toussaint, 348
Industrie Africaine du Disque (IAD), 285, 292, 296, 350, 356, 359, 377
Industrie Zaïroise du Son (IZASON), 285, 356
'Infidélité Mado' (a/c Bitshoumanou), 181
Innovation series records, 260–61, 269, 270, 325
International African Association, 7
International Association of the Congo, 9
International Federation of the Phonographic Industry (IFPI), 322
International Monetary Fund (IMF), 218
International Pelgrims Group. See Fonior
International Salsa Musique, 261–2
International Sam Mangwana, 268
International-Disques-Akué, 190
Isa label, 172
Islam, 233, 364
Island Records, 261–3, 290, 335, 387
Itela Boketsu 'Baniel,' 329, 356, 357, 360
Iyole (Kanda Bongo Man), 268
Izeidi, Augustin Futu 'Faugus,' 116, 123, 127, 138, 141, 142, 180
Izeidi Mokoy (Roger Dominique), 151, 180, 276; African Fiesta and, 111–12, 114–15, 126–7; African Fiesta (66) National and, 127–8, 141–2, 143; African Jazz and, 66, 83–4, 111–12; CEFA and, 41–4, 104–5, 150; Fonior and, 56, 96, 104–5, 112, 129,

274–5; record labels of, 114, 128, 150

'Jacky' (a/c Franco), 231–2, 355
Jadot Sombele 'le Cambodgien,' 224, 306
Jadotville, 92, 119
Jambo Jambo (night club and orchestre), 222–3
Jamel (band), 124, 175
Janssens, Emile, 92
Janssens, Fernand, 24, 32, 106
Japan, 206, 333, 335, 343–4, 388
Les Jardins Fleuris (night club), 252
Jazz, 16, 45, 57, 76
Jazz African (band), 84, 88, 116, 163
Jazz Bohème, 20
Jazz Mango, 72. See also Bukasa, Léon
JBZ studio, 279, 315
Je Suis Fâché (Abeti), 319
Jerk (dance), 136, 156
Jeronimidis, Alexandros, 24, 26, 33, 47, 143, 273
Jeronimidis, Nicolas, 23–8, 30, 47, 70. See also Ngoma
Jeunesse Mouvement National de la Révolution (JMNR), 162
Jhimmy. See Elenga, Zacharie
Jhimmy Chante (film), 36
João, André 'Depiano,' 72
Jobs (dance), 136
Josky. See Kiambukuta Londa
'J.T.' (a/c Kanda Bongo Man), 326
Juju, 262, 290, 291, 335

Kaba, Joseph, 49–50
Kabako, Lambert, 236, 352
Kabamba, William 'Serpent,' 141, 183
Kabasele Tshamala (Joseph) 'Le Grand Kalle,' 90, 108, 136, 139, 178, 316; African Jazz and, 44–6, 49–50, 63–7, 83–90, 91, 95, 96–8, 111–14, 116, 167, 235; African Team and, 134, 167, 184; background of, 36–8, 62–3; CEFA and, 41, 44; creates Surboum African Jazz label, 98, 150; death of, 276–8, 296, 299; decline of, 210, 244, 276; Esengo and, 63–7, 93, 116; helps O.K. Jazz record at Fonior, 98–9; made grand maître, 276; marriage of, 110–11; Opika and, 36–40,

44–6; as president of SONECA, 197; vocal style of, 88, 203, 215, 225, 391. Works written or recorded by: 39, 40, 44, 86, 91, 97–8, 110
Kabasele Yampanya (Jean) 'Pepe Kalle,' 177–9, 285, 300–302, 334, 348–9, 381, 383
Kabila, Laurent, 1, 391–2
Kadimoke, Adamo, 202
'Kaful Mayay' (a/c Tabu Ley), 208–10
Kahamba Uzalu 'Shaba,' 211, 253, 268, 372, 389
Kala-yi-Boeing (Wenge Musica), 372
'Kale-Kato' (a/c Kabasele), 40, 44, 110
Kalle, Pepe. See Kabasele Yampanya
Kalombo, Albino, 72
Kalombo 'Didi,' 160
Kalonji, Raymond 'Ray Braynck,' 72, 124, 138, 170, 202
'Kamalé' (a/c Nyboma), 178
Kamalé (band), 250, 270
Kamalondo (night club), 223
Kamani Mado (Kosmos), 265
'Kamavasthy' (a/c Soki Dianzenza), 212
Kamba, Paul, 19–20, 22, 27, 30
'Kambile' (a/c Dilu Dilumona), 301
Kambite, Andre 'Damoiseau,' 116
Kamenga Kayobote 'Jolie Detta,' 340, 354, 356
Kami (Tshala Muana), 318
Kamikaze Loningisa (band), 350–51, 377. See also Youlou Mabiala
Kanda Bongo Man, 266–8, 313, 320–22, 325–8, 383, 384, 387
Kanyama Moya Lotula 'Ringo Moya,' 245–50, 257, 261, 269, 279, 320, 348, 383
Kanza, Daniel, 83
Kanza, Thomas, 75, 83, 86, 91, 94
Kapitena Kasongo, 202
Kara (band), 249
Karawa Musica, 224, 302, 306, 307
'Karibou ya Bintou' (a/c Tabu Ley), 210
Kasanda wa Mikalayi (Nicolas) 'Docteur Nico,' 93, 139, 146, 161, 172, 273, 276, 278; African Fiesta and, 114–15, 126–27, 144; African Fiesta Sukisa and, 127–8, 129, 136–41, 182–4, 252; African

Index

Jazz and, 44–6, 66, 83–4, 95, 97, 111–14, 143, 296; background of, 35–6, 38–9; comeback of, 252–3, 294–8; death of, 298–99; decline of, 182–4, 210, 252, 298; Esengo and, 66, 138; guitar playing style of, 88–9, 115, 138–9, 215, 225, 247, 299, 300; legacy of, 299, 300; uses Hawaiian steel guitar, 114, 115, 138, 139, 297. *See also* Nico's works listed by title
Kasavubu, Joseph, 63, 79, 84, 90, 94, 119–20, 148
Kashama, Oscar, 56–7
Kasongo, Antoine, 22
Kasongo wa Kasongo (Jean Marie) 'Rondot,' 202, 382
Kassanda, Rene 'Karé,' 127, 141, 142, 208
Kassav', 322
Kasseya Seyo 'Souzy,' 314, 316, 318
Katanga (Shaba) Province, 16, 17, 90, 92–3, 101, 119, 242, 391
Kaya, Antoine 'Depuissant,' 46, 67, 88, 114, 127, 142
Kazadi, Etienne 'Chantal,' 137, 139
Kebano, Freddy, 162, 220, 377
Kebo (dance), 15, 29, 301
'Kebo' (a/c Dilu Dilumona), 301
Keïta, Salif, 323
Keje, Editions, 151, 186
'Kelhia' (a/c Tabu Ley), 282
Kengo wa Dondo, 226, 278, 283
Kenya, 329. *See also* Nairobi
Kiabelua, Afi, 340
Kiadaka, Samuel 'Samy,' 100
Kiambukuta Londa 'Josky,' 141, 183, 201, 204, 289, 357, 371
Kiambukuta, N'Lemvo 'Serge,' 351
Kiamuangana Mateta (Georges) 'Verckys,' 172, 207, 233, 240, 241, 243, 274–5; Anti-Choc and, 340; background of, 151–2; Bella Bella and, 177–8, 211; contracts of, 310–11; Empire Bakuba and, 177–9, 301, 349; enterprises of, 152, 177–9, 235, 251, 255, 280, 285, 375; at Franco's funeral, 366, 367; Grands Maquisards and, 153, 179; Langa Langa Stars and, 306; Lipua Lipua and, 178; 'Nakomitunaka,' 173–4, 177, 178; O.K. Jazz and, 117, 118, 125, 129, 152, 229;
Orchestre Vévé and, 152–4, 177, 251; Trio Madjesi and, 175; UMUZA and, 197, 251, 276; Victoria Eleison and, 307. *See also* Vévé, Editions; Vévé, Orchestre
Kiesse Diambu (André), 210, 253, 282, 292
Kiland, L.M., 261. *See also* Loukelo Menayame
Kilo-Moto mines, 23–4
Kimbangu, Simon, 60–61, 152, 171
Kimbembe, Jacques, 135
Kimoko, Dally. *See* Ndala Kimoko
Kimpa Vita (Dona Beatriz), 61
'Kimpiatu' (a/c Emeneya), 336–7
Kimpwanza (night club), 346
Kin-Bantous (band), 146
Kindoki Ndoki (Jean), 151, 186
King, Ben E., 380
King, Don, 207
King, Rachid, 315
Kinshasa (Léopoldville): Bandalungwa district of, 149, 161; bars in, 11, 52, 74, 75, 149; Barumbu district of, 32; Citas neighborhood of, 15; *cité indigène* of, 5, 11, 32, 52, 74, 122; CNL attack on, 119; conditions in, 80, 350, 375; description of, 3–5, 11, 52, 122, 149–50, 375; Foncobel district of, 32, 54; founded as Léopoldville, 9; Gombe (Kalina) district of, 4–5, 71; Kalamu district of, 74, 122; Kasavubu (Dendale) district of, 74, 122; Kingabwa district of, 150, 362; Kinshasa district of, 5, 11, 32, 74, 122; Kintambo district of, 5, 74, 122, 149; Limete district of, 54, 95, 122, 182, 298, 356, 366; Lingwala (St. Jean) district of, 32, 358; map of, 12; as market for Brazzaville bands, 238–9; Matonge (Renkin) neighborhood of, 142, 149, 157–8, 176, 183, 195, 219, 251, 309, 342, 343, 346, 375; name changed from Léopoldville, 122; Ndjili district of, 122; Ngiri-Ngiri district of, 52, 74, 122; number of bands in, 187, 197, 225; population of, 12, 30, 122, 149, 238, 284; racial segregation in, 4–5, 58; riots in, 79–80, 374, 375; rural
people move to, 4, 5, 17–18, 30, 67; *ville* of, 4–5, 11; Yolo district of, 55; Zone Annexe of, 122. *See also* Congo, Democratic Republic of the
Kinzonzi, André 'Du Soleil,' 170
Kiri-kiri (dance), 136
'Kiri-Kiri Mabina ya Sika' (a/c Nico), 136
Kisangani (Stanleyville), 20, 75, 86, 94, 120, 131, 190, 374
Kisangani Djenga 'Prince Espérant,' 224, 305–6, 310, 311
Kisatu, Bébé, 177
Kishila Ngoyi 'Faya Tess,' 329–30, 372, 389
Kisola Nzita, 211
Kitoto, Marie, 68
Kiwakana Kiala 'Aime,' 371, 382
Kizita Yal, 390
'Kobeta Mwasi Te' (a/c Bukasa), 72
Kola Ntalulu 'Philo,' 208, 245, 246
Kolamoy, Lambert 'Vigny,' 127, 137
Kolelas, Bernard, 376
Kolosoyi, Antoine 'Wendo,' 22, 24, 26–30, 70, 73, 141, 170, 207, 296
Kombo, Blaise, 371–2
Kongi Aska, 202, 372, 389
Kongo Bar, 11, 104, 117
Kongo Bina label, 24
'Kongo Dipanda' (a/c Bukasa), 90
Kongo people, 5, 11, 20, 61, 63, 66, 79, 90
Kosmos. *See* Moutouari, Côme
Kossa Kossa (band), 210, 230, 339, 340
'Kotiya Zolo Te' (a/c Bowane), 32
Kouka, Célestin 'Célio,' 49, 52, 68, 80, 82, 106, 129–30, 186, 352, 377
Kouka, Mathieu, 116
Kounkou, Théo Blaise, 186, 236, 246–9, 257–5, 279, 320
Krubwa, Bibi, 334
Kulthum, Umm (Om Kalsoum), 273–4, 281
Kuntima, Dominique 'Willy' (a.k.a. Willy Mbembe), 67, 97, 114, 116, 127, 141, 142, 180
Kwamy. *See* Munsi Diki
Kwassa Kwassa (Kanda Bongo Man), 328
Kwassa-kwassa (dance), 327

Labbé, Claude, 278
Laboga, Marcelin, 38
Le Laboureur et Ses Enfants (La Fontaine), 334
LaCoste, Colette, 263–5, 271, 318, 321–2. *See also* Safari Ambiance
Lagos, 103–4, 247, 249. *See also* Nigeria
'Lagos Night' (a/c Lokassa), 379
Laila, Sophie, 189
'Laissez-Nous Tranquilles' (a/c Franco), 361n
Lamy, Benoît, 334
Landa Bango label, 146
Lando, Philippe 'Rossignol,' 56–7, 59, 65–6, 123, 170, 188, 270, 358
Landu, François 'Franchard,' 146
Landu, Lessa 'Lassan,' 139, 140–41, 183
Landu, M'Pongo 'M'Pongo Love,' 220–22, 233, 263–5, 295, 314, 315, 318, 321, 369–70
Langa Langa Stars, 305–6, 308, 310–11, 338, 339
Lari people, 20, 81
Lassa Ndombasi 'Carlito,' 292, 339, 371, 389
Lassan, Franc. *See* Fariala ya Yembo
Lassan, Lessa. *See* Landu, Lessa
Lela-Lela (Kanda Bongo Man), 326–7, 328
Lema-a-Nsi (Ray Lema), 222, 314
Lengi Lenga. *See* Nsumbu Lenga
Leopold II (king of Belgium), 7–11
Léopoldville. *See* Kinshasa
'Lettre à Mr. le Directeur Général' (D.G.) (a/c Franco), 283–4
'Libala ya 8 Heures du Temps' (a/c Rochereau), 142
'Libanga na Libumu' (a/c Bavon), 160
Libanko (band), 223, 224, 302
Liberia, 107, 110, 315
'Liberté' (O.K. Jazz), 226
Lidjo Kwempa. *See* Pangu Nguisi
Liengo, Honoré, 32, 41, 66
Lignanzi, Lea, 250, 259, 261
'Likambo Oyo' (a/c Boukaka), 166
Likembe (sanza), 14, 71, 164. *See also* Marimbula
Likinga Mangenza 'Redo,' 217, 302, 304, 344, 347
'Limbisa Ngai' (a/c Ngwalali), 139

'Lina' (a/c Emile Soki), 159
Linaud, Ange, 162, 186
Lingala, 14, 77–8, 108, 316
Lipua Lipua (Lipwa Lipwa), 178, 179, 210, 250, 270, 339
Lisala Bar, 84
Lisanga, Pauline, 68
'Lisanga Bambanda' (a/c Tabu Ley), 282
'Lisolo' (a/c Emile Soki), 157, 159
Lissouba, Pascal, 376, 377, 392
Lita Bembo (Gaby), 210–11
Litemo Luciana, 333, 335
Livre d'Or (Empire Bakuba), 348
'Liwa' (a/c Bowane), 32
'Liwa ya Champagne' (a/c Kwamy), 99
'Liwa ya Niekesse' (a/c Mangwana), 279
'Liwa ya Somo' (a/c Shungu), 215
'Liwa ya Wechi' (a/c Franco), 99
'Liza' (a/c Kanda Bongo Man), 327
Lô, Ismael, 323
Loboko, Albert, 19
'Locataire' (a/c Franco), 278
Lokassa Kasia (Denis) 'ya Mbongo,' 142, 167, 180, 208, 245–50, 257, 269, 279, 319, 320, 327, 378–80
Loketo, 325, 328, 378, 380
Loko Massengo (Marcel), 153, 172, 175–7, 227
Lokole Isifi, 216–17, 223, 224, 302, 305
Lokombe Nkalulu (Camille), 144, 210, 371
Lola Djangi (Camille) 'Checain,' 123, 124, 181, 201, 204, 282, 371, 382
Lomé, 103, 249, 250, 268, 269, 297, 318. *See also* Togo
Lomeka label, 24
Lomingo Alida, 211, 362, 371, 378
London, 291, 361, 364
Longomba, Awilo, 333
Longomba Besange Lokuli (Victor) 'Vicky,' 42–3, 161, 181, 210; African Jazz and, 83–7, 95; death of, 358, Négro Succès and, 100, 117, 124; O.K. Jazz and, 56–8, 59, 68–70, 82, 117–18, 129, 145, 181, 188, 227; vocal style of, 69–70, 215
Loningisa, 31–2, 41, 47, 54–9, 68, 70, 106, 116, 123, 196, 381

'Lopango ya Bana na Ngai' (a/c Franco), 99
Los Angel (band), 154
Los Batchichas (band), 144
Loubassou, Denis, 238
Lougah, François, 317, 383
'Louise Mungambule' (a/c Bukasa), 72
Loukelo Menayame (Charles Pierre) 'Loukelo Samba,' 151, 157, 260–61, 269
Lourdes, 364
Lovanium University, 62, 148
Lovy du Zaïre (band), 181, 210, 249
Luambo Makiadi (François) 'Franco,' 107, 146, 164, 172, 186, 243, 274–5, 299, 313; awarded gold record, 283, 286, 354; awarded Maracas d'Or, 278–9, 286; background of, 52–4, 381; banned in Brazzaville, 101, 145; Bavon Marie Marie and, 124, 161–2; best musician of 1976, 226; changes in music of, 182, 286; children of, 182, 282, 286, 367; consolidates power in music business, 205, 225, 226–7, 231; converts to Islam, 233, 364; death of, 365–8; discusses AIDS, 355, 363; estate of, 382; feuds with Kwamy and African Fiesta, 125–6, 128, 131; feuds with the press, 353, 354, 357; final performance of, 364; guitar playing style of, 88–9, 124, 225; health of, 356, 358–9, 361–2; helps launch Operation Africa, 314–15; interviewed for Zaïrean television, 362–3; jailing of, 82, 232–3; legacy of, 367; lifestyle of, 182; Loningisa and, 54, 56–9; made grand maître, 276; Madilu and, 287–8, 291, 292–3, 353–4; MAZADIS and, 198–201, 217–18, 225, 229, 233, 241–2, 285, 355–6; misogynistic tendencies of, 287, 288, 291, 292; Mobutu and, 195, 199–200, 205, 232–3, 278, 366; in National Order of the Leopard, 228, 233, 366; Ngoma and, 53; obscene songs of, 125, 146, 201, 226, 231–3, 239, 240; as O.K. Jazz boss, 98–9, 129, 145, 181–2, 183, 204–5, 227–8, 230, 235, 254–5, 282–3,

Index

291–2, 355–6; as O.K. Jazz member, 56–9, 68–9, 83, 116–18; performs in the U.S., 288–90; plays the Hammersmith Palais, 291; record labels of, 186, 195, 232, 254–5, 278, 283, 306, 320; records at Fonior, 98–9; records with Feruzi, 173; responds to talk of exile, 283; Sam Mangwana and, 203, 229, 278–9, 360–61; singing of, 57, 288; SOPHINZA and, 242, 355–6; Tabu Ley and, 225, 229–31, 234, 283–4, 367–8; tours Rwanda and Burundi, 357–8; Trio Madjesi and, 226–7; as UMUZA president, 194, 195, 197–8, 225–7, 229, 233, 358; Verckys and, 152; Vicky and, 83, 100, 117, 181–2, 358; Victoria Eleison and, 337, 355, 356, 357; wives of, 182, 282, 286–7, 359, 364–5. *See also* Franco's works listed by title; O.K. Jazz; Un-Deux-Trois; *Ye! magazine*
Luampasi, Albert, 53
Lubadika, Pablo 'Porthos,' 249, 256, 258, 259, 261–2, 268, 269, 320, 325, 327
Lubelo, Daniel 'De La Lune,' 56, 58, 59, 80, 82, 104, 117, 118, 120, 170
Lubumbashi (Elisabethville), 46, 92, 94, 119, 131, 374, 392
'Lucie Tozongana' (*a/c* Bavon), 125
Lukau, Julios, 260, 268
'Lukoki' (*a/c* Franco), 361
Lukombo Mayemba 'Djeffard,' 309, 342, 372, 390
Lukombo Nzambi 'Shimita,' 309, 342, 379
Lukunku Sampu, 362
Lulonga, 118
Lumi-Congo (night club), 238
Lumingu, André 'Zorro,' 127, 137, 146
Lumumba, Patrice, 75–6, 79, 84–6, 90–94, 118
Lundula, Victor, 92
Lutula, Edouard 'Edo Clari,' 97, 163
Lutumba Ndomanueno Massiya (Simon) 'Simaro,' 202, 204, 357, 367; as O.K. Jazz leader, 368, 371, 382; as O.K. Jazz member, 117, 129, 138, 201–4, 208; as O.K. Jazz vice-president, 282–3, 291–2, 356.

Works written by: 181, 202–4, 279, 291–2, 371
Luvemba, Dju Dju 'Dju Dju Chet,' 336
Luwowo, Gaspard 'Gaspy,' 100, 124

Ma Coco (Pablo Lubadika), 261–2, 269
'Ma Hele' (*a/c* Simaro), 181
Ma-Elika (night club), 343
Mabele, Aurlus, 323–4, 325, 328, 380, 383
'Mabele' (*a/c* Simaro), 203–4
Macauley (night club), 11
'Madeleina' (*a/c* Pablo Lubadika), 262
Madiata Madia (Gerard), 197, 202, 358
Madibala, Martha, 68
Madilu Bialu 'System,' 287–9, 291, 292–3, 353–4, 357, 362, 367–8, 371, 382–3, 389
Madilu System (band), 288
Mageda Nsingi, 267
Maiga, Boncana, 263
Maika (band), 216
Makaba, Alain, 371
Makanga 'Juslain,' 177
Makeba, Miriam, 207, 279, 281
Makengela, Etienne 'Diamant,' 146
Makfé (band), 230
Makiadi 'Kelly,' 177
'Makiadi' (*a/c* Nico), 297
Makiesse (Franco's mother), 367
Makola Dialuliba 'Makolin,' 336
Malage de Lugendo, 354, 371
Malambu ma Kizola, 228, 254–5, 282, 355, 356, 359, 362, 364–5, 367
Malao, Augustin 'Hennecy,' 208
Malapet, Jean Dieudonné 'Nino,' 56, 238, 366; background of, 51–2; Bantous de la Capitale and, 80–81, 102–7, 130, 133, 184, 186, 236, 352, 377; Esengo and, 66, 89; Negro Jazz and, 49–50, 49, 52
Malebo (Stanley) Pool, 3, 4, 7, 9, 172
Malekani, Justin 'Jerry,' 107–8, 134, 170, 244
Malembe 'El Chanto,' 336
Mali, 110, 262, 263, 266, 315, 323, 349
Malinga (Kanda Bongo Man), 325–6, 327
Malinga (style of music), 16
Maloko (band), 380
Malonga, Samuel 'Samy

Trompette,' 238
Malula, Joseph, 37, 62–3, 97n, 110, 171, 277
Mama Kulutu (night club), 195
Mama Kusala (night club), 382
'Mama-Iye-Ye' (*a/c* Nyboma), 270
Mambenga (dance), 136
Mampouya, Albert, 164
Mandelson, Ben, 262
Mandiangu, Paul 'Dercy,' 162, 176, 238
Mandjeku Lengo 'Dizzy,' 280, 371, 378, 389; African All Stars and, 245–50, 269, 279–80; Afrisa and, 230, 245; Festival des Maquisards and, 144–5; Grands Maquisards and, 145, 210; Kossa Kossa and, 210, 230; O.K. Jazz and, 292, 357, 362
Mando Négro Kwala Kwa (band), 162, 258
Mango Records, 323
Mangwana, Sam (Mangwana Mayimona, a.k.a. Sam Moreno), 235, 268, 279, 280–81, 378; African All Stars and, 244–50, 279–80; African Fiesta (66) National and, 127, 141; Afrisa and, 229, 244; background of, 144; Eddy'Son and, 256–7; Festival des Maquisards and, 141–2, 144–4; O.K. Jazz and, 201–4. *See also* Mangwana's works listed by title
Maniatakis, Charles, 263–5, 271, 318, 322. *See also* Safari Ambiance
Mansiamina Mfoko (Paul) 'Bopol,' 268, 273, 320, 369, 385–6; African All Stars and, 249; African Fiesta Sukisa and, 141; Afrisa and, 268; Bamboula and, 146; Continental and, 183; Eddy'Son and, 256; Innovation series and, 260–61, 268; Quatre Etoiles and, 269–71, 324–5; Ya Tupas and, 222
Mantuika Kobi 'Thierry,' 230, 362, 371
Manuaku Waku (Félix) 'Pepe Felly,' 157, 213, 216, 222, 300, 303, 309–10, 313, 342, 344, 346, 380, 389
Manufacture Zaïroise du Disque (MAZADIS, formerly

Index 429

MACODIS), 98, 107, 150; abandoned by Fonior, 241–2; becomes MAZADIS, 172; decline of, 218, 221, 254, 356; established as MACODIS, 95; Franco and, 198–201, 217–18, 225, 229, 233, 241–2, 285, 355–6. See also Fonior
Manzenza Sala Musala, 226, 230, 294, 362, 364
'Manzeta' (a/c Nico), 294
'Manzil-Manzil' (a/c Mbilia Bel), 331
Maracas d'Or, 278–9, 286, 324, 328
Maria, Maria (Sam Mangwana), 244–5
'Maria Tchebo' (a/c D'Oliveira), 248, 268
Maria Tebbo (Sam Mangwana), 268–9
'Marie Clara' (a/c Rochereau), 390
'(Tu m'as déçu) Marie-Jeanne' (a/c Bopol/L.M. Kiland), 261
'Marie Lompengo' (a/c Jhimmy), 34
'Marie-Louise' (a/c Wendo/Bowane), 28–30, 73, 76
'Marie Pauline' (a/c Mizele), 139
Marimbula, 21. See also Likembe
Maringa, 16, 20
'Mario' (a/c Franco), 292–4, 336, 353, 354
'Martin Luther King' (a/c Rochereau), 136
Martiniquais, Orchestre, 22
Martinique, 134
'Maseke ya Meme' (a/c Bavon), 160
Masela, Didier, 371
Massaka 'Djo Mass,' 348
Massamba, Bernard, 20
Massamba, Fidèle 'Sammy,' 263, 265, 268
Massamba-Debat, Alphonse, 102, 119, 120, 132, 162, 376
Massengo, Rigobert 'Max,' 81
Massu (O.K. Jazz), 354
Master Mwana Congo. See Nkounkou, Ignace
'Masuwa' (a/c Pablito), 133–4, 136
Matadidi Mabele 'Mario,' 153, 175–7, 227
Matandu, Pedro 'Cailloux,' 137
'Matata Masila na Congo' (a/c Kabasele), 97–8
Matchatcha (band), 380
'Matebu' (a/c Papa Wemba), 309
Matima Mpioso Kinuani, 158, 213, 300, 303–4, 342, 345–6, 381
Matinda (African All Stars), 249
Matolu Dode 'Papy Tex,' 179, 300–302, 348–9
Matonge (Renkin). See Kinshasa
Matsoua, André, 61, 81
Matumona Lulendo 'Defao,' 309, 311, 338, 380–81
Mavatiku Visi (Michel) 'Michelino,' 142, 144, 149, 180, 208, 230, 283
Mavuela Somo (Siméon), 158, 213, 216–17, 223, 344
'Maya' (a/c Simaro), 291–2, 371
Mayaula Mayoni, 222, 226
'Mayele Mabe' (a/c Tino Baroza), 97
'Mbanda Akana Ngai' (a/c Franco), 361 n
Mbanda Matière (Tshala Muana), 318
Mbanza, 5, 63
Mbarga, Prince Nico, 246, 249, 379
'Mbele-Mbele' (a/c M'Pongo Love), 265
M'Bemba, Yves André 'Pablito,' Pamelo Mounk'a, 195, 377; Bantous de la Capitale and, 104, 124, 129–30, 133–4, 236–8, 258, 265, 352, 377; becomes Pamelo Mounk'a, 258; death of, 381; Eddy'Son and, 258–9, 261, 272, 352; Trio CEPAKOS and, 186, 236–8. Works written or recorded by: 133–4, 136, 258–9, 261, 352
Mbembe Mbilia 'Joe Nickel,' 309, 342
M'Benza, Syran, 249, 256, 268, 269–71, 320, 324–5, 380, 389
Mbenzuana Ngamboni 'Bozi Boziana,' 213, 216–17, 223, 303, 306, 310–11, 338, 340–41, 344, 346
'Mbeya-Mbeya' (a/c Evoloko), 214
Mbilia, Casimir 'Casino,' 107, 134
Mbilia Mbuyo 'Mbilia Bel,' 280–82, 287, 290, 329–32, 343, 344, 385–6
Mbole Tambwe, 176
'Mbongo' (a/c Losimba), 310
'Mbongwana' (a/c Espérant), 310
Mbumba, Pierre 'Attel,' 142, 180
Mbuta Mashakado, 223, 303, 344, 346
'Mbuta' (a/c Nyboma), 270
Megamix (Sam Mangwana), 380
Megamix Vol. 1 (Lokassa), 379, 380
Meissonnier, Martin, 335, 388
Mekanisi Zemba (Modeste) 'Modero,' 208, 245, 372, 389
'Melia' (a/c Kosmos/Massamba), 265
Melo-Congo (band), 22, 51
Mélodie distributors, 321–2, 323, 387
Menace de Divorce (Grand Zaïko), 342
Menga, Andre, 66, 100
'Mère Supérieure' (a/c Papa Wemba), 224
Merengue, 138
'Merengue President' (a/c Nico), 138
'Merengue Scoubidou' (a/c Nico), 138
Meridjo Belobi, 158, 213, 304, 342, 345
'M'Fono Yami' (a/c Papa Wemba), 335
Mfumu Muntu Bambi, 151, 200, 251. See also Parions ou Mondenge, Editions
Mi-composé, 34, 38, 115, 142, 247
Mi-solo, 138, 268
'Micky Me Quiero' (a/c Malapet), 89
Micra Jazz (band), 202
'Mikalayi' (a/c Nico), 297
Milanda Nkutu Azowa 'Baramy,' 202
Mingiedi 'Jeef,' 114, 127, 137
Minzoto Kulutu (band), 213
Minzoto Wella Wella (band), 222, 315, 346. See also Etoiles, Les
Missamou, Joseph 'José,' 186
Missia, Albert 'Robin Mopepe,' 154, 155
Mission, Fernand, 96
'Mista John' (a/c Pepe Kalle), 301
Miyalu Kayonda, 284
Mizele, Paul 'Paulins,' 116, 127, 137, 140, 146
Moanda, Vital 'D.V.,' 157–9, 213, 216, 303–4, 313, 342–3, 344–6. See also Zaïko Langa Langa
'Mobali na Ngai' (a/c Franco), 146
'Mobembo Eleki Tata' (a/c Izeidi), 114
Mobutu Sese Seko (Joseph-Désiré), 132, 141, 194, 298;

driven from power, 1, 391–2; elected president, 148, 285–6; forms MPR, 132; Franco and, 195, 198–201, 205, 232–3, 278, 366; as kleptocrat, 242–3, 284, 350; Lumumba and, 92, 94; pressured to reform political system, 373–5; seizes control of government, 94, 120. *See also* Congo, Democratic Republic of
Mobutu Sese Seko Fund, 236, 276, 298
Mode Succès (band), 260
Mofude 'Fifi,' 340, 381
Moke, Simon, 202
'Mokili Makalamba' (a/c Eyenga), 68
'Mokitani ya Wendo' (a/c Tabu Ley), 390
'Mokolo Nakokufa' (a/c Rochereau), 128–9
Moleka Nzoko, 346
Molenga, Seskain, 177, 244
Mon Mari est Gabonais (Anti-Choc), 341
'Mongali' (a/c Tabu Ley), 173, 180, 208
Mongo Ley, 307
Mongombe, Henri, 157
Moniania ma Muluma (Augustin) 'Roitelet,' 41–2, 44, 48, 56, 58–9, 65–6, 72, 146, 170, 196–7, 382
Monsengwo Pasinya, Laurent, 374–5
Monsieur, Carlos, 55, 59
Montreal World's Fair, 134
'Monzo' (a/c Simaro), 204
Morocco, 242, 392
Mose Se Sengo 'Fan Fan,' 244
'Mosinzo Nganga' (Zaïko Langa Langa), 159
Mossaka (dance), 136
Moumpala, Michel, 238, 250
Mounk'a, Pamelo. *See* M'Bemba, Yves André
Moutouari, Côme 'Kosmos,' 129–30, 133, 136, 170, 186, 236–7, 265, 352
Moutouari, Pierre, 136, 162, 265
Mouvement Congolais pour la Démocratie et le Développement Intégral, 376
Mouvement National Congolais (MNC), 79, 90
Mouvement National de la Révolution (MNR), 132, 162
Mouvement Populaire de la Révolution (MPR), 132, 141, 148, 198, 206, 373–4

Mouvement Socialist Africain (MSA), 81
Moya, Ringo. *See* Kanyama Moya Lotula
Moyen-Congo. *See* Congo, Republic of
Moyibi (Nyboma and Pepe Kalle), 349
Mozambique, 280
Mpasi Samba 'Patcho Star,' 307, 311, 346
Mpassy, Alphonse 'Mermans,' 130, 138, 186, 352, 377
'Mpeve ya Longo' (a/c Tabu Ley), 281
Mpiana Mukulumpa 'J.P.,' 371
Mpiso Mati 'Annie,' 282, 286, 359, 365
M'Pokolo (Tshala Muana), 318
M'Pongo Love. *See* Landu, M'Pongo
Mpoyi Kaninda 'Djo,' 280, 382
'M.P.R.' (a/c Mujos), 132
Mpudi zi Kisala 'Deca,' 201, 291
Muaka Mbeka 'Bapuis,' 158, 213, 303, 342, 345
Muanda 'Thylon,' 346
Mubiala Bakiemen 'Joly,' 307, 336
Mubiala Emeneya (Jean) 'Jo Kester,' 306, 307, 311–12, 313, 336–8, 355, 370, 383. *See also* Victoria Eleison
Muchacha (band), 223, 302
Mujos. *See* Mulamba Pania
Mukangi 'Déesse,' 340
Mulamba Pania (Joseph) 'Mujos,' 120–21, 129, 131–2, 183, 184, 235–6, 238
Mulele, Pierre, 148, 185
Mulembu 'Tagar,' 178
Mumbata Mambu 'Joe Poster,' 309, 342, 381
Munange 'Maproco,' 152
Mundanda, Antoine, 71
'Munga Josephine' (a/c Didi Kalombo), 160
Munoko Gisalu 'Dodo,' 372, 390
Munsi Diki (Jean) 'Kwamy,' 238, 253, 278, 280; African Fiesta and, 125–6, 229; African Fiesta Sukisa and, 127–8; O.K. Jazz and, 98, 99, 116; Révolution and, 131–2, 151
Musekiwa, Isaac, 46, 93, 98, 113, 131, 225, 278; African Jazz and, 46–7, 52; O.K. Jazz and, 68–9, 98, 129, 152, 202, 228, 362, 368, 370
La Musette label, 151, 157, 260
Music: animation in, 158, 308;

bands decline, 378; bands form, 19–20, 22; bass used in, 41, 155; brass bands and, 14, 17, 22; censorship of, 133, 145–6, 201, 225–6, 232, 239, 278; Christian, 14, 76; conga drums, 56–7; Congolese entrepreneurs in, 150–51; evolves from traditional to modern, 4, 16–17, 19, 32–3; guitar acoustic introduced in, 14, 15, 17; guitar electric introduced in, 41–4; guitar steel (Hawaiian) used in, 114, 115, 138, 139, 297; horns used in, 40–41, 116, 158, 279, 308, 385–7; independence and, 93; influence of foreign styles on, 13, 14, 15–16, 18, 19, 20–21, 40–42, 46–7, 69–70, 114, 134, 154–6, 158, 160, 174–7, 222, 265–6, 316, 335, 337–8, 384–7, 388–9; influence of recording studios on, 32–3, 37–8, 73–4; instruments of, 14, 16–17, 18, 20–21, 32, 33, 136, 155 (*see also* bass, horns, etc. under Music); languages of, 13, 16, 77–8, 104, 108–9, 305, 316; Latin American, 1 3–14, 20–21; medley style of, 379–80; Paris soukous versus Congo rumba, 273, 383–5; pirating of, 240–41, 285, 321–3; promotion of, 43–4, 47–8, 186–7, 271; recording of, 18–19, 24–6, 31–2, 42, 96, 150, 163, 177, 181, 186, 285, 350, 375, 377, 385–6; roles in traditional life of, 36, 67; show style performance of, 174–5, 181, 219, 225, 285; spread of Congolese style of, 102–4, 107–9; stylistic schools of, 88–9, 203, 225, 230, 299, 300, 313, 391; synthesizer used in, 194, 261, 319, 338, 348, 385–7; traps used in, 88, 136, 155, 158, 297; vocal groups in, 19–20, 22; women in, 43, 67–8, 188–9, 194. *See also* Musicians; Recording Technology; Records
Musicians: authenticity and, 172–4, 208; author's rights and, 43, 58–9, 97, 195–6, 243, 274–5; business practices of, 387; competition among, 70, 73–4, 98, 225; conflict with producers and, 271–2, 320–21, 323; instability of

Index 431

bands and, 146–7; migration to Brazzaville of, 238, 244; migration to Brussels of, 1–2, 267, 371, 378; migration to East Africa of, 244; migration to Paris of, 1–2, 243–4, 256–8, 263, 265–6, 267, 270, 272–3, 317, 318–19, 320, 328, 335–6, 338, 372, 378; migration to West Africa of, 107–8, 244–6, 249, 250, 272–3, 315; migration to U.S. of, 389; money and, 113–14; quest for international sound by, 384, 386, 388; recording contracts of, 28, 58–9, 271, 311; separation from roots of, 378; social status of, 36, 67; stage names of, 169–70; unionization of, 146, 194, 195–98, 352 (*see also* Union des Musiciens Zaïrois)
Les Mustangs (band), 155, 156
Mutombo Nyamabo 'Ben,' 306, 310–11, 338, 340, 380–81
Mutshipule, Casimir 'Casino,' 116, 163
Mutuashi (dance), 315–16
Mutuashi (Tshala Muana), 389
Muzina (Afrisa), 389–90, 391
M'vogo, Roland, 246, 248, 279
Mvuemba 'Chiro,' 346
Mwamba Mongala (Charles) 'Dechaud': African Fiesta and, 115; African Fiesta Sukisa and, 127, 137–8, 140–41; African Jazz and, 44–6, 66, 83, 95, 96–7, 116, 143; 'African Jazz Mokili Mobimba,' 97, 248, 275, 390; background of, 35–6, 38; with Nico in Lomé, 297
'Mwambe' (a/c Bokelo), 123–4
'Mwana Nsuka' (a/c Miyalu Kayonda), 284
Mwanga, Paul, 35, 36, 39, 47
'Mwasi Abandaka' (a/c Rochereau), 114
Mwena, Joseph, 46, 72, 116, 127, 141, 142, 180
Mwinkwa, Tino, 183, 238, 320, 352
Les Myosotis (band), 156, 157
Myosotis, Photas, 116, 188
'Myriam Immortelle' (a/c Olomide), 348

'Na Kombo ya Jhimmy Putulu' (a/c Jhimmy), 34
'Na Mokili Tour à Tour' (a/c Franco), 283–4

'Nadina' (Afrisa), 329
Nairobi, 240, 354. *See also* Kenya
'Nairobi Night' (a/c Lokassa), 379
'Nakeyi Abidjan' (a/c Chantal), 139
'Nakobala na Ngai ata Mbwa' (a/c Franco), 201
'Nakoma Mbanda na Mama ya Mobali Ngai' (a/c Franco), 226
'Nakomitunaka' (a/c Verckys), 173–4, 177, 178
Nana. *See* Akumu Wakutu
Nana Music, 255
National Order of the Leopard, 228, 233, 299, 358, 366
'Nato Mama' (a/c Wendo/Bowane), 30
Ndaiye, Amadou, 377
Ndala Kimoko 'Dally,' 250, 270, 319, 320, 379
'Ndaya' (a/c Mayaula), 222
'N'daya Paradis' (a/c Rochereau), 115
'N'Djoli' (a/c Olomide), 251
Ndombe Opetun (Paul) 'Pepe,' 142, 180, 191, 230–31, 233, 280, 329, 371
Ndombe label, 102
Nedule Montswet (Antoine) 'Papa Noël,' 44, 66, 72, 89, 116, 124, 210, 378, 387, 389; Bamboula and, 146, 189, 270; Bantous de la Capitale and, 102, 106; Franco and, 362, 365–6; O.K. Jazz and, 230, 283, 292
Negro Band, 81, 107, 144, 162, 163, 186
Negro Jazz, 49–50, 52, 56, 68
Négro National, 162
Négro Succès, 100, 117, 124–5, 135, 160, 162, 175, 176, 178, 180, 238, 244, 314
Neves, Lopes, 241
New York, 283, 289
'Ngai Marie Nzoto Ebeba' (a/c Franco), 118
'Ngala ba Petit Mbongo' (a/c Franco), 56
Ngaliema (Téké king), 9
'Nganda Renkin' (a/c Michelino), 149
Ngando, Fredo 'Tete Fredo,' 259, 266, 325, 380
'Nganga' (a/c Soki Dianzenza), 212
Ngangura Mwenze, 334
Ngiama Werason, 371
Ngiandu Kanza, 202

Ngizulu Kubiala 'Fafa de Molokai,' 333
Ngoma, 41, 48, 71, 88, 155; death of Nicolas Jeronimidis and, 47, 70; expands into pressing and distribution, 47, 273; founding of, 24–6; musicians of, 28, 30, 53, 68, 70–73, 97, 116, 127; pay for musicians of, 28; Sonodisc and, 273–4; stays in business, 106, 143, 273
Ngonda 'Wally,' 340, 381
'Ngonga Ebeti' (a/c Depuissant), 114
Ngoss Club, 343, 346
Ngouabi, Marien, 162–3, 184–5, 236, 350
Ngouma Lokito, 340
Ngoy, Eugene 'Gogene,' 65, 66
Nguesso, Denis Sassou, 236, 350, 376, 392
Nguini, Vincent, 380
Ngwalali, Michel, 137, 139, 146
Ngwango Isionoma 'Seli-Ja,' 221
Nickel, Joe. *See* Mbembe Mbilia
Nicoletta, Fille des Antilles (Aurlus Mabele), 323
Nigeria, 110, 118, 123, 188, 244, 247, 262. *See also* Lagos
Nkounkou, Freddy 'Freddy Mars,' 107, 134, 244
Nkounkou, Ignace 'Master Mwana Congo,' 258–9, 261, 340–41
'Non' (a/c Franco), 287–8, 291
'Nora Mensah' (a/c Pamelo), 352
Novelty label, 24
Nseka Bimwela (Joseph) 'Huit Kilos' (a.k.a. Fatima Lola), 307, 312, 329, 336, 372, 389
N'Sele, 344, 346
Nsimba, Simon 'Diana,' 142, 144–5, 230
Nsumbu Lenga 'Lengi,' 217, 302, 303, 342, 345
Ntembo Pinos, 307
Ntesa Nzitani (Daniel) 'Dalienst,' 142, 145, 153, 210, 230, 233, 244, 282, 289, 292, 378, 382
'Ntoni' (a/c Simaro), 203
N'vondo, Jimmy, 259, 266, 325
Nyamabo, Ben. *See* Mutombo Nyamabo
Nyboma Mwan Dido, 178, 250, 270–71, 325, 349, 384–5
Nyoka Longo 'Jehrsy Jossart,' 157, 213, 216, 303–4, 342–7, 381, 382
Nzaya Nzayadio, 339

Index

Nzenze, Jean Pierre 'Jean Trompette,' 141, 208
Nzenze Mongengo, 309–10, 342
Nzinzi (Emeneya), 337–8
Les Nzoi (band), 186, 237
Nzola Ndonga 'Petit Prince,' 306–7, 338–9
Nzungu, Samuel 'Colon Gentil,' 170, 196

O.D. Jazz (band), 175
Odéon Kinois (band), 22, 24, 116
Office de Cooperation Radiophonique (OCORA), 164
Office National des Droits d'Auteur (ONDA), 196
Office Togolais du Disque (OTODI), 297, 318
'Ohé Suka ya Rumba' (a/c Eyenga), 68, 77
O.K. Bar, 52, 56–7, 58, 149
O.K. Jazz: adds T.P. initials, 145; anniversaries of, 277–8, 353, 354; banned in Brazzaville, 101, 145; best band of 1980, 278; competition with African Jazz and, 98; at Dakar festival, 129, 130–31; dancers (Francolettes) of, 182, 188; demise of, 382–3; deserters of form Révolution, 131, 145; discipline in, 204–5; expansion of, 117–18, 181–2, 201–2, 205, 230; faces urban guerrillas, 119; feuds with African Fiesta, 125–6; formation of, 56–8, 381; Franco's death and, 367–8; horn section loaned to Victoria Eleison, 337, 355; mentioned, 208, 343; musical arrangements of, 57–8, 69–70, 116, 182, 286; musicians of, 56–7, 59, 65, 68, 82, 98, 116–18, 120, 125, 129, 145, 181, 188, 201–2, 227, 229–31, 235, 244, 270, 279, 280, 282–3, 289, 291–2, 339, 340, 350, 356–8, 362, 366, 368, 370, 371, 382; musicians of expelled from Congo-Léo, 120; musicians of jailed, 233; obscene songs of, 125, 146, 201, 226, 231–2, 239–40; Operation Africa and, 315–16; record labels of, 118, 164, 186, 195, 232, 255; records at Fonior, 98–9, 117; stylistic school of, 88–9, 225, 230; survives in Kinshasa, 355–6, 375; tours of, 238, 288–90, 291, 354, 357–8, 361, 362; two wings of, 282–3, 291–2, 361; as victim of pirating, 322; at Zaïko's tenth anniversary, 303; at Zaïre 74 festival, 207. *See also* O.K. Jazz works listed by title
Okabando, Jean Jules, 352
Olomide, Koffi. *See* Agbepa Mumba.
Olympia (Paris concert hall), 167, 174, 188, 191–2, 220, 226, 227, 383
Olympia label, 24–5, 27, 106
'Les On Dit' (a/c Franco), 356
'On Entre O.K. On Sort K.O.' (a/c Franco), 59
'Onassis ya Zaïre' (a/c Evoloko), 215
Onyx (night club), 195
Opangalut, Jacques, 81
Opango, Yhombi, 236, 376
Operation Africa, 314–15
Opika, 33, 34–41, 44–5, 46, 48, 52, 63, 68, 106, 296
Order of Devoted Service to Congo, 236
The Original Innovation (Bopol), 260
OTC (band), 38, 44
Ouattara Moumouni, David, 266–71, 322, 324, 380
Oubangui-Chari. *See* Central African Republic
Ouedraogo, Ram, 315–17, 349
'Ozali Suka ya Mobali' (a/c Nico), 139

Pablito. *See* M'Bemba, Yves André
Paiement Cash (Zaïko Langa Langa), 343
Palais de Congrès, 352
Palais du Peuple, 253, 329, 334, 346, 347, 366, 368
Palladium Theater, 176, 192, 219, 220, 223, 227, 329
Palthe, Z. van Wulfften, 242
Pamba-Pamba (band), 288
'Pambu' (a/c Nzenze), 310
Pan-African Cultural Festival (Algiers), 165, 189
Pandi, Saturnin 'Ben,' 51, 56, 59, 65–6, 80–82, 102–3, 130, 133, 186, 352, 366
Pangu Nguisi 'Lidjo' Kwempa, 313, 333, 340
Panthères (band), 155
Papa Noël. *See* Nedule Montswet
Papa Wemba. *See* Shungu Wembadio
Papa Wemba, 335
Papadimitriou, Athanase, 30–32, 54, 381
Papadimitriou, Basile, 30–32, 47, 51–5, 58–9, 106, 381
'Paquita' (a/c Rochereau), 104
Para Fifi (night club), 210
'Para-Fifi' (a/c Kabasele), 39, 40, 44
Parions ou Mondenge, Editions, 151, 200, 216, 223, 251
Paris: Akueson in, 190, 191; Congolese musicians in, 134, 167, 184, 191, 243–4, 254–73, 276, 282, 317–28, 331–2, 335–6, 338, 349, 355, 359, 372, 378; production of Congolese music in, 254–73, 295, 316, 317–28, 335, 348, 384–7
Partager (M'Pongo Love), 369
Parti Congolais du Travail (PCT), 163, 185, 186, 236, 376
Parti National du Progrès (PNP), 90
'Pas Possible Maty' (a/c M'Pongo Love), 222
Le Passeport label, 255
Patcho Star. *See* Mpasi Samba
Patenge (drum), 16
Pathé Marconi, 107, 118, 136
Patou (of Olympia label), 24, 27
Patrice and Mario, 69–70, 76
Paulina (Franco's wife), 286–7
'Pauline' (a/c Nico), 139
'Pauline' (a/c Zaïko Langa Langa), 159
Pela Nsimba 'Jack,' 244
Pelgrims de Bigard, Eugene Willy, 95, 107, 150, 198, 254–5. *See also* Fonior
People's Revolutionary Party, 391
Perruche Bleue (night club), 156, 160, 223
Perse, Marcel, 273–5. *See also* Sonodisc
'Pesa le Tout' (a/c Rochereau), 114
Petit Bois (night club), 110, 117
Petit Prince. *See* Nzola Ndonga
'Peuple' (a/c Rochereau), 142
Le Peuple (band). *See* Trio CEPAKOS
Phénomène (Mbilia Bel), 331, 385
Philips (includes Phonogram, Polydor, Polygram), 47, 106, 150, 157, 159, 189, 199, 239, 240, 242. *See also* Société Phonographique et Industrielle du Zaïre
Phonogram-Kenya (Polygram-Kenya), 240, 354

Phonograph, 13
Pickett, Wilson, 380
Pierrot (musician), 72
Pilaeis (of Ngoma), 47, 72
Pirès (musician), 288
'Pitié, Je Veux la Reconciliation' (a/c Bopol), 260
Pointe Noire, 17, 350, 378
Polar beer, 74, 75
Pôle Position (Papa Wemba), 389
Polydor/Polygram. See Philips
'Pont Sur le Congo' (a/c Boukaka), 164, 166
Popolipo Zanguila, 305, 310, 311, 342, 344–5
Populaires, Editions, 186, 195, 232, 255
Portugal, 5, 11, 144, 304, 344, 347
Post, François, 321
Poster, Joe. See Mumbata Mambu
Pouéla, Jean Félix 'Du Pool,' 145, 202
Les Presets (singers), 337
Price, Lloyd, 207
Primus beer, 74, 75
'Proclamation' (a/c Papa Wemba), 309
'Pusana Moke' (a/c Guy-Léon Fylla), 43

Quartier Latin, 347–8, 378
'Quatre Boutons' (a/c Franco), 125, 145
Les Quatre Etoiles, 270–71, 313, 325, 378, 380
4 Grandes Vedettes de la Musique Africaine, 270
'Quelle Mechanceté' (a/c Dino Vangu), 282
Quist (night club), 11, 52, 56, 149

Radio, 18–19, 26, 27, 38, 68, 74, 108
Réal, Jean, 19
Real World Records, 389
Recording technology: cassette tapes, 239–40, 321–3, 356, 375, 377; compact disc, 350, 377; direct-to-disc recording, 24, 25, 32, 47; effects on music of, 26, 29, 106, 136, 286, 297, 348, 385–7; recording tape introduced, 47. See also Music; Records
Records: as disposable commodity, 33; distribution of, 47, 95–6, 98, 105, 107, 108, 186–7, 199, 273–4, 321, 323, 343, 387; forty-five r.p.m., 97, 106, 136, 143, 286; pirating of, 240–41, 285, 321–3; pressing of, 24, 32, 47, 95, 98, 163, 198–200, 218, 221, 222, 239–42, 245–6, 273, 285, 350, 355–6; promotion of, 43, 47–8, 186, 271; sales of, 25, 47, 143, 159, 175, 218, 254, 259, 285, 293, 308, 316, 319, 321, 401, 402, 403; seventy-eight r.p.m., 13, 18, 24, 32, 33, 74, 97, 286; shortage of, 217–18, 221, 222, 239–42, 285; thirty-three and one-third r.p.m., 143, 255, 286; vinyl's dominance ends, 239–40, 356. See also Music; Recording technology
Redding, Otis, 155, 380
Les Redoutables. See Abeti Masikini
Reggae, 76, 261, 262, 265, 323, 387
'La Reine de Sabah' (a/c Boziana), 341
La Reine du Soukous (Abeti), 383
Renkin neighborhood. See Matonge
La Réponse de Mario (O.K. Jazz), 360, 361n
'Requisitoire' (a/c Tabu Ley), 391
Restaurant of the Zoo, 111, 117
'Retroussons les Manches' (a/c Nico), 128
Révolution (band), 131–2, 145, 151, 195, 227
'Riana' (a/c Nyamabo), 339
Ringo Star (Rigo Star), 320
Roboti robota (dance), 311
Rock'a Mambo, 66, 75, 80, 82, 89, 102, 120, 123, 124, 188, 270
Roitelet. See Moniania ma Muluma
Roosevelt, Eko, 263
Rossi, Tino, 39, 76, 88, 215
Rossignol. See Lando, Philippe
'La Roue Qui Tourne' (a/c Nico), 297
Round Table conference, 83–6
Rounder Records, 389
Rue d'Amour (Koffi Olomide), 348
Rumba, 21–2, 76–7, 136, 246–7
Rumba Music (Sam Mangwana), 389
Rumba rock, 300
'Les Rumeurs (Baiser ya Juda)' (a/c Franco), 359–60, 361n
Rwanda, 329, 357, 391–2
Ry-Co Jazz, 107–8, 123, 134,
184, 190, 244, 266, 319, 380, 381
Rykodisc, 387–8

Saak Saakul. See Bonghat Tshekabu
SABAM, 43, 196
Sabena airlines, 40
SACEM, 169–70, 243, 272
Sacré Marpeza, 308
'Sadou' (a/c Franco), 361n
Safari Ambiance, 263–5, 271, 318, 321, 322, 343, 369
Safari Sound label, 263
Safro. See Boloko Manzangi
Sai-Liza (Kanda Bongo Man), 321–2, 327–8
Saint Hilaire (night club), 156
Sala, Gilles, 84, 86, 108, 164, 278
'Salima' (a/c O.K. Jazz), 226
Salsero, Domingo, 258, 259, 261, 268, 325–6
Sam Mangwana et l'African All Stars, 247
Samantha (Pamelo Mounk'a), 259
Samba, Joseph 'Mascott,' 130, 138
Sambat, Alexandre, 318
Samu Bakula (Armand-Louis), 127, 141, 142, 197, 210
Samunga Tediangaye, 211, 235
San Salvador (band), 30
Sangana Yala Elefo (Valentin), 137, 183, 252
'Sango ya Mawa' (a/c Matolu Dode), 301
Sangua Mbaya 'Maray,' 306
Sans Commentaire (Madilu System), 389
Sans Issue (Zaïko Nkolo Mboka), 389
'Sans Préavis' (a/c Emeneya), 312
Sanza. See Likembe
La sape, 308–9, 328
Sapeurs, 308–9, 328
Saturne (studio), 377
Seaman, Norman, 193
Seba, Georges, 319
Sebene, 28–9, 77
Le Sebene (night club), 228
Seli-Ja, 221
Senegal, 107, 110, 191, 226, 323, 334. See also Dakar
Service Technique Africain de Radiodiffusion (STAR), 156
'Sex Machine' (a/c James Brown), 176
'Sex Madjesi' (a/c Matadidi), 176
'Sex Vévé' (a/c Verckys), 177
Sexteto Habanero, 13, 21

Shaba Province. *See* Katanga Province
Shanachie Records, 290
Shimita. *See* Lukombo Nzambi
Show Boat (night club), 156
Shungu Wembadio (Jules) 'Papa Wemba,' 251, 313, 383; in film *La Vie est Belle*, 334–5; Lokole Isifi and, 216–17, 223; as sapeur, 224, 308–9, 328; solo career of, 335–6, 338–9; Tabu Ley and, 252; tours Japan, 333–4, 335; Viva La Musica and, 223–4, 229, 304–7, 313, 333–4, 335, 336, 388; vocal style of, 224; Yoka Lokole and, 223; Zaïko Langa Langa and, 157–9, 213–16, 344. *See also* Papa Wemba's works listed by title
Sierra Leone, 15, 107–8, 139, 315, 380
Siluvangi (bar), 11, 16
Singapore, 322
Sinza (band), 135–6, 154, 162
Siscala, Didi, 162
Sita Malukisa 'Thamar,' 183
Slave trade, 5–6, 393
Smurf (dance), 311
Société Amicale des Originaires de l'Afrique Equatoriale Française, 61
Société Belge du Disque (SOBEDI), 24, 32
Société Congolaise du Disque (SOCODI), 163, 184, 186–7, 238, 285, 297
Société des Artistes et Compositeurs Congolais (SACCO), 196
Société des Editions de Disques Boboto (SOCEDIBO), 132, 142, 151
Société Française du Son (SOFRASON). *See* Fonior
Société Nationale des Editeurs Compositeurs et Auteurs (SONECA), 196–7, 210, 229, 236, 241, 243, 274
Société Phonographique et Industrielle du Zaïre (SOPHINZA, formerly SOPHINCO), 150, 172, 199, 221, 239, 242, 285, 355–6
Soki Dianzenza (Emile), 147, 156–7, 159, 177–8, 188, 211–12, 266–7, 370–71
Soki Vangu (Maxime), 156–7, 177–8, 211–12, 267, 240, 288, 370–71
Solovox organ, 39, 394

Son, 20–21, 76
Sonodisc, 273–5, 321–2
Soro (Salif Keïta), 323
'Sosoliso na Sosoliso' (a/c Matadidi), 176
Sosoliso (band). *See* Trio Madjesi
Soukous, 4, 135–6, 249, 262–3, 291, 325, 349, 380, 383–5
Soukous Stars, 378–80
Soukouss Vibration (Afro Rythmes), 380
Soul on Fire (Maloko), 380
Soum djoum, 180
Sound D'Afrique (Island), 262–3
'Sous-Alimentation Sexuelle' (a/c Franco), 231–2
South Africa, 242, 280, 333
Soviet Union, 93, 206, 237
Spanish, 13, 89, 104, 106, 108
Stadium 20 May, 207
'Stand By Me' (a/c King/Lieber/Stoller), 380
Stanley, Henry Morton, 6–10, 14
Stanley Pool. *See* Malebo Pool
Stanleyville. *See* Kisangani
Star Musique label, 260
Star, Rigo. *See* Bamundele, Rigobert
Stein (owner of STENCO), 106–7
STENCO, 106–7
Stino Mubi 'Stino As,' 333, 335
Stukas Boys, 155, 207, 210–11, 213, 235, 340, 362
'Suavilo' (a/c Nico), 139
'Suite Lettre No. 2' (a/c Franco), 283–4
Sukami, Teddy, 159, 213, 215, 216, 304
Suke Bola, 211
Sukisa label, 127
Super Band, 135
Super Bella Bella, 177. *See also* Soki Dianzenza
Super Boboto (band), 162
Super Fiesta (band), 142
Super Jazz (bar), 107
Super K (Diblo Dibala), 325
Surboum African Jazz label, 98, 99, 113, 114, 150. *See also* African Jazz label
'Suzana Coulibaly' (a/c Mangwana), 249, 256–7, 261, 262
Suzanella Maison Blanche (night club), 210
'Sweet Mother' (a/c Nico Mbarga), 246, 379
Sylla, Ibrahima, 322–3, 325, 349, 369, 378–80, 389
Symba (band), 151, 288

Sympathique Jazz (band), 163
Syndicat des Artistes Membres de la SONECA, 196
'Synza' (a/c Olomide), 251
Système Art Musique (SAM) label, 268

'Table Ronde' (a/c Kabasele), 86
Tabu Ley (Pascal) 'Rochereau,' 75, 135, 161, 163, 172, 188, 243, 273; African Fiesta and, 114–15, 127; African Fiesta (66) National and, 127–9, 141–3, 167–8; African Jazz and, 89–90, 96–7, 111–14, 235, 276; Afrisa and, 172, 173, 208–10, 221, 243–5, 252–3, 280–82, 328–31, 372, 378, 389–90; awarded gold record, 283; background of, 89–90, 170; enterprises of, 228–9, 255, 281; Franco and, 225, 229–31, 234, 283–4, 367–8; legacy of, 390–91; Mbilia Bel and, 280–82, 328–31, 343, 345; moves to Paris, 372; moves to U.S., 389; on loan to O.K. Jazz, 89–90; Pablito and, 104; Papa Wemba and, 252; performs in the U.S., 290–91, 389–90; plays at Montreal World's Fair, 134; plays the Olympia, 167–8; as president of SONECA, 229, 236; reunion with Docteur Nico, 252–3, 280, 294; sale of Fonior Congolese music catalog and, 274–5; Sam Mangwana and, 141–2, 144, 229, 244; setbacks following Olympia, 180, 208; show style of performance and, 174–5; style of, 115, 229, 313; suspended for slighting Mobutu, 141–2. *See also* Tabu Ley's works listed by title
'Tailleur' (a/c Franco), 278
Taloulou, Alphonse, 130, 186, 352, 377
Tam-tam (drums), 46, 56–7
Tam Tam (night club), 123
Tam Tam Bantou (night club), 110
'Tam-Tam Pour l'Ethiopie' (a/c Dibango), 314
Tanzania, 329, 391
Taumani, Albert, 41, 46, 67, 278
TBK label, 320
Tcha Tcho (Koffi Olomide), 348
Tchadé (musician), 72
Tcheza label, 150

Index 435

Tchicaya, Pambou 'Tchico,' 186, 236
'Tchimurenga Zimbabwe' (a/c Mangwana), 269
Téké people, 7–9
Télé-Music (band), 378
Tembo (band), 120, 144, 162
Théâtre de Verdure, 174
Thu Zaina, 155, 157, 159, 230, 244, 303, 339
Tiers Monde Coopération, 280, 356
Tiers Monde Révolution, 280
'Tika-Bazuwa' (a/c Mbilia Bel/Rigo Star), 331
Tingaut (Franco's employee), 255
Tip Top Jazz (band), 170
Tofolo Kitoko 'Tofla,' 307, 311–12, 336
Togo, 190–91, 249, 260, 261, 266, 297, 298, 322, 349, 373. *See also* Lomé
'Tokumisa Congo' (a/c Essous), 105–6
Totem Music label, 323
'Toujours O.K.' (a/c Mangwana), 361
Toulmonde, Editions, 221
Touré, Aladji, 318
Toure Kunda, 334
'La Tout Neige' (a/c Nyoka Longo), 159
'Toyokana Tolimbisana na Congo' (a/c Kabasele), 98
'Toyota' (a/c Rochereau), 143
'Trahison' (a/c M'Pongo Love), 264
Trautman, Paul, 290
Tres (musical instrument), 21
'Très Fâché' (a/c Franco), 286–7
Trio BOW, 70, 170
Trio CEPAKOS (and Le Peuple), 186, 237, 258, 265
Trio Los Makueson's, 190
Trio Madjesi (and Sosoliso), 175–7, 179, 188, 207, 210, 226–7
Trio Matamoros, 13
Trois Amies, 32, 68
Les 3 Caballeros, 43
Trouble (Loketo), 325
Tshala Muana (Elisabeth), 315–18, 349, 389
Tshamala, Jean 'Picollo,' 129, 131
'Tshebele' (a/c Tshala Muana), 316
Tshiluba language, 316
Tshimanga, Assosa, 178
Tshimpaka, Roxy 'Niawu,' 300,

303–4, 306, 310–11, 338–9, 381
Tshisekedi, Etienne, 374
Tshombe, Moïse, 90, 92, 94, 101, 119–20
'Tu Silencio' (a/c Malapet), 106
'Tu Vois?' (a/c Franco), 291–2
Tumba Ayila (Pierre) 'Emoro,' 302, 334, 381
Tutsi people, 391–2
Twist, 108, 119, 123
'Twist à Leo' (a/c Dibango), 122–3
'Twist With the Docteur' (a/c Freddy Nkounkou), 108
Type K (night club), 228–9, 238, 251, 252–3

Uganda, 116, 267, 391
Un-Deux-Trois (night club), 195, 200, 225, 232, 238, 251, 291, 356, 361, 375, 382
Union de la Jeunesse Socialiste Congolaise, 184
Union Démocratique de Défense des Intérêts Africains, 81
Union des Musiciens Congolais (UMC), 352
Union des Musiciens Zaïrois (UMUZA), 194, 195–8, 225–7, 229, 233, 236, 251, 276, 358
Union Minière du Haut Katanga, 17, 90, 206
Union National des Travailleurs Congolais (UNTC), 196
Union Panafricaine pour la Démocratie Sociale, 376, 377
United Nations, 93, 94, 119, 149
United States of America, 9, 93, 120, 126, 196, 206, 242, 389–90
Upper Volta. *See* Burkina Faso
Urbanization 4, 17–18, 30, 32, 67

Vadio Mabenga, 217, 223
Van Bilsen, A.A.J., 62–3
Vangu, Dino, 177, 230, 253, 279, 282, 329
Vangu, Jean Paul 'Guvano,' 127, 129, 138, 141–2, 145
Vedette Jazz (band), 98
Verckys. *See* Kiamuangana Mateta
Véritable Victoria (band), 312
'La Vérité de Franco' (a/c Franco), 146
Vévé Centre, 251, 276, 307, 375
Vévé, Editions, 152–4, 175, 177–9, 216, 251, 301, 311
Vévé, Orchestre, 152–4, 175, 177, 179, 210, 238, 251, 303,

339. *See also* Kiamuangana Mateta
Vicky. *See* Longomba Besange Lokuli
Victor (recording company), 13
Victoria Brazza (band), 20, 22, 27, 30
Victoria Coquilhatville (band), 22
Victoria Eleison, 285, 307, 308, 311–12, 329, 336–8, 339, 346, 355, 356–7, 370. *See also* Mubiala Emeneya
Victoria Kin (band), 22, 24, 27
'La Vie des Hommes' (a/c Franco), 353–4
La Vie est Belle (film), 334–5, 349
'La Vie est Belle' (a/c Papa Wemba), 334
'La Vie est un Combat' (a/c Nico), 297
'Vie ya Mosolo' (a/c Sukami), 215
Vipères Noirs (band), 155
VISA 1980 label, 255, 278, 306, 320
Vis-à-Vis (night club), 89, 117, 142, 149, 152, 161, 176, 183, 346, 351, 375
Vita label, 114, 150
Viva La Musica, 224, 251, 252, 255, 302, 388; dissolution of, 335; formation of, 223, 224, 229; musicians of, 224, 305–7, 311, 313, 320, 333, 340, 346; style of, 308; tours Japan, 333–4, 335. Works recorded by: 224, 305–6, 309, 333, 335, 388–9
'Vive Lumumba Patrice' (a/c Vicky), 86
Vocal groups, 19–20, 22
Vog Cinema, 281, 296
Voice of America, 108, 138, 249, 289, 298
Voice of Zaïre, 172, 225, 276, 306
Voix de la Concorde, 38
La Voix du Zaïre (M'Pongo Love), 264
Vonga Ndayimba 'Vonga Aye,' 264, 295, 296
Vox Africa, 116, 142, 146, 152, 163, 175, 210, 267
Le Voyageur (Papa Wemba), 388

Warnant, Gilbert, 40
Washington, D.C., 289, 298, 380
Wassa (band), 383
Watam (band), 53
Wateto, Henri, 130

Watoto wa Katanga (band), 72. *See also* Bukasa, Léon
Wela Kingana 'John Payne,' 131
Wendo. *See* Kolosoyi, Antoine
Wenge Musica (band), 371–2, 375
'While She's Away' (a/c Musekiwa), 46
Women in music, 43, 67–8, 188–9, 194
Women's mutual assistance associations, 50, 67
World beat, 1, 383, 388–9
World Festival of Black Arts (Dakar), 129, 130–31, 133
World Festival of Youth (Havana), 237
Wuta Yundula Mayanda (Blaise Pasco) 'Wuta Mayi,' 146, 183, 201, 230, 270–71, 272, 324–5, 389

Ya Tupas (band), 222, 249, 303
Yaba, Jimmy, 381
Yamba, Miguel, 326, 389
Yamba-Yamba, Albert, 35, 38
'Yambi Chérie' (a/c Michelino), 144
Yancomba Dibala 'Diblo,' 266–8, 273, 320, 323–4, 325–8, 380, 384, 386
Yantula, Pierre 'Petit Pierre,' 83, 88
'Ye' (a/c Franco), 201
Ye! magazine, 228, 230, 234
Yéké yéké (dance), 136
Yé-yé groups, 154–6
Yo La! (Ry-Co Jazz), 380
Yoka Lokole, 223, 224, 302, 333

Yondo Kusala (Denise) 'Yondo Sister,' 379
Yossa Taluki, 288
Youlou, Fulbert, 81, 94, 101–2, 120
Youlou Mabiala (Gilbert), 145, 152, 172, 201, 230, 244, 350–51, 358, 366, 377
Youth bands, 154–60, 174, 210, 246, 300, 308, 313, 337. *See also* individual bands by name, Zaïko Langa Langa, etc.
Yss Boys (band), 155
Yvorra, Charly, 51

ZADIS label, 235, 251
Zaïko Langa Langa, 188, 207, 210, 211, 251, 255, 302–3, 322, 343; administration of, 216, 303, 342–3; anniversaries of, 303, 344; criticism of, 214–15; dances of, 158, 214, 304; formation of, 157–9; Isifi singers of, 213, 215, 216, 223; mourns D.V. Moanda, 313; musicians of, 157–9, 213–14, 216, 302–4, 306, 310, 311, 339, 342, 344, 345–6; Ngoss and, 329, 343–6; recording output of, 339, 343; revises meaning of name, 172; splits within, 216, 223, 344–6; style of, 158, 215, 246–7, 304, 308. Works recorded by: 159, 214, 215, 304, 343
Zaïko Langa Langa Familia Dei, 344–7, 375, 378, 381
Zaïko Langa Langa Nkolo Mboka, 344–7, 371, 375, 378, 381, 389
Zaïre. *See* Congo, Democratic Republic of the
Zaïre (currency), 132, 218, 238, 241, 284–5, 350, 372, 375, 401
Zaïre Club, 183–4
Zaïre River. *See* Congo River
Zaïre 74 festival, 207–8, 211, 219
Zaïreanization, 198–200, 206, 217–18, 219, 222, 225, 239, 240, 242, 373
'Zamba' (a/c Soki Vangu), 211–12
Zamuangana 'Enock,' 158, 213, 303, 304, 342, 345, 346, 381
'Zando ya Malonga' (a/c Rochereau), 128
Zanzibar, 8, 236
'Zeke ya Pamba' (a/c Joe Poster), 310
Zekete zekete (dance), 304
'Zela Ngai Nasala' (a/c Mangwana), 145, 248
Zemanont Kanza, 339
Zenaba (African All Stars), 248, 257
Le Zénith (Paris concert hall), 383
Zing, Pierre Claver, 322
Zinga Botao, 274
Zitany, Neil, 379
Zizi, Fidèle. *See* Babindamana, Fidèle
Zouk, 134, 319, 327, 349
'Zouké Zouké' (a/c Pepe Kalle), 349